THE PAPERS OF
GEORGE MASON

Sponsored by

THE NATIONAL SOCIETY OF
THE COLONIAL DAMES OF AMERICA,

THE BOARD OF REGENTS OF GUNSTON HALL,
and
THE INSTITUTE OF
EARLY AMERICAN HISTORY AND CULTURE

THE UNIVERSITY OF NORTH CAROLINA PRESS
Chapel Hill, 1970

THE PAPERS OF

GEORGE MASON

1725–1792

VOLUME I *1749–1778*

ROBERT A. RUTLAND, *Editor*

Standard Book Number 8078-1134-3
Copyright © 1970 by The University of North Carolina Press
All rights reserved
Library of Congress Catalog Card Number 70-97016
Printed by Kingsport Press, Inc., Kingsport, Tennessee
Manufactured in the United States of America

TO *Peggy*

George Mason

Painted in 1811 by Dominic W. Boudet, after the lost portrait by John Hesselius. Courtesy of the Virginia Museum of Fine Arts, Richmond; photograph courtesy of Colonial Williamsburg, Inc.

ACKNOWLEDGMENTS

The Regents of Gunston Hall and their parent organization, the National Society of the Colonial Dames of America, have provided the necessary financial aid from the outset of the Mason Papers project in 1963. Hopefully, these volumes will contribute substantially to a broadening knowledge of Mason's role in American history and increased attention for Gunston Hall, Mason's restored home near Lorton, Virginia, which is administered by the Regents on behalf of the Commonwealth of Virginia.

The Institute of Early American History and Culture and its former director, Dr. Lester J. Cappon, have performed a vital role in all stages of the editing and publication. The present director, Dr. Stephen Kurtz, has been a good friend as well as editorial consultant. Joy Dickinson of the Institute staff has completed the difficult and demanding work of copy editor with patience and skill. Dr. Philip Hamer, who included the Mason Papers in the National Historical Publications Commission Report of 1954, and his successor as director of the Commission, Dr. Oliver W. Holmes, furnished indispensable support. Members of both the editorial committee and administrative board have been generous in permitting infringements upon their time and have contributed immeasurably to the accuracy and documentation of various state papers and private letters.

The support and many courtesies of Lambert Davis and his staff at The University of North Carolina Press have been in the finest traditions of the great university presses. Help and condolence has come from Julian Boyd, editor of the monumental *Papers of Thomas Jefferson*, Lyman Butterfield of *The Adams Papers*, and editors William T. Hutchinson and William M. E. Rachal of *The Papers of James Madison*, who have blazed editorial pathways that will serve untold generations of historians.

Among private collectors of manuscripts, no assistance has exceeded that afforded by Mr. R. Carter Pittman of Dalton, Georgia. Mr. Pittman's long-standing interest in Mason resulted in an extensive collection of microfilm and documentary reproductions which he generously offered the editor at the inception of the present work.

[ix]

Later, his editorial comments and guidance were of marked assistance. Most conspicuous among the many librarians who have assisted in the preparation of these volumes are Mrs. Dorothy Eaton of the Division of Manuscripts, Library of Congress; Miss Ruth Salisbury, coordinator of special collections at the University of Pittsburgh library; and Mrs. Virginia Gray, manuscripts section, Duke University library. Great courtesy has been shown by Mr. John Alden, Boston Public Library; Mr. James R. Short, Colonial Williamsburg, Inc.; Mr. John W. Dudley, Virginia State Library; Messrs. Edmund Berkeley, Jr., Richard E. Jenkins, Jr., and Robert E. Stocking of the University of Virginia library; Miss Josephine L. Harper, State Historical Society of Wisconsin library; Messrs. Nicholas Wainright, John D. Kilbourne, and R. N. Williams II of the Historical Society of Pennsylvania; Messrs. Fred Shelley and Leonard Rapport of the National Archives; Mr. Robert F. Clayton, Marietta College library; Mr. Francis S. Ronalds, Morristown National Historical Park; Mr. Greer Allen, editor of *Manuscripts;* Mr. Robert W. Hill and Mrs. Maud D. Cole of the New York Public Library; Mr. Herbert Cahoon, Pierpont Morgan library; Mr. Robert O. Dougan, Henry E. Huntington library; Mrs. H. Nelson Kilbourn and Miss Mabel E. Winslow of the Daughters of the American Revolution Archives; Mr. William H. Bond, Houghton library, Harvard University; Mr. Archie Motley, Chicago Historical Society; Mr. James M. Babcock, Detroit Public Library; Dr. Clifford K. Shipton, American Antiquarian Society; Mrs. Dorothy Thomas Cullen, Filson Club library of Louisville; Mr. Wilmer Leech, New-York Historical Society library; Mr. Robert L. Scribner, *The Papers of James Madison;* Miss Elizabeth Baer, John Work Garrett library of Johns Hopkins University; and especially Mrs. Cassie Rankin of the Warrenton, Virginia, library. Private aid has come from Mr. George H. S. King, Mr. Nathaniel E. Stein, Dr. Samuel W. Thomas, Mrs. Thomas Riggs Cox, Dr. Robert E. Cushman, Dr. John Carter Matthews, Miss Dorothy E. Marshall, Professor Leo Kaiser, and Dr. Alfred P. James.

Extraordinary assistance was provided by Mrs. Sandra Dresbeck, who compiled the biographical-geographical glossary and performed many other tasks with good humor and sound scholarship. Mrs. Sarah H. Hogan, Gene Larson, and Mr. Robert Oaks also aided with the project at various stages of the collecting and editing process, and made signal contributions to the overall work. By preparing the manuscript for the printers, Mrs. Lallé Hoffman and Miss Yolanda Victoria expanded their knowledge of American history and absorbed some of the determination that was characteristic of George Mason.

CONTENTS

1769

1770

1771

1772

AN EXPLANATION OF
THE EDITORIAL GUIDELINES

The decision to publish *The Papers of George Mason* was the result of a conviction, held by historians and interested laymen, that George Mason needed to be reintroduced to American history. In the years since 1892, when Kate Mason Rowland's *The Life of George Mason, 1725–1792* first appeared, many new manuscripts have been discovered, while editorial standards have advanced to make nineteenth-century collections of papers hopelessly outmoded. To correct the record and to add to that record, these volumes contain all public and private papers that were written by Mason, or addressed to him, and available in 1969. These volumes contain documents that illustrate his private and business affairs, and certain conjectures have been made in the assumption that an editor's intuition and experience ought to be shared—that to suppress a well-grounded speculation might indeed be a disservice to scholarship. In addition, the speeches Mason delivered at the Federal Convention in 1787 and at the Virginia ratifying convention in 1788 have been included. Although not falling into the strict "papers" category, they contribute enormously to a total understanding of what Mason did and said at an important juncture in our history. A discouraging number of documents, now lost to history, are noted by brief entries and when possible their contents reconstructed. In a few instances documents long thought to have been written by Mason alone are described as either the result of a combined (or committee) effort or work incorrectly and often circumstantially ascribed to him. Old claims of authorship, sometimes based on nothing more than local tradition, have been challenged.

Routine business papers and memoranda have been accorded brief entries only, but an appendix in Volume I selectively calendars Mason's transactions not covered by the main text. Identification of persons and places mentioned has been attempted, oftentimes with great trepidation, in a biographical-geographical glossary which follows in this volume. The annotations and introductory essays for certain groups of papers enlarge upon the contextual meaning of the papers or speeches. The aim throughout these volumes has been to eschew cumbersome detail and still give the reader useful information, following the guidelines established by Julian P. Boyd as editor of *The Papers of Thomas Jefferson*. Hopefully, Boyd's happy avoidance of the pedantic style will also be apparent here.

The spelling, punctuation, and grammar of the papers published in these volumes are those of the original, unless otherwise stated in the textual notes. An exception, however, is the silently inserted period in place of many a semicolon or colon that the writer obviously intended to function as a break rather than a pause. The literal form has been retained for places, salutations, and complimentary closings, but the dateline will always head the document regardless of its location in the original. Capitalization follows the original, when ascertainable, except that Mason's habit of capitalizing pronouns has led to a general rule that pronouns (except the first person singular) invariably begin with a lower-case letter. To correct inconsistencies, the first word in each sentence is always capitalized. Mason often omitted periods and substituted long dashes, but to establish clarity the dash is replaced with a period and superfluous dashes omitted entirely. Mason often neglected to indent the beginning of a paragraph, a stylistic quirk that is remedied when there is a clear break in the thought. Mason's peculiar spelling of such words as "immediately" and "settled" is inconsistent, but in most cases he was spelling words in 1792 about the way he had in his earliest letters. On occasion, he would spell the same word differently in a single sentence. These and other distinctive features of his correspondence have been reproduced as written, and only the infrequent slips of the pen (such as repeating a word)—"it will be to your your advantage"—are corrected silently.

Similarly, the original use of contractions and abbreviations has been allowed to stand, but raised letters have been lowered. The ampersand, the symbol ⅌ for per, monetary designations, and contractions appear as written. The only exception to this is the eighteenth-century printer's thorn which, to avoid "ye" and "yt," is expanded to the modern form: the, that, or their. Blank spaces or short gaps are retained in the printed text as they appear in the original document. Minor additions made by the writer in the margins or above the line appear without comment. Words or sentences crossed through by the writer ordinarily will not be printed, but if significant will be noted in the textual explanation.

Words and sentences in a foreign language are printed as written, with pertinent translations in the textual notes. Brackets have been employed to restore words missing in damaged manuscripts or to make conjectures on those gaps caused by time or carelessness. These surmises will be duly noted, but where missing portions defy editorial speculation they will be marked with an ellipsis (. . .) or deemed illegible. Mason's additions to certain public documents are printed in italics or within angle brackets, as textual notes explain. Missing manuscripts are calendared and whatever knowledge exists of their contents will be summarized within double brackets.

Legislation in Mason's handwriting poses no problem, but there is little doubt that many resolutions and bills he drafted or helped write disappeared long ago. Their loss may be due to circumstances, such as when a clerk sent a resolution to the printer and the original then became scrap paper, or to the conflagration at Westham early in 1781 when British troops destroyed a portion of the Virginia archives. A clue to Mason's participation in drafting a bill was the Speaker's order for a particular member to carry a measure to the Senate from the House of Delegates. Usually this courtesy was accorded the drafter of a bill, but this was not always the case and in Mason's situation ill health often forced him to miss days or weeks while a session progressed. When Mason presented a bill and was ordered to carry it to the Senate, the editorial assumption herein has been that Mason was the principal author of the measure even though a manuscript for the legislation is missing or exists only in a clerk's handwriting. In a few cases, where Mason presented a bill but someone else was ordered to carry it to the Senate, the measure is still printed because of circumstances which point to Mason as the chief author. The editor has attempted to justify such decisions in textual notes accompanying the document. This process creates a divergence between these volumes and Kate Mason Rowland's *Life of George Mason . . .* , and while all such discrepancies are noted, the editorial standards of her day need not be belabored.

The papers ordinarily bear only the name of the addressee or the author. Legislation is usually headed by the title designated by the *Journal of the House of Delegates*, or as it appears in Hening's *Statutes at Large . . . of Virginia*. However, when the original title is adjudged too cumbersome or obscure, a modern heading has been substituted; in such cases the original title is carried in the explanatory notes. Business papers and Ohio Company correspondence are headed according to the direct purpose of the document. Convention speeches are headed by the subject under discussion.

ANNOTATION

The descriptive note appearing beneath the document states whether the manuscript (letter, speech, bill, etc.) still exists and in what form, such as RC (recipient's copy), FC (file copy), or Tr (transcription). The designation Ms (manuscript) is broad, but elaboration will ordinarily follow in the note. Usually, a recipient's copy is in the handwriting of the sender and ordinarily the documents are also in the author's hand. Circumstances made it impossible to use primary sources throughout the work, however, and in some cases only a printed text is now available, but any variation (such as a clerk's preparation) will be noted and, if possible, explained. File copies usually were made by clerks or retained in letterbooks. Transcriptions will bear the name of the transcriber and the date of his transcription whenever possible. Most other documents will be arbitrarily classified as manuscripts. The location of the document will be made by using the National Union Catalog symbols (with those most frequently used set forth below). The address, endorsements, signatures or lack of signatures, enclosures, and other pertinent information will follow. The note summarizing a document will also tell the number of written pages, including address and endorsements. For brevity's sake, GM will be substituted for George Mason throughout these notes.

The second paragraph below the document will contain those brief comments necessary for clarity and understanding. Identifications will be made only when the material is not covered in the biographical-geographical glossary. Instead of numbered footnotes the pertinent words will be printed in this note in small capitals. Cross-references to other materials will appear in this paragraph, as well as printed sources that relate to the document.

Textual notes will in most cases follow important documents to indicate significant corrections, deletions, or variations in the original or printed texts. Mason's insertion of words, or phrases, will be pointed out, and the handwriting of others identified if known. Noteworthy variants of the document from previously printed versions, particularly those in Kate Mason Rowland, *Life of George Mason* . . . , will be cited in the third paragraph below the document.

DATES

A word about the shift from the Old Style to the New Style calendar in 1752 is in order. On 2 September 1752 Great Britain and her colonies officially abandoned the Julian calendar and adopted the Gregorian, used on the continent, by legally declaring the following day to be 14 September 1752. Prior to that time the calendar conversion was further complicated by the designation of March 25 as the first day of the new year. The change came while Mason was still a young man and thus the altered calendar is mainly a historical curiosity in these volumes, rather than a tedious, recurring problem. The date of each printed document, therefore, is that which appears on the original.

LOCATION SYMBOLS

Most of the institutions or libraries possessing the materials printed in these volumes are listed below with their National Union Catalog symbol. The only exception for the provenance of materials will be the citation of Gunston Hall, Lorton, Virginia. The Regents of Gunston Hall have a manuscript collection maintained there as part of their restoration and exhibition project.

For the sake of brevity these symbols, from the National Union Catalog in the Library of Congress, will indicate the location of documents held by public institutions. The location of documents in private collections or the use of texts from printed sources will be explained in a descriptive note.

CSmH	Henry E. Huntington Library, San Marino, Calif.
CtY	Yale University
DLC	Library of Congress
DNA	The National Archives
ICHi	Chicago Historical Society
ICU	University of Chicago Library
KyLoF	Filson Club Library, Louisville
MB	Boston Public Library
MH	Harvard University Library
MHi	Massachusetts Historical Society
MdAA	Maryland Hall of Records, Annapolis
MeHi	Maine Historical Society, Portland
MWA	American Antiquarian Society
MiD	Detroit Public Library
NcD	Duke University Library
NHi	New-York Historical Society, New York
NN	New York Public Library
NNC	Columbia University Library
NNP	Pierpont Morgan Library, New York
PHC	Haverford College Library
PHi	Historical Society of Pennsylvania, Philadelphia
PP	Free Library of Philadelphia
PPiU	University of Pittsburgh Library
Vi	Virginia State Library, Richmond
ViHi	Virginia Historical Society, Richmond

ViU	University of Virginia Library
ViW	College of William and Mary Library
ViWC	Colonial Williamsburg, Inc.
WHi	Wisconsin State Historical Society, Madison

SHORT TITLES

The following printed works are cited with frequency in the annotation, and are listed here in their expanded form:

Ballagh, *Lee Letters*	James Curtis Ballagh, comp., *The Letters of Richard Henry Lee*, 2 vols. (New York, 1911–1914)
Boyd	Julian P. Boyd, ed., *The Papers of Thomas Jefferson*, 17 vols. (Princeton, 1950—)
DAB	*Dictionary of American Biography*
Elliot, *Debates*	Jonathan Elliot, ed., *The Debates of the Several State Conventions on the Adoption of the Federal Constitution*, 5 vols. (Philadelphia, 1901)
Farrand, *Records*	Max Farrand, ed., *The Records of the Federal Convention of 1787*, 4 vols. (New Haven, 1911–1937)
Force, *American Archives*	Peter Force, ed., *American Archives*, 4th Ser., 6 vols. (Washington, 1837–1846)
Grigsby	Hugh Blair Grigsby, *The History of the Virginia Federal Convention of 1788 . . .* , 2 vols. (Richmond, 1890–1891)
Harrison	Fairfax Harrison, *Landmarks of Old Prince William*, 2d ed. (Berryville, Va., 1964)
Hening	William Waller Hening, ed., *The Statutes at Large; Being a Collection of All the Laws of Virginia . . .* , 13 vols. (Richmond, 1819–1823)
Hutchinson-Rachal	William T. Hutchinson and William M. E. Rachal, eds., *The Papers of James Madison*, 5 vols. (Chicago, 1962—)
JHB	*Journals of the House of Burgesses of Virginia, 1619–1776*, 13 vols. (Richmond, 1905–1915)

JHD
: *Journal of the House of Delegates of the Commonwealth of Virginia* (Richmond, 1827; 2d ed., 1828), cited by edition and date of session

Madison
: *Notes of Debates in the Federal Convention of 1787, Reported by James Madison* (Athens, Ohio, 1966)

Mulkearn
: Lois Mulkearn, comp., *George Mercer Papers relating to the Ohio Company of Virginia* (Pittsburgh, 1954)

Robertson
: David Robertson, comp., *Debates and Other Proceedings of the Convention of Virginia . . . June, 1788 . . .* , 2d ed. (Richmond, 1805)

Rowland
: Kate Mason Rowland, *The Life of George Mason, 1725–1792*, 2 vols. (New York, 1892)

Sabin
: Joseph Sabin, *et al.*, comps., *Bibliotheca Americana. A Dictionary of Books relating to America . . .* , 29 vols. (New York, 1863–1936)

Swem
: Earl G. Swem, comp., *Virginia Historical Index . . .* , 2 vols. (Roanoke, 1934–1936)

Tyler
: Lyon G. Tyler, *Encyclopedia of Virginia Biography*, 5 vols. (New York, 1915)

Va. Gaz.
: *Virginia Gazette* (Williamsburg [1751–1780] and Richmond [1780–1781]). To distinguish between the several newspapers bearing the same name, the publisher's name will be placed in parentheses.

VMHB
: *Virginia Magazine of History and Biography*

WMQ
: *William and Mary Quarterly*

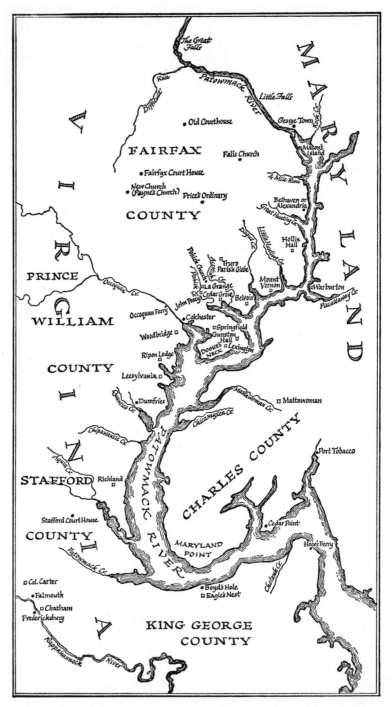

The region of the upper Potomac as George Mason knew it. Place-names and spellings largely conform to those of the Fry-Jefferson map (1755). Locations of plantations (□), and town sites, ferries, and public buildings (•) are approximate.

Prepared by Richard J. Stinely of Colonial Williamsburg, Inc.

BIOGRAPHICAL-GEOGRAPHICAL
GLOSSARY

Compiled by Sandra Ryan Dresbeck

The purpose of this glossary is to limit identifications in the annotations following a document to the bare essentials and also to furnish a convenient aid for persons working in the general field of study. Mrs. Dresbeck encountered numerous errors of fact in many standard genealogical and biographical works which she has endeavored to correct. When possible, cross-references were checked to verify conflicting statements. Admittedly, the early American penchant for the repeated use of traditional Christian names has brought on much confusion. Within the relevant branch of the Mason family there were six George Masons in a row, and the problem of identification is compounded by numerous uncles and cousins also known as George Mason. The brothers Jenifer of Maryland (both named Daniel) are another case in point. In these circumstances, the authority of such experts as George H. S. King of Fredericksburg, Virginia, has been extremely helpful in untangling family relationships. Mrs. Dresbeck has also been assisted in her endeavors by Sarah Hogan, the staff of the Papers of James Madison, the UCLA Research Library, the Montana State University Library, and her husband, Mr. Leroy Dresbeck.

R. A. R.

[Entries marked with an asterisk (*) are more fully reported in DAB, and those marked with a dagger (†) in the *Dictionary of National Biography*. A guide to the short titles cited is found on pages *xxvi–xxvii*. All counties cited are in Virginia, unless otherwise noted.]

ACCOTINK, Fairfax County: name of both a creek and bay entering the Potomac River; Accotink Bay is a part of Gunston Cove.

ADAM, ROBERT (1731–1789): born at Kilbride, Scotland; partner, Alexandria shipping firm, Carlyle and Adam, wheat and tobacco agents, 1760, Robert Adam and Co., 1771; Fairfax County justice of the peace, 1770; Alexandria trustee, succeeding George William Fairfax; Fairfax committee of safety, 1774; subscriber to Ballendine's project for clearing

Potomac navigation, 1774; laid Alexandria Academy cornerstone, 1785; founder of Alexandria Masonic Lodge.

ADAMS, GABRIEL: father of William Adams; owned lands in Prince William and Fairfax counties; 1st Truro Parish vestry, 1732, but not reelected, 1744; voted for Fairfax burgess, 1744; exempted from paying any future parish levies, 1745.

* ADAMS, JOHN (1735–1826): born at Quincy, Mass.; led resistance to Stamp Act; served in Continental Congress, 1774–1778; commissioner to France and Holland, 1777–1779, 1780–1782; signed Treaty of Paris, 1783; minister to Great Britain, 1785–1788; vice-pres. of U.S., 1789–1797; pres. of U.S., 1797–1801; father of John Quincy Adams, 6th pres. of U.S. A definitive edition of Adams's papers is in progress under the general editorship of Lyman H. Butterfield.

ADAMS, RICHARD (1726–1800): born in New Kent County; brother, Thomas Adams; Richmond residence was on Adams (Church) Hill; New Kent County burgess, 1752–1765; Henrico County burgess, 1769–1775; Va. committee of safety, 1774–1775; del. to all Va. conventions, 1775, 1776; House of Delegates, 1776–1778; Va. Senate, 1779–1782; signed Williamsburg Association, 1776; joined John Ballendine in experiments on air furnace and canal building, 1775–1781.

ADAMS, THOMAS (1730–1788): born in New Kent County; brother of Richard Adams; attended William and Mary, 1756; resided in England, 1762–ca. 1774; clerk, Henrico County; signed Articles of Association, 1774; New Kent County committee of safety chairman, 1774; del. to Continental Congress, 1778–1780, where he signed Articles of Confederation; served Va. Senate for Augusta, Rockingham, Rockbridge, and Shenandoah counties, 1783–1786; died on Augusta County estate, Cowpasture.

ADAMS, WILLIAM: son of Gabriel Adams; father-in-law of Rev. William Watters and Rev. John Childs, Methodist preachers; Truro Parish processioner, 1755; Fairfax Parish vestry, 1765; Fairfax sheriff, 1768; Fairfax justice of the peace, 1770; Methodist preaching established at his home, 1773.

ALEXANDER, CHARLES (1737–1806): son of John Alexander and Susanna Pearson; born St. Paul's Parish; married Frances, daughter of Dr. Richard Brown, half brother of Dr. Gustavus Richard Brown; unsuccessful candidate for Fairfax parish vestry, 1765; Fairfax committee of safety, 1774; Fairfax commissioner for state aid, 1780; Fairfax board of overseers of the poor as pres., 1797.

ALEXANDER, PHILIP (1704–1753): called "capt."; of Chotank, Stafford County; son of Philip Alexander and Sarah Ashton; married Sarah, daughter of Col. Rice Hooe, 1726; Alexandria built on land owned jointly with John Alexander and Hugh West; GM succeeded Alexander as Alexandria trustee, 1753; his descendant, Philip of Chotank, was killed in duel with Lawrence Washington. See GM to George Washington, 19 Mar. 1783.

ALEXANDER, PHILIP (1742–1790?): apparently 2d son of Capt. Philip Alexander (1704–1753) and Sarah Hooe; Fairfax County committee of safety, 1774; with GM, elected to House of Delegates, 1777; subscriber to Christ Church of Alexandria, 1785.

ALEXANDER, PHILIP (1760–1783): of Chotank; son of John Alexander and Lucy Thornton; probably served in militia, ca. 1780–1783; married Jane, daughter of Col. Lewis Willis and Jane Champe; fatally wounded in duel with Lawrence Washington, 1783.

ALEXANDER, SAMUEL: probably a Fairfax County planter; although a Samuel Alexander was an associator, supporting the Frederick County, Md., committee of observation, 1775.

ALEXANDER, WILLIAM: 2d son of William Alexander, lord provost of Edinburgh; had financial dealings with Benjamin Franklin before Revolution;

left London for France, 1776; daughter Miriamne married Franklin's grandnephew Jonathan Williams, 1779; secret agent of Sir William Pulteney, who tried to bring peace through personal negotiations with Franklin; left Nantes, 1783; settled in Richmond, Va., as Messrs. William Alexander and Co., 1784, 1788; Va. tobacco agent of the French Farmers' General, 1785.

ALEXANDRIA: Fairfax County; Potomac River town founded in 1749 in vicinity of Hunting Creek warehouse, on lands purchased from Philip Alexander, John Alexander, and Hugh West; originally known as Belhaven or Belle Haven; renamed in 1752; in 1789 part of the land Va. ceded to the U.S. for a federal district; in 1845 formally returned to the jurisdiction of Va.

ALLISON, WILLIAM: Fairfax County freeholder; signed Fairfax petition against British debts, 1783; possibly a lieut. col., 1st Va. Regt., 1779–1780; became partner of John Mason in plan to manufacture snuff.

AMBLER, JACQUELIN (1742–1798): Yorktown merchant; son of Richard Ambler; William and Mary, 1753–1760, College of Philadelphia, 1761; joined his father in business at Yorktown; married Rebecca, daughter of Pres. Lewis Burwell of Kingsmill, and subject of Jefferson's "Belinda"; York River naval officer; York County justice of the peace during early years of Revolution; chairman, Va. board of trade, 1779–1780; Va. Council, 1780–1782; Va. treasurer, 1782–1798; Henrico Parish vestryman after Revolution; daughter Elizabeth Jacqueline married Col. William Brent, son of William Brent of Richland; daughter Mary Willis married Chief Justice John Marshall.

AMBLER, JOHN: son of Richard Ambler and brother of Jacquelin Ambler; educated at Cambridge; inherited all his father's lands on Jamestown Island, ferry house, and Powhatan Swamp plantation; owned much land on Va. Peninsula,

1786–1787; married Frances, daughter of Gill Armistead and Betty Allen.

ANALOSTAN ISLAND. See MASON'S ISLAND.

ANDERSON, CAPT. [JOHN]: possibly the ship master who loaded tobacco from Va. ports aboard ship *Chatham*, 1769–1770; a Capt. John Anderson served with Va. troops at Winchester, 1783.

ANTHONY, JOSEPH: probably a mercantile shipowner prior to Revolution; John Mason, GM's merchantson, had friend who may have been an ardent abolitionist Va. del. to antislavery convention, 1798.

AQUIA CHURCH: Overwharton Parish, Stafford County; built in 1757, located about three miles north of Stafford Court House; was the original parish church when Overwharton was established.

ARELL (ARREL, ARRIL, ARROL), DAVID: Alexandria tavernkeeper, 1768; capt., Va. troops in Continental line, and presumably the "Lt. Arril" GM refers to in Apr. 1776, although there are apparently two others, Samuel and Richard, of the same surname in Alexandria recorded in the 1770s and 1780s.

ATHAWES, EDWARD: London merchant prominent in the Va. tobacco trade, succeeded by his son, Samuel. See his correspondence, "Letters and Other Papers, 1735–1829," VMHB, XXIII (1915), 162–172.

ATHIE (ATHEY, ATHY), SAMUEL: Fairfax County planter and tenant of William Fitzhugh of Millmont, 1787; paid by Truro Parish vestry for upkeep of poor, 1774.

ATHIE (ATHEY, ATHY), THOMAS: apparently a small planter of Fairfax County who lived near GM; signed GM's petitions to separate the jurisdictions of Alexandria and Fairfax, 1787, and to move the courthouse, 1789, 1790.

AUGUSTA COUNTY: named after Princess Augusta (1719–1772) of Saxe-Gotha, who married the Prince of

Wales in 1736; the largest and western-most county when created in 1738, but had no county government until 1745; later subdivided into several counties.

AYLETT, WILLIAM (1743–1781): of Fairfield, King William County; son of Philip Aylett; burgess, 1771–1775; del. to all Va. conventions, 1775–1776; signed nonimportation assn., 1774; married Mary, daughter of Col. James Macon, 1776; Va. commissary, 1776–1777; Continental army deputy commissary-gen. for Southern Dept., 1777–1780; died suddenly at Yorktown, mid-Apr. 1781.

BAILEY, WILLIAM (d. *ca.* 1782): possibly a planter-merchant with interests on both sides of the Potomac who resided in the Northern Neck; posted executor's bond for GM in probate of French Mason's estate, 1748.

BAKER, JERMAN [d. 1799]: Petersburg or Blandford tobacco merchant, 1769; turned to law by 1772, settled estate of William Byrd III, 1777; clerk, Chesterfield County committee of safety, 1775; Chesterfield del. to General Assembly, 1779, and apparently at other times, considered good speaker.

BALLENDINE, JOHN (d. 1782): of Lancaster County; ship capt., promoter, builder-owner of saw mills, forges, iron works; wrote *Proposals for opening the navigation of the River Potowmack* (London, 1773); GM was trustee of his Potomac canal company, 1774; began construction of James River canal and Westham iron works, 1776; sought subsidies from Va. General Assembly for canal and weapons manufacture; married Frances, daughter of Charles Ewell; various enterprises were in financial difficulty at Ballendine's death. See Harrison, 435*n*–436*n*.

BALLUSE. See BAYLIS.

BALMAIN, WILLIAM (d. 1784): Alexandria merchant in firm of Henderson & Balmain; signed Fairfax County nonimportation agreement, 1770, but complained of inequities in enforce-ment, 1771; died in Alexandria. See *Virginia Journal* and *Alexandria Advertiser,* 22 June 1770.

BANISTER, JOHN (1734–1788): of Hatcher's Run, near Petersburg; lawyer, burgess, 1765–1775; del. to Va. conventions, 1775, 1776; Dinwiddie County del. to Va. General Assembly, between 1776–1783; Va. del. to Continental Congress, where he supported R. H. and Arthur Lee, 1778–1779.

BANKS, HENRY: son of Gerard Banks and Frances Bruce of Green Bank, near Fredericksburg; lawyer, merchant, head of Banks & Co., Richmond; owned over 77,000 acres of Va. lands, moved to Ky. after death of wife, Martha, probably *ca.* 1790.

BARBOUR, JAMES (*ca.* 1734–1783): son of James Barbour, reputedly the 1st settler in Culpeper County, served under Col. Thomas Slaughter in the Culpeper militia, 1756, and in an expedition against Indians above Winchester; Culpeper burgess, 1761–1765; Culpeper lieut., 1775; his brother, Capt. Philip Barbour, visited the region around the mouth of the Ohio River, 1780. See Hutchinson-Rachal, I, 222*n;* III, 106*n*–107*n.*

BARBOUR, THOMAS (1735–1800?): son of James Barbour of Culpeper County; born near Barboursville, Orange County; Orange justice of the peace, 1768 to death; married Mary Thomas, 1771; Orange burgess, 1769–1776; Orange committee of safety, 1774; del. to Va. conventions, 1775; Orange lieut.; father of Gov. James Barbour (DAB, *q.v.*) and U.S. Supreme Court Justice Philip Pendleton Barbour.

BARCLAY, THOMAS (1728–1793): Philadelphia merchant; Va. supply agent in France, 1782; commissioner to settle U.S. accounts in Europe, 1782–1787; consul gen. in France, authorized to appoint U.S. commercial agents or vice consuls there, 1783–1787; agent of John Adams, Jefferson, Franklin to conclude treaty of friendship and commerce with Morocco, 1785–1787; Jefferson appointed him consul for

Morocco, 1791; died in Lisbon. See Hutchinson-Rachal, IV, 291, 326.

BARNES, CAPT. ———: probably the New Englander, Corbin Barnes, who commanded American ships trading between France and U.S. in 1778/1779; also commander of the privateer, *General Lincoln*, 1779. See Lyman H. Butterfield, *et al.*, eds., *The Diary and Autobiography of John Adams* (Cambridge, Mass., 1961), II, 335, 402; IV, 171, 192.

BARNES, JOHN: of Port Tobacco, Md.; son of Maj. Abraham Barnes and Sarah Ball of Fairfax County; brother-in-law of GM's brother, Thomson Mason; married Elyn, daughter of Benjamin Harrison (d. 1790) of Brunswick County; probably signed GM's petition to move the Fairfax courthouse, 1790.

*BARNEY, CAPT. JOSHUA (1759–1818): naval and merchant marine officer from Baltimore; served aboard the ship *Hornet*, commanded by Commodore Hopkins, 1775; commissioned lieut., Continental navy, 1776; lieut. of the frigate *Virginia*, 1777; carried from France to Philadelphia news of the loan from King Louis XVI and preliminary peace articles, 1783; active Federalist, 1787, 1788; served in War of 1812.

BARRON, JAMES (1740–1787): son of Capt. Samuel Barron, brother of Capt. Richard Barron; married Jane Cowper, father of Commodore James Barron (DAB, *q.v.*); apprenticed by his guardian in the James River–London trade, *ca.* 1750, and later entrusted with command of one of his own vessels, by 1769; arrogance of British naval officers toward Americans caused his refusal of a merchant command, 1774; as capt. in Va. navy, patrolled Chesapeake and convoyed stores ships; succeeded Commodore Walter Brooke as commander of Va. navy, 1780; his ship, *Liberty*, was sole survivor of Arnold's attack on Va. fleet in James River, 1781; member of the national board of war; commanded Va. revenue fleet (two vessels), 1783–1787. See Robert A. Stew-

art, *History of Virginia's Navy in the Revolution* (Richmond, 1933), 144–146.

BARRON, RICHARD: younger brother of James Barron; capt., Va. navy during Revolution; commanded armed boat *Patriot* in his brother's fleet.

BARRY, JOHN (d. 1775): son of Edward Barry, former clerk of Truro Parish vestry; Truro vestry clerk, 1765–1775; partner in McCarty & Barry; collector of tithes for Truro Parish, 1740, 1742; became clerk of Pohick Church, 1743, and of Pohick and New Church, 1744, both of Truro Parish; an original trustee of Colchester, Va., 1753; contended with George Washington over property lines. See Douglas S. Freeman, *George Washington* (N.Y., 1948–1953), III, 287–288.

BARRY, WILLIAM: small-scale planter and merchant of Fairfax County; possibly a limited partner in McCarty & Barry; signed GM's petition favoring removal of Fairfax courthouse from Alexandria, 1789.

BASSETT, FRANCES: called "Fanny"; daughter of Burwell Bassett of Eltham, and Anna Maria Dandridge, the sister of Martha Washington; married George Augustine Washington at Mount Vernon, 1785; later married Tobias Lear, whose 1st wife had died, 1793.

*BASSETT, RICHARD (1745–1815): born Cecil County, Md.; capt., Del. Light Horse during the Revolution; Del. council of safety, constitutional convention, legislator, 1776–1786; del. to Annapolis Convention; inactive member of the Federal Convention, 1787, but leader in the Del. ratifying convention; U.S. Senate 1789–1793; chief justice, court of common pleas, 1793–1799; gov. of Del., 1799–1801; Adams's "midnight appointee" to the U.S. Circuit Court seat which was soon legislated out of existence.

BAXTER, JAMES (d. 1763): administrator of the will of GM's father and guardian of GM, 1735; undersheriff to Augustine Washington in Westmoreland County, 1727; owned lands in

[xxxiii]

Prince William and Fairfax counties; Truro Parish vestry, 1734, 1736; capt., French and Indian War; high sheriff, Cecil County, Md., 1760–1762; apparently also a member of the Md. legislature. See Harrison, 54.

BAYLY (BAYLEY, BAYLIE), PIERCE: Fairfax County subsheriff, 1768; sheriff, 1769; Truro Parish collector of tithes, 1767–1772; favored separation of Fairfax County jurisdiction from Alexandria township, 1787.

BAYLEY (BAYLY), SAMUEL: neighbor of GM's; paid by overseers of poor for caring for indigent parishioners, 1792.

BAYLEY (BAYLIE, BAYLY), WILLIAM: Fairfax County resident in 1780s; signed GM's petition for removal of Fairfax courthouse, 1790.

BAYLIS, JOHN (d. 1765): with GM was one of the original trustees of Dumfries, Prince William County; burgess, 1761–1765; killed in duel with Cuthbert Bullitt.

BEALL, SAMUEL (d. 1792?): Williamsburg merchant; son of Col. Samuel Beall; served on Washington County, Md., committee of observation, 1776; appears to have moved to Va., 1777; partner in Norton & Beall with John Hatley Norton, until ca. 1783; married Nancy Booth of Md., 1779; member, Williamsburg Masonic Lodge, 1778–1782.

BECKLEY, JOHN JAMES (1757–1807): legislative clerk, politician, of Henrico County; clerk, Henrico committee of safety, 1774; a founder of Phi Beta Kappa, 1776; asst. clerk, Va. committee of safety, 1776; clerk, Va. Senate, 1777–1779; clerk, House of Delegates, 1779–1789; clerk, high court of chancery and court of appeals, 1782; clerk, Va. ratifying convention, 1788; clerk, U.S. House of Reps., 1789–1797, 1801–1807; 1st librarian of Congress, 1802–1807. See Hutchinson-Rachal, I, 319n; N. E. Cunningham, Jr., "John Beckley: An Early American Party Manager," WMQ, 3d Ser., XIII (1956), 40–52.

BELVOIR, Fairfax County: home of the Fairfax family; built in the 1740s by William Fairfax, pres. of the Va. Council; on Rankin's Point, on the Potomac halfway between Mt. Vernon and Gunston Hall; home of George William Fairfax (1724–1787), one of the major centers of social and political life of colonial Virginia.

BENEZET, DANIEL: son of Jean Étienne Benezet, a Huguenot, who fled Picardy for Rotterdam, 1715, then migrated to London; family moved to Philadelphia, 1731, where Daniel and his brothers successfully imported London goods; signed the Philadelphia nonimportation agreement of 1769. See DAB under "Anthony Benezet."

BERKELEY, EDMUND (1730–1802): of Barn Elms, Middlesex County; son of Edmund Berkeley and Mary Nelson; married Judith, daughter of William Randolph of Tuckahoe, 1757, then Mary, daughter of Carter Burwell of The Grove, 1768; Middlesex burgess, 1771–1776; del. to Va. conventions, Mar. and Dec., 1775, May 1776.

*BINGHAM, WILLIAM (1752–1804): British consul at St. Pierre, Martinique, 1770–1776; Continental agent in West Indies, 1776–1780; owned privateers; founder, director, Pa. Bank, incorporated as the Bank of North America, 1781; associated with Robert Morris; Pa. del. to Continental Congress, 1786–1789; Pa. Assembly, 1790–1795; U.S. Senate, 1795–1801.

BIRD, WILLIAM: Alexandria flour merchant, 1792; married Catherine, daughter of John Dalton; subscriber to Christ Church, Alexandria, 1785.

BLACKBURN, EDWARD: married Margaret Harrison, 1757; Fairfax Parish vestry, 1765; Prince William County justice of the peace, 1775.

BLACKBURN, RICHARD (1706–1757): born at Ripon, Yorkshire, England; married Mary Watts; brother of Edward Blackburn; father of Thomas Blackburn; settled near Dumfries, Prince William County, where he built Ripon Lodge, and was a planter and building contractor; contracted with Truro vestry to build a church, 1733; Prince William burgess, 1745,

1746, 1747; with GM was an original trustee of Dumfries, 1749; Prince William justice of the peace, 1751. See Tyler, I, 187.

BLACKBURN, THOMAS (*ca.* 1740–1807): son of Richard Blackburn of Ripon Lodge, near Dumfries, Prince William County; married Christian, daughter of Rev. James Scott and cousin of GM; Prince William justice of the peace, 1769; burgess, 1772–1776; committee of safety, 1774–1775; del. to Va. conventions, 1775; lieut. col., 2d Va. Regt., 1776–1777; severely wounded at Germantown; trustee for Dumfries, 1776; original trustee for Newport, 1787, and Centerville, 1792. See obituary in Richmond *Virginia Gazette*, 29 Aug. 1807.

BLADEN, THOMAS (1698–1780): son of Md. secy. and atty. gen., William Bladen; married Barbara, sister-in-law of Charles Calvert, 5th Lord Baltimore, 1731; Md. gov., 1742–1747; disposed of Md. properties, moved to England and became member of Parliament; Bladensburg, Md., named for him.

BLADEN, THOMAS: Fairfax County resident and signer of GM's petition for removal of the courthouse in 1790; does not appear related to Md. family of same name.

BLADEN, WILLIAM: Fairfax County freeholder; possibly son of Thomas Bladen of Fairfax County, although there were two William Bladens (one Jr.), of Fairfax, both listed as heads of households, 1782; a William Bladen was supported by the Fairfax overseers of poor, 1797–1801.

*BLAIR, JOHN (1687–1771): attended William and Mary; deputy auditor-gen. *pro tem.*, 1713; naval officer, upper James River district, 1727; deputy auditor-gen., 1728–1771; burgess, 1734–1740; Va. Council, 1745–1771; acting gov., 1758 and 1768; with associates received from the Council a 100,000-acre grant, west of Fairfax County, 1745; advocated religious toleration.

*BLAIR, JOHN (1732–1800): born in Williamsburg, son of John Blair; married Jean Balfour; attended William and Mary, Middle Temple, 1755; college burgess, 1766–1770; clerk of Council, 1770–1775; college del. to convention of 1776, served on committee to frame constitution and declaration of rights; executive council, 1776, 1777; judge, 1778, and later chief justice of Va. General Court; member, high court of chancery, 1780, and justice of 1st Va. Court of Appeals; del. to Federal Convention, 1787, signer of Constitution; Federalist del. to Va. ratifying convention for York County; associate justice, U.S. Supreme Court, 1789–1796.

*BLAND, RICHARD (1710–1776): son of Richard Bland; attended William and Mary; Prince George County burgess, 1742–1775; wrote *An Inquiry Into the Rights of the British Colonies*, early defense of colonial position on taxation, 1766; opposed Henry's Stamp Act resolutions, 1765; signed Va. nonimportation assn., 1769; del. to Va. conventions, 1775, 1776; Va. committee of safety, 1775; House of Delegates, 1775; Continental Congress, 1774, 1775.

*BLAND, THEODORICK (1742–1790): born in Prince George County; attended school in Yorkshire, 1753–1758; Univ. of Edinburgh, M.D., 1763; practiced medicine in Va., 1764–1771; as "Cassius" attacked Lord Dunmore in *Va. Gazette*, 1775; capt., 1st Va. cavalry, 1776; col., 1st Continental dragoons, 1779; served in N.J., Pa. campaigns; Va. del. to Continental Congress, 1780–1783; House of Delegates, 1786–1788; Antifederalist del. to Va. ratifying convention, 1788; U.S. House of Reps., 1789–1790.

BLAND, WILLIAM: born in Va.; attended William and Mary, 1758–1763; ordained and licensed for Anglican ministry, 1767; minister of James City Parish, 1771, 1774; opposed clerical project to introduce an American bishop, 1771; signed nonimportation assn., 1774; chaplain, 1st Va. Militia Regt., 1775–1776; minister of Warwick Parish, 1785.

BOGGESS, ROBERT (d. *ca.* 1773): lived at La Grange; Fairfax County sheriff, 1739; Truro Parish tithe collector, 1743–1744; Truro Parish vestry, 1745–1773; churchwarden, 1748–1749, 1754–1755, 1759–1761; apparently, name was pronounced "Bogg's." See Harrison, 421, 497.

BONDFIELD, JOHN: American merchant based at Bordeaux, France, 1778; acted as U.S. commercial agent at ports of Bordeaux, Bayonne, Rochefort, and La Rochelle, 1778; partner in firm of Bondfield & Girardeau, 1785; U.S. vice-consul, Bordeaux, 1786, 1787.

BOONE, SAMUEL (b. 1728): born in Oley, Pa., son of "Squire" Boone and Sarah Morgan; brother of Daniel Boone (DAB, *q.v.*); possibly a blacksmith and Quaker; married Sarah Day, educated Quaker who taught Daniel Boone reading and writing; moved to Md. about 1758.

BOSMAN, THOMAS: Fairfax County freeholder, 1744.

*BOUDINOT, ELIAS (1740–1821): began N.J. law practice, 1760; Princeton trustee, 1772–1821; Essex, N.J., committee of correspondence, 1774; N.J. provincial congress, 1775; commissary gen. for American prisoners, 1777; del. to Continental Congress, 1777–1784, and its pres., 1782; secy. of foreign affairs, 1783–1784; supported ratification of the Constitution, 1787; U.S. House of Reps., 1789–1795; director, U.S. Mint, 1795–1805.

BOYD'S HOLE: King George County; a ferrying point on Potomac which was also a seaport for 18th-century Va. tobacco trade; the port was about 16 miles east of Fredericksburg.

*BRADDOCK, EDWARD (1695–1755): commander-in-chief of British forces in North America, 1754; arrived Hampton, Va., 1755; his troops cut wilderness road from Ft. Cumberland toward Ft. Duquesne; fatally wounded when British-American forces were routed by the French, Indians, and Canadians near the Ohio, 9 July 1755.

BRADFORD, WILLIAM: served in 3d Va. Regt., 1775.

BRADLEY, JAMES: possibly William and Mary student, 1763; member of Williamsburg Masonic Lodge, 1778; possible signer of GM's Fairfax County petitions in 1787, 1789.

*BRAXTON, CARTER (1736–1797): born at Newington, King and Queen County, son of George Braxton; attended William and Mary, later served on College Board of Visitors; lived in England, 1758–1760; King William County burgess, 1761–1775, except for brief term as sheriff in early 1770s; signer of Burgesses' resolution claiming sole right to tax Virginians, 1769; signed nonimportation assn., 1769; King William del. to Va. conventions, 1775; Va. committee of safety, 1775; Va. del. to Continental Congress, 1776; signer of Declaration of Independence; Va. House of Delegates and Council, *ca.* 1776–*ca.* 1797; supported Act to Establish Religious Freedom, 1785.

BRENT, DANIEL CARROLL: lived at Richland, Stafford County; son of William Brent (1733–1782) of Richland, and Eleanor Carroll; Stafford del. to Va. lower house, 1759–1814; married Anne Fenton, daughter of Thomas Ludwell Lee, 1782; owned stone quarry on Aquia Creek, and Brent Town Dividend, 1804; brother of Senator Richard Brent.

BRENT, ELIZABETH (d. 1778): youngest daughter of George Brent of Woodstock, sister of GM's wife; died unmarried. See W. B. Chilton, comp., "Genealogy," VMHB, XIX (1911), 94–95.

BRENT, GEORGE (d. 1778): of Woodstock, Stafford County; oldest son of Robert Brent and Susannah Seymour; married Catherine Trimmingham, in Bermuda; served on Stafford committee of correspondence, signed Stafford Resolves, 1774; children included Sarah, GM's 2d wife.

BRENT, JOHN (d. 1813): lived at Norfolk and in Charles County, Md.; son of Sarah Brent Mason's brother, Robert Brent of Woodstock, and Anne Carroll; married a distant relative, Anne, daughter of William Brent of Charles County, Md.

BRENT, RICHARD (1757-1814): lawyer, son of William Brent of Richland, and Eleanor Carroll; brother of Col. Daniel Carroll Brent; Stafford County del. to Va. House of Delegates, 1788, del. for Prince William County, 1793, 1794, 1800, 1801; U.S. House of Reps., 1795-1803; Va. Senate, 1808-1810; U.S. Senate, 1809-1814.

BRENT, ROBERT (ca. 1730-1780): of Woodstock, Stafford County; son of George Brent of Woodstock and Catherine Trimmingham; brother of GM's 2d wife; attended College of St. Omer, Flanders; married Anne, sister of John Carroll; original member, Mississippi Co., 1763; Stafford committee of safety, 1774; owned Aquia quarries; commissioner to locate land for James Hunter's ironworks, 1777; among his children were George and Mayor Robert of Washington, D.C.

BRENT, ROBERT (1764-1819): son of Robert Brent of Woodstock, and Anne Carroll; married Mary, daughter of Notley Young, of Prince Georges County, Md., 1787; 1st mayor of Washington, D.C., serving ten successive terms; orphans' court judge until 1819; U.S. Army paymaster-gen. until 1819. See Chilton, "Genealogy," VMHB, XIX (1911), 96.

BRENT, SARAH (ca. 1730-1806): GM's 2d wife, married Apr. 1780; oldest daughter of George Brent of Woodstock.

BRENT, WILLIAM (1733-1782): of Richland, Stafford County; son of Capt. William Brent of Richland and Hannah Neal; married Eleanor, daughter of Daniel Carroll (1730-1796); Stafford justice of the peace; Stafford committee of safety, 1774; del. to Va. convention, 1776; del. to Va. House of Delegates; father of Sen. Richard Brent, Col. Daniel Carroll Brent.

BRENT, WILLIAM, JR. (ca. 1755-1786): son of William Brent of Richland, Stafford County; capt., Prince William militia, 1776; lieut. col., 1st Va. Regt., 1777; col. 2d Va. Regt., 1778-1781; married Eliza Jacqueline, daughter of Jacquelin Ambler; brother of U.S. Senator Richard Brent and Col. Daniel Carroll Brent. See John H. Gwathmey, Historical Register of Virginians in the Revolution . . . (Richmond, 1938), 91.

BROADWATER, CHARLES (d. 1806): of Springfield, Fairfax County; son of Charles Broadwater; capt., Fairfax militia; served Braddock's campaign, 1755; Truro Parish vestry, 1732-1765, Fairfax Parish vestry, 1765, 1775, 1787; Fairfax justice of the peace, 1770-1789; Fairfax burgess, 1774, 1775; Fairfax committee of safety, 1774; maj., col., Fairfax militia; del. to Va. House of Delegates, 1781.

BROADWATER, GUY: son of Charles Broadwater; brother of Col. Charles Broadwater of Springfield; Truro Parish processioner, 1743, 1751, 1755; surveyed Hampshire County land deeded to GM by Lord Fairfax, 1754.

BROOKBANK, THOMAS: apparently a small planter of Fairfax County; headed a household of nine whites, owned one dwelling in 1785.

BROOKE, HUMPHREY (ca. 1730-1802): of Fauquier County and Dumfries; son of Humphrey Brooke, Sr., and Elizabeth Braxton; Fauquier clerk, 1759-1793, when his son Francis succeeded him; Va. Senate clerk, 1786-1790; Prince William County circuit court clerk, 1789-1793; voted for ratification of the Federal Constitution; Va. Senate, 1791-1802. See Grigsby, II, 198.

BRONAUGH, JEREMIAH (1702-1749): son of Jeremiah Bronaugh of Stafford County; married Simpha Rosa Enfield Mason, aunt of GM, widow of John Dinwiddie who was brother of Gov. Robert Dinwiddie; Truro Parish vestry, 1733-1749, churchwarden, 1734-1735, 1736-1737, 1742-1744; Prince William County sheriff, 1734-1735; Fairfax County justice of the peace, 1742, 1743.

BRONAUGH, WILLIAM (1730-1800): eldest son of Col. Jeremiah Bronaugh; married Margaret Murdock (1760), Mary Cooke (after 1761), Rebecca Craine (1783); ensign, 1754, lieut., capt.; served with Va. troops in the French and Indian War; Stafford County justice of the peace, 1765–1769; member of the Stafford commission of peace; signed Westmoreland County protest against the Stamp Act, 1764; Shelburne Parish vestry, Loudoun County, 1771–1800; trustee of Middleburg, Va., 1787. See Tyler, I, 196.

BROWN, GUSTAVUS RICHARD (1747–1804): born at Rich Hill, Charles County, Md., son of Gustavus Brown, half brother of Frances (Brown) Moncure; married Peggy Graham; physician, botanist, graduate of Univ. of Edinburgh, 1768; Md. Prov. Council, 1774; Charles County committee of correspondence, 1774; judge, Charles County, 1776–1784; supported Constitution in Md. ratifying convention, 1788; visitor, gov. of St. John's College, Annapolis, 1789; attended Washington's last illness.

*BROWN, JAMES (1766–1835): brother of John Brown; practiced law in Ky., where he settled, 1789; Ky. sec. of state, 1792; district atty., Orleans Territory, and prepared its civil code, 1808; U.S. senator, La., 1813–1823; minister to France, 1823–1829.

BROWN, JEAN (1728–1784): daughter of Gustavus Brown and Frances Fowke, cousin of GM, sister of Mrs. John Moncure, Mrs. James Scott, Mrs. John Graham, half sister of Gustavus Richard Brown, Mrs. Thomas Stone; married Rev. Isaac Campbell before 1755; owned large estates in Prince William County, and lived in Charles County, Md.

*BROWN, JOHN (1757–1837): brother of James Brown; settled at Danville, Ky., 1782, but soon moved to Frankfort; Va. senator, Ky. district, 1784–1788; rep. of Ky. district of Va. to Continental and U.S. congresses, 1787–1792; U.S. senator, Ky., 1792–1805.

*BROWN, WILLIAM (1752–1792): grandson of Gustavus Brown and Frances Fowke; Univ. of Edinburgh, M.D., 1770; married Catherine, daughter of Rev. James Scott; settled at Alexandria, Va.; Fairfax County committee of safety, 1774; 2d Va. Regt. surgeon, 1775–1776; Middle Dept. surgeon-gen., 1776–1778, physician-gen. 1778–1780; wrote 1st pharmacopeia published in U.S., 1778; chairman, Alexandria Academy trustees; Fairfax justice of the peace, 1787; Fairfax overseer of poor, 1788.

BROWNE, EDWARD: English clerk, friend and business partner of William Lee. See Worthington C. Ford, *Letters of William Lee* (Brooklyn, 1891), I, 105.

BROWNE, JOHN (d. *ca.* 1793): son of William Browne of James City County; married Sarah, daughter of John Cooper; Va. commissary-gen. during Revolution.

BROWNE, WILLIAM (d. *ca.* 1810): son of William Browne, brother of commissary-gen. John Browne; possibly attended William and Mary, 1754; married Alice Eaton; James City County deputy sheriff, 1789.

BUCHAN, ROBERT: schoolmaster, minister, of Stafford County; rector of Potomac and Aquia parishes, also taught school attended by GM's sons, John and Thomas, 1784–1785.

BUCHANAN, ANDREW: Fredericksburg resident and possibly a lawyer; elected with GM as Stafford County delegate to Va. ratifying convention, 1788, voted against Constitution. See Grigsby, I, 345n.

BUCHANAN, JAMES (d. 1787): Richmond merchant, long engaged in mercantile business on James River; Henrico County committee of safety, 1774; Richmond del. to General Assembly; board of directors, state board to erect public buildings, 1785.

BUCKLAND, WILLIAM (1734–1774): London joiner who left England under indenture to GM's younger brother, Thomson Mason; supervised construction of Gunston Hall, 1755–1758; became independent architect, noted for the Hammond-Harwood house, Annapolis, Md., 1774; completed Truro Parish glebe buildings, 1759-1760.

BUCKNER, PHILIP (1747-1820): known as "capt."; son of John Buckner; married Tabitha Ann Daniel; left his home in Port Royal, Caroline County, for Ky.; founded Augusta, on Ohio River, 1797. See William Buckner McGroarty, "The Family Register of Nicholas Taliferra with Notes," WMQ, 2d Ser., I (1921), 162.

†BURGOYNE, JOHN (1722-1792): British general who commanded troops defeated at Saratoga, 17 Oct. 1777.

BURWELL, LEWIS (1716-1784): of Kingsmill, James City County; son of Lewis Burwell, builder of Kingsmill, grandson of Maj. Lewis Burwell, of the Council, and cousin of Lewis Burwell, Council pres.; married Frances Thacker, widow of James Bray, 1745; James City burgess, 1758-1775.

BURWELL, LEWIS (ca. 1747-1779): son of Council pres. Lewis Burwell; Balliol College, Oxford, 1765; studied law in London at Inner Temple, 1765; Gloucester County sheriff, 1767; Gloucester burgess, 1769-1775; del. to Va. conventions, Mar. and July 1775, May 1776; married Judith, daughter of Mann Page.

BURWELL, NATHANIEL: of Carter's Grove, James City County; son of Carter Burwell; attended William and Mary, 1772; married Susanna Grymes of Middlesex County, 1772; then Mrs. Lucy Page Baylor; appraiser of Peyton Randolph's estate, 1775; apparently member, James City County committee of safety, 1774; James City burgess, 1781; James City del. to Va. ratifying convention, 1788. See Grigsby, II, 376-377.

BUSHROD'S CORNER: Fairfax County; part of GM's holdings on Pohick Creek; originally the dividend of Thomas Speke (1603-1659), passed to Thomas Brererton, clerk of the Council (1657), and Richard Bushrod of Gloucester (1660, 1662), and ultimately to GM's grandfather, George Mason.

BUTLER, PIERCE (1744-1822): born in Ireland; stationed in Boston as an officer in the British army before the Revolution; settled in Charleston, S.C.; del. to Continental Congress, 1787, 1788; del. to Philadelphia Convention, 1787; U.S. senator, 1789-1796, 1802-1804.

BUTLER, WILLIAM (1759-1821): born in Prince William County; son of James Butler, and presumably a distant relative of GM; moved to S.C., 1770; lieut., capt. in Revolution, 1775-1782; del. to S.C. ratifying convention, 1788; S.C. House of Rep., 1787, 1788; sheriff, 96th district, 1794; militia maj. gen., 1796; U.S. House of Reps., 1801-1813; maj. gen. in defense of S.C., War of 1812.

BYRD, WILLIAM III (1729-1777): lived at Westover, Charles City County; commanded 2d Va. Regt., 1755, and assumed Washington's command when latter resigned; Lunenburg County burgess, 1752-1754; Council, 1754-1776; Indian commissioner, built Forts Chiswell and Robinson; married Elizabeth Carter, 1748, and later Mary Willing of Philadelphia, cousin of Mrs. Benedict Arnold; brother-in-law of Landon Carter. See Tyler, I, 161-162; Gov. Francis Fauquier to Hon. William Byrd, Dec. 10, 1760, VMHB, VII (1900), 444-445.

*CABELL, WILLIAM (1730-1798): of Union Hill, Amherst County; son of William Cabell; Amherst County, 1st presiding magistrate of Amherst; 1st county lieut., 1st surveyor, 1st coroner, vestryman, churchwarden, burgess, all by 1761; signed nonimportation assn., 1769; del. to Va. conventions, 1775, 1776; Amherst committee of safety; Va. committee of safety, 1775-1776; served on convention committee for declaration of rights and constitution, 1776; Va. Senate, 1776-1781; House of Delegates, 1781-1783, 1787-1788; opposed Constitution in Va. ratifying convention, 1788; trustee of Hampden-Sydney College.

†CAMERON, ALAN (1753-1828): born in Errach, Scotland, and headed Cam-

eron clan; emigrated to S.C., served as Indian agent and carried royalist dispatches to Va., 1775; served under John Connolly and captured by Md. militia, Nov. 1775; after escape attempts released, 1778; returned to Scotland, later raised "Cameron Highlander" regt., served in Flanders, 1794–1795, Egypt, 1801, Denmark, Sweden, Portugal; knighted, 1815; promoted to lieut. gen., 1819. See obituary in *Gentleman's Magazine*, XCVIII, Pt. I, 367.

CAMPBELL, ARTHUR (1743–1811): born in Augusta County; at 14 captured by Indians and lived with tribe for three years; escaped to British military force, 1759; for services as guide, received land grant near Falls of Ohio; moved to Royal Oak, on Holston River, 1769; col., militia, Washington County, and involved in separatist movement proposing state of Franklin, 1785; died at Middleborough, Ky. See Tyler, II, 239–240.

CAPE CHARLES: southern tip of Northampton County, Va., on Eastern Shore; entrance to Chesapeake Bay lies between Cape Charles at the north and Cape Henry on south.

CARLYLE, JOHN (1720–1780): son of Dr. William Carlyle of Carlisle, England; married Sarah, daughter of Hon. William Fairfax, and later Sybil, daughter of Hugh West; Dumfries agent for a Scottish shipping firm, 1740; business partner of John Dalton at Belle Haven (later Alexandria), 1744–1777; original trustee of Alexandria, 1749; resigned from Ohio Co., 1749; commissary for the Ohio expedition, 1754; succeeded father-in-law, William Fairfax, as South Potomac customs collector, 1758; Fairfax County justice of the peace, 1770; Fairfax committee of safety, 1774–1775. See Gay Montague Moore, *Seaport in Virginia: George Washington's Alexandria* (Richmond, 1949), 14, 17, 21, 62–70.

CARR, WILLIAM (d. 1791): Dumfries merchant, an original incorporator and trustee of Dumfries, 1749, 1761; commissioner to divide Truro Parish property with the newly created Fairfax Parish, 1765; Prince William County committee of safety, 1774; rent collector for Robert Carter's "Frying Pan Tract," 1785–1791; an original trustee of Carrborough, Va., 1788.

* CARRINGTON, PAUL (1733–1818): son of George Carrington of Cumberland County; married Margaret, daughter of Clement Read, Lunenburg County clerk, with whom he studied law; king's atty., Bedford, Mecklenburg, Botetourt, and Lunenburg counties; maj., Lunenburg militia; Charlotte County burgess, 1765–1776; Charlotte lieut., presiding justice; Charlotte committee of safety; Va. conventions, 1775, 1776; convention committee for declaration of rights and constitution; Va. committee of safety, 1775, 1776; Va. senate, 1776–1778; justice of general court, 1779; Va. chief justice, 1780; court of appeals, 1789–1807.

* CARROLL, DANIEL (1730–1796): of Upper Marlborough, Md.; merchant, son of Keene Carroll and brother of Archbishop John Carroll; married Elizabeth W. Carroll of Duddington; shareholder, Mississippi Land Co., 1767; with GM, was supporter of scheme to clear Potomac for navigation, 1774; Md. Council, 1777–1781; Md. Senate, 1781; del. to Continental Congress, 1781–1787; del. to Federal Convention, 1787.

CARTER, CHARLES (*ca.* 1728–1796): called "Jr.," of Nanzatico, King George County, and Ludlow, Stafford County; son of Charles Carter of Cleves and Mary Walker, and grandson of Robert "King" Carter; married Elizabeth (1722–1776), daughter of Col. John Chiswell and Elizabeth Randolph; King George burgess, 1756–1771, Stafford burgess, 1773–1776, and del. for Stafford, 1781; signed nonimportation associations, 1769, 1774; an owner of "Frying Pan Tract." See Jack P. Greene, ed., *The Diary of Landon Carter* (Charlottesville, 1965), 130*n*, 463*n*, 641*n*.

CARTER, CHARLES (1732–1806): of Corotoman, Lancaster County, and after 1771 Shirley, Charles City County;

eldest son of John Carter and Elizabeth Hill, daughter of Col. Edward
Hill; grandson of Robert "King"
Carter; married Mary W. Carter,
daughter of Col. Charles Carter of
Cleve, and later Ann Butler Moore,
daughter of Bernard Moore; brother
of Edward, brother-in-law of William Byrd III, nephew of Landon
Carter, cousin of Robert Carter of
Nomini; attended William and
Mary, 1753, 1754; Lancaster County
burgess, 1758–1776; signed nonimportation assn., 1769, 1774; board of visitors, William and Mary, 1769, 1772;
Lancaster County committee of
safety, 1775; del. to Va. conventions,
1775; state council, 1776; daughter
Ann Hill married "Lighthorse Harry"
Lee. See Tyler, I, 204.

CARTER, LANDON (1709–1778): son of
Robert "King" Carter and Elizabeth
Landon, brother of Robert Carter of
Nomini; lived at Sabine Hall on the
Rappahannock; Richmond County
burgess, 1748–1765; served on committee preparing remonstrance against
Stamp Act, 1764; Richmond committee of safety; married Elizabeth (d.
1740), daughter of John Wormeley,
then Maria (d. 1744), daughter of
William Byrd, and finally Elizabeth,
daughter of Thomas Beale; eldest son
was Robert Wormeley Carter. See
Greene, ed., *Diary of Landon Carter*.

CARTER, ROBERT (1728–1804): of Nomini Hall, Westmoreland County; son
of Robert Carter of Nomini and
grandson of Robert "King" Carter;
married Frances Ann (d. 1787),
youngest daughter of Hon. Benjamin
Tasker of Md., 1754; lived in Williamsburg, 1761–1772; admitted to
Inner Temple, 1764; Council,
[1758–1776]; member of Ohio Co.;
possessed one of the finest private
libraries in America; died in Baltimore. Louis Morton, *Robert Carter
of Nomini Hall* (Williamsburg,
1945).

CARTER, ROBERT WORMELEY
(1734–1797): of Sabine Hall; eldest
son of Landon Carter of Sabine Hall
and 1st wife, Elizabeth Wormeley;
Richmond County burgess, 1769–1776;

del. to Va. Conventions, 1775; House
of Delegates, 1776–1787; married
Winifred Travers Beale, daughter of
Capt. William Beale of Richmond
County. See Louis Morton, "Robert
Wormeley Carter of Sabine Hall:
Notes on the Life of a Virginia Plan-
ter," *Journal of Southern History*,
XII (1946), 345–365.

CARTWRIGHT, THOMAS: tavern-keeper
living at Burwell's Ferry, 1775; moved
to Thomas Doncastle's Ordinary by
Jan. 1776; probably moved to Williamsburg by 1780; member, Williamsburg Masonic Lodge, 1775–1781;
went to Nova Scotia, 1783, and entered a claim as a loyalist.

* CARY, ARCHIBALD (1721–1787):
known as "Old Iron," "Old Bruiser";
married Mary Randolph; Goochland
County burgess, 1748–1749; moved to
Ampthill after father (Henry Cary)
died; Chesterfield County burgess,
1756–1776; opposed Henry's Stamp
Act resolutions, 1765; but signed nonimportation assns., 1769, 1770, 1774;
del. to Va. conventions, 1775, 1776;
lay del. to convention to reorganize
the Protestant Episcopal Church,
1785.

CASWELL, RICHARD (1729–1789): N.C.
lawyer; N.C. House of Commons,
1754–1771, speaker, 1769–1771; Continental Congress, 1774–1776; commander at Battle of Moore's Creek
Bridge, N.C., Feb. 1776; brigadier
gen., New Bern militia district,
1776; pres. N.C. constitutional convention, 1776; N.C. gov., 1776–1780,
1785–1788; commanded N.C. troops at
Camden, 1780; comptroller gen., 1782;
N.C. Senate Speaker, 1782–1784; N.C.
ratifying convention, Fayetteville,
1789; Speaker, N.C. lower house, 1789.

CHAMPNEY, WILLIAM: Fairfax County
freeholder; Truro Parish processioner, 1743; clerk, New Church,
Truro Parish, 1746. See Philip Slaughter, *History of Truro Parish*, ed. Rev.
E. L. Goodwin (Philadelphia, 1908),
19, 25, 128.

CHANTILLY: Westmoreland County;
home of Richard Henry Lee.

CHAPMAN, CONSTANTIA PEARSON (*ca.* 1714–*ca.* 1791): daughter of Simon Pearson of Overwharton Parish, Stafford County; wife of Nathaniel Chapman; Pearson Chapman (d. 1784) was her son; daughter Lucy was 3d wife of Col. Samuel Washington.

CHAPMAN, NATHANIEL (*ca.* 1710–*ca.* 1760): son of Jonathan Chapman; married Constantia, daughter of Simon Pearson; Fairfax County merchant; lived in Charles County, Md., also owned large tracts in Prince William and Fairfax counties; Ohio Co. treasurer until Sept. 1749, when succeeded by GM; directed the Principio Iron Works in Md.; executor for both Lawrence and Augustine Washington.

CHAPMAN, PEARSON (1745–1784): son of Nathaniel Chapman; married Susanna Alexander; ancestor of Dr. Nathaniel Chapman (1780–1853), distinguished physician. See Harrison, 262–263.

* CHASE, SAMUEL (1741–1811): Annapolis lawyer; Md. Assembly, 1764–1774; member of Annapolis Sons of Liberty; Md. committee of correspondence, 1774; del. to Continental Congress, 1774–1778, 1780; Md. convention, 1775; Md. council of safety, 1775; signer of Declaration of Independence, 1776; attended with GM, Mount Vernon convention, 1785; del. to Federal Convention, 1787; Baltimore chief criminal justice, 1788; Md. General Court chief justice, 1791; opposed ratification of the Constitution under the signature "Caution," but later turned Federalist; named to U.S. Supreme Court, 1796, impeached, tried, acquitted, 1804–1805.

CHEW, LARKIN: son of Col. Thomas Chew of Orange County; lieut., Byrd's 2d Va. Regt. and wounded, 1754; pensioned, and still on rolls, 1785.

CHICHESTER, RICHARD (*ca.* 1736–1796): Col. of Fairfax County; son of Richard Chichester and Ellen Ball; married Ann, daughter of Col. James Gordon of Lancaster County, 1759, and later Sarah, daughter of Col.

Daniel McCarty, *ca.* 1766; moved to Fauquier County, 1765, and then to Fairfax County, probably shortly after his 2d marriage; Fairfax lieut.; commissioner of specific tax for Fairfax, 1781; signed GM's Fairfax petitions to separate Fairfax and Alexandria jurisdictions (1787) and to move county courthouse (1789, 1790); Fairfax justice of the peace, 1789–1790; daughter Sarah married GM's son, Thomson Mason, of Hollin Hall. See Horace E. Hayden, *Virginia Genealogies* (Washington, 1931), 107.

CHILTON, STEPHEN: ship captain, son of Capt. Thomas Chilton of Westmoreland County; sailed on the *Liberty*, 1771; apparently worked with William Lee, brother of R. H. Lee. See James C. Ballagh, comp., *The Letters of Richard Henry Lee* (N.Y., 1911–1914), I, 60.

CHIPAWANSIC (CHAPPAWAMSIC, CHOPAWANSICK): creek, part of which is a swamp, entering the Potomac River near Dumfries; forms the boundary between Prince William and Stafford counties; also, a plantation which was the dower land of GM's mother; GM lived there some time after the death of his father, in 1735.

CHISWELL'S MINES: Wythe County; also known as "The Lead Mines," located on west bank of the New River in what was then Augusta County; discovered by Col. John Chiswell (1726?–1766); important sources of lead in munitions manufacture; Fort Chiswell was built a few miles west of the mines in 1758; were still in production as late as 1893.

CHOTANK PARISH: Stafford County; lower parish of Stafford, south of Potomac Creek; name derived from the creek which drained the area; at the beginning of the 18th century, name officially changed to St. Paul's Parish. See also OVERWHARTON PARISH and POTOMAC CREEK.

*CHRISTIAN, WILLIAM (*ca.* 1743–1786): capt. in Col. William Byrd's Va. regt., 1755; studied law under Patrick Henry, and married his sister, Anne; Fincastle County burgess,

1773–1775; commanded Fincastle militia in Dunmore's War, 1774; committee of safety, 1775; Va. convention, Mar., July 1775; lieut. col., 1st Va. Regt., Continental line, Feb. to Aug., 1776; col., Va. militia; led successful expedition against Cherokees in Holston and Watauga valleys; commissioner to treat with Cherokees, 1777; Botetourt-Fincastle senator, 1776, 1780–1785; moved to vicinity of present-day Louisville, Ky., 1785; died in raid against Wabash Indians.

CHRISTMASS, CHARLES: Fairfax Cty. freeholder; Truro Parish sexton, 1733, 1734. See Truro Parish Vestry Book (DLC), 10 June 1733, 18 Nov. 1735.

CHURCH, ROBERT: Fairfax County freeholder; official of Truro Parish vestry; signed Madison's "Memorial & Remonstrance" against Assessment bill which GM circulated, 1785; signed GM's petition to remove courthouse, 1789, 1790; worked with county overseers of the poor, 1795.

* CLARK, GEORGE ROGERS (1752–1818): born in Albemarle County; surveyed Ohio region, 1772–1774; militia capt., Dunmore's War, 1774; wanted Ky. under Va. jurisdiction; encouraged by GM, led a Va. expedition against British, Indians in the West, 1777–1779; Va. commissioner to allot Illinois lands, treat with Northwest Indians, until 1786; deeply involved in various western colonization schemes, particularly with the French, 1788–1798.

CLARK, THOMAS: Fairfax County freeholder and apparently a friend of GM's; witnessed marriage contract between GM and Sarah Brent, 1780; sided with GM in battle over repeal of the act against extensive credit, 1783.

CLARKE, [JOSEPH?]: ship captain, commanded the ship *Tom* in Va.-London tobacco trade before Revolution; apparently returned to the sea after the war as skipper of the *Commerce*, which sailed between London and the Potomac ports.

*CLINTON, GEORGE (1739–1812): N.Y. gov., 1777–1795, 1800–1804; opposed legislative grant of N.Y. port import duties to Congress, 1781; secured law enabling N.Y. state officials to collect duties, 1783; strong opponent of Constitution; pres., N.Y. ratifying convention, June 1788; finally acquiesced in ratification by N.Y. after Constitution had been ratified by nine states; U.S. vice-pres., 1804–1812.

COCKBURN, MARTIN: born in Jamaica; married Ann Bronaugh, cousin of GM's; his estate Springfield adjoined Gunston Hall; Truro Parish vestry, 1774; Fairfax county committee of safety, 1774; Cockburns were godparents to Elizabeth, GM's youngest daughter; executor of GM's will.

COF(F)ER, JOHN: ensign, George Mason, Jr.'s minuteman company, 1776; as 2d lieuts., he and Charles Lewis Broadwater were court-martialed, dismissed from the 10th Va. Regt. for illegally procuring clothing from the Va. state military stores, 1778; possibly charter trustee of Occoquan, Va., 1804. See Harrison, 667.

COFFER, THOMAS WITHERS (1713–1781): son of Francis Coffer and Mary Littlejohn Withers; married Mary Farguson (1715–1758); Truro Parish vestry, 1765–1781, and churchwarden, 1768–1769, 1771–1772. See Philip Slaughter, *A History of Truro Parish*, ed. Rev. E. L. Goodwin (Philadelphia, 1908), 118.

COLVILLE, JOHN (d. 1755): son of John Colville, born at Newcastle-on-Tyne, England; captain of one or more Potomac trade ships by 1733; Truro Parish vestry, 1734, 1744; churchwarden, 1740–1741; Prince William County justice of the peace, 1734–1742; Fairfax County justice of the peace, 1742–1755; Prince William militia col., 1740; Prince William burgess, 1743–1747; commissioner for selecting site for Prince William courthouse, 1740.

CONEMAUGH RIVER (CONEMACH, CONEMOUGH, CONIMUCH, CONNUMACH, KUNNUMAX): river with headwaters in Cambria County, Pa., which unites with the Loyalhanna River at Saltsbury, Indiana County, Pa., to form the Kiskiminetas River.

CONNER (CONNOR), SAMUEL: was paid by Truro Parish for upkeep of a poor child, 1741–1758; possibly a member of the Occoquan Baptist Church, Prince William County, 1776.

CONNER, [TERRENCE?]: capt. of the ship Industry, registered out of Petersburg, Va.; may have resided in Fairfax County in 1780s.

CONNOCOCHEEGE (CONOCOCHEAGUE) CREEK: stream originating in south-central Pa. flowing south into Potomac at Williamsport, Md.

CONNOLLY, JOHN (b. ca. 1750); frontier agent, loyalist; born in Lancaster, Pa.; close associate of George Croghan, who saved him from debtor's prison; appointed by Gov. Dunmore as agent in Va.-Pa. boundary dispute and arrested by Pa. officials for claiming disputed area; released, he returned with 80 men and arrested the Pa. authorities, occupied Fort Pitt and renamed it Fort Dunmore, 1774; appointed by Dunmore to head secret western mission, 1775, but was captured in Md., jailed in Philadelphia; escaped to Canada, 1781; led force which destroyed Hannastown, 1782; testified before commissioners on loyalist claims, London, 1784; for involvement in British intrigues to capture New Orleans, 1788–1789, was expelled from Ky. See Nicholas B. Wainwright, George Croghan, Wilderness Diplomat (Chapel Hill, 1959), 286–295.

CONSTABLE, DAVID: born County Fordyce, Scotland; apparently a longtime friend of Rev. John Scott, son of Rev. James Scott; M.A., King's College, Aberdeen, 1770; tutor, Gunston Hall, 1774–1781; surveyed GM's lands, 1780; went to St. Christopher's, B.W.I., 1781; commanded a trading ship in 1782, 1783, sailing between West Indies, southern U.S. ports, and Scotland. See Royal Gazette (Jamica) 8 June 1782; Hayden, Virginia Genealogies, 614.

CONTEE, THOMAS: of Brookfield, Prince Georges County, Md.; Md.

council of safety, 1776–1777; often chairman of Patuxent Associators, 1781. See Richard Henry Spencer, "Hon. Nicholas Thomas," Md. Hist. Mag., VI (1911), 159; "Minutes of the Board of Patuxent Associators," ibid., 305, 306–308, 317.

CONWAY, RICHARD: son of John Conway and Frances Sinah Span(n); married Mary, daughter of John West and Margaret Pearson Terrett; settled in Alexandria, commanded a trading vessel by 1771; Fairfax County committee of safety, 1775; signed Alexandria petitions of merchants and sea adventurers to General Assembly, for a naval office, 1779, also petitions to increase the power of Congress over commerce, 1785, and on the establishment of bank discounts, 1792; Fairfax justice of the peace, 1787; mayor of Alexandria, 1800.

CONYNGHAM (CUNNINGHAM), GUSTAVUS (1747–1819): born in Ireland; married Anne Hockley, daughter of Philadelphia merchant, 1773; Revolutionary blockade runner and privateer on ships Charming Peggy, Surprise, and Revenge; raided enemy ships in English channel; commanded brig Maria during Quasi-War with France. See R. W. Neeser, ed., Letters and Papers . . . of Gustavus Conyngham (New York, 1915).

COOKE, JOHN (1755–1823): born in Stafford County, son of Travers Cooke and Mary Doniphan; married GM's daughter, Mary Thomson; lived at West Farm, Stafford County; Aquia vestry, 1815–1823.

CORBIN, FRANCIS (1759–1821): of Buckingham Lodge, Middlesex County, then The Reeds, Caroline County; son of Richard Corbin, councillor and receiver general; studied in England at Canterbury school, Cambridge, Inner Temple; returned to Va. after Revolution; married Ann Munford, daughter of Robert Beverly; Middlesex del. to Va. lower house, 1784–1794; Federalist in the Va. ratifying convention, 1788; rector, William and Mary, 1790; fought Edmund Pendleton's Memorial against the Alien and Sedition Acts, 1798.

CORBIN, GAWIN (d. 1760): son of Gawin Corbin, of King and Queen County, and Jane Lane; lived at Pekatone, Westmoreland County, and Laneville, King and Queen County; married Hannah, daughter of Thomas Lee of Stratford; King and Queen burgess, 1736–1740; Middlesex burgess, 1742–1747; executor of Thomas Lee of Stratford.

CORBIN, RICHARD (1708–1790): of Buckingham House and Corbin Hall, Middlesex County, and Laneville, King and Queen County; son of Gawin Corbin, brother of Gawin Corbin of the Ohio Co., brother-in-law of John Tayloe, father-in-law of Carter Braxton; attended William and Mary; married Betty, daughter of John Tayloe; executor of Thomas Lee of Stratford; Middlesex burgess, 1748–1749; Va. Council, 1751–1776; receiver-general for Va. quit-rents, 1754–1776; Board of Visitors, William and Mary, 1776; Stratton Major Parish vestry, King and Queen County, 1739, churchwarden, 1760; influential in procuring Washington's 1st military commission; fought paper money emissions in "The Palladium of Virginia's Credit," 1764; intermediary between Dunmore and Va. committee of safety, Jan. 1776; widely known as a loyalist, but retired at the beginning of the war; after Dunmore resigned, received a commission to be royal gov., but Corbin hid it; signed loyalist petition, 1778. See his Letter Books, 1758–1768 (ViWC); David John Mays, Edmund Pendleton; a Biography, (Cambridge, Mass., 1952) I, 152; II, 87–90.

COTTON, JOHN: of Fairfax County and an acquaintance of GM; signed petition against repeal of an act to prevent extensive credits, and Madison's petition "Memorial & Remonstrance" against Assessment bill of 1785.

CRAFTS, THOMAS: sailmaker, Fairfax County, 1778; may later have located in Norfolk.

*CRAIK, JAMES (1730–1814): born near Dumfries, Scotland; married Marianne Ewell; University of Edinburgh, M.D.; emigrated, 1750; practiced in West Indies, Norfolk, and at Winchester, where he was fort surgeon; commissioned surgeon of Col. Fry's regt., 1754; became Washington's chief medical officer; served with army as asst. director-gen. of hospitals from 1777; promoted to chief physician and surgeon of the army, 1781–1783; director-gen. of hospital department, 1798; physician-gen., 1798–1800; attended Washington's last illness.

*CRAWFORD, WILLIAM (1732–1782): farmer, frontiersman, surveyor; served with Washington in Braddock's campaign, 1755; active in capture of Fort Duquesne and in Pontiac's rebellion; succeeded Christopher Gist as Ohio Co. surveyor, 1759; land agent for Washington; officer Va. regts., 1776–1777; served under Gen. Lachlan McIntosh, 1778; resigned in 1781, but later joined punitive expedition against Indians in Ohio valley; captured by Delawares and burned at the stake, 1782.

CRESAP, DANIEL: called "col."; oldest son of Thomas Cresap; lived near Old Town, Washington County, Md.; served in French and Indian War; sold lands in Hampshire County, 1777. See Kenneth P. Bailey, The Ohio Company of Virginia and the Westward Movement, 1748–1792 (Glendale, Calif., 1939), 49.

*CRESAP, THOMAS (1702–1790): born Yorkshire, England; emigrated to Md., ca. 1717; married Hannah Johnson, ca. 1727; father of Col. Daniel Cresap; moved to area near present-day Wrightsville, Pa., where settlers disputed Md. jurisdiction and burned his home; served as Md. militia capt., later moved to Shawnee Oldtown, the western-most Md. settlement; had trading post on Iroquois-Cherokee war trail; commissioned by GM and Ohio Co. shareholders to clear passage from Wills Creek to junction of Redstone and Monongahela rivers.

*CROGHAN, GEORGE (d. 1782): born near Dublin, Ireland; emigrated to frontier area near Carlisle, Pa., 1741, and established a trading base; expert in Iroquois and Delaware languages and customs, a leading Indian agent for Pa.; Indian scout with Washington and Braddock, 1755; deputy to Sir William Johnson, northern superintendent of Indian affairs, 1756–1772; built Croghan Hall, 1758, and patented thousands of acres in N.Y. and Pa.; member of Indiana and Illinois companies, charter member of Vandalia company; Revolution wrecked his land schemes, and he was impoverished for the rest of this life. See Wainwright, *Croghan.*

CUSTIS, JOHN PARKE (1755–1781): son of Martha Washington by her 1st husband, Daniel Parke Custis; tutored by Rev. Jonathan Boucher at Annapolis; attended King's College, N.Y.; married Eleanor, daughter of Benedict Calvert of Mount Airy, Prince Georges County, Md., and granddaughter of Charles Calvert, 6th Lord Baltimore; wealthy and owned many slaves; member of the Va. House of Delegates; died of fever during the Yorktown campaign.

CUSTIS, MARTHA (*ca.* 1756–1773): daughter of Martha Washington by her 1st husband, Daniel Parke Custis; called "Patsy"; died of epilepsy, 1773. See Mount Vernon Ladies Association of the Union, *Annual Report, 1960,* 21, 27.

DADE, TOWNSHEND, JR. (d. 1781): Fairfax County freeholder, 1744; Fairfax Parish vestry, 1765; Fairfax justice of the peace; Fairfax committee of safety, 1774; rector of Christ Church, Alexandria, 1765–1778; possibly minister in Truro Parish, 1774; (not the Townshend Dade of Chotank, a Stafford justice of the peace and St. Paul's Parish vestryman). See . . . *Industrial and Historical Sketch of Fairfax County* . . . (Falls Church, Va., 1907), 47.

DALTON, JOHN (d. 1777): business partner in Carlyle and Dalton, longtime agents for Mt. Vernon; Alexan-

dria trustee, 1750; committee to superintend completion of the Alexandria courthouse, 1754; Truro Parish processioner, 1755; Fairfax Parish vestry, 1765, 1773; signed Fairfax County nonimportation agreement, 1770; a Va. trustee for John Ballendine's project for clearing Potomac navigation, 1774; Fairfax committee of safety, 1774–1775; committee for the defense of the Potomac with GM; Potomac agent for purchasing commodities for the export trade with the West Indies to supply Va. military forces, 1776. See Moore, *Seaport,* 71–72.

DANDRIDGE, BARTHOLOMEW (1737–1785): son of Col. John Dandridge of New Kent County, and brother of Martha Washington; married Elizabeth Macon, sister of Mrs. William Aylett; successful lawyer in county court practice; New Kent burgess, 1772–1776; del. to Va. conventions, 1775, 1776; member of convention committee to draft constitution and bill of rights, 1776; Va. Council, 1776; House of Delegates; justice, Va. General Court, 1778, 1781, 1782.

DANIEL, PETER (b. 1706): son of James Daniel, father of Travers Daniel; married Sarah Travers Pearson, daughter of Rawleigh Travers, widow of Capt. Christopher Pearson, 1736; settled in Northumberland County area which became part of reorganized Stafford County; Stafford justice, 1744 until death; Aquia vestry, 1757; first signer of Stamp Act protest, 5 Oct. 1765; Stafford committee, 1774. See Hayden, *Virginia Genealogies,* 295–297.

DANIEL, TRAVERS SR. (1741–1824): son of Peter Daniel; born at Mt. Pleasant, lived at Tranquility, Stafford County; married Frances Moncure, daughter of Rev. John Moncure and Frances Brown, goddaughter of GM, 1762; Stafford justice of the peace, 1765, and then presiding justice; Stafford committee of safety, 1774; among children was Travers (married to Mildred, daughter of Hon. Thomas Stone of Md.), House of Delegates,

1790–1793, and a Stafford justice, 1788.
DARNALL, JOHN (d. 1768): of Frederick County, Md.; related to the Carroll family; member, Frederick County Associates, Frederick committee of observation, 1775–1776. See "Extracts from the Carroll Papers," *Md. Hist. Mag.*, XI (1916), 264, 326.

DARRELL, SAMPSON: son of William Darrell and Ann Mason, GM's aunt; descended from Sir Marmaduke Darrell, a member of the Va. Company, and prominent Stafford County family; processioner for Truro Parish, 1743–1751; unsuccessful candidate for Fairfax Parish vestry, 1765; Fairfax sheriff, 1767; Fairfax justice of the peace, 1770. See Slaughter, *Truro Parish*, ed. Goodwin, 19, 29, 44–45, 129.

DAVIDSON, JOHN: Scottish tutor who apparently taught at Gunston Hall around 1770–1773 and had been brought to America by GM.

*DAVIE, WILLIAM RICHARDSON (1756–1820): born in Egremont, Cumberland, England; brought to America in 1763 and adopted by relative; attended Queen's Museum College, Charlotte, N.C., and College of New Jersey (Princeton); served in cavalry during Revolution, severely wounded near Charleston, 1779; studied law and licensed in Salisbury, N.C., 1780; del. to N.C. ratifying convention, 1788, and served N.C. legislature, where was instrumental in chartering Univ. of N.C.; gov. of N.C., 1798; Federalist, appointed brig. gen. in Quasi-War with France, peace commissioner on delegation sent to France, 1799.

DAVIS, AUGUSTINE: born at Yorktown; married Martha Davenport, 1778; partner of John Clarkson in publishing the *Va. Gazette*, Williamsburg, 1778; they were state printers, 1779; 1st newspaper printer-editor in Richmond, 1779; Federalist, postmaster in John Adams's administration.

*DAWSON, JOHN (1762–1814): of Spotsylvania County; graduated Harvard, *ca.* 1782; House of Delegates for Spotsylvania, 1786–1789; Antifederalist Spotsylvania del. to Va. ratifying

convention, 1788; Va. executive council; presidential elector, 1793; carried ratified convention to France, 1800; Republican congressman, 1797–1814.

DEAKINS, WILLIAM (d. *ca.* 1816): Georgetown, Md., merchant; a Md. trustee for Ballendine's project for clearing Potomac navigation, 1774; owned Revolutionary War privateers through firm of O'Neal, Deakins & Co.; collected Georgetown Hundred subscriptions for arms, 1775; a William Deakin, Jr., was delegate to the Md. ratifying convention, 1788. See J. T. Scharff, *History of Baltimore* (Philadelphia, 1881), 100–104.

DELAP and HANS: Bordeaux mercantile firm operated by S. Delap and John Hans; served as commercial agents for U.S., 1778; claimed Continental Congress and private U.S. citizens had unpaid balances, 1787.

DENEALE, WILLIAM: of Fairfax County; Truro Parish vestry, 1781–1785; Fairfax sheriff, 1799–1802; signed Fairfax petition against British debts, 1783, and GM's petition to move the county courthouse, 1789, 1790; related to George Deneale, Fairfax clerk, 1798–1801.

D'ESTAING, COMTE. See ESTAING, COMTE D' (Charles Hector).

DETTINGEN PARISH: Prince William County; divided from Hamilton Parish, 1744; used old Overwharton Parish chapel at Quantico until a new parish church was built at Dumfries in 1752.

DICK, CHARLES (1715–1783): of Spotsylvania County; married Mary Roy, a distant cousin of GM's; resided in Fredericksburg, associated with Col. Fielding Lewis in weapons factory that was subsidized by Va.

*DICK, ELISHA CULLEN (1762–1825): born in Pa.; attended Philadelphia Pequa Academy; medical studies with Dr. Benjamin Rush, 1780; entered office of Dr. William Shippen; M.B., U. Pa., 1782; settled in Alexandria; led cavalry in Whiskey Rebellion, 1794; Alexandria mayor, 1804; an attending physician during Washington's final illness.

DICK, JAMES: emigrated from England, 1734; slave dealer and merchant at Londontown, Md., 1734; partner of son-in-law Anthony Stewart in James Dick and Stewart, Annapolis, *ca.* 1764; signed Annapolis nonimportation assn., 1769; defended John Buchanan in case of violation of nonimportation assn., 1770; shared financial interest in the *Peggy Stewart,* owned by Anthony Stewart. See Elihu S. Riley, *A History of Anne Arundel County* (Annapolis, 1905), 58–60.

*DICKINSON, JOHN (1732–1808): born in Md.; studied law in England and practiced in Philadelphia; his *Letters from a Farmer in Pennsylvania* (1767–1768) were classic exposition of colonial rights; del. to Continental Congress, 1775–1777, 1779–1780, but voted against Declaration of Independence; served as pres. of Del., 1781–1782 and Pa., 1782–1785; Del. rep. at Federal Convention, 1787; urged adoption of the Constitution under the pen name "Fabius."

DIFFICULT RUN: northern boundary of Fairfax County when Loudoun County was first created; boundary was later (1762) moved north leaving Difficult Run entirely in Fairfax County; enters the Potomac about ten miles northwest of Alexandria.

DIGGES, COLE (b. 1748): son of Dudley Digges (1718–1790) and Martha Armistead; married Margaret, sister of Col. William Walker.

DIGGES, COLE (1754–1817): of Warwick County; maj. in Spotswood's Legion, 1781; Va. General Assembly, 1778–1783; Va. ratifying convention, 1788.

DIGGES, DUDLEY (1718–1790): of York County and Williamsburg; son of Col. Cole Digges and Elizabeth Power; lawyer; col. of horse and foot, 1748; York receiver of military fines, 1749; York burgess, 1752–1776; del. to Va. conventions, 1775, 1776; Va. committee of safety, 1775–1776; Va. Council, 1776–1780; state examiner of claims during war.

DIGGES, WILLIAM: of Warburton, Prince Georges County, Md., nearly opposite Mount Vernon, and site where Fort Washington was built.

DIGGES, WILLIAM (1742–1780): called "col.," of Bellfield; married Elizabeth, daughter of William Digges of Denbigh.

*DINWIDDIE, ROBERT (1693–1770): born near Glasgow, Scotland; merchant, customs collector, surveyor-gen. for southern colonies, 1738; lived in Va., became *ex officio* member of Va. Council, 1741; royal gov. of Va., 1751–1758; quarreled with House of Burgesses over pistole fee and land patents, Board of Trade ruled against him; supporter of Ohio Co. petition for royal grant in Ohio valley; helped Gen. Braddock prepare for campaign against Fort Duquesne, 1755; was distant relative of GM's; left Va., 1758.

DIXON, JOHN (d. 1791): Williamsburg printer; married Rosanna, daughter of William Hunter, 2d printer of the *Va. Gazette* and widow of Joseph Royle (d. 1766); partner of Alexander Purdie in the *Gazette,* from Hunter's death until 1774, when formed a new partnership with William Hunter, Jr.; died in Richmond. See Tyler, I, 224.

*DOBBS, ARTHUR (1689–1765): born in Ireland; high sheriff of Antrim, 1720; engineer-in-chief and surveyor of Ireland, 1730; actively promoted exploration for northwest passage, from 1730; published *An Account of the Countries Adjoining to Hudson's Bay,* 1744, favoring dissolution of the Hudson Bay Co.; as gov. of N.C., 1754, brought the colony into mainstream of intercolonial affairs. See Clarke Desmond, *Arthur Dobbs Esquire, 1689–1765* (Chapel Hill, 1957).

DOGUES (DOEG'S, DOGUE'S) NECK: a jut of land in Fairfax County between Occoquan and Pohick creeks that extends into the Potomac; large areas of the neck were acquired by GM and his father; GM was born on the neck and he built Gunston Hall here (1755–1758); identified as "High P[oin]t." on Fry-Jefferson map (1794 ed.); by mid-twentieth century the area was popularly known as Mason

Neck, and the older name is known only to antiquarians.

DONALD, ALEXANDER: probably a Scottish tobacco merchant who moved to Va. before 1775; Richmond merchant after 1781; carried on slave transaction, Hanover County, 1785. See James H. Soltow, *The Economic Role of Williamsburg* (Williamsburg, 1965), 51.

DONALDSON, ROBERT: Alexandria merchant and former business partner of William Hartshorne, 1792; perhaps the merchant Robert Donaldson, from Fayetteville, N.C. (1764–1808); buried in Petersburg, Va. The Brock Collection (CSmH) has the papers dissolving the partnership of Hartshorne and Donaldson of Alexandria.

DONELSON, JOHN (*ca.* 1724–1783): of Pittsylvania County; Camden Parish vestry, 1769; county surveyor, 1767–1779; burgess, 1769–1774; county militia lieut., 1775–1777; worked with James Robertson, Richard Henderson in western land colonization schemes, 1778–1779; helped establish Nashborough on Cumberland River; moved to Ky., supported petition to Congress for separate statehood; killed by Indians; daughter, Rachel, married Andrew Jackson (1767–1845). See Dale Van Every, *A Company of Heroes: The American Frontier, 1775–1783* (New York, 1962), 223–227.

DOUGLASS, ROBERT: Fairfax County freeholder, performed minor services for Truro Parish vestry, father of William Douglass.

DOUGLASS, WILLIAM: of Fairfax County; son of Robert Douglass; resident of Truro Parish, dealt with Dumfries merchant Daniel Payne. See Henry J. Berkley, "The Port of Dumfries, Prince William County, Virginia," WMQ, 2d Ser., IV (1924), 99–116.

DRIVER, JOHN: of Suffolk County; active in tobacco shipping trade, *ca.* 1767; probably served on Isle of Wight County committee of safety, 1775; sold supplies to Southampton County militia, 1776; may have been

Upper Nansemond Parish vestryman, 1777–1785.

*DULANY, DANIEL (1722–1797): son of Daniel Dulany, Sr.; studied at Eton, Cambridge, Middle Temple; admitted to Md. bar, 1747; married Rebecca, daughter of Benjamin Tasker, 1749; Md. Assembly, 1751–1754, 1756; Md. Council, 1757–1776; commissary-gen., 1759–1761; Md. secy., 1761–1774; wrote *Considerations on the Propriety of Imposing Taxes in the British Colonies . . .* (1765); retired as a loyalist to Hunting Ridge, near Baltimore, when Revolution began; nearly all his property was confiscated; died in Baltimore. See A. C. Land, *The Dulanys of Maryland* (Baltimore, 1955).

DUMFRIES: Prince William County; shipping and commercial center; GM a trustee when town incorporated, 1749; became county seat of Prince William in 1759; when tobacco trade fell during the Revolution, Dumfries commercial activity declined rapidly; the decay was hastened by the silting of the wharves on the Potomac so that large ships could no longer dock; the county seat was removed to Brentsville in 1822.

DUNBAR, ROBERT: Scottish merchant based at Falmouth, on Rappahannock River; married Elizabeth Gregory, daughter of Francis Thornton (d. 1795) and Ann Thompson, of Spotsylvania County; probably assisted county committee of safety in purchases of saltpeter and sulphur, 1775.

DUNLAP, JAMES: factor for Dunlap, Cross & Co., 1776, whose business centered in Falmouth–Fredericksburg area; made a deposition in an Essex County stolen tobacco case, 1772–1773.

*DUNMORE, JOHN MURRAY (1732–1809); 4th Earl of, also Viscount Fincastle; Scottish peer; gov. of N.Y., 1771; royal gov. of Va., 1771–1775; rebuilt Fort Dunmore (later Pittsburgh), 1773; launched attack from there against the Shawnees in Dunmore's War, 1774; clashed with House of Burgesses; removed his fam-

ily to *HMS Fowey* at outbreak of Revolution; declared martial law, encouraged slaves to desert, Nov. 1775; bombarded and burned Norfolk, Jan. 1776; gov. of Bahamas, 1787–1796; died in England.

DUVALL, JOHN PIERCE (*ca.* 1751–1792): Monongalia County rep. in House of Delegates, 1777–1779; state senator, 1780–1791; successively lieut., Monongalia, Harrison counties; Randolph Academy trustee. See Hutchinson-Rachal, I, 260*n*.

EAGLE TAVERN, Richmond, Va.; in 18th century, located on slope of Shockoe hill, later on Main St. between 12th and 13th streets, on David Ross's lot; between James River and capitol.

EARP, CALEB: Fairfax County deputy sheriff; signed Fairfax petition to separate the jurisdictions of Fairfax and Alexandria, 1787.

EDDENS (EDDINS), SAMUEL (d. 1803): capt., Va. troops in Continental line, 1781; officer, Va. chapter, Society of the Cincinnati, *ca.* 1789.

*EDEN, ROBERT (1741–1784): born Durham, England; British army officer; married Caroline Calvert, sister of Lord Baltimore, proprietor of Md.; gov. of Md., 1768–1776; supposedly sympathized with colonial viewpoint; Germain-Eden letters, Apr. 1776, cast suspicion on his friendship for colonies; Gen. Charles Lee ordered Baltimore committee to arrest Eden, but Md. Council refused, instead asked him to leave colony; departed June 1776; died at Annapolis while attempting to recover his confiscated property.

EILBECK, SARAH EDGAR (d. 1780): GM's mother-in-law, wife of William Eilbeck, Charles County, Md., merchant-planter (d. 1765); their home, Mattawoman, was across Potomac from the peninsula owned by GM's father and later site of Gunston Hall, on Mattawoman Creek.

EILBECK, WILLIAM (d. 1765): GM's father-in-law; wealthy merchant and land owner of Charles County, Md.; married Sarah Edgar (d. 1780).

*ELLSWORTH, OLIVER (1745–1807): Conn. lawyer, political leader; del. to Continental Congress, 1777–1783; del. to Federal Convention, 1787; ardent Federalist, attacked GM personally in his "Letters of a Landholder," published from Nov. 1787 to Mar. 1788; elected to U.S. Senate, 1789–1796; chief justice of U.S., 1796–1800; U.S. commissioner to France, 1799–1800.

ELLZEY, THOMAZIN: Fairfax County land owner, atty.; apparently a friend of GM's; Truro Parish vestry (*ca.* 1765) and churchwarden, 1772–1777, 1781–1782; conducted surveys for parish, 1765–1767; supported GM's act to limit extensive credit, 1783; signed GM's petitions to remove courthouse from Alexandria, 1789, 1790; county board of overseers of the poor, 1795.

ELLZEY, WILLIAM: GM's atty. before Revolution; trustee, town of Colchester, 1753; Va. trustee for Ballendine's project to clear Potomac, 1774; Loudoun County committee of safety, 1774; married Frances Westwood; represented Loudoun in Va. General Assembly after 1783.

EPPES, FRANCIS (d. 1776): Prince George burgess, 1736–1749; lieut. col., Byrd's 2d Va. Regt., French and Indian War; maj., Col. Patrick Henry's 1st Va. Regt., 1775; col., 2d Va. Regt., 1776; not to be confused with Francis Eppes of Eppington.

ESTAING, CHARLES HECTOR, COMTE D' (1729–1794): French admiral; his fleet prevented from effective operations by storms and poor strategy, 1778–1780; executed by French radicals.

FAIRFAX, BRYAN, (1736–1802): 8th Lord Fairfax, son of William Fairfax, half brother of George William Fairfax, and brother-in-law of John Carlyle; attempted careers in trade and army, inherited large tracts from Fairfax estate in Fauquier and Fairfax counties; married Elizabeth, daughter of Wilson Cary, then Jane, daughter of James Donaldson of Fairfax County, 1780; lived at Towlston Grange, 1759; Fairfax justice of the peace, 1770; opposed Stamp Act; arrested in Pa. for reconciliation efforts, 1777, but released by Washington; helped organize Protestant Episcopal Church in Va.; ordained, 1786, and officiated at Christ Church, Alexandria, and Falls Church, 1789–1792.

FAIRFAX, GEORGE WILLIAM (1725–1787): eldest son of Hon. William Fairfax and his 1st wife, Sarah Walker; cousin of Thomas, 6th Lord Fairfax, half brother of Bryan Fairfax; educated in England, *ca.* 1745; married Sarah (1730–1811), daughter of Col. Wilson Cary, 1748; Frederick burgess, 1748–1755, Fairfax burgess, 1756–1758; Council, 1768–1773; Fairfax justice of the peace; original trustee of Alexandria, 1748; Truro Parish vestry, 1757–1776, and churchwarden, 1763–1764; resigned from the Ohio Co., 1749; executor of Lawrence Washington estate, 1752; col., Va. militia, during the French and Indian War; customs collector for the port of South Potomac; left Va., 1773, to take possession of Toulston, Yorkshire, England, which he inherited from his uncle; died in Bath, England.

FAIRFAX, ROBERT, (1706–1793): 7th lord Fairfax, son of Thomas, 5th lord Fairfax, and Catherine Culpeper; officer, Horse Guards, 1737–1739; married Martha Collins (d. 1744), and Sarah Best (d. 1750); succeeded to title, 1781, but Va. confiscated his estate; died in poverty.

*FAIRFAX, THOMAS, (1693–1781): 6th lord Fairfax of Cameron, proprietor of the Northern Neck of Va.; migrated to Va., 1747; lived on the Potomac until 1752, when he moved to Greenway Court in the Shenandoah Valley; only peer resident in America; neutral during Revolution.

FAIRFAX, WILLIAM (1691–1757): of Belvoir, Fairfax County; born in England; married Sarah Walker, then Deborah Clarke, mother of Bryan, 8th lord Fairfax; became agent for his first cousin, Thomas, 6th lord Fairfax, for Northern Neck estates, 1734; county militia lieut.; served on Truro Parish vestry; Prince William burgess, 1742–1743; member, pres., Va.

Council, 1743–1757; charter trustee of Alexandria, 1749.

FAIRFAX COUNTY: formed 1742 out of Prince William and part of Loudoun counties, between Potomac and Occoquan Creek; where GM was born and resided; represented by GM in House of Burgesses, 1758–1761, the Va. conventions, 1775, 1776, and House of Delegates, 1776–1780, 1787–1788.

FAIRFAX COURTHOUSE: Fairfax County; site changed from Spring Field to Alexandria, 1752; GM's movement to transfer the site of new courthouse to a more central location led to prolonged disagreement; was finally located on the Fairfax and Loudoun turnpike; new courthouse was completed and occupied in 1800. See Harrison, 323–325.

FAIRFAX PARISH: Fairfax County; divided from Truro Parish in 1764; contained Alexandria and vicinity; built Fall's (1767) and Alexandria (Christ's) churches.

FALCONER, NATHANIEL: capt. of ship *Friendship* on Philadelphia-to-London run, 1760; sought and may have obtained command in U.S. navy during Revolution.

FALLS WAREHOUSE: (Falls of the Potomac), Fairfax County; about one mile north of Difficult Run; built by Thomas Lee in 1742 as a public tobacco warehouse, it had little success.

FARGUSON, JOHN: Fairfax County freeholder; Truro Parish vestry, 1733–1744.

*FAUQUIER, FRANCIS (1704?–1768): royal gov. of Va. 1758–1768; popular official who warned William Pitt of colonial resistance to taxation, 1760; dissolved House of Burgesses for passing the Stamp Act Resolves, 1765.

*FEBIGER, CHRISTIAN (1746–1796): Continental army officer, 1775–1783; 2d Va. Regt., 1778–1779; provisioning officer for Southern Army under Gens. Gates and Greene, 1780; aided Col. Daniel Morgan in suppressing Hampshire County, Va., loyalist insurrection, 1781; commanded Va. recruits in Lafayette's army; officer, Va. line, 1781; later treasurer of Pa.

FENDALL & HIPKINS: Alexandria mercantile firm specializing in flour trade, 1792; [Thomas] Fendall may have been a ship captain who also owned a large Fairfax County estate, *ca.* 1782–1785.

FENWICK, JAMES (d. 1823); ship captain in Potomac trade during 1780s; may have been son of Ignatius Fenwick and Sarah Taney; owner of Pamonky; after 1789 aided brother Joseph Fenwick, business partner of GM's son, John Mason, in Bordeaux.

FENWICK, JOSEPH: business partner of GM's son, John Mason, in Bordeaux, 1788–1791; served as U.S. consular official in France and remained in France after the firm of Fenwick & Mason was dissolved.

FITZGERALD, JOHN (d. 1800): emigrated from Ireland before Revolution; married Jane, daughter of Jerome Digges, Prince Georges County, Md.; wheat merchant in Alexandria, by 1775; partner of Valentine Peers, by 1779; aide to Washington during Revolution; director, Potomac Navigation Co., 1785, and its pres., 1793–1796; Fairfax justice of the peace, 1787; Alexandria committee for ratification of Constitution, 1788; collector of customs, Alexandria, 1791; mayor of Alexandria.

FITZHUGH, GEORGE (d. 1722): of Stafford County; son of Colonel William Fitzhugh of Bedford and Sarah Tucker; married Mary, daughter of George Mason II of Stafford; Stafford burgesses with GM's father; inherited his father's Stafford lands.

FITZHUGH, HENRY (1687–1758): son of William Fitzhugh of Bedford, King George County; Stafford County sheriff, 1714; tobacco inspector for Westmoreland, Stafford counties, 1714; quorum justice of the peace, Stafford; married Susanna Cooke, daughter of Mordecai Cooke of Gloucester County, 1718; Stafford County burgess, 1712–1714, 1736.

FITZHUGH, HENRY (1706–1742): oldest son of William Fitzhugh of Eagle's

Nest and Anne Lee, daughter of Richard Lee of Stratford; studied at Christ Church, Oxford, 1722; married Lucy, daughter of Hon. Robert Carter of Corotoman, 1730; Stafford County burgess, 1736–1747; lieut. col., Stafford militia.

FITZHUGH, HENRY (1723–1783): 2d son of William Fitzhugh of Bedford; married Sarah Battaile, daughter of Capt. Nicholas Battaile, 1746; col., Stafford County militia, 1752; may be the Henry Fitzhugh who was charter member of the Mississippi Co., 1763; furnished supplies to the American army, 1782; bequeathed all his Stafford and King George County lands to his grandson, Henry.

FITZHUGH, HENRY: son and heir of William Fitzhugh of Eagle's Nest, and grandson of William Fitzhugh (d. 1701); was probably among the wealthiest Virginians of the 1780s.

FITZHUGH, WILLIAM (1721–1798): of Rousby Hall, Calvert County, Md.; son of George Fitzhugh and Mary Mason, GM's aunt; 1st wife, Martha Lee Turberville (1744), 2d wife, Mrs. Ann Frisby Rousby (1752); first lived in Stafford County; served with Lawrence Washington under Admiral Vernon at Carthagena, 1740; Stafford burgess, 1748–1758; sold provisions to Chesapeake trading vessels; officer, French and Indian War; moved to Rousby Hall, 1759; Md. Council, 1769–1774; del. to Md. convention, 1776; Calvert committee of vigilance; blind and infirm after 1781. See Richard Beale Davis, ed., *The Colonial Virginia Satirist: Mid-Eighteenth-Century Commentaries on Politics, Religion, and Society* (American Philosophical Society, *Transactions*, LVII [Philadelphia, 1967]), pt. 1, 12–13.

FITZHUGH, WILLIAM (1725–1791): son of Maj. John Fitzhugh (d. 1733), of St. Paul's Parish, Stafford County; home was Marmion in Stafford, now King George County; married 1st Ursula Beverley, daughter of Col. William Beverley of Blandfield, Essex County, then Hannah; Stafford burgess, 1748, 1751, 1761–1765; probably maj. of Stafford militia, 1752; furnished supplies for the American army, 1782.

FITZHUGH, WILLIAM (1741–1809): only son of Henry Fitzhugh (1706–1742) and Lucy, daughter of Robert Carter of Corotoman; married Ann, daughter of Peter Randolph of Chatsworth, Henrico County; owned Eagle's Nest and Somerset, King George County, Chatham, Stafford County, and Ravensworth, Fairfax County; lived at Chatham, near Fredericksburg; trustee and director of Dumfries, Va., 1749; possibly charter member of Mississippi Co., 1763; King George burgess, 1772–1776; King George committee of safety, 1774–1775; del. to Va. conventions, 1775–1776; commissioner for establishing an arms factory at Fredericksburg, 1775; commissioner to locate land for iron works, 1777; del. to 2d Continental Congress, 1779–1780; Va. House of Delegates, 1776, 1777, 1780, 1781, 1787, 1788; Va. Senate, 1781–1785; Federalist candidate for Congress, 1788; sold Chatham, 1796, and moved to Ravensworth near Alexandria.

FITZHUGH, WILLIAM (1761–1839): son of William Fitzhugh of Rousby Hall and Ann Frisby Rousby; served with Continental dragoons, 1779–1782; settled near Hagerstown, Md., after war; moved to New York, 1816; married Ann Hughes.

*FITZSIMONS, THOMAS (1741–1811): born in Ireland; Philadelphia business man, legislator, built fire ships and other equipment for American forces during Revolution; Pa. del. to Continental Congress, 1782; del. to Federal Convention, 1787; supported Alexander Hamilton's program in U.S. House of Reps., 1789–1795; trustee, Bank of North America, 1781; went bankrupt, 1805.

FLEMING, THOMAS: Annapolis shipfitter and merchant in 1750s and 1760s; apparently moved to Alexandria around 1770, began shipbuilding activity and served as Fairfax County ship's carpenter during Revolution;

overseer, Alexandria academy. See Arthur Pierce Middleton, *Tobacco Coast; a Maritime History of Chesapeake Bay in the Colonial Era* (Newport News, Va., 1953) 24.

FORD, THOMAS (d. 1776): Fairfax County freeholder; Truro Parish vestry, 1765–1776.

FORREST, URIAH (1756–1805): born near Leonardstown, St. Marys County, Md.; officer, Md. Regt., ca. 1776–1777; wounded at Germantown and Brandywine; business partner of Benjamin Stoddert in Forrest and Stoddert; del. to Continental Congress, 1786, 1787; married Rebecca Plater, daughter of Gov. George Plater of Md.; Federalist member of U.S. Congress, 1793–1794, resigned; maj.-gen., Md. militia, 1795; clerk of the District of Columbia circuit court, 1800–1805.

FOUSHEE, WILLIAM: a surviving partner in the firm of Ramsay, Taylor & Foushee; may have been a Prince William County justice of the peace.

FOWLER, JOHN: co-owner of sloop *Liberty*, which was sold to Va., 1776; probably also owned plantation in Fairfax County; Fairfax overseer of poor, ca. 1787–1789; Fairfax justice of the peace, 1799, 1801.

FRANCIS, TENCH (1730–1800): Philadelphia merchant, signer of the 1769 Philadelphia nonimportation resolution; married Anne Shippen Willing; reportedly helped enforce test oath against Quakers, 1779–1781; first cashier, Bank of North America.

*FRANKLIN, BENJAMIN (1706–1790): printer, essayist, scientist, statesman; born in Boston; made Philadelphia *Pa. Gazette* into leading colonial newspaper; helped found American Philosophical Society (1743); served as loyal deputy postmaster general (1753–1775); Pa. agent in London; served in Continental Congress; represented U.S. at French court (1776–1785) where he was signer of peace treaty with Great Britain; del. to Federal Convention, 1787. See Leonard W. Labaree, *et al.*, eds., *The*

Papers of Benjamin Franklin, 12 vols. (New Haven, 1959–).

FREDERICKSBURG ACADEMY: grammar school attended by GM's sons and other Northern Neck young men in 1770s and possibly later; located on Prince Edward St., Fredericksburg. See S. J. Quinn, *History of the City of Fredericksburg* (Richmond, 1908).

FRENCH, DANIEL (d. 1771): of Fairfax County; son of Daniel French of King George County; married Penelope Manley, daughter of Harrison Manley; lived at Rose Hill, west of Alexandria; Truro Parish vestry, 1744–1746; Fairfax Parish vestry, 1765; repaired Pohick Church, 1751 and contracted to build new Pohick church, 1769. See Truro Parish Vestry Book (DLC), 8 Aug. 1743, 18 Feb. 1744, 15 Feb. 1774.

FUGATE, JEREMIAH: probably GM's overseer at Gunston Hall; signed GM's Fairfax County petitions to move the county courthouse, 1789, 1790.

*GAGE, THOMAS (1721–1787): British army officer; wounded at Braddock's defeat, 1755, and served throughout the French and Indian War; commander-in-chief of North America, 1763–1773; royal gov. of Mass., 1774–1776; left Boston and continued military service.

GARDNER, JOSEPH: Fairfax County planter; signer of Madison's "Memorial & Remonstrance" against the assessment bill, which GM circulated in 1785.

*GATES, HORATIO (1728–1806): British army officer, 1749–1765; wounded in Braddock's defeat, 1755; moved to Traveller's Rest, Berkeley County, 1772; Continental army adjutant gen. with rank of brigadier gen., 1775; maj. gen., 1776; commanded Northern army during Saratoga compaign, 1777; pres., board of war, 1777–1778; after Lincoln's surrender at Charleston, S.C., Gates took command of the Southern army; defeated by Cornwallis in the Battle of Camden, 16 Aug. 1780; relieved by Nathaniel Greene at Charlotte, 2 Dec. 1780; served at

Newburgh under Washington, 1782–1783; returned to Va., where he was pres. of the Va. Society of the Cincinnati, 1783; moved to Rose Hill Farm in present New York City, 1790; N.Y. legislator, 1800–1801.

GATES, ISAAC (d. 1790): Fairfax County farmer, ward of Truro Parish, 1784–1790.

*GATES, SIR THOMAS (*ca.* 1585–1621): member of the Va. Company who brought fleet to Jamestown, 1609; lieut. gov. under Baron De La Warr, 1611–1614.

†GERMAIN, LORD GEORGE (1716–1785): disgraced at battle of Minden, 1759; appointed to British cabinet as sec. for American affairs; GM wrote a resolution condemning the intercepted Germain-Eden correspondence, 1776.

GIBSON, JOHN: merchant of Colchester, Va., 1774; elected to Truro Parish vestry, resigned 1784; Fairfax County justice of the peace, 1785; signed GM's petition against repeal of act to prevent extensive credits.

GIBSON, JOHN (1729–1782): Philadelphia merchant, favored use of economic restrictions on British trade until colonial rights were established, 1770; Philadelphia mayor, 1771–1772.

GILES, JACOB: Md. land speculator, merchant; charter member of the Ohio Co.; was probably associated with Principio Co., *ca.* 1775–1777.

*GILMAN, NICHOLAS (1755–1814): born at Exeter, N.H., served in state regiments during Revolution; del. to Continental Congress, 1786–1788; del. to Federal Convention, 1787; Federalist in U.S. House of Reps., 1789–1797; served in N.H. Senate, 1804–1805; U.S. Senate, 1804–1814.

GILPIN, GEORGE: Alexandria merchant; signed nonimportation association in Fairfax County, 1770; Fairfax committee of safety, 1774, 1775; inspector of tobacco at Alexandria; flour inspector and wheat purchaser, 1775; Fairfax justice of the peace, 1781, 1782, 1785; director, Potomac Navigation Co., 1785–1786; signed petition to establish a bank at Alexandria, 1792; original trustee of towns of Matildaville, 1790, Occoquan, 1804.

*GIST, CHRISTOPHER (1706–1759): explorer, lived in N.C.; explored north of the Ohio from Shannopin's Town (Pittsburgh) to the mouth of the Scioto, 1750; explored south of the Ohio from the Monongahela to the Great Kanawha for Ohio Co., 1751; accompanied Washington to Fort Duquesne, 1753; guided General Braddock on his expedition to Fort Duquesne; died of smallpox, 1756 in either South Carolina or Georgia.

GLASSFORD, JOHN: Glasgow, Scotland tobacco lord who owned stores along the Potomac and other streams in Va. and Md.; operated valuable business during the French and Indian War; had an outlet in Dumfries after 1750. See Glassford Account Books, DLC.

*GODDARD, WILLIAM (1740–1817): Baltimore printer; came to Md. after printing newspapers in R.I. and Pa.; publisher of *Md. Journal & Baltimore Advertiser.*

GOODRICH, JOHN (1722–1785): Norfolk merchant and shipowner at outbreak of Revolution; became loyalist during Revolution; was captured and imprisoned, later released after his property was confiscated. See "Virginia Legislative Papers," VMHB, XVII (1909), 171–172, 249–250, 253–257.

GOOSLEY, WILLIAM (1748–1809): Yorktown merchant; capt., York County minutemen; met Philip Mazzei in London, 1770; York justice of the peace, 1789, and sheriff, early 1790s. See Hutchinson-Rachal, I, 297n.

GORDON, JACOB (d. 1817): Fairfax County resident and probably listed in the Truro Parish records as Angel Jacobus Jourdan, 1775; he and his wife lived for a time at Gates County.

*GORHAM, NATHANIEL (1738–1796): Charlestown, Mass., merchant; Mass. legislator, justice; Continental Congress, 1782, 1783, 1785–1787; del., Federal Convention, 1787; a Federalist leader in Mass. ratifying convention, 1788; bought the Genessee country

from Mass. in a corporate syndicate which probably included, among others, Robert Morris, 1788.

GOSNELL, JOHN: Fairfax County resident; owned lands immediately below the mouth of Accotink, adjoining Mason estate; tract later site of Pohick tobacco warehouse.

GOSNELL'S PATENT: Fairfax County; oldest of three patents for land on Pohick Creek, issued in 1657; immediately below the mouth of Accotink Creek.

GRAHAM, GEORGE: oldest son of Richard Graham of Dumfries and Jane Brent, sister of GM's wife Sarah; del. to Va. General Assembly; Prince William County justice of the peace, 1790; commanded Fairfax County light horse, War of 1812; commissioner gen., U.S. land office; acting secy. of war under Madison and Monroe; 1st married the widow of GM, Jr., then Miss Watson of Alexandria.

GRAHAM, JOHN (1711–1787): born in Perthshire, Scotland; emigrated as a merchant, but left mercantile business shortly after; Dumfries, Va., of which he was an original trustee, built on his land, 1749; Fairfax County clerk, 1746–1752; Prince William County clerk, 1752–1777; married Christian, daughter of Dr. Gustavus Brown, 1742, then married, Elizabeth Catesby, daughter of Catesby Cocke, 1746. See Harrison, 394–395.

GRAHAM, RICHARD (d. 1796): born in Scotland, merchant at Dumfries; married Jane Brent, daughter of George Brent of Stafford County, sister of GM's wife Sarah; one of the earliest land speculators on the Ohio; affiliated in business with Michael Gratz, who emigrated to Fredericksburg from Philadelphia, 1776, dealt in ships, and also promoted exploration, survey, and settlement of Kentucky country; Prince William County justice of the peace and sheriff, 1784. See DAB under "John Graham."

GRAYSON, BENJAMIN SR. (d. 1757): called "capt."; Scotch emigrant; settled on the Occoquan; wealthy merchant with extensive local business; married Susanna Monroe (d. 1752); Prince William County justice of the peace, 1731, 1734 (?), 1744, 1751, 1753; his lands held later became the foundation of Henry Lee's Leesylvania.

GRAYSON, BENJAMIN JR.: son of Capt. Benjamin Grayson, brother of Rev. Spence Grayson and William Grayson; followed his father's mercantile business, but failed; partner of John Ballendine in wheat milling and bread baking near Occoquan Falls, 1762; rejected in election of Truro Parish vestry, 1765; close friend of Washington.

GRAYSON, REV. SPENCE (1734–1798): son of Capt. Benjamin Grayson, brother of Benjamin, Jr., and William Grayson; inherited Belle Air, Prince William County, his father's Potomac residence; married Mary Elizabeth, daughter of Dr. Peter Wagener; began theological studies in England, where he had been educated, perhaps at Oxford; Prince William County justice of the peace, 1769; minister of Cameron Parish, Loudoun County, *ca.* 1771–1784; chaplain, Grayson's Regt., 1777–1779; close friend of Washington; daughter, Susannah Monroe Grayson, married Postmaster General Lund Washington.

*GRAYSON, WILLIAM (1736–1790): born in Prince William County; Dumfries lawyer; lieut. col., aide-de-camp to Washington, 1776; col., 1777–1779; Va. board of war, 1779–1781; Va. House of Delegates, 1784–1785; 1788; Va. del. to Continental Congress, 1785–1787; Prince William del. to Va. ratifying convention, 1788; U.S. Senate, 1789–1790; Antifederalist.

GREAT HUNTING CREEK: Fairfax County, near Alexandria; name appears in 1695; earlier known as Mussel Creek, also Indian Cabin Creek.

GREEN, CHARLES (d. 1765): Anglican minister, M.D.; ordained as first incumbent minister of Truro Parish, 1737–1765; apparently in poor health in his later years; began preaching in Alexandria, 1753; acquired considerable land in Fairfax, Prince William, Loudoun counties. See Slaughter, *Truro Parish,* ed. Goodwin, 10–11, 13.

*GREEN, JONAS (1712–1767): son of Boston printer Timothy Green; worked as printer in Boston, Philadelphia; Md. public printer, 1738; established *Md. Gazette,* 1745.

GREEN, WILLIAM: overseer on GM's Fairfax County lands; was qualified as freeholder and signed GM's petitions for removing the county courthouse in 1789, 1790.

GREEN RIVER: flows westerly course through central Ky. then north into the Ohio near Evansville, Ind., and Henderson, Ky.

*GREENE, NATHANAEL (1742–1786): brig. gen., Continental army, 1775; quartermaster gen., 1778–1780; commander of the Southern army, 1780–1783; defeated by British at Guilford Courthouse, and Camden, S.C., 1781; beseiged Charleston, Dec. 1781–Dec. 1782, when the British evacuated; bankrupt from spending his personal fortune in the war effort, settled near Savannah, Ga., 1785.

GREGORY, STEPHEN: ship owner, capt. of the *Commerce;* may have served earlier (*ca.* 1779) as jr. officer on the U.S. frigate *Confederacy;* appears to have been employed by Robert Morris of Philadelphia; sailed on Potomac in 1786 as master of the *Comte d'Artois.*

GREY, STEPHEN (d. *ca.* 1724): of Stafford County; worked a tract on Four-Mile Run; was deeded land on the Potomac in Westmoreland County, 1724.

GRIFFIN, CORBIN (d. 1813): son of Leroy Griffin and Mary Anne Bertrand; lived in Yorktown; studied medicine; York County committee of safety, 1775–1776; surgeon in the Va. line Regt. during Revolution; Va. senator, 1780; married Mary Berkeley, daughter of Col. Edmund Berkeley of Barn Elms, Middlesex County.

*GRIFFIN, CYRUS (1748–1810): brother of Dr. Corbin Griffin; studied law at Edinburgh and Middle Temple; returned to practice law in Va., 1774; Lancaster County del. to Va. General Assembly, 1777–1778, 1786–1787; del. to Continental Congress, 1778–1780, 1787, where he served as pres. 1788, until the new government under the Constitution supplanted it; 1st federal judge for the Va. district, presided over the James Callender libel trial, and the Aaron Burr treason trial; died at Yorktown.

GRIFFIN, SAMUEL (d. 1810): son of Le Roy Griffin and Mary Anne Bertrand; brother of Dr. Corbin Griffin and Cyrus Griffin; lived at Williamsburg; col., "Flying Camp," Continental line; Va. board of war, 1781; House of Delegates, 1787, 1788; served U.S. House of Reps., 1789–1795. See Gwathmey, *Virginians in Revolution*, 328.

GRIFFITH, DAVID (1742–1789): born in N.Y., studied medicine in England; surgeon with British army, American militia in Indian wars, 1764–1765; private medical practice, 1765–1770; ordained in England, 1770; rector of Shelburne Parish, Loudoun County, 1771–1776; signed nonimportation agreement, 1774; preached before the Va. convention, 31 Dec. 1775; chaplain and surgeon of the 3d Va. Regt., 1776–1779; rector of Fairfax Parish, Fairfax County, 1779–1789; secy., 1785, and pres., 1786, of Va. general convention of Protestant Episcopal Church (1785–1789); elected 1st Va. bishop, but resigned (1789) before consecrated for financial reasons.

GRUELL, MESSRS. JAMES, & Co.: French mercantile branch of the Nantes house of Penet D'Acosta Frères & Cie.; represented Va. in various business dealings, 1777–1779, although William Lee insisted (1777) that Gruell was a lone-handed operator and the "firm is not known here."

GUNNELL, HENRY: Fairfax County freeholder, 1744; Truro Parish vestry, 1756–1765, churchwarden, 1761–1763; unsuccessful candidate for Fairfax Parish vestry, 1765; Fairfax committee of safety, 1774; signed Fairfax petition against repeal of an act to prevent extensive credits (1783), and GM's petition to move the county courthouse (1789, 1790).

GUNNELL, JOHN: Fairfax County freeholder; collector of Truro Parish tithes, 1773–1774.

GUNSTON HALL: Fairfax County, Va.; GM's plantation seat on Dogue's (now Mason) Neck; finished in 1758, partly designed by architect William Buckland; after GM's death, estate was eventually divided and the house sold to a succession of owners until purchased by the late Louis Hertle, whose wife was a member of the National Society of Colonial Dames; deeded by Hertle to the Society and the Commonwealth of Va. as a national historic shrine; opened to public after completion of restoration, 1952; located 16 miles south of Alexandria, Va.

GWINN'S (also GWYNN'S) ISLAND: offshore area of approx. 2,000 acres near mouth of Piankatank River; adjacent to Gloucester (now Mathews) County; used by Lord Dunmore until midsummer, 1776, as base for raids up the Potomac and in the Chesapeake Bay. See H. Howe, *Historical Collections of Virginia* (Charleston, S.C., 1845), 376; John Daly Burk, *History of Virginia* (Petersburg, Va., 1805–1814), IV, 172–175.

HAMILTON, ALEXANDER: of Piscataway; Md. tobacco merchant; headquarters on Piscataway Creek, which empties into the Potomac six miles above Gunston Hall and Mason Neck, nearly opposite Mount Vernon; his storehouse may have been located above the present Farmington Landing, and at time of GM's dealings (1784) shared much of the western shore tobacco trade with Port Tobacco. See Lewis Evans, *Map of the Middle British Colonies* (London, 1755); also Glassford Account Books, DLC.

HANBURY, CAPEL (d. 1769): brother of John and Osgood Hanbury; partner in London merchant shipping firm of John and Capel Hanbury, and later (1766) in Capel and Osgood Hanbury; member of the Ohio Co., but not an original petitioner; the Hanburys acquired the company shares of London merchant Samuel Smith (1763) and Hanbury's shares were still held by his heirs, 1778; influential in colonial political appointments; opposed Stamp Act.

HANBURY, JOHN (1700–1758): Quaker merchant and banker; brother of Capel and Osgood Hanbury; member of London-based firm of John Hanbury, later John and Capel Hanbury, with extensive colonial trade, especially in Va. and Md.; an original Ohio Co. patentee, and first London representative, although distrusted by John Mercer; in Va., misused Ohio Co. information to acquire 130,000 acres in Augusta County; also interested in the Vandalia Co.; politically influential with British leaders, especially of the Newcastle and Pelham administration; suggested Va. as base of operations during the French and Indian war, and recommended Horatio Sharpe as commander; died at Coggeshall, Essex, England.

HANBURY, OSGOOD: London tobacco merchant in firm with his brother Capel Hanbury, from 1766; later known as Hanbury and Lloyd (1774), which became the great banking company of Lloyd's (1908); executor with London merchant Samuel Athawes of Lady Rebecca Gooch, widow of Gov. William Gooch, 1773; London trustee during the Revolution of the Bank Stock Co. for the province of Md.

*HANCOCK, JOHN (1737–1793): patriot leader, Revolutionary War, after he inherited Boston mercantile firm and lost ship Liberty when British customs officials seized it; del. to Mass. General Court; pres., Mass. Prov. Congress, 1774–1775; pres., Continental Congress, 1775–1777; signer, Declaration of Independence; gov. of Mass., 1780–1793.

HANOVER TOWN: Hanover County seat; on Pamunkey River about ten miles north of Richmond; the Va.

committee of safety met there in Sept. 1775.

HANSON, ALEXANDER CONTEE (1749–1806): of Frederick County, Md.; son of John Hanson and Jane Contee, daughter of Alexander Contee; attended Philadelphia College, then studied law in Annapolis; aide to Washington for several months in 1776; associate justice of the Md. General Court, 1778; Federalist pamphleteer, 1788, and as "Aristides" wrote for Md. Journal; Md. chancellor, 1789–1806; compiled "Hanson's Laws," for the Md. legislature; married Rebecca Howard of Annapolis.

HARDY, [JOHN?]: ship's officer aboard the General Washington, which carried marque authorization to attack enemy vessels, ca. 1781–1782.

*HARDY, SAMUEL (1758–1785): of Isle of Wight County; William and Mary, 1778; admitted to the Va. bar, 1 Oct. 1778; immediately elected to the House of Delegates, served 1778–1781; escheator, 1779–1780; Va. Privy Council, 1781; Va. lieut. gov., 1782; Continental Congress, 1783–1785; chairman of committee which handled congressional business during recess, 1784.

HARPER, JOHN (1728–1804): wealthy Philadelphia Quaker, partner of William Hartshorne in Alexandria shipping firm; agent for Washington at Mount Vernon; procured military stores for Prince William and Fairfax militia; religious convictions barred combat role during war; married Sarah Wells of Pennsylvania (20 children), and Mary (Cunningham) Reynolds (9 children).

HARRISON, BENJAMIN (1726?–1791): born in Charles City County; attended William and Mary, 1745; Charles City burgess, 1749–1775, served on correspondence committee (1773); del. to Va. convention, 1775/1776; Charles City County del. to House of Delegates, 1776–1781; Continental Congress, Aug. 1774–Oct. 1777, except for brief interval; served on the committee for secret correspondence (Nov. 1775), marine committee (Mar. 1776), board of war and ordinance (June 1776), and many committees concerned with finance; signed Declaration of Independence; Speaker, House of Delegates, 1778–1781; gov. of Va., 1781–1784; House of Delegates, 1784–1791; del. to Va. ratifying convention, 1788.

HARRISON, NATHANIEL (*ca.* 1708–1791), "Col." of Brandon, Prince George County; oldest son of Nathaniel Harrison of Wakefield, from whom he inherited land in Charles City, Prince George, and New Brunswick counties, and many slaves; 1st married Mary Digges (d. 1744), then in 1748 married Lucy, daughter of Robert Carter of Corotoman, widow of Henry Fitzhugh of Eagle's Nest, Stafford, now King George County; Prince George justice of peace and militia before the Revolution; Prince George committee of safety, with his son, Benjamin; elected to the Va. state council, 1776–1778, when his son refused to accept election; Va. Senate, for the district of Isle of Wight, Surry, Prince George counties.

HARRISON, RICHARD (1750–1841): born in Md.; agent for the Va. committee of safety at St. Pierre, Martinique; merchant at Cadiz, where he performed consular duties without formal congressional appointment, 1780–1786; recommended by GM and nominated by Madison for Spanish consulate, 1781, but final action was never taken; Washington appointed him, and the Senate confirmed, his appointment as consul for the port of Cadiz, 1790, while he was a merchant at Alexandria; auditor of the federal treasury, 1791–1836; married Nancy, daughter of Dr. James Craik; their daughter married George Mason (1797–1870), of Hollin Hall. See Hutchinson-Rachal, II, 53.

HARRISON, ROBERT HANSON (1745–d.1790): son of Richard Harrison and Dorothy Hanson; practiced law at Alexandria before the Revolution; signed Fairfax County nonimportation assn., 1770; member, clerk, Fairfax committee of safety, 1774; private secretary with rank of lieut. col. on Washington's staff, 1775–1781;

chief justice of Md. General Court, 1781; declined appointment by Washington to the 1st U.S. Supreme Court, to become chancellor of Md., 1789; died at his home at Port Tobacco, Md.

HARRISON, THOMAS (d. 1774): called "Jr." or "the younger"; son of Thomas Harrison of Chipawansic; Prince William County sheriff, 1733; Prince William justice of the peace, 1734–1746; succeeded his father as 1st justice and probably also as county lieut. 1746, 1752; 1st presiding justice of newly formed Fauquier County, 1759; Fauquier County lieut. 1761; Fauquier burgess, 1760–1769; trustee of Dumfries, 1749. See Harrison, 331, 338–339, 345–346, 387.

HARTSHORNE, WILLIAM (d. *ca.* 1802): Alexandria merchant; Fairfax County committee of safety, 1774; dealt in wheat and flour, first as partner in Harper & Hartshorne (1775), and later Hartshorne & Donaldson (until 1792); treasurer, Potomack Navigation Co., 1785; trustee, Alexandria Academy, 1786.

*HARVIE, JOHN (1742–1807): married Margaret, daughter of Gabriel Jones; col., Va. militia, 1775–1776: Augusta, West Augusta del. to Va. conventions, 1775, 1776; del. to Continental Congress; Va. purchasing agent, 1778; longtime register of the Va. land office, from 1780; Richmond mayor, 1785–1786.

HARWOOD, JOHN: of Charles City County; apparently son of Thomas Harwood, a vintner of King and Queen County; ensign, Charles City militia, 1776, 1778; owned lands in King and Queen and King William counties.

HARWOOD, WILLIAM (d. *ca.* 1780): probably son of William Harwood (d. 1737) of Warwick County; Warwick justice of the peace, 1753; Warwick burgess, 1742–1776; signed Va. nonimportation assn., 1769; del. to Va. conventions, 1775–1776; House of Delegates, 1776; chairman, Warwick committee of safety, 1774–1776.

HAWKINS, GEORGE FRAZER (d. *ca.* 1791): of Prince Georges County, Md.; appears to have been involved in Ohio Co. litigation with GM in the 1790s.

HEDGES, ROBERT: sold land tract to GM's father; rented portion of a 700-acre tract on Hallowes' Creek, west of Mattox Creek, from John Washington, *ca.* 1668.

HEDGMAN, PETER (d. 1765): son of Nathaniel Hedgman; studied law; Stafford County justice of peace, 1745; Prince William burgess, 1736–1740; Stafford burgess, 1742–1758; royal commissioner for surveying the back line of the Fairfax grant, 1746–1747; trustee for Dumfries, Va., 1749; his father bought Accokeek, the residence of the 1st George Mason (1629–1686), on Potomac Creek; he and his wife, Margaret, had three sons—William, George, and John.

HENDERSON, ALEXANDER: emigrated from Scotland, 1756, settled as merchant at Colchester; Fairfax County justice of peace from 1770 until after 1785; Truro Parish, Pohick vestry, 1773; del., Fairfax County, House of Delegates, 1781, 1783; Fairfax County trustee for road repair; served with GM as Va. commissioner at Mount Vernon convention, 1785; Va. commissioner for Potomac navigation, 1784; one of the committee GM appointed in his will to ensure the proper division of his estate.

*HENDERSON, RICHARD (1735–1785): judge, land speculator; associate justice, superior court, 1768–1773, which the Regulators closed; after retirement employed Daniel Boone as his agent, in Richard Henderson and Co., by 1764; organized the Louisa Co., renamed the Transylvania Co., to settle a proprietary colony; his Treaty of Sycamore Shoals on the Watauga, if legal by precedent of the Treaty of Ft. Stanwix (1768), cleared the region of Indian titles by buying Cherokee lands between the Kentucky and Cumberland Rivers, March 1775; established Boonesborough; Revolution prevented recognition of claims by either England or Congress, and both Va. and N.C. claimed jurisdiction, so his project collapsed; later, Va. reimbursed with large tract; N.C. commissioner for survey of the border with Va., 1779–1780; promoted and established a colony at French Lick, later Nashville; N.C. legislature, 1781; N.C. council of state, 1782.

HENLEY, DAVID (1748–1823): col., Continental army; court-martialed in Boston on charges brought by Gen. Burgoyne, 1778, but apparently absolved; merchant, Boston firm of Otis & Henley, 1780; served as congressional commissioner for settling Illinois accounts, 1787.

HENRY, JAMES (1731–1804): of Accomack County; burgess, 1772, 1773–1776; del. to Va. General Assembly, 1778–1779; del. to Continental Congress, Dec. 1779–July 1780; Va. Court of Admiralty, 1782–1788; Va. General Court, 1788–1800; an active legislator, careless historians have mistakenly credited some of his work to Patrick Henry.

*HENRY, PATRICK (1736–1799): born in Hanover County; won fame trying "Parson's Cause" against established church, 1760; Louisa County burgess, 1765–1769; Hanover County burgess, 1769–1776; Va. del. to Continental Congress, 1774–1776; close political ally of GM; del. to Va. conventions of March 1775, May 1776; Va. gov., 1776–1779, 1784–1786; encouraged George Rogers Clark to lead Illinois country expedition, 1777–1779, with GM as corroborator; Va. General Assembly, 1780–1784; declined appointment to Federal Convention, 1787; with GM, led Antifederalist opposition to Constitution at Va. ratifying convention, 1788; dominant figure in Va. politics, he declined U.S. senate seat and Washington's appointments as secy. of state, chief justice, 1795; refused to serve as gov., 1796; converted to Federalist party, he opposed Va. and Ky. resolutions; died in Charlotte County.

HERBERT, WILLIAM: Alexandria merchant, born in Ireland; married Sarah

Carlyle, daughter of John Carlyle; succeeded John Muir as Alexandria flour inspector, *ca.* 1775; subscriber of Christ Church, Alexandria, 1785; Fairfax County justice of peace, 1787; supported Constitution in 1787–1788; founder, Washington Society in Alexandria, 1800; mayor of Alexandria. See "Patents Issued during the Regal Government," WMQ, 1st ser., IX (1901), 139.

HEREFORD, JOHN (1690–1743): son of James Hereford, Westmoreland County; married Jane Barnes, 1721; Truro Parish vestry, 1732–1743; Truro Parish churchwarden, 1732–1734; owned 300 acres on the Accotink, which he offered to sell to the parish as glebeland, 1734; owned lands in Prince William County, which he sold to Dennis McCarty (d. 1742).

HEREFORD, JOHN (b. 1725): presumably son of John Hereford and Jane Barnes; Truro Parish processioner, 1751, 1755; signed Fairfax petitions to separate the jurisdiction of Alexandria and Fairfax counties, 1787, and GM's petition to move the county courthouse, 1790; witnessed the will of Col. Daniel McCarty, 1791.

HEREFORD, ROBERT (1769–1831): presumably the son of John Hereford (b. 1725); married an otherwise unidentified Mary Mason (1770–1831).

HETH, WILLIAM (1735–1808): served as officer in Montgomery's Regt., wounded at Quebec, 1775; lieut., Daniel Morgan's riflemen; col., 3rd Va. Regt., during the Revolution; taken prisoner at Charleston, 1780, and held until war's end; applied to Gov. Garrison for a collectorship of customs, 1783; collector for Bermuda Hundred, the most important port in Va., 1791; commissioner for settling the Illinois accounts, 1787; held lucrative office during Washington presidency.

HILL, WHITMEL (1743–1797): (N.C. planter born in Bertie County, N.C.; graduated College of Philadelphia, 1760; col., during Revolution; N.C. conventions, 1775–1776; N.C. constitutional convention, 1776; N.C. House of Commons, 1777; del. to Continental Congress, where he was member of the Admiralty Board, 1778–1781; N.C. Senate, 1778–1780, 1784, 1785; died at his plantation, Hills Ferry, near Hamilton, N.C. See Hutchinson-Rachal, II, 92*n.*

HIPKINS, LEWIS: of Fairfax County; probably a partner in Fendall and Hipkins, Alexandria flour buyers.

HODGSON, WILLIAM: Alexandria merchant; London resident and member, "The Honest Whigs," London supper club to which Franklin belonged; aided the American commissioners at Paris through correspondence with Franklin; served two years in Newgate prison for anti-British sentiments; in 1790 established dry goods business and counting house in Alexandria, Va.; Hodgson and Co. signed Alexandria petition for a branch of Bank of the U.S., 1792; his four large account books, covering 1792–1801, were filed in the Court of Claims with regard to French Spoilation Claims, and are now in the National Archives; married Portia Lee, daughter of William Lee, 1799.

HOLMES, JOHN: an Anglican minister, briefly served as rector of Truro Parish, 1736.

HOOE, JOHN (*ca.* 1700–1766): of Hooe's Ferry, Stafford County; son of Col. Rice Hooe of Barnesfield, who owned the ferry that crossed Potomac to Port Tobacco, Md.; Stafford County justice of peace, 1745; St. Paul's Parish vestry, King George County; may have been maj. in Stafford militia, *ca.* 1750–1751.

HOOE, JOHN (b. 1728): son of Howson Hooe and grandson of Col. Rice Hooe of Barnesfield; the owner of Hooe's Ferry opposite Port Tobacco on Potomac; Prince William County justice of peace, 1769; Prince William committee of safety, 1774; managed the John Parke Custis plantations in New Kent and King William counties, 1790.

HOOE, ROBERT TOWNSEND: originally of Charles County, Md., which he represented in Md. conventions, 1775–1776; partner in firm of Hooe, Harrison & Co., Alexandria wheat buyers; owned shares in privateers operating on Potomac during Revolution; Alexandria mayor, 1780; Fairfax County court, 1782–1790; trustee for Alexandria lottery, 1789; trustee, Alexandria banking firm, 1792; was member of Fairfax Parish vestry, but donated land in Alexandria to St. Mary's Catholic Church, 1793; married Margaret, daughter of Landon Carter of Pittsylvania County.

HOOMES, BENJAMIN: Va. officer in Continental line, 1775–1778; wounded at battle of Monmouth; GM apparently acted on his behalf when Hoomes sought return to active duty as maj., Dec. 1778; received military bounty of 5,333 acres.

HOPKINS, JOHN (ca. 1757–1827): known as John Hopkins, Jr., Richmond merchant, and Va. commissioner of Continental loans, 1780–ca. 1794; earlier a clerk in the office of the state treasurer; accused of malfeasance in office, but found innocent, 1781; founding director, Bank of Richmond, state chartered, 1792; moved to Alexandria, ca. 1805, soon thereafter to plantation Hill and Dale, Frederick County.

HOUGH, JOHN: of Loudoun County; among the original trustees of Leesburg, 1758; owned a mill on Goose Creek, Loudoun County; agent for Robert Carter of Nomini Hall for rents from Frying Pan Tract, 1767–1777; Loudoun County justice of peace, 1762; made field survey notes for Washington's land on Four-Mile Run, 1766; a manager for Thomas Johnson, Jr.'s Potomac navigation project; trustee for Ballendine's Potomac project, 1774; commissioner for roads to connect coast with the N.W. mountain gaps, 1772; owned, sold Alexandria lots, 1771, 1772; guided Potomac Co. party, bound for the mouth of the Shenandoah River, from Leesburg over the Short Hills, 1788. See Louis Morton, *Robert Carter*, 76, 279, 129; Moore, *Seaport in Virginia*, 157.

HUBBARD, BENJAMIN: merchant, tavern-keeper, Caroline County; by 1770, Hubbard's Ordinary was familiar gathering place, probably on route between Fredericksburg-Williamsburg; Caroline County committee of safety, 1774; married Elizabeth Todd.

HUGHES, DANIEL: associate of Samuel Hughes during the Revolution in the manufacture of cannon, Frederick County, Md.; among Md. trustees of Ballendine's Potomac navigation project, 1774; Washington County, Md., committee of safety, 1776, 1777; St. Paul's vestryman, ca. 1780. See Scharf, *History of Baltimore*, 519.

HUGHES, SAMUEL: among Md. trustees of Ballendine's Potomac navigation project, 1774; probably a member of Washington County, Md., committee of safety, 1775–1777; member, Md. legislative committee sent to New Orleans in search of arms and clothing, 1778; state senator, 1781–1783; owned Md.-based privateers during the Revolution; associated with Daniel Hughes in Messrs. Samuel and Daniel Hughes, cannon manufacturers of Frederick County, Md., during the Revolution; cast shot for the U.S. Navy at Mt. Pleasant Iron Foundry, with financial aid through the policy of navy secretary Robert Smith, 1805. See Scharf, *History of Baltimore*, 79, 100–104, 193, 205, 424.

HUNTER, ALLISON & Co.: Alexandria merchants, specialized in wheat trade, 1775 and later; partners were John Allison and probably William Hunter.

HUNTER, JAMES (1721–1784): migrated from Scotland, 1746; operated an iron works in Stafford County near Falmouth, from about 1750; managed public stores at Fredericksburg, 1776; during Revolution the works was vital to the American war effort, being a rolling and slitting mill working 600 to 800 tons of iron each year. See O. H. Darter, *Colonial Fredericksburg . . .* (N.Y., 1957), 201–204, 231.

HUNTER, JOHN (1733–1795): merchant, lived at Little England, near Hampton, Va.; son of William

Hunter and half brother of Williams-burg printer-postmaster William Hunter; directed building of Cape Henry lighthouse, 1752; army com-missary-gen., French and Indian War, when associated with John Carlyle of Alexandria; evidently sold business to Capel and Osgood Hanbury and Richard Goslin, all London mer-chants; beneficiary and executor of Gov. Dinwiddie's will.

HUNTER, WILLIAM (b. 1748?): Alex-andria merchant, probably a partner in the wheat-flour firm of Hunter & Allison; active on behalf of a petitions favoring Potomac naval force (1779), increased congressional powers for Congress (1785), wheat inspection (1788).

HUNTER, WILLIAM (d. 1761): Wil-liamsburg printer-postmaster; son of William Hunter, Hampton merchant; bought printing business from daugh-ter of William Parks, first newspaper printer in Williamsburg, and con-tinued publication of the *Va. Gazette*, 1751–1761; acted as official printer for colony; friend of Benjamin Franklin, who appointed him deputy postmas-ter-gen., 1753–1761; in his will, pro-vided wages for teacher in a Negro school. See Isaiah Thomas, *History of Printing in America* (Albany, 1874), II, 163–165.

*HUTCHINS, THOMAS (1730–1789): military engineer, typographer; officer, colonial troops, 1757–1759; later joined regular British army, but resigned, 1780; prepared *A Topo-graphical Description of Virginia, Pennsylvania, Maryland and North Carolina* (1778); *An Historical Nar-rative and Topographical Description of Louisiana and West Florida* (1784); geographer of the U.S., 1781–1789; supervised survey of the Northwest Territory under Ordi-nance of 1785, his surveying system is still used for platting public lands in the U.S.; died during his 3d expedi-tion to complete plat of the seven ranges.

ILLINOIS COUNTY: in Va.; created in Dec. 1778, by the General Assembly;

encompassed the region north of the Ohio, much of it still controlled by the British or Indians; the legislation asserted Va. control over the area conquered by G. R. Clark's troops; the county was dissolved by the Va. western land cession which Congress accepted in Mar. 1784.

*IMLAY, GILBERT (*ca.* 1754–*ca.* 1828): known as capt., but uncertain whether he attained this rank during his Revolutionary War service; bought Ky. tract, by 1783; deputy surveyor, speculator on large scale in Ky., 1784; encountered financial, legal difficulties, left Ky., and probably North America, Nov. or Dec., 1785; despite repeated efforts, Ky. courts were unable to locate him; wrote *A Topographical Description of the Western Territory of North America* (London, 1792), novel *The Emigrants* (1793); while in Ky., had dealt with James Wilkinson and Benjamin Sebas-tian, who were secretly plotting with Spain; became politically important in France for his involvement with Bris-sot in plans to seize La. from Spain, 1793; formed liaison with Mary Wall-stonecraft, and was father of her daughter Fanny. See R. L. Rusk, "The Adventures of Gilbert Imlay," *Indiana University Studies*, X (1923).

"INDIAN QUEEN": famous Philadelphia tavern at corner of High Street and South Fourth; was meeting place for delegates to the Federal Convention (May–Sept. 1787).

INDIANA COMPANY. See VANDALIA COMPANY.

*INNES, HARRY (1753–1816): practiced law in Bedford County; administered state-owned powder mills and lead mines, 1776–1777; claims commissioner for Abingdon area, 1779; Bedford County escheator, 1779; tax commis-sioner 1781–1784; atty. gen., Va. west-ern district, 1784; moved to Ky., 1785; opposed ratification of the Federal Constitution, 1788; U.S. district judge, Ky., 1789–1816; active advocate of Ky. statehood; possibly associated with Benjamin Sebastian and Gen. James Wilkinson in their Spanish intrigues; bitter personal and political enemy of Humphrey Marshall.

*IZARD, RALPH (1742–1804): born in S.C., attended school in Hackney, England; married Alice DeLancey, niece of James DeLancey, chief justice, and lieut. gov. of N.Y., 1767; lived in London as patron of literature and art, 1771; toured continent with Arthur Lee, 1774–1775; Congress elected him commissioner to Tuscany, 1777; S.C. congressman, 1782; Federalist U.S. Senator, 1789–1795; pres. *pro temp.* of the 3d Senate; invalided by paralytic stroke, 1797.

*JACKSON, WILLIAM (1759–1828): known as "Major Jackson"; born in Cumberland, England; brought to S.C.; served in Gadsden's regiment, 1775; lieut. in expedition against St. Augustine, Fla., 1778; asst. secy. war dept. under Gen. Lincoln, 1782–1783; secy., Federal Convention, 1787; personal secy. to Washington, 1789–1791; declined appointment as adj. gen., 1791; business partner of William Bingham; married Elizabeth Willing, daughter of Thomas Willing, pres., Bank of North America, 1795; assisted surviving Continental officers in adjustment of their half-pay claims, 1818–1819.

JAMES, ABEL: Philadelphia Quaker merchant, partner of Henry Drinker; close friend and correspondent of Benjamin Franklin; partner in attempt to establish a linen manufactory, 1764, financial supporter to Philadelphia Academy, 1755, and Library Co. of Philadelphia.

*JEFFERSON, THOMAS (1743–1826): lawyer, born in Albemarle County; 3d pres. of U.S.; burgess, 1769–1775; del. to Continental Congress, 1775–1776; drafted Declaration of Independence; del. to Va. General Assembly, 1776–1778; often exchanged ideas with GM, wrote a draft of Va. constitution that was influential in shaping final document, 1776; gov. of Va., 1779–1781; congressman, envoy to France, cabinet minister under Washington, 1783–1794; elected vice-pres. of U.S., 1796; pres. of U.S.,

1800–1809; wrote Va. bill establishing religious freedom and was founder of Univ. of Va., 1817–1826; buried near Monticello, elegant home he designed. A definitive edition of his papers is being published under the editorship of Julian P. Boyd (Princeton, 1950—).

JENIFER, DANIEL (1727–1795): of Charles County, Md.; brother of Daniel of St. Thomas Jenifer; may have been partner in Md. firm of Jenifer & Hooe, Potomac and Chesapeake Bay merchants; commissary of purchases for Charles County, *ca.* 1776–1781.

*JENIFER, DANIEL OF ST. THOMAS (1723–1790): owner of Stepney, in Charles County, Md.; brother of Daniel Jenifer; commissioner, Del.-Pa. boundary dispute, 1760; rec.-gen. for proprietors; Gov.'s Council, 1773–1775; pres., Md. council of safety, 1775 and Md. Senate, 1777; del. to Continental Congress, 1778–1782; served with GM as commissioner at Mount Vernon Convention, 1785; Md. intendant of revenue; del. to Federal Convention, 1787.

JETT, THOMAS (d. 1785): merchant of Leedstown, Westmoreland County; lived at Walnut Hill, represented London factors Perkins, Buchanan & Brown and later Barley, Wigginton & Francis; King George County committee of safety, 1775.

JOHNS, AQUILA: ship capt., may have been skipper of the *Dolphin;* commanded the *Buckskin,* 28-gun privateer owned by Samuel and Robert Purviance and other Baltimore residents, 1779; married Hannah Bond, 1757; Baltimore town undersheriff, 1780.

JOHNS, THOMAS: Georgetown, Md., merchant; named as Md. trustee in project for clearing and navigating the Potomac, 1774.

JOHNSON, JOSHUA: (b. 1742), merchant, brother of Gov. Thomas Johnson of Md.; born in Calvert County, Md.; worked in London counting house, eventually became a large tobacco dealer, and was apparently with firm of Wallace, Davidson & Johnson, and later of Wallace, Johnson & Muir; lived at Nantes, 1776, and served as an American agent, 1776–1781; handled order for engraving GM's coat of arms, *ca.* 1784; 1st American consul at London, 1790–1797; his 2d daughter, Louisa Catherine, married John Quincy Adams; returned to America, appointed to minor post by Pres. John Adams. See Esmerelda Boyle, *Biographical Sketches of Distinguished Marylanders* (Baltimore, 1877).

JOHNSON, RINALDO: of Prince Georges County, Md.; married GM's daughter, Ann Eilbeck Mason; authorized to sign money during the session of Continental Congress at Baltimore; member of the Patuxent Associators, served on the committee of purchases, 1781; postmaster at Acquasco, Md., before 31 Dec. 1811, when Thomas Rinaldo Johnson was appointed deputy postmaster; his relationship with other Md. Johnsons is uncertain. See Scharf, *History of Baltimore*, 74.

*JOHNSON, THOMAS (1732–1819): born in Calvert County, Md.; practiced law in Annapolis; served as Anne Arundel County rep. in Md. Gen. Assembly; del. to Continental Congress, 1774–1775; active in Potomac navigation scheme, 1775, 1785, and pres. of Potowmack Co., 1789; Md. gov., 1777–1779; urged ratification of Articles of Confederation by Md. legislature conditioned on surrender of western claims by Va. and other states, 1780–1781, 1786–1787; del. to Md. ratifying convention, 1788, supported Constitution; assoc. justice, U.S. Supreme Court, 1791–1793. See Harrison, 404–405.

*JOHNSON, SIR WILLIAM (1715–1774): land speculator and Indian agent; one of largest land owners in North America; his intimate knowledge of the Six Nations, especially the Mohawks, enabled him to bind this alliance to the English; N.Y. provincial council, 1750–1774; royal agent for Six Nations, 1754; built Fort William Henry, 1755; created baronet, 1755; royal agent for all tribes north of the Ohio, 1756; captured Fort Niagara,

1759; established fur trade, 1761; deputized George Croghan agent for Pa. and Ohio valley tribes, 1756; favored a boundary of settlement, which was accomplished through the Treaty of Fort Stanwix, 1768, which Indiana Company used as basis for claims against GM's Ohio Co. interests.

*JOHNSON, WILLIAM SAMUEL (1727–1819): of Stratford, Conn.; known as Dr. Johnson, from his honorary LL.D., Oxford, 1766; lawyer; Conn. House of Reps., 1761, 1765; 1st Anglican in the Conn. upper house, 1766–1775; Stamp Act Congress, 1765; Continental Congress, 1784–1787; Federal Convention, 1787, and signer of Constitution; supported adoption in Conn. ratifying convention; U.S. Senator, 1789–1791; pres. of Columbia College, 1787–1800; active in drafting the Judiciary Act, 1789.

JOHNSTON, ARCHIBALD: GM's neighbor, son of George Johnston (d. 1766), an Alexandria lawyer, and Sarah McCarty; may have served with 12th Va. Regt., Continental line; brother of Lieut. Col. George Johnston.

JOHNSTON, GEORGE (1750–1777): called Col. George Johnston, Jr.; son of George Johnston, Fairfax County burgess and confidant of Patrick Henry; his 2d wife, Sarah McCarty, sister of GM's friend Daniel McCarty (d. 1792); served at the battle of the Great Bridge, 9 Dec. 1775; capt. 2d Va. Regt. operating against Dunmore, May 1776; maj., 1776; lieut. col., aide-de-camp, confidential military secretary to Washington, 1776–1777.

JOHNSTON, ZACHARIAH (1742–1800): son of Irish immigrant; inherited estate near Fisherville; sent from Augusta County to House of Delegates, 1778–1791; supported act establishing religious toleration, 1785; Augusta del. to Va. ratifying convention, 1788; supported Constitution; del. from Rockbridge County to Va. General Assembly, 1792, 1797, 1798. See Grigsby, I, 341.

JONES, CHARLES: Alexandria coach maker; owned eight slaves in 1782.

JONES, GABRIEL (1724–1806): born near Williamsburg; educated in England, served law apprenticeship under John Houghton; king's atty. for Frederick and Augusta counties; Frederick burgess, between 1748 and 1754; Hampshire burgess, 1754–1755, 1758–1761; Augusta burgess, 1757, 1758, 1769–1771; sponsored Washington's 1st candidacy as Frederick burgess, 1758; prosecutor, Rockingham County; Va. commissioner to investigate disaffection near Fort Pitt, 1777; elected twice to Continental Congress but refused to serve, 1779; headed list of judicial appointments in Va. state system, but refused to serve, 1788; House of Delegates, 1783; strongly Federalist Rockingham County del. to Va. ratifying convention, 1788.

*JONES, JOSEPH (1727–1805): lawyer, politician, born in King and Queen County; studied law in England, admitted to practice there, 1751; moved to Fredericksburg, then to King George County, where he was elected burgess, 1772; served on Va. committee of safety; del. to Va. conventions, 1775–1776; served with GM on committee to draft a declaration of rights, 1776; del. to Continental Congress, 1777–1778, 1780–1783; worked with GM in establishing Va. claims to western territory and Va. cession to Congress; justice, Va. General Court, 1789–1805; was uncle of James Monroe.

JONES, WALTER (1745–1815): son of Thomas Jones (d. 1757) and Elizabeth Cocke; of Hayfield in Lancaster County; studied at William and Mary, and at Univ. of Edinburgh with Dr. William Cullen, where he graduated, 1769; married Alice, daughter of Dr. William Flood; appointed Physician Gen. to the Continental army, but declined; longtime member of Va. legislature; del. to Va. ratifying convention of 1788; congressman, 1797–1799, 1803–1811; father of Walter Jones; personal physician of Robert Carter of Nomini Hall.

JUNIATTA RIVER (CHONIATA, CHINIOTTA, CHINIOTTE, JONIADY, JOHNDACHQUANAH): sources in Bedford and Blair counties, Pa.; enters the Susquehanna River at Logania, Perry County, near Harrisburg; identified on Lewis Evans's 1755 map as "Juniata R."

KEITH, JAMES (1734–1824): called "Major"; oldest son of Rev. James Keith of Hamilton Parish, and Mary Isham Randolph; Hampshire County burgess, 1761–1762; resigned to become Frederick County clerk, 1762–1824; moved to Alexandria after Revolution, served as mayor, 1784; urged GM to support ratification of the Constitution, 1787; actively promoted turnpikes, industries and towns dependent upon Alexandria's commerce; among the original promoters of Potomac navigation improvements, and was among the Fredericktown Adventurers of Thomas Johnson's plan of 1762; an early subscriber of the Potowmack Co. and held directorship and presidency, 1798; uncle of John Marshall.

*KENTON, SIMON (1755–1836): frontiersman, alias Simon Butler; hunter along the Ohio, Great and Little Kanawha rivers, 1771–1774; scout, Dunmore's War, 1774; moved to Boonesborough, appointed scout, 1775; served Clark expedition to Kaskaskia, 1778; captured by Ohio Indians, taken to the British at Detroit, and escaped, 1779; scouted for Clark on the Ohio, 1780, 1782; lived at Maysville, Ky., 1785; served with Gen. Shelby's Kentuckians during the War of 1812; moved to Zanesfield, Logan county, ca. 1820, where he died.

*KING, RUFUS (1755–1827): Newburyport, Mass., lawyer; rep. to Mass. general court, 1783–1785; moved to allow neither "slavery nor involuntary servitude" in the Northwest Territory, while in Continental Congress, 1784–1786; del. to Federal Convention, where he served on the committee on style, 1787; del. to Mass. ratifying convention, 1788; moved to N.Y., and elected to N.Y. Assembly; U.S. senator from N.Y., 1789–1795, 1813–1825; minister plenipotentiary to Great Britain, 1796–1803, 1825–1826; last Federalist candidate for pres., 1816.

KIRK, JAMES: Alexandria merchant; migrated from Derbyshire; perhaps married Mary Norris, Lancaster County, 1762; later married Lucy Carter, daughter of Edward Carter and Catherine Brent, 1768; listed by Robert Carter of Nomini Hall as Alexandria wheat buyer, 1775; signed Fairfax nonimportation assn., 1770, Fairfax County committee of safety, 1774–1775; Fairfax committee of correspondence; signed Alexandria petition seeking to increase the power of Congress over commerce, 1785.

KIRKPATRICK, THOMAS: Alexandria merchant; signed Fairfax County nonimportation assn., 1770; wheat buyer and flour inspector, 1775; also spelled "Kilpatrick."

KISKOMINETO RIVER (KISKIMINETAS): in Pa.; formed by the union of the Conemaugh and Loyalhanna Rivers; enters the Alleghany opposite Freeport, Armstrong County, Pa.; called Romanettoes by the Ohio Company. See Lewis Evans's *Map of the Middle British Colonies in America* (London, 1755).

*LAMB, JOHN (1735–1800): son of a convict transported to N.Y. City, who later manufactured mathematical instruments; prospered as a wine merchant; led N.Y. Sons of Liberty after the Stamp Act; signed nonimportation assn.; capt., N.Y. artillery co., 1775; commanded artillery at West Point, 1779, 1780; brevetted brig. gen., 1783; served in N.Y. legislature; appointed collector of customs for the Port of N.Y., 1784; chairman, "Federal Republicans" Society opposing the Constitution; died in poverty.

LANCASTER: Pa. site of Indian treaty conference in the summer of 1744 where the Six Nations (Iroquois) recognized the king's right to all lands in Va.; this enabled Va. to make land grants on south side of Ohio River; Va.'s rep. to conference was Thomas Lee of the Ohio Co.

LANE, JAMES HARDWICK: of Stafford and Loudoun counties; possibly the agent for Robert Carter's Frying Pan Tract, 1762–1766; overseer of the estate of Col. William Steptoe, 1771; possibly member of Loudoun County committee of safety, 1775; brothers were John and William; "Hardwick" often appears in other spellings, e.g., Hardidge, Hardage.

LANE, WILLIAM: Alexandria merchant in firm of William Lane & Co., 1792; may have been the father of John Lane (1789–1855), Methodist minister and founder of Vicksburg, Miss.

*LANGDON, JOHN (1741–1819): Portsmouth, N.H., businessman; speaker, N.H. legislature, 1775, 1777–1781, 1786–1787, 1803–1805; Continental Congress, 1775–1776, 1783, 1788; N.H. Senate, 1784; N.H. pres., 1785, 1788; Federal Convention, 1787; N.H. ratifying convention, 1788; pres. *pro tempore* during the 1st and most of the 2d congresses in the U.S. Senate, 1789–1801; heavy speculator in Continental securities; opposed Jay Treaty, 1795; strongly Francophile, he opposed the Quasi-War against France, 1798–1799; N.H. gov., 1805–1811, except 1809.

LANGHORNE, WILLIAM: of Gambell, Warwick County; called "Major"; Warwick burgess, 1772–1775; signed Va. nonimportation agreements, 1769, 1774; Warwick committee of safety, 1774; del. to Va. convention, 1775.

LANGSTONE, THOMAS: apparently of Upper Parish, Nansemond County, where he witnessed the agreement of Rev. Patrick Lunan to relinquish his rectorship there, 1775.

LAURASON, JAMES, JR.: resident of Alexandria, probably associated with the mercantile firm, Laurason & Scott, also Laurason & Shreve; petitioner on behalf of Alexandria Academy, 1786, and for wheat inspection, 1787; also spelled "Lawrason."

*LAURENS, JOHN (1754–1782): Middle Temple-educated son of Continental Congress pres., Henry Laurens; Revolutionary War lieut. col.; wounded

Gen. Charles Lee in a duel issuing from Lee's "constant personal abuse" of Washington, 1778; after being exchanged following the surrender of Charleston, Congress commissioned him envoy extraordinary to France, 1780, to express the needs of the army; he succeeded by appealing directly to King Louis XVI, 1781; returned to America and negotiated the terms of capitulation after the Yorktown campaign, 1781; killed in guerrilla combat; GM alluded to him as "Col. Lawrence" in letter to his son, 3 June 1781.

LAWSON, ROBERT (1748–1805): of Prince Edward County; maj. 4th Va. Regt., 1776, col., 1777; brig. gen. by 1780; during Gen. Leslie's invasion of Va., Lawson raised a militia legion, chose his own officers, among them Lt. Col. John Francis Mercer and James Monroe, 1780; this troop joined Gen. Muhlenberg near Smithfield, Isle of Wight County, but disbanded when Leslie joined Cornwallis by water; served in House of Delegates, 1779; Va. Privy Council, 1781; his brigade was noted for its desertions during harvest season, 1781; battle of Guilford Court House, 1781; Va. Society of the Cincinnati, without brevet; Hampden-Sidney College trustee, 1783; del. to Va. ratifying convention, 1788; moved to Ky., 1789; died in Richmond.

*LEAR, TOBIAS (1762–1816): born in Portsmouth, N.H.; attended Harvard, 1783; travelled and studied in Europe; private secy. to Washington, 1785–ca. 1792; settled at Alexandria, 1794; pres., Potomac Canal Co., 1795; his 2d wife was the widow of George Augustine Washington; Washington's military secy., 1798; consul gen. at Algiers, ca. 1802; negotiated with Morocco and Tripoli, 1803–1805; left Algiers, 1812; committed suicide.

*LEE, ARTHUR (1740–1792): son of Thomas Lee of Stratford, brother of Richard Henry Lee, William Lee; studied at Eton and Edinburgh University, 1764; began medical practice in Williamsburg, 1766; left medicine for law, 1768, studying in Lincoln's Inn and Middle Temple; admitted to London bar, 1775; wrote newspaper essays on behalf of colonial resistance, 1768–1775; appointed to join Franklin and Deane as commissioner to France, 1776; feuded with Deane and Franklin over conduct in France; appointed to Spanish mission, but remained in Paris, where William Lee and Ralph Izard joined him, 1777; signed treaty with France; Lee's charges caused Congress to recall Deane, but later Congress split between Lee and Deane, Lee was dismissed in 1779 and returned to Va., 1780; del. to Va. House of Delegates, Continental Congress, 1781–1784; commissioner to treat with Indians at Ft. Stanwix, 1784, at Ft. McIntosh, 1785; appointed by Congress to the treasury board, 1785–1789; opposed Constitution; retired to Lansdowne, Middlesex County.

*LEE, CHARLES (1731–1782): English-born professional army officer whose first battle was Braddock's defeat, 1755; fought in America, Portugal; considered a plan for establishing colonies in the Illinois country; settled in Berkeley County, 1775; violently anti-Tory; 2d ranking Continental maj. gen.; visited Williamsburg, March–May 1776, and became involved in controversy over Gov. Eden of Md.; worked on the defenses of Charleston, S.C., and Ga., 1776–1777; strongly criticized Washington, and was challenged by John Laurens; captured and held British prisoner, 1777–1778; court martialled, convicted for retreating without apparent cause from battle of Monmouth, 1778; his one-year suspension from the army was followed by dismissal.

LEE, FRANCIS (d. ca. 1794): plantation owner, Warwick County; son of Francis Lee (d. 1753) of Chiskiak, York County; as orphan lived with brother William; filed claim for enemy depredations on Peninsula, 1781.

*LEE, FRANCIS LIGHTFOOT (1734–1797): son of Thomas Lee of Stratford; settled in Loudoun County, where he was burgess, 1758–1768, and original trustee of Leesburg, 1758; member, Mississippi Co., 1763; signed Westmoreland assn. against the Stamp Act, 1766; married Rebecca Tayloe, daughter of John Tayloe of Mt. Airy, and settled at Menokin, Richmond County, 1769; Richmond burgess, 1769–1776; del. to Va. convention, 1775; when GM declined nomination to Continental Congress, he recommended Lee, who served, 1775–1779; signed Declaration of Independence, helped frame Articles of Confederation, and advocated free navigation of the Mississippi, free northern fisheries, and a peace treaty with Great Britain as a necessity; supported the Constitution, 1787–1788.

LEE, HANCOCK (1740–1819): son of Hancock Lee of Ditchley and Mary Willis, daughter of Henry Willis of Fredericksburg; his home, Greenview was on the Rappahannock, in Fauquier County; with brother Willis Lee, and cousin Hancock Taylor, explored in Ky., where Indians killed both companions and captured him, *ca.* 1771–1774; supervised Ohio Co. surveyors, 1775; Ohio Co. failed to secure their grant because Lee was not legally certified surveyor; married Winifred Eustace Beale, 1776; founded Leestown on the Kentucky River, one mile below the future site of Frankfort, 1776; friend of Daniel Boone; commissioner of the Rappahannock Co., 1811; his children were Willis, Hancock, Thomas Ludwell (not to be confused with the son of Thomas Lee of Stratford), Emeline, Elizabeth; died in Ky.

LEE, HENRY (1729–1787): of Leesylvania, near Dumfries, Prince William County; son of Henry Lee and Mary Bland; brother of "Squire" Richard Lee of Lee Hall; married Lucy Grymes, daughter of Charles Grymes and Frances Jenings, 1753; attorney, Prince William justice of peace, county lieut., burgess, 1758–1776; del. to Va. conventions, 1775–1776; Dumfries trustee, 1761; Va. Senate, 1780; among the wealthiest Virginians, 1787,

1788; his children included Henry ("Light Horse Harry"); grandfather of Robert E. Lee.

*LEE, HENRY (1756–1818): known as "Light Horse Harry," son of Henry Lee of Leesylvania, where he was born; attended College of New Jersey (Princeton), 1773; spectacular cavalry officer; his "Lee's Legion" was created after earlier service with Va. regts., 1778; joined Gen. Greene in southern campaign and was at Yorktown, 1781; married cousin Matilda Lee, heiress of Stratford; del. to Va. House of Delegates, 785; Continental Congress, 1785–1788; Federalist at Va. ratifying convention, 1788; Va. gov., 1792–1795; U.S. House of Reps., 1799–1801; 2d wife was Anne Hill Carter of Shirley, and their 5th child was Robert E. Lee (1807–1870); injured in riot, his health failed after 1811; died at Cumberland Island, Ga.

LEE, JOHN (d. 1777): 8th son of Philip Lee of Md., where he was born; settled in Essex County, where he succeeded his cousin Col. John Lee of Cabin Point (d. 1767), as county clerk, 1761–1777; son, Hancock Lee, succeeded him; married Susannah Smith, cousin of Mrs. John Lee of Cabin Point.

LEE, JOHN (1709–1789): bachelor son of Hancock Lee and Mary Kendall, known as Capt. John Lee of Chapawamsic; uncle of Ohio Co. surveyor Hancock Lee; inherited 1,750 acres on Chapawamsic Creek, Stafford County, and patented 240 acres on Cedar Run, a branch of the Chapawamsic, adjoining a tract of his brother Hancock, 1724; may have been Aquia Parish vestryman, 1757; died at the Orange County home of his nephew, John, son of Hancock Lee.

LEE, JOHN (1743–1802): son of Hancock Lee and Mary Willis; brother of Ohio Co. surveyor Hancock Lee; ensign, 1775; capt. of marines aboard the Va. state sloop Liberty, 1776; Continental line lieut., capt., 2d Va. Regt., 1776; maj., Va. state line, 1778; retired from service, 1782, after serving under Gen. Gates in the Carolinas, and received a large service bounty; settled in Woodford County, Ky., 1792.

LEE, JOHN; called John Lee, Jr., of Orange County; son of Hancock Lee; cousin of Richard Henry Lee, nephew of Col. John Lee (1709–1789); possibly a signer of the Westmoreland Resolves.

LEE, LUDWELL (1760–1836): 2d son of Richard Henry Lee and Anne Aylett; educated in England and France; returned to America, practiced law, but soon became a planter; Va. Senate, 1793, and sometime pres.; an original trustee of Newport, Va., 1787; married cousin Flora Lee, daughter of Philip Ludwell Lee of Stratford, 1788; married 2d wife, Elizabeth, 1797; he had nine children; member of Fairfax Parish, 1789; lived at Shooter's Hill, near Alexandria, later at Belmont, near Leesburg, Loudoun County, where he died.

LEE, PHILIP LUDWELL (1727–1775): oldest surviving son of Thomas Lee of Stratford, Westmoreland County, and Hannah Ludwell; inherited Stratford; educated in England, and studied law, Inner Temple, 1749; accompanied his father and William Beverley when they went to treat with Indians in Pa., 1744; his father gave him a 2/40 share of Ohio Co. stock, 1749, which his estate or heirs still held in 1778; Westmoreland burgess, 1756, succeeded father on the Gov.'s Council, 1757, and was pres., 1758, 1759; original trustee, Leesburg, 1758, and of Philee, 100 acres adjoining the warehouse at the Falls of the Potomac, 1772; married Elizabeth, daughter of Col. James Steptoe of Westmoreland County, ca. 1761; active turfman; inherited lands in Westmoreland and Northumberland counties, on the Md. Eastern Shore, above the Falls of the Potomac, and two islands in the Potomac; appraisal of his estate, filed 1782, enumerates 6,595 acres, including Stratford.

LEE, RICHARD (1726–1795): Squire of Lee Hall, Hague, Va.; son of Henry and Mary Bland Lee of Leesylvania;

married Sarah Poythress, 1786; Westmoreland justice of peace; Cople Parish vestry, 1755, 1785; Westmoreland burgess between 1757 and 1774; del. to Va. conventions, July, Dec. 1775; House of Delegates, between 1777 and 1793; naval officer for South Potomac dist.; member, Ohio Company; brother of Col. Henry Lee of Leesylvania.

*LEE, RICHARD BLAND (1761–1827): son of Henry Lee, brother of Henry "Light-Horse Harry" Lee; Loudoun del. to Va. General Assembly, 1784–1788, 1796; Federalist, Va. ratifying convention, 1788; Va. rep. in Congress, 1789–1795, where he switched to favor assumption of state debts in exchange for location of the national capital on the Potomac, 1789; moved to Washington, D.C., 1815.

* LEE, RICHARD HENRY (1732–1794): son of Thomas Lee; born at Stratford; Westmoreland justice of peace, 1757; charter member, Mississippi Co., 1763; Westmoreland burgess, 1758–1776; opposed tax plans by Parliament; organized Westmoreland nonimportation assn., 1766; possibly drafted nonimportation resolves, 1769, which GM approved; drafted plans for committees of correspondence with Jefferson and Patrick Henry, 1773; Va. del. to Continental Congress, 1774–1779, 1784–1787; Va. conventions, Mar. 1775, May 1776; Va. House of Delegates, 1780; declined election to the Constitutional Convention, 1787; opposed ratification of the Constitution, and wrote Antifederalist "Letters of the Federal Farmer"; U.S. Senate, 1789–1792.

LEE, THOMAS (1690–1750): born at Mt. Pleasant, Westmoreland County, 4th son of Richard Lee; reputedly taught himself Latin and Greek; married Hannah Philippa, 2d daughter of Col. Philip Ludwell of Greenspring, James City County, Lee's associate on the Va. Council, 1722; by shrewd moves built small paternal inheritance into a large fortune; managed Fairfax family properties in Va., 1713–1747; Westmoreland burgess, 1726, 1727–

1728, 1732, but judged unduly elected, 1720, 1722; his house, Mt. Pleasant was robbed, burned apparently in revenge for signing a criminal warrant; received grant from Queen Caroline's privy purse to compensate for loss; moved to Stratford, on the Potomac; Va. del. to Lancaster Indian conference, where crown bought title to western lands and secured Ohio Valley tribes as allies; Va. Council, from *ca.* 1732 onward, where he served as acting gov. and commander-in-chief, 1749–1750; died before commission as Va. gov. reached him, 1750; apparently initiated the organization of the Ohio Co., 1748–1749; while acting gov., corresponded on western lands and the boundary dispute between Va. and Pa. with Gov. Hamilton, 1749–1750; named among debtors of Speaker Robinson's estate, 1749; father of Philip Ludwell, Thomas Ludwell, Richard Henry, Francis Lightfoot, William, Arthur, and two daughters.

LEE, THOMAS LUDWELL (1730–1778): 4th son of Col. Thomas Lee of Stratford; admitted to Inner Temple, 1748; married Mary, daughter of William Aylett of Westmoreland; Stafford burgess, 1758–1765, 1768; inherited Ohio Co. shares from his father, 1750; charter member, Mississippi Co., 1763; signed Westmoreland address and resolves against the Stamp Act, 1766; Va. conventions, 1775–1776; Va. committee of safety, 1775, 1776; served on convention committee to prepare a bill of rights, and original draft is in the handwriting of Lee and GM, 1776; a political ally of Patrick Henry, he was a nominee for pres. of the General Assembly, 1776; justice, Va. General Court, 1777–1778; committee to revise Va. laws, 1777–1778; died of rheumatic fever at his home, Bellevue, Overwharton Parish, Stafford County, three months after the committee of revisors met at Fredericksburg, and without having completed his, the 5th, portion of the revision; his children were Thomas Ludwell, William Aylett, George, Anne Fenton (who married Col.

Daniel Carroll of Richland), Lucinda, Rebecca.

*LEE, WILLIAM (1739–1795): 10th child of Col. Thomas Lee of Stratford; charter member, Mississippi Co., 1763; associated with his brother Arthur, the Dennys, DeBerdts and Stephen Sayre in London business, 1768–1776; sheriff of London, 1773; alderman of London, 1775; GM believed Lee cheated him on 1775 tobacco transaction, led to bitter lawsuit; U.S. commercial agent at Nantes, 1777; U.S. commissioner to Berlin, Vienna, Holland, 1777–1779; remained in Brussels until 1783, when he retired to his Va. home Green Spring; married in London to Hannah Philippa Ludwell, daughter of Philip Ludwell of Green Spring, 1769.

LEETE, DANIEL: surveyed Ohio Co. lands with Hancock Lee; brigade master, quartermaster, and paymaster, Va. troops in the Continental line.

*L'ENFANT, PIERRE CHARLES (1754–1825): French military engineer, served without pay in American Revolution, and retired as a maj., 1777–1784; settled in N.Y.; member, designer of the Society of the Cincinnati eagle; designed the remodelling of government buildings when capital was in N.Y. City; planned the District of Columbia, 1791.

LEWIS, STEPHEN: of Fairfax County; voted in 1774 election of burgesses; apparently served in 8th Va. Regt., Continental line, or with light dragoons, during Revolution; probably married Elizabeth Offutt.

LEWIS, THOMAS: of Fairfax County; Truro Parish vestryman, 1733, churchwarden, 1735, and replaced on the vestry by Col. John Colville, 1740; Thomas Lewis and Thomas Lewis, Jr., both voted in the Fairfax election for burgesses, 1744; presumably, one of them served on the Fairfax County committee of safety, 1774.

LEWIS, THOMAS (1718–1790): called "Col."; born in Ireland, and migrated with his father, John, to Augusta County; brother of Andrew Lewis; 1st Augusta County surveyor, *ca.*

1750; married Jane Strother, sister of Mrs. Gabriel Jones, 1749; apparently practiced law; served in Va. conventions, 1775–1776; favored independence, 1776; on committee to draft declaration of rights, state constitution, 1776; Augusta County committee of safety, 1776; state accounts commissioner; led Va. commissioners in arbitration of boundary dispute with Pa., 1779; Rockingham County del. to Va. ratifying convention, where he favored adoption of the Constitution, 1788; his estate was on the Shenandoah River. See Grigsby, II, 20–24.

LEXINGTON: a plantation owned by GM, on Dogue's or Mason Neck, and named about the time of the battle (19 Apr. 1775); later, GM gave the plantation to his oldest son, George Mason, Jr., who resided there until his death in 1796.

LICKING, WATERS OF: Ky. river which flows northwest, entering the Ohio River in Fayette County, Ky. between the Little and Big Miami rivers.

LIMOZIN, ANDRE: French merchant at Havre de Grace, appointed American agent there by William Lee, 1778; GM's dealings with him in 1778 were lengthy and unfortunate; appointed U.S. consul, 1787.

*LINCOLN, BENJAMIN (1733–1810): of Mass.; maj. gen. who commanded American forces at Charleston, S.C., 1778–1780, where he was replaced, after he and his forces had been captured, by Gen. Horatio Gates; served at Yorktown, 1781; sec. of war, 1781–1783; put down Shays's Rebellion, 1787; supported Constitution in Mass. ratifying convention, 1788; negotiated with Creek Indians in southern states, 1789, and with the Indians North of the Ohio, 1793.

LINTON, MR.: possibly John Linton or William Linton, both of Prince William County, and probably both related to Truro Parish vestryman (1765–1770) and longtime Prince William justice of peace William Linton (d. 1770); John Linton was a lieut., William an ensign in Va.

troops, Continental line; both were charter trustees of Carrborough, Va., 1788.

LITTLE, CHARLES: of Fairfax County; called "Col."; married Mary Manley; lived at Cleesh, which had belonged to John Colville, ca. 1765; lived in Pittsylvania County, 1767; Fairfax County justice of peace, 1782; commissioner for road to the northwestern mountain gaps, 1785; urged GM to support Constitution, 1787; original trustee of South Haven, Va., 1798, built on John Mason's land; trustee of Providence, Va., 1805; with Capt. William Henry Terrett, helped Washington survey land on Four Mile Run, 1799.

LITTLE HUNTING CREEK: Fairfax County; flows into the Potomac near Alexandria.

LITTLE, JAMES: possibly a merchant or planter, Anne Arundel County, Md.; GM and Little were involved in efforts to collect debts owed them by Thomas Rutland (d. ca. 1790), 1788.

LLOYD, THOMAS: shorthand reporter who sought clerkship at Pa. ratifying convention, 1787; lost bid for position, but some of his notes were printed; reported Md. ratifying convention, 1788, but Antifederalists believed he was bribed to suppress his notes; published *Congressional Register*, 1789, and was accused of misrepresenting House of Reps. debates in resolution presented to 1st Congress; Elliot, *Debates*, uses his reports, although their accuracy has been questioned.

LOGSTOWN: important Indian settlement in Pa. during migration of Delaware and Shawnee tribes, ca. 1725–1727; treaty signed here in 1752 was considered vital to Ohio Co. plans as it confirmed English right to build two trading posts on the Ohio and make settlements south of Ohio; situated on north bank of Ohio, about 18 miles below old Fort Duquesne.

LOMAX, LUNSFORD (1705–1772): of Portobago, Caroline County; son of John Lomax and Elizabeth Wormeley; crown commissioner for survey of Fairfax land grant, 1735–1737; Caroline burgess, 1742–1756; director, Cape Henry lighthouse, 1752; Va. commissioner, Treaty of Logstown, 1752.

LOMAX, THOMAS (1746–1811): planter of Portobago or Port Tobago on the Rappahannock, Caroline County; known as "Maj." involved with the Ohio Co.; married Ann Corbin, daughter of John Tayloe of Mt. Airy, 1773; brother-in-law of Francis Lightfoot Lee, and of Landon Carter of Sabine Hall; Caroline County committee of safety, 1774–1776; Caroline County justice of peace, 1776; Va. Senate, 1776; House of Delegates, 1778–1782; Va. Council, 1781–1783.

LOUDOUN, FORT: frontier outpost built 1756–1757 under command of Col. George Washington, on site of Winchester, Va.; held a garrison of 450 men and was equipped with 24 field guns; never attacked by French, who reported it impregnable; named to honor John Campbell, Earl of Loudoun, commander of British army in North America in early stages of French and Indian War, gov. gen. of Va., 1756–1759.

LOWNDES, ELIZABETH (1726–1789): daughter of Benjamin Tasker of Annapolis, pres. of the Md. Council; married Christopher Lowndes, merchant, at Bladensburg, 1747; among children was Rebecca (Mrs. Benjamin Stoddert); died at Bladensburg.

LOYALHANNA CREEK (LOWEATHAN-NING, LAELHANNECK, LEWLHANNON, LOYALHANNEN): in Pa., tributary of the Kiskiminetas rising in Westmoreland County, midway between the waters of the Juniata and the Ohio rivers on the trail from Raystown (Bedford) to Shannopins Town (Pittsburgh); united with the Conemaugh at Saltsburg, Pa., to form the Kiskiminetas.

LOYAUTÉ, MONSR. (also LOYEAUTÉ): Frenchman who as inspector gen. was to command and train a Va. corps of 100 men drafted from the state artillery, 1778; encountered trouble with

the Va. legislature when he conceived that his office included command over the military officers of Va. at large, and the Assembly directed him to confine command to his own corps; R. H. Lee had helped obtain support for him in Va. General Assembly in 1777.

LYLES, WILLIAM: of Prince Georges County, Md., and Alexandria; known as "Col."; partner of John Fitzgerald in Lyles & Fitzgerald, shippers, 1783–1789; served on Alexandria committee of safety during Revolution; member, Alexandria Sun Fire Co.; owned privateer schooner *Sally*, commissioned, 1782; commanded by Capt. T. Conway, was owned at Baltimore by W. and H. Lyles of Alexandria; may have owned New Tavern in Alexandria, 1785; supporter of Alexandria Academy, 1786; returned to Md., 1789. See Moore, *Seaport in Virginia*, 92.

MCATEE, WILLIAM: a small householder of Fairfax County, probably having settled there before Revolution; he appears on the 1785 county census in GM's precinct as head of a family of seven whites, but owned no dwelling house.

MCCABE, HENRY: Alexandria businessman before Revolution; may have signed Fairfax nonimportation assn., 1770.

MCCARTY, DANIEL (d. 1791): called "Col." and "the elder," of Fairfax County; GM's friend; son of Major Dennis McCarthy (d. 1743) and Sarah Ball; born at Pope's Creek, Westmoreland County, home of his grandfather, Col. Daniel McCarthy, Speaker, House of Burgesses; his uncle Daniel, was also Westmoreland burgess; married Sinah Ball (1728–1798) *ca.* 1742; apparently executor for Augustine Washington, Sr., with Lawrence Washington and Nathaniel Chapman, 1743; Truro Parish vestry, 1750–1791; with GM supervised construction of new glebe buildings, 1754; Colchester, Va., trustee, 1753; with GM, a Va. trustee for Ballendine's Potomac navigation project,

1774; Fairfax justice of peace, 1770, 1781, 1782; apparently Westmoreland County committee of safety, 1775; gave supplies to Revolutionary army, 1782; his children included Sarah (2d wife of Col. Richard Chichester), Daniel, Jr. (married GM's daughter Sarah), Sinah (married Peter Wagener, 1809); apparently lived and is buried at Mt. Airy, Fairfax County, near Cedar Grove.

McCARTY, DANIEL, JR. (1759–1801): called "Col.," "younger"; son of GM's friend, Col. Daniel McCarty of Pope's Creek and Sinah Ball; lieut., 1775; served at Brandywine, Germantown; married GM's daughter Sarah 1778, settled at his grandfather's estate, Cedar Grove, as one of GM's closest neighbors, between Pohick and Accotinck creeks; elected to Truro Parish vestry, 1779, but refused to serve; board of overseers of the poor, 1793, 1795; perhaps trustee of South Haven, Va., built on John Mason's land, 1798; lived for a time with his son Daniel in Md.; children were Daniel, born about 1780, settled in Charles County, Md., 1800; Edgar, Sarah, George (1786–1808); John, who killed his cousin Stevens Mason in a famous duel, 1818; William Mason, congressman.

McCARTY, THADDEUS (d. 1812): of Loudoun County; son of Maj. Dennis McCarty and Sarah Ball; brother of GM's friend and neighbor, Daniel McCarty; owned 1,220 acres on Goose Creek; married Sarah Elizabeth Richardson, niece of Peter Wagener, 1768; another Thaddeus McCarty was on the Lancaster County committee of safety, 1775, and county court clerk, 1778–1787.

McCLURE, JOHN (d. 1825): leading Baltimore merchant; actively supported nonimportation, 1770; Baltimore Independent Cadets, 1774; in Whig Club mob which menaced *Md. Gazette* Editor William Goddard in his house, 1777; subscribed £5,000 to buy salt for redistribution as price control measure, 1779; bought confiscated loyalist property; pledged large

sum to aid Lafayette, 1781; owned privateering vessels during Revolution; committee to build market house, 1784; contributed to building a courthouse, 1784.

*McCLURG, JAMES (*ca.* 1746–1823): M.D., Univ. of Edinburgh, 1770; Revolutionary wartime physician-gen. and director of hospitals for Va.; del. to Federal Convention, after Patrick Henry and Richard Henry Lee had declined appointment, 1787; there he advocated life term for pres., federal veto of state laws; Va. executive council.

McCREA, ROBERT: Alexandria merchant, in firm of McCrea & Mease; acted as commercial agents for Fairfax County, 1775; patron of Alexandria Academy, 1786; Fairfax County court, 1781, 1782; mayor of Alexandria.

MACCUBBIN, NICHOLAS: Annapolis merchant, active in provisioning ships; son of Zachariah Maccubbin; married Mary, daughter of Dr. Charles Carroll, 1747; St. Ann's parish vestry, 1747–1750, 1768, 1769; was paid for French and Indian War services; served, Md. General Assembly, 1780, 1781; committee to superintend Associators of Annapolis, 1781. See Middleton, *Tobacco Coast*, 235.

McDANIEL, [WILLIAM]: operated tavern in Dumfries, 1789; active in Dumfries Masonic lodge, 1797.

*McHENRY, JAMES (1753–1816): migrated from Ireland to Baltimore, via Philadelphia, where he studied medicine under Dr. Benjamin Rush; practiced medicine, served as surgeon in Revolutionary army, but abandoned medicine when he became secy. to Washington, *ca.* 1779; Md. Senate, 1781–1786, 1791–1796; Congress, 1783–1786; Federal Convention, 1787, where he kept private journal of the proceedings, 1787; Federalist, Md. ratifying convention, 1788; Md. Assembly, *ca.* 1788–1791; U.S. Secretary of War, 1796–1800; political ally of Alexander Hamilton; Federalist opponent of the War of 1812.

McLEAN, LAUGHLIN or LOCHLAN (b. 1731): Scotch immigrant who enlisted in Col. Washington's Prince William County detachment, 1755; may have been the Scotsman mentioned by GM in letter to P. Henry, 6 Apr. 1777.

McPHERSON,———: John Mason recalled that the 1st Scotch tutor at Gunston Hall was a Mr. McPherson, of Maryland, which means that he probably taught GM's children ca. 1767–1770; apparently travelled to England in winter, 1770–1771. See Rowland, I, 97, 151.

*MADISON, JAMES (1751–1836): legislator, of Orange County; 4th pres. of U.S.; educated at College of New Jersey (Princeton); entered Va. convention of 1776 and was instrumental in rewording of Article XVI in GM's Declaration of Rights; thereafter served in Va. legislature, Continental Congress and U.S. House of Reps.; drafted "Memorial & Remonstrance" against religious assessment bill, 1785, which GM helped circulate; member of Va. delegation, Federal Convention, 1787, and his notes are primary source of information about its proceedings; del. to Va. ratifying convention, 1788; supported Jefferson's program, helped prepare Ky. and Va. resolves, sec. of state, 1801–1809; elected pres. of U.S., 1808; reelected during War of 1812; retired to Montpelier, 1817. A definitive edition of his papers is being published under the editorship of William T. Hutchinson and William M. E. Rachal (Chicago, 1962—).

MALUND, JOHN: probably the John James Malund of Kinsale, Northumberland County, who migrated from Wales; married Harriot Lucy, daughter of Robert Carter of Nomini Hall; agent for Thomas, 6th Lord Fairfax; possibly Northumberland justice of peace; Va. state senator, 1793; maintained correspondence with Robert Carter, 1790–1802.

MANLEY, HARRISON (d. ca. 1773): of Fairfax County; married Sarah Massey; father of John Harrison; daughter, Penelope, married Daniel French;

fox-hunting companion of Washington; was security for Peirce Bayly as Truro Parish tithe collector, 1772.

MANLEY, JOHN: Fairfax County freeholder, 1744; son and heir of Harrison Manley; Truro Parish processioner in precinct between Pohick and Dogue's creeks, 1743; paid by parish for helping poor, 1743; bought a Pohick church pew 1773; married Sarah, daughter of Dade Massey and Parthenia Alexander, apparently the sister of Rev. Lee Massey, GM's cousin and widow of William Triplett.

MARKHAM, JAMES: capt., Va. state naval force, commanded Dragon, 1779, after earlier service aboard the Page on the Rappahannock; received 6,591 acres as military bounty; married Catherine Kenner of Fairfax County, 1770.

MARLBOROUGH, (also MARLBRO and MARLBORO): Stafford County; originally a town authorized by the Va. General Assembly which never prospered; purchased by John Mercer and converted into a plantation; often visited by GM during his youth.

*MARSHALL, THOMAS (1730–1802): father of Chief Justice John Marshall; closely associated with Washington and the Fairfax family, he aided Washington in survey of Fairfax lands; Fauquier burgess, 1761–1767, 1769–1778, 1775–1776; del. to Va. convention, 1775; surveyed in Ky. to locate land warrants, 1780; commissioner to examine and settle public accounts in the West, 1781; moved family to Ky., 1783; assisted GM in legal matters; Ky. del. to Va. General Assembly.

*MARTIN, JOSIAH (1737–1786): British army officer, 1737–1769; gov. of N.C., 1771–1775; commanded British and Loyalist troops in the South, 1776–1781.

*MARTIN, LUTHER (ca. 1748–1826): lawyer, Somerset County, Md., until he moved to Baltimore, 1778; Md. Convention at Annapolis, 1774; Md. atty. gen., 1778–1805, 1818–1822; untiring prosecutor of Loyalists; served in Continental Congress, 1785; Federal

Convention, 1787, where he walked out with John Francis Mercer and refused to sign the Constitution; opposed ratification as a member of the Md. convention, 1788; defended Aaron Burr in his treason trial at Richmond; chief judge of the court of oyer and terminer, City and County of Baltimore, 1813–1816; strong opponent of slavery; died in Aaron Burr's home.

MARTIN, THOMAS BRYAN (1731–1798): of Greenway Court; son of Denny Martin and Frances, sister of Thomas, 6th Lord Fairfax; migrated to Va., 1751, and was established on William Fairfax's quarter, The Manor of Greenway Court, Frederick County, where Lord Fairfax lived with him; Frederick justice of peace, ca. 1752–ca.1776; Hampshire County lieut., 1755; Hampshire burgess, 1756–1758; Frederick burgess, 1758–1761; succeeded George William Fairfax as Lord Fairfax's land agent for the Northern Neck, 1762; trustee for Winchester, Bath, and Warm Springs, 1758–1776; retired from public life at the beginning of the Revolution; Martinsburg, (W.) Va., named for him when it was laid out by Col. Adam Stephen, 1778; executor, beneficiary of Lord Fairfax, 1781; died unmarried, leaving Greenway Court estate to his housekeeper, and other effects to relatives in England; will was challenged by Va. because beneficiaries were aliens, but was upheld by U.S. Supreme Court.

MASON, ANN EILBECK (1755–1814): 2d surviving child of GM and Ann Eilbeck; married Rinaldo Johnson of Prince Georges County, Md.; after her mother died (1773), she was housekeeper at Gunston Hall until her marriage; lived at Aquasco.

MASON, DAVID (1733–1792): Sussex County burgess, 1758–1775; Va. conventions, 1775, 1776; House of Delegates, 1780, 1781; col., 15th Va. Regt., resigned 1778; commanded Va. regt. in N.C., 1779; involved in case of alleged disloyalty, 1782; held many local offices; no evidence to indicate

kinship with GM. See Hutchinson-Rachal, I, 282n.

MASON, ELIZABETH (b. 1768): GM's 8th surviving child; married William Thornton of Society Hill, King George County, who was del. to Va. ratifying convention, 1788; their sons were George Francis and William Mason.

MASON, FRENCH (d. 1748): of Truro Parish, Prince William County; son of Col. George Mason and Mary Fowke, GM's grandparents; Truro Parish processioner, 1734; offered land for a glebe in Truro Parish, 1734; GM was his executor.

MASON, FRENCH: GM's cousin, possibly the son of French Mason (d. 1748), although GM's uncle Gerard Mason also had children; signed GM's Fairfax County petitions to move the county courthouse, 1789, 1790.

MASON, GEORGE (1690–1735): GM's father, sometimes called George Mason III; son of Col. George Mason (ca. 1660–1716) of Stafford County; accompanied Gov. Spotswood on "golden horseshoe" expedition, 1716; Stafford County burgess, 1720–1735; county militia lieut., 1720; honorary burgess of Glasgow, 1720; probably was merchant and factor as well as planter; Stafford court clerk, 1722; married Ann Thomson, 1721, niece of Sir William Thomson; their children were GM, Thomson, and Mary Thomson (1731–1758); drowned in Potomac when a ferry overturned.

MASON, GEORGE: of Pohick, GM's cousin and probably a neighbor; probably the George Mason, Sr., of Pohick was GM's contemporary and son of French Mason, GM's uncle; census records indicate both a father and namesake lived in Pohick Creek area and by 1782 owned a single slave. See Fairfax County entries in U.S. Bureau of the Census, Heads of Families at the First Census taken in the Year 1790 (Washington, 1908).

MASON, GEORGE, JR. (1753–1796): of Lexington, GM's oldest son; suffered from nervous or rheumatic disorder; married Elizabeth Mary Ann Barnes;

visited European spas in search of cure, 1779–1782; six children included George Mason VI (1786–1834) of Gunston Hall, Ann Eilbeck Mason, and Gen. Richard Barnes Mason; was chief beneficiary and executor of GM's estate, 1792–1793.

MASON ISLAND: in Potomac River opposite Rock Creek, Md., adjacent to Washington, D.C., and Arlington, Va.; known in 1969 as Theodore Roosevelt Island, but in 18th century was variously called Barbadoes and Analostan Island; GM's father obtained the 75-acre patent in 1717.

MASON, JOHN (1766–1849): of Analostan and Clermont, GM's 7th child; born in Charles County, Md., educated at Gunston Hall by Scot tutors and at Robert Buchanan's Stafford County Academy, 1783–1785; in William Hartshorne's Alexandria trading firm, 1786–1787, then accompanied GM to Federal Convention; with James and Joseph Fenwick of Md. formed trading firm of Fenwick, Mason & Co.; represented firm at Bordeaux, 1788–1791; there witnessed Girdonist activities and recorded his impressions of French Revolution; inherited over 2,000 acres on left bank of Potomac, opposite Georgetown, Md., where he engaged in mercantile and banking business after GM's death; director, Potowmack Navigation Co., 1802; supt. of Indian trade, 1807; served in War of 1812, commissary gen. of prisoners; later moved to Clermont, near Alexandria; married Anna Maria Murray; their ten children included James Murray Mason (1798–1871) and Sarah, who married Gen. Samuel Cooper (C.S.A. adjt.). See John Mason Papers, DLC.

MASON, MARY THOMSON (b. 1762), 6th of GM's surviving children; married Col. John Travers Cooke, of Stafford County.

MASON NECK: five-mile long peninsula in Fairfax County jutting into the Potomac between Pohick and Occoquan creeks about 15 miles south Alexandria; undoubtedly the original Dogue's or Doeg's Neck, GM's birth-place; site of Gunston Hall, finished in 1758, and Lexington, built on southern end as home for GM's oldest son, George Mason, Jr.; remained in family hands until early 19th century; still called "Dogue Neck" in 1924.

MASON, SARAH EILBECK (1760–1823): GM's 5th surviving child; married Daniel McCarty, Jr., son of GM's old friend and neighbor; among their seven children were John, who killed his cousin Stevens Mason in a duel, and William Mason, a congressman.

MASON, THOMAS (1770–1806): of Woodbridge, GM's 9th surviving child; married Sarah Barnes; his godparents were Martin Cockburn, Capt. John Lee, Mrs. Lee Massey, and Mrs. Ann Cockburn; studied at Rev. Robert Buchan's Stafford County Academy, 1784–1785; attended Fredericksburg Academy, 1788; worked for William Hartshorne, Alexandria merchant; inherited most of GM's Prince William County lands, including the Occoquan ferry.

MASON, THOMSON (1733–1785): of Raspberry Plain, Loudoun County; GM's younger brother, for whom GM was later a guardian, and paid for part of his education; Middle Temple, 1751; Stafford County burgess, 1758–1761, 1765–1772; Loudoun County burgess, 1772–1774, 1777–1778, Elizabeth City County, 1779; commissioner of road to connect Alexandria and Colchester with N.W. mountains, 1772; wrote nine "British American" letters, 1774; refused to sign nonimportation assn., 1774; with GM was Va. trustee for Ballendine's project to clear the Potomac, 1774; in House of Delegates, drafted bill to organize the Northwest Territory as the Va. County of Illinois, sought exclusion of loyalists from citizenship, favored regulations for paying foreign or domestic debts by cancelling wartime interest and measures allowing for currency depreciation; failed to benefit politically from GM's prominence.

MASON, THOMSON (1759–1820): of Hollin Hall, GM's 4th surviving child; partner with William Allison in snuff factory, 1783; married Sarah Chichester; among their eight children was Ann Eilbeck (1787–1845), who married Samuel Dawson; was sometimes known as Thomson, Jr., to distinguish him from GM's brother; served briefly with James River militia during Revolution; collector of customs, Alexandria, after 1789; Fairfax County overseers of poor, 1795; charter trustee of South Haven, Va., 1798.

MASON, WILLIAM (1757–1818): of Mattawoman, GM's 3d surviving child; capt., Fairfax County militia, 1778; Gen. Henry Lee offered him commission with his southern command, but GM interceded, 1780; brief service during S.C. campaign; married Ann Stuart of King George County; their four children included George Mason (1797–1870) of Hollin Hall and Spring Bank, who married his cousin, Elizabeth.

MASSEY, LEE (1732–1814): trusted friend of GM; son of Dade Massey and Parthenia Alexander of Stafford County; half brother of Rev. Townsend Dade; his 3d wife was GM's cousin, Elizabeth (daughter of Col. Jeremiah Bronaugh and Simpha Rosa Enfield Mason); brother-in-law of Martin Cockburn; lived at Bradley on the Occoquan; inherited Springfield from the Cockburns; a lawyer, was persuaded by his friends, including GM and Daniel McCarty, to seek and gain ordination by the Bishop of London, 1766; Truro Parish minister, 1767–1777, succeeding Rev. Charles Green; Fairfax County committee of safety, 1774; parish vestry clerk, 1775–1777; committee to prepare a plan for care and provision for the poor of the parish, 1775; studied medicine, practiced among the poor without fee; GM nominated him to a vacancy on the Va. General Court; was a legal adviser to GM and is prominently mentioned in GM's will.

MAY, GEORGE: land speculator, Ky.; may have served in 3d Va. Regt., Continental line; Jefferson County surveyor by 1780; with brother, John,

apparently used his office to survey and patent large tracts of land upon Ohio and its tributaries; GM tried to exchange some of his lands on Green River for May's acreage adjacent to the Ohio; his holdings appear to have exceeded 200,000 acres. See W. R. Jillson, *Old Kentucky Entries and Deeds* (Louisville, 1926), 247–248.

MAY, JOHN: of Jefferson County, Ky.; with brother George, a certified surveyor, patented several hundred thousand acres of Ky. lands adjacent to Ohio; GM attempted an exchange of land with the May brothers, 1785–1786.

*MAZZEI, PHILLIP (1730–1816): physician, merchant, horticulturist, author, agent for Va. in Europe, 1779; visited Va. to introduce vine culture, olives, and fruits expected to flourish there, 1773; failure of agricultural experiments at Colle, near Monticello, followed by his energetic support of the Revolution; undertook unsuccessful mission to borrow money for Va. from the Duke of Tuscany, 1779; paid for gathering European political and military information for Gov. Thomas Jefferson, 1779; a naturalized Virginian, he corresponded with many Virginians.

MEASE, JAMES: merchant with interests in Philadelphia, Alexandria; with Va. firm of McCrea & Mease, which acted as commercial agents for Fairfax County, 1775; assisted quartermaster gen. in procurement of clothing during Revolution.

MEASE, ROBERT: partner in Alexandria mercantile firm, McCrea & Mease; active on behalf of Potomac naval force, 1779; supported Alexandria Academy, 1786; his firm procured supplies for Fairfax County, 1775 and perhaps later.

MERCER, GEORGE (1733–1784): oldest surviving son of John Mercer of Marlborough and Catherine Mason, GM's aunt; brother of James Mercer, half brother of John Francis Mercer, cousin of GM; studied at William and Mary; aide-de-camp to Washington and wounded at Fort Necessity,

1754; lieut., capt., in 1st Va. Regt., then lieut. col. of William Byrd's 2d Va. Regt., 1754–1760; commissioned by William and Mary to survey Ohio River lands, 1759; Frederick burgess, 1761–1765, but spent 1763, 1764 sessions in England as agent for Ohio Co.; treasurer for Thomas Johnson, Jr.'s, company to clear Potomac navigation, 1762; appointed stamp distributor under Stamp Act, 1765, and returned to Va. with stamps for Md. and Va.; burned in effigy at Westmoreland County courthouse, for which the Mercers blamed Richard Henry Lee; entrusted stamps to the commander of H.M.S. *Rainbow*, and returned to England; testified to House of Commons that the Stamp Act could be enforced only with troops, 1766; married Mary Neville, 1767; appointed by Lord Hillsborough lieut. gov. of N.C., but never took office; surrendered Ohio Co. claims in 1770 for share of Grand Ohio Co., an act GM repudiated; his share in John Mercer's estate was sold to meet his London expenses; after 1776 had moved to Paris, apparently with a British pension; returned to London and died there while under treatment for mental illness. See Alfred P. James, *George Mercer of the Ohio Company* (Pittsburgh, 1963).

*MERCER, JAMES (1736–1793): son of John Mercer of Marlborough and Catherine Mason, GM's aunt; brother of Col. George Mercer, half brother of John Francis Mercer; studied at William and Mary; capt., commander of Ft. Loudoun at Winchester, during French and Indian War; married Eleanor, daughter of Charles Dick of Fredericksburg; Hampshire burgess, 1762–1776; del. to Va. conventions, 1775, 1776; drafted Fredericksburg Resolutions; Burgesses committee of correspondence, 1774; Va. committee of safety, 1775–1776; member, committee to draft declaration of rights, state constitution, 1776; Va. del. to Continental Congress, 1779; Va. General Court, Court of Appeals, 1779–1789; member of reorganized Va. Court of Appeals, 1789–1793.

MERCER, JOHN (1704–1768): of Marlborough, Stafford County; born in Dublin; son of John Mercer and Grace Fenton; studied at Trinity College; migrated to Va., 1720, and for a time was a merchant; began law practice, 1728; Prince William County court disbarred him until he was reinstated by the Council; compiled *An Exact Abridgement of all the Public Acts of Assembly, of Virginia*, (Williamsburg, 1737; 2d ed., Glasgow, Va., 1759); copies of the *Abridgement* were ordered by the General Assembly for each of the county justices; a guardian of GM, 1735; secretary, Ohio Co.; great business and landed interests in Va. and Ireland; owned Marlborough Town in Potomack Neck; Aquia Parish vestry, 1757; wrote early tract opposing Stamp Act; member of Stafford County court which resigned in protest against Stamp Act after Mercer addressed Gov. Fauquier; indebted to Speaker John Robinson and to his estate, partly from establishing a brewery, 1767; owned a notable library of 1,500 volumes, a third of them on law; married Catherine Mason, sister of GM's father, 1725, then married Ann, daughter of Dr. Roy, 1750; died at Marlborough.

*MERCER, JOHN FRANCIS (1759–1821): son of John Mercer of Marlborough, and Ann Roy; half brother of Col. George Mercer and James Mercer; served with 3d Va. Regt. 1776–1777; aide-de-camp to Gen. Charles Lee, 1778–1779; lieut. col. under Gen. Lawson, 1780; raised cavalry troop to aid Lafayette, 1781; raised corps of militia grenadiers, 1781; studied law under Jefferson's tutelage, 1779–1780, and practiced briefly at Fredericksburg, Va. House of Delegates, 1782, 1785–1786; Continental Congress, 1782, 1783; Md. delegate to Philadelphia Convention but left before it ended, 1787; opposed Constitution in Md. ratifying convention; Md. House of Delegates, 1788–1789, 1791–1792, 1800–1801, 1803–1806; U.S. House of Reps. 1791–1794; Republican gov. of Md., 1801–1803.

MERIWETHER, T[HOMAS]: presumably Thomas Meriwether, maj., Va. troops, Continental line, and member of the Va. Society of the Cincinnati; a Thomas Meriwether was also Va. Council clerk.

*MIFFLIN, THOMAS (1744–1800): Philadelphia merchant; favored nonimportation agreements and drafted the Philadelphia Assn., 1774; Continental Congress, 1774, 1775; Continental army quartermaster gen., 1775–1778; deeply involved in the Conway Cabal; War board, 1777–1778; favored amending the Pa. Constitution of 1776; sympathized with the aims of the Federal Convention, 1787, but was an inactive delegate; Pa. Supreme Executive Council, 1788, pres., 1788–1790; Pa. gov., 1790–1799; Jeffersonian in politics.

MILLS, JOHN: GM's neighbor; signed an Alexandria petition for a naval office on the Potomac, 1779; signed a Fairfax petition to separate Alexandria from the county, 1787.

MINNIS, CHARLES (d. 1778): contractor for building Yorktown barracks, 1777, but died before it could be completed. See Hutchinson-Rachal, I, 242n.

MINOR, GEORGE: Fairfax County justice of peace, 1784; supported ratification of Constitution, 1787; Fairfax County overseer of poor, 1788, 1794; original trustee, South Haven, Va., 1798; as col., commanded militia regt. at Washington, D.C., Baltimore, during War of 1812.

MITCHELL, [BENJAMIN]: GM's overseer on lands adjacent to Little Hunting Creek, Fairfax County, 1791; a William Mitchell was an overseer for Robert Carter of Nomini some time earlier, in Fairfax and Prince William counties; a Benjamin Mitchell was compensated by Fairfax overseers of poor for services rendered, 1801.

MONCURE, FRANCES BROWN (1713–ca. 1775): 2d daughter of Gustavus Brown and Frances Fowke, a relative of GM's, of Rich Hill, Charles County, Md.; probably goddaughter of GM's father; half sister of Gustavus Richard Brown; married Rev. John Moncure; with him, was keenly interested in floriculture, horticulture; incurably grieved by her husband's death, never overcame her depression so that management of the family fell to her son, John, and daughter, Anne.

MONCURE, REV. JOHN (ca. 1709–1764): b. in Scotland; studied medicine; emigrated to Va., ca. 1733; tutored in Northumberland County, and studied divinity; ordained by the Bishop of London, 1737; his intimate friend was Rev. James Scott, brother of Rev. Alexander Scott (whom Moncure assisted, then succeeded in 1738 as rector of Overwharton Parish, Stafford County); trustee of Dumfries, Va., 1761; bought large tract on the Potomac, which he named Clermont, and much of which he settled with tenants before 1738; gov. and Council ruled that he could not discharge both pastoral and justice of peace duties, and therefore revoked his justice commission from Stafford County, 1752; GM an executor, guardian of his children, and godfather of several Moncure children; the five Moncure children included Frances, goddaughter of GM; John, godson of GM, and Anne, goddaughter of GM; buried under the chancel of Aquia Church, Stafford County. See Hayden, *Virginia Genealogies*, 262–263; 424–427.

MONTGOMERIE, THOMAS: of Fairfax County, probably a collector for Truro Parish, for he gave churchwardens £189 for 27,001 pounds of tobacco taken in tithes, 1774–1775; friend of Richard Graham (d. 1796).

MONTOUR, ANDREW: son of Madam Montour, a Huron half-breed daughter of a Frenchman, and friendly to the English; involved with Christopher Gist, Michael Cresap, Thomas Cresap, Jr., in seeking 80,000 acres near Ohio Co. lands, 1752; commissioned by Va. as an interpreter, Logstown conference, 1752; Gov. Dinwiddie sent him with a captain's commission to command friendly Indian scouts with Washington, 1756–1757.

MOORE, CLEON (d. 1808): Colchester resident; capt. of Va. troops, Continental line; severely wounded at battle of Brandywine; received 4,000 acres as military bounty; elected to Truro Parish vestry, 1781; signed Fairfax County petition against repeal of an act to prevent extensive credits (1783); supporter for the Alexandria Academy, 1786; bonded as a notary public, 1793; moved to Alexandria, 1800, where he was Register of Wills until his death; neighbor and particular friend of GM; involved with the Norfolk Packet.

MOORE, JEREMIAH (1746–1815): originally from Chappawamsic; of Moorefield, Fairfax County; early Baptist preacher in Fairfax County, signed Madison's "Memorial and Remonstrance" circulated by GM in Fairfax County, 1785; opposed religious assessment bill; criticized disqualification of clergymen from public office in 1776, 1800. See *Washington Star*, 15 July 1917.

MOORE, WILLIAM: of Fairfax County, Truro Parish processioner, 1743; was GM's bondsman in settling estate of French Mason, 1748; possibly the father of the William Moore who signed Madison's "Memorial and Remonstrance" against the assessment bill, which GM circulated, 1785.

*MORGAN, GEORGE (1743–1810): partner in Philadelphia mercantile firm, Baynton, Wharton, and Morgan, 1763–ca.1768; visited Illinois country as their representative, dealt in the western fur trade, traded Indian goods; leader in movement to establish civil government in Illinois; the trading venture failed, and the partnership went into voluntary receivership; the largest remaining asset was its share in the Indiana grant, 2,862 square miles of present W. Va.; Indiana Co. reorganized with Morgan as sec.-gen. and supt. of the land office, with headquarters at Ft. Pitt, 1776; Va. claimed jurisdiction over the area, with consequent conflict in the Va. General Assembly, Congress, and the U.S. Supreme Court; the 11th Amendment to the Constitution ended Morgan's quest for his claim, 1798; served during the Revolutionary War as Indian agent for the middle dept., deputy commissary gen. of purchases for the western district, 1775–1776; with Spanish aid, settled the colony of New Madrid in Spanish La., 1789; testified against Aaron Burr at his trial in Richmond.

*MORRIS, GOUVERNEUR (1752–1816): N.Y. lawyer; drafted N.Y. Constitution, 1776; N.Y. council of safety, 1776–1777; Continental Congress, 1778–1779; moved to Philadelphia, became asst. to financier Robert Morris, 1781–1785; planned decimal coinage system; Pa. del. to Federal Convention, 1787, where he drafted the Constitution in its final literary form; returned to N.Y., 1788; agent of Robert Morris in France, where he pressed tobacco contract claim against the Farmers-General, 1789; appointed minister to France, 1792–1794 despite Senate opposition; deeply involved in plot to rescue King Louis XVI; recalled *quid pro quo* for Citizen Genet; U.S. Senate, 1800–1803; chairman, commission for Erie Canal; Hartford Convention, 1814.

MORRIS, RICHARD (ca. 1746–1821): known as "Col.," merchant-planter, operated in Prince George, Louisa, Hanover counties; Va. state treasury official, commissary, paymaster, 1776; provisioner for Continental troops, 1778–1780; state coordinator of specific grain tax, 1781–1782; Louisa del. to House of Delegates, 1788; probably associated with firm of Morris & Richards, which sold military equipment to Va., 1775–1776.

*MORRIS, ROBERT (1734–1806): Philadelphia merchant, initially associated with the Willing family, from 1754; signed nonimportation agreement, 1765; Continental Congress, 1775–1778; opposed independence, but signed the Declaration, 1776; signed Articles of Confederation, 1778; Pa. Assembly, 1775–1781, 1785–1786; superintendent of finance, 1781–1784; heavy subscriber to the Bank of North America, 1782; Annapolis Convention, 1786; signed controversial contract with French Farmers-General to monopolize the tobacco trade with France, 1785; Federal Convention, 1787; Pa. sent to U.S. Senate, 1789–1795; speculated heavily in lands in western N.Y. and elsewhere; owned a large portion of the site of the future federal capital; but overextended his credit and was imprisoned for debt, 1798–1801; remainder of his life spent supported by his wife's annuity.

Moss, John (1750–1809): of Fairfax County; may have been officer, Va. regt., Continental line; commissary agent for equipping Continental troops, and was to supply Va. troops en route to Charleston, 1780; apparently owned a tavern after the war, when he was designated "col."; signed Fairfax constituents letter in favor of the Constitution, 1787; Fairfax County board of overseers of the poor, 1788–1791. See Hutchinson-Rachal, II, 9n.

*Moultrie, William (1730–1805): S.C. Commons House, 1752–1770; prov. congresses, council, senate, 1775–1780; brig. gen. of Continental troops after defending Sullivan's Island, 1776; captured at Charleston, and a prisoner, 1780–1782; a moderate whose brother was a Loyalist, the British unsuccessfully urged Moultrie to change sides; maj. gen., 1782; S.C. House of Rep., 1783; lieut. gov., 1784; gov., 1785–1787, 1792–1794; state senate, 1787–1791; S.C. ratifying convention, 1788; pres., S.C. Society of the Cincinnati, until 1805.

Mount Vernon: George Washington's Fairfax County home on the Potomac built by his half brother Lawrence in the 1730s and early 1740s; the estate was named in honor of Admiral Edward Vernon, under whom Lawrence had served in the Cartagena campaign, 1740–1741.

*Moylan, Stephen (1737–1811): muster master, American troops at Cambridge, Mass., 1775; secy. to Gen. Washington, 1776; quartermaster gen., 1776; commanded light dragoons, 1777–1781; court martialed for quar-

relling with Polish officers, exonerated; brevetted brig. gen., 1783; commissioner of loans in Philadelphia, 1793.

Muir, John: Alexandria merchant, handled British goods and bought tobacco; fox-hunting companion of Washington, 1768; signed Fairfax nonimportation agreement, 1770; Alexandria wheat inspector until 1777; Fairfax County committee, 1775; signed Alexandria petitions for naval office on the Potomac, 1779, and to urge an increase in the power of Congress over commerce.

*Munford, Robert (d. 1784): of Richlands, Mecklenburg County; capt., 2d Va. Regt. under Col. William Byrd III, 1758; Mecklenburg County lieut., 1765–1784; burgess, 1765–1775; Va. General Assembly, 1779–1781; signed Williamsburg nonimportation assn., 1770; recruiting officer during Revolution; his *Collection of Plays and Poems* (1798) published posthumously; death prevented completion of his rhymed translation of Ovid's *Metamorphoses*, Bk. I.

Murry, Patrick: owned property in Alexandria, 1774–1786, when finances forced him to sell; the firm of Murray and Wheaton, signed Alexandria merchants' petition for a branch of the Bank of the U.S. at Alexandria, 1792.

Nelson, Hugh (1750–1800): of Yorktown; son of William Nelson (1711–1772); attended William and Mary, 1769–1771; a leading merchant in Yorktown before war began; lieut. col., Va. troops, 1775; brother of Gen. Thomas Nelson.

*Nelson, Hugh (1768–1836): of York, Albemarle counties; Va. state senate, 1786–1791; Speaker, House of Delegates, 1793; presumably York County justice of peace, 1789; Va. General Court justice; U.S. House of Reps., 1811–1823; U.S. minister to Spain, 1823–1824.

Nelson, James: probably a native of Culpeper County, son of Joseph Nelson; migrated to Fayette County, Ky., *ca.* 1807; married Elizabeth, daughter of Maj. William Boone.

NELSON, THOMAS (1716-1782): called "Secy."; lawyer, merchant, planter of Yorktown; son of Thomas Nelson, Sr., of Yorktown; Va. secretary, 1742-1776; York County burgess, 1745-1749; Va. Council, 1749-1776; of which he became pres. when his brother William died; secretary of the Commonwealth of Va.; unsuccessful conservative candidate for gov. against Patrick Henry, 1776; declined appointment to the first Va. state executive council, 1776; retired, lived at Yorktown until it was occupied by British forces; during battle of 1781, his house was nearly levelled, and Nelson was brought out by flag of truce; married Lucy Armistead; uncle of Thomas Nelson (1738-1789). See Emory G. Evans, The Nelsons: A Biographical Study of a Virginia Family in the Eighteenth Century (unpubl. Ph.D. Diss., University of Virginia, 1957).

*NELSON, THOMAS (1738-1789): called "Jr."; York County burgess, 1761-1775; Va. conventions, Aug. 1774, Mar. 1775, July 1775, May 1776; col., 2d Va. Regt.; Cont. Cong., 1775-1777, 1779; introduced resolution for independence in Va. convention, 1776, and carried it to Congress; signed Declaration of Independence; opposed Va. act to sequester British property, 1777; brig. gen. and commander of Va. forces; succeeded Jefferson as gov., but forced to resign by illness before the end of his term, 1781; financially ruined by the Revolution.

*NELSON, WILLIAM (1711-1772): York County merchant; York County burgess, 1742-1744; Va. Council, 1744-1772, of which he was pres., acting gov., 1770-1771; opposed Great Britain's taxation policy, and supported colonial manufacturing; helped GM's widowed mother.

NELSON, WILLIAM (1746-1807): lawyer, of The Dorrill, Caroline County; married Lucy, daughter of Col. John Chiswell and Elizabeth Randolph,

1771; served at Yorktown, 1781; Caroline County judge.

*NESBITT, JOHN MAXWELL (1730-1802): partner in Philadelphia shipping firm of Redmond, Conyngham & Nesbitt, from 1756; Pa. Bank director, 1780; Bank of North America director, 1781-1792.

NICHOLAS, GEORGE (1754?-1799): born in Williamsburg; son of Robert Carter Nicholas, attended William and Mary; army capt., col. during Revolution; studied law; del. from Albemarle County, House of Delegates, 1781, where he moved to investigate Gov. Jefferson's conduct during the Arnold invasion; cooperated with Madison on religious liberty statute; opposed issuance of paper currency; Federalist, Va. ratifying convention, 1788; moved to Ky., 1790 and became involved in Spanish trade at New Orleans and land speculation; represented GM in Ky. land title litigation, 1790; 1st atty. gen. of Ky.; leader in Ky. resolutions of 1798; in political activities, he cooperated with his brother, Wilson Cary Nicholas, who was gov. of Virginia, 1814-1816.

*NICHOLAS, ROBERT CARTER (1728-1780): Williamsburg; attended William and Mary, married Anne Cary; leading lawyer in colonial Va.; York and James City burgess, 1756-1775; del. to Va. conventions, 1775, 1776; Va. treas., 1766-1776; close friend of Jefferson, he took moderate stance regarding resistance measures to royal authority; member, Va. committee of safety, 1775-1776; opposed Declaration of Independence; favored church establishment; elected to High Court of Chancery, 1778; died at The Retreat, Hanover County.

*NICHOLAS, WILSON CARY (1761-1820): son of Robert Carter Nicholas; born in Williamsburg; reared in Hanover County; attended William and Mary but withdrew to serve in army, 1779; returned to Albemarle County, married Margaret Smith, elected del. to Va. General Assembly, 1784-1789, 1794-1799; del. to Va., ratifying con-

vention, 1788; U.S. Senate, 1799–1804; House of Reps., 1807–1809, where supported embargo; campaign aid to Madison in 1808 presidential race; re-elected to Congress, 1809, but resigned because of ill health; as gov. of Va., 1814–1816, worked with Jefferson in creating Univ. of Va.; in 1819 panic he defaulted on $20,000 note which Jefferson had endorsed; died at home of Thomas Jefferson Randolph, his son-in-law, and was buried at Monticello.

NIMMO, WILLIAM (d. 1748): emigrated from Linlithgow, Scotland; qualified as attorney-at-law in Va. general court, 1743; had a large practice at Williamsburg; member of the Ohio Co., he made no mention of its stock in his will.

NISBET, JAMES (d. ca. 1784): Prince William County justice of peace, 1751; apparently the Dr. James Nisbet[t] who was paid by Truro Parish vestry for tending the sick, 1766, 1775.

NORMANSELL, RICHARD: owned 2,550 acres on both sides of the main run of the Pohick Creek tributary, Accotink, 1666; his dividend was later included in Hereford Manor, site of 1st chapel above Occoquan; William Fairfax purchased this tract and consolidated it with other titles, 1738–1741.

NORTHERN NECK: the tidewater and inland area between the Rappahannock and Potomac rivers in Va.; granted by Charles II to a group of proprietors in 1649; eventually became property of the Fairfax family.

NORTON, JOHN HATLEY (1745–1797): son of merchant John Norton; married Sarah, daughter of Robert Carter Nicholas, 1772; partner, John Norton & Sons of Norfolk, Va.; although his business was located in Philadelphia by 1782, he lived near Winchester, Frederick County, 1785. See Hutchinson-Rachal, I, 318n; IV, 252n.

OCCOQUAN FERRY: act of 1684 (Hening, III, 21) required the 1st George Mason to provide ferry for soldiers and horses near mouth of Occoquan Creek, but David Strahan, was 1st

contractor for the service in 1691; by 1744 ferry privilege belonged to the Masons (Hening, V, 252); after 1795, GM's son Thomas, to whom GM granted the rights to the ferry in his will, built a toll bridge at the spot. See Harrison, 496.

OGLE, ANNE TASKER: daughter of Benjamin Tasker and Anne Bladen; sister of Mrs. Robert Carter of Nomini; married Samuel Ogle, Md. gov., 1741; brought as a dowry Belair, a 3,600-acre estate in Prince Georges County, Md.; among her five children was Benjamin, gov. of Md., 1798–1801; widowed, 1752; family allied with the Carrolls in politics and business. See DAB under "Samuel Ogle."

O'NEALE, CHARLES: Alexandria resident, overseer of GM's quarter at head of Little Hunting Creek, 1781; sought a veteran's pension and may have been enlisted in a Va. regt., Continental line; signed Madison's "Memorial & Remonstrance" against religious assessment bill, which GM circulated in Fairfax County, 1785.

OUTRAM,——: ship capt., commanded the Liberty, which sailed between Va. ports and London in 1770s, 1780s.

OVERWHARTON PARISH: in Stafford County, extended well above Occoquan Creek and was GM's home parish until 1731, when reorganization led to the creation of Truro Parish; Aquia Church was original seat of parish, but Pohick Church seems to have become center of newly created parish in 1733.

OWEN, [DAVID]: Indian trader, reportedly murdered his Indian wife and their five children for scalp bounties during Ponitac's rebellion; accompanied George Rogers Clark on western expedition to Falls of the Ohio, 1772; a Robert Owen was employed as bookkeeper for the Easton Indian conference, 1756.

OWSLEY, THOMAS: migrated to Va. from Dorset County, England, 1692; apparently made trip to Va. in 1677 as collector of debts for English merchant; settled on Little Hunting Creek, later part of Fairfax County, and traded with Piscataway Indians; Stafford County clerk, justice of peace; Ousley's Creek, a tributary of Little River at head of Bull Run mountains, was named for him.

PAGAN, JOHN: (d. *ca.* 1776): related to the Pagan merchant family of Glasgow, Scotland; an original trustee of Alexandria, 1749; managed lottery to provide a church and market house at Belle Haven, 1751, for which GM was subscriber. See Harrison, 405, 662.

*PAGE, JOHN (1743–1808): of Rosewell, Gloucester County; House of Burgesses; Va. committee of safety, 1776; Va. lieut. gov. under Patrick Henry; Gloucester County del. to General Assembly, 1781–1783, 1785–1788, 1797, 1798, 1800, 1801; Congress, 1789–1797; Commissioner to determine Va.-Pa. boundary, 1784; Va. gov. 1802–1805; brother of Mann Page, Jr.

PAGE, MANN, JR. (1749–*ca.* 1810): planter, lawyer; home at Mannsfield, near Fredricksburg; William and Mary, 1763–1765; Spotsylvania County committee of safety, 1775; Va. conventions, 1775, 1776; House of Delegates, 1776–1787, 1795, 1796; Continental Congress, 1776–1777; apparently son-in-law of John Taylor of Mt. Airy; brother of John Page of Rosewell. See Hutchinson-Rachal, IV, 137*n*–138*n*.

PANTHER CREEK: Ky. tributary of the Green River running east to west and entering the Green at about Curdsville, Davies County, Ky.

PARKER, HUGH (d. 1751): apprentice to Philadelphia merchant Edward Shippen; Frederick County, Md., merchant, and operated trading post at Kuskuski, on the Pa. frontier, by 1748; Ohio Co. agent, *ca.* 1748–1751; with Thomas Cresap, acquired the Wills Creek lands at the head of the Potomac River, site of present-day Cumberland, Md., and on Braddock's route, 1755; advertised among Indians the great advantages of dealing with the Ohio Co., and brought enmity of Pa. and French traders; explored

Ohio Co. grant to determine best survey sites, although Indian and Pa. opposition hindered project, 1749.

*PARKER, JOSIAH (1751–1810): of Macclesfield, Isle of Wight County; col. in Revolution and commander of Va. militia south of the James River, *ca.* 1779; Va. convention, 1775/1776; on committee with GM to confer on the state of troops of the Va. line, 1778; House of Delegates, 1780, 1781; a strong Antifederalist, he was defeated as a candidate for the Va. ratifying convention, 1788; Congress, 1789–1801; Va. General Court justice, 1789–1791. See Grigsby II, 376.

*PATERSON, WILLIAM (1745–1806): N.J. lawyer, atty. gen., 1776–1783; del. to Philadelphia Convention, 1787, where he introduced "New Jersey Plan"; signed Constitution, and supported it in N.J. ratifying convention; U.S. Senator, 1789–1790; 1st nine sections of the Judiciary Act of 1789 are in his hand; gov. and chancellor of N.J., 1790; U.S. Supreme Court, associate justice, 1793–1806.

PAYNE, EDWARD: Fairfax County freeholder; owned site of Payne's Chapel (or New Church), built near present Fairfax County courthouse, 1766, and destroyed in Civil War; Truro Parish vestry, 1765–1774; churchwarden with GM, 1765, 1774; commissioner for Alexandria and Colchester road to the northwest mountain gaps, 1772; Fairfax County committee of safety.

PAYNE, WILLIAM: probably son of William Payne, Sr., with whom he served on Truro Parish vestry, 1756–1765; Truro Parish churchwarden, 1761, 1764; Fairfax Parish vestry, 1765; Fairfax County justice of peace, 1770, 1785; Fairfax County committee of safety, 1774; supported ratification of Constitution, 1787; Fairfax County sheriff, 1796–1799; original trustee, Providence, Va., 1805. See Slaughter, *Truro Parish*, ed. Goodwin, 44–45.

PEAKE, WILLIAM (d. *ca.* 1761): Fairfax County planter; lived in the Fork of Little Hunting Creek; Washington's closest neighbor; Truro Parish vestry, 1733–1761; possibly a Fairfax County militiaman, 1755, 1756.

PENDLETON, EDMUND (1721–1803): lawyer; Caroline County burgess, 1752–1776; pres., Va. conventions, Dec. 1775, May 1776; pres., Va. committee of safety, 1775–1776; served with GM on committee of revisors of Va. statutes, 1777–1779; Speaker, House of Delegates, 1776; presiding judge, Va. Chancery Court, 1777; pres., Va. Supreme Court of Appeals, 1779–1803; pres., Va. ratifying convention, 1788; supported Constitutional ratification, 1788. See Mays, *Pendleton.*

PENDLETON, HENRY: son of James Pendleton, nephew of Edmund Pendleton; Culpeper County burgess, 1769–1776; Va. conventions, Mar., Dec. 1775; signed nonimportation assns., 1769, 1774.

PENDLETON, HENRY (1750–1789): son of Nathaniel Pendleton, nephew of Edmund Pendleton; justice, S.C. Court of Common Pleas, 1771; captured in fall of Charlestown, 1780. See Hutchinson-Rachal, II, 105n.

PENDLETON, JOHN, JR. (1749–ca. 1807): of Henrico County; nephew of Edmund Pendleton; clerk, Va. committee of safety, 1775–1776; clerk, Va. Senate, 1777; Richmond common council, 1783–1784. See Hutchinson-Rachal, I, 190n.

PENET, J. PIERRE: West Indies ship's surgeon, turned Nantes shipper and merchant in various partnerships; by 1779, operated as Penet d'Acosta Frères et Cie.; congressional agent to collect munitions in France, 1775; appointed brevet aide-de-camp to Washington's staff, 1776; requested by Congress to send 200 workmen to man a small arms factory in the U.S., 1779; GM may have written resolution which would have enabled Penet to operate foundry in Va., 1779; commercial agent, furnished Va. with military supplies, 1779–1782.

PEYTON, FRANCIS (1748–ca. 1814): of Loudoun County; son of Valentine Peyton; born in Prince William County; burgess, 1769–1774; Loudoun County justice of peace, 1770; Shelburne Parish vestry, 1770–1807, trustee, Colchester, Alexandria, 1775, Middleburg, 1787; Loudoun committee of safety, 1774–1775; del. to Va. conventions, 1775, 1776; col., Loudoun militia, 1781; Va. General Assembly, 1780; Loudoun County lieut., 1781, 1782, 1789, 1790; cited for failing to make a militia return, 1789; state commissioner to settle Indian expedition business, 1785; road commissioner, 1772, 1785; Va. Senate, 1791–1811; married Frances Dade; had a namesake nephew, Francis Peyton of Alexandria.

PEYTON, FRANCIS (d. 1836): known as Francis, Jr., of Alexandria; nephew of Col. Francis Peyton of Loudoun County; son of Craven Peyton of Loudoun County; commissioner to settle militia accounts, 1775; in business as Francis Peyton & Co. of Alexandria, by 1787; Fairfax County justice of peace by 1790; with Andrew Peyton signed petition for Alexandria branch of the Bank of the U.S., 1792; Alexandria trustee, 1795; commissioner for unsuccessful Fairfax and Loudoun Turnpike Road Co., 1796; coroner, 1797; married Sarah, daughter of Hugh West and Elizabeth Minor, ca. 1786; she later married Maj. Henry Gunnell.

PEYTON, HENRY (d. 1781): called Col., of Prince William County; son of Valentine Peyton; born in Stafford County; Prince William County sheriff, 1750, 1779; justice of peace, 1754–1761; led Prince William militia, 1755; County lieut., 1755–1756, 1761; burgess, 1756–1761; longtime member of the Dettingen Parish vestry, churchwarden, 1769–1780; trustee, Dumfries, 1761; tithe collector, 1780.

PEYTON, HENRY (ca. 1744–1814): of Prince William County; son of John Peyton; Prince William County justice of peace, 1769, 1770; county commissioner to ascertain pay due militia and amount of damages due the Indians, ca. 1758; married Mary Tassaker Fowke of Gunston Hall, Stafford County.

PEYTON, SIR JOHN (*ca.* 1720–1790): of Iselham, Gloucester County; son of Thomas Peyton; baronetcy recognized in Va. by 1756; capt., Gloucester County militia, 1758; North Run Parish vestry until 1787; churchwarden, 1759; county lieut., 1775–1782; sheriff, 1782–1783; supported Revolution; financially distressed, 1781–1786; while sheriff neglected his duties, resulting in a general court judgment against him; 2d wife was Mary Taliaferro, widowed daughter of Charles Dick (*q.v.*)

PEYTON, YELVERTON (*ca.* 1735–*ca.* 1794): of Stafford County; son of John Peyton; Fauquier County justice of peace, 1759; lived in Fauquier but moved to Stafford County when his father died; kept tavern at Aquia, 1768; Stafford justice of peace, 1769; Stafford burgess, 1772; Stafford County committee expressing sympathy for Boston citizens, 1774; married Elizabeth Heath of Stafford County.

PHILLIPS, WILLIAM (1731–1781): British army maj. gen.; negotiator for prisoner of war exchanges; commanded British troops in Va., succeeding Benedict Arnold, 1781.

PICKETT, MARTIN (1740–1804): of Fauquier County; son of William Pickett; Fauquier undersheriff, 1759; lieut., French and Indian War, 1761; lieut. col., col., Fauquier militia, 1777–1781; del. to Va. convention, 1776; an original settler of Warrenton; Fauquier County tax commissioner, 1782; coroner, 1783; sheriff, 1785, 1789–1790; del. to Va. ratifying convention, 1788; served on Warrenton vestry.

PIERCE, JOHN (d. 1788): of Conn.; asst. paymaster, Continental army, 1776–1781; paymaster gen., 1781; commissioner of army accounts, 1783–1786; appointed by Congress as commissioner for settling the Illinois account, 1787.

*PIERCE, WILLIAM LEIGH (*ca.* 1740–1789): won distinction at battle of Eutaw Springs, 1781; brevet maj., 1783; Savannah, Ga., merchant in William Pierce & Co.; Congress, 1787; Ga. del., Federal Convention, 1787; left during the convention, did not sign Constitution, although he favored ratification. See Farrand, III, 94.

*PINCKNEY, CHARLES (1757–1824): 2d cousin of Charles Cotesworth Pinckney and Thomas Pinckney; S.C. lower house, 1779–1780; del. to Continental Congress, 1784–1787; led opposition to measure conceding U.S. navigation privileges on the Mississippi in return for Spanish commercial privileges, 1786; early advocate of a convention to amend the Articles of Confederation; attended Federal Convention of 1787; S.C. gov., 1789–1792, 1796, 1806; alienated from Federalists by 1795; Jeffersonian U.S. Senator, 1798; U.S. Minister to Spain, 1801–1805; U.S. House of Reps., 1818–1820.

*PINCKNEY, CHARLES COTESWORTH (1746–1825): brother of Thomas Pinckney; English-trained lawyer; S.C. council of safety, 1776, 1779; S.C. Senate pres., 1779; brevetted brig. gen. after Revolution; attended Federal Convention of 1787 and supported the Constitution in the S.C. ratifying convention; succeeded Monroe in mission to France, 1796; involved in XYZ Affair; Federalist vice-pres. candidate, 1800; Federalist candidate for pres., 1804, 1808.

*PINCKNEY, THOMAS (1750–1828): brother of Charles Cotesworth Pinckney; English-trained lawyer; Royal Military Academy, Caen, France; aide to Count d' Estaing; staff officer of Gen. Horatio Gates; wounded, captured at battle of Camden; recruited in Va., served with Lafayette at Yorktown; S.C. gov., 1787–1789; pres., S.C. ratifying convention; minister to Great Britain, 1792–1795; envoy extraordinary to Spain, where he negotiated the Treaty of San Lorenzo el Real, 1795–1796; U.S. House of Reps., 1797–1801.

PIPER, HARRY: Scottish merchant based in Alexandria by 1757, purchased tobacco for Scottish houses, also arranged for trans-Atlantic passage for indentured servants,

1765–1772; sold GM headrights for 377 persons brought from Great Britain and Ireland in June, 1773; signed Fairfax County nonimportation assn., 1770. See Soltow, *Economic Role of Williamsburg*, 162, 177.

POHICK BAY: Fairfax County; Potomac inlet where Pohick Creek enters Gunston Cove, north of Mason Neck; location of Daniel McCarty's Pohick tobacco warehouse, *ca.* 1732.

POHICK CHURCH: Fairfax County; 1st Pohick Church was in use as early as 1715 on south side of Dogue Creek; before 1730 2d church was built above the Occoquan ferry in old Overwharton Parish and renamed Pohick Church in 1733; used until 1772; Washington, GM disagreed on location of 3d structure; Washington's plan prevailed, and new church was built at the crossroads of the Occoquan-Alexandria and Ravensworth rolling roads, more convenient to Mount Vernon than to Gunston Hall. See Harrison, 285–286; Meade, *Old Churches of Virginia*, II, 227.

POLLARD, THOMAS (b. 1741): son of Joseph Pollard, who bequeathed him lands in Fairfax County, and Priscilla Hoomes; Fairfax County committee of safety, 1774; Truro Parish vestry, 1774–1784, churchwarden, 1774–1776, 1778–1779; supported Constitution, 1787; Fairfax County board of overseers of the poor, 1793, 1795; moved to Ky., *ca.* 1798.

POPE, JOHN: of Prince William County; may have served with Va. regt. in Continental line, 1776–1777; del. to Va. General Assembly, 1792, 1798, 1800; trustee, town of Dumfries, 1786.

POPE, NATHANIEL: of Chilton, Hanover County; may have served with Nelson's light dragoons during Revolution; apparently owned lands along South Anna River, 1787; as practicing lawyer in Hanover County, 1788/1789, his clients included William Duval, Parke Goodall, and William Fontaine.

PORTER, THOMAS: of Spotsylvania County; may have been officer in the Va. regt. guarding the British troops captured at Saratoga known as "Convention prisoners," 1779; possibly the partner of Porter & Ingraham, Alexandria merchants by 1787 who dealt in wheat and flour trade.

POSEY, JOHN: of Fairfax County; capt., French and Indian war, 1758; Truro Parish processioner, 1751–1755; Truro Parish vestry, 1765–1770; ferry on his property below Mount Vernon crossed Potomac to Md. lands owned by Thomas Marshall, 1753–1769; Washington acquired ferry and adjacent lands as result of an earlier unpaid loan to Posey; for £11 Washington bought Posey's rights to 3,000 acres of unlocated western lands; was eventually sent to debtor's prison. See Freeman, *Washington*, III, 94–100, 293–294.

POTOMAC CREEK: runs through the middle of Stafford County and flows into Potomac River; was old boundary line between Overwharton and St. Paul's parishes.

POWELL, LEVIN (1737–1810): deputy sheriff, Prince William County; married Sarah, daughter of Burr Harrison, 1765; settled in Loudoun County, where he was a merchant, owned a flour mill, and acquired large tracts, Loudoun County justice of peace, 1769; Shelburne Parish vestry, 1771; Loudoun committee of safety, 1775; maj., Loudoun County minutemen in battles at Norfolk, Hampton, 1775; lieut. col., 16th Va. Regt., 1777–1778; acquired more than 60,000 acres in the West; visited Ky., *ca.* 1780; Boonesborough trustee, 1779; Middleburg, Va., Centerville, Va., incorporated on his properties, 1787, 1792; charter trustee, Matildaville, Va., 1790; commissioner, unsuccessful Fairfax and Loudoun Turnpike Road Co., 1796; Va. House of Delegates, 1779, 1787, 1788, 1790, 1791; Va. ratifying convention, 1788; only Va. presidential elector to favor John Adams over Thomas Jefferson, 1796; Federalist congressman, 1799–1801.

POWELL, ROBERT (d. 1829): of Fairfax County; lieut., 3d Va. Regt., 1776;

resigned as capt., 1779; maj., Va. militia, 1781; received military land bounty of 4,666 acres. See Gwathmey, *Historical Register of Virginians in the Revolution*, 635.

PRENTICE (also PRENTIS) JOHN: served with 1st and 10th Va. regts., Continental line.

PRENTIS, JOSEPH (1754–1809): of Williamsburg; member of Va. council of state, 1778; del. to Va. General Assembly, 1777–1788; Speaker, House of Delegates, 1788; judge, Va. General Court, 1788–1809. See Mays, *Pendleton Papers*, I, 257, 138–139.

PRESTON, WILLIAM (1729–1823): of Greenfield, Botetourt County; born in Ireland, parents emigrated to Va., 1735; ranger capt., French and Indian war; clerk, war council, 1756; surveyor, county lieut., Fincastle and Montgomery counties, 1775; made surveys for Loyal Co.; burgess from Augusta County, 1765–1768, from Botetourt, 1769–1771; Fincastle County committee of safety, 1775; served in southern campaigns under Gen. Greene, 1780; married Susannah Smith of Hanover County; children were Elizabeth, Gen. John (Va. treasurer), Gen. Francis (U.S. congressman), and James Patton (Fla. gov.).

PRICE, BENONI: owner of Price's Old-Fields ordinary, near GM's proposed site of Fairfax County courthouse; county freeholders met there to draft a resolution addressed to GM and David Stuart, 2 Oct. 1788, and Fairfax County overseers of the poor met at Price's Ordinary between 1788 and 1796; county overseers of the poor paid for use of his house, 1795; signer of Fairfax Memorial and Remonstrance, 1785, the petitions to separate the jurisdictions of Fairfax County and Alexandria, 1787, and GM's petition to move the county courthouse, 1789, 1790.

PURDIE, ALEXANDER (d. 1779): printer, born in Scotland; joined Joseph Royle on the *Va. Gazette* and succeeded Royle as editor, 1766; shortly thereafter entered partnership with John Dixon, who had married Royle's

widow, Rosanna Hunter; partnership lasted until 1774; final partnership with William Hunter, 1774; Purdie was regarded as controlled by the colonial government, and William Rind established a rival *Va. Gazette*, 1766–1773; appointed public printer to the colony, 1775.

PURVIANCE, SAMUEL, JR.: born in Donegal, Ireland; emigrated to America *ca.* 1754 and resided at Philadelphia until 1768 (had been active against Stamp Act there) when he moved to Baltimore; Baltimore merchant, served on committee of correspondence, 1774; chairman, Baltimore committee of safety which Gen. Charles Lee ordered to arrest Gov. Robert Eden, Apr. 1776; Md. council of safety took affront, thwarted Eden's arrest, and successfully sought censure of Purviance's conduct, though GM wrote resolve which seemed to vindicate him; corresponded with GM about western land grants and titles; land speculator; member of expedition to lower Ohio in 1788, which was attacked by Indians; Purviance was among those captured and his subsequent history is a mystery. See Robert Purviance, *A Narrative of Events . . . in the Revolutionary War* (Baltimore, 1849), 32–33.

QUANTICO CREEK: Prince William County; enters Potomac River at Dumfries; silted Dumfries's wharves so badly that by the time of the Revolution larger ships could no longer dock.

QUIN (QUYNN, QUINN), ALLEN: of Annapolis, Md.; served in French and Indian War; as a bachelor lived at Mr. Swan's; his house had been site of William Rind's circulating library before Rind went to Williamsburg, 1766; St. Ann's Parish vestry, 1774–1777, probably later, and churchwarden, 1776; Md. General Assembly, 1780, 1781; committee to superintend Annapolis Associators, 1781; committee to chart the Severn River; committee to direct fortifications of Annapolis; mayor of Annapolis during 1790s.

RAMSAY, WILLIAM (1716–1785): born in Kirkcudbright, Scotland; apparently business partner of John Carlyle at Belhaven, later Alexandria; friend of GM, and probably responsible for GM becoming an Alexandria trustee; original trustee on committee to lay out town of Alexandria, 1747; owned Royal George Tavern by 1760; manager of lottery to build Belhaven church and market house, 1751; committee to superintend completion of courthouse, 1754; adjuster of weights and seals with John Carlyle at Hunting Creek Warehouse, 1754; business partner of John Dixon until 1757; incurred heavy debts in buying out Dixon's interests; commissary of troops, 1756–1758; overseer of Alexandria Academy, 1756–1760; first and only Lord Mayor of Alexandria, 1761; visited Scotland, made a burgess by Dumfries, Kirkcudbright, 1765; signed Fairfax County nonimportation agreement, 1770; Fairfax justice of peace, 1770, 1781, 1782; Alexandria postmaster, 1772; commissioner for Alexandria-Colchester road to the northwestern mountain gaps, 1772; with GM, a Va. trustee for Ballendine's plan for clearing Potomac navigation, 1774; Fairfax County committee of safety, 1774, 1775; Freemason; member, Sun Fire Co.; signed Alexandria petition for a naval office on the Potomac, 1779; married Ann, daughter of GM's friend George Johnston of Fairfax County and Sarah McCarty, sister of GM's friend, Daniel McCarty; they had eight children. See Moore, *Seaport in Virginia*, 52–61.

RANDOLPH, BEVERLEY (1754–1797): born at Chatsworth, Henrico County; son of Col. Peter Randolph; graduated William and Mary, 1771; Williamsburg Masonic Lodge, 1773–1783; represented Cumberland County in Va. House of Delegates, 1777–1780; commanded regt. in Gen. Lawson's brigade, 1780; lieut. gov., 1784; Va. executive council, 1781, pres., 1787–1788; Va. gov., 1788–1791; married Martha, daughter of Auditor James Cocke of Williamsburg, See Tyler, II, 45–46.

*RANDOLPH, EDMUND (1753–1813): of Williamsburg, del. to Va. convention, 1776; Va. atty. gen., 1776; Williamsburg mayor; Continental Congress, where he favored five percent impost, 1779; elected gov., defeating Richard Henry Lee and Theodorick Bland, 1786–1787; Annapolis convention, 1786; Antifederalist member of the Philadelphia Convention, 1787, where he proposed the Virginia Plan; agreed with GM about faults in Constitution and refused to sign it, later criticized the Constitution in *Letter . . . on the Federal Constitution*, 1787; however, advocated adoption in the Va. ratifying convention, and clashed with GM, 1788; U.S. atty. gen., 1789; U.S. sec. of state, 1794–1795; returned to law practice; senior counsel for Aaron Burr in treason trial; wrote a history of Revolutionary Va.

*RANDOLPH, PEYTON (1721–1775): eminent Williamsburg lawyer; king's atty. gen., 1748–1766; burgess, 1748–1775; Speaker, House of Burgesses, 1766–1775; Burgesses's agent in England opposing pistole fee, 1753; pamphleteered for paper money; opposed Patrick Henry's Stamp Act resolutions, but wrote moderate protest against Stamp Act, 1764; Va. convention pres., Mar., July 1775; Continental Congress pres., 1774–1775.

RANSOM, JOSEPH: Fairfax County resident, millwright on Washington's Muddy Hole Farm, 1764; Truro Parish vestry gave him money for upkeep of his child, 1774.

RAPPAHANNOCK RIVER: flows southeast through Va. into the Chesapeake Bay; regarded as southern boundary of the Northern Neck.

RAWLINGS, MOSES: commanded Rawlings's Continental Infantry, whose nucleus was Stephenson's Md. and Va. rifle regt. of 1776, 1777–1779; consolidated with Gist's Continental Infantry, 1779–1781; charged with prisoners of war after Burgoyne's defeat.

RAYS TOWN: in Pa., prominent place on Indian trails between the Ohio and Susquehanna rivers; located on the Juniatta River; now Bedford, Bedford

County, Pa., See also JUNIATTA RIVER.

READ, GEORGE (1733–1798): born in Cecil County, Md.; practiced law, New Castle, Del., 1752; Lower Del. atty. gen. 1763; Continental Congress, 1774–1777; signed Declaration of Independence; pres. of Del. constitutional convention, 1777; Del. vice pres.; Del. House of Reps., 1779–1780; admiralty justice, U.S. Court of Appeals, 1782; Del. rep. to Philadelphia Convention, 1787; U.S. senator, 1789–1793; Del. chief justice, 1793–1798.

*READ, JACOB (1752–1816): lawyer of S.C. and Savannah, Ga.; capt., Charleston militia, captured when the city fell, exiled to St. Augustine, then Philadelphia, 1780–1781; Charleston rep. to the S.C. Assembly, served on the committee to amerce loyalists; Speaker, 1787–1794; state privy council, 1783; Continental Congress, 1783–1786; Federalist delegate to S.C. ratifying convention, 1788; Federalist U.S. senator, 1795–1801.

REARDON, JOHN: of Loudoun County; signed Loudoun County resolves, 1774; possibly moved to Fairfax County in 1780s; a John Reardon signed GM's petition to move the county courthouse, 1790.

REARDON, WILLIAM: of Fairfax County; freeholder and voter in 1744 election for county burgesses; Truro Parish processioner, 1751; probably was William Reardon, Jr., who signed GM's circulating copy of Madison's "Memorial & Remonstrance" against assessment bill, 1785, and GM's petitions to remove courthouse, 1789, 1790.

REDD, WILLIAM: of Caroline County; may have been a student at Donald Robertson's school in King and Queen County, 1763; owned 14 slaves in 1783 census enumeration.

REDSTONE FORT: near Brownsville, Fayette County, Pa.; at confluence of Redstone Creek and Monongahela River; an expedition authorized by Ohio Co. had built a storehouse at mouth of Dunlap's Creek, on the trail from Wills Creek, Md., where the name "Redstone Old Fort" was given

to an ancient Indian mound; Gov. Dinwiddie sent force two years later (1754) with orders to fortify the Red Stone-Monongahela "forks," but French forces interrupted their work; Col. James Burd began another fort at site, 1759, which was officially named Fort Burd; town of Brownsville incorporated there, 1815. See George P. Donehoo, *History of the Indian Villages and Place Names in Pennsylvania* . . . (Harrisburg, Pa., 1928), 170–173.

REINTZELL, [ANTHONY]: tanner and dealer in hides; an Anthony Reintzell was a member of the Frederick County, Md., associators, 1775.

REVELEY, (also REEVELEY) JOHN: ironmonger, associated with the promoter John Ballendine in erecting Buckingham furnace, 1776–1778, to produce pig iron; partner with Ballendine at Westham foundry and ordinance works, ca. 1779–Jan. 1781, when British raiders destroyed the facility. See Boyd, III, 125–147.

REYNELL, JOHN: Philadelphia merchant; Quaker signer of antiwar petition, 1756; shareholder, Library Co. of Philadelphia; member, American Philosophical Society; chairman, committee of agreement for Philadelphia nonimportation assn., 1769.

RICHARD, GEORGE: Alexandria printer, founder of *Va. Journal & Alexandria Advertiser*, 5 Feb. 1784.

RICKETTS, BENJAMIN: Alexandria flour merchant, partner in firm of Stump and Ricketts, 1792; favored establishment of a state branch bank in Alexandria; married Mary Stuart.

RIDDICK, LEMUEL (1711–1775): Nansemond County planter, lawyer; Upper Parish vestry, ca. 1733–1773; director, Cape Henry lighthouse, 1757; burgess, 1736–1775; signed Va. nonimportation agreement, 1769; may have joined with Patrick Henry and James Mercer in address to the royal gov. about certain western land grants, requesting discouragement of all land monopolies within Va., Nov. 1769.

RIDOUT, THOMAS (1754–1829): born in Dorsetshire, England; half brother of

John Ridout, secretary to Md. gov., Horatio Sharpe; taught school, 1772–1774; settled on one of his half brother's tracts on the Md. Potomac frontier, 1775–1778; sailed to St. Eustatia, 1778; on return, ship ran ashore at Cape May and most of the cargo was lost, 1778; ran goods between the U.S. and West Indies, in a career notable for catastrophe, 1778–1779; after much financial difficulty, joined Joshua Johnson's firm as agent in Bordeaux, 1780; visited Annapolis and met Washington, LaFayette, 1784; failed in tobacco shipping venture financed by half brother, 1785; had dealings with GM in 1786 as capt. of ship *Fanny;* in deep financial trouble, he sailed between Bordeaux and Norfolk, 1786–1787; unable to recoup his losses, he left for Ky. and later New Orleans, carrying Washington's letters of introduction to Gen. Wilkinson and others; apparently returned to England after American ventures failed; granddaughter was Lady Matilda Ridout Edgar, British writer (1844–1910). See Mrs. Russell Hastings, "Calvert and Darnall Gleanings from English Wills," *Md. Hist. Mag.,* XX (1927), 215–235.

RIGG, JOHN: of Fairfax County; may have commanded ship which carried flour in Chesapeake Bay during Revolution; signed Madison's "Memorial & Remonstrance" against religious assessment bill, which GM circulated in Fairfax County; signed GM's petition to move the county courthouse, 1790.

ROANE, WILLIAM (d. 1785): of Essex County; son of William Roane and Sarah Upshaw; Essex County justice of peace, 1751; militia capt., 1765; burgess, 1769–1774; signed Va. nonimportation agreements, 1769, 1774; deputy atty. gen., 1768; Essex clerk; Essex committee of safety, 1774; militia col., 1777, but too old for active service; married Betty, daughter of Spender Mottrom Ball; their children were Thomas, Spencer (the jurist), Judith, and Sarah; survived by 2d wife, Anne.

ROBERTS, JOHN: Fairfax County freeholder; tithed in Truro Parish, 1734,

and apparently served on Fairfax Parish vestry.

ROMANETTOES CREEK: the name used by Ohio Co. in reference to the Kiskimenetas Creek (*q.v.*).

RONALD, WILLIAM: born in Scotland; apparently a merchant of William Ronald & Co., in copartnership with Aitchison and Parker and John Thompson & Co., 1777; possibly Northampton County committee, 1774; Powhatan delegate to Va. lower house, 1781, 1785; Va. del. to Annapolis Convention, 1786; Va. ratifying convention, 1788; his property included 11,944 acres in Powhatan, Chesterfield, Goochland, Surry counties, and 200 slaves in 1787–1788. See Hugh Blair Grigsby, *The History of the Virginia Federal Convention of 1788* . . . (Richmond, 1890–1891), II, 380n.

ROOTES, GEORGE: called "col."; son of Maj. Philip Rootes of Rosewall, King and Queen County, and Mildred Reade; moved to western Va.; Augusta burgess, 1744–1776; Va. convention, 1775.

ROSS, DAVID: doctor, of Bladensburg, Md; gave testimony in Md. council's investigation of Thomas Cresap, ca. 1740; married Ariana, eldest daughter of John Brice of Annapolis, 1750; Md. subscriber to Thomas Johnson's plan to open Potomac canal, 1762, and Md. trustee for Ballendine's Potomac project, 1774; involved in litigation with GM over lands.

ROSS, DAVID (*ca.* 1736–1817): business man, land speculator, of Petersburg and Richmond; Va. state commercial agent, 1780–1782, and forwarded large tobacco shipments to France; invested in flour mills, iron foundries, coal pits, in vicinity of James River; director, James River Co.; owned over 100,000 acres in Henrico, Fluvanna, Cumberland, and other counties during the 1780s; also reputed to own 400 slaves, 254 horses, and 806 head of cattle, 1787, 1788; severe floods along James River in 1786 caused enormous losses and he later lost much of his property; Fluvanna del., Va. General Assembly, 1781–1783; Va. Senate, 1786; appointed to Annapolis Convention, but declined to serve, 1786.

Ross, HECTOR: Colchester merchant with other business interests at Dumfries, 1758–1761; apparently acted as commercial agent for Truro Parish, 1765, 1767, in disposing of tobacco paid for tithes; Fairfax County justice of peace, 1770; signed petition GM favored against repeal of act to prevent extensive credits, 1783; favored separation of Alexandria city and county jurisdictions, 1787.

Ross, JOHN (1729–1800): Scotland-born Philadelphia merchant, ship-owner, lawyer; agent to settle the business of Thomas Morris, deceased half brother of Robert Morris, 1777; congressional agent in France to buy clothing, munitions, 1777–1780; there he clashed with William and Arthur Lee; alleged he spent nearly £20,000 sterling from his own pocket for military supplies in his frequent requests for reimbursement to Congress, 1780–1784.

ROUSBY HALL: large Md. plantation near mouth of Patuxent River and Solomon's Island; owned in GM's time by his cousin, William Fitzhugh, who was described in the 1770s as a famous host; the Rousbys married into several great Md. and Va. families; destroyed during the War of 1812. See William Eddis, *Letters from America* (London, 1792), 27–28.

ROUSSEAU, HENRY: probably the Henry Russaw or Russau listed as heading a Fairfax County household of seven whites, three blacks, 1782; and seven whites, one dwelling, seven other buildings, 1785.

RUMNEY, WILLIAM: Alexandria physician who migrated from England, 1763; retained by Washington for Mount Vernon; also paid on account by Truro Parish vestry, probably for attending the parish sick, 1764; Fairfax County committee of safety, 1774; surgeon, Va. troops, Continental line; may have been a capt. in the Fairfax militia, 1777; received a military land bounty.

RUSSELL, WILLIAM (1687–1759): of Culpeper County; born in England; migrated to Va. as a clerk to Lieut. Gov. Spotswood, 1710; bought land on Branch of Mattapony in Spotsylvania County, 1724; sent by Spotswood to negotiate with Pa.'s Gov. Gordon on postal service details, 1730; joined Larkin Chew, Jr., in promoting settlement of land in Spotsylvania County on lands against which Robert Carter, as agent for the Northern Neck proprietors, entered caveats, 1729; licensed to keep a ferry on the Shenandoah, 1736; Orange County justice of peace, 1736, when he was living north of the Rapidan; St. Mark's Parish vestry, 1740; lieut. col., Culpeper militia, 1756; buried in Buck Run Church, Culpeper County; father of Gen. William Russell, Jr., grandfather of William Russell III, both distinguished frontiersmen.

RUTHERFORD, ROBERT (1728–1803): born in Scotland; studied Royal College of Edinburgh; settled in Berks County, Pa., then moved to Va.; Frederick County high sheriff, 1743–1744; ranger capt., 1758; unsuccessful candidate for Frederick burgess, 1761; Frederick burgess, 1766–1771, when he resigned to become coroner; signed nonimportation agreements, 1769, 1774; Berkeley burgess, 1772–1776; with GM was a Va. trustee for Ballendine's plan to clear the Potomac, 1774; del. to Va. conventions, 1775, 1776; on committee to draft declaration of rights, Va. constitution, 1776; Hampshire County state senator, 1776–1790; U.S. House of Reps. 1793–1797; defeated for 3d term, 1796; married Mrs. Mary Howe; settled on estate, Flowing Spring, near Charlestown, (W.) Va.

RUTLAND, THOMAS (d. *ca.* 1790): merchant-planter of Annapolis, Md.; son of Thomas Rutland of Anne Arundel County, Md.; "Rutland's Purchase" was large tract of land between Laurel and Annapolis once held by the family; appears to have operated importing business in Annapolis, built houses there, and owned privateers outfitted during Revolution; his transactions with GM are obscure, but his dealings in land, tobacco, and commerce must have been extensive; married Ann Hall, *ca.* 1784.

*RUTLEDGE, EDWARD (1749–1800): Charleston, S.C., lawyer, trained in England; delegate to Continental Congress, and signed the Declaration of Independence, 1774–1776; S.C. provincial congresses, 1775, 1776; S.C. House of Reps., 1778, 1782–1796; drafted bill to confiscate Loyalist-owned properties; S.C. ratifying convention, 1788; S.C. Senate, 1796, 1798; S.C. gov., 1798; brother of John Rutledge, and brother-in-law of Charles Cotesworth Pinckney, his law partner.

*RUTLEDGE, JOHN (1739–1800): Charleston, S.C. lawyer, del. to Continental Congress, state legislator and gov., 1774–1782; S.C. chancery court, 1784; del., to Federal Convention, 1787, where he opposed GM in consideration of restrictions on slavery; associate justice, U.S. Supreme Court, 1789–1791; S.C. chief justice, 1791; U.S. Senate rejected Washington's nomination of Rutledge as Chief Justice of U.S. 1795; brother of Edward Rutledge.

ST. EUSTATIA (ST. EUSTATIUS): island colony in the Dutch West Indies important as a trading outlet during Revolution.

SANDFORD, JOHN: ship captain, operating from the port of Alexandria, *ca.* 1770–1779; commanded the schooner *Sidney*, sloop *Flying Fish*.

SANDFORD, LAWRENCE: ship captain from Port of Alexandria, 1764–1779; commanded brig *Adventure* as capt. in Va. state navy, 1776; since he was also trading on own account, he was not entitled to land grant for his wartime services.

SAVAGE, WILLIAM: physician, of Dumfries, Prince William County; married widow of Rev. Charles Green, Margaret, *ca.* April 1767, when her estate was temporarily entrusted to George Washington and Bryan Fairfax; a settlement of the affair strained

relations between Dr. Savage and the trustees; he later owned the brigantine *Success*, which was seized at Quantico by the commonwealth for use of Va. state naval force, 1778, and GM became involved in a final settlement of the damages; he appears to have been an aggressive, contentious man. See Freeman, *Washington*, III, 182–184, 279–280.

SAXTON, JOHN: Fairfax County freeholder; may have been tenant of William Fitzhugh of Millmont, who signed GM's petitions to move the county courthouse, 1789, 1790.

SCHWEIGHAUSER & DOBREE: Nantes mercantile firm that carried on extensive wartime business with Va. planters, probably dealt mainly in tobacco; John Daniel Schweighauser was partner; one of the few firms GM had confidence in, a rarity in 18th-century Va. trans-Atlantic affairs.

SCIOTO RIVER: tributary of the Ohio River; flows south through the center of present-day Ohio, through Columbus, and into the Ohio at Portsmouth.

*SCOTT, CHARLES (*ca.* 1739–1813): noncommissioned officer in Braddock's campaign, 1755; lieut. col. 2d Va. Regt.; col. 5th. Va. Regt.; col. 3d Va. Regt., 1776; Continental brig. gen., 1777; captured at Charlestown, S.C., 1780; brevetted maj. gen., 1783; Society of the Cincinnati; commissioner to appoint surveyors for western military bounty lands, 1783; settled in Woodford County, Ky., 1785; Ky. del. to Va. Assembly, 1789, 1790; commandant, Ky. district, 1791; engaged in various Indian battles; Ky. gov., 1808–1812.

SCOTT, GUSTAVUS (1753–1801): of Montgomery County, Md.; son of Rev. James Scott and cousin of GM; fled to Scotland after the celebrated Bullitt-Baylis duel, and studied at King's College in Aberdeen, and Middle Temple, 1765–1771; settled, practiced law in Somerset County, Md.; Md. conventions, 1774, 1775, 1776; signed Md. Assn., 1775; moved to

Dorchester County, *ca.* 1776; Md. Assembly, 1776, 1780, 1784; Annapolis meeting with Va. commissioners to settle Potomac-Pocomoke navigation, 1784; Continental Congress, 1784–1785; Md. Assembly committee on war prizes, 1776; favored James Rumsey's monopoly in Md. for steamboat invention; moved to Annapolis, then to Montgomery County, near Georgetown, where he built Rock Hill, which he later sold to Joel Barlow; District of Columbia commissioner, 1795; made various reports to Congress, the 1st of which sought a national university, 1796–1799; owned shares in the Potomac Co., Potomac Bridge Co., North American Land Co.; inherited his father's Stafford and Fairfax properties, also owned lands in Fauquier, Loudoun, Alleghany counties, Va., and adjacent areas; Uriah Forrest was friend and executor; married Margaret Hall, daughter of Hall Caile of Annapolis. See Hayden, *Virginia Genealogies*, 623–629, 593*n*–595*n*.

SCOTT, JAMES (d. 1782): born in Dipple Parish, Morayshire, Scotland; son of John Scott, brother of Rev. Alexander Scott; ordained as Anglican, licensed for Va., *ca.* 1735; married Sarah, daughter of Dr. Gustavus Brown and Frances Fowke of Rich Hill, Charles County, Md., a cousin of GM, *ca.* 1738; freeholder, Fairfax County, 1744; inherited Rev. Alexander Scott's estate, Dipple, Stafford County, and lived there until he became rector of Dettingen Parish, Prince William County, 1745–1782; lived then at Westwood, Prince William County; parish bought a 400-acre glebe for him on Quantico Creek; active Ohio Co. member; appointed GM agent for his shares in his will; often officiated in Truro Parish, 1765–1767, between the rectorships of Rev. Charles Green and Rev. Lee Massey; Dumfries trustee, 1761; Prince William County, justice of peace, 1769, 1770; owned land in Stafford, Fauquier, Fairfax counties, and on Carter's Run; he and his wife were buried at Dipple.

SCOTT, SARAH BROWN (1715–1784): daughter of Dr. Gustavus Brown of Rich Hill, Charles County, Md., and Frances Fowke, daughter of Col. Gerard Fowke, GM's great uncle; married Rev. James Scott, *ca.* 1738; her sisters included Frances, wife of Rev. John Moncure; Christian, wife of John Graham; Jean, wife of Rev. Isaac Campbell; and Margaret, wife of Hon. Thomas Stone; inherited Westwood and 500 acres; buried at Dipple.

SEATON, [GEORGE]: tobacco shipper in trans-Atlantic trade; operated in Fairfax County, may have been associated with Uriah Forrest, *ca.* 1790; a George Seaton had business interests in Amherst and King William counties, 1766–1768.

*SEBASTIAN, BENJAMIN (*ca.* 1745–1834): Va. clergyman who moved to Ky. district; practiced law at Louisville, 1784; advocated immediate statehood and free navigation of Mississippi at Ky. convention, 1788; became involved in intrigues with Spanish officials in La.; served on Ky. bench with George Muter in 1790s; his Spanish connections were exposed and he retired from public life to run a gristmill and sawmill in Grayson County, Ky.

SELDEN, MARY THOMSON MASON (1731–1758): only sister of GM; married Col. Samuel Selden, son of Joseph Selden and Mary Cary, 1751; of Salvington, Stafford County, across Potomac Creek from John Mercer's Marlborough; children were Samuel, Mary Mason (married Mann Page of North End, then Dr. Wilson Cary Selden), Miles Cary; Selden's 2d wife was Ann, daughter of John Mercer of Marlborough, and Catherine Mason, GM's aunt.

SELDEN, MILES (d. 1811): of Henrico County; sought boundary lines between Henrico and Hanover counties, 1774; capt. in Revolution; Henrico justice of peace; Henrico del. to Va. General Assembly; Va. Council, 1784–1785; Henrico vestryman after 1783; married Elizabeth, daughter of

Col. Gill Armistead, and Elizabeth Allen.

SHEILD, ROBERT: known as "col.," of York County; son of Rev. Samuel Sheild (d. 1803) and Molly Hansford; married 1st his cousin, Rebecca Sheild; 2d wife was Mary Reade; York County del. to Va. General Assembly; York County justice of peace.

SHELBY, EVAN: Indian fighter, frontier legislator; served on punitive expedition in Lord Dunmore's war, 1774; col., commanding Va. troops that destroyed pro-British Cherokee villages, 1779; del. to Va. General Assembly, 1780s; speculated in western lands, worked for Cumberland Gap roadways, and later settled in Tenn. See Boyd, II, 285–286.

SHORE, HENRY SMITH: merchant from Petersburg, associated with brother Thomas Shore in trans-Atlantic trade; apparently traded in Bordeaux and London, 1790–1793; wife Martha d. 1803 in Richmond.

SHORE, THOMAS (d. 1803): of Violet Bank, near Petersburg, where he was the business partner of David Ross, 1782; state purchasing agent for the James River district, 1776; brother of H. S. Shore.

SHURTEES CREEK (also CHARTIERS, CHURTREES): enters the Ohio from south in area west of Pittsburgh; Ohio Co. ordered a fort built at confluence with the Ohio in 1753. See Mulkearn, 147–148.

SIMM(E)S, CHARLES: of Alexandria; lieut. col., 6th Va. Regt., Continental line; Va. Society of the Cincinnati; Fairfax del., to Va. General Assembly, 1785; member, Alexandria committee to support Constitution, 1788; Fairfax del. to Va. ratifying convention, 1788; handled business and mortgages of Col. George Mercer, 1788; Alexandria common council chairman; customs collector for port of Alexandria, 1795–1814; pres., Potowmack Navigation Co., 1807–1814, in which he had been active since about 1785; son was Hon. John Douglas Simm(e)s.

SIMPSON, FRENCH: Fairfax County freeholder; known as "capt.," and signer of the petitions to separate jurisdiction of Alexandria and Fairfax County, 1787, and GM's memorial urging removal of the courthouse from Alexandria, 1789, 1790.

SIMPSON, WILLIAM: apparently worked for Edward Washington at Belmont during the 1760s; at least four William Simpsons headed Fairfax County households, 1782, 1785; two of them evidently lived in the vicinity of Belmont in the 1780s, two of the others trespassed on GM's property, 1763; one signed Fairfax "Memorial & Remonstrance," 1785; and a William Simpson was supported by Truro Parish, 1785.

SKINNER, WILLIAM: ship capt., Va. state naval force, 1776; served aboard the sloop *Congress;* awarded military land bounty of 5,333 acres.

SMITH, JOHN: of Loudoun County; lieut., Va. rifle co. attached to Stevenson's (Stinson's) battalion, in regt. commanded by Col. Moses Rawlings; among the Virginians captured at the fall of Fort Washington, 1776.

SMITH, JOHN M. (d. 1794): Baltimore merchant, legislator; invested in Baltimore waterfront property, 1759; founding elder, Baltimore Presbyterian church, 1762; Baltimore County committee on nonimportation, 1770; Baltimore committee of correspondence, 1774; served on local committee to observe nonimportation, 1774, 1775; Md. constitutional convention, 1776; Md. House of Delegates, 1776–1778; state senator, 1781, 1786; his sons were John, Jr., Gen. Samuel, and sec. of navy, Robert.

*SMITH, MERIWETHER (1730–1794): signed Westmoreland Assn., 1766; Va. conventions, 1775, 1776; on convention committee to draft declaration of rights, 1776; Madison mistakenly recalled that Smith prepared the first draft of the Va. constitution, but the weight of evidence is with GM; Va. House of Delegates, 1776, 1778, 1781–1782, 1785–1788; Continental Congress, 1778–1779, 1780–1781; delegate to Annapolis Convention, which he refused to attend, 1786; opposed Constitution in the Va. ratifying convention, 1788; Va. Council; his eccentricities gained him nicknames, such as "the Oddity of Virginia," and "Fiddlehead."

*SMITH, SAMUEL (1752–1839). Baltimore merchant, officer in Revolution, investor in confiscated loyalist lands; director of Bank of Md., he speculated in lands and lost a fortune in panic of 1819; state legislator, ship owner, he regained political power and commanded the militia in riots that followed failure of Baltimore bank, 1835; Baltimore mayor, 1835–1838.

SMYTH, JOHN FERDINAND DALZIEL: Md. loyalist; born in Scotland; lived on Port Tobacco Creek, Charles County, Md.; gave up plans to flee to Miss. at start of revolution, instead joined Dunmore at Norfolk; appointed surgeon of Dr. John Connolly's regt. by Dunmore; captured with Connolly's party beyond Hagerstown, Md., Nov., 1775; escaped but was captured, 12 Jan. 1776, and returned as a prisoner to Philadelphia; Congress offered him parole; severely injured in attempt to escape, Dec. 1776; imprisoned in condemned felons' dungeon and later transferred to prison in Baltimore; wrote full account in *A Tour of the United States of America* (London, 1784).

SPEAKE, ROBERT: apparently a Fairfax County planter; listed as heading a Fairfax County household of eight whites, 1782; signed petitions to separate the jurisdictions of Fairfax and Alexandria, 1787, and GM's petitions to move the county courthouse, 1789, 1790.

SPOTSWOOD, ALEXANDER (1751–1818): of Newpost and Nottingham, Spotsylvania County; son of Col. John Spotswood and Mary Dandridge; grandson of Gov. Alexander Spotswood, whose land and mining interests he continued; married Eliza, daughter of William Augustine Washington, a niece of George

Washington, 1769; maj., 2d Va. Regt., 1775; lieut. col. 1777; resigned after the battle of Germantown; appointed brig. gen. to command Va. troops, but too few were recruited; commanded in Va. militia during Gen. Alexander Leslie's invasion of Va. 1780; an army camp was established at Nottingham, near Fredericksburg; received 10,000 acres for his war services; owned 47,262 acres and much property in Spotsylvania, Orange, and Culpeper counties. See Darter, *Colonial Fredericksburg*, 117, 119, 211.

SPRINGFIELD: Fairfax County home of Martin Cockburn, near Gunston Hall on Dogue's Neck.

STAFFORD COURT HOUSE: Va. town, served as seat after Stafford County was created in 1664 from part of Westmoreland County; about 25 miles south of Gunston Hall.

STANWIX, FORT: near present-day Rome, Oneida County, N.Y.; treaty signed here in 1768 was denounced by GM as usurpation of Va. rights to western lands; colonial administrators persuaded Six Nations, or Iroquois tribe, to relinquish claims from area near Lake Ontario to Tennessee River; treaty closed west to colonization, but favored speculators friendly to Sir William Johnson; Vandalia or Grand Ohio Co. shareholders based their hopes on treaty's validity, while Ohio Co. claims would have been invalid if treaty had been upheld in London. See Sosin, *Whitehall in the Wilderness*, 173–177.

STARK, BOLLING (1733–1788): son of William Stark of York, then Prince George County, and Mary Cocke Bolling; Dinwiddie burgess, 1769–1771; Va. convention, May 1776; Dinwiddie County committee of safety, 1776; partner in Alexander, Glass, Strachan & Co., apothecaries, for which he was collecting debts, 1775; House of Delegates, 1777; council, 1781; Va. state auditor, 1781, 1786; owned property in Prince George, Dinwiddie, and Norfolk counties.

STEPHEN, ADAM (1730–1791): born in Va.; Ohio Valley expedition, 1754;

lieut. col., served under Washington at Winchester, and present at Braddock's defeat, 1755; on expedition against Creeks on S.C. frontier, 1756; charter member, Mississippi Co., 1763; brig. gen., 1776; maj. gen., 1777; held responsible for mistaken attack on troops of Gen. Anthony Wayne in fog at Germantown; accused of drunkenness, dismissed from service; lived in Berkeley County near Shenandoah Junction after the war, near Horatio Gates and Charles Lee, both of whom were also court martialed, dismissed from service; del. to Va. ratifying convention, where he supported the Constitution, 1788.

STEPHENSON (also STINSON), HUGH: capt., later col., commanded Md.-Va. riflemen who entered Continental line, June 1776; he apparently died of natural causes, but a large part of his force, serving under Col. Moses Rawlings, was captured by British at fall of Fort Washington, 16 Nov. 1776; his heirs were awarded 6,666-acre military land grant.

STEPTOE, GEORGE (d. 1784): physician of Westmoreland County; son of Col. James Steptoe and Elizabeth Eskridge Aylett; M.D., University of Edinburgh, 1767; Westmoreland County committee of safety, 1775; brothers were James, Thomas (d. ca. 1785), and William.

STEPTOE, WILLIAM: of Hewick, Middlesex County; son of Col. James Steptoe and Elizabeth Eskridge Aylett; probably attended William and Mary College, 1772–1776; married Elizabeth, daughter of Christopher Robinson and Sarah Wormeley, 1782; correspondent of William Lee, 1786.

STEWARD, [HUGH]: also Stewart; ship capt., commanded brig Mercury, 1789; may have been partner in Alexandria firm of Stewart & Hubbard; a Hugh Stewart was original trustee of the town of Centerville, 1792.

STEWART, ANTHONY (d. ca. 1791): loyalist merchant from Annapolis; charter member, Mississippi Co., 1763; married Jane, daughter of James Dick, 1764; partner of James Dick in the case of ship Good Intent, when they attempted to land goods in violation of nonimportation assn., 1769; owned Peggy Stewart, that carried tea on which he had paid duty, Oct. 1774; mob forced him to burn the brig; presented for high treason, 1781, and his properties confiscated by state; later testified before commissioners of United Empire Loyalists at Halifax, Nova Scotia, 1785.

STEWART, (also STEUART) WILLIAM: Annapolis merchant, of St. Ann's Parish; Anne Arundel sheriff, 1768, 1769; signed Annapolis nonimportation agreement.

STINSON. See STEPHENSON.

*STITH, WILLIAM (1707–1755): Oxford-educated author of History of the First Discovery and Settlement of Virginia (Williamsburg, 1747; London, 1753), the earliest important secondary treatment of the origins of Va. to 1624; his interpretation, strongly opposing King James I, proved most influential on subsequent historians; while pres. of William and Mary, 1752–1755, his opposition to Governor Dinwiddie's pistole fee cost him concurrent appointment as commissary of the Bishop of London and member of the Council; GM cited Stith in support of his claims to headrights (50-acre grants for each person imported into colony).

STOCKTON, SAMUEL WITHAM (ca. 1747–1794): of N.J.; secy. to William Lee, 1778–1779; secretarial account settled by Congress, 1780; secy. of N.J. ratifying convention, 1787; N.J. secy. of state, 1794.

*STODDERT, BENJAMIN (1751–1813): capt. in Revolution, 1777; secy., Board of War, 1779–1781; married Rebecca, daughter of Bladensburg, Md., merchant Christopher Lowndes; successful merchant at Georgetown, Md., in Forrest, Stoddert, & Murdock, a firm in the Potomac trade, with branches at London and Bordeaux established by Uriah Forrest; with William Deakins purchased privately blocks of land in the federal district, which were then ceded to the government;

the land transactions were handled by the Bank of Columbia, of which Stoddert was an incorporator, 1794; U.S. secy. of the navy, 1798–1801; his business suffered during the War of 1812; died heavily in debt.

*STONE, THOMAS (1743–1787): of Havre de Venture, near Port Tobacco, Charles County, Md.; studied law under Thomas Johnson; married Margaret, daughter of Dr. Gustavus Brown, and GM's cousin; served in Continental Congress, 1775–1778, where he helped draft Articles of Confederation, signed Declaration of Independence; Charles County del. to Md. Senate, 1776–1787; del. to Va.-Md. commission on Chesapeake jurisdiction; appointed to Federal Convention, 1787, but declined the appointment because of wife's illness; deeply depressed, he died suddenly at Alexandria while waiting to sail for England.

STONE, WILLIAM: of Fairfax County; probably father and son, Sr., and Jr., with one owning five slaves and the other two slaves in 1782 enumeration; one was among the signers of GM's petition for removing the county courthouse from Alexandria, 1789.

STREET, J.: ship capt., commanded a vessel, *Two Brothers,* in trans-Atlantic trade; also was master of *Two Friends;* carried cargo for Wallace, Johnson, & Muir, a firm which dealt with GM in 1780s.

*STRONG, CALEB (1745–1819): Mass. lawyer; county atty., 1776–1790; drafting committee, Mass. constitutional convention, 1779; state senate, 1780–1789; Mass. supreme judicial court, 1783; Federal Convention, 1787; Federalist in Mass. ratifying convention, 1788; U.S. Senator, 1789–1796; active framer of the Judiciary Act, 1789; reported Hamilton's plan for a national bank, 1791; Federalist gov. of Mass., 1800–1807, 1812–1816; opposed War of 1812, supported Hartford Convention, 1814.

STUART, DAVID (1753–): Alexandria doctor, close friend of George Washington; attended William and Mary,

studied medicine in Edinburgh and Paris; practiced in Fairfax County; married Eleanor Custis, widow of Washington's adopted son; served, with GM, in House of Delegates, 1787; del. to Va. ratifying convention, 1788; Federalist, he was named to 1st commission for the District of Columbia; wrote an agricultural treatise; trustee for Centerville, 1792, and Providence, 1805.

*SULLIVAN, JOHN (1740–1795): of Portsmouth, N.H.; Continental Congress, 1774, 1775; Continental brig. gen., 1775; maj. gen., 1776–1779; Continental Congress, 1780–1781; N.H. constitutional convention, 1782; N.H. atty. gen., 1782–1786; Speaker of N.H. Assembly, 1785, 1788; N.H. pres., 1786–1787, 1789; chairman, N.H. ratifying convention, 1788; judge, U.S. district court, N.H., 1789–1795.

SUMMERS, GEORGE (d. 1818): of Fairfax County; son of John Summers, early settler of Alexandria area; militia officer, helped prepare defenses around Alexandria, 1776; he and son, George, Jr., signed Madison's "Memorial & Remonstrance" against religious assessment bill, which GM circulated in county, 1785; served on Fairfax board of overseers of the poor, *ca.* 1795–1802; married Anne Smith Radcliffe; a son, William, was elected to House of Reps. from western Va.

TALBOT, DANIEL: of Fairfax County; agent for Col. Nathaniel Harrison; signed petition against British debt repayments, 1783; married Ann, daughter of John West, GM's friend and Fairfax burgess from 1755 to 1775.

TALBOT, JOHN: legislator, of Bedford County; House of Burgesses, 1761–1775; del. to Va. conventions, 1775–1776; del. to Va. General Assembly; chairman, Bedford County committee of safety, 1775; son of Matthew Talbot (d. 1758); married Sarah Anthony of Bedford, and later Phoebe Mosby of Henrico County; moved to Wilkes County, Ga., 1784, and served in Ga. state legislature.

[xcix]

TASKER, BENJAMIN (*ca.* 1690–1768): of Belair, Prince Georges County, Md.; son of Thomas Tasker, a Md. merchant; member of Md. Provincial Council for 32 years and pres., acting gov. of Md., 1752–1753; del., Albany Congress, 1754; leading horse breeder; owned Petapsco iron works, Baltimore County; married Anne, daughter of Md. secy. and atty. gen. William Bladen; their children were Benjamin, Jr., Anne (married Gov. Samuel Ogle), Rebecca (married Daniel Dulany, Jr.), Elizabeth (married Christopher Lowndes), and Frances (married Robert Carter of Nomini).

TASKER, BENJAMIN, JR. (*ca* 1720–1760): of St. Anne's Parish, Anne Arundel County, Md.; son of Benjamin Tasker and Anne Bladen; member, Md.-Pa. border commission, 1750, 1760; Md. provincial secy., council member; renowned horseman.

TAYLOE, JOHN (1721–1779): of Mt. Airy, Richmond County; known as "col." and John II; son of John Tayloe, member of the Va. Council; Richmond County justice of peace, 1742; Lunenburg Parish vestry, 1743; among his land dealings were membership in the Ohio Co. from 1749 to 1778, and a 100,000-acre grant in Augusta County which expired after a two-year extension, 1749; owned Neabsco iron furnace, Prince William County; Va. Council, 1757–1776; completed Mt. Airy, on the Rappahannock, 1758; owned a house in Williamsburg; raised notable race horses; Dumfries, Va., a trustee, 1761; apparently retired from public life at onset of war, and ignored his election to Va. Council, 1776; married Rebecca, sister of George Plater, St. Mary's County, Md., 1747; their children were Elizabeth, Rebecca (Mrs. Francis Lightfoot Lee), Ann Corbin (Mrs. Thomas Lomax), Eleanor, Mary (Mrs. Mann Page of Mannsfield); his friend Presley Thorton, married Tayloe's adopted daughter, Charlotte Belson; brother-in-law of Col. Richard Corbin and Mann Page of Rosewell; friend, neighbor of Landon Carter of

Sabine Hall; owned lands in Prince William, Fairfax, Loudoun counties, Va., and Baltimore County, Md., also numerous cargo vessels.

*TAYLOR, JOHN (1753–1824): of Hazelwood, known as John Taylor of Caroline (County); reared and trained in law by Edmund Pendleton; maj., lieut. col., Va. troops, Revolution; Va. House of Delegates, 1779–1782, 1783–1785, 1796–1800; U.S. Senate, 1792–1794, 1803, 1822–1824; worked on land laws to benefit settlers; advocate of states' rights, he agreed with GM and Henry that Constitution infringed on both rights of citizens and states; opposed Hamilton's funding measures; supported Jefferson for presidency, 1800; active in passage of 12th Amendment, 1803; opposed War of 1812; his political writings influenced generations prior to Civil War.

*TAZEWELL, HENRY (1753–1799): married Elizabeth, daughter of Benjamin Waller; studied law under his uncle, John Tazewell; Brunswick County burgess, 1775–1778; raised, commissioned capt. of cavalry troop, but hoped for reconciliation; Va. convention committee to draft constitution and bill of rights, 1776; Williamsburg delegate to Va. House of Delegates, 1778–1785; general court justice, 1785–1793; opposed ratification of Constitution; U.S. Senator, 1794–1799.

TAZEWELL, JOHN (*ca.* 1741–1781): Williamsburg lawyer; uncle of Henry Tazewell; attended William and Mary, 1758–1762; Williamsburg city council, 1767; college counsel, 1771; Bruton Parish vestry, 1774; city committee of safety, 1774; clerk, House of Burgesses committee of correspondence, 1773; clerk, Va. conventions, 1775–1776; House of Delegates, 1776–1777; assoc. justice, Va. General Court, 1778; married a daughter of John Bolling of Chesterfield County.

TERRETT, WILLIAM HENRY (d. 1758): freeholder, Prince William County, 1740; original member of the Fairfax County court, 1742; Truro Parish vestry clerk, 1745; married Margaret, daughter of Simon Pearson, sister of Constantia Pearson Chapman, 1735; she later married her cousin Col. John West, the elder; may have been the father of Capt. George Hunter Terrett, and Capt. William Henry Terrett, both of Fairfax County. See Harrison, 139, 321.

TERRY, NATHANIEL (d. 1780): of Halifax County; son of Benjamin Terry and Elizabeth Irby; member, House of Burgesses, 1758–1775; del. to Va. conventions, 1775–1776; signed Va. nonimportation agreements, 1769, 1774; Antrim Parish vestry, 1763; Halifax justice of peace, 1773; probably his son, Nathaniel (d. 1834), who served in Revolution and was captured at Charleston, 1780, then paroled until 1783, and awarded 5,166-acre military land bounty.

THOMPSON, WILLIAM: of Colchester, Fairfax County; served in militia co. with GM's son, William, and rose to rank of capt., possibly served from 1777 to 1781 with later military bounty award of 4,000 acres; signed GM's petitions to remove courthouse from Alexandria, 1789, 1790; opposed GM on issue of Constitution, favored ratification, 1787–1788; married Ann Washington (b. 1768), daughter of Robert Washington and Alice Strother of King George County.

*THOMSON, CHARLES (1729–1824): Philadelphia schoolmaster turned merchant; kept records of negotiations for the Treaty of Easton, 1757; secy. to Continental Congress, 1774–1789; retired to his estate, Harriton, near Philadelphia; translated Septuagint and New Testament, ca. 1789–ca.1815.

THORNTON, ANTHONY (1695–1757): of St. Paul's Parish, Stafford County; son of Francis Thornton of Stafford County, grandson of William Thornton, immigrant; married Winifred, daughter, heiress of Col. Peter Presley of Northumberland House, Northumberland County; their four sons were Col. Presley of Northumberland House; Col. Francis of Society Hill;

Peter of Rose Hill, Caroline County; and Anthony of Ormsby, Caroline County. See "Virginia Council Journals, 1726–1753," VMHB, XXXII (1924), 63–64.

THORNTON, FRANCIS (d. 1784): of Society Hill, Stafford and King George counties; son of Anthony Thornton and Winifred Presley, brother of Col. Presley Thornton and Peter Thornton; married Sarah Fitzhugh, who probably was GM's cousin, from St. Paul's Parish, Stafford County, 1747; King George justice of peace, militia col.; King George County committee of safety, 1774; active Va., Md. turfman from 1752; children included Winifred (wife of Capt., later Col., Daniel McCarty, of Pope's Creek, Westmoreland County), and Elizabeth (wife of her cousin Presley Thornton).

THORNTON, GEORGE: of Spotsylvania County; son of Francis Thornton of Fall Hill, near Fredericksburg, and Frances Gregory; business partner of William Triplett in Thornton & Triplett, from ca. 1772; visited England to open correspondence with merchants, 1772; Spotsylvania County del., to Va. convention, 1776; House of Delegates, 1777; one of his ships was sold by the state, 1776; children were Lucy Francis (wife of Capt. John Posey), Reuben, George Washington; a maj. in the Continental army, he died during a forced march; his widow married Gen. Thomas Posey.

THORNTON, PETER: of Rose Hill, Caroline County; son of Anthony Thornton and Winifred Presley, brother of Col. Presley Thornton and Francis Thornton; married Ellen Bankhead.

THORNTON, PETER PRESLEY (1750–1811): of Northumberland House, Northumberland County; son of Col. Presley Thornton, nephew of Peter Thornton, Francis Thornton; inherited Ohio Co. stock from his father, 1769; married Sally, daughter of Maj. Robert Throckmorton, Gloucester County, 1771; Northumberland justice of peace; Northumberland burgess,

[ci]

1772–1775; Va. convention, 1775; col., Va. minute regt., 1775–1777. See Gwathmey, *Virginians in Revolution*, 771.

THORNTON, PRESLEY (1721–1769): of Northumberland House, Northumberland County, on the Potomac; son of Col. Anthony Thornton and Winifred Presley, brother of Francis Thornton and Peter Thornton; inherited most of the Presley family's large estates; St. Stephen's Parish vestry, Northumberland County, 1749; Northumberland burgess, 1748–1761; Va. council, 1761; partner in Ohio Co., 1749–1769, when his son Peter Presley inherited his share; Dumfries, Va., trustee, 1761; Mississippi Co., 1763; married adopted daughter of John Tayloe of Mt. Airy, who took their children to England before the Revolution; his estate was still indebted to Speaker Robinson's estate in 1792. See Bishop [William] Meade, *Old Churches, Ministers, and Families of Virginia* (Philadelphia, 1901), II, 143.

THORNTON, WILLIAM (d. 1800): son of Francis Thornton of Society Hill, King George County, which William inherited; also owned The Cottage, King George County; married GM's daughter Elizabeth; Va. House of Delegates, 1784–1786; Va. ratifying convention, 1788. See W. G. Stanard, "Thornton Family," WMQ, 1st Ser., XXV (1916), 124–125.

TILGHMAN, JAMES (1716–1793): lawyer from Talbot County, Md.; son of Col. Richard Tilghman; Md. Assembly, 1762–1763; moved to Philadelphia, where he was a member of the common council, 1764; served as Ohio Co. attorney, 1767; Pa. Council, 1767–1776; secy., Pa. land office, 1769–ca. 1777; suspected of loyalism, he apparently retired from public life, settled at Camel's Worthmore, Kent County, Md.; married Anna, daughter of Tench Francis of Fausley, Talbot County, Md.; uncle of Pa. chief justice Edward Tilghman, brother of Md. Council pres. Matthew Tilghman, and of Col. Richard Tilghman, who married Susan Frisby, apparently sister of Mrs. William Fitzhugh of Rousby Hall, who was GM's cousin.

TILLET (T), JOHN: apparently a Fairfax County blacksmith or gunsmith; possibly related to Giles Tillett, Truro Parish vestryman, who lived on the Occoquan Back (rolling) Road, 1706; signed Fairfax County petitions against British debts, 1783, and for separate jurisdictions of Fairfax County and Alexandria, 1787.

*TRENT, WILLIAM (1715–1787?): Indian trader, interpreter, land speculator; partner of George Croghan in Indian trade, 1749–1754; suffered losses from French and Indian raids along Ohio, built Ohio Co. outpost on Redstone Creek, 1754; dispatched by Gov. Dinwiddie to Forks of the Ohio to build fort, and was blamed when French captured site in his absence; later joined Pa. traders and speculators, sought confirmation of Treaty of Fort Stanwix; accompanied Samuel Wharton to England on behalf of Indiana grant, 1769–1775; presented Indiana or Grand Ohio claims to Va. General Assembly, 1779, when GM advocated opposite viewpoint; then sought aid from Continental Congress with several unsuccessful petitions, 1779–1783. See James, *George Mercer*, 100, 106ff.

TRIPLETT, REUBEN: midshipman, clerk, Va. state naval force; served aboard *Tempest*, 1778; son of Francis Triplett (d. 1757) and Mildred, of Washington Parish, Westmoreland County; may have been master of the *Ann*, sailing in Va. waters, 1789; for three years of naval service he received land bounty of 2,424 acres; moved to Loudoun County.

TRIPLETT, THOMAS (d. 1780): of Fairfax County; son of Francis Triplett, brother of William Triplett; French and Indian war service, 1756; Fairfax County justice of peace; Fairfax committee of safety, 1774; Christ Church (Alexandria) vestryman; lived at Round Hill, across the road from the Truro Parish glebe, had various Fairfax County lands, including some GM apparently later acquired.

TRIPLETT, WILLIAM (d. 1803): of Truro Parish; son of Francis Triplett, brother of Thomas Triplett; parish processioner, 1767, 1771; executor for Harrison Manley, 1774; reconstructed, from the original building, the main house at Mount Vernon which still stands; Truro Parish vestry, 1776–1785, and churchwarden, 1777–1778; original pew holder of old Pohick church; was close friend of Washington; married Sarah, daughter of Dade Massey and Parthenia Alexander, apparently the sister of Rev. Lee Massey, and distant cousin of GM. See Slaughter, *Truro Parish*, ed. Goodwin, 118–119.

TRIPLETT, WILLIAM: of King George and Westmoreland counties; son of Francis Triplett; probably the merchant partner of George Thornton living near Fredericksburg, Va., who deeded Thornton 300 acres, 1775, and who is mentioned in the letters of merchant and relative, Thomas Jett.

TRIST, NICHOLAS (d. 1783): probably from Devonshire, England; served in British army; married Eliza House of Philadelphia; died at his settlement on the Mississippi, near Natchez, where he planned to retire; son was Hore B. Trist (b. 1778); Thomas Jefferson managed his widow's interests.

TRURO PARISH: in Fairfax County; GM's home parish, organized from Hamilton Parish in 1732, with Overwharton Chapel as 1st church and in continuous use until Pohick Church was occupied in 1772; GM was vestryman or churchwarden from 1749 until 1784. See Slaughter, *Truro Parish*, ed. Goodwin.

TUCKER, ST. GEORGE (1752–1827): lawyer; Annapolis Convention, 1786; Va. General Court justice, 1788, Va. Supreme Court of Appeals, 1803–1811; Va. federal district court, 1813–1827.

TURBERVILLE, JOHN: planter of Hickory Hill, Westmoreland County; at William and Mary, 1753, 1754; married Martha, daughter of Col. John Corbin of Portobago; bred, raced horses; capt., *ca.* 1770; member Westmoreland County committee of safety, 1775; Turberville, Va. built on his Fairfax County land near the Little Falls, 1798.

TWIGTREE TOWN (also TWIGHTWEE TOWN): Miami settlement on the Great Miami River, located near present site of Piqua, Ohio; the tribe, under the leadership of Chief Pickawillany, was friendly toward the English traders; attacked in June 1752 by Ottawa, Chippewa Indians led by French; raid prompted Virginians to plan the ouster of French forces in the Ohio valley. See Mulkearn, 491.

*TYLER, JOHN (1747–1813): of Greenway, Charles City County; studied law under Robert Carter Nicholas; Charles City committee of safety, 1774; judge, high court of admiralty, 1776; strong political ally of Patrick Henry; Charles City del. to Va. lower house, 1777–1780; Va. Council, 1780–1781; Speaker, Va. House of Delegates, 1781–1785; Antifederalist delegate, Va. ratifying convention, 1788, Va. General Court, 1789–1808; Va. gov., 1808–1811; U.S. judge, Va. district, 1811; father of U.S. pres. John Tyler.

VAN BIBBER, ISAAC (*ca.* 1736–1825): Baltimore merchant; Baltimore County justice of peace; Baltimore committee of correspondence, 1774; committee to superintend nonimportation in Baltimore, 1774; owned privateering vessels in Md. and Charleston, S.C., during the Revolution; became co-partner of Richard Harrison, in Van Bibber & Harrison, traded from St. Eustatia for the Va. committee of safety, 1776; county orphans' court justice, 1779, 1786; part-owner, Baltimore Iron Works; director, Baltimore Manufacturing Co. (textiles), 1789; helped organize Bank of Md., 1784; captain of the watch, Fells Point.

VANDALIA COMPANY: also Indiana Co., Walpole Co., and Grand Ohio Co.; project of Philadelphia merchants and land speculators; involved leading British politicians, from 1769 until Revolution; sought a royal grant encompassing much of present-day

W. Va. and part of eastern Ky. on basis of Treaty of Fort Stanwix (1768); the claim overlapped with the previous grant to the Ohio Co. of Va., which brought GM into the controversy; after 1776 the American promoters, chiefly Samuel Wharton and William Trent (*q.v.*), sought a Va. confirmation of their claims, but later shifted their battle to the Continental Congress after an unsuccessful hearing before the Va. General Assembly, 1779; the dispute carried into Congress when the public domain was being created by western land cessions from Va. and other states.

*VARNUM, JAMES MITCHELL (1748–1789): lawyer, infantry, R.I. militia officer, during Revolution; sometime congressman, 1780–1787; active interest in Northwest Territory; director, Ohio Co. of Associates, 1787; U.S. judge, Northwest Territory; actively assisted drafting territorial legal code.

WABASH (also OUBACHE) RIVER: principal waterway through Illinois country above Ohio, British post at Fort Sackville (Vincennes), captured by George Rogers Clark's expedition, Feb. 1779; also name for the land company, formed by speculators from Pa., Md., and elsewhere, who sought huge grant in Ohio Valley in 1770s; later the group merged their claims to form Illinois-Wabash Co., which unsuccessfully sought congressional recognition of their Indian land purchases north of the Ohio.

WAGENER (WAGGONER), PETER (1717–1774): called "maj."; lawyer; son of Rev. Peter Wagener; born at Sistend, Essex, England; married Catherine, daughter of Speaker John Robinson, 1739; home on north bank of Occoquan Creek; Prince William County clerk, 1742–1752; Fairfax County clerk, 1752–1774; town of Colchester, Va., was built on his land in 1753; Truro Parish vestry, 1770–1774, and churchwarden, 1771–1772.

WAGENER, PETER, JR. (1742–1798): son of Maj. Peter Wagener; succeeded his father as Fairfax County clerk, and as Truro Parish vestryman, 1774; Truro Parish churchwarden, 1776–1777; Fairfax County overseer of the poor, 1787–1795; married Sinah, daughter of Col. Daniel McCarty (d. 1791); Fairfax lieut. during Revolution; signed Fairfax petition against repeal of the act to prevent extensive credits, 1783; favored adoption of Constitution, 1787; son Peter served under George Rogers Clark in the Illinois Regt.; good friend of GM. See Harrison, 433–434.

WAITE, THOMAS: Fairfax County freeholder who contracted with Truro Parish vestry to construct glebe buildings, 1752, but lost contract for failure to complete the work, 1758. See Truro Parish Vestry Book (DLC), 2 Oct. 1752, 27 Oct. 1758.

WAITE, WILLIAM: with James Wren, was paid for plans for Truro Parish glebe buildings, 1769; may have married Jane, GM's niece, daughter of Simpha Rosa Enfield Mason and John Dinwiddie.

WALKER, JOHN (1744–1809): lawyer; son of Dr. Thomas Walker; born at Castle Hill, Albemarle County; graduated William and Mary, 1764; moved to Belvoir, Albemarle County; Albemarle burgess, 1773–1776; commissioned with his father to negotiate with Ohio Indians at Fort Pitt, 1775; Continental Congress, 1780; land speculator; appointed U.S. senator, 1790, to fill vacancy left by William Grayson's death; married Elizabeth, daughter of Bernard Moore of Chelsea, 1764. See Hutchinson-Rachal, II, 138*n*.

*WALKER, DR. THOMAS (1715–1794): practiced medicine in Fredericksburg; main agent of Loyal Land Co. in southern valley of Va.; 1st white man to have recorded an expedition to Ky., 1750; commissary-gen. to Va. troops under Braddock's command, 1755; speculated in business and land with Andrew Lewis; served in House of Burgesses for various counties; moved to Castle Hill, Albemarle County, where was a neighbor of Jefferson's father and later guardian for

Jefferson; Va. commissioner at Fort Stanwix meeting with Indians, 1768; commissioner to negotiate with Ohio Indians at Pittsburgh, 1775; Va. committee of safety, 1776; Va. executive council, 1777–1781; led Va. commission to extend westward its border with N.C., 1779; father of John Walker.

WALLACE, CHARLES: merchant, Annapolis, Md.; St. Ann's Parish vestry, 1757–1758; served in French and Indian War; sent with Mordecai Gist to bring Anthony Stewart, owner of tea ship *Peggy Stewart*, before a mob, 1774; owned privateers registered in Md. during the Revolution.

WALLACE, JOHNSON & MUIR: mercantile firm in Nantes during American Revolution, later shifted offices to London, *ca.* 1784–1785; apparently Joshua Johnson was partner in firm, which owned the privateer *Favorite*, commissioned at Baltimore in 1782 and commanded by Capt. James Buchanan; GM enjoyed good relations with the firm.

WALLER, BENJAMIN (1716–1786): son of Col. John Waller; lived in Williamsburg; attended William and Mary; practiced law in James City County; Bruton Parish vestry, Williamsburg, 1744; James City County burgess, 1744–1761; clerk, Va. General Court, 1745–1776; had a leading role in exposing the Speaker Robinson fraud, 1766; Williamsburg committee of safety, 1774; judge of the state admiralty and general courts, 1776–1785; married Martha Hall, 1746. See Hayden, *Va. Genealogies*, 382–383.

WALLER, JOHN, JR.: son of Col. John Waller of Newport, Spotsylvania County; brother of Benjamin Waller.

WALLER, JOHN (b. 1753): son of Benjamin Waller; Spotsylvania County clerk, 1774–1786; active in Spotsylvania Baptists' Assn., 1780; clerk, Essex County Baptist Assn.; House of Delegates, 1791.

WALLER, ROBERT HALL (b. 1764): son of Benjamin Waller; York County clerk; married Nancy Camm (d.

1800), and later Martha Langhorne Crafford.

WALLER, WILLIAM (1762–1841): born on Va. peninsula, son of Benjamin Waller of Williamsburg; may have served as enlisted man in 2d Va. Regt., 15th Va. Regt., and other units of Continental line; possibly a York County justice of the peace.

WALPOLE, THOMAS: London banker, nephew of Sir Robert Walpole; member of the Grand Ohio Co., which in early 1770s was identified as "the Walpole Co." and attracted investment by influential British politicians.

WARDROP, JAMES (d. 1760): merchant in Upper Marlborough, Md.; Meadow Land surveyed for him, 1744; died in N.Y. after long illness; his heirs in Great Britain still held one share of Ohio Co. stock, 1778. See William B. Marye, "The Old Indian Road," *Md. Hist. Mag.*, XV (1920), 383.

WASHINGTON, AUGUSTINE (b. 1720): youngest son of Augustine Washington and Jane Butler; brother of Lawrence Washington, half brother of George Washington; studied at Appleby School; inherited Wakefield, Westmoreland County, from his father; Ohio Co. member, sold shares to Robert Carter of Nomini, before 1768; Westmoreland County burgess, 1754–1758; married Anne, daughter of William Aylett.

WASHINGTON, CHARLES (1738–1799): son of Augustine Washington and Mary Ball; brother of George Washington; married Mildred, daughter of Col. Francis Thornton.

WASHINGTON, EDWARD, SR. (d. 1792): of Fairfax County; described as a planter in land grants issued in his name in 1737 and afterwards; subsheriff, Prince William County, 1737; tobacco inspector, during 1730s; an inspector at Occoquan and Pohick warehouses, 1748; acquired Belmont on the Occoquan River from Catesby Cocke, *ca.* 1742; possibly connected with the estate office of the Northern Neck proprietors, probably as a collector; an original trustee of

Colchester, 1753; unsuccessful candidate for Truro Parish vestry, 1765. See Davis, ed., *The Colonial Virginia Satirist*, 14–15.

WASHINGTON, EDWARD, JR. (d. 1813): inherited Belmont from his father, Edward, Sr.; Truro Parish vestry, 1779–1785; signed Fairfax County petitions against British debts and against the repeal of an act preventing extensive credits, 1783; signed Fairfax County "Memorial & Remonstrance," circulated by GM, 1785; an original trustee of Occoquan, Va., 1804. See Harrison, *Old Prince William*, 275–276, 662.

*WASHINGTON, GEORGE (1732–1799): commanding gen., Continental army, American Revolution, 1775–1783; 1st pres. of U.S., 1789–1797; son of Augustine Washington and Mary Ball; surveyor, militia officer, burgess from Fairfax County; inherited Mount Vernon, 1752; close friend of GM's until resentment over ratification struggle of 1787–1788; buried at Mount Vernon.

WASHINGTON, JOHN AUGUSTINE (1736–1787): called "Jack"; son of Augustine Washington and Mary Ball; brother of George Washington; managed Mount Vernon while Col. Washington participated in French and Indian War campaigns; married Hannah, daughter of Col. John Bushrod of Bushfield, Westmoreland County, 1756; inherited his father's shares in the Principio Iron Co. before 1757; moved to Bushfield, 1758, which he owned, 1774–1787; col., militia; Westmoreland justice of the peace, 1777; charter member, Mississippi Co., 1763; Westmoreland committee of safety, 1775. See Mount Vernon Ladies' Assn. *Annual Report 1964*, 18–21.

WASHINGTON, LAWRENCE (1718–1752): oldest surviving son of Augustine Washington and Jane Butler; half brother of George Washington; studied at Appleby School, England; capt., colonial troops reinforcing Gen. Wentworth, served under Admiral Vernon in the West Indies,

Cartagena, 1741; settled on Hunting Creek Plantation, Fairfax County, 1740, which he renamed Mount Vernon; later a militia maj.; Fairfax County burgess, 1742–1749; charter member, Ohio Co.; interested in Va.-Md. iron works; married Anne, oldest daughter of Hon. William Fairfax of Belvoir, 1743.

WASHINGTON, LUND (1737–1796): planter, plantation manager, of Fairfax County; son of Townsend Washington and Elizabeth Lund of Chotank Creek, King George County; cousin of George Washington; married his cousin Elizabeth Foot; managed large estates in Albemarle and Orange counties, then took over Col. Henry Fitzhugh's Ravensworth in Fairfax County; manager of Mount Vernon during Gen. Washington's absence, and continued until 1785 in his employ; replaced Daniel McCarty on Truro Parish vestry, 1784.

WASHINGTON, MARTHA (1732–1802): daughter of Col. John Dandridge of New Kent County; married Daniel Parke Custis, 1749; married George Washington, 1759; remained at Mount Vernon through most of war, 1775–1783; is buried at Mount Vernon.

WASHINGTON, SAMUEL (1734–1781): of Harwood, Berkeley County; son of Augustine Washington and Mary Ball, George Washington's brother; Continental army col.; married five times; 1st wife, Jane, daughter of Col. John Champe; 2d, Mildred, daughter of Col. John Thornton; 3d, Lucy, daughter of Nathaniel Chapman; 4th, Anne, daughter of Col. James Steptoe, widow of Willoughby Allerton; 5th, Susannah, daughter of John Perrin, widow of George Holden.

WASHINGTON, WILLIAM AUGUSTINE (1752–1810): cavalry officer, nephew of George Washington, native of Va.; served at Long Island, Trenton, 1776; led cavalry under Gates and Greene in N.C., cited for bravery at Cowpens, 1781; led light dragoons at Guilford Court House, 1781; captured at Eutaw Springs, 1781, and paroled;

brigadier gen., U.S. army, 1798, retired, 1800.

WATERS, (WATTERS), WILLIAM (1751–1833): 1st native American Methodist itinerant preacher; raised near Baltimore, Md., attended Philadelphia conference of Methodists, 1775; married Sarah, daughter of William Adams, granddaughter of Gabriel Adams, 1778; attended Methodist conference at Brokenback Church, Fluvanna County, 1779; Baltimore circuit, 1779; settled near Alexandria, 1783; rode circuits, 1786, 1801; supported adoption of the Constitution, 1787.

WAUGH, TYLER (b. 1740): Fairfax County planter; son of William Waugh and Margaret Tyler of Stafford County; married Mary Crump in Fauquier County, 1773.

WEBB, GEORGE (1729–ca. 1786): called "col."; admiralty commissioner, 1776; Va. treasurer, 1777–1779; Va. executive council, 1780–1782; receiver of Va. taxes for continental use, 1782, 1783. See Hutchinson-Rachal II, 31n; III, 173n, 182n.

WEST, HUGH, SR. (d. 1754): son of John West and Susanna Pearson; married Sibyl, daughter of William Harrison; Truro Parish vestry, 1744–1754; churchwarden, 1746; owned lands, ferry, and warehouses at site of Alexandria, Va., and was an original trustee of the town, 1749; supervisor with GM of construction of new glebe buildings, 1754; Fairfax County burgess, 1752–1754.

WEST, HUGH, JR. (d. 1767): Alexandria lawyer; son of Hugh West, Sr., and brother of Capt. John West, Jr.; married Elizabeth, daughter of John Minor; Fairfax County burgess, 1754–1755, Frederick County burgess, 1756–1758. See Harrison, 138–140.

WEST, JOHN (d. 1777): son of Hugh West, Sr.; married Catherine, daughter of Maj. Thomas Colville and Mary Foster, before 1755; Truro Parish vestry clerk, 1756–1764; Fairfax County justice of the peace, 1764–1777; longtime Fairfax surveyor; signed Fairfax nonimportation assn., 1770; nephew of Col. John West, whom he succeeded as Fairfax delegate to the Convention of 1776.

WEST, JOHN (d. 1777): Fairfax County soldier, merchant; son of John West and Susanna Pearson; lived at West's Grove, near Alexandria; married Mary (d. ca. 1748), and later Margaret Pearson; lieut., served under Washington at Great Meadows, 1754; sent to Winchester with French prisoners in his charge; Truro Parish vestry, 1744–1765; militia maj., col.; Fairfax Parish vestry, 1765; succeeded his brother, Hugh, as Fairfax burgess and held seat at intervals between 1755 and 1776; Fairfax sheriff before 1761; Fairfax justice of the peace, 1764–1777; signed Fairfax nonimportation assn., 1770; Fairfax committee of safety, 1774; often confused with his namesake nephew, who also died in 1777.

WEST, ROGER (ca. 1755–1801): son Col. John West, and his 2d wife, Margaret Pearson Terrett; of West Grove, Fairfax County; married Nancy, daughter of Dumfries merchant Allan Macrae, and later to Marianne, daughter of Dr. James Craik; supported Constitution, 1787; Fairfax justice of the peace, ca. 1787–1799; signed GM's Fairfax petition to move the courthouse; pres., Fairfax board of overseers of the poor, 1793, 1795; an original trustee of South Haven, Va., built on John Mason's land, 1798; a founding member and vice-pres., Washington Society, Alexandria, 1800.

WEST, STEPHEN: merchant of Prince Georges County, Md.; member of Annapolis committee on the case of the ship *Good Intent;* resided at Woodyard, which was purchased from the Darnall family; married Hannah Williams, 1753; Md. agent for securing army provisions during the Revolution; issued his own currency, called Stephen West's money; owned popular Annapolis coffee house; succeeded Daniel Carroll on the Md. council, 1781, after serving in the Md. assembly.

WEST, THOMAS: Alexandria, Va., resident, son of Capt. John West, Jr., and Catherine Colville; apparently captain of the ship *Cameron;* one of two Fairfax County Thomas Wests, and probably headed a household of five whites, ten blacks, 1782; signed Fairfax petitions against British debts, 1783; supported ratification of Constitution, 1787.

WESTCOTT, [WRIGHT?] (d. 1784): probably the ship captain who commanded the *Potomack,* Dec. 1776; after the galley *Revenge* was sunk, he moved to command of the ship *Henry;* guardian and near relative of Stephen Wright, who sailed for Martinique with him; they were captured by the ship *Ceberus* and imprisoned; married Fanny, daughter of Queen Annes County, Md., merchant Thomas Walke.

WESTERN, WILLIAM: (probably also spelled "Weston") of Fairfax County; probably did minor repairs to Pohick vestry house, 1768; welfare recipient, 1793, 1795, 1797; signed Fairfax petition against British debts, 1783, and petitions for removal of the courthouse, 1789, 1790.

WESTHAM FOUNDRY: Henrico County; located above the Falls of the James near Richmond; destroyed by Benedict Arnold's troops in Jan. 1781.

WETHERBURN, HENRY (d. 1760): Williamsburg tavern-keeper; bought Bland house in 1738 and ran it along with three other ordinaries.

*WHARTON, SAMUEL (1732–1800): Philadelphia-based land speculator, Indian trader; accompanied William Trent to England, ostensibly to have Indiana Tract validated, 1769; organized Grand Ohio Co. with English associates, 1769–1775; joined Benjamin Franklin in France, 1779; portions of his tract, *Plain Facts* (Philadelphia, 1781), attacked GM's advocacy of Ohio Co. claims; Del. rep. to Continental Congress, 1782–1783.

WHITESIDE, PETER (1752–1828): Philadelphia merchant; clerk for Willing, Morris & Co., *ca.* 1774–1777; formed own firm thereafter, and appears to have undertaken business for Continental Congress.

WHITING, THOMAS (*ca.* 1712–1781): merchant of Gloucestertown, Va.; son of Henry Whiting and Ann Beverley; Gloucester County burgess, 1755–1776; del. to Va. conventions, Mar. and Dec., 1775, May 1776; signed Va. nonimportation agreement, 1769; Gloucester committee of safety, 1775; lieut. col., militia, 1775; chairman, Va. admiralty board, 1776; commissioner, board of trade, 1779; married Molly, daughter of James Hubard; grandfather of John C. Fremont. See Hutchinson-Rachal, I, 299*n.*

*WILKINSON, JAMES (1757–1825): served in Revolutionary War as aide-de-camp to Gen. Horatio Gates and was involved in Conway Cabal; forced to resign commission, 1781; moved to Ky. and worked for immediate separation of Ky. from Va., 1785; served in U.S. army after 1791; chief witness at Aaron Burr's trial; was court martialed but acquitted in 1811; served in War of 1812, and died in Mexico.

*WILLIAMS, JONATHAN, JR. (1750–1815): native of Boston, grandnephew of Benjamin Franklin; commercial agent at Nantes for U.S. envoys in France, 1779; his actions deepened the Lee, Deane-Franklin factionalism in Congress; maj. gen., superintendent of West Point.

*WILLIAMSON, HUGH (1735–1819): mathematician, physician, scientist, who studied in Europe, practiced in Philadelphia, carried news of Boston Tea Party to England; returned to Carolinas, traded with French sugar islands, gave medical attention to troops; elected to N.C. Commons House, 1782, 1785; del. to Continental Congress, 1782–1785, 1787; replaced Willie Jones as del. to Federal Convention, 1787; del. to N.C. 2d ratifying convention, 1789, and favored adoption of Constitution; later moved to N.Y.: member of American Philosophical Society and founder of Literary and Philosophical Society.

WILLS CREEK: flows through Pa., empties into Potomac on Md. side; site of Ohio Co. trading post and storehouse; Braddock's road to Fort Pitt passed by here, 1745–1760; now site of Cumberland, Md.

WILSON, CUMBERLAND: of Dumfries, Prince William County; may have been associated with GM in a land or mercantile transaction, *ca.* 1790; was intimate friend of their mutual acquaintance, Richard Graham (d. 1796).

WILSON (WILLSON), GEORGE: apparently a surveyor or deputy surveyor in Ky., *ca.* 1785–1786; GM condemned the practice of certified surveyors who made entries in their own name, and may have had Wilson in mind, since the two became involved in a bitter legal struggle over a large tract of Ky. acreage; the lawsuit which resulted was not settled until 1804, in Wilson *v.* Mason (1 Cranch 45).

WILSON, WILLIAM: Alexandria merchant who dealt in tobacco, wheat, and British imports, 1775; after war favored increased power of Congress over commerce, and signed petition for branch bank in Alexandria, 1792.

WOOD, JAMES (d. *ca.* 1777): Orange County surveyor, 1738; Frederick County clerk, 1743–1760; asst. to Va. commissary gen., John Carlyle, 1754–1755; founded Winchester, Va., 1758; Frederick Parish vestry, 1764–1774; vestry clerk, 1764; churchwarden, 1765; Frederick burgess, 1766–1776; signed Va. nonimportation agreement, 1769; Frederick justice of the peace, 1770; Va. convention, 1776; father of Gov. James Wood.

WOOD, JAMES (1750–1813): born in Frederick County; son of Col. James Wood; Frederick Parish vestry, clerk; capt., Dunmore's War, 1774; Frederick burgess, 1775; Va. convention, May 1776; commissioner with Thomas and John Walker, Andrew Lewis, Adam Stephen, to treat with Ohio Indians at Pittsburgh, 1775; col., 8th Va. Regt., engaged in frontier defense, 1776; served at Brandywine;

superintendent of all war prisoners in Va., 1781; pres., board of arrangements to reduce Va. infantry, artillery, 1782–1783; Va. brigadier gen., 1783–1784; Va. Society of the Cincinnati, vice-pres., 1789, pres., 1802–1813; Va. executive council, 1784–1813; Va. lieut. gov., 1784; Va. gov., 1796–1799; presidential elector, 1789; Va. abolitionist society, vice-pres., 1797, pres., 1801; married Jean, daughter of Rev. John Moncure; died at Olney, near Richmond; Wood County (W. Va.) named for him. See Hayden, *Virginia Genealogies,* 428–437.

WOOD, JEAN (1753–1823): daughter of Rev. John Moncure and Frances Brown; related to GM through the Fowke family; born at Clermont; inherited half of her father's Fairfax County lands; married James Wood (see above); musician and poetess; founder, "Female Humane Association of Richmond," for indigent widows, orphans; 1811; Jean Wood Society to benefit indigent theological students founded in her honor.

WOODFORD, WILLIAM (1734–1780): of Caroline County; officer, French and Indian War; Caroline justice of the peace; Caroline committee of correspondence, 1774; committee to enforce the nonimportation assn., 1774; intimate friend of Edmund Pendleton; 3d Va. Regt., 1775; defeated Lord Dunmore at Great Bridge, and forced him to abandon Norfolk, Dec. 1775; col., 2d Va. Regt., 1776; brigadier gen. with Continental army, Feb. 1777; N.J. and Philadelphia-area campaigns, 1778–1779; sent to aid Charleston, Dec. 1779; captured when Charleston fell; died a prisoner in N.Y.

WREN, JAMES: of Fairfax County; married Catherine, daughter of Charles Brent and Hannah Innes, 1753; related to Truro Parish vestryman Thomas Wren; built present Falls Church; with William Waite, was paid for plans for Truro Parish glebe buildings, 1769; supported ratification of Constitution, 1787; collector and receiver of parish tobacco and money, 1788; Fairfax County poor rate collector, 1793, 1795; original trustee of Turberville, Va., 1798.

*WYTHE, GEORGE (1726–1806): lawyer; Williamsburg burgess, 1754–1755, 1758–1768; clerk, House of Burgesses, 1769–1775; Va. del. to Continental Congress, 1775–1776; signer of Declaration of Independence; committee for revisal of laws, 1777; Speaker, House of Delegates, 1777; Va. Court of Chancery, 1778–1806; del. to Federal Convention, 1787; offered resolution for adoption at Va. ratifying convention, 1788.

YELLOW BANK: shown about 20 miles north of mouth of Ohio River in Thomas Hutchins's 1778 map; placed on left bank, 200 miles from mouth, 45 miles east of Henderson, Ky., on Zadok Cramer's *Navigator* (1814 ed.).

YOHOGANIA COUNTY: created by the General Assembly in 1776, the county extended Va.'s jurisdiction over an extensive area between the Ohio and Monongahela then in dispute between Va. and Pa.; the county was dissolved upon settlement of the boundary controversy in 1786, when most of the area was ceded to Pa.

YOUGHIOGHENY RIVER (also YOUGHYAGENI, YAWYAWGANEY): enters the Monongahela from the south at McKeesport, Allegheny County, Pa.

YOUNG, NOTLEY: of Prince Georges County, Md.; his oldest daughter Mary married Robert Brent, 1st mayor of Washington, D.C., and nephew of Sarah Brent Mason; owned land in new federal capital.

YOUNGHUSBAND, PLEASANT (d. 1808): operated a Richmond boarding house, *ca.* 1788; possibly the widow of Isaac Younghusband, who had served on the Henrico County committee of safety, 1774.

ZANE, ISAAC (d. 1795): called "Jr."; born in Pa.; merchant, distiller, miller in Frederick, Shenandoah counties; burgess, 1773–1775; Va. conventions, Mar. and July 1775, May 1776; House of Delegates, 1776–1795; militia col. See Hutchinson-Rachal, I, 185n; II, 127n.

GEORGE MASON OF GUNSTON HALL
AN INTRODUCTION

George Mason was that rare type of public man who disdains personal power. Other players on the stage of Virginia and national politics between 1765 and 1788 easily upstaged this crotchety plantation owner from Fairfax County. Even so, Mason's intellect contributed a distinctive quality to the leadership of the Revolutionary generation. In George Mason's character a strong but abstract sense of justice was fused with a practical concern for everyday life. Some of Mason's contemporaries believed he was brilliant—"of the first order of greatness" as Jefferson said—while others thought Mason's political ideas were too advanced. Still a third group considered him priggish and intractable. In some measure, there was truth in all these judgments.

Mason was a Virginian. Unquestionably, his Northern Neck origin was a controlling fact in his life. Mason's father and grandfather had been frontiersmen as well as gentlemen-planters. Father, son, and grandson had been born, raised, and had died in a thirty-square-mile microcosm. Washington was an American, and then a Virginian. Jefferson was a man of the world, an American, and a Virginian. Madison was a scholar, an American, and only incidentally a Virginian. In the company of these demigods, Mason was never ashamed to confess his primary allegiance to the colony and later the commonwealth of Virginia. But he also lacked Washington's vanity, Jefferson's dilettantism, and Madison's timidity on the slavery issue. At the right moment, this quartet of Virginians sensed a high obligation to all Americans, and this characteristic redeems their imperfections.

Historians rely on records, and until 1892 the Mason ledger was scarcely discernible. Then Kate Mason Rowland's two-volume *Life of George Mason, 1725–1792* was published, and for the past eight decades it has been the major source of Mason materials. However, vestiges of southern mythology along with some Victorian-styled censorship in Miss Rowland's incomplete work combined to obfuscate Mason's contributions to Revolutionary statecraft. Barring the appearance of some long hidden copybook or sheaf of letters, the present work represents the total picture of Mason's involvement in the many endeavors which claimed his attention between 1750 and his death.

The plain facts about Mason's life do not make breathless reading.

Rather, from his youth onward there is a stolid quality about his life that sets him apart from the military adventurers, world travelers, and frontier swashbucklers who were among his friends and neighbors. Many questions can be asked about Mason's early life for which our answers can only be intuitive, because the evidence is buried forever. How helpful it would be to know more about the impact on the nine-year-old Mason of his father's drowning in the nearby Potomac. We can only speculate upon the tutelage Mason received during his formative years or the guidance afforded by a scholarly uncle as Mason neared his maturity, with its burden of responsibilities. His attitude toward women, learned from a widowed mother, seems to have been typical of the era—marked by a tender sentimentality that never bothered him in business or political dealings.

Reaching manhood was no sudden and sobering experience for the young Mason, for he moved readily into the workaday world of midcentury Virginia. It is unlikely that Mason missed the camaraderie of college life at William and Mary, for with Washingtons, Lees, and Mercers for companions he acquired lasting friendships at an early age. The availability of John Mercer's well-stocked library had an impact on the young Virginian, who learned Latin as he discerned the value of sandy loams and timbered backlands. Mason came to respect intellectual values more highly than material ones, a man's intelligence more highly than the quality of his tobacco leaf—though both were important.

Much idle speculation could arise over the sources of Mason's ideas, but such exercises often proceed on thin historical evidence. Besides his mother's guidance Mason studied under a private tutor, a circumstance that hardly pleased his choleric uncle though it was the prevalent system of plantation education. When Mason was forty-two John Mercer recalled that most tutors he had known were "without either religion or morals, & I attribute it to George Mason's tutor that I have long doubted with a good deal of concern, that he had very little improved in either." [1] Mercer's skepticism might have been based on nothing more than a borrowed book which Mason forgot to return, for both men looked upon books as their most valued possessions.

Little is known of Mason's personal library, but his interest in self-education was manifested in 1747 when he purchased a twenty-volume set of *An Universal History, from the Earliest Account of*

1. John Mercer to George Mercer, 22 Dec. 1767–28 Jan. 1768, Mulkearn, 211–212.

Time (Dublin, 1745), a compendium work mainly devoted to the glories of ancient Greece and Rome. Two volumes of Cicero's essays on morality and a magnificent Bible were certainly on the shelves at Gunston Hall. Mason's letters and public papers clearly reveal that he was familiar with the books which most educated men knew, from Lucretius to Locke. His library was not large, but the books were carefully selected and often read. The gracious plantation home-headquarters in which Mason housed his books, sheltered his family, and entertained his friends bore the stamp of quality. With his neighbor, Washington, he exchanged ideas, cherry tree graftings, and warm hospitality. Rather than attempting to do many things, Mason eschewed the dilettante's role and concentrated on relatively few endeavors with a patient thoroughness.

Indeed, Mason was more patient with carpenters and bricklayers than with his peers in politics. Irritable by inclination and health, he was not marked for a political career, so that only the obligations imposed by wealth and intellect (not to mention family tradition) forced him into such demanding duties as a justice of the peace or a burgess undertook. In business dealings, family affairs, and political matters it was Mason's habit to be forthright, even blunt. This characteristic allowed those around him to always know where he stood on a given issue—hardly the best qualification for a diplomat. In his straightforward approach Mason sometimes lost friends, but he was never challenged for his honesty.

Possibly a touch of humor would have helped Mason bear life's burdens with more ease; however, the eighteenth century was more noted for its satires than its comedies. We do not know whether Mason ever attended a theater, played a musical instrument, or gambled at cards or horses. We know he liked madeira and other good wines, though his taste for them probably did little to relieve the tortures of gout which plagued him throughout his adult life. Some of the impatience and irritability may be understandable in the light of Mason's medical history, which qualified him as a valetudinarian of the first rank. His personal health and the well-being of a large family constituted a major concern of Mason's life; and the constant allusions to health and the self-diagnosis in which he indulged became a dominant theme in his relations with others. On the other hand, Mason found ill health a handy plea for nonattendance at meetings or for avoidance of public business. The caution of one friend to another, to consult Colonel Mason "if he is well," tells us that by fellow Virginians Mason was regarded as a brilliant man, but also a sick one.

Beyond Mason's parochial interests the two major areas of his involvement were the Ohio Company and service in Revolutionary politics from 1765 onward. His life tenure as treasurer of the Ohio Company brought him duties that Mason fulfilled, not without complaint, but with a sense of hope. The first part of Volume I deals with this complex story. What was to have been a profitable land speculation dragged on and on, until it finally became a burden that Mason patiently bore. The facts necessary to an understanding of the Ohio Company documents are provided in a lengthy headnote, so let it only be mentioned here that Mason's determination alone seems to have held the company together after the first crush of disappointment following the French and Indian War.

Politics beckoned Mason while he was still learning to manage a plantation. He lost his first attempt to win a House of Burgesses seat from Fairfax County in 1748, but within two years he had been elected a vestryman of Truro Parish, admitted to the Ohio Company partnership, and married to dainty Ann Eilbeck. The pace of his life quickened during the next decade, for Mason was chosen as a justice of the peace (a demanding and important office) and, in 1758, a burgess. Bumper tobacco crops, lean years, Ohio Company business, private land dealings, and a multitude of vestry and county demands kept Mason occupied. He kept his own account and copy books, but these have never been found. Still, enough of his correspondence has survived to prove that Mason rarely delegated responsibility. Beyond a trip to Alexandria (where he was a town trustee) or the several journeys to Williamsburg, Mason developed no taste for travel. Between 1753 and 1772 Ann Eilbeck Mason gave birth to twelve children, nine of whom survived, and this large family was supplemented by dozens of slaves, all of whom were dependent upon the master of Gunston Hall for their welfare. Though Mason took the title of "Colonel" which his father and grandfather had carried—apparently by a militia commission long since lost—military duties were out of his line. The demands of plantation and family were conveniently invoked when Mason was pressed to consider further public service. Until 1765, he had no reason to suspect he would ever have to participate in the colony's affairs again. The mere notion of dull men arguing fine points of law or passing bills to keep livestock off the Williamsburg streets (while the candles grew shorter all the while) was repulsive to him.

Beginning in 1763, rude shocks upset the sedate worlds of George III and George Mason. The Proclamation of 1763 frustrated the Ohio Company's plans of western settlement. The Stamp Act signaled a new direction in British-American relations. The impact of events at Whitehall in London now affected the lives of men along the Potomac. Consider Mason's dilemma.

Tradition, religion, and royal favors had long nurtured the roots of loyalty in colonial Virginia. Mason drew allegiance to the Crown with his first breath, when George I sat on the throne. During his formative years, George II was his sovereign. The coronation of George III came after Mason's judgment, habits, and outlook on life had matured. In those slow-moving days, it seemed that the young monarch had barely settled in his seat of power when irritating incidents began to occur with disturbing regularity. Nothing like this had upset the Virginians under George II. Ultimately, it was easier to forsake an allegiance to this misguided grandson of a great and good man. Oaths meant more to eighteenth-century Americans by far than any affirmations we make now. To Mason, the many signs of fealty to George II were genuine; but after 1765 it obviously was harder for Americans to look upon George III as a wise, benevolent, and compassionate king. Though Mason wrote in 1766 that he was "unalienably affected to his Majesty's sacred Person & Government," in that same letter he warned, "Such another Experiment as the Stamp Act wou'd produce a general Revolt in America."

Thus it took little urging from Washington and other Northern Neck neighbors who sought Mason's help in shaping a resistance movement. A decade passed before arguments changed to musket balls, but at each halting step Mason counseled patience mixed with firmness. Mason's reluctance to fill a number of public offices might be blamed on his family concerns or his illness, but not upon an indifference to public affairs. In his own mind Mason drew a sharp line between personal involvement and his public duty. For a time in 1773, his wife's death caused him to withdraw from worldly affairs. Slowly the melancholy wore off.

On matters concerning human rights Mason was ever ready to do battle, but when the focus shifted to petty local matters he was easily bored and inclined to curtness. At such times his acute gout was paraded as a curse, but perhaps it was easier to bear the gout than the harangues of small-minded men—the "Bablers" as he called them—whose vision was limited to crossroads politics.

Though Mason's vision on one scale was parochial, on the slavery issue he took an early, outspoken stand. During the Stamp Act crisis he denounced human bondage as a corrupting influence "upon the Morals & Manners of our People." His state papers from that time onward show Mason's chronic uneasiness about slavery. It was an intellectual discomfort Mason tried to share with other southerners, but with little success. Entrapped by the system and his moderate nature, Mason sensed what should be done about slavery but would not tread beyond denunciations and clairvoyant pronouncements.

When the critical moment arrived at the Virginia convention in 1776, Mason's role was determined by his willingness to act decisively and his articulate expression of Revolutionary aspirations in such documents as the Fairfax Resolves. Along with the Declaration of Independence, Mason's draft of the Virginia Declaration of Rights stands as a major achievement of the Revolution. Both of these state papers gave expression to the emerging American consensus that independence and personal freedom ought to be permanently established. This was proved by the rapid infiltration of the Masonian concepts into other state constitutions between 1776 and 1780. The document and its various texts are printed in a separate section of this volume.

Both Mason and Jefferson shaped proposals for a Virginia constitution, and though the final draft bore more of Mason's imprint than Jefferson's, the two men complimented each other in their comprehension of Revolutionary problems and their solution. Mason lacked Jefferson's majestic concept of mankind's potential, but he had more real experience with the faults which the Revolution might correct. On occasion Mason transcended the workaday world when he pondered the fate of "generations unborn" or the pathetic field hands who trudged tired bodies toward their shacks in the twilight. Though Mason deemed as a basic right "the means of . . . pursuing and obtaining happiness and safety," yet lofty, high-minded prose was not his forte. In contrast to Jefferson's ennobling words, there is a flinty quality about Mason's state papers.

Convinced that corruption had seized the minds of Britain's leaders, Mason and the other American Whigs (patriots) believed destiny had called them to carry aloft the rights of man. When reports from England intimated that a Revolution was "the Work of a Faction, of a Junto of ambitious Men against the Sense of the People of America," Mason was incensed. "On the Contrary," he insisted, "nothing has been done without the Approbation of the People, who have indeed out run their Leaders. . . ." To combat the conspiracy theory of the Revolution, Mason by 1778 viewed the question as specious. "It is a Matter of Moonshine to us, whether Independence was at first intended, or not, and therefore we may now be believed." [2] In short, Americans were involved in the most

2. GM to [Mr. ——— Brent?], 2 Oct. 1778, below.

justifiable of all battles, a fight for self-preservation, with an antago-
nist as venal as was Rome in its last stages of decay. Mason and his
co-adjutors were confident that the Revolution would succeed, for
in their readings of history a dissolute tyranny could not long
survive in a battle with virtuous, embattled freemen.

With unaccustomed energy, then, Mason served on the Council
of Safety, worried about enemy forays upon the Potomac shores,
wrote enabling legislation for the infant commonwealth, and still
found alibis to keep him away from the Continental Congress. The
scope of Mason's wartime interests ranged from sending a son into
the army to making plans for keeping troops in the field. No
account books survive to tell how much grain Mason turned over to
army commissaries, but in the Committee of Safety account book
for 1775–1776 there are entries showing that Mason bought supplies
worth £857.17s.7d for the Fairfax County militia.[3] In short, Mason
combined some duties of an ordnance officer and quartermaster
during the crucial first years of the war.

Still, Mason's reluctance to serve in the larger arena of national
affairs disconcerted his friends. It was a troubled Washington who
in 1779 wrote Mason a long letter of lament over the low caliber of
congressmen then in the state delegations. "Where are our Men of
abilities?" he asked. "Why do they not come forth to save their
Country? Let this voice my dear Sir call upon you—Jefferson &
others—do not from a mistaken opinion that we are about to set
down under our own Vine and our own fig tree let our hitherto
noble struggle end in ignom[in]y." [4] To another Virginian, Washington wrote that each state should "not only choose, but absolutely
compel their ablest Men to attend Congress." [5] Whatever Mason
thought of such entreaties, he found the annual trip to Richmond
sufficiently taxing on his health. Moreover, the Northern Neck
plantations seemed to be open to attack by British marauders, and on
more than one occasion Mason packed his silverware and furniture
and prepared to flee inland when rumors of an invasion seemed
creditable. Even closer to Mason's heart than the Commonwealth of
Virginia was the safety of Gunston Hall and its inhabitants.

Unquestionably, Mason avoided duties that demanded his physical
presence, though his intellectual resources were always on call.

3. Entry for 1 Dec. 1775, Account Book, Virginia Committee of Safety,
1775–1776 (Vi).
4. Washington to GM, 27 Mar. 1779, below.
5. Washington to Benjamin Harrison, 18[–30] Dec. 1778, John C. Fitzpatrick, ed., *The Writings of George Washington from the Original Manuscript Sources, 1745-1799* (Washington, 1931–1944), XIII, 462–468.

When the war began Mason was fifty—an advanced age as he calculated it—and his infirm body lacked the adamantine quality of his political convictions. Few patriots outdid Mason in his optimistic view that America would triumph, maintained such determined consistency of purpose, or were so disinterested in personal gain. Mason's sense of personal honor, combined with his broader reflection upon the goals of the Revolution, permitted him to survey the actions of others dispassionately. While many of his planter friends would have escaped responsibility for prewar debts to British merchants through a flimsy legislative dodge, Mason denounced and helped defeat an effort to use the war as an excuse for dishonesty. While still in mourning for his wife in 1773, Mason expressed his philosophy about public service in a will which was expected to carry a message from the grave for his sons. They should, he cautioned, "prefer the happiness of independance and a private station to the troubles and vexation of publick business." However, if they became public servants neither "motives of private interest or ambition . . . nor the terrors of poverty and disgrace, or the fear of danger or of death" should deter them from passing on the heritage of "those sacred rights to which they themselves were born."

Concern for future generations was a common denominator with the Revolutionary leaders. Steeped in classical history and moral essays, they were convinced that through the exercise of his natural rights man could be rational and just. Jefferson, Mason, and like-minded patriots were committed to a blending of statecraft with justice—a secularized justice that would guarantee to the citizen his rights to revolutionary ideals: life, liberty, and the pursuit of happiness.[6] Jefferson strove for justice at all levels (social, economic, educational) and in every facet of government. Mason's ideas were hardly so encompassing, which may mean that he was of a more practical turn of mind. As Mason's concept of the purpose of government evolved, he focused upon political justice. If every man had a vote he would communicate and participate with other citizens in frequent elections, insuring the survival of the first principles of government. What were those fundamental principles? Mason spelled them out in Article XIII of the Virginia Declaration of Rights, and their order is important—justice, moderation, temperance, frugality, and virtue.

With customary impatience Mason tried to retreat from active

6. As distinguished from god-ordained justice, or the justice derived from Jehovah in the Old Testament. See Georges Gurvitch, "Justice," *Encyclopedia of Social Sciences*, VIII, 509–514.

politics after the Revolution, but the goal of retirement proved elusive. His interest in the waning fortunes of the Ohio Company, the pressure for cession of Virginia's western lands, and the current economic stresses all demanded Mason's attention. Members of the Congress and the Virginia legislature sought his opinions, and British merchants found that Mason was their ally on the vexing question of debt recovery. Court clerks in Fairfax and surrounding counties became familiar with his name as he sued for the recovery of debts, both privately and as the Ohio Company treasurer. Mason shed the widower's role in 1780 but was careful to protect his heirs with a marriage settlement, then watched his children marry and leave for their own plantations.

The events between 1781 and 1786 proved there was no weather-cock quality in Mason's political convictions. As is often the case, some disillusionment must follow a revolution when war's momentum is lost in postwar realities. The 1783 treaty ending the war brought a favorable boundary settlement and established the paramount issue of independence beyond all question. Americans soon learned, however, that rather than solving their problems, national sovereignty only magnified them. State finances, state boundaries, state currencies, state customs—all provoked endless discussion among the former thirteen dependencies. Entreated to return to the House of Delegates and seek solutions for scores of vexing problems, Mason withdrew with predictable petulance. When Fairfax County voters planned a canvass on his behalf in the spring of 1784, Mason's reaction was unequivocal. "I have repeatedly declared that I can not serve the County, at this time, as one of it's Representatives," he wrote. "I shou'd look upon such Attempt, in no other Light than an oppressive & unjust invasion of my personal Liberty; and was I to be elected . . . I shou'd certainly refuse to act, be the Consequences what they will." [7] Mason's friends took the hint.

However, Mason's isolation from legislative business was far from complete. An assessment bill providing for state support for "Teachers of the Christian Religion," favored by Henry and opposed by Madison, brought Mason out of his shell. Madison wrote an attack upon the bill which Mason regarded as unanswerable. He paid for a broadside edition of the protest, then sent the handbill to friends and pleaded for its circulation as a petition. Public opinion was thus mobilized, the bill was defeated, and in 1786 the backlash brought passage of Jefferson's bill "Establishing Religious Free-

7. GM to Martin Cockburn, 18 Apr. 1784, below.

dom." Besides this involvement, Mason's previous service on a committee appointed to settle disputes between Virginians and Marylanders fishing or sailing on the Potomac was recalled when a new body was created. Edmund Randolph, Madison, Alexander Henderson, and Mason were appointed commissioners charged with framing "such liberal and equitable regulations . . . as may be mutually advantageous to the two States." Mason accepted this job, and in circuitous fashion the conference wound its way to an enlarged view of interstate problems, far beyond seines or shoals. This discussion of specie, paper money, and commercial regulations expanded until it blossomed into the Annapolis Convention of 1786—the seedling of the federal gathering of 1787.

Mason never attended the Annapolis Convention, although he was chosen as a Virginia delegate. Nor did he serve in the House of Delegates in 1786, despite Washington's influence that persuaded him to allow a successful canvass that spring. Gout sent Mason to his bed, so he excused himself from both chores. By this time the debility of the Continental Congress was notorious, and Madison was in that group which believed only federal regulatory and taxing powers could save the Republic. By late 1786 the strong nationalists had finally accomplished what had been on their minds for several years. Late in 1783 Madison had sounded Mason out on the idea of revising the patchwork Articles that held the Union together. While the controversy over a national treasury financed by customs raged, Madison learned that Mason was lukewarm in his opposition to a federal impost. When Madison broached the concept of a federal conference "for *revising our form of government he was sound and ripe. . . . His heterodoxy lay chiefly in being too little impressed with* either the *necessity* or the *proper means of preserving the* confederacy." [8] Madison slipped the conversation held at Gunston Hall into a convenient pocket of his memory and waited.

The passage of three years only confirmed the nationalists' fears. After visiting Mason, Madison reported to Jefferson a fear "concerning his federal ideas." Mason conceded that Congress might regulate commerce. "But he has been led so far out of the right way, that a thorough return can scarcely be hoped for." [9] What exactly did Madison mean by "a thorough return"? Perhaps Madison meant a return to the days of '76, when every patriot's first concern was independence and local interests were of less importance. If so, this

8. Madison to Jefferson, 10 Dec. 1783, Boyd, V, 377.
9. Madison to Jefferson, 12 May 1786, *ibid.*, IX, 518–519.

was wishful thinking on Madison's part, for by 1786 Mason took a suspicious view of a national government. Nothing seemed certain, however. Thus, when the abortive Annapolis Convention issued a call for a national conference and Virginia again chose Mason as a delegate, he accepted the appointment. "Col. Mason will pretty certainly attend," Madison noted in April. Moreover, Madison added, Mason had renounced "his errors on the subject of the confederation, and means to take an active part in the amendment of it." [10]

The decision to travel 140 miles to visit Philadelphia—to take the longest trip of his lifetime—indicates the importance Mason attached to the coming Federal Convention. Shays's Rebellion during the past winter had excited many Americans beyond all proportion. "We are fast verging to anarchy and confusion!" was Washington's reaction.[11] Since Washington's return to Mount Vernon the two neighbors had resumed their old cordiality. Strong hints must have been directed at Mason from his fellow delegate that unless they rewrote the Articles of Confederation, the Republic was doomed. Moreover, Mason well knew the baneful effects of depreciating currency, Spanish threats to the Mississippi, and interstate quibbling. So he packed a trunk and headed for the Indian Queen Tavern, with enough hope to lighten the inconvenience of hard saddles and the risk of dangerous ferry crossings. Safe in Philadelphia, Mason reported to his family on his forthcoming mission: "The expectations and hopes of all the Union centre in this Convention." By this time the delegates headed for Philadelphia knew what was afoot even though the general public did not. The Continental Congress had taken the bait from Annapolis and called the meeting to recommend amendments for the Articles of Confederation. From the outset the delegates accepted the crystallized opinions of the "energetic government" clique (Hamilton, Madison, Gouverneur Morris, Rufus King, and others) that favored abandoning the Articles and starting afresh. Mason accepted this approach, but he also believed that the contemplated federal plan would not reserve "to the State Legislatures a sufficient Portion of Power for promoting & securing the Prosperity and Happiness of their respective citizens." [12] It was this concern which caused Mason to break with his old friends and refuse to sign the Constitution four months later.

10. Madison to Jefferson, 23 Apr. 1787, *ibid.*, XI, 309–310.
11. Washington to Madison, 5 Nov. 1786, Fitzpatrick, ed., *Writings of Washington*, XXIX, 51–52.
12. GM to George Mason, Jr., 20 May 1787, below.

Much of Volume III tells the story of Mason's participation in the tense struggle to write and ratify the Constitution, from the first personal letters through his final Richmond speech. Mason's principles forced him to join Randolph and Gerry as they stood aside while their colleagues signed the engrossed copy. In the haze of history, Mason's contributions to the Constitution became misty, while his Antifederalist stand seemed to tarnish the sterling character of his Revolutionary patriotism. The Federalist school of nineteenth-century historians tended to overlook Mason, while the southern apologists overemphasized his weakest points and forgot his noblest efforts. For slaveholder Mason to declare (on 22 August 1787) that "every master of slaves is born a petty tyrant" took courage. For Mason to continue with a warning that slavery, unless it was strangled by restrictions, would bring "the judgment of heaven on a Country" was indeed prophetic. Even in twentieth-century America, there is a pitiable ring to Mason's prediction in the same antislavery speech: "As nations can not be rewarded or punished in the next world they must be in this. By an inevitable chain of causes & effects providence punishes national sins, by national calamities." [13] Thus Mason could rise above personal interests to make a plea for the rights of man. Since 1765 he had been excoriating slavery for its pernicious, degrading effects upon America. The speech, as Madison's notes reveal, made no converts.

The record also shows that Mason fought for taxes on luxuries, insisted that every voter should cast a ballot in electing congressmen, and when few others agreed, at first supported popular election of the president. As the thermometer in Philadelphia rose, old friends became remarkably frank. Madison, arguing that the re-election of congressmen should not be prohibited, asked Mason "to vouch another fact not less notorious in Virginia, that the backwardness of the best citizens to engage in the legislative service gave but too great success to unfit characters." [14] So there was sniping and perhaps some snarling, but the main business proceeded. On the minor compromises Mason gave ground as he declared their work was so important "he would bury his bones" in Philadelphia "rather than expose his Country to the Consequences of a dissolution of the Convention without any thing being done." [15]

The pressure to accomplish something durable, to preserve the gains of the Revolution, was tremendous. It made some delegates

13. Madison, 503.
14. *Ibid.*, 178.
15. *Ibid.*, 244.

think and act, on occasion, in ways that can only be explained by the tension. One of Madison's speeches was downright foolish. Luther Martin made a boorish spectacle of himself. Mason and Randolph promoted the idea of a three-man presidency, with each section choosing an executive who would have a veto power. There were many interests and many prejudices that had to be accommodated.

No delegate outdid Mason in his insistence upon the provision that all appropriation bills originate in the House, or that state legislatures be allowed to tax exports. Mason conceived the first idea as a safeguard against a scheming Senate, the latter as an effort to prevent manufacturing states from shifting tax burdens to agricultural areas. He served on the committee that recommended the large national and state debts might be assumed by the emerging federal government—a measure Mason could approve because it seemed to deal with the inherent honesty of a government to keep its promises. (Unlike some other delegates, Mason did not use this secret knowledge to buy depreciated securities at bargain prices.) Mason's interests ranged from defining treason to keeping the military under civilian control, but as the Constitution took its final form he saw a dangerous tendency to favor northern interests over those of the South. This was an obstacle that Mason could not overcome, for he suspected that on vital matters the northern states would control Congress. "The Southern States had therefore good ground for their suspicions." [16]

The sine qua non for Mason became his proposal that a two-thirds majority of Congress must approve an act regulating commerce between the United States and foreign powers. The point may seem abstract in the twentieth century, but to many Americans in 1787 it represented a check on the hated "navigation laws" of colonial days, when all products had to be carried back and forth across the Atlantic in British ships. As Mason and many other southerners believed, without this safeguard the northern shipping interests would gain subsidies for their freighting—subsidies that would be paid mainly by the South. When the convention voted to strike this provision on August 29, Mason's course of opposition was fixed, and nothing in the intervening two weeks shook his determination to work for amendments prior to ratification. Even Mason's belated attempt to add a bill of rights to the Constitution was a half-hearted effort, compared to his feelings about northern domination. Those who asked Mason to sign the Constitution, after he had vowed on

16. *Ibid.*, 501.

August 31 "that he would sooner chop off his right hand than put it to the Constitution as it now stands," did not know him well.

"Col. Mason left Philada. in an exceeding ill humour indeed," Madison observed. "A number of little circumstances arising in part from the impatience which prevailed towards the close of the business, conspired to whet his acrimony." [17] Mason's patience had worn terribly thin by mid-September. His pamphlet—*Objections to the Constitution*—recited Mason's list of imperfections in the final draft and gave the Antifederalists a rallying slogan: "There is no bill of rights." Meager as it was, the hue and cry against the Convention because there was no bill of rights proved to be the Antifederalists' strongest argument. Mason's other indictments, including the unfettered regulation of commerce, usually fell on barren ground. The whole business became more disagreeable for Mason, and a carriage accident on the return trip to Gunston Hall did nothing to relieve his irritation over the final days of defeat at Independence Hall.

Back in Fairfax County, Mason dismissed rumors that a public meeting in Alexandria had condemned his convention conduct. He wrote Washington a conciliatory note, assuring the general that his opposition to the Constitution was based solely upon principle, but a notable coolness drifted between the ridges separating Gunston Hall from Mount Vernon. Washington concluded that Richard Henry Lee and Mason were in league to defeat the Constitution, and his correspondents promoted this notion. To a neighbor, Washington wrote that Mason's pride and "want of manly candor" would keep him from admitting "an error in his opinions . . . though conviction should flash on his mind as strongly as a ray of light." [18] Certainly Mason served as an Antifederalist in the Richmond convention called to consider the Constitution and with Patrick Henry directed the opposition so skillfully that they lost by only a handful of votes in June 1788. Dispirited and defeated, Mason angrily lashed out with a list of recommended amendments and returned home, unconvinced that his efforts had been worthwhile. Mason's reaction to Washington's snub—the general later classified him as his "quondam friend"—is not recorded.

Although the Constitution was ratified by Virginia and soon became the supreme law of the land, the Antifederalists remained a powerful element in commonwealth politics. In 1790, Patrick Henry saw to it that his old friend was chosen a United States senator, but

17. Madison to Jefferson, 24 Oct. 1787, Boyd, XII, 280.
18. Washington to Dr. James Craik, 8 Sept. 1789, Fitzpatrick, ed., *Writings of Washington*, XXX, 396.

Mason had not sought the honor and refused the appointment. Even though it meant a chance to serve with Richard Henry Lee in the new body, Mason refused the Senate seat without a moment's hesitation. He turned instead to domestic affairs and showed more concern about the location of a county courthouse than he had over a national capital. To a homesick son (his much beloved favorite, John) in faraway France, Mason dispatched a Virginia mockingbird and plenty of fatherly advice. Mason continued his worry over bodily ills, his own and his family's, and as an amateur apothecary he advised a large brood to always keep plenty of calomel on hand. In semi-retirement Mason reread the classics, pored over history and law books, supervised tobacco sales, cared for slaves, and insisted on a simple elegance that modern visitors to the restored Gunston Hall still sense.

Time erased most of the bitterness engendered by the ratification battles. Madison's determination to see a bill of rights enacted drew Mason's approval. Several additional amendments, including one limiting the jurisdiction of federal courts to admiralty cases, would have pleased him vastly. Then, he wrote, "I cou'd chearfully put my Hand & Heart to the new Government." Mason worried about old friendships and was pleased to hear assurances that Madison regarded him with "undiminished . . . complete esteem." A gossiping relative of Washington's turned tatler in 1789 to repeat a slur allegedly made by Mason about the general's efforts to pay old debts in depreciated paper money. A formal note to Washington evoked a stiff, formal answer, but Jefferson went out of his way to be kind to the elder statesman. In the fall of 1792, the secretary of state visited Gunston Hall and found its master "just recovering from a dreadful attack of the cholic," but still "perfectly communicative." [19] Mason kept abreast of the political scene through the newspapers, and was convinced that Hamilton had "done us more injury than Great Britain and all her fleets and armies." The failure to meet slavery issues head-on at Philadelphia in 1787 still troubled Mason, and the two old friends shared a conviction that the potentially explosive question of the black man's place in America could rock the Republic to its very foundation.

Mason was not much of a dreamer, however, and there was plenty still to be done. The Ohio Company business dragged on, there were law suits pending in Kentucky, new farm lands were needed as

19. Jefferson to Madison, 1 Oct. 1792, Paul Leicester Ford, ed., *The Writings of Thomas Jefferson* (New York, 1892–1905), VI, 114.

tobacco stalks relentlessly sucked fertility from the soil. Between-times, there were sick children to tend, and that oldest of Mason's enemies—the gout—would not surrender to any known treatment.

And then, on an autumn Sunday afternoon in 1792, all of George Mason's anxieties disappeared—forever.

VOLUME I

1725. Born at Mason family home on Dogue's Neck, then in Prince William County, now Fairfax County, Virginia.

1735. Father died in ferry accident.

1748. Unsuccessfully sought seat in House of Burgesses from Fairfax County.

1749. Elected vestryman of Truro Parish. Admitted to the Ohio Company partnership.

1750. April 4. Married Ann Eilbeck of Charles County, Maryland.

1751. Appointed treasurer of reorganized Ohio Company.

1754. Appointed Town of Alexandria trustee.

1758. Gunston Hall completed.

1758–1761. Served as Fairfax County delegate in House of Burgesses.

1765–1766. Participated in efforts to resist enforcement of Stamp Act. Wrote letter to London *Public Ledger* disclaiming American ambitions for independence.

1769. Active in shaping nonimportation agreements as resistance measure against Parliamentary taxation.

1773. Wrote historical treatise on "Extracts of Virginia Charters" to buttress land claims.

1773. March 9. Ann Eilbeck Mason died.

1774. Assisted patriots who planned passive resistance toward British measures. Wrote Fairfax Resolves.

1775. Wrote Fairfax County Committee Resolutions. Served on county Committee of Safety and as Fairfax County delegate to Virginia Convention. Refused to serve in Continental Congress.

1776. Served in Virginia Convention. Prepared drafts of Declaration of Rights and Constitution which were adopted after committee alterations.

1777–1778. Represented Fairfax County in Virginia House of Delegates.

THE PAPERS OF

GEORGE MASON

1749–1778

The Ohio Company of Virginia

[21 June 1749–16 October 1792]

EDITORIAL NOTE

George Mason's involvement with land began the moment he reached his majority and was to both please and plague him until he died. His love for the land was without reservation, but the total experience had a bittersweet quality about it. As often happens in great speculations, the profits on paper resist efforts to turn hard cash. Mason's land ventures were complicated by the additional element of political favoritism as men in high places spent much of their waking hours devising ways and means of acquiring staggering amounts of land for virtually no cash outlay. Then as now, such men tended to identify their own best interests with those of their country.

Land acquisition and management demanded a major share of Mason's time, but he tried to keep in balance the public good and his own desires. His involvement in the Ohio Company was a separate concern from his private land business, as were the speculations in the fifty-acre importation rights that were redeemable in land warrants, and his legislative activity to maintain the western land claims of the Commonwealth of Virginia. A brief account of the Ohio Company—its formation, structure, goals, successes, and failures—is presented in this volume although the story of Mason's direct concern continues to the time when his company shares became part of his estate in 1792.

The situation vis-à-vis land speculation and land grants in eighteenth-century America has been oversimplified to make it appear that huge tracts were doled out to royal favorites, colonial cliques, and scheming individuals. To be sure, the common denominator was greed; vast profit at little risk the goal. However, the drive for western lands also involved vision, sacrifice, and determination. Many of the largest speculators ultimately fell into a morass of debt, but there were others such as Mason who had the combined instincts of the statesman and the entrepreneur. They financed the explorations and surveys that made settlement of the West relatively safe and absolutely certain.

Mason caught the land fever early in life, and indeed few of his contemporaries were immune to the malady. Paper claims to thousands of acres were too tempting to forego. The anguish of litigation, double-dealing in the legislative halls, and frustration in establishing clear titles were experiences Mason shared with many citizens who looked westward for fortunes and a secure estate. That Mason was not ruined by his speculations is in part a tribute to his prudence for he sank hundreds of pounds into his schemes, but it was money he could afford to speculate with, because he ran his plantations and other business affairs along sound principles. Mason also appears to have been successful enough in local land speculation that he could indulge in remote

[3]

ventures involving great risk. On the lands that he inherited or bought and cultivated, Mason made money. On the lands that he dreamed of as the basis for a western estate, his gamble was essentially futile. The Ohio Company scheme was in the latter category.

As Shaw Livermore points out, the restless energy and land hunger of Virginians were directed toward the area between the coast and the piedmont of the colony until the 1740s.[1] French traders moving south from Canada into the Ohio Valley posed a direct threat to the expansionist plans of Virginians who heard stories of verdant acres beyond the mountains. Exploration confirmed reports of rich soil, abundant water, and waterways leading to the outer world. Thomas Lee, a member of the Governor's Council in Virginia and a delegate to the Indian conference at Lancaster in 1744, was impressed with these reports. Lee, who had served Lord Fairfax as a land agent and was behind no other Virginian in his desire to accumulate a vast personal estate, concocted a plan whereby both he and his friends might gain while the king's interest in blocking the French might also be served.

By 1747 Lee's scheme had taken shape as the Ohio Company of Virginia, a trading partnership with twenty shares, formed to obtain a land grant in the area ceded by the Iroquois on the south side of the Ohio River. The ultimate purpose of the plan was to make money—not a small sum, but fortunes for all the original partners or their heirs. An experienced frontiersman estimated that by 1763 the Indian trade "in Furs, Skins, & Peltry" would reach £150,000.[2] The plan was to establish a trading monopoly with the Indians who inhabited the area until such time as they could be persuaded to move on and allow the land to be sold in parcels large and small. The size was not important as long as the profits were assured.

Though land speculation in the eighteenth century has been compared to stock-market ventures in the twentieth, the analogy is in part faulty. The eighteenth-century speculators conceived that wealth and power were related by immutable forces to landholding. Thus the Virginia gentry who looked upon land speculation as a healthy outlet for surplus cash were only pursuing a well-traveled road. No Virginian was more aware of this potential profit than Thomas Lee. Lee used his position on the Council as a sounding board and probably persuaded Governor William Gooch to explore the crown's attitude toward a 500,000-acre grant south of the Ohio. Lee gathered into the partnership such Virginia worthies as George William Fairfax, Lawrence Washington, and Augustine Washington. He also made overtures to John Hanbury, a London merchant presumed to have considerable influence with British political figures. To make the plan more palatable in London, Lee encouraged the idea that the royal treasury would benefit if a private company built settlements and erected a buffer between the established English colonies and the encroaching French. "The public good and the Kings service I have cheifly in Veiw, to make a strong

1. Shaw Livermore, *Early American Land Companies; Their Influence on Corporate Development* (New York, 1939), 75-77.
2. Adam Stephen to R. H. Lee, 24 Feb. 1760, Lee Papers (microfilm, ViU).

settlement and carry on a fair and extensive trade by these means to gain the Indians to Brittish intrest," Lee repeatedly told correspondents.[3]

To serve "the Brittish intrest" as well as his own and that of his partners, Lee forwarded a request to the crown for 500,000 acres of land south of the Ohio River—200,000 to be granted immediately with 300,000 more pledged if the company built a fort and settled a hundred families in the territory within seven years. The Board of Trade recommended approval of the petition, declaring "it was their opinion it would be for his Majesty's Service to grant the Prayer of the Company, as such a Settlement would be a proper Stop towards checking the Incroachments of the French . . . by Means of which the British Settlements were much exposed" and the Indian trade jeopardized.[4]

To complicate the problem, traders from neighboring Pennsylvania were moving among the savages in the Ohio country that was disputed territory because of confusion over the charters of 1609 (Virginia) and 1681 (Pennsylvania). Nobody was certain which colony had a clear title to the area around the forks of the Ohio. "Your Traders have prevail'd with the Indians on the Ohio, to believe that the Fort is to be a bridle for them, & that the Roads which the Company are to make is to let in the Catawbas upon them to destroy them," Lee complained to the governor of Pennsylvania.[5] In a sense, the Ohio Company's fight to control the area became Virginia's fight, for although the 1609 grant was of the sea-to-sea variety, it needed reinforcement by that clearest of all frontier titles: possession. The larger quarrel with the French soon turned the dispute with Pennsylvania aside, but only temporarily. Meanwhile Virginians took the initiative in establishing their claims, and Washington's western journeys in 1753–1754 helped force the issue with the French.

In June 1749, a few months after Sir William Gooch was ordered to grant the company its first tract of 200,000 acres, George Mason became a partner in the enterprise. It was soon apparent that fairly large cash outlays would be required to launch the company's first phase of storehouse-building and Indian-trading, and several of the original partners excused themselves after the call for a hundred pounds from each member was sounded. When Nathaniel Chapman stepped down as treasurer three months later, Mason was elevated to the post in what proved to be a lifetime appointment. Thus Mason became a custodian of Ohio Company affairs years before the outbreak of fighting with the French. He found plenty of company business to divert him from plantation affairs. Plans were made to build storehouses, and goods costing two thousand pounds were ordered to stock the trading posts. Surveys were ordered, roads cleared, and at first it seemed likely that

3. Thomas Lee to Conrad Weiser, 27 Feb. 1749/1750, Lee Papers (microfilm, ViU).
4. Undated memorandum, Shelburne Papers, Clements Library, University of Michigan. See also Leonard Woods Labaree, ed., *Royal Instructions to British Colonial Governors 1670–1776* (New York, 1935), II, 645–647.
5. Thomas Lee to Governor Hamilton, 22 Nov. 1749, Lee Papers (microfilm, ViU).

the partners would profit enormously. There was some talk that the lands alone would bring them nearly twenty thousand pounds, less surveyor's fees and trifling sums for legal paperwork.

Even Thomas Lee's death in 1750, though it removed a powerful figure from the partnership, failed to dampen enthusiasm. Although several partners sold their shares, the company's prospects seemed bright enough to lure other investors into the scheme. In 1751 Mason's uncle, John Mercer of Marlborough, joined the partners and drafted formal articles of agreement. Mercer, a lawyer given to meticulous detail, provided that the new and the old partners would have three hundred pounds invested and be entitled to two shares each in the reorganized company.

One provision in the new agreement fell hard on Mason. Each partner was enjoined—but in practice the business fell mainly on Mason—to practice diligence "in all their Buyings Sellings Accounts Reckonings Disbursements & Dealings . . . & promote the said joint Trade & Stock without Fraud or Deceit & give their Attendance upon the said Companies Affairs as often as shall be necessary or they shall be required so to do in such Parts & places as the said Partners respectively live and reside." Since several of the partners lived in Great Britain, the nonresident partners obviously expected "all just Care & Diligence" in the management of company affairs. The fourteen Americans who signed the agreement were Virginians and Marylanders, most of them friends and neighbors. But from 1751 onward, it was Mercer and Mason who kept the Ohio Company in business. Christopher Gist went to the Logstown Conference in June 1752 on Mason's orders. The resulting Logstown Treaty seemed to confirm the 1744 pact and apparently cleared the company's Indian land title as far west as the Kanawha River.

By late 1752 the company outlook seemed bright indeed. However, as often happens in speculative enterprises, circumstances beyond one man's control may alter everything. In the Ohio Company's case, the continued frontier skirmishes between French traders and soldiers and their British-American counterparts were ominous. Nevertheless, the company opened a trading post on the Potomac, near the mouth of Wills Creek. Here the goods dispatched by Hanbury's firm—kettles, blankets, flints, knives, hardware, and trading trinkets—were stored or sold to traders and settlers. Another storehouse was built at Rock Creek (site of present-day Washington, D.C.) and a road cleared from the Wills Creek station through the wilderness to the headwaters of the Monongahela. Although larger plans were in view, Mason soon pursued a plodding course of litigation against many company customers who were poor credit risks. The early hopes for huge profits from the fur trade faded while squatter's rights were exerted by settlers who moved into the bottom lands of the Ohio tributaries, ignoring "the prior claims of the Ohio Company of Virginia." [6]

While Mason was occupied in the mundane role of bill-collector, the

6. Alfred P. James, *The Ohio Company, Its Inner History* (Pittsburgh, 1959), 113.

French swooped down into the Ohio country and for several years the company was in some ways a military appendage of the colony of Virginia. The road between Wills Creek and the Monongahela was used to move military stores to the west, a post built on Redstone Creek by Ohio Company employees became a fort, and a trading post established at the forks of the Ohio River (which in time became Fort Duquesne, still later Fort Pitt) was also considered a military outpost. In a vain effort to check the French advance, Gist and other company agents served as military advisors for the militia venture which ended with Washington's surrender at Fort Necessity in July 1754. Though Governor Robert Dinwiddie of Virginia was concerned about the far-reaching implications of the French invasion, the lands immediately involved were part of the Ohio Company's hoped-for tract and the governor himself was a stockholder. Indeed, opponents later charged that the war between 1754 and 1758 was fought to pull Ohio Company chestnuts out of the fire.

After British forces under Forbes occupied the French Fort Duquesne, various Virginia groups became restless and sought further western land grants. Seeds of dissension were sown aplenty as conflicting military and private land grants overlapped, surveys were run along ill-defined boundaries, and high politics in Williamsburg, Philadelphia, Annapolis, and London thwarted the issuance of clear titles. Even before the French ouster, the company partners complained, they had invested heavily in the project "with a view of making fortunes for their children, in a very hazardous undertaking," while their rivals were characterized as rapacious "landmongers." [7] Just exactly when a speculator became a landmonger is not clear, but at least in the minds of the company partners, their motives deserved encouragement by the governor and Council. Other Virginians with equally presentable political credentials were anxious to gain grants from the governor and Council for transmontane tracts. Few requests were modest. For example, Councilman John Lewis and his friends had been granted 800,000 acres. Then there were the conflicting claims of the Indiana, Mississippi, Transylvania, and Vandalia companies in the region south of the Ohio.

Complicating the picture was the overlapping 200,000-acre grant Governor Dinwiddie promised Virginians who served in the French and Indian campaigns as a military bounty, "on the east side of the river Ohio." Mason and his colleagues considered Dinwiddie's generosity as in fact a military necessity, but also hoped that if the terms of the original grant were thus altered they might claim a series of one thousand-acre tracts along the seventy-five-mile company road westward from Wills Creek. To keep the Indians calm, Colonel Bouquet at Fort Pitt issued a proclamation forbidding any English subject from settling or hunting "to the west of the Alleghany mountains." If that were not sufficient cause for alarm among the Ohio Company partners, the unsettled Pennsylvania-Virginia boundary dispute led to claims that

7. *Case of the Ohio Company* . . . [n.p., 1769?], 8; reproduced in Mulkearn, 326–393.

the lands around Fort Pitt had never been Virginia's to give away. In time Mason explained the effects of the French and Indian War and its aftermath upon the company's fortunes as disastrous.

From 1763 onward Mason was a member of the five-man executive committee, participating in or guiding a series of petitions, remonstrances, and other maneuvers designed to reaffirm the original company charter. All hope for profits from the fur trade had now been abandoned.[8] The committee decided to hire a London solicitor to plead their cause. Clearly, the partners believed their troubles grew from intentional delays fomented by rivals on the governor's Council. Not so easy to explain, however, was General Jeffrey Amherst's refusal to allow the sale of company lands around the Wills Creek storehouse, which was now a dilapidated military post known as Fort Cumberland. On every side, thwarted partners believed that their next move had to come from the king's chambers or failure was imminent. Moreover, a royal grant would reinforce the company's hand in any argument with rival claimants in either Virginia or Pennsylvania. To accomplish this end, Mason's kinsman and John Mercer's son, Colonel George Mercer, was dispatched to London in 1763 with instructions to press the company claims at Whitehall. Unfortunately, Mercer arrived in London too late. In October the king took his ministers' advice and signed the Proclamation of 1763, which forbade colonial settlement on Indian lands west of the Alleghany mountains. Tired of a long, expensive war, the British mood was conciliatory toward the frontier Indians. The overseas reaction to Pontiac's rebellion, far from calling for vengeance against the Indians, restricted colonial expansion into the West.[9]

Unhappily for the Ohio Company and the settlers who were eager to push westward, British policy from 1763 consistently discouraged both land settlement and speculation. George Mercer is seen in perspective as a pitiful, ineffectual lobbyist who petitioned on the company's behalf more in resignation than in hope. When the Earl of Shelburne finally sought an account of the company's claims from Governor Fauquier in Williamsburg, it meant more frustration and disappointment. For by 1767 the company no longer had a Lee or Dinwiddie on the Council to support its vast claims. The net result was a large bill from Mercer for futile services rendered.[10]

After John Mercer's death in 1768, Mason's knowledge and stamina were the company's main assets. There is no record of any profits—only delay, frustration, and more assessments. Yet the prospects took an upward swing in the late 1760s when a few British courtiers and Philadelphia speculators easily convinced fashionable Englishmen that a verdant paradise awaited the venturesome in the Ohio Valley. In April 1769 readers of a Williamsburg newspaper learned that "Mrs. Macaulay, the celebrated female historian, talks of ending her days on the banks of the Ohio," and in time trans-Atlantic gossip had placed a fourteenth colony where the Scioto and Kanahwa emptied their waters into the

8. Jack M. Sosin, *Whitehall and the Wilderness; The Middle West in British Colonial Policy, 1760-1775* (Lincoln, Nebr., 1961), 62–69.
9. *Ibid.*, 136–137.
10. James, *Ohio Company*, 153.

[8]

fabled *rivière belle.* By 1773 Washington was half convinced that he might own the very townsite of the future colony's capital, and his correspondence with Mason and others reveals a heady optimism.

Then Ohio Company affairs took a downward turn through an unlucky circumstance. The Vandalia Company, spawned in Philadelphia but backed by influential Englishmen, seemed verging on dishonesty to some scrupulous men in Whitehall. Lord Hillsborough's disdain for the Vandalia proposal (that would have swallowed most of present-day West Virginia) helped bring on his removal as secretary of state for the American colonies, but the Vandalia partisans were so anxious to bribe or bargain that eventually their project foundered in British bureaucratic channels. The bad name of Vandalia did nothing to help further the overlapping Ohio Company claims, and powerful forces close to George III favored a wilderness buffer zone rather than a land boom as a means of maintaining peace on the Indian frontier. If the Vandalia group, with all its wealth and prestige, could not win royal favor, there was little hope for the Ohio Company with its lonely representative—a man barely able to pay his bills, much less bribe a weak-willed undersecretary. George Mercer's 1770 scheme to merge Ohio and Vandalia claims was a fiasco which Mason testily repudiated.

Some of Mason's early enthusiasm was dampened, but he was too deeply involved to withdraw from the Ohio enterprise. He filed suits by the dozen to collect company debts for goods sold on credit and pored over royal charters and land grants until he became an expert, not only on the Ohio Company situation, but also on the royal charters and land grants affecting Virginia from 1609 onward. Prior to the Revolution, Mason's knowledge of land law (already extensive, since he handled his own leases and deeds without a lawyer's aid) became so respected that until his death colleagues deferred to his expert legal knowledge. From 1775 until his death Mason exerted himself repeatedly to salvage some assets from the floundering enterprise.

During the period from 1775 to 1779 Mason worked in the Virginia Convention and House of Delegates for confirmation of the original terms of the company grant. As an influential legislator in the patriot group that directed the Revolution, Mason fought the claims of rival companies and wrote laws which would have permitted a final settlement of the company's claims. His history of the enterprise was carefully detailed in the petition to the General Assembly of 20 November 1778 (*q.v.*). A pair of land laws drafted by Mason (with Jefferson's aid) were finally passed in June 1779, but the Ohio Company's western claims were waylaid by a vindictive opposition in the process. A specific clause validating the claim was defeated, and a technical flaw in the surveys ultimately forced Mason to abandon hope for legal recognition of the old 1749 claim.

Even as Mason clung to that earlier dream (which was probably given the *coup d'grace* by the Virginia Court of Appeals on 29 Apr. 1783), his confidence was shared by other partners. Mason was not alone in mentioning the company shares in his will, yet the major legacy of the Ohio Company was tiresome litigation which dragged on into the nineteenth century. It is possible that Mason had liquidated some old

Ohio Company properties in Maryland in the 1780s and distributed the proceeds to the shareholders, but the evidence for this is circumstantial. No records remain to show whether the investors ever realized any profits. However, Professor James observes that any gains made in selling goods or real estate probably were spent on lawyer's fees. The only losses "were in fact not real but losses of possible speculative profit." [11]

Mason's dealings on behalf of the Ohio Company are treated here selectively. The Company minutes, resolutions, and other official matters were published in Lois Mulkearn, comp., *George Mercer Papers Relating to the Ohio Company of Virginia,* and will not be repeated here. However, official orders, notices of meetings, letters, petitions, and commentaries prepared or signed by Mason (either as treasurer or a member of the executive committee) have been included, even when they duplicate items in the *Mercer Papers* and elsewhere, for the sake of continuity. Legal actions in debt litigation, powers of attorney, court processes to recover lands, and other routine materials have been calendared in Alfred P. James, *The Ohio Company, Its Inner History* (Pittsburgh, 1959), 300–353; but in Appendix A a few items are included because the line between Mason's private dealings and those on the company's behalf is not always clear. The totality of the company's business that Mason conducted reveals a high sense of responsibility, considerable fortitude, and great expectations.

Personal relationships stemming from company affairs, matters of historical and geographical importance, and such other information as will enlighten Mason's role in the Ohio Company from 1749 to 1792 will appear in explanatory notes following particular documents.

The Ohio Company to John Hanbury

Potomack, 21 June 1749. The company minutes indicate that GM was admitted to full partnership on 21 June and their letter to John Hanbury was discussed later the same day. The partners report the receipt of Hanbury's petition to the king of 11 January 1749, requesting a 500,000-acre land grant on the left or south bank of the Ohio. They have heard that the Duke of Bedford was active on their behalf, and the partners want him to join them with a full share, if Hanbury thinks such a gesture proper. The partners also want the king to send a letter of instruction to Governor William Gooch, so that the survey of their grant may proceed. Goods worth two thousand pounds are ordered for delivery by late November, preferably at a Potomac port, for use in the Indian trade. A second cargo is to be shipped in time to reach America by 1 March 1750. They consider Hanbury a full partner and are deducting his share (£125) from their remittance.

FC (Mercer Papers, PPiU). This is taken from a Ms in the handwriting of Richard Rogers, John Mercer's clerk, titled "Orders and Resolutions of the Ohio Company, 1749–1761." The letter is printed in Mulkearn, 140–141.

11. *Ibid.,* 184.

To Lawrence Washington

SIR   May 27th: 1750

As the Gentm. Mr. Parker offers for Security are utter Strangers to me, I can not take upon me to say whether I think him sufficient or not; but as Mr. Parker's affairs are circumstanced, I imagine they are the only Security he can at this Time give, & therefore I most readily concur in the same Opinion with you, that it's better to accept them than Delay sending up the Goods any longer; for we have already given our Rivals the Pensilvns. too many advantages over us, by suffering them to engage the Interest of the Indians, & raise in them numberless Prejudices agst. the Ohio Compy while we, instead of fulfilling our Engagements & complying wth. our Promises in Supplying them wth. Goods, have lain quite still, as if we were altogether unconcerned in the Matter; for these Reasons I shou'd look upon anything that put a Stop to the Trade for this Season, as utterly destructive of our whole Scheme, & think it ought carefully to be avoided; & I have really so good an Opinion of Parker that I can hardly think he'll offer to defraud us; besides I believe his All depends upon his discharging this Trust with Honour & Integrity. But as the Company have ordered that he shou'd give Security, & have relyed upon us to take it, we ought by all Means to observe their Directions; & I make no doubt let the Event be what it will, that they will approve what we have done; as they must be convinced we act upon no other Motive than the Interest of the Company. I therefore agree to accept the Security Mr. Parker offers till a Genl. Meeting of the Company at wch. Time they may accept or reject them, as they think proper—but I hardly think the Instrument of Writing Mr. Parker shewed me authentic, & am of Opinion they ought to bind themselves wth. him in a Penal Bond under their Hands & Seals; but as this can not be Done imediatly, I suppose there can be no Risque in letting him have a Load of Goods now, & desiring him to have such Bond signed agst. [the goods until] he comes down again. Had Mr. Chapman been at home, I shd. have consulted him upon it; as he is not, I give you my own Sentiments, & am wth. my Compl. to the Ladys Sr Yr. most humble Servt

GEORGE MASON

[P.S.] I wrote to stop our second Cargoe till next Spring

RC (Morristown, N.J., National Historical Park). An inaccurate version appeared in Moncure Daniel Conway, *Barons of the Potomack and the Rappahannock* (New York, 1892), 280-281.

Lawrence Washington had traveled to England during the summer of 1749, and may have ordered goods for the Ohio Company account then. HUGH PARKER was hired on 21 June 1749 to carry the company's goods to the projected trading post opposite the mouth of Wills Creek. Parker and Thomas Cresap bought the land on the company's behalf, and the Wills Creek "Factory" was authorized early in 1750. The two traders were also charged with building roads from the Potomac storehouse to other posts planned between the upper Potomac and the forks of the Ohio. GM succeeded Nathaniel Chapman as treasurer on 25 Sept. 1749, and was soon forced into a decision-making role. At an executive committee meeting on 29 Mar. 1750 which Lawrence Washington and GM attended, it was agreed that Parker would forward the company's trading goods to Christopher Gist on an Ohio tributary. A short time later, Parker began doing a sizeable credit business at Wills Creek on the company's behalf. OUR SECOND CARGOE was due 1 Mar. on an order to John Hanbury in London, which GM wanted to delay until the first order was sold or distributed.

Agreement with Christopher Gist

[11 September 1750]

Agreement made with Christopher Guist by the Committee of the Ohio Company the 11th day of September 1750. for the greater Encouragement of the first Setlers upon the Company's Lands.

Whereas Mr. Christopher Guist proposes to remove one hundred and fifty or more Family's to the Ohio Company's Land on the Branches of the Mississippi to the Westward of the great Mountains. We hereby agree and oblige ourselves that all such persons as will remove themselves to, and settle upon the said Lands contiguous to each other, within two Years from the Date hereof shall have a Fee simple in any Quantity of the Companys Land not exceeding fifty acres for every person they remove more than four, or one hundred Acres for every person less than four upon the following Terms.

To pay the Ohio Company after the Rate of four pounds Sterling for every hundred Acres within three years after seating upon the Land to have their Title Deeds sign'd and acknowledged upon payment of the Consideration money. To hold their Lands five years Quit Rent free and then to pay the usual Quit Rent of Virginia. In Witness whereof we have hereunto set our Hands this 11th. day of September 1750.

JAMES SCOTT   NATH CHAPMAN
RICHARD LEE   GEORGE MASON

Ms (Mercer Papers, PPiU). In the handwriting of John Mercer.

Gist was instructed by the company's executive committee on this same day to proceed westward at once "in Order to search out and discover the Lands upon the River Ohio, & other adjoining Branches of the Mississippi down as low as the great Falls thereof." The point was to "find a large Quantity of good level Land, such as you think will suit the Company" for its initial 200,000-acre grant (Mulkearn, 7–8). Gist was to be paid £150 for this service, which was to include preparation of a map and journal, with an advance of £30 from GM. Gist, who also carried a message from Thomas Lee for the Ohio country Indians, started west on 31 Oct. 1750 and returned to Roanoke on 19 May 1751. His journal is printed in Mulkearn, 8–31. Gist delivered Lee's invitation to a conference at Fredericksburg, but to no purpose (Lee died suddenly on 14 Nov. 1750, and the Indians seemed disinterested). What Gist obviously learned was that any thought of settling families along the Ohio tributaries was, to say the least, premature—the first warning shots of the French and Indian War had already been fired. Lee, as acting governor of Virginia, was trying to win over the Indians and kept prodding the company for action on the land grant until his death. The USUAL QUIT RENT OF VIRGINIA was two shillings per 100 acres. The Virginians' anxiety increased, and Gist received more instructions from GM on the company's behalf on 16 July 1751 and 28 Apr. 1752 (q.v.).

Articles of Agreement for the Ohio Company

[*Stafford Court House, 22–24 May 1751.*] From its inception the Ohio Company had been a trading partnership of petitioners and grantees operating on an ad hoc basis. The deaths of Thomas Lee and Hugh Parker created legal problems which forced the partners to consider a more formal arrangement. John Mercer probably wrote this agreement and at this meeting he became a full partner. The articles recognized 20 full partners in the Ohio Company, whose purpose was "the taking up and settling a Tract" of 500,000 acres in the Ohio Valley, "and for the carrying on a Trade with the INDIANS in those Parts." The agreement in fact created a joint stock company, with each partner holding two shares in the enterprise, which was expected "to be compleat and ended" by 1771. It also made possible the legal conduct of business by an executive committee or—as it happened—by GM alone when circumstances dictated. Ten of the partners, including GM, were present when this agreement was discussed and signed.

Ms (Vi). The document consists of two vellum sheets taped together with seals attached. The entire text is printed in Appendix A of James, *Ohio Company*, 205–219.

Instructions to Christopher Gist

[16 July 1751]

After you have returned from Williamsburg and have executed the Com'ission of the President & Council, if they shall think proper to give you One, otherwise as soon as you can conveniently, you are to apply to Colo. Cresap for such of the Company's Horses, as you shall want for the Use of yourself and such other Person or Persons you shall think necessary to carry with you; and you are to look out & observe the nearest & most convenient Road you can find from the Company's Store at Will's Creek to a Landing at Monhongeyela; from thence you are to proceed down the Ohio on the South Side thereof, as low as the Big Conhaway, and up the same as far as you judge proper, and find good Land. You are all the Way to keep an exact Diary & Journal & therein note every Parcel of good Land; with the Quantity as near as you can by any Means compute the same, with the Breadth, Depth, Course and Length of the several Branches falling into the Ohio, & the different Branches any of them are forked into, laying the same as exactly down in a Plan thereof as you can; observing also the Produce, the several Kinds of Timber and Trees, observing where there is Plenty and where the Timber is scarce; and you are not to omit proper observations on the mountainous, barren, or broken Land, that we may on your Return judge what Quantity of good Land is contained within the Compass of your Journey, for we would not have you omit taking Notice of any Quantity of good Land, tho not exceeding 4 or 500 Acres provided the same lies upon the River Ohio & may be convenient for our building Store Houses & other Houses for the better carrying on a Trade and Correspondence down the River.

In Witness whereof we have hereunto set our hands the day and year above

Lawe. Washington
James Scott
George Mason
J Mercer

Ms (Mercer Papers, PPiU). In the handwriting of John Mercer, and printed in Mulkearn, 31–32 and 175, under Mercer's title: "Instructions given to Mr. Christopher Gist by the Com'ittee of the Ohio Company July 16th. 1751."

Gov. Dinwiddie commissioned Joshua Fry, Lunsford Lomax, and James Patton to represent Virginia at an Indian conference called for "the full Moon in May" at Logstown because of rumblings from the Indians about the land cessions in the Treaty of Lancaster and reports of increased French activity in the Ohio Valley. Despite the precarious situation with the French, the company was still intent on establishing settlements. Gist was sent to Logstown on behalf of the company, but he departed on a preliminary mission from the storehouse opposite the mouth of Wills Creek on 4 Nov. 1751, headed for the BIG CONHAWAY (Kanawha) River country on the south side of the Ohio. Gist traveled via A LANDING AT MONHONGEYELA, near the point where Red Stone Fort was built later by the company. When Gist and his party encountered Indians they were invited to the Logstown meeting and promised "a Present from the King of Great Britain" (Mulkearn, 32–36). Gist took note of the terrain, waterways, timber lands, and soil conditions. The company's envoys also gathered samples of pelts, mineral ores, and soil from a salt lick. On 29 Mar. 1752 the Gist party returned to the factory at Wills Creek along a route Gist recommended for "a tolerable good Road from Wills's Creek to the upper Fork of Mohongaly, from whence the River is navigable all the Way to the Ohio for large flat bottomed Boats" (Mulkearn, 39). Gist estimated the roadway would extend "about 70 M[iles]," a fairly accurate estimate. After Gist returned to Virginia he was given a new set of instructions by GM dated 28 Apr. 1752 (q.v.).

Ohio Company Advertisement

[7 April 1752]

By the Committee of the Ohio *Company.*

THE several Members of the said Company, in *Virginia* and *Maryland,* are desired to meet at Mr. *Wetherburn's,* in the City of *Williamsburg,* on *Thursday* the 7th Day of *May* next. *April* 7, 1752.

> *George Mason,*
> *James Scott,*
> *John Mercer.*

Printed from *Va. Gaz.* (Hunter), 10 Apr. 1752.

This seems to have been the first public notice or call for a company meeting under the terms of the 1751 articles of agreement. MR. WETHERBURN'S was the popular tavern (now restored by Colonial Williamsburg) on Duke of Gloucester street, a favorite meeting place until Henry Wetherburn's death in 1760.

Instructions to Christopher Gist

[28 April 1752]

Whereas the Governor has been pleased to grant you a commission empowering and requiring you to go as an Agent for the Ohio company to the Indian treaty to be held at Logstown on the sixteenth day of May next, you are therefore desired to acquaint the chiefs of the several nations of Indians there assembled that his Majesty has been graciously pleased to grant unto the Honble Robert Dinwiddie Esquire Governor of Virginia and to several other gentlemen in Great Britain and America by the name of the Ohio company a large quantity of land on the river Ohio and the branches thereof thereby to enable and encourage the said company and all his Majesties subjects to make settlements and carry on an extensive trade and commerce with their brethren the Indians and to supply them with goods at a more easie rate than they have hitherto bought them. And considering the necessities of his children the [six nations and the other Indians to the Westward of the English settlements and the hardships they labour under for] want of a due

[15]

supply of goods and to remove the same as much as possible his Majesty has been pleased to have a clause inserted in the said companys grant obliging them to carry on a trade and commerce with their brethren the Indians and has granted them many priviledges and immunitys in consideration of their carrying on the said trade and supplying the Indians with goods. That the said company have accordingly begun the trade and imported large quantitys of goods, but have found the expence and risque of carrying out the goods such a distance from the inhabitants without having any place of safety by the way to lodge them at or opportunity of getting provisions for their people so great that they cannot afford to sell their goods at so easy a rate as they would willingly do nor are they at such a distance able to supply their brethren the Indians at all times when they are in want for which reason the company find it absolutely necessary immediately to settle and cultivate the land his Majesty has been pleased to grant them which to be sure they have an indisputable right to do as our brethren the six nations sold all the land to the westward of Virginia at the treaty of Lancaster to their father the King of Great Britain and he has been graciously pleased to grant a large quantity thereof to the said Ohio company yet being informed that the six nations have given their friends the Dellawars leave to hunt upon the said land and that they still hunt upon part thereof themselves and as the settlements made by the English upon the back land may make the game scarce or at least drive it further back the said company therefore to prevent any difference or misunderstanding which might possibly happen between them and their brethren the Indians touching the said lands are willing to make them some further satisfaction for the same and to purchase of them the land on the East side the river Ohio and Allagany as low as the great Conhaway providing the same can be done at a reasonable rate and our brethren the six nations and their allies will promise and engage their friendship and protection to all his Majesties subjects setling on the said lands, when this is done the company can safely venture to build factorys and storehouses upon the river Ohio and send out large cargoes of goods which they cannot otherwise do. And to convince our brethren the Indians how desirous we are of living in strict friendship and becoming one people with them you are hereby empowered and required to acquaint and promise our brethren in the name and on behalf of the said company that if any of them incline to take land and live among the English they [may purchase] the said companys lands upon the same terms and conditions as the white people have and enjoy the same priviledges which

[16]

they do, as far as is in the companys power to grant. And that you may be the better able to acquaint our brethren the Indians with these our proposals, you are to apply to Andrew Montour the interpreter for his assistance therein and the company hereby undertake and promise to make him satisfaction for the trouble he shall be at. If our brethren the six nations approve our proposals the company will pay them whatever sum you agree with them for, and if they want any particular sort of goods you are to desire them to give you an account of such goods and the company will immediately send for them to England and when they arrive will carry them to whatever place you agree to deliver them at. If our brethren the Indians do not approve these proposals, and do refuse their protection and assistance to the subjects of their father the King of Great Britain, you are forthwith to make a return thereof to the said Ohio company that they may inform his Majesty thereof. You are to apply to Colo. Cresap for what wampum you have occasion of on the company's account for which you are to give him a receipt.

You are also to apply to him for one of the companys horses to ride out to the Logstown.

As soon as the treaty is over you are to make an exact return of all your proceedings to the company.

GEORGE MASON Treasr.

Additional Instructions given Christopher Gist Gent on a Seperate Paper.

Upon your Arrival at the Treaty if you find the Commissioners do not make a general Agreement with the Indians in behalf of Virginia for the Settlement of the Land upon the Waters of the Ohio and Mississippi or that in such Agreement there are any doubtful or ambiguous Expressions which may be prejudicial to the Ohio Company you are then to endeavour to make purchase of the Land to the Eastward of the River Ohio and Allagany and procure the Friendship and protection of the Indians in Setling the said Land upon the best Terms you can for a quantity of Goods.

You are to agree with them to deliver the said Goods at the most convenient place you can if Possible at the Forks of Mohongaly, if the Indians give you a list of Goods which they desire to be sent for in return for their Land you are to enquire and find out as near as you can the usual prices of such Goods among the Indians, that we may be as near the Sum you agree with them for as possible.

You are to Engage Andrew Montour the Interpreter in the Companys Interest and get him to assist you in making a purchase of the

Indians, and as the Company have great Dependance and Confidence in the said Andrew Montour they hereby not only promise to make him satisfaction for his trouble, but if he can make an Advantageous Bargain for them with the Indians they will in return for his good Offices let him have a handsome Settlement upon their Land without paying any purchase money upon the same Terms which the said Company themselves hold the Land, and without another consideration than the Kings Quit rents. If you can obtain a Deed or other written Agreement from the Indians, it must be taken in the names of the Honble. Robert Dinwiddie Esqr. Govr. of Virginia, John Hanbury Esqr. of the City of London Mercht. Capel Hanbury of the said City of London Mercht. John Tayloe, Presly Thornton, Philip Ludwell Lee, Thomas Lee, Richard Lee, Gawin Corbin, John Mercer, George Mason, Lawrence Washington, Augustine Washington, Nathaniel Chapman Esquires and James Scott Clerk, all of the Colony of Virginia, James Wardrop, Jacob Giles & Thomas Cresap Esqrs. of the province of Maryland and their Associates Members of the Ohio Company, in the said Deed or Agreement you are to mention the Bounds of the Land as expresly as possible that no dispute may arise hereafter, and we would have the Indians clearly understand what Land they sell us, that they may have no Occasion to complain of any Fraud or underhand dealings, as is often the Custom with them.

The said Ohio Company do hereby agree and oblige themselves to make you satisfaction for the Trouble and Expence you shall be at in Transacting their Affairs at the said Treaty pursuant to the Instructions by them Given you. Given under my hand in behalf of the Ohio Company this 28th. day of April 1752.

GEORGE MASON Treasr.

Ms (Mercer Papers, PPiU). In the handwriting of John Mercer, the first part designated by Mercer as "Instructions given Christopher Gist Gent by the Ohio Company April 28th. 1752."

GM probably was in Williamsburg witnessing the activities related to the forthcoming Indian conference, since the Ohio Company meeting had been called for 7 May 1752 in the capital. The purpose of Gist's western trips and the results of various Indian conferences seem confusing if the sources are not consulted. The immediate problems in 1752 were French interference in the Ohio Valley and deteriorating Indian relations because of intercolonial rivalries. In the hands of some historians this matter became inordinately complex and hence their secondary accounts have not always clarified the situation. As GM and the other company partners must have seen it, the impending crisis with the French might be averted if the Iroquois tribes withdrew to new hunting grounds and allowed King George's subjects to gradually settle the trans-Allegheny country below the Ohio. Thus Gov. Dinwiddie, GM, and other company partners were anxious to erase any cloud on their Indian title so that settlement could begin on lands on the right bank of the Kanawha River. The Virginia commissioners received numerous instructions regarding their mission, including reassurances to the Indians that the Lancaster treaty was in their best interests. To keep the matter in perspective, it is useful to recall that a 1748 census made by the interpreter, Conrad Weiser, showed that there were only about 800 warriors living in the upper Ohio hunting grounds. Dinwiddie also charged the commissioners with securing "a quiet and peaceable Possession to his Majesty's Subjects of this Colony of all the lands" presumably ceded in 1744. Apparently, the Indians believed their earlier cession was of lands along the Cheat, Monongahela, and Youghiogheny rivers, while the Virginians thought they had won a clear title to all lands between the Alleghenies and the Ohio. It is likely that Pennsylvania traders had aroused the Indians' fears with stories of more settlers coming into the area who would drive away game—orderly settlements were an anathema to the traders. Part of the problem also centered around the uncertain boundary between Pennsylvania and Virginia, a delicate matter that was not settled until 1785. Pennsylvania officials dispatched Lewis Evans on a scouting trip similar to Gist's journeys of 1750–1751, and in a memorandum of 26 June 1760 offered Evans 100 guineas for gaining "Intelligence of the Southern & Western Bounds of Pennsylvania, where not yet settled" (Samuel Hazard, comp., *Colonial Records of Pennsylvania*, 1st Ser. [Harrisburg, 1851–1853], II, 47–49). More specifically, Evans was to "Get informed of the Stock and Scheme of the Virginia Co., trading to Ohio, and what Disadvantages they labour under, or advantages they now or hereafter may enjoy more than we from their Situation." The Iroquois tribes harassed by the French in 1750–1751 reportedly asked their "English brothers" to build a fort in the area, but neither Pennsylvania nor Virginia officials were anxious to erect a stockade that would have shown their determination to defend the Ohio Valley. Dinwiddie's instructions on this point have a devious ring, for he claimed that since France and England were not—technically speaking—at war, the Ohio Company ought to be excused from the earlier royal order to build a fort ("The Treaty of Logg's Town, 1752," vmhb, XIII [1905], 143–152). The Ohio Company minutes of 22 May 1751 show that the partners blamed Sir William Gooch for the King's order because the governor had conveyed the impression to London that the company would erect a military base. What they intended to build was "only a small fort for the security of their Goods and people and not a regular Fort and Garrison for the protection of the Countrey . . . with such a charge as no private Company could support" (Mulkearn, 142). In short, the company only wanted a warehouse, and if a military fort "should be insisted on in such a sense it must in the end entirely ruin and disappoint the whole undertaking." Nor could Gov. James Hamilton of Pennsylvania kindle enthusiasm for a fort. When Hamilton sympathized with the Indians' request and turned to the Quaker-dominated legislature for funds, he was rebuffed by lawmakers who favored lip service to fort-building. In the circumstances, Hamilton candidly advised the Iroquois and their allies to seek aid from Virginia. The Six Nations' friends, THE DELLAWARS (Delaware tribe), were believed to have 165 warriors in the area. ANDREW MONTOUR had succeeded Conrad Weiser, Thomas Lee's favorite, as the company interpreter, because Gist's knowledge of Indian languages was reportedly scanty. The covert instructions ON A SEPERATE PAPER indicate a wariness of the commissioner's intentions, and may have been directed toward Col. James Patton. Patton and his Virginia partners had a 100,000-acre grant "on the three branches of the Mississippi" dated 26 Apr. 1745, in a region south of the Ohio Company grant. The commissioners proceeded, however, to make a general agreement in which the Six Nations confirmed the Virginia title to the south side of the Ohio so that a separate deed listing each company partner was not made. The Indians at

Logstown did say they had "not the full power in our hands here on Ohio; [and] we must acquaint our council at Onandago of the affair," (*Case of the Ohio Company*, 21–22; facsimile in Mulkearn). The upshot of this reservation was that the conference was a failure, since the Onandago council never ratified the agreement made on 13 June 1752. Undaunted by the uncertainty of the Indian negotiations, the Ohio Company proceeded on 19 Sept. 1752 to order a survey of 200,000 acres between the Kiskomineto River and the mouth of the Kanawha (Mulkearn, 175–76).

To George Washington

SIR   Dogues N[e]ck, July 29. 1752
   I came Home f[rom . . .] Yesterday, when I re[ceived your letter informing] me with the time of yr Brother['s fu]neral, & desiring my Attendance. I am very sorry it did not come to [my] Hands sooner; had I known it in [time] I wou'd by no Means have refused the last Peice of Respect to the Memory of a Gentleman, for whom, when alive, I had a sincere Regard—
   I most heartily condole you on the Loss of so worthy a Brother & Friend & am Sir Yr. most hble Sert.

                                                    GEORGE MAS[ON]

   RC (Washington Papers, DLC). A facsimile reproduction of this letter was used for the frontispiece of Stanislaus Murray Hamilton, ed., *Letters to Washington* . . . (Boston, 1898–1902), I. Douglas S. Freeman, *George Washington, a Biography* (New York, 1948–1957), I, 264*n*, states that the letter "is supposed to have been addressed" to Washington.
   Lawrence Washington was George Washington's half-brother. He died on 26 July 1752. Col. Lunsford Lomax, who had served as a Virginia commissioner at the Logstown Indian conference, bought Lawrence Washington's share in the Ohio Company from the estate's executors.
   Portions of the letter along the upper right margin are missing. Missing words have been conjectured and placed in brackets.

Ohio Company Advertisement

                                                    [5 October 1752]

THE Ohio Company are desired to meet at *Stafford* Court-House on *Monday* the 20th of *November* next.

                                                    George Mason,
                                                    James Scott,
October 5, 1752.   *John Mercer.*

   Printed from *Va. Gaz.* (Hunter), 6 Oct. 1752.

Petition to the Governor and Executive Council of Virginia

[6 November 1752]

The Petition of the Ohio Company.

Sheweth,

That the said company, having at their great charge and expence, employed persons for above these two years past, to search and view the lands on the *Ohio*, alias *Alligany River*, as far westward as the *Twigtree Town*, and to cultivate trade and friendship, with the several nations and tribes of Indians, inhabiting those parts, in order to seat the same, according to the condition of his Majesty's instruction, communicated to this Honourable Board, by his honour the late governor; and having also, at their great charge, cleared a *waggon road, from their storehouse at Will's Creek, to one of the branches of the Ohio, navigable by large flat-bottomed boats,* which is the nearest, best, and almost only passage, through the great ridge of mountains, and consequently is of great benefit to the public: Your petitioners pray leave to survey and take up *their first two hundred thousand acres, between Romanettos, alias Kiskaminettas Creek, and the fork of the Ohio, and the great Conhaway, alias New River, alias Wood's River, on the south side of the said River Ohio, in as many surveys, as they shall think fit, your petitioners understanding the Indians are not willing any settlements, on the north side thereof, should be yet made;* and as your petitioners make no doubt, but that they shall be able, not only to comply with the conditions of their first grant, in one year from this time, but to seat a much greater number of families, than they are obliged to, if your honours would permit them to take up *such small tracts of land, not exceeding one thousand acres, as lie in spots interspersed between the company's surveys, as they shall cause to be actually seated on, before the 25th of December, 1753, on the terms of your petitioners grant, or such other terms and conditions, as your Honours shall think reasonable,* which your petitioners apprehend would be of great advantage, to his Majesty and his plantations, as it would be the most effectual means, to increase and secure their first settlements, which the encroachments of the French, and especially, the new fort built by them on the west end of Lake Erie, and on the south side thereof, the last year, render necessary, the same manifestly tending to interrupt your petitioners grant; and your petition-

[21]

ers, in order to settle a sufficient force, must, without such permission, be obliged to part with all their own lands, to encourage the settlement, contrary to the intent and agreement of the company, who did not enter into so expensive an undertaking, with a view of setting up for a company of landmongers, though several companies, of that sort, now trade in this colony, but with a view of making fortunes for their children, in a very hazardous undertaking, at a very great and certain expence, whereas *the landmongers, by procuring an order of council, for a certain quantity of land, make surveys at so unreasonable a distance, as might include five hundred times the quantity, and it is presumed, under their grant, no person can interfere; when they meet with purchasers, so much land is taken up, and his Majesty's land is granted, to his subjects, not by a purchase from himself, but persons, who substitute themselves [as] his brokers, and receive the full value of them.*

Your petitioners therefore hope, that your Honours will think it reasonable, they should reap some of the advantage the public will receive, by their great expence, and not allow private persons to interfere with their bounds, or to take up large tracts of the lands, they have been at the charge of discovering, till they may have time to apply to his Majesty, and know his pleasure, as your petitioners are so far from setting up for an engrossing company, that they are willing to receive any new members into it, on the same terms they ho[l]d their several shares, which from thirteen at the time of his Majesty's grant, now amount to twenty, *yet have not so much land among them, as some persons, who are so far from being at any expence, or procuring any public advantage, that they have made large fortunes by selling his Majesty's lands.*

And your petitioners shall ever pray.

Printed in *Case of the Ohio Company* (NHi), 7-8, with the partners' signatures omitted. The Ms has not been found. This rare pamphlet is reproduced in Mulkearn, 326-393.
The hysterical and somewhat bitter tone of this petition (which may have been prepared by John Mercer) was in part caused by misinformation and partly attributable to growing anxieties. Approval of the Executive Council was required for surveys of more than 400 acres. The petition overstates the company's progress and makes innuendoes that could not be supported by evidence. Some work may have been done on clearing A WAGGON ROAD from the Wills Creek storehouse to the confluence of the Monongahela and Youghiogheny rivers, but on 4 Nov. 1751 Christopher Gist left the storehouse and reported the path "is now very full of old Trunks of Trees and stones, but with some pains might be made a very good Wa[gon] Road." In late Apr. 1752, Colonel Cresap had been authorized to spend company funds for clearing this road, but its completion by 6 Nov. 1752 was unlikely. Ignorant of regional geography beyond the Alleghenies, the partners were led to believe that

surveys by other speculators, i.e., A COMPANY OF LANDMONGERS, were endanger-ing their own claims. In 1751 the company minutes noted that James Patton and his partners had made surveys "far without their Limits and within those allowed to the Company" (Mulkearn, 143). In fact, the activities of Patton, Dr. Thomas Walker, and Speaker John Robinson (Greenbrier Company) were related to lands south of the company grant. Moreover, time was slipping by and the company had not yet surveyed a single acre of ground, hence the self-imposed deadline of Christmas 1753, which was well in advance of the seven-year limitation in the original grant of 1749. There is no record that the Council acted on this petition.

Land Lease to Thomas Halbert

[29 December 1752]

THIS INDENTURE, Made this twenty ninth Day of December in the Year of our Lord, One Thousand Seven Hundred and fifty two BETWEEN George Mason of the Parish of Truroe & County of Fairfax Gent: of the one Part, and Thomas Halbert of the same Parish & County Planter of the other Part;

WITNESSETH, That the said George Mason for and in Consideration of the Rents, Duties, Reservations, and Covenants herein after re-served and mentioned, on the Part and Behalf of the said Thomas Halbert his Heirs and Assigns, to be paid, done, and performed, HATH demised, granted, and to Farm let, unto the said Thomas Halbert his Heirs and Assigns, one certain Messuage Tenement, or Parcel of Land, in the Tenure and Occupation of the said Thomas Halbert now being; containing two hundred Acres, one hundred Acres thereof being that Plantation whereon John Drakeford lately lived, & the other hundred Acres adjoinging & convenient thereto between a certain Branch called Hat Marked Branch & a small Branch called Nelson's Spring Branch & one of the out Lines of the pattent running from the sd. Hat Marked Branch towards the Branches of Difficult Run, if so much can be found without in-croaching upon the Tenants already setled upon the sd. George Mason's Land—Together with all the Profits, Commodities, and Appurtenances, to the same belonging, or in any-wise appertaining: Reserving and excepting unto the said George Mason his Heirs and Assigns, the Liberty of getting Timber, on any Part of the hereby demised Land and Premises; as also all Mines, Minerals, and Quar-ries, and the Use of them; with free Ingress, Egress and Regress, in, to, and from the said demised Premises, and the Privilege of Hunt-ing, and Fowling, in or upon any Part thereof: TO HAVE AND TO HOLD the said Messuage Tenement, or Parcel of two hundred Acres of

Land, with the Appurtenances, (except as before excepted) unto the said Thomas Halbert his Heirs and Assigns, from the Day of the Date hereof, for and during the natural Lives of him the said Thomas Halbert Lydia his Wife & John his eldest Son and the longest Liver of them; YIELDING AND PAYING unto the said George Mason his Heirs, Executors, Administrators, or Assigns, Yearly, and every Year, for and during the Space and Term before-mentioned, on the First Day of *December,* the Rent of one thousand & fifty Pounds of good merchantable crop Tobacco clear of Caske in one Hogshead, in any one Warehouse in the sd. County of Fairfax except that at the Falls of Potomack River commonly called the Falls Warehouse and if it happens, That the said reserved Yearly Rent, or any Part thereof, be in Arrear or unpaid, for the Space of one Kalendar Month next after the Day whereon the same ought to be paid, That then, and so often as it shall so happen, it shall and may be lawful to, and for the said George Mason his Heirs, Executors, Administrators, or Assigns, into the said demised Premises, or any Part thereof, to enter and destrain, and the Distress or Distresses, then and there found, to take, lead, drive, and carry away, and thereof to dispose, according to Law: And if no sufficient Distress, or Distresses, can or may be found, in or upon the said demised Premises wherewith the said Rent and Arrears, if any there happen to be, may be fully satisfied and paid, That then it shall and may be lawful, to and for the said George Mason his Heirs, Executors, Administrators, or Assigns, into the said hereby demised Premises, or any Part thereof, in the Name of the Whole, without Demand, to re-enter, and the same to have again, repossess and enjoy, as in his or their first or former Estate; any Thing herein to the contrary thereof, in any-wise, notwithstanding. And the said Thomas Halbert for Himself, his Heirs, Executors, Administrators, and Assigns, DOTH covenant, promise, and agree, to and with the said George Mason his Heirs Executors Admrs & Assigns that he the sd. Thos. Halbert his Heirs, Executors, Administrators, and Assigns shall, and will Yearly, and every Year, during the Continuance of this Demise, pay unto the said George Mason his Heirs, Executors, Administrators, or Assigns, the before reserved Rent of one thousand & fifty pounds of good merchantable Crop Tobo. clear of Caske in one Hogshead on the Day whereon the same ought to be paid, and in the Manner as before reserved and mentioned: And the said Thomas Halbert for Himself, his Heirs, Executors, Administrators, and Assigns, doth further covenant, promise, and agree, to and with the said George Mason his Heirs Executors Admrs. & Assigns that He the said

[24]

Thomas Halbert his Heirs, Executors, Administrators, or Assigns, shall not tend, or suffer to be tended, on the said demised Premises, above a full and sufficient Crop, for five able, working Hands, in any one Year; and if at any Time it shall appear, that there is more than a full and sufficient Crop for five able, working Hands, tended on the hereby demised Premises, that then the said Thomas Halbert his Heirs, Executors, Administrators, or Assigns, shall and will pay unto the said George Mason his Heirs, Executors, Administrators, or Assigns, the Sum of Two Hundred Pounds of Tobacco over and above the before reserved Yearly Rent, for every and each Hand's Crop more than five and so in Proportion, Yearly, and every Year, while the same is continued or suffered to be done; and that the said Thomas Halbert his Heirs, Executors, Administrators, or Assigns, shall not make, or suffer to be made, any Manner of Waste of any Sort of Timber, on any Part of the hereby demised Land and Premises; and if at any Time any Timber, fit for Carpenters or Coopers Use, or Rails should be cut down, in clearing Ground or otherwise, the same shall all be worked up, and not suffered to rot or perish, under the Penalty of One Hundred Pounds of Tobacco, over and above the Value of such Timber, to be paid by the said Thomas Halbert his Heirs, Executors, Administrators, or Assigns, to the said George Mason his Heirs, Executors, Administrators, or Assigns, for every such Offence: And that the said Thomas Halbert his Heirs, Executors, Administrators, or Assigns, shall not use, sell, or otherwise dispose of, or suffer to be sold, used, or otherwise disposed of, any Sort of Timber, or Wood, from off any Part of the hereby demised Land and Premises, in any Manner whatsoever, (except for the proper Use and Benefit of the hereby demised Land and Premises) without the Consent of the said George Mason his Heirs or Assigns first obtained, under his or their Hand: And further, the said Thomas Halbert for Himself, his Heirs, Executors, Administrators, and Assigns, doth covenant, promise, and agree, to and with the said George Mason his Heirs Executors Admrs. or Assigns that he the sd. Thos. Halbert his Heirs, Executors, Administrators, or Assigns, shall and will, within the Space of Seven Years at farthest, from the Date hereof, build or cause to be built, on some convenient Part of the hereby demised Land and Premises, two Well framed dwelling Houses at least sixteen feet square each with out Side Chimneys & two well framed Tobacco Houses or Barnes at least thirty two feet long & twenty feet wide each or other Houses and Buildings equal thereto; and the said Thomas Halbert his Heirs, Executors, Administrators, and Assigns, shall, and will, always, during the Continuance of this Demise, keep the said Houses or Buildings in good Order and Repair, and if at any Time any of them should go to Decay, or happen to be destroyed by any Accident, shall build others as good in the Room of them: And that the said Thomas Halbert his Heirs, Executors, Administrators, or Assigns, shall and will also, within the before-mentioned Space of Seven Years, plant, on some convenient Part of the hereby demised Land and Premises, an Orchard of two hundred *Winter* Apple Trees, at thirty feet Distance every Way from each other, and eight hundred Peach Trees, at fifteen Feet Distance every Way from each other, and keep the same always during the Continuance of this Demise well trimmed, pruned, fenced in, and secured from Horses, Cattle, and other Creatures; and if any of them should die or decay, that the said Thomas Halbert his Heirs, Executors, Administrators, and Assigns, shall plant others of the same Kind in the Room of them, so as during the Continuance of this Demise, always to keep up the same Number. And further the said Thomas Halbert for himself, his Heirs, Executors, Administrators, and Assigns, doth covenant, promise, and agree, to and with the said George Mason his Heirs & Assigns, that no Assignment, Transferrance, or other Conveyance whatsoever, of the hereby demised Land and Premises, or any Part thereof, shall be made by the said Thomas Halbert his Heirs or Assigns, or any other Person or Persons whatsoever, without the Consent of the said George Mason his Heirs or Assigns first obtained, under his or their Hand and Seal, otherwise such Assignment, Transferrance, or Conveyance, to be void and of no Effect. And further the said Thomas Halbert for Himself, his Heirs, Executors, Administrators, and Assigns, doth covenant, promise, and agree, to and with the said George Mason his Heirs Executors Admrs. & Assigns that he the sd. Thomas Halbert his Heirs, Executors, Administrators, and Assigns, shall and will, always, during the Continuance of this Demise, keep the hereby demised Land and Premises, with the Appurtenances, in good and sufficient Order and Repair; and at the Expiration of the said Demise, whenever it shall happen, shall and will deliver the same in good, sufficient, tenantable Order, Repair, and Condition, unto the said George Mason his Heirs, Executors, Administrators, or Assigns. And the said George Mason for Himself, his Heirs, Executors, Administrators, and Assigns, doth covenant, promise, and agree, to and with the said Thomas Halbert his Heirs Executors Admrs. & Assigns that he the sd. Thos. Halbert his Heirs and Assigns, and all and every other Person and Persons who by Virtue of this Demise shall be legally and justly possessed of the hereby demised Land and

[26]

Premises, shall and may, under the Rents, Payments, Penalties, Reservations, Restrictions, Provisoes, Conditions, and Agreements, herein before mentioned, peaceably and quietly have, hold, use, occupy, possess, and enjoy the said hereby demised Land and Premises, with the Appurtenances, during the before mentioned Space and Term of three Lives without any Trouble, Molestation, or Interruption, from Him the said George Mason his Heirs, Executors, Administrators, or Assigns, or any other Person or Persons, claiming, or to claim, by, from, or under him, them, or any of them. IN WITNESS whereof, the said Parties have hereunto interchangeably set their Hands, and affixed their Seals, the Day, Month and Year first above-written.

Signed, Sealed, and Delivered,

in the Presence of

[his] Mark
Thomas Halbert
T

WILLIAM BRONAUGH
G MERCER
JEAN BROWN

Memorandum

That it is agreed between the within mentioned Partys that the within mentioned Thomas Halbert is to have one hundred Acres of the within mentioned Land three Years Rent free, & that he is to pay only six hundred & thirty Pounds of Tobacco untill the first Day of December which shall be in the Year of our Lord one thousand seven hundred & fifty six, at which time he begins to pay the full Rent within mentioned—

[his] Mark
Thomas Halbert
T

Printed document (Gunston Hall). GM wrote in the name and identification of the binding parties, the description of the property, special conditions, and the memorandum on the reverse side. GM also noted on the reverse side: "Counterpart of George Mason to Thomas Halbert—Lease for 200 Acres of Land at Accotinck for three Lives dated the 29th: Decemr. 1752—Rent 1050 lbs. Crop Tobo. clear of Caske pble on the first Day of December."

This is the first known land lease which GM arranged. Subsequent leases will be calendared in Appendix A. In the 18th century the word "indenture" was used for most agreements involving two or more parties. The lease was in the time-honored form that emerged from English land transactions in the Middle Ages, and follows the wording of "A Demise for three Lives of a Tenement" found in Orlando Bridgman, *Conveyances* (London, 1682), 15–17. A calendar of GM's land transactions is found in Appendix A of this volume.

[27]

Proposal to Settle Foreign Protestants on Ohio Company Lands

[6 February 1753]

At a Committee of the Ohio Company at Mr. Mercers at Marlborough in Stafford County February 6th. 1753.

On the Application of Mr. John Pagan Mercht. to know what Encouragement the Company would give to German Protestants who would come into this Colony to settle their Lands on the Ohio, he being now on a Voyage to Great Britain and intending to Germany from thence in Expectation of Engaging a great number of families to remove for that purpose in Case the Prejudices that have been artfully propagated among those people can be effectually removed and they can be convinced they may on equal if not better terms settle in this Colony than in Pensylvania or the other adjoining provinces. The Committee being satisfied that a large Accession of foreign Protestants will not only be advantageous to this Colony but the most effectual method of promoting a speedy Settlement on the Ohio, and extending and securing the same, before mentioning their own proposals think proper to observe.

That with regard to their religious Liberties, all foreign Protestants may depend on enjoying in this Government the Advantage of the Acts of Toleration in as full and ample manner as in any other of his Majesties plantations whatsoever, as great numbers of them have already experienced.

As to their civil Rights, they will be entitled to Naturalization which will be attended with all the Priviledges and Advantages of English natural born Subjects which are too many to be here enumerated. That of electing their Representatives in the Legislature is the greatest can be enjoyed by any Subjects, And the English Laws of Liberty and property are universally allowed to be the best in the World for securing the peoples lives and fortunes against Arbitrary power or any unjust Encroachments whatsoever.

The Levies in this Government which will be better understood by the name of Taxes are of three kinds Public, County, and Parish, The first of which is imposed by Act of Assembly on every person in the Colony liable to pay Levies for defraying the public Charge of this Colony once in two or three years, the second for defraying each County's Charge by the people living therein which is annually imposed, as is the last on the parishoners for maintaining the Minister and other parochial Charges. All these are paid in Tobacco the Staple of the Countrey, but no Male under sixteen years of Age or any white Woman is obliged to contribute thereto. These however are so moderate that we can venture to affirm that taking them all together one Year with the other they don't amount to above the Value of eight shillings Sterling per poll, and no Tax or Imposition is laid on anything necessary for food or raiment or the Subsistence of Life, Officers fees of all kinds and Law charges amount to little more than one half of the Charge of that Sort in the adjoining Colonies, Nor do we know any single place in his Majesties Dominions where the Subject is supported in all his Rights at so easy an Expence, Our Militia renders Soldiers useless and we have no Ecclesiastical Courts.

The Legislature by an Act made last year hath exempted all foreign protestants coming to Settle West of our Great Mountains from paying Levies of all kinds for the term of ten Years from their Settlement As by a Copy of the Act hereto annexed.

As the Committee looks on these Advantages to be sufficient to invite any Strangers not bypassed by some Prejudice to settle in this Colony preferably to any other of his Majesties plantations, which they are very desirous of, so for a further Encouragement they propose and undertake in behalf of the Company.

That as the said Company is intitled to five hundred thousand Acres of Land upon the River Ohio which is exempted from Quit rents for ten years after which term the Quit rent is no more than two Shillings Sterling yearly for every hundred Acres, Every foreign protestant coming in to Settle on the said Land shall have a good title made to him for as much as he desires at the rate of five pounds Sterling for every hundred Acres discharged of Quit rents for the same time allowed to the Company.

That all such as come in on those terms shall be supplied with Warehouses for their Goods convenient carriages for removing them to their Lands and such Quantity of Wheat Flour and Salt as they may want for their present Subsistence at the same Rates the Company pays for them, And such of them as have not ready money to pay for the Lands they desire to purchase shall be allowed two years Credit paying five per cent per Annum Interest.

As no Countrey in the world is better or more conveniently watered than Virginia the most convenient Passage will be into Potomack River which is Navigable by the largest Ships within ten Miles of the Falls. The Companys Store house at Rock creek where they may land and have their Goods secured is sixty miles from

Connococheege a fine road from whence they may go by Water in the Companys Boat to their Store house at Wills Creek about forty miles and from thence the Company have cleared a Waggon Road about sixty miles to one of the head branches of the Ohio navigable by large flat bottomed boats where they proposed to build Store-houses and begin to lay off their Lands. From this place there is no Obstruction to prevent such Vessels passing into the Mississippi which by the best Calculation is near a thousand miles, and as the Ohio from thence branches all the way down in numberless Branches it not only affords the convenience of making most of the Settlements by Water carriage but will enable the Settlers by the same carriage to carry on their Trade and supply themselves with every produce of those parts. The Rivers are Stocked with fine Fish and wild Fowl and the Woods abound with Buffaloes Elks Deer wild Turkeys and other Game of divers kind. The Land itself is universally allowed to be as good as can be far exceeding any Lands to the East of the great Mountains well Stocked with Timbers of all kinds and Stone for building, Slate Limestone Coal, Salt Springs and various Minerals. In short it is a Countrey that wants nothing but Inhabitants to render it one of the most delightful and valueable Settlements of all his Majesties plantations in America, And as the Value of those back Lands is now discovered and all the nations of Indians in those parts and for some hundred miles round are not only in Strict Amity and friendship with this Government but have faithfully promised to Assist and protect this English Settlement on the Ohio which has tempted many other persons to take up Lands in those parts and people are daily going to Settle them, there can be no doubt but the Settlement in those parts will soon be a very considerable one.

The Committee further Engages in behalf of the said Company for the greater Encouragement of such foreign protestants to lay off two hundred Acres of Land for a Town to be called Saltsburg in the best and most convenient place to their Settlement to be divided into Lotts of one Acre each, Eight of which to be appropriated for a Fort Church and other public buildings and every Tradesman or other person Settling and living three Years in the said Town to have one Lot forever paying the Quit rent of one farthing a Year,

JAMES SCOTT
GEORGE MASON
J MERCER

Ms (Mercer Papers, PPiU). Copied by Richard Rogers, Mercer's clerk, with "Signed by" preceeding the signatures. The postscript to Christopher Gist's instructions of 28 Apr. 1752, relating to the road from Wills Creek to the Monongela, was copied by Rogers following this proposal.

There is no evidence that Pagan was able to create any interest in this scheme, which growing tension between the French and English in the Ohio valley made impracticable. The legislation WHICH HATH EXEMPTED ALL FOREIGN PROTESTANTS from quitrents for ten years was passed in 1752—"An Act for encouraging persons to settle on the waters of the Mississippi"—(Hening, VI, 258) evidence that the House of Burgesses and Council were ready to compete with Pennsylvania and Maryland for the immigrating Germans. Meanwhile GM and his partners believed their own propaganda, for in July 1753 they authorized Gist, Cresap, and Capt. William Trent to erect a fort and lay off a townsite of 200 acres.

From Robert Dinwiddie to the Committee of the Ohio Company

[15 February 1753]

[. . .] I am sorry to hear by a letter from Mr. Trent, that some of the *Twigtwees* are gone over to the French, and that some French officers, &c. are at Logstown building of houses, &c. and that there are many others at their forts on the lakes, which he calls an army, but hope they are only trades from Canada. This information I had last week by express, which I returned, and desired him to get what farther intelligence he possibly could, between this and May, when I shall send some powder, arms, &c. to Winchester, a present to the Indians.

Printed in *Case of the Ohio Company* (NHi), 9–10. The Ms has not been found.

Trent and Cresap wrote Dinwiddie on 22 Jan. 1753 that some Indians had defected to the French, who were at Logstown and building a settlement. Dinwiddie had previously instructed Andrew Montour to invite the Six Nations' principal men to a council at Winchester scheduled for May, but Montour reported the Indians were intimidated by the French and would not be at Winchester for the promised doling out of royal presents (Mulkearn, 428–429). The tribe here referred to as the Twigtwees was an Algonquian tribe, the Twightwees. Frederick W. Hodge, ed., *Handbook of American Indians North of Mexico*, Smithsonian Institution Bureau of American Ethnology, Bulletin 30 (Washington, 1907), Pt. 1, 852.

Instructions to Christopher Gist

27 July 1753. Gist obtained a surveyor's commission from the College of William and Mary, and was ordered to measure the distance from the storehouse at Wills Creek to the forks of the Monongahela along "the Road clear'd by the Company." Gist was to learn what he could about the activities of William Russell, survey a townsite where Shurtees

Creek entered the Ohio, and make other surveys totaling 200,000 acres. Gist was cautioned to survey only the best lands, seek sites for company storehouses along the river, and "keep an exact Journal."

FC (Mercer Papers, PPiU). In Richard Rogers' handwriting, without the usual indication that committee members signed the instructions. The entire text is printed in Mulkearn, 149–150.

To John Hanbury

[[? *July 1753*. Minutes of the Ohio Company meeting of 23 July show that GM reported "that he has wrote to Mr. Hanbury for twenty Swivel Guns and other Arms and Ammunition for the Use of the Fort." See Mulkearn, 149. Not found.]]

Dogues Neck Survey Notes

[February 1754]

Begin at the head of the main S. Et. Fork of Baxter's als. Holt's Creek just in a small Fork of the sd. Creek at or near the place where Bushrod's back Line crosses the sd. Branch (NB close by the place is a large white Oak broke down) from thence run down the Meanders of the sd. Branch S 60. W. (at 57. ps. came to the head of the Creek as high as the Tide Water flows & the Marsh reaches, at which place it forks & a small Branch runs up towards the Neck Gate) Course continued in all 77 p. as far as the Bridge over the Creek to the Spring; thence going thro' the Marsh & Creek (they being hard frozen)—& over an Ivy Point S 55.W. 57. p. S 61 Wt. (Xing the Mouth of a Jut at 29 p) in all 37. p. then N 39. Wt. 40 p. N 69. Wt. 32.p. S 46 Wt. 50 p to the top of a long Point opposite the Mouth of the Mill Creek then S 81. W. (Xing a Jut at 16 p) in all 58 p. Then West (Xing a very short fork'd Jut at 70 p) Xing the Mouth of a large Jut at 150 p Xing a short bit of Marsh about 4 Chains wide at 184. ps. Xing another bit of Marsh wch. fork'd about 10 Chains wide at 210 P—in Xing this Marsh we were about 5 Chains from the Creek Side & about 2 Chains below the fork of sd. marsh. West Course continued in all 246. p to the Water Side at a Steep Bank at a Bay in the Mouth of the Creek, from whence the Point wch. makes the Mouth of the Creek on the other Side bore N 16. E. & the Distance about three hundred Yards NB in Xing several of the points upon the West Course we were at some Distance from the Creek sometimes near 20 poles thence down the Meanders of Occoquan Bay S 38. W. 18 p. to a small ps. of Marsh

[32]

abt. 5 Chains wide wch. forks abt. 50 yds. higher up thence, Xing the sd. marsh S 75. Wt. 24 p. to the Edge of the Bank at the upper End of Ward's old feild (NB from this place Mr. Cocks Fish House bore N 6. Wt. his Dwelling House N 12. Wt. Mr. Peakes House N. 54. Wt. the point above Mr. Peakes wch. makes the Narrows of Occoquan River bore N. 62. Wt. [. . .] the Main Road line N [59?] Wt. John Linton's plantation & House on the lower Side [of Occoquan?] 71 Wt. along point in Linton's Neck on the lower Side of Occoquan opposite to Sandy point bore S 69. Wt.) Thence down the The Meanders of Occoquan Bay along the Bank thro' Ward's old feild S 29. Wt. 100 ps. to a little bit of sunken ground by a Landing, then along the Shore (the Tide being very low) S 46. W. (Xing the Mouth of Ward's Jut at 160 p.) in all 178 p. West 51. P. N 61. W. 43. p. opposite to the Tump Island (from this Place Mr. Cock's Fish House bears N 31. E. his dwelling House N 21. E Mr. Peakes House N 9. Wt. the point above Mr. Peakes wch. makes the Narrows of Occoquan River N 14. W. the ferry House upon the Main Road on the lower Side of Occoquan N 36. W. John Linton's House on the lower side of Occoquan N 43. W. the Point on the lower Side of Occoquan opposite Sandy point bears S 84. Wt.) Thence along a Beach of Sand along the outside of the Horse Marsh S 67. Wt. 71 p. to Sandy Point viz. abt. 2 chains on the lower side thereof thence, still along the Sand beach between the Horse Marsh & the River, S 33. E. 64 p to the end of the Horse Marsh then along the Shore S 1. Wt. 32. p. S 27. E 42 p to the Half Way Landing (from wch. place a pocorsin runs a good Way up into the Woods) the same Course continued in all 76. P thence along the Bank Side thro' Dogues Island old feild S 44. E. 50. P. to the place where my Granfather formerly lived course continued in all 58 ps. to the old plantation Landing thence along the Shore S 47 E 68 p. to a porcorsin wch. runs a good Way into the woods commonly called the Short Marsh then S 32 E 27 p. S 13. E 40 p. to the lower Side the Mouth of high point Creek S 21 Wt. 94 ps. S 13. E 25 p. to the middle of high point Cliffs wch. make the Mouth of Occoquan on the upper Side (from this place free-stone point wch. made the Mouth of Occoquan on the lower Side bore S 54 Wt. Cockpit point S 37 W.—Stump Neck Point S 24 Wt.) then still along the Shore up the Meanders of Potomack River S 53. E 54 p. to the lower End of the Ash pocorsin, thence along the Outside of sd. Pocorsin (the Tide being very low) N 76 E 38 P. N 57 E 60 P. about 4 Chains above the upper End of the Ash pocorsin thence East 90 ps. S 78 E 41 p. to stony point (from whence Free-stone point bears S 62. p. w.

Cockpit Point S 44 Wt. Stump N[eck poi]nt S 31 Wt. Cornwallis's Point on the upper Side the Mouth of Mattawoman Creek S 19. Wt. the young Widow Pye's House S 9. E * John Pye's House S 66. E—Mr. Chapman's House East Crain Island N 84 E. Mr. Geo. Parker's House on the upperside of pomonkey Creek N 74 E) from stony point run up the River still along Shore—N 55 E 19 P N 35 E 28 p. N 83 E 126 P. within two Chains of Gabriel's Tobo. Bed Landing, then N 54. E 62. ps. N 86 E 33 P. N 67 E 34 p. six Chains below Miall's Landing then along the Shore & up the Bank N 89 E 44 p. then along the Bank Side N. 84 E. (at 60 ps. came to my dwelling House) Course continued in all 95. poles to the lower End of the great Marsh at the Foot of the Causeway just above the Causeway Landing thence along the Causeway & the high Land (NB from my House Cornwallis's Point on the upper side of Mattawoman Creek bears S 32. Wt. young Widow Pye's House S 24 Wt. the point right across from my House bears S 2. E. John Pyes House S 39 E Mr. Chapman's House S 83. E. Crain Island S 88 E Mr. Parker's house on the upper Side Pamonkey Creek bears N 75 E. right over Hollowing Point) from the foot of the causeway run up the Meanders of the marsh & the high Land thro' the edge of the Marsh N 12 E 62 p. N 2 E. (Xing Roberts's Jut at 15 p.) in all 86 p near the Side of the Causeway Creek a little below Crawford's Landing then Xing the sd. creek N 20 E 53. p. opposite the upper End of a little Island wch. is about 150 yards long & abt. 50 yds. from our course. the upper part of the sd. Island ends in a narrow point) then still thro' the Marsh N 36 p E (Xing a small Arm of the Marsh wch. runs a little into the woods at 26 p.) at 40 p. come opposite to the first fork of the middle creek Xing a Jut of the Middle Creek wch. runs abt. 200 yards into the Lands & forks, at 84. p. course continued in all 122 Poles to a hill Side in the Edge of the Woods (NB about the middle of this last Course runs thro' the Marsh a good way from the high Land) then down the river Side & thro' the Marsh S 86 E. 78 p. to the Side of the Creek about 12 Chains above Wm. Bronaugh's Landing (NB from this place to where the Course of Bushrod's back Line from Heryford's Corner Tree Xes this Creek is N 14 E 77 p. abt. two chains from the Creek side & 16 P. from Heryfords corner tree wch. stands upon the End of an Ivy Point by the Marsh on the other Side the Creek) from the Side of the Creek just above Wm. Bronaugh's landing run Xing the Creek & close by the tip Ends of several points S 27 E 85. p to the Sand Beach at the upper End of the great Marsh just above the Mouth of a small Jut wch. runs between Bosman's & Moores from this place the end of the Cause way point bore S 36 Wt. & the Edge of the Marsh at the Mouth of the middle Creek bore S 66. Wt. Then up the Meanders of potomack River S 30 E 32. p. S 73 E passing by a Valley wth. a sunken Marshy Place in it at 40 ps. Course contd in all 66 p. then S 80 E 27 P. to the edge of a Bank just above a Valley & a little peice of Marsh where formerly stood a Poplar the lower Corner of Bushrod's pattent upon Potomack River thence running wth. the Course of Bushrod's [. . .] xing [. . .] Wt. 29 p (passing by Bosmans [lower?] about 4 Chs. to the left at 50 p Xing the head of the little Jut between Bosman's & Moores 6 P passing by Wm. Moore's House abt. 150 yards to the Right at 135 p. Xing a miry Jut a Branch of Wm. Bronaugh's Creek at 150 P) at 222 P came opposite Heryford's Corner Tree upon the Creek Side 4 Chains to the left (Xing the sd. creek at 230 poles Xing the new Road to the Neck at 430 ps) 483 poles in all to the main S.E. fork of Baxter's Creek where we first begun to survey the Neck.—

To know the Quantity of Acres contain'd in the great Marsh we run from the lower end of the Marsh at the foot of the Causeway up the Meanders of potomack River along the sd. Causeway on Sand beach N 48 E 20 p. N 39 E (Xing a sand Jut that breaks thro' the Causeway at 40 p) in all 46 p then N 57. E 80 P N 19 E 38 P N 13 E 16 P. to the End of the Causeway Point at the Mouth of the Causeway Creek from whence the Mouth of the Middle Creek & the edge of the Marsh bore N 5. E. the edge of the Marsh at the Mouth of Wm. Bronaughs Creek bore N 23 E & the Sand Beach at Bosman's point at the upper End of the Great Marsh bore N 36. E.—

To survey the 300 acres wch. my Father purchased of Holt's Heirs in the Fork of Baxter's Creek (being a part of Drayton's Pattent sold by old Baxter to Wm. Holt) we estended Bushrod's back Line from the Place where it struck the S.E. fork of Baxter's Creek at the end of 483 Poles (viz from the Place from whence we begun to survey Dogues Neck) N 29 p Wt.—Xing a small Drein of the sd. Creek by the foot of the Hills at 77. ps. Xing a Branch of the Mill Creek at 290 poles in all 360 ps. (from the sd. S.E. fork of Baxters Creek & 843 poles from Bushrod's lower Corner upon Potomack River) to the Cool Spring Run about 150 yards from the Spring Head it being the main N Wt. fork of Baxter's Creek commonly called the Mill Jut or Creek & thence down the Meanders of the sd. Cool Spring Run S 3. Wt. at 70 ps. pass'd by the Mouth of the Fork wch. we before x'd wth. the back Line; Course continued in all 105. poles then S 26. W Xing the Neck old path abt. 100 yds. above the old Mill Dam at 72. ps. Course continued in all 146 ps. to the Si [de] of the Mill Creek abt. 150 Yards below where the Tide Water flows (NB—about the latter half of this Course we were generally about Six Chains from the Side of the Branch viz. to the left Hand of it) then S 23½ E Xing a small Jut & Marsh at 23 ps. in all 60 Ps—then S 4. Wt. 66 poles to a Landing at a point right in the Fork [. . .] the Mouth of the small Drein [. . .] flows into Baxter's of the creek—from thence up the Meanders of the SE fork of Baxter's Creek to Bushrod's Line —which having run in surveying Dogues Neck there was no Occasion to do over again—NB. just above the Mouth of the Mill Jut a large miry Jut makes out of the S.E. fork of Baxter's Creek wch. runs a good Way almost parrallel to the Mill Creek & makes the point between them very narrow—

Ms (Mason Papers, DLC). In GM's hand, endorsed "Feild Notes upon a Survey of Dogues Neck & the Land bought of Holt's Heirs in the fork of Baxter Creek—1754 G M"; the top of page one is titled "Notes upon a Survey made of Dogues Neck by George Mason in February 1754—."

Now known as Mason's Neck, DOGUES NECK extends into the Potomac channel between Occoquan and Pohick creeks. For detailed information on this ancestral property and identifications of persons mentioned in the manuscript, see the glossary in the front matter of this volume. The area is also described in Harrison, 41–56. A POCOSIN, variously spelled by GM, is a wooded marsh.

In the margin of the second page, near the asterisk, GM wrote: "* point opposite to my House bears S 51 E." On the third page, GM's marginal note reads: "NB course corrected from the poplar on the River [to?] Heryford's Spanish Oak N. 31. Wt."

For the sake of clarity, GM's original brackets have been altered to parentheses throughout. In the Ms he used both marks interchangeably. The portions with ellipses in brackets are illegible folds in the Ms.

To Thomas Waite

MR. WAITE   [21 June 1754]

The vestry are of Opinion that none of the bricks of the two first kilns are fit to be put into the Walls of the Glebe House but that what is done be pulled down & done with good bricks & that the Cellar windows be done with good ring oak or Locust & that in Case you begin a New that they will allow you Six months further than the time mentioned in our Bond to compleat it.

G MASON   JAMES HAMILTON
HUGH WEST   JOHN WEST
ABRAHAM BARNES   ROBERT BOGGESS
JOHN TURLEY   THOMAS WREN
CHARLES BROADWATER

FC (Truro Parish Vestry Book, DLC). Presumably the clerk copied this letter as ordered and it was signed by the vestrymen present.

GM had served on a committee with Daniel McCarty and Hugh West charged with superintending construction of buildings on the glebe lands—a parsonage and certain outbuildings. At the 21 June 1754 meeting the committee reported that Waite had not kept the terms of their agreement, for "the bricks whereof the dwelling House is at present done are very bad & not fit to be used." A year later, the vestry book records that McCarty was ordered to pay Waite £39 13s. as a first installment on their contract. GM objected and insisted that the minutes show: "NB that George Mason before Signing this order desired that his Dissent might be entered thereto."

Deed from Thomas Lord Fairfax

25 October 1754. A deed of land in Hampshire County, then a part of the Proprietor's Grant adjoining Frederick County in the colony of Virginia, to GM for 329 acres as surveyed by Guy Broadwater. Under terms of the deed, GM, his heirs and his assigns would hold the property forever, providing they paid the annual quitrent of one shilling for every fifty acres "yearly and every year on the Feast Day of St. Michael the Arch Angel."

Ms (Gunston Hall), and registered in the *Proprietor's Office Book M*, Fol. 508 (Vi). GM probably bought this tract for £2 or less, as Lord Fairfax sought "purchase money that was in most cases less and never more than that charged for crown lands." See Beverly W. Bond, Jr., *The Quit-Rent System in the American Colonies* (New Haven, 1919), 68ff. Northern Neck landholders paid a propriety quitrent until 1785, when the Virginia legislature abolished the system and placed all land titles on the same footing. GM's later land transactions are calendared in Appendix A of this volume.

To George Washington

DR SIR   Dogues Neck Augt. 21st: 1755.

I fully intended to have waited on you this Evening at Belvoir, but find my self so very unwell after my Ride from Court, that I am not able to stir abroad.

I have taken the Liberty to inclose you two Bills for £300 . . . Ster: drawn by Mr. Paymaster Genl. Johnston on Colo. Hunter, & an Ordr. on Govr. Dobbs from his Son for £18..15. Ster: also a Letter for Colo. Hunter, & another for his Honr. our Govr. If Colo. Hunter shou'd be in Town whilst you stay there, I shou'd esteem it a particular Favour if you'll be so kind to negotiate the Affair wth. him: it is indifferent to me whether he pays Cash or Bills, pble in London, at the prevailing Exchange at the time: 'tis probable it may suit him to take up the Ordr. on Govr. Dobbs. If you shou'd not see Colo. Hunter, please to leave the Bills wth. Govr. Dinwiddie—

I beg you'll excuse the Trouble I have taken the Liberty to give you on this Occasion, & give me Leave to assure you that Nothing wou'd give me more sensible Pleasure than an Opportunity of rendering you any acceptable Service.

I heartily wish you Health & every Felicity, & that you may find the new Regulations in our Milatary Affairs agreeable to yr. Wishes, & such as will enable you to accept the Command of our Troops with Honour—

I am wth. my Comps. to all at Belvoir Dr Sir Yr. most obdt. Hble Sert

G Mason

RC (Washington Papers, DLC). Addressed to "Geo: Washington Esqr." The version printed in Rowland, I, 62, is incorrectly dated 1 Aug. 1755.

BELVOIR was the home of William Fairfax, built on a bluff overlooking the Potomac, half way between Dogue's Neck and Mount Vernon. Washington was about to depart from Williamsburg at the urging of friends who favored his appointment as commander of a 4,000-man defense force. The General Assembly had voted a military appropriation of £40,000 as frontier conditions worsened after the fall of Fort Necessity. Washington was offered the command, refused it for a time, and then finally accepted. See Freeman, *Washington*, II, 106–13.

To George Washington

DEAR SIR   Dogues Neck June 12th. 1756

I take the Liberty to address you on Behalf of my Neighbour & your old School-fellow, Mr. Piper: who, without duly considering the Consequences, when he was at Winchester enlisted as a Searjeant in Capt. Mercer's Company; he has been down to consult his Father upon it, & finds him excessively averse to it, & as his principal Dependance is upon the old Man (besides the Duty naturally due to a parent) his disobliging him in an Affair of this Nature cannot but be highly detrimental to him. I need not then say that it wou'd be an Act of Humanity in Colo. Washington to discharge him! Mr. Piper tells me that he has never yet been attested, which seems so essential a Part of the Enlisting that I conceive he cou'd not be legally detain'd against his Will, but has still a Right to depart upon returning whatever Money he may have received. This I only hint, & submit it to your better Judgement. Be that as it will, Mr. Piper wou'd much rather chuse to receive his Discharge from you as a Favour than insist upon it as a Matter of Right. It wou'd be superfluous to add that your good Offices to Mr. Piper on this Occasion will ever be esteem'd the greatest Obligation on Dr Sir Yr. most obdt Servt.

G. MASON

RC (Washington Papers, DLC). Sent to Washington at the headquarters of the Virginia Regiment at Winchester. Endorsed.

CAPT. MERCER'S COMPANY was either the 2d Company, commanded by GM's cousin George, or the 8th Company, commanded by another cousin, John Mercer. The General Assembly act which raised the Virginia Regiment provided for a sergeant's daily pay of 18 pounds of tobacco, or the cash equivalent, so Piper would have to return WHATEVER MONEY HE MAY HAVE RECEIVED. See Hening, VI, 549.

From George Washington

[[*29 Aug. 1756*. Washington wrote GM regarding the pending arrival of Catawba and Cherokee warriors, who had agreed to join the Virginia Regiment on the frontier by terms of a treaty signed that spring. Apparently Washington wanted GM to procure presents for the Indians, judging from GM's reply of 13 Sept. 1756 (*q.v.*). Not found]].

To George Washington

DR. SIR   Dogues Neck Sept. 13th: 1756

Your Favour of the 29th. Augt. did not come to my Hands till Yesterday: as I did not see the Messenger who brought it, who I understood call'd at my Building on his Way to Fredericksburg, I shall keep this, a Day or two, to see if he will call for an Answer as he returns from thence; if he does not, I shall send it to Mount Vernon, & beg the favr. of yr. Brother to convey it by the first Safe Hand to Winchester.

By the inclosed List you will be able to judge whether we can furnish such Goods as will be necessary for our Friends the Catawba & Cherokee Indians.

The principal Articles wanting are Kettles & strip'd Duffeilds: I much doubt whether they can be got on this Side [of] Philadelphia, & perhaps not there; as the Indian-Trade has been at a Stand a good while.

The Goods are all chd. at the genuine fst. Cost & Shop Notes; upon which, I think, we can't afford to take less than 100 per Ct. Virga. Cury—which I hope will not be thought unreasonable; considering the Height of Freight & Insurance, & the high Exchange we shall be obliged to pay in papr. Cury. for Bills to make a Remittance. I hope I shall not have any thing to do with the C[olone]l, or C[om]m[itt]ee for tho' I have no Objection to any of the Gentlemen, in their private, yet they are the last People in the World I shou'd chuse to have any Concern with in their public Capacity! An uncontroulable Power of delaying, altering, or rejecting the Accts. of private persons, for Articles furnish'd, or Services done, by their own Orders, is a very discouraging Circumstance, 'tis a power which I dare say none of the Government's Officers in England wou'd offer to assume, & I am mistaken if the frequent Exercise of it here has not been highly detrimental to the Public, as well as greatly injurious to many private People!

My Friend Capt. Mercer gave me Reason to flatter myself with the Thoughts of having your Company in Dogues Neck some time this Month; but I am afraid, if you wait the Arrival of the Warriours of the South, I shall not have the Pleasure of seeing you [for] a long time. We have been often made to expect great Matters from these Cherokees; & yet I stedfastly believe they have no Thoughts of giving themselves any further Trouble than to get what they can from us, by amusing us with fair Promises!—

I very sincerely wish you Health, Success, & every Felicity & am Dr Sir Yr. most obdt. Hble Servt.

G MASON

RC (MH). Addressed and endorsed: "From Colo. Geo: Mason/13th Sepr. 1756/Enclosing a list of India Goods."
Washington apparently made arrangements with GM regarding supplies for the frontier during this period, and it may have been connected with the appointment of GM as a militia colonel. On 8 Oct. 1755 Washington instructed Capt. Thomas Waggener that "If Powder and Lead can not be had in Alexandria, you are to apply to Mr. George Mason, who will Supply you with what you think proper." Eleven months later, after the 29 Aug. 1756 letter had been dispatched with its order for goods, Washington informed Gov. Dinwiddie he had "Not yet heard from Colonel Mason." This seems to be the first use of a title GM was to carry the rest of his life. Dinwiddie had dispatched two commissioners to the Catawba and Cherokee tribes who successfully negotiated a treaty in the spring of 1756. The Indians were to be protected by Virginia and to send warriors who would join Virginia in attacks on the French and their allied tribesmen. GM's skepticism regarding the Indians was warranted by the facts, for although 400 warriors responded to Dinwiddie's call, they were unreliable, caroused a good deal, and incessantly demanded presents (see R. A. Brock, comp., The Official Records of Robert Dinwiddie, . . . [Richmond, 1883–1884], II, 641). Meanwhile, Washington had returned about 15 Sept. from the frontier to Fairfax County for a meeting of Lawrence Washington's heirs.

To George Washington

DEAR SIR   Dogues Neck 4th Jany 1758

The Bearer (my Cousin French Mason) waits on you with an Acct. I recd. from Capt. Trent, amounting to £165..12..2¾ as I have an imediate Call for a pretty large Sum, you will particularly oblige me in sending the Cash per this Bearer; who will give a Rect. for what he receives—if you happen not to have the Cash at Home, I must beg the favour of you to order it for me by the first safe Hand from Winchester. I intended to have waited on you myself this Day or Tomorrow, with this Acct. bu[t] am prevented by an Express this Morning from Chappawamsic, to acquaint me that my Sister Selden (who has been ill along time) is now given over by her Physician, & not expected to live Many Hours; & I am just setting off upon the Melancholly Errand of taking my last Leave of her!

I hope you will comply with the Opinion & Advice of all your Friends, & not risque a Journey to Winchester till a more favourable Season of the Year, or a better State of Health, will permit you to do it with Safety; & give me Leave Sir to mention another Consideration, which I am sure will have Weight with you—in attempting to attend the Dutys of your Post at a Season of the Year when there is no Room to expect an Alarm; or any thing extraordinary to require your Presence, you will, in all probability, bring on a Relapse, & render yourself incapable of serving the public at a time when there may be the utmost Occasion; & there is nothing more certain than that a Gentleman in your Station owes the Care of his Health & Life not only to himself & his Friends, but to his Country. If you contin[ue] anytime at Mount Vernon, I will do myself the pleasure of spending a Day or two with you very soon.

I am wth. Mrs. Mason's Comps & my ow[n] to yr. Brother, his Lady, & yrself. Dr. Sir Yr. affecte. hble Sert

G. MASON

P. S.

You will be pleased to return the Acct. per the Bearer; for I have not any Copy of it; & if it's necessary for you [to] take it in, I will enter it in our Books, & send it [to] you again—

RC (Washington Papers, DLC). Addressed to "George Washington Esqr." The version printed in Rowland, I, 65–66, omits the postscript.

Washington was convalescing at Mount Vernon from an attack of dysentery when GM wrote this letter. GM's SISTER SELDEN was his only sister, Mary Thomson Mason Selden, whose predicted death soon sent GM into mourning.

To George Washington

DEAR SIR

Race Ground at Boggess's Saturday 6th May 1758—5 o'Clock P: M:—

 The Bearer French Mason, a Relation of mine, has an Inclination to serve his Country upon the intended Expedition; I recommended him to the president for a Lieutenancy in the Regiment now raising; but unfortunately before he reachd Wmsburg every Commission was disposed of; otherwise he was sure of succeeding, as the President wou'd have done him any Service in his Power—as there are some Vacancys in yr. Regiment, his Honour has been so kind to give him a Letter of Recommendation to you. Had I known of these Vacancy's, I shou'd have taken the Liberty of applying to you sooner on his Behalf; for as he purposes to continue longer in the Service than this Campaign, & push his Fortune in that Way of Life, he wou'd prefer a Commission in yr. Regiment; & it wou'd give me great Satisfaction that he was under the imediate Command of a Gentleman for whom I have so high an Esteem—you may be assured, Sir that I wou'd not recommend a person to your Favour who I did not, from my own Knowledge, believe to be a Young fellow of Spirit & Integrity. He has lived a good while with me, & if I am not greatly deceived; he has personal Bravery that will carry him thro' any Danger with Reputation, & this Opinion I am the more confirm'd in, as he never was a flashy fellow. He has been but little in Company, & has not that Address which is requisite to set a Man in an advantageous Light at first, but he is a very modest Lad, & does not want parts; & I am confident will endeavour to deserve your good opinion, as well as to support the Character I have given him. He this Moment came up from Wms.burg, & found me here, & as I thought there was no time to be lost, I advised him to set off instantly for Winchester, as soon as I cou'd procure this Scrap of paper, & get a place in the Croud to sit down to write. If he fails in a Commission, he had Thoughts of going out a Voluntier but as he has but a small Fortune, I advised him against it. Whatever you are so kind to do for him on this Occasion I shall always regard as a particular Obligation on me. I beg you'll excuse this Trouble & believe on all Occasions very sincerely Dear Sir Yr. most obdt. Hble. Sert.

G MASON

I have really wrote this in such a Hurry, that I am afraid it's hardly intelligible

RC (Washington Papers, DLC). Addressed "To Collo George Washington/ Fort Loudon."

The RACE GROUND AT BOGGESS'S was a field belonging to the Robert Boggess family, located near Pohick Church, Fairfax County. The PRESIDENT was John Blair, head of the Virginia Council and acting governor of the colony between Jan. and June 1758. French Mason, GM's cousin, apparently was not destined for an ensign's commission in Washington's regiment. See Blair's letter dated 3 May 1758 in Hamilton, ed., *Letters to Washington*, II, 283–84, and Washington's reply in Fitzpatrick, ed., *Writings of Washington*, II, 197. GM's letter to Blair has not been found.

From George Washington

[[*8 May 1758*. Washington replied to GM's letter of 6 May (*q.v.*) which recommended French Mason for a commission in the Virginia regiment under his command. GM read Washington's reasons for rejecting his cousin and declared he was "perfectly satisfied." Not found]].

To George Washington

DEAR SIR   Dogues Neck 16th May 1758—

I am favour'd wth. yrs. of the 8th Inst. per French Mason, & am perfectly satisfied wth. the Justice of yr. Reasons for not providing for him in yr. Regiment at this Time. I am convinced, from yr. State of the Case, that it cou'd not well have been done without prejudicing the Service. He tells me you were kind enough to promise him a Commission the next Vacancy that happens. I shou'd have been very glad his Fortune wou'd have supported him as a Volunteer: both he & I were very fond of his entering as such in yr. Regiment; but I really did not think it advisable that he shou'd run his own little Estate in Debt upon the Occasion: you know what kind of an Establishment our Virga. Troops are on—Nobody can tell how soon they may all be disbanded, without any Provision for a broken Leg, or a shortned Arm! or if they shou'd happen to be kept up for a good many Years, how possible is it for an Officer to be reduced without being guilty, or so much as accused of any Misbehaviour? Faith these are discourageing Circumstances. On the British Establishment a young fellow may venture to dip his Estate a little on the Road to Preferment, where he is sure, if he behaves well, that a Commission is some sort of a Provision for Life; but here I really

[43]

think a young Man who enters into the Service, & has but a small Estate of his own ought if possible to preserve it unimpair'd, to return to, in Case of a Disappointment, or an Accident. These Reasons have influenced me to dissuade French Mason from entering as a Volunteer, & as he is very fond of trying a Soldier's Life, & indeed I found it absolutely necessary that he shou'd do so, as the only Means of getting him clear of a very foolish Affair he is likely to fall into with a Girl in this Neighbourhood, I have advised him to enlist in the new Regiment, if he can be made a Serjeant: My Reason for advising him to enlist in that Regiment, is that if he shou'd be disappointed in getting a Commission, he may if he pleases, quit the Service the first of December next; whereas from the Act of Assembly, it appears to me that the Men who enlist in the old Regiment may be detain'd as long as any Troops are kept up in the Pay of this Government; at least it may admit of a Dispute. I speak this to you only as my own private Opinion, without any Intention of making it public to the prejudice of the recruiting Service.

If he shou'd have the good fortune to get a Commission, tho' he will accept of the first that offers in either Regiment, he will prefer an Ensignsy in yr. Regiment to a Lieutenancy in the other, & I have advised him if he shou'd get a Comn. in Colo. Byrd's Regiment to exchange it if he can by any Means for one in yours. I shall relye Sir on your good offi[ces] in his Favour whenever a Vacancy happens, & I flatter myself that, by a strict A[d]herence to hi[s] Duty, he will strive to deserve your good Opinion. I very sincerely wish yo[u] Health & every Felicity & am Dr. Sir   Yr. most obd. Ser

G. MA[SON]

RC (Washington Papers, DLC). Addressed to Washington at "Fort Loudoun."

THE JUSTICE OF YR. REASONS appears to have extinguished French Mason's ambitions for a military career, despite GM's continued flattery. THE NEW REGIMENT was authorized by the House of Burgesses in Apr. 1758, and was under the command of William Byrd III of Westover. The two regiments were to join Gen. Forbes in his attack on Fort Duquesne, but, so far as we know, without French Mason in the ranks.

A portion of the last paragraph is missing because of a tear along the right margin of the final page.

A Loan Agreement for Maurice Pound

Fairfax County October 1759

Maurice Pound a Native of Germany having setled at Colchester in the said County about three years since on two Lotts which he purchased (one of which he has improved according to Law) and

planted a Vineyard on them; during which time he has lived at his own Expence without any profit from his Vineyard having been much retarded in his Undertaking by these two last dry summers, & having one of his Lots yet to save by building the legal Improvements; with a Winepress & other Conveniencys, proposes to any Gentlemen who are desirous to help him, & encourage & promote an Undertaking likely to be so usefull, & beneficial to this Colony to oblige himself to improve his other Lott, & to mortgage both the said Lotts to any Gentlemen who will advance him one hundred pounds Current money the Interest of which he proposes to pay Yearly & the principal sum Advanced within five Years, & the whol time to prosecute with Industry all measures possible to bring his Vineyard to perfection, (a thing not [to] be done at once) of which he has a most encouraging prospect if seasons will permit.—
N.B. the Lotts to be mortgaged to any one or more of the Subscribers in Trust for all—I have known Maurice Pound ever since he lived in Colchester he has the Character of a very honest industrious Man: I have been frequently in his Vinyard upon which he has an infinite deal of Labour, & I realy believe if our Soil & Climate is capable of producing good Wine that he will, wth. proper Encouragement, bring it to perfectin tho' I don't think less than £150 will do as I am sensible that his present Circumstances are too low to carry on his undertaking without assistance & from my Opinion of the Intigrity a Capacity of the Man, I will advance him ten Pounds upon the above mentioned Terms, & I wil[l] readily join with the other Subscribers in making up whatever Sum they shall judge necessary for the Purpose.

G:MASON

Ms (PHi). In a copist's handwriting, and signed first by GM, then by Charles [Grayson?], Daniel French, George William Fairfax, Spence Grayson, Thomson Mason, Benjamin Grayson, and George Washington.

By the autumn of 1759 GM was well settled in his new home, Gunston Hall, which provided ample room for bottled goods in its wine cellar. The agreement resulted in loans totaling £118 for Pound. The Virginians' belief that their colony might somehow become a vast vineyard is also reflected in "An act for encouraging the making [of] Wine" in Hening, VIII, 364–366.

The Ms is torn or faded in several places, which accounts for the doubtful signature and blank spaces.

Endorsement on William Buckland's Indenture to Thomson Mason

8th. Novr. 1759

The within named William Buckland came into Virginia with my Brother Thomson Mason, who engaged him in London, & had a very good Character of him there; during the time he lived with me he had the entire Direction of the Carpenter's & Joiner's Work of a large House; & having behaved very faithf[ully in] my Service, I can with great Justice recommend him, to any Gentleman that may have Occasion [to] employ him, as an honest sober diligent Man, & I think a complete Master of the Carpenter's & Joiner's both in Theory & Practice.

G Mason

Ms (photostat, DLC; original owned by Daniel R. Randall, Annapolis, Md., 1933). In GM's handwriting, on the reverse side of Buckland's indenture dated 4 Aug. 1755.

Buckland signed the indenture as a carpenter and joiner on 4 Aug. 1755 in London, agreeing to serve four years at £20 per annum salary. He arrived at Gunston Hall after work on the main building had begun but rapidly impressed GM with his skill and subsequently supervised construction until the house was finished in 1758. Buckland went on to achieve considerable success as an architect in the Virginia-Maryland tidewater (see R. R. Beirne and J. H. Scarff, *William Buckland, Architect of Virginia and Maryland* [Baltimore, 1958], especially the chapter on Gunston Hall).

Portions of several words obscured by a blotch on the document have been restored within brackets.

To Robert Dinwiddie

Sir
Sept. 9. 1761.

As we may expect a peace next Winter and have no reason to doubt North America will be secured to the British Government, and then Liberty will be granted to his Majestys Subjects in those Colonies to Settle the Lands on Ohio, we the Committee of the Ohio company think it a proper time as soon as peace is concluded to apply for a Grant for the Lands intended us by his Majestys instructions to Sir William Gooch, and have for that purpose sent over a Petition to his Majesty, and a large and full State of our Case and have employed Mr. Charlton Palmer a Man we are inform'd of great capacity and diligence to Solicit our cause and Endeavour by all means to get us a patent in England. He will be directed to apply to our Members in London for their Advice and Assistance, and as no Person knows the Affair better than Mr. Dinwiddie, nor can it be imagined any of the Company have such an acquaintance or interest with Persons in Power, let us beg you will please exert yourself in getting us a patent by natural bounds on the best terms possible for rather than be remitted to the Government here, who from jealousy or some other cause have ever endeavoured to disappoint us in every design we could form to settle and improve the Lands. We will agree to any reasonable consideration for such a Deed from England, but if this cannot be obtained then the most plain and positive instructions to the Governor of Virginia be procured on terms the most advantageous to the Company

We are Sir, with the greatest esteem and regard Yr. very huble. Servts.

Committee $\left\{\begin{array}{l} \text{JAMES SCOTT} \\ \text{G MASON} \\ \text{THOS. LUD. LEE} \\ \text{RICHARD LEE} \end{array}\right.$

Ms (Mercer Papers, PPiU). Addressed: "To Robert Dinwiddie Esqr, London." In the handwriting of Richard Rogers, John Mercer's clerk.

Dinwiddie left Virginia in 1758, but he retained his full share in the Ohio Company and was therefore personally interested in a successful renewal of the original 1749 grant. Following years of inactivity, the company affairs were revived by the French withdrawal from the Ohio valley. Both George Mercer and Thomas Cresap sought Col. Henry Bouquet's aid "in procuring German and Swiss settlers" for company lands. Bouquet, the commandant at Fort Pitt, rebuffed them and in Oct. 1761, issued a proclamation which banned white settlements west of the Alleghenies (see Sosin, *Whitehall and the Wilderness,* 42–43). Meanwhile, John Mercer began corresponding with the London solicitor, Charlton Palmer; and in Oct. 1760, GM authorized Edward Athawes, a London merchant, to pay Palmer's fees "and all other Expences attending the said Application" for a confirmation of the earlier grant.

Petition to King George III

[9 Sept. 1761]

The petition of the committee of the Ohio Company, in your Majesty's colony and dominion of Virginia, in behalf of themselves, and the rest of their partners

Most humbly sheweth,

THAT your Majesty's late royal grandfather, (of blessed memory) was graciously pleased, by his additional instruction, to his lieutenant governor of Virginia, dated at his court at St. James's, the sixteenth day of March, in the twenty second year of his reign, for the considerations therein mentioned, to direct, and require his said lieutenant governor forthwith, to make a *grant or grants to your petitioners and their associates, of two hundred thousand acres of land, betwixt Romanetto and Buffalo Creeks, on the South-side of the river Alleghany, otherwise Ohio, and betwixt the two Creeks and Yellow Creek, on the North-side of the said river; or in such other parts to the West of the Great Mountains, in the said colony*

[47]

of Virginia, as should be adjudged most proper by your petitioners,
for making settlements thereon, and extending the British trade in
those parts, free from the payment of any rights, as also from the
payment of any quit-rents, for the space of ten years, from the date
of their grants; at the expiration of which term your petitioners
were to pay the usual quit-rents, for so much of the said lands as
they should have cultivated within that time. Provided, that such
grant or grants, should be inserted a clause or clauses, declaring, that
if your petitioners and their associates did not erect a fort on the said
lands, and place a sufficient garrison therein, for the security and
protection of the settlers, and likewise seat at their proper expence
an hundred families thereon, in seven years the said grant or grants
should be void. And the said lieutenant governor was thereby authorized and required as soon as the said two hundred thousand
acres should be settled, a fort erected, and a sufficient garrison
placed therein, to make a farther grant or grants to your petitioners
and their associates, of three hundred thousand acres more, under
the like conditions and restrictions, as the first two hundred thousand acres, and adjoining thereto, within the said limits.

That your petitioners upon the first notice of his majesty's said
instruction, not only applied to the said lieutenant governor, for the
said grant or grants, but at their own expence employed proper
persons to discover the lands upon the Ohio, and cultivate a friendship with the Indians on that river, and advanced several thousand
pounds to begin and carry on a trade with them; besides taking
every other step to comply with the conditions of their said grant,
according to the true intent and meaning of the said instruction,
until the French encroachments upon your majesty's dominions in
those parts, brought on a war, in which your petitioners effects were
indifferently plundered, by their pretended Indian friends, and the
French and Indian enemy; and their debtors in those parts, were for
the most part either killed, dispersed, or ruined. Notwithstanding
which endeavours, expences, and losses, your petitioners have hitherto been unable to obtain any grant, or grants for any part of the
lands mentioned in the said instruction; but have been from time to
time put off, by divers pretences, particularly, that the Indians
would not suffer the said lands to be settled; though the Indians
consent to settle thereon, had been obtained at the treaty at Loggs-
town, in June 1752, and your petitioners caused several families to
settle, and soon after set about building a fort, at the place now
called Pittsburg. And although the government of Virginia pitched
upon the same place as most convenient to build a fort on, at the

governments expence, and took the possession thereof from your petitioners, engaging by proclamation, to give one hundred thousand acres of land contiguous thereto, and one hundred thousand acres more, on or near the Ohio, without any rights, or paying any quit rents, for the term of fifteen years, for the encouragement of such officers and soldiers, (over and above their pay) as should enter into his majesty's service, to erect and support the said fort. Yet no other fort was ever built, or undertaken there, but that begun by your petitioners, till the same was retaken from the French, in one thousand seven hundred and fifty eight. Your petitioners having been at the whole expence of that building there, when the French took possession of the Ohio, in April 1754.

That your petitioners have applied to the government here several times, since the possession has been regained, for leave to survey their lands, in order to obtain their grants, but without any manner of success: And at the same time they have great reason to believe, that divers persons are soliciting for grants of the same lands from Pennsylvania, and other places; but as they are conscious, that besides the advantage of his late majesty's instruction in their favour, they cannot be justly charged with either having done, or omitted any thing, to forfeit their right under the same; they most humbly submit their case to your majesty's consideration, and pray that you will be graciously pleased, in consideration of their great losses and expences, and to avoid any farther charges or contestations, by some positive and direct instruction to your governor here, to order your petitioners may have a grant or grants for the said lands, upon the terms aforesaid, or such others, as to your majesty, in your great wisdom shall seem just. And your petitioners will ever pray.

PHIL. LUD. LEE,
G. MASON,
JAMES SCOTT,
J. MERCER,
THOMAS LUD. LEE.

Text printed here is from *The Case of the Ohio Company*, 25-26. The Ms is missing. A search for the original in the P.R.O., London, was unavailing.

The petition might have been strengthened with details of how the company property had been used by the crown or destroyed by the enemy. Besides the pivotal fort which the French seized at the forks (Fort Duquesne), the British had commandeered the storehouse at Wills Creek and it was now part of Fort Cumberland. Meanwhile, the storehouse William Trent built on the Redstone (Redstone Old Fort) had been seized by the French. The company never used these outposts for its purposes when the British and Virginians later reoccupied the area. The DIVERS PERSONS seeking land grants from Pennsylvania were a group of Lancaster and Philadelphia merchants and their agents, who eventually designated themselves as the "Suffering Traders" and began open competition with the Ohio Company for conflicting land claims in the Ohio valley.

To Capel and Osgood Hanbury

GENTM,   Virginia Sepr. 10th. 1761.

As we have reason to expect a peace soon, and think it will be then practicable to prosecute our intended Settlements upon the Ohio, we have thought it absolutely necessary to employ some Person in England to make application at the proper Boards on our behalf, as well as to present a Petition to his Majesty shewing the Reasons why we have hitherto been disabled to comply with the Terms mentioned in the royal Instructions and praying some further Indulgency's and for this purpose we have transmitted to Mr. Charlton Palmer a full State of the Companys Case and have directed him to confer with you upon the Subject

We have met with so many Discouragements from the Government in Virginia (many of the Council being concerned in large Entries of Land themselves) that rather than have any further Altercation here we would willingly pay any reasonable Consideration for a Patent in England by natural bounds which we hope will not be thought unreasonable when the expence we have been at is considered, and the great benefit that will result to the public from our Discovery's, and there cannot be a stronger proof of the public principles upon which the Company have acted than that they have expended a much larger Sum in searching and discovering the inland parts of this Continent to the Westward than the Composition of all our Lands would have amounted to according to the common Rules of granting Lands the inhabited parts of the Colony and it is notorious that till our Discovery the Countrey upon the Ohio, and the fatal Consequences of the French Incroachments then were altogether unknown or unattended to. The Inhabitants even of this Colony being utterly unacquainted with the Geography of that Countrey, as is plain from all the late Maps published either here or in England—which are actually laid down from the Journals and Discovery's of our Agents, but if a Patent cannot be obtained in England, we then hope that by a fresh Instruction to the Governor of Virga. we may have our time for Settling the Lands prolonged. The Article of the Fort altered, or at least mitigated that we may be allowed to contract with a Surveyor of our own without being liable to the high fees settled by Law, and that we maybe permitted to Survey our Lands in small Tracts. We think there cannot be any just Objection to prolong our time for making Settlements, as the Incroachment of the French and the War have hitherto rendered it impossible to proceed in them. And we are at this time told that the Governor has Instructions to grant no Lands upon the Ohio for fear of giving Offence to the Indians. Upon the whole we make no doubt of your Assisting and supporting us in every thing that you judge conducive to our common Interest and are, Gentlemen, Yr. most Hble Servts.

> JAMES SCOTT
> J MERCER
> G MASON
> THOS. LUD LEE
> RICHARD LEE

Committee

Ms (Mercer Papers, PPiU). Addressed: "To Messrs Capel & Osgood Hanbury/Merchts. in London." In the handwriting of Richard Rogers, John Mercer's clerk.

Capel and Osgood HANBURY may have held an interest in the Ohio Company, for their brother John Hanbury, an original shareholder, died in 1758. The Virginia partners apparently believed that they retained some of the influence at Whitehall held by their late brother. THE LATE MAPS PUBLISHED EITHER HERE OR IN ENGLAND included the Fry-Jefferson map (1751) and Lewis Evans map (1755). Both indicated increasing knowledge of the transmontane region and its waterways. THE ARTICLE OF THE FORT was a key provision in the 1749 grant. It charged the company with building a fort and providing "a sufficient garrison therein for the security and protection of the settlers." Once the fort had been built and garrisoned, an additional 300,000 acres were to be added to the first 200,000 acres. Apparently the company sought permission to make independent surveys, thus avoiding payment of established fees (Hening, III, 329-33). Gov. Fauquier had been instructed by the Board of Trade in June 1760, to make no land grants in the Ohio Valley "untill His Majesty's further pleasure be known." See Sosin, *Whitehall and the Wilderness*, 45. Sosin points out that the British administrators believed the best way to keep the frontier Indians quiet was to deny permission for white settlements in "open Violation of our late solemn Engagements." The Treaty of Easton (1758) had promised the Indians undisturbed possession of their hunting grounds west of the Alleghenies.

Ohio Company Advertisement

[17 February 1763]

A GENERAL MEETING of the OHIO COMPANY is desired at *Stafford* Court-House, in *Virginia*, on Tuesday the fifth of March next. It is hoped that the several members, who are able to attend then, will not fail, as the Business of the Company has suffered very much from their neglecting to meet for so long a time. To prevent the trouble of Law-Suits, and further Notice, those who have any accounts to settle with the Company are also requested to attend at the time and place above-mentioned.

By order of the Committee of the OHIO COMPANY.

Printed from Annapolis *Maryland Gazette*. Also in *Pennsylvania Gazette*, 24 Feb. 1763.

GM was conducting business as the company treasurer and presumably drafted this notice. THE TROUBLE OF LAW-SUITS is demonstrated by the calendar of legal actions GM pursued on the company's behalf.

Power of Attorney to George Mercer

[29 March 1763]

At the request of George Mason the following Power of Attorney was recorded March the 30th. one thousand seven hundred and sixty Three To Wit, To All whome these presence shall or may concern I George Mason of the County of Fairfax in the Colony and Dominion of Virginia send Greeting—

Whereas the committee of the Ohio company by their resolve of the second day of this Instant March did agree and direct that about Fifty Acres of the said Companies Land at Wills Creek adjoining to Fort Cumberland [shou]ld be laid off into Town Lotts with about Two hundred and fifty acres of the Adjacent high Land for out Lotts to be Annexed to the Town (which is to be called Charlottesburg) in such a manner that one such out Lott shall forever belong to, and be deemed appurtenance to the Town Lott to which it was at first annexed and on no Account separated from it & that Colo George Mercer be Impowered to lay off and dispose of the same upon the Companies Account either by Leases for Three lives with privilege of renewing the said Leases for two Lives more upon paying a fine of twenty Shillings sterling for each life so renewed or for the term of fifty years at an Annual Ground rent of Ten shillings sterling or if the purchasers insist upon having a fee simple estate in their Lotts that the said Lotts be sold to the highest bidder reserving in the Deeds an annual Ground Rent of Five Shillings Sterling Money. That the persons who take lotts either by Leases or Deeds be obliged to Build on each Town Lott within Three years from their Respective Titles one House at least Twenty feet long and sixteen feet wide with a Brick or Stone Chimney which is always to be kept in repair under penalty of forfeiting their Lotts and that no house or Buildings whatsoever shall be erected on the out Lotts except stables or Cow Houses and that the usual covenants for distress and reentry upon the nonpayment of the [recorded?] Rent be inserted in the said Deeds and Leases. And as the land upon which the said Lotts are to be laid off or pattented in the name of me the said George Mason in Trust for the said [Ohio Company, the said George Mercer is hereby impowered and required to execute deeds and leases] As above mentioned to the persons purchasing and taking the *said* Lotts or that I should make a power of Attorney to the said George Mercer to execute and acknowledge the said Deeds and Leases in my Name. Know ye therefore that I the said George Mason in pursuance of the said resolve have made ordained constituted and appointed and by these presents Do make ordain Constitute and appoint the said George Mercer my true and Lawfull Attorney for me and in my name but in trust for the said Ohio Company to make seal and deliver as my Deeds all and every such Deeds and Leases as maybe Necessary to grant and Demise unto all and every person or persons willing to Lease and purchase the same all or any of the Lotts in the said Town of Charlottesburg and the out lotts appurtenant to the same at and under the several Rents purchases Conditions and Agreements mentioned in the above recited resolve of the said Committee of the Ohio Company and also for me in my Name to acknowledge all and every such Deeds and Leases by him so made Sealed and Delivered pursuant to the Laws and practices of the Province of Maryland, so as to render the same Valid and Effectual to all intents and purposes to the several purchasers and Lessees and to receive from the several purchasers the purchase Money for such Lotts and the Counterparts of their several Deeds and Leases to be signed Sealed Executed and Acknowledged by the several purchasers and Leases and generally for me and in my Name to do perform and execute all & every such Act and Acts thing and things as shall or may be requisite and Necessary on or about the premises in as full and ample manner to all intents Constructions and purposes as I myself might or could if I was personally present Ratifying confirming and holding for good and Valid whatsoever my said Attorney shall lawfully do or cause to be done in or about the premises by Virtue of these presents. In Witness whereof I have hereunto set my hand and Affixed my Seal this Twenty ninth day of March in the Year of our Lord one thousand Seven hundred and sixty three.

G MASON

Sealed and Delivered in Presence of ⎫

George Heryford   Robert R. Haskins ⎭

Tr (Frederick County Land Records H, MdAA).
Frustrated in their efforts to have their original grant confirmed, the Ohio Company shareholders resolved on 2 Mar. 1763 to lay out a town on their property adjoining the Wills Creek storehouse and sell or lease lots. Their resolution, printed in Mulkearn, 181–182, is followed verbatim in many portions of this document. James says (*Ohio Company*, 106) that the proposed town site was part of the Walnut Bottom Tract acquired by GM in 1753 for the company's use. George Mercer proceeded to Fort Cumberland and made a survey in the spring of 1763. A sale of lots was scheduled when rumors cast a cloud over their endeavor. Mercer then traveled to New York and sought permission from General Amherst for the company *"to build a town on their own lands,* not suspecting a possibility of a denial, as the fort was in a ruinous condition" (*Case of the Ohio Company*, 29). Amherst denied Mercer's request on the grounds that the proposed town site was of strategic importance to the crown. Thus thwarted, Mercer returned to Virginia and in July 1763, the impatient shareholders met and voted to dispatch Mercer to London, hoping to settle their problem by obtaining an unimpeachable confirmation of the 1749 grant (Mulkearn, 182; Alfred P. James, *George Mercer of the Ohio Company: A Study in Frustration* [Pittsburgh, 1963], 40–44).
The wording in faded portions in the document has been restored from the company minutes. The Ms is endorsed: "March the 30th: 1763. Came before me the Subscriber one of his LShips Justices of the Provincial Court of Maryland Geor Harford and Robert Haskins Subscribing Witnesses to the within power of Attorney and made oath on the Holy Evangs. of Almighty God that they saw the within Named Geo Mason sign and execute the within power of attorney and that they Subscribed their Names as Witnesses thereto. JOHN DARNALL."

To Francis Fauquier

[[*Williamsburg, 27 May 1763.* "The address of the house of Burgesses." This 12-page Ms is a reply from the House of Burgesses to complaints from British merchants who protested the use of Virginia Treasury Notes as legal tender. Written in an unidentified hand and now in the Washington Papers, DLC, the document is incorrectly said to be in GM's handwriting in Rowland, I, 381. The document also has been attributed to Richard Henry Lee, and was printed among the "Selections and Excerpts from the Lee Papers" in *Southern Literary Messenger*, Feb. 1860, 128–133, where it was misdated 1765. However, Charles Carter, Edmund Pendleton, and George Wythe were on the committee appointed to prepare the address, which is printed in JHB, 1761–1766, 188–192. Washington's endorsement gives no hint of the authorship, but he and Lee were attending members of the House of Burgesses in 1763. GM was not.]]

Ohio Company Advertisement

[16 June 1763]

A GENERAL MEETING of the *OHIO* COMPANY is desired at *Stafford* Court-House, on Patowmack Creek, in *Virginia*, the first Monday in July next. The General-Assembly of *Virginia* being unexpectedly called, will prevent the Committee of the *Ohio* Company from meeting on the first Monday in *June*, as was formerly advertised; and as there are Matters of the greatest Importance to the Company to be settled at their next Meeting, this Notice is ordered to be published in the *Virginia, Maryland* and *Pennsylvania* Gazettes, that the several members may be informed of it.
By order of the Committee of the OHIO COMPANY.

Printed from Annapolis *Md. Gaz.*
THE GENERAL ASSEMBLY OF VIRGINIA BEING UNEXPECTEDLY CALLED met in Williamsburg on 19 May. Gov. Fauquier had hoped the burgesses would stabilize the Virginia Treasury Notes, which depreciated to the point that British merchants had complained to the Board of Trade. The somewhat defiant response from the burgesses on 27 May 1763 (*q.v.*) has been mistakenly attributed to GM. Fauquier prorogued the burgesses on 31 May. The partners involved were Richard Lee and Thomas L. Lee, burgesses, and councillors John Tayloe, Jr., and Presley Thornton, and possibly Philip Ludwell Lee. Moreover, George Mercer had returned from his disappointing meeting with Gen. Amherst and was a burgess from Frederick County.

From George Washington

DEAR SIR,   Mount Vernon 17th. July 1763
We were a good deal disappointed in the promised Visit. A constant Watch was kept until The accustomed Bell gave The signal for Dinner, and said it was time to look no more. We do not readily comprehend The cause of The disappointment, but as Water seems nor to be the Element favourable to our wishes, we hope you will no longer trust to so uncertain a conveyance, but give us The pleasure of securing a visit at the next appointment. I am u[nder] a necessity of going to Fredericksburg early in next Week (i.e. about The 26th) for a Weeks stay, to which please if you have any commds. I shoud be glad To execute them. Our Compliments I mean Mrs. Green's, he is at Church, Mr. & Mrs. Fairfax and Mrs.

Washington's, are tendered along with those of Sir Yr Most Obedt. Hble Servt.

G. WASHINGTON

RC (Gratz Collection, PHi). Fitzpatrick, ed., *Writings of Washington*, II, 401–402, reproduces this letter and speculates that it was addressed to GM. "Supposed to be intended for G. Wm Fairfax Esqr" has been written on the back of the letter in an unidentified hand.

To Alexander Henderson

DR SIR   Gunston Hall 18th. July 1763

I wou'd advise you to have your Cellars quite up to the Water-Table laid wth. sound Bricks; Salmon Bricks are very apt to moulder in a Cellar when there is any Dampness, wh. few are without: it is usual wth. workmen to stowaway their bad Bricks in the Cellars, not because they will last better there than in the other parts of the Building, but because they are more out of Sight. Salmon Bricks [ma]y do very well for Inside-work above the Water-table, & in the Breasts & bulky parts of Chimneys. When I built my House I was at [some?] pains to measure all the Lime & Sand as my Mortar was made up, & always had two Beds, one for outside-Work ⅔ds. Lime & ⅓d. Sand, the other equal parts of Lime & Sand for Inside-work—it is easily measured in any old Tub or Barrel, & there is no other way to be sure of having your mortar good without Waste, & the different parts of yr. Building equally strong. The above proportion of Lime is greater than is generally used; but when you consi[der] how much heavier the Sand is, & how much closer it lies in measuring than the Lime you will find it not too much. If you have any good pit-sand, out of your Cellars or Well, it will make your mortar much tougher & stronger than it will be wth. other sand, & in that Case the proportion of Lime may be something less. Next to pit sand the River Shoar Sand on fresh Water is best, & the Sand in the Roads worst of all; as being very foul & full of Dust.

I wou'd by no means put any Clay or Loam in any of the Mortar; in the first place the Mortar is not near so strong, & besides from its being of a more soft & crumbly Nature, it is very apt to nourish & harbour those pernicious little Vermin the Cockroaches, who can't so easily penetr[a]te into the strong harsh Mortar made wth. [L]ime & Sand only; & this I assure you is no slight Consideration; for I have seen some brick Houses so infested wth. these Devils that a Man had better have lived in a Barne than in one of them.

[56]

I am afraid you will have but an indifferent Acct. of Richd. Masons & Robt. Speake's Crop of Tobo. tho' it is not all yet prized up, so that I can't be certain as to the Quantity: I think Speake's Share will not exceed five or six hundred, & his Balce. upon my Books is at this time 66/6 after giving him Crd. by You for 84/. Whatever Dick Mason's Share is will be entirely coming to him, as he has no Acct. wth. me; but he had handled his Tobo. in so careless & slovenly a Manner that more than half of it is rotten, & even the best of it I doubt will run some Risque at the Ware house.

I send you all the Hair I have except a little I kept in Case we shou'd have any small Job to do. Melford tells me there is 18 Bushels of it. I am Dr Sir Yr. most Hble Sert.

G. MASON

RC (Gunston Hall).
The version of this letter printed in Marietta M. Andrews, *George Washington's Country* (New York, 1930), 54–56, has modernized spelling in some cases and has misspelled Robert Speake's name.

To George Mercer

[[*20 Oct. 1763.* A memorandum of Col. Theodorick Bland, copied by Charles Campbell and now in the Campbell Papers (NcD), includes a sentence: "G Mason's letter to G Mercer, Octobr. 20, 1763: Compensation." Mercer had gone to England in Sept. 1763, as instructed by the Ohio Company shareholders at their July meeting. GM apparently did not attend that meeting, for the Ohio Company petition to the king (*Case of the Ohio Company*, 30–31) does not bear GM's signature. Bland's memorandum relates to Indian lands west of the Alleghenies. Not found.]]

Indemnity Bond to Thomas Bladen

8 November 1763. GM promises to pay Thomas Bladen £960 10s. in currency, or £464 10s. in pieces of eight worth "Seven Shils. & Six pence each" if paid "at or upon the first Day of June 7 next ensuing the Date hereof, wth. Legale Interest for the same," for 1,310 acres in Maryland near the Wills Creek storehouse property owned by the Ohio Company.
Printed document (Mason Papers, DLC). The filled-in portions of the document are in a handwriting identified as that of Benjamin Tasker by James, *Ohio Company*, 237–238, where the entire document is reprinted.
In a notable understatement, Prof. James calls this document "a highly complex manuscript." The document carries four endorsements. Chronologically, the first reads: "2 June 1763/Colo. Geo: Mason/Bond £464:10:ps. 8/at

the 6." The second is dated 8 Nov. 1763 and signed by Tasker as a witness. This endorsement allows GM to deduct the value of the 300-acre Pleasant Valley Tract if he does not obtain a patent for it. The third endorsement of 11 Jan. 1792 acknowledges the receipt of £692 10s. "in discharge of the within Bond," and is signed by "Danl. Dulany/Admr. of the/within Obligee." In this transaction GM was acting on behalf of the Ohio Company despite the fact that it appears to be a private contract between two persons; and from the 2 June 1763 endorsement it seems part of a scheme then afoot to buy a considerable amount of land around Wills Creek storehouse, build a town, and sell townsite lots. The initial failure of the plan is explained in the notes following the power of attorney of 29 Mar. 1763 (q.v.). Litigation involving the tracts continued beyond GM's death and kept his heirs in the courts until 1821.

GM's signature has been mutilated. The fourth endorsement, the only one in GM's handwriting, explains the document's presence in his papers. It reads: "discharged, and a Rec[e]ipt endorsed from Daniel Dulany Esqr. Admr. to Thos. Bladen Esqr. The Obligee. dated January 11th. 1792."

To John Mercer

[[6 Dec. 1763. "Colo. Mason wrote me the 6th. of last December that he had by several opportunities wrote to Mr. Athawes to pay you and Colo. Mercer £290 Sterling on the companies account which I suppose has been complied with. . . ." Mercer to Charlton Palmer, 17 Apr. 1764 (Mulkearn, 185). Not found.]]

To John Mercer

[[11 Jan. 1764. "Colo. Mason wrote me . . . Jan' 11th. last after having seen the Kings proclamation he declares his opinion to be that the proclamation was an express destruction of our grant and that we ought not to be concerned with any lands in those parts except we could have some effectual and real security, against the Indians and therefore advised that we should sollicit to be recompensed for the great trouble and expence we had been at. . . ." Mercer to Charlton Palmer, 17 Apr. 1764 (Mulkearn, 185). The 7 Oct. 1763 proclamation signed by George III forbade royal governers to grant warrants or surveys on lands west of the Alleghenies which were reserved for the Indian tribes. Not found.]]

From James Scott

[[10 Mar. 1764. GM reported a letter from the Rev. James Scott "the day before" he received Mrs. John Moncure's letter of 11 Mar. Both concerned the death and burial of GM's dear friend, John Moncure, the rector of Overwharton parish. Not found.]]

From Mrs. John Moncure

[[*11 Mar. 1764*. Mrs. Moncure was the wife of the Rev. John Moncure, the rector of Overwharton Parish and GM's close friend. She apparently sought advice about the funeral arrangements for her deceased husband. See GM's letter of 12 Mar. Not found.]]

To Mrs. John Moncure

DEAR MADAM: Gunston [Hall], 12th March, 1764

I have your letter by Peter yesterday, and the day before I had one from Mr. Scott, who sent up Gustin Brown on purpose with it. I entirely agree with Mr. Scott in preferring a funeral sermon at Aquia Church, without any invitation to the house. Mr. Moncure's character and general acquaintance will draw together much company, besides a great part of his parishioners, and I am sure you are not in a condition to bear such a scene; and it would be very inconvenient for a number of people to come so far from church in the afternoon after the sermon. As Mr. Moncure did not desire to be buried in any particular place, and as it is usual to bury clergymen in their own churches, I think the corpse being deposited in the church where he had so long preached is both decent and proper, and it is probable, could he have chosen himself, he would have preferred it. Mr. Scott writes to me that it is intended Mr. Green shall preach the funeral sermon on the 20th of this month, if fair; if not, the next fair day; and I shall write to Mr. Green tomorrow to that purpose, and inform him that you expect Mrs. Green and him at your house on the day before; and, if God grants me sufficient either to ride on horseback or in a chair, I will certainly attend to pay the last duty to the memory of my friend; but I am really so weak at present that I can't walk without crutches and very little with them, and have never been out of the house but once or twice, and then, though I stayed but two or three minutes at a time, it gave me such a cold as greatly to increase my disorder. Mr. Green has lately been very sick, and was not able to attend his church yesterday, (which I did not know when I wrote to Mr. Scott:) if he should not recover soon, so as to be able to come down, I will inform you or Mr. Scott in time, that some other clergyman may be applied to.

I beseech you, dear madam, not to give way to melancholy reflections, or to think that you are without friends. I know nobody that has reason to expect more, and those that will not be friends to you and your children now Mr. Moncure is gone were not friends to him when he was living, let their professions be what they would. If, therefore, you should find any such, you have no cause to lament the loss, for such friendship is not worth anybody's concern.

I am very glad to hear that Mr. Scott purposes to apply for Overwharton parish. It will be a great comfort to you and your sister to be so near one another, and I know the goodness of Mr. Scott's heart so well, that I am sure he will take a pleasure in doing you every good office in his power, and I had much rather he should succeed Mr. Moncure than any other person. I hope you will not impute my not visiting you to any coldness or disrespect. It gives me great concern that I am not able to see you. You may depend upon my coming down as soon as my disorder will permit, and I hope you know me too well to need any assurance that I shall gladly embrace all opportunities of testifying my regard to my deceased friend by doing every good office in my power to his family.

I am, with my wife's kindest respects and my own, dear madam, your most affectionate kinsman,

GEORGE MASON

Printed in Bishop [William] Meade, *Old Churches, Ministers, and Families of Virginia* (Philadelphia, 1901), II, 201–202. The original letter has not been found.

GM considered the Rev. John Moncure one of his closest friends, and when drafting his own will in 1773 provided "a Mourning ring of three Guineas Value" for Moncure's son, "which I desire him to wear in memory of my Esteem for my much lamented friend his Deceased Father." YOU AND YOUR SISTER TO BE SO NEAR is an allusion to Mrs. James Scott, who was Mrs. Moncure's sister. Both were GM's cousins.

To George William Fairfax and George Washington

GENTLEMEN   Gunston-Hall 23d. Decemr. 1765.

Inclosed is the Scheme I promised you for altering the Method of replevying Goods under Distress for Rent: I thought it necessary to explain fully the Land-lord's Right by the common-Law, to shew that our Act of Assembly was a mere Matter of Indulgence, & that an Alteration of it now will be no Incroachment upon the Tenant: the first Part of it has very little to do with the Alteration proposed,

& only inculcates a Doctrine I was always fond of promoting, & which I cou'd wish to see more generally adopted than it is like to be: the whole is indeed much longer than it might have been, but that you will excuse as a natural Effect of the very idle Life I am forced to lead. I beg you will alter such Parts of it as either of you think exceptionable.

If I had the Act of Assembly obliging our Vestry to pay for the Glebe &c. I wou'd prepare a Petition for Redress, & get it signed in Time.

Wishing the Familys at Belvoir & Mount Vernon all the Mirth & Happiness of the approaching Festival, I am Gentm. Yr. most obdt. Hble Sert.

G MASON

RC (Washington Papers, DLC). Addressed: "To Colo. Geo: Fairfax & Colo. Geo: Washington," with the "Scheme for Replevying Goods and Distress for Rent" enclosed.

GM apparently discussed the problems created by the Stamp Act which would devolve on landowners with Fairfax and Washington. The enclosed SCHEME was GM's solution, a means whereby landlords could collect rents from uncooperative or improvident tenants without using stamped legal documents. The implications are set forth in the textual note accompanying the entire document (q.v.). The ACT OF ASSEMBLY was the 1748 statute, "An act for the better securing the payment of rents, and preventing the fraudulent practices of Tenants" (Hening, VI, 9–13). THE FIRST PART OF IT is GM's earliest recorded disdain for slavery. THE VERY IDLE LIFE was an allusion to GM's health, which was affected by attacks of gout from early manhood until his death. The ACT OF ASSEMBLY was probably the 1752 act which impowered the Truro Parish Vestry to sell its glebe lands and share the proceeds with Cameron parish (Hening, VI, 270–272). Fairfax and Washington had been churchwardens in 1763 and 1764. GM was appointed a Truro Parish churchwarden in Nov. 1765, and seems to have been a prime mover in completing the long-delayed transaction (Hening, VIII, 202–203). The glebe lands and church silver plate were finally sold at auction on 22 May 1767 (Truro Parish Vestry Book, DLC).

Scheme for Replevying Goods and Distress for Rent

[23 Dec. 1765]

The Policy of encouraging the Importation of free People & discouraging that of Slaves has never been duly considered in this Colony, or we shou'd not at this Day see one Half of our best Lands in most Parts of the Country remain unsetled, & the other cultivated with Slaves; not to mention the ill Effect such a Practice has upon the Morals & Manners of our People: one of the first Signs of the Decay, & perhaps the primary Cause of the Destruction of the most flourishing Government that ever existed was the Introduction of great Numbers of Slaves—an Evil very pathetically described by the Roman Historians—but 'tis not the present Intention to expose our Weakness by examining this Subject too freely.

That the Custom of leasing Lands is more beneficial to the Community than that of setling them with Slaves is a Maxim that will hardly be denyed in any free Country; tho' it may not be attended with so much imediate Profit to the Land-holder: in Proportion as it is more useful to the Public, the Invitations from the Legislature to pursue it shou'd be stronger:—no Means seem so natural as securing the Payment of Rents in an easy & effectual Manner: the little Trouble & Risque attending this Species of Property may be considered as an Equivalent to the greater Profit arising from the Labour of Slaves, or any other precarious & troublesom Estate. The common-Law (independant of any Statute) gives the Land-lord a Right to distrain upon anything on his Land for the Rent due; that is, it puts his Remedy into his own Hands: but as so unlimitted a Power was liable to be abused, it was found necessary to punish the Abuse by penal Statutes, made in terrorem, to preserve Justice, & prevent the Oppression which the Poor might otherwise suffer from the Rich, not to destroy the Land-lord's Right, which still remained unimpeach'd, and has not only been exercised in this Colony from it's first Settlement, but has obtained in our Mother-Country from Time immemorial. Uninterrupted life & long Experience carry with them a Conviction of general Utility.

The fluctuating State of our Trade, the Uncertainty of our Markets & the Scarcity of Money frequently render it impracticable for the Debtor to raise Money out of his Effects to discharge a sudden & perhaps unexpected Judgement, & have introduced a Law giving the Debtor a Right to replevy his Goods under Execution by Bond with Security (approved by the Creditor) to pay the Debt & Costs with Interest in three Months; which Bonds are returnable to the Clerk's Office whence the Execution issued, to remain in the Nature of Judgements, & final Executions may be obtain'd upon them when due by a Motion to the Court, with ten Days Notice to the Partys. The Legislature, considering Distresses for Rents in the same Light with Executions for common Debts, has thought fit to extend the same Indulgence to them; tho' it wou'd not be hard to shew that the Cases are by no Means simular, & that the Reasons which are just in the former do not hold good in the latter: by comparing the Laws there also appears such an Inconsistency in that relating to replevin

Bonds for Rent as may render the Method prescribed difficult if not impracticable; there being no previous Record (as in the Case of Executions) the Bonds do not seem properly returnable to the Clerk's Office, nor is that Matter clearly express'd or provided for in the Act. This has not hitherto been productive of much Inconvenience; tho' contrary to the Course & Spirit of the common-Law, the Land-lord may thereby be brought into a Court of Judicature before he can get the Effect of a just & legal Distress; but in our present Circumstances it will occasion manifest Injustice.

If the Officer making a Distress, upon being offered Security, refuses to take a Bond for Want of Stamp'd Paper, the Goods of the Tenant must be imediatly exposed to Sale, & he deprived of the Indulgence intended by the Act of Assembly.

If the Officer takes a replevin Bond as usual, the Land-lord will lose his Rent, the Tenant then having it in his Power to keep him out of it as long as he pleases; for in the present Confusion & Cessation of Judicial proceedings the Land-lord will not have an Opportunity of applying to Court for an Execution when the Bond becomes payable, or if he does, the Clerk will not venture to issue one. In either Case there is such a Hardship as calls for the Interposition of the Legislature.

These Inconveniencys it is conceived may be obviated if the Tenant, instead of replevying his Goods by Bond, had a Right to supersede the Distress for three Months by Application to a single Magistrate, who shou'd be empowered & required, upon the Tenants producing under the Hand of the Person making the Distress a Certificate of the Rent distrained for & Costs, to take from the Principal & good Securitys a conditional Confession of Judgement, in the following or some such Form.

"Virginia . . . . County sct.

You A. B.—C. D.—& E. F. of the sd. County do confess Judgement unto G. H. of the County of . . . for the Sum of . . . due unto the sd. G. H. for Rent, for which Distress has been made upon the Goods of the sd. A. B. and also for the sum of . . . the Costs of the sd. Distress: which said Sums of . . . and . . . Costs with legal Interest from the Date hereof to be levyed of your and either of your Bodys Goods or Chattels for the Use of the sd. G. H. in Case the sd. A. B. shall not pay & satisfy to the sd. G. H. the said sums of . . . and . . . Costs with Interest thereon as aforesaid within three Months at furthest from the Date hereof—Taken & acknowledged the . . . Day of . . . before me one of his Majesty's Justices of the

Peace for the sd. County of . . . Given under my Hand the Day & Year aforesaid.—To J. K. Sherif—or Constable (as the Case is)"

Which Confession of Judgement shou'd restore to the Tenant his Goods, & be return'd by the Officer to the Landlord, who at the End of the three Months (giving the Partys ten Days Notice) shou'd be entitled to an Execution thereon, to be awarded by a single Magistrate also.

This Method will protect the Tenant from Oppression by confirming the Indulgence the Act of Assembly formerly gave him, at the same Time that it secures the Land-lord in the Payment of his Rent; & it can hardly be objected to as giving a single Magistrate a new & dangerous Jurisdiction, when it is considered that the Application to a Court on replevin Bonds for Rent was mere Matter of Form, in which the Court cou'd exercise no judicial Power, and that an Execution might as safely be awarded by a Magistrate out of Court in the Case of Rents, where (as has been before observed) there was no original Record or Jurisdiction in the Court, but by the common-Law the sole Power vested in the Land-lord; who, shou'd the proposed Alteration take place, will be as liable to be punished for the Abuse of it as he was before. If the Form of the Judgement recommended is objected to as subjecting the Body to Execution in a Case where the Goods only were originally liable; let it be considered that it is at the Tenant's own Request the Nature of his Debt is changed, that when the Land-lord sues for Rent, he may upon a Judgement order a Fi: fa: or a Ca: sa: at his own Option, & that he may do the same thing in the Case of replevin Bonds.

If some such Alteration as is here proposed shou'd be thought necessary, any little Errors or Deficiencys in this Scheme may be easily corrected in drawing up the Law.

Ms (Washington Papers, DLC). Enclosed with the letter of 23 Dec. 1765 to George William Fairfax and George Washington. Endorsed in unidentified hand; "From Colo Geo: Mayson to Colo G: Fairfax & Colo G. Washington /23 Dec 1765/ Inclosing a scheme for replevying goods under distress for rent."
This four-page document marks GM's transition from the role of a passive spectator to that of a concerned participant in the protest movement against British colonial regulations. Since the spring of 1765, Virginians and other Americans had been concerned about enforcement of the Stamp Act, and an active majority was determined to evade its provisions as an act of patriotic faith (Edmund and Helen S. Morgan, *The Stamp Act Crisis* [Chapel Hill, 1953], 88–89). On 20 Sept. 1765, Washington assumed that one of "the first bad consequences attending it [the Stamp Act]" was that "Our Courts of Judicature must inevitably be shut up" (quoted in David Mays, *Edmund Pendleton* [Cambridge, Mass., 1952], I, 167). Many Virginia courts did close on 1 Nov. 1765, but not all of them, since several proceeded in matters where stamped paper might be avoided. Washington was a burgess and if not actually present

when the House assembled in June 1765, was sympathetic to the resolutions which declared that Virginians were "not bound to yield Obedience to any Law or Ordinance" imposing taxes unless passed by the General Assembly. As GM explained in his accompanying letter (*q.v.*), his plan was not a finished draft for possible legislation but rather a summary view of the existing situation with a suggested form for obviating anticipated legal difficulties. GM's obiter dictum on slavery is the first indication of his hostility to human bondage, the final echoes of which he sounded in Philadelphia in 1787. In the light of his own large slaveholding interests, GM's expressions against slavery make it obvious that he held to a double standard on slavery. GM condemned slavery on moral and economic grounds, but since others would not heed his advice (or predictions) about the baneful effects of slavery, he tended to disregard it himself as did his sons. GM's remarks upon the common law of land tenancy reveal his considerable legal knowledge which was a product of reading and experience. Indeed, GM has often been mistakenly identified as a lawyer because of his public papers and his leadership in the General Assembly on matters related to land ownership. The influence of his uncle, John Mercer, can only be surmised; but GM did have access to Mercer's large library and hence to all the standard law books of the day. Thus GM acquired what is rare in a layman, a lawyer's vocabulary and understanding of the law. The underlying basis for this draft was an assumption that Virginians would not use stamped paper and therefore needed a device to circumvent the law. The scheme centered around distresses (property seizures) by landlords for non-payment of rent, and replevins (recovery of goods pledged as security) by well-intentioned tenants. Fairfax, Washington, and GM assumed that THE PRESENT CONFUSION & CESSATION OF JUDICIAL PROCEEDINGS would lengthen into months or years, but repeal of the Stamp Act was rumored in the *Va. Gaz.* (Purdie), 31 Oct. 1765, and became a fact on 4 Mar. 1766. Accordingly, Washington was spared the further effort of introducing GM's plan to the House of Burgesses.

To the Committee of Merchants in London

GENTLEMEN   Virginia Potomack River June 6th 1766.

There is a Letter of yours dated the 28th of Febry last, lately printed in the public Papers here; which tho' addressed to a particular Set of men, seems intended for the Colonys in general; and being upon a very interesting Subject, I shall, without further Preface or Apology, exercise the Right of a Freeman, in making such Remarks upon it as I think proper.

The Epithets of Parent & Child have been so long applyed to Great Britain & her Colonys, that Individuals have adopted them, and we rarely see anything, from your Side of the Water, free from the authoritative Style of a Master to a School-Boy.

"We have, with infinite Difficulty & Fatigue got you excused this one Time; pray be a good boy for the future; do what your Papa and Mamma bid you, & hasten to return them your most grateful Acknowledgements for condescending to let you keep what is your own; and then all your Acquaintance will love you, & praise you, & give you pretty things; and if you shou'd, at any Time hereafter, happen to transgress, your Friends will all beg for you, and be Security for your good Behaviour; but if you are a naughty Boy, & turn obstinate, & don't mind what your Papa & Mamma say to you, but presume to think their Commands (let them be what they will) unjust or unreasonable, or even seem to ascribe their present Indulgence to any other Motive than Excess of Moderation & Tenderness, and pretend to judge for yourselves, when you are not arrived at the Years of Discretion, or capable of distinguishing between Good & Evil; then every-body will hate you, & say you are a graceless & undutiful Child; your Parents & Masters will be obliged to whip you severely, & your Friends will be ashamed to say any thing in your Excuse: nay they will be blamed for your Faults. See your work—See what you have brought the Child to—If he had been well scourged at first for opposing our absolute Will & Pleasure, & daring to think he had any such thing as Property of his own, he wou'd not have had the Impudence to repeat the Crime."

"My dear Child, we have laid the Alternative fairly before you, you can't hesitate in the Choice, and we doubt not you will observe such a Conduct as your Friends recommend."

Is not this a little ridiculous, when applyed to three Millions of as loyal & useful Subjects as any in the British Dominions, who have been only contending for their Birth-right, and have now only gained, or rather kept, what cou'd not, with common Justice, or even Policy, be denied them? But setting aside the Manner, let me seriously consider the Substance & Subject of your Letter.

Can the Honour of Parliament be maintained by persisting in a Measure evidently wrong? Is it any Reflection upon the Honour of Parliament to shew itself wiser this Year than the last, to have profited by Experience, and to correct the Errors which Time & endubitable Evidence have pointed out? If the Declaratory Act, or Vote of Right, has asserted any unjust, oppressive, or unconstitutional Principles, to become "waste paper" wou'd be the most innocent use that cou'd be made of it: by the Copys we have seen here, the legislative authority of Great Britain is fully & positively asserted in all Cases whatsoever. But a just & necessary Distinction between Legislation & Taxation hath been made by the greatest & wisest Men in the Nation; so that if the Right to the latter had been disclaimed, it wou'd not have impeached or weakened the Vote of Right; on the contrary it wou'd have strengthened it; for Nothing (except hanging the Author of the Stamp Act) wou'd have contributed more to restore that Confidence which a weak or corrupt Ministry had so greatly impaired.

We do not deny the supreme Authority of Great Britain over her Colonys, but it is a Power which a wise Legislature will exercise with extreme Tenderness & Caution, and carefully avoid the least Imputation or Suspicion of Partiality. Wou'd to God that this always had been, that it always may be the Case! To make an odious Distinction between us & your fellow Subjects residing in Great Britain, by depriving us of the ancient Tryal, by a Jury of our Equals, and substituting in its' place an arbitrary Civil Law Court— to put it in the Power of every Sycophant & Informer ("the most mischievous, wicked abandoned & profligate Race" says an eminent writer upon British Politics, "that ever God permited to plague Mankind") to drag a Freeman a thousand Miles from his own Country (whereby he may be deprived of the Benefit of Evidence) to defend his property before a Judge, who, from the Nature of his office, is a Creature of the Ministry, liable to be displaced at their Pleasure, whose Interest it is to encourage Informers, as his Income may in a great Measure depend upon his Condemnations, and to give such a Judge a Power of excluding the most innocent Man, thus treated, from any Remedy (even the recovery of his Cost) by only certifying that *in his Opinion* there was a *probable* Cause of Complaint; and thus to make the property of the Subject, in a matter which may reduce him from Opulence to Indigence, depend upon a word before an unknown in the Language & Style of Laws! Are these among the Instances that call for our Expression of "filial Gratitude to our Parent-Country?" These things did not altogether depend upon the Stamp-Act, and therefore are not repealed with it.

Can the Foundations of the State be saped, & the Body of the People remain unaffected? Are the Inhabitants of Great Britain absolutely certain that, in the Ministry or Parliament of a future Day, such Incroachments will not be urged as Precedents against themselves?

Is the Indulgence of Great Britain manifested by prohibiting her Colonys from exporting to foreign Countrys such Commoditys as she does not want, & from importing such as she does not produce or manufacture & therefore can not furnish but upon extravagant Terms? One of your own Writers (I think it is Bishop Burnett) relates a remarkable peice of Tyranny of the Priesthood in Italy. "They make it an Article of Religion" says he "for the People to mix Water with their Wine in the Press, by which it is soured; so that the Laity can not drink a Drop of good Wine, unless they buy it from the Convents, at whatever Price the Clergy think fit to set upon it." I forbear to make the Application.

Let our fellow-Subjects in Great Britain reflect that we are descended from the same Stock with themselves, nurtured in the same Principles of Freedom; which we have both suck'd in with our Mother's Milk: that in crossing the Atlantic Ocean, we have only changed our Climate, not our Minds, our Natures & Dispositions remain unaltered; that We are still the same People with them, in every Respect; only not yet debauched by Wealth, Luxury, Venality, & Corruption; and then they will be able to judge how the late Regulations have been relished in America.

You need not, Gentlemen, be afraid of our "breaking out into intemperate Strains of Triumph & Exultation" there is yet no Cause that our Joy shou'd exceed the Bounds of Moderation.

If we are ever so unfortunate to be made Slaves; which God avert! what Matter is it to us whether our chains are forged in London, or at Constantinople? Whether the Oppression comes from a British Parliament, or a Turkish Divan?

You tell us that "our Task-Masters will probably be restored." Do You mean the Stamp-Officers, or the Stamp-Ministry? If the first, the Treatment they have already found here will hardly make them fond of returning—If the latter, we despise them too much to fear them.—They have sufficiently exposed their own Ignorance, Malice, & Impotence—The Clovenfoot has been too plainly seen to be again concealed; They have rendered themselves as obnoxious to Great Britain as to America.

If the late Ministerial Party cou'd have influenced the Legislature to have made so cruel & dangerous an Experiment as attempting to enforce the Stamp-Act by military Power, wou'd the Nation have engaged heartily in such an execrable Cause? Wou'd there have been no Difficulty in raising & transporting a Body of Troops sufficient to occupy a Country of more than two thousand Miles in Extent? Wou'd they have had no Dangers to encounter in the Woods & Wilds of America. Three Millions of People driven to Desperation are not an Object of Contempt. America, however weak in herself, adds greatly to the Strength of Great Britain, which wou'd be diminished in Proportion by her Loss: with prudent Management she might become an impenetrable Bulwark to the British Nation, and almost enable it to stand before the Stroke of Time.

Say there was not a Possibility of failing in the Project; what then wou'd have been the Consequence? Cou'd you have destroyed us without ruining yourselves? The Trade of Great Britain is carryed on & supported, principally by Credit. If the American [British?] merchant has an hundred thousand pounds due to him in the Colonys, he must owe near as much to his Woolen-Draper, his Linnen-Draper; his Grocer, &c. and these again are indebted to the Manufacturer, & so on: there is no determinate End to this Commercial Chain; break but one Link of it, and the whole is destroyed. Make a Bank[r]upt of the Merchant by stopping his Remittances from America, and you strike at the Credit of every Man who has Connections with him: there is no knowing where the Contagion wou'd stop. You wou'd overturn one another, like a Set of Nine Pins. The Value of your Lands & Produce wou'd fall, your Manufacturers wou'd starve for want of Employment, your Funds might fail, your public-Credit sink. And let but the Bubble once burst; where is the Man who cou'd undertake to blow it up again?

These Evils are, for the present, removed. Praised be Almighty God! Blessed be our most gracious Sovereign! Thanks to the present mild & prudent Temper of Parliament. Thanks to the wise & honest Conduct of the present Administration. Thanks to the unwearied Diligence of our Friends the British Merchants, & Manufacturers; Thanks to that happy Circumstance of their private Interest being so interwoven with ours, that they cou'd not be separated. Thanks to the spirited & disinterested Conduct of our own Merchants in the northern Colonys; who deserve to have their Names handed down, with Reverence & Gratitude to Posterity. Thanks to the Unanimity of the Colonys themselves. And many Thanks to our generous & able Benefactor, Mr. Pitt; who has always stood forth a Champion in the Cause of Liberty & his Country. No Thanks to Mr. Grenville & his Party; who, without his Genius or Abilitys, has dared to act the part that Pericles did, when He engaged his Country in the Peleponesian War; which, after a long & dreadful Scene of Blood, ended in the Ruin of all Greece, and fitted it for the Macedonian Yoke. Some Bungler in politics will soon, perhaps, be framing Schemes for restraining our Manufacturers. Vain Attempt! Our Land is cheap and fresh, we have more of it than we are able to employ; while we can live in Ease & Plenty upon our Farms, Tillage, & not Arts, will engage our Attention. If by opening the Channels of Trade, you afford Us a ready Market for the Produce of our Lands, and an Opportunity of purchasing cheap the Conveniencys of Life, all our superfluous Gain will sink into Your Pockets, in Return for British

Manufactures. If the Trade of this Continent with the French & Spaniards, in their Sugar-Islands, had not been restrained, Great Britain would soon have undersold them, with their own Produce, in every Market of the World. Until you lay Us under a necessity of shifting for ourselves, You need not be afraid of the Manufactures of America. The ancient Poets, in their elegant Manner of Expression, have made a kind of Being of Necessity, and tell Us that the Gods themselves are obliged to yield to her. It is by Invitations & Indulgence, not by Compulsion, that the Market for British Manufactures is to be kept up, & increased in America:—without the first, you will find the latter as ineffectual, as destructive of the End it aims at, as Persecution in Matters of Religion, which serves not to extinguish, but to confirm the Heresy. There is a Passion natural to the Mind of Man, especially a free Man, which renders him impatient of Restraint. Do you, does any sensible Man think that three or four Millions of People, not naturally defective in Genius, or in Courage, who have tasted the Sweets of Liberty in a Country that doubles it's Inhabitants every twenty Years, in a Country abounding in such Variety of Soil & Climate, capable of producing not only the Necessarys, but the Conveniencys & Delicacys of Life, will long submit to Oppression; if unhappily for yourselves, Oppression shou'd be offered them? Such another Experiment as the Stamp-Act wou'd produce a general Revolt in America.

Do you think that all your rival Powers in Europe wou'd sit still, & see you crush your once flourishing & thriving Colonys, unconcerned Spectators of such a Quarrel? Recollect what happened in the Low-Countrys a Century or two ago. Call to Mind the Cause of the Revolt. Call to Mind too the Part that England herself then acted. The same Causes will generally produce the same Effects; and it requires no great Degree of Penetration to foretell that what has happened, may happen again. God forbid there shou'd be Occasion, and grant that the Union, Liberty, and mutual Happiness of Great Britain, & her Colonys may continue, uninterrupted, to the latest Ages!

America has always acknowledged her Dependence upon Great Britain. It is her Interest, it is her Inclination to depend upon Great Britain. We readily own that these Colonys were first setled, not at the Expence, but under the Protection of the English Government; which Protection it has continued to afford them; and we own too, that Protection & Allegiance are reciprocal Dutys. If it is asked at whose Expence they were setled? The Answer is obvious at the Expence of the private Adventurers our Ancestors; the Fruit of whose Toil and Danger we now enjoy.

We claim Nothing but the Liberty & Privileges of Englishmen, in the same Degree, as if we had still continued among our Brethren in Great Britain: these Rights have not been forfeited by any Act of ours, we can not be deprived of them, without our Consent, but by Violence & Injustice; We have received them from our Ancestors, and, with God's Leave, we will transmit them, unimpaired to our Posterity. Can those, who have hitherto acted as our Friends, endeavour now, insidiously, to draw from Us Concessions destructive to what we hold far dearer than Life!

—If I cou'd find Example
Of thousands, that by base Submission had
Preserv'd their Freedom, I'd not do't; but since
Nor Brass, nor Stone, nor Parchment bears not one;
Let Cowardice itself forswear it.—

Our Laws, our Language, our Principles of Government, our Inter-marriages, & other Connections, our constant Intercourse, and above all our Interest, are so many Bands which hold us to Great Britain, not to be broken, but by Tyranny and Oppression. Strange, that among the late Ministry, there shou'd not be found a Man of common Sense & common Honesty, to improve & strengthen these natural Tyes by a mild & just Government, instead of weakening, & almost dissolving them by Partiality & Injustice! But I will not open the wounds which have been so lately bound up, and which still require a skilful & a gentle Hand to heal them.

These are the Sentiments of a Man, who spends most of his Time in Retirement, and has seldom med[d]led in public Affairs, who enjoys a moderate but independent Fortune, and content with the Blessings of a private Station, equally disregards the Smiles & Frowns of the Great; who tho' not born within the Verge of the British Isle, is an Englishman in his Principles, a Zealous Assertor of the Act of Settlement, firmly attached to the present royal Family upon the Throne, unalienably affected to his Majesty's sacred Person & Government, in the Defence of which he wou'd shed the last Drop of his Blood; who looks upon Jacobiteism as the most absurd Infatuation, the wildest Chimæra that ever entered into the Head of Man; who adores the Wisdom & Happiness of the British Constitution; and if He had his Election now to make, wou'd prefer it to any that does, or ever did exist. I am not singular in this my Political Creed; these are the general Principles of his Majesty's Subjects in America; they are the Principles of more than nine-tenths of the People who have been so basely misrepresented to you, and whom you can never grant too much; because you can hardly give them any thing, which will not redound to the Benefit of the Giver.

If any Person shou'd think it worth his while to animadvert upon what I have written, I shall make no Reply. I have neither Abilitys nor Inclination to turn Author. If the Maxims have asserted, & the Reflections I have made, are in themselves just, they will need no Vindication; if they are erronious, I shall esteem it a Favour to have my Errors pointed out; and will, in modest Silence, kiss the Rod that corrects me. I am, Gentlemen, Your most obdt. Servt.

A VIRGINIA PLANTER.

Ms (Mason Papers, DLC). Endorsed by GM: "Copy of a Letter to the Committee of Merchants in London in June 1766.—by a Virginia Planter. & published in the Public Ledger."

GM's ire was raised by the publication of "*A letter from the Committee of Merchants in* London, *trading to* North America, *directed to the merchants in* New York, *dated Feb. 28,* 1766," which appeared in the *Va. Gaz.* (Purdie), 16 May 1766. Presumably, GM wrote this rebuttal to the London merchants and dispatched it through an agent to the London *Public Ledger,* but a search of its extant files in the British Museum and other depositories does not reveal that the letter ever reached its intended audience. The AUTHORITATIVE STYLE of the schoolmaster's charge was GM's idea of British arrogance, and not—as the quotation marks might indicate—borrowed from another source. The Declaratory Act as "WASTE PAPER" was the merchants' own term, paraphrasing those who had opposed repeal of the Stamp Act and who had stated that "the Parliamentary vote of right will be waste paper, and that the colonies will understand very well that what is pretended to be adopted on mere commercial principles is really yielded through fear, and amounts to a tacit, but effectual surrender" of Parliamentary power. Substitution of the Admiralty courts—AN ARBITRARY CIVIL-LAW COURT—for trial by jury in the vicinity was one of the most obnoxious features of the Stamp Act. The merchants' letter pleaded for Americans to "strengthen the hands of your advocates" by prompt expressions of "filial duty and gratitude to your parenty country." BISHOP BURNET was Gilbert Burnet (1643–1715), Bishop of Salisbury, whose observations on continental travel were popular and who also wrote a *History of His Own Time* (London, 1724). Burnet's leanings were certainly anti-Catholic, but GM either heard a garbled account, or quoted inaccurately, from *Three Letters Concerning the Present State of Italy . . . Being A SUPPLEMENT to Dr. Burnets Letters* (n.p., 1688) by an author identified as "a person of known Integrity." In this account (136–137) the author reports that at Parma residents watered their wine because they "were possessed with this *Superstition,* that it was Indispensably necessary to mix it with *Water* in the *Cask. . . .* Yet the *Excise* that is laid on the *Wine* in *Florence,* has taught the Inhabitants a point of Wisdom . . . the *People* who have no mind to pay *Excise* for *Water,* keep their *Wine* pure. . . ."

GM's assertion that IN CROSSING THE ATLANTIC Americans had changed only their climate, not their minds, is a rephrasing of Horace (*Epistles,* I, xi): "Not their own passions, but the climate changed." (See Richard M. Gummere, *The*

American Colonial Mind and the Classical Tradition [Cambridge, Mass., 1963], 2). GM loosely quoted from the merchants' letter an admonition against TRIUMPH AND EXALTATION. The letter read: "But if violent measures are continued, and triumphs on the point gained; if it is talked of as a victory . . . your friends must certainly lose all power to serve you; your taxmasters probably be restored. . . ." TO ENFORCE THE STAMP-ACT BY MILITARY POWER was to attempt the impossible, as some Englishmen predicted four decades earlier. GM appears to have been familiar with Gordon and Trenchard's *Cato's Letters,* and No. 67 (published 8 Dec. 1722) warned against using arms to command American obedience. "Force can never be used effectually to answer the End, without destroying the Colonies themselves. Liberty and Encouragement are necessary to carry People thither, and to keep them together when they are there; and Violence will hinder both." OUR OWN MERCHANTS IN THE NORTHERN COLONIES were the Boston, New York and Philadelphia groups which signed nonimportation agreements, and commercial boycotts enforced by the Sons of Liberty that gave "British merchants an urgent reason to wish for repeal" (Morgan, *Stamp Act Crisis,* 295). THE ANCIENT POETS . . . MADE A KIND OF BEING OF NECESSITY was a fixed idea in GM's mind and reappears verbatim in a letter of 2 Oct. 1778, so it may have been copied from a secondary work on classic poets. Unfortunately, a search of their works as well as the foremost English writers did not yield the source for the blank verse: "If I could find example. . . ." At any rate, GM's angry reaction to the letter may have been rejected by the *Public Ledger* because GM eschewed the London merchants' advice "to inculcate the propriety of the conduct we recommend."

The seven-page Ms is entirely in GM's handwriting. The punctuation for quotations has been modernized. On the fourth page, the Ms has been altered by an unknown writer so that the word "American" is bracketed. Obviously GM meant to write: "If the British Merchant has an hundred thousand Pounds due to him . . . ," but his mind was ahead of his pen, and so it came out "American Merchant." The modernized text printed in Rowland, I, 381–389 is not free from errors, both editorial and typographical.

Memorandum to James Tilghman

[March, 1767]

Upon being informed that Mr. Croghan claimed some Credit on his Bond to the Ohio Company for part of the Money recovered by Captain Trent from Governor Dinwiddie, George Mason sent to Mr. John Mercer (who managed the Suit for Capt. Trent) desiring a particular Accot. of the matter, and received from Mr. Mercer the following Answer and Account.

(copy)

"Dr. Sir

Your memorandum by my son gave me a good deal of trouble to search for Captain Trents papers, tho' I was almost certain that they would not turn to Mr. Croghans advantage any further than by returning an Account of his which our Assembly refused to allow"

"Captain Trents claim for his own £35..4..2 and his
Men's pay in the whole   £222. .18. .0
for Provisions for himself and Men   68. . 7. .9
for going out with the first present, himself £100
Horses £90. .16. .0   Wampum £16. .4—
Provisions £11. .14. .9—Owens £6. .11. .4—
bringing in Skins £6. .9. .0—Interpreter £5. .16. .0 } 247. .18. .10
—an Express £5—French Deserters Express 40/,
Half thicks 38/9   A ruffled shirt 15/—one Ps.
ribbon 9/, a Skin for Belts 5/.
For going out with the second present, himself £50
—Horses £37. .2. .—presents £9. .15. .0
Wampum £8. .9. .6—Match Coats £7. .10. .0   } 126. .11. .5
Expresses £6. .12. . Skins for Belts £4. .10
Half thicks £2. .12. .11

                                                        £665. .16. .0

"Of that Sum £321..11..2 was due to himself, and £344..4.. [torn] to his Men. [He] offered me any part of what I could recover of it, and I realy believe it would have been lost, if I had not by a good [Fee?] procured Mr. Dinwiddie to be arrested at York. Even afterwards the Court put me upon such proof of the Account as they were almost certain I could not procure—but meeting Colo. Washington and Colo. Mercer, who recommended me to some other witnesses then luckily in Town and having a good Jury who resented the Treatment Trent met with; they not only allowed the whole Accot. but gave such Damages as satisfied me, and therefore I according to Capt. Trents order gave the Ohio Company Credit for the whole £665..16..0. I hope this will be satisfactory, & am Dr Sir Your most Obedient Servant

JOHN MERCER

March 1st. 1767."

George Mason was also at the Expence and trouble of procuring from the Secretarys Office Authentic Copys of all Capt. Trents Accots. &c. in the Suit with Mr. Dinwiddie and found them to agree exactly with the above state of Mr. Mercer's except the Article for Provisions of £68..7..9 which in the Office Copy is £70..9..9 —but whence this difference of £2..2 arises, is not apparent. This it is presumed will be sufficient to satisfie both Capt: Trent & Mr. Croghan, that Mr. Croghan is not entitled to any Credit from the Ohio Company on this Accot. and if by any private agreement between Mr. Trent and Mr. Croghan the latter has a right to any part of it (which does not appear to be the case from the Papers in the Suit) Capt. Trent ought to pay Mr. Croghan himself, as Mr. Mercer has given Capt. Trent Credit for the whole [sum to] the Ohio Company.

Mr. Croghans Accot. Certificates, for which the Virginia Assembly refused to make him any Allowance are inclosed herewith, Colo. Tilghman will be pleased to return them to [torn] And oblige his most Hble. Servt.

G: MASON

Tr (Cadwallader Papers, PHi). In the reprint of this transcript appearing in James, *Ohio Company*, 239–240, it is not made clear that this is written in an unidentified hand, probably Tilghman's clerk's.

William Trent's ventures as an Indian trader, part-time soldier, and full-time speculator led to a variety of endeavors. After the Logstown conference (1752) Trent was sent to the Miami tribe bearing the FIRST PRESENT from the colony of Virginia as part of Gov. Dinwiddie's scheme to undermine French influence in the Ohio valley. In the same year, the Ohio Company employed Trent as a factor responsible for building storehouses on Ohio tributaries and trading with friendly Indians. In 1753 Dinwiddie authorized Trent to distribute the SECOND PRESENT among well-disposed Indians on the Virginia frontier. Trent continued to serve the company but was commissioned a captain of the Virginia militia in Jan. 1754, and charged with building a fort at the forks of the Ohio. Capt. Trent and Maj. George Washington both drew on supplies from company storehouses as they readied defenses against the encroaching French forces. While the dual agent of the company and the colony, Trent "was Obliged to make use of the Company's money as well as Goods Such as Blankets, Guns, Powder, Lead &c to pay the Workman And furnish them with Provisions for that Purpose as appears in the Company's Books Charged to the Government of Virginia." (T. Cresap to [James Tilghman], 20 May 1767, in James, *Ohio Company*, 241–242). The copied letter from John Mercer relates to Trent's law suit against Dinwiddie, who probably posted a bond for the funds claimed before he departed for London early in 1758. In 1761 the House of Burgesses rejected a proposal that the colony assume part of the £800 judgment because "Application was never made . . . for Payment of the said Money; and it was a Transaction entirely between" Dinwiddie and Trent (JHB, 1758–1761, 255). John Mercer had won the judgment in the fall of 1760 (James, *Ohio Company*, 232). George Croghan was a frontier crony of Trent's and seems to have bought company goods under a £1,000 bond signed in 1752. In 1767 Tilghman was hired by GM to recover that amount and this memorandum was sent to Philadelphia, where the case was tried. Croghan apparently hoped to reduce his company debt with counter claims that GM denied. Tilghman won the law suit, but Croghan's fortunes were so low that any recovery of actual money is doubtful (Nicholas Wainwright, *George Croghan: Wilderness Diplomat* [Chapel Hill, 1959] 249).

[From George Washington]

[[5 Apr. 1767. John C. Fitzpatrick's . . . *List of the Washington Manuscripts from the Year 1592 to 1775* (Washington, 1919) identifies a letter from Washington for this date, but in 1968 the item could not be found in the Library of Congress as it was cited (Volume XII, 1374), and the editor believes its inclusion was a clerical error. No other trace of such an item has been found.]]

Private Boundary Award
Fairfax County

[15 July 1767]

To ALL CHRISTIAN people to whom this present writing of award shall Come

George Mason of Gunston Hall in the parish of Truro & County of Fairfax Sendeth greeting whereas Peter Smith late of Westmorland County Died Seized of Certain Lands Situate lying & being upon bull Run Now in the sd. parish of Truro & County of Fairfax which by his last will & Testament he Devised to several of his Children & whereas Divers disputes & Controversies touching & Concerning the Division of boundaries of the sd. Lands have been heretofore Moved & Depended between Elizabeth Landman the widow & Peter Smith & William Smith the sons & heirs of James Smith Decd. who was one of the sons of & Devisees of the above named Peter Smith the Testator of the one part and James Jinnings son & Devisee of Daniel Jennings Decd. (who purchased from Thomas Smith another of the sons & Devisees of the said Peter Smith the Testator) of the other part for the appeasing Ending & finally Determining whereof the said parties have submitted themselves & are become bound Each to the other by their Several Obligations dated the 11th. day of June 1767. in the sum of one hundred pounds with Conditions thereunder written for the performance of the award arbitrament & Determination of Howson Hooe & John Hooe of the County of Prince Wm. Gent. & in Case they should Disagree in their opinion then for the performance of the award arbitrament & Determination of Colo. George Mason as umpire between them as by the sd. obligations & Conditions doth & may more fully and at large appear & whereas the said Howson Hooe & John Hooe Gent have Disagreed in their Opinion & have Certified the same under their hands the 3d. day of this present Month of July NOW KNOW YE that I the said George Mason having Taken upon myself the Charge & burden of the said award & arbitament & having fully & Deliberately heard & Examined the

[76]

allegations & Evidence of both the said Parties Concerning the premises Do by these presents arbitrate Determine award & order that a Certain Branch or run running thro' the said Lands from the Back part thereof into bull Run Generally Called the Dividing branch (the same lying & being between the sd. James Jenning's Spring branch & a run Called the Mill branch) is & shall be a boundary & Division between the said Lands now held by the sd. parties under the will of the before mentioned Peter Smith late of Westmorland County Decd. Namely the said Elizabeth Landman Peter Smith & Wm. Smith as Claimers from the sd. James Smith one of the sons & Devisees of the said Peter Smith the Testator & the sd. James Jennings as a Claimer under the purchas[e] from Thomas Smith another of the sons & Devisees of the said Peter Smith the Testator as afsd. the sd. Branch or run having been formerly Marked agreed upon & Settled as a Division & boundary between the Said Lands by the Mutual Consent and agreement of the before Mentioned James Smith & Thomas Smith two of the sons & Devisees of the sd. Peter Smith the Testator before the sd. Thomas Smith sold his part thereof & I do further arbitrate determine award & Order that the said Elizabeth Landman Peter Smith & Wm. Smith their heirs or Assigns on their part shall not hereafter have use occupy or Claim any of the sd. Land Lying & being above or on the upper side of the sd. Dividing branch or run, & that the said James Jinnings his heirs or assigns on his part shall not hereafter have use Occupy or Claim any of the said Land Lying & being below or on the Lower side of the sd. Dividing Branch or run but that the same shall be & Remain a perpetual division & boundary between the sd. parties & their heirs & Assigns for ever. In Witness whereof I have hereunto Set my hand & Affixed my seal This 15 Day of July in the year 1767.

GEORGE MASON

FC (Edmund Jennings Lee II Papers, NcD). Endorsed: "At a Court Continued & held for the County of Fairfax 22d. Sept. 1767. This award made by George Mason Gent. Between Peter Smith & James Jennings is ordered to be Recorded."

From Robert Carter

[[*11 Dec. 1767.* Carter wrote GM asking for a loan. GM sent his regret, on 23 Jan. 1768, that he "had some little Time before let out what Cash I had bye me upon Maryland Bonds. . . ." Not found.]]

From John Mercer

[[*ca. 21 Dec. 1767*. In a letter to George Mercer begun 22 Dec. 1767 and finished 28 Jan. 1768, John Mercer explains that when he received George Mercer's letter of 18 Sept. 1767, he relayed "copies of that part of your letter relating to the Compy" to GM, John Tayloe, Philip Ludwell Lee, and Robert Carter. George Mercer's letter of 6 Sept. 1767 apparently reported more fully the action of the Board of Trade in seeking Governor Fauquier's advice on a policy for western land grants, but John Mercer noted that it arrived on 3 Jan. 1768, after the copied earlier letter had been sent to GM and the other shareholders. See Mulkearn, 211–212. Mercer reported that he gave the letter to his head overseer on 23 Dec. 1767 "& he promised it a safe & immediate passage, but it, as it seems, miscarried." Not found.]]

From Presley Thornton and Richard Lee

[[*8 Jan. 1768*. John Mercer wrote George Mercer some time between 22 Dec. 1767 and 28 Jan. 1768 (Mulkearn, 186–220) that Thornton and Lee "had on the 8th. wrote to Colo. Mason" urging GM to call a meeting of the Ohio Company shareholders. Their action was based on news of the queries about the company addressed to Gov. Fauquier. Not found.]]

To John Mercer

[[*ca. 10 Jan. 1768*. Mercer wrote his son George a long letter between 22 Dec. 1767 and 28 Jan. 1768 (Mulkearn, 186–220) in which he reported that pertinent parts of George Mercer's letters from London had been communicated to GM, John Tayloe, Philip Ludwell Lee, and Robert Carter. In mid-Jan., John Mercer noted that his letter to GM had miscarried. Mercer then reported that "on the 12th. to my great surprize, I rec'ed a letter from him [GM] inclosing their's [Presley Thornton and Richard Lee] & desiring me to acquaint him with their motives, which from their letter he found they rec'ed from me." Thornton and Lee wanted GM to call an Ohio Company meeting. GM's letter to Mercer has not been found.]]

To Robert Carter

DEAR SIR: Gunston Hall, January 23d, 1768
  The Ohio Company, being informed that their case is referred by order of his Majesty and Council to the consideration of the Gover-

nor and Council of Virginia, who are to make a report thereon, I have, at the instance of several members, wrote to his Honor the Governor, to desire the favor of him to inform us of the purport of this order &c.; what is expected from the Company in consequence thereof. I have taken the liberty, Sir, to enclose the letter under cover to you and must beg the favor of you to make such inquiries and procure such copies as you think necessary for the Company's information, as well as forward any answer the Governor may think fit to favor us with.

There is to be a meeting of the Company at Stafford Court House on Tuesday, the 23d of February next, where we expect the have the pleasure of your company. I enclose an advertisement to give notice of it, which you will please to have inserted in the VIRGINIA GAZETTE. One is already sent to the printer at Annapolis.

I received your favor of the 11th December last and wished it was in my power to oblige you with the sum you desire, but I had some little time before let out what cash I had by me upon Maryland bonds, with a promise to the gentleman who borrowed it not to call for it soon. I made some large purchase. If I should be lucky enough to receive any considerable sum next summer, I will let you know it.

I beg my compliments to your lady, and am, Sir,

Your most obedient humble servant,

G. MASON.

RC (Darlington Collection, PPiU). Addressed: "To the Hon. Robert Carter, Esq.:/Williamsburg."

GM and the other shareholders had learned by this date that the Board of Trade was seeking answers to certain questions about the Ohio Company's activities before acting on the renewed company petition of 1765. By this time Gov. Fauquier probably also had received Lord Shelburne's letter of 8 Oct. 1767. Shelburne's queries were similar to the Board's, of course. What was the nature of the company claim? How was the company formed? How much money had the company actually spent "in consequence of the first Cession of Land . . . by the Indians," or the king's instructions of 1749? (See the letter quoted in Mulkearn, 641, from P. R. O., C. O. 5: 1345/385–90). The enclosed letter to Gov. Fauquier from GM has not been found. The company advertisement GM sought appeared in the *Va. Gaz.* (Rind) on 11 and 18 Feb. 1768, and in the Annapolis *Md. Gaz.* on 4, 11, and 18 Feb. 1768.

To Francis Fauquier

[[*Jan. 1768*. George Mercer arrived in England in Sept., 1763, and finally presented a petition to George III in 1765 asking that the Ohio Company either be compensated by Parliament for its past endeavors and losses in the Ohio valley or receive a definitive land grant "in some other part of your majesty's American dominions" (*Case of the Ohio Company*,

32–33). The king sent this petition to the Lords of Trade, who waited until 26 June 1767 to act. They sent a recommendation, which the Secretary of State forwarded to Gov. Fauquier, asking for a full report on the company's efforts and expenses, the present situation in the Ohio country vis-à-vis the Proclamation of 1763, "and upon the effect which the encouragement of such settlements may have on the temper of the Indians." Moreover, Fauquier's opinion was sought on a plan to discourage further settlements in the region. GM heard about this report and in his letter to Robert Carter of 23 Jan. 1768 indicates that he wrote Fauquier a query about "the Purport of the sd. Order, & what is expected from the Company in Consequence thereof." Presumably, Carter was to deliver GM's letter and return with the governor's reply. GM's letter has not been found.]]

From Robert Carter

SIR   Wm'sburg 10th Febry 1768
Your friendly Letter inclosing one for his honor the Governor, also a Notification (which will be published to-morrow in both Gazettes) was put into my hands this day. His honor doth not open Letters after Candles are alighted, therefor the Consideration of yours & a large Packet are postponed, till Sol's rays shall re-illuminate our Atmosphere.

I have before me a transcript of part of Col: Geo: Mercer's letter dated the 18th day of last Sepr, which is addressed to his Father. It is annexed to a letter, written by mr Mercer of Malbrough; who saies thou hast a Copy of the same. The Copy of the Report of the Lords recommended to his Majesty, & the Order in consequence thereof, I fear are lost. For neither the former, nor the latter have been received: And our only expectation, is on the Duplicates. The Company will have a firm Basis to build on when the Report & order shall arrive; and not otherwise. I apprehend every Resolution, every Request without them, will be premature. I beg leave to remark that the expected order issued on Account of our own Memorial. Can we consistently echo it, or necogitate anew, without considering the royal Order? I think we cannot. But what ever shall be determined by the Gentlemen who shall attend, I shall submit to, believing they will deliberately attend to the Papers & Information, that will be layed before them.

I would cheerfully have obeyed the summons if my state of health would have allowed me, so Sir, be pleased to present my Compliments to those Gentlemen who shall attend.

[80]

Mr Mercer begs leave to resign his Place, & recomends Col: Tho Lee, as a very proper Person to act in that office; if the Col will Do the business, he hath my Vote freely.

12th day—

The Packet mentioned above, inclosed a Copy of an order of his Majesty relative to the Ohio-Company. I asked for a Copy of said transcript, but it was thought uncivil to give one before it was communicated to a full Council. His honor comprises in the inclosed letter the general purport of the whole Order in two words, Viz: Proceedings, & Circumstances. See his Letter.

The Governor is also directed to run a line from the lead-mine (commonly called Chiswell's) to the Place the late commissioners ended at; who were employed by the Lord Baltimore & Messrs Penn.

It is said that two, or three new Governments will be created to the West & north-west of the presen[t] ones; & if neither of them shall include the territory situate betwixt this Government, and Ohio-river, then the Restrictions in his Majesty's Proclamation published in the year 1763, will be taken off.

Intelligence from London. It is said the following Interrogatories will shortly transpire.

Who were the first Advisers, & Establishers of the Ohio-Company?

Have the Company ever given any Consideration to the Indians for the Land they are claiming? And was the Cession made to Governt, or to the Company.

What sum of money have they imbursed?

Do the Company say his late Majesty directed either of his Governors to grant 500,000 acres of Land to them, in the year of 1748? And if that shall be insisted on, they must produce the Warrant.

I design, that this article of news shall be imparted to a few Gentlemen only, & not made public. I read it only once, & write fm memory, therefor make a proper allowance. Pray furnish me with Answers to these Questions. I am, Sir, Your most obednt & very hum Sert

ROBT CARTER

P.S.

I shall answer the last Paragraph of your Letter, when I have more Leisure. R.C.

[81]

Will not the Govr's Report necessarily require the Company to meet?

RC (Dreer Collection, PHi). Addressed: "To Col: Geo: Mason."

Carter lived in Williamsburg and in 1768 was a member of the Council as well as a major shareholder in the Ohio Company. THE COPY OF THE REPORT was the 26 June 1767 recommendations of the Board of Trade to Lord Shelburne, and Shelburne's queries were dated 8 Oct. 1767. OUR OWN MEMORIAL to George III was prepared by George Mercer and referred by the king to the Board of Trade on 21 June 1765. John Mercer had written Carter on 21 Dec. 1767 informing him of the events in London affecting the company, and also of Mercer's desire to decline further involvement. "It is now above two years since I gave notice to the other members of Committee that my ill State of health & private Affairs would not permit me to attend the Company's business any longer & recommended Colo. Thos. [Ludwell] Lee as a very proper person to be appointed in my stead. . . ." (James, *Ohio Company*, 253). THE PACKET MENTIONED ABOVE, i.e., the Shelburne queries bearing the king's seal, arrived in Williamsburg before Carter dispatched his letter. Now the Board's wishes were known, thus ending speculation over the various reports and recommendations. Gov. Fauquier's letter presumably clarified matters by addressing certain questions to GM. A LINE FROM THE LEAD-MINE to the end of the Mason-Dixon Line would have extended a boundary from Fort Chiswell to the western Maryland border. Such a boundary would have overlapped the Proclamation Line of 1763, which was a barrier to western settlement. This order, along with the rumor that TWO, OR THREE NEW GOVERNMENTS WILL BE CREATED was based on more than hearsay. Shelburne had been developing a plan for the West during the summer of 1767, and on 11 Sept. 1767 had actually broached this new scheme to the cabinet. Shelburne sought and received cabinet approval for a policy that would permit the establishment of two transmontane colonies, "retain a few of the principal forts, and return control of Indian affairs to the provinces. . . ." (Sosin, *Whitehall in the Wilderness*, 156–164). Shelburne's proposal would have obliterated the Proclamation Line of 1763, and by his instructions to Sir William Johnson the new policy was implemented, resulting in the Treaty of Fort Stanwix. (See map in H. H. Kagan, *et al.*, eds., *American Heritage Atlas of U.S. History* [New York, 1966], 77.) On the face of it, Shelburne's cabinet proposal (along with the questions about the company) would indicate that the Ohio Company was to be a partner in developing western settlements. But Prof. Sosin takes the contrary view and presumes that Shelburne was actually using dilatory tactics toward the company "because, under the terms of its prewar grant, it enjoyed an immunity from quitrents for ten years from the time the lands were settled." (See Sosin, *Whitehall in the Wilderness*, 137–138.) Shelburne's scheme was offered as a means of holding down imperial expenses on the frontier, and thus quitrents would have accrued to the Crown rather than to private companies. However, Shelburne was relying on Benjamin Franklin for much advice as he formulated this policy, and Franklin was heavily involved in the Vandalia Company. George Mercer seemed to know what was afoot, but did not have easy access to Shelburne's office, as did the Vandalia promoters. This may account for Mercer's eventual decision to merge the Ohio Company claims with the Vandalia group, but does not necessarily mean that Shelburne was hostile to the Ohio Company. It is quite possible that Benjamin Franklin was simply a more charming person to deal with than George Mercer.

Numerous superscript letters in the original manuscript have been lowered. Carter also placed the tilde ∼ on "recomended," "sumons," and "comonly"—

and these words were expanded as though written fully. Several colons have been reduced to periods for clarity's sake.

Ohio Company Advertisement

[11 February 1768]

A FULL MEETING of the OHIO COMPANY is desired, on *Tuesday* the 23d day of *February,* at Stafford court-house, on business of importance.

G. MASON, Treasurer.

Printed from *Va. Gaz.* (Rind), 11 Feb. 1768. On the same day the Purdie and Dixon *Va. Gaz.* printed a similar advertisement but with the date of "*Thursday* the 25th of this instant. . . ." Other notices in the Rind edition and those of 11 and 18 Feb. 1768 in the *Md. Gaz.* indicated the meeting was scheduled for 23 Feb. The BUSINESS OF IMPORTANCE was related to rumors that Gov. Fauquier had been asked to report on the company's affairs.

From Francis Fauquier

[[*ca. 11 February 1768.* Gov. Fauquier was carrying on his duties under the strain of illness, but he apparently tried to follow Lord Shelburne's instructions regarding the Ohio Company. Fauquier died on 3 Mar. 1768, but his temporary successor (John Blair) reported that Fauquier had written to GM requesting answers to Shelburne's queries "to enable me to comply the best I can." Blair wrote Shelburne on 21 Mar. 1768 and noted that he had seen a copy of this document in Fauquier's letterbook. (Quoted in Mulkearn, 638, from Blair to Shelburne, P.R.O., C. O. 5:1346/13–16.) Robert Carter's letter to GM, 10 and 12 Feb. 1768, contained Fauquier's letter as an enclosure and explained that the governor's query related to "two words, Viz: Proceedings, & Circumstances." Not found.]]

Ohio Company Proposal

[*ca.* 15 February 1768]

The following Proposals I think might be proper on Behalf of the Ohio Company—

If the original instructions from his late Majesty to Sr. Wm. Gooch, then Governor for Virga. are insisted upon, & no other Indulgencys are to be granted the Company in Consideration of the Expence we have been at, & the Discoverys we have made, then we have certainly a Right to the 500,000 Acres therein mentioned in as many different Surveys as the Company think fit; the Words "Grant or Grants" plainly bea[r]ing that Meaning, & being no Way inconsistent wth. the Laws & Customs of Virga.—but if the Words of the Instructions are to be taken in the confined Sense recommended by a former Report of the Lords of Trade, & we must take the Land in Tracts of 20,000 Acres, the Breadth ⅓d. of the Length; then Lands will not be worth our Acceptance, as we cou'd have taken them up upon much better Terms here, without any Application in England.

If the Government in England shou'd think the Company deserve further Indulgencys, & shou'd be inclined to make us an extensive Grant; then I shou'd approve of the following Terms—A Grant to be made the Company (naming the Members) according to the following Bounds—To begin where the pensilvania Line crosses the River Monongahaly, to run with the Pesilvania Line a due West Course to the River Ohio, & down the River Ohio to the Mouth of the great Conhaway, alias New River, or Woods River, & up the sd. River Conhaway to the Mouth of the Green Briar River, & from thence by a straight Line to the Beginning upon the River Monongahaly: in Consideration of which the Company will pay a Yearly Acknowledgment to the Crown in Lieu of Quit Rents, will make a Purchase of the Lands at their own Expence from the Indians, & procure their Protection & Influence in setling them; & will engage to settle 500 Familys thereon within the space of seven Years from the Date of their Grant. It is to be observed that these Bounds are as nearly comformable to the original Bounds mentioned in the Ohio Company's first Petition & the Royal Instructions as they can be, without interfering with Mr. Penn's Grant; which according to the Line lately run by the Commissioners between the Proprietors of Maryland & Pensilvania, includes part of the Lands formerly ordered to be granted to the Company, & at the same time is so contiguous to Virginia as to admit of being under the same Government.

The Pesilvania Charter (according to the Line lately run by the sd. Commissioner's) includes the Lands actually discovered & setled by the Company—between the River Monongahaly & Youyuagaine; & tho' the Proprietors of Maryland & Pesilvania both promised Mr. Hanbury decd. that they wou'd grant any of their Lands in that Country, that might happen to fall within their Limits, to the Company upon the same Terms that the Crown did; yet these Promises can't now be relyed on: which is the Reason we now propose to bind our Grant upon the Pensilvania Line.

[84]

RC (Henry Papers, 1762–1881, DLC). In 1965 this two-page manuscript by GM was found among the miscellaneous Henry Papers, where it had been placed by mistake. In the upper right-hand corner of the first page "P Henry" has been written in pencil. At the lower left-hand corner of the second page, an archivist has written "Ac. 2850."

GM wrote this memorandum after the company shareholders learned that the Board of Trade had delayed action on George Mercer's 1765 petition to await news and recommendations from Gov. Fauquier. By the time GM had attended the company meeting at Stafford Court House, his thinking on the matter had been somewhat clarified, but GM still repeated a portion of this proposal in his enclosure to John Mercer on 26 Feb. 1768. A FORMER REPORT OF THE LORDS OF TRADE was the restrictive Board of Trade report of 25 June 1754, which altered the original plan of western settlement, as GM explained. THE LINE LATELY RUN was the boundary between Pennsylvania and Maryland surveyed by Charles Mason and Jeremiah Dixon in 1766. Since the extended Pennsylvania-Virginia border was not yet determined, GM's remarks about the western extension of the Pennsylvania line were highly conjectural. That he soon realized this is made clear in GM to John Mercer, 26 Feb. 1768.

The Ms gives the appearance of being a rough draft. Three repetitious lines on page two have been crossed through, as have several other words whose inclusion would not have altered the essential meaning. See GM's revisions and addenda in his MEMORANDUM UPON THE BOUNDARIES . . . , *ca.* 20 Feb. 1768.

From Robert Carter

[[*19 Feb. 1768*. Carter sent this letter by an express rider, which GM acknowledged in his reply of 24 Feb. 1768. Perhaps Carter had fresh news about the request from Whitehall to Gov. Fauquier relating to the Ohio Company petition for western lands. It appears from GM's reply that Carter sought answers to questions about company expenditures and agents, the company's involvement in the Treaty of Logstown, and the whereabouts of the original warrant for the land grant of 1749. GM received the letter at Stafford Court House while waiting for enough company shareholders to assemble so that they might conduct business. Not found.]]

Memorandum on the Boundaries Proposed by the Ohio Company

[*ca.* 20 February 1768]

I think the following or some such Proposals would be proper on behalf of the Ohio Company.

If the Instructions from his late Majesty are insisted on, and the Company are thought to deserve no further Favours in Consideration of the great Charge they have incurred the Discoveries they have made, and the Informations they have from time to time given to the Government; then we ought at least to have Liberty to

Survey our 500,000 Acres in as many different Tracts as we please, the words Grant or Grants plainly bearing that Meaning and being no way inconsistent with the Laws and Customs of Virginia, where the Patentees have never been obliged to make large Surveys for any particular Quantity, but if the words "Grant or Grants" are to be understood in the limitted Sense recommended some time ago by the Board of Trade, and we are obliged to take the Lands in Tracts not less than 20,000 Acres, the breadth to be ⅓ the length, We have been deceived by an unnatural Construction of the Words in the Royal Instructions into a very heavy and useless Expence, as such Grants would not be worth our Acceptance, and what his late Majesty out of his Bounty, intended as a Favour and Encouragement to the Petitioners, would be turned into a real Injury, as we could have taken up the Lands upon better Terms here, without making any Application in England as many others have done in very large Quantities on this side the Allighany Mountains. Our Proposal was to take our Lands on the other side the Allighany Mountains in a Country then unknown, which we have since discovered and opened a Road of Communication to it, at our own private Expence.

The first Adventurers in such an Enterprise as this have certainly a just Right to the Prefference in taking up the Lands they at so great Expence discovered; When the Ice is once Broke, and the Settlement made practicable, those who came after will readily take such Lands as the first Adventurers refused, which in fact will be more valuable than the very best are now and the very additional Expences attending small Surveys will sufficiently restrain the Company from making more Surveys than they find absolutely necessary. As there is not the same necessity for the Company's building a Fort now as formerly, and as a Fort we had begun, and a great many other of our Buildings and Effects were destroyed by the War; We have reason to hope that Article will be remitted; and also that the Company may be indulged with appointing and employing a Surveyor of their own; the legal Fees to Surveyors of the Counties being exceeding high, nor would the Surveyor of Augusta County (at several hundred Miles distance from the place, tho it now falls within his District) be able to execute it, consistent with the duty's of his Office in that part of his Country that is already inhabited— the only Reason why it may be thought to belong to his Office is, that the County of Augusta has no Bounds to the Westward; but as this is to be a new Settlement, and at present disjoined from Virginia he can't be thought to be injured by such Appointment.

[86]

The Proprietor of the Northern Neck has always exercised the right of appointing his own Surveyor for taking up Lands not withstanding there was a commissioned Surveyor in each County, whom he has employed or not as he thought convenient.

If it should be thought proper to grant greater Indulgencies to the Company, and recompence them with a more extensive Grant, then I should think a Grant upon the following, or some such Terms, and by the following Boundaries might answer.

To begin on the River Mohongahaly where the Pennsylvania line crosses the said River [and run] with the Pensylvania line a due West Course to the River Ohio, and down and with the River Ohio to the Mouth of the great Canhaway, alias Woods River or New River, and up the said Canhaway River binding with the same to the Mouth of the Green Briar River, and from thence by a streight Line to the Beginning on the River Mohongahaly. In consideration of which the Company to pay a yearly Acknowledgment in Lieu of Quitrents, to purchase the Lands of the Indians at their own Expence, and procure their Countenance and Protection to the Inhabitants, and to Settle 500 Families on the Land within seven years from the date of their Patent. In this Case it might be proper for the Ministry to recommend it to Sir William Johnston to use his Interest and good Offices with the Indians in assisting the Company to make a Purchase of the Lands; which they would propose to do in plain and express Terms, without the least Fraud or Deception, that the Indians may have no Cause to complain hereafter that they had been imposed upon, as has too frequently been the Case, and been attended with very fatal Consequences.

It is to be observed that these Bounds mentioned in our first Petition, and his late Majesty's Instructions without interfering with the Bounds of Mr. Penn's Grant, or without going to the Westward of the River Ohio; which would at present give great Umbrage both to the six Nations and the Western Tribes of Indians.

The Line lately run by the Commissioners between the Proprietors of Maryland and Pensylvania will cross the Mohongahaly, and strike the Ohio many Miles below Pitsburg, consequently include all the Lands the Ohio Company had Settled, and though both the Proprietors of Maryland and Pensylvania promised the late Mr. Hanbury that they would grant to the Company any vacant Lands, convenient to them, which might fall within their respective Provinces; Yet we don't know how far such Promises are now to be relied on; which is the Reason for ascertaining the Boundaries as before mentioned, to avoid a possibility of any Dispute. The Lands are also so convenient to Virginia, that they may well be under the same Government at least for the present.

It will be best to obtain a Grant in England instead of referring Us to the Governor and Council for the names of the present Company should lie inserted to prevent Disputes with such as were merely nominal, and have not advanced a single Shilling, nor been at the least Trouble.

FC (Mercer Papers, PPiU). In John Mercer's handwriting and endorsed: "Boundaries proposed by the Ohio Company when their grant is renewed."

GM had digested the rumors of a requested report from Lord Shelburne and had obviously given the idea more thought, as a comparison with the earlier (*ca.* 15 Feb.) draft indicates. The Ohio Company shareholders, including GM, assumed that the desired governor's report was a straight-forward action by Lord Shelburne, and that the report would become the basis for final settlement of their claims. Prof. Jack Sosin, however, believes that when Shelburne took the Board of Trade recommendation and relayed it to Fauquier he "practically buried" the Ohio Company claim (Sosin, *Whitehall and the Wilderness,* 136–138). Sosin suggests that Shelburne had access to a complete file on company affairs dating back to 1757, so that answers to the questions asked of Fauquier were already available in London. "Perhaps the Secretary of State [Shelburne] did not respond enthusiastically to the Ohio Company because, under the terms of its prewar grant, it enjoyed an immunity from quitrents for ten years from the time the lands were settled." Fauquier took on the assignment in good faith, and naturally turned to GM for the necessary information. Bad weather had delayed the scheduled company meeting from 23 Feb. until the 25th, when GM met with John Mercer and Richard Lee at Stafford Court House. Despite the newspaper advertisements and personal entreaties the meeting lacked a quorum. John Mercer wrote George Mercer on 3 Mar. 1768 with caustic comments on company affairs (Mulkearn, 221–228), including the poor attendance at meetings. GM and Mercer were circumspect in their dealing with Lee, because Lee was on the Council. When Lee left the meeting Mercer and GM "were very glad of [it] for we cou'd not talk before him of anything that cou'd promote the company's interest which he would begrudge to advance ones shilling for & he had no right to expect we should communicate our Sentiments to him." When Mercer and GM finished their talks "Colo. Mason enquir'd if I had his memorandum of the bounds, I cou'd not find it on which we searched every paper over & found Dick [Lee] according to his old Custom had pocketed it. . . . Colo. Mason was however able to supply the Loss but it cost him above two hours to do it." Thus this memorandum passed into Mercer's hands. The three shareholders took no umbrage at the Board of Trade report but on the contrary had a copy "which they read & commended extremely." GM's suggestion that the SURVEYOR OF AUGUSTA COUNTY would not resent the appointment of company surveyors was asking a good deal of human nature. Augusta County indeed had no western boundary, so that legal surveys in the Ohio Valley were under that county's jurisdiction. Moreover, Augusta County residents were in no mood for friendly negotiations with the Company, as their petition to the House of Burgesses of 24 Nov. 1766 showed (JHB, 1766–1769, 37). The petitioners complained that their hopes of "settling on the Waters of the *Ohio,*" had been deterred "by reason of the Claims sundry Companies set up by Virtue of some old Grants . . . the Terms of which have never been complied with." If

Shelburne ever saw this petition he found reinforcement for his ideas, since the Augusta residents claimed that but for the company grants the frontier "would have been so well peopled that the Inhabitants would have been able to have repelled the Incursions of the *Indians,* and saved immense Sums to the Colony." The petition was tabled but caused uneasiness among company shareholders. GM pondered the boundary problem between Pennsylvania and Virginia overnight and wrote John Mercer a letter on 26 Feb. 1768 concerning his apprehensions (*q.v.*).

John Mercer sent a copy of this memorandum to George Mercer with a letter dated 3 Mar. 1768 (Mulkearn, 227). GM's original Ms has not been found.

To Robert Carter

SIR   Stafford Court House Febry, 24th: 1768

I have your Favour of the 19th. Inst. ♉ Express, & am obliged to you for the Pamphlets you was so kind to send me, which I have not yet had time to peruse. Your's of the 10th Inst. inclosing a Letter from his Honour the Governor to which you refer, is not come to Hand. To my great Mortification we are disappointed in the Compy's. Intended Meeting, not a Member but Mr. Mercer Colo. Richd. Lee & myself attending; so that we are unable to proceed upon any Business. I presume when his Majesty's Instructions arrive, his Honour the Governour will favour us with proper Information; or will let us know the purport of those already received, when they shall have them communicated to the Council; tho' it does not appear from the Papers we have received from England that the Matter is referred to the Council, but to the Governour only.

Most of the Interrogatories you mention may be easily answered. Our Petitions to his Majesty & applications to the Board of Trade as well as our own Books & Proceedings, & above every thing else, the Sums of Money actually advanced in the Prosecution of the Scheme, will shew who were the first advisers & Establisher of the Ohio Company; not one Man except the present Members, & those of whom they purchased & under whom they claim, having ever advanced a single shilling; except two or three Gentlemen who were at first concerned, & upon refusing to continue in the Company, or be any longer concerned, were repaid what they had advanced.

The Company had not only an Agent at the Treaty of Logg's Town, but actually ingaged Andrew Montour, the famous Indian Interpreter, (who was himself one of the Onandagoe Council & a Chief of the Six Nations) by a considerable Present to prevail on the Indians to make the Cession they did; which was to have been made in the Company's Name, but that Governor Dinwiddie thought it was irregular or illegal to do so.

The Sum advanced by the Company wth. Interest from the respective Dates, is near £10,000-Sterling: it can be exactly ascertain'd from our Books.

His late Majesty's Instructions to Sir Wm. Gooch relative to our Grant are entered in the Council Books, & we have a copy of them. The original Warrant can not be required of us; that being an Act of Government, was transmitted to the Governor himself, & not to us. My Paper gives me no room to add, but that I am very respectfully, Sir Yr. most Hble. Sert

G. Mason

Yr Letter to Mr. Hough shall have the first safe Conveyance

RC (MeHi).

GM's bad luck with the mails was typical and creates much sympathy for the patient 18th-century businessman. THE COMPY'S INTENDED MEETING has been called after several partners received copies of George Mercer's letter, which also had miscarried before it reached Gunston Hall. GM called the meeting and then was denied the useful information contained in Carter's 10 Feb. 1768 letter, though it would appear Carter has repeated MOST OF THE INTERROGATORIES in this letter. THE ORIGINAL WARRANT was the royal grant of 23 Feb. 1749.

To John Mercer

DEAR SIR.   Mrs. Moncures 26th Feb. 1768

Since I parted with you, I have upon reflecting on the Bounds proposed in my Memorandum for the Ohio Grant, apprehended that in one particular I am wrong. I have mentioned "Beginning on the River Mohongahaly where the Pensylvania Line crosses the said River; and runing with the Pensylvania Line a due West Course to the Ohio River." Now as we are not certain where Mr. Penns five Degrees of Longitude will end, this description may be disadvantageous to us. If his five Degrees of Longitude reach over the Ohio upon extending his lower West Course, then I am right; but on the contrary, if his five degrees of Longitude are out before his lower West Line reaches the Ohio, then I apprehend Mr. Penn must run a North Course from the end of his West Line; which will strike the Ohio River much higher up than to continue the West Course would do, and take in some very valuable Lands that the Bounds before mentioned would leave out. It is indeed said that the five degrees of Longitude on his lower West Course will reach over the Ohio; but as this is not absolutely certain, we should be cautious in our Descriptions. I therefore think it will stand much better thus, "Beginning on the River Mohongahaly where the Pensylvania Line crosses the said River, and running with the Lines or Boundaries [of] Pensylvania to the Ohio River &c" as before, this will answer in either Case. As I desire Mr. Daniel to whose care this is directed to [leave] immediately, I hope it will come to your hands before you dispatch your Letters to England; for I think the Alteration very material, for some other Reasons which I have not now time to mention.

G. MASON

[P.S.] Or as Mr. Penn's Bounds are yet so uncertain, perhaps the Boundaries of a Grant to the Ohio Company would be better expressed as follows

"Beginning upon the East side of the River Ohio or Allaghany where the Pennsylvania Line crosses the said River, and running down and with the said River Ohio to the Mouth of the Great Conhaway River, alias New River or Woods River, and up and with the said Great Conhaway River to the Mouth of the Great Briar River, from thence by a streight Course to the nearest part of the Boundaries of Pennsylvania, and with the Boundaries or Lines of Pennsylvania to the Beginning upon the Ohio River."

All that Country or tract of Land bounded on the West and North West by the Ohio or Allaghany River; on the South and South West by the Great Conhaway River, otherwise called New River or Woods River; on the East and South East by the Green Briar River and the Allaghany Mountains, on the North and North East by the Mohongahaly River and the Boundaries of Pennsylvania to the Ohio or Allaghany River.

FC (Mercer Papers, PPiU). The copy is in John Mercer's handwriting, and appended to his file copy of GM's "Boundaries proposed by the Ohio Company," *ca.* 20 Feb. 1768.

Ambiguities in the 17th-century charters of the two colonies led to misunderstanding over whether the forks of the Ohio lay in Virginia or Pennsylvania. Obviously, the Ohio Company shareholders had assumed from 1749 onward that jurisdiction for this area rested with Virginia. A compromise on the western boundary of Pennsylvania was arranged in 1779, but final surveys were not completed until 1785. Meanwhile, GM perceived the implications of extending the Mason and Dixon line westward. MR. PENNS FIVE DEGREES OF LONGITUDE granted by the 1681 charter extended the Pennsylvania southern boundary west from the Delaware River. After the Mason and Dixon survey of 1766, GM at first assumed an extension of the Pennsylvania-Maryland boundary would become the Virginia-Pennsylvania line until it reached beyond the Ohio, since neither colony had a clear conception of its western limits. GM's second thoughts were well-founded but of no practical use to the company, since the possibility of a land grant to the company was certainly remote after 1779. In fact, the Pennsylvania line did turn northward about 15 miles east of the Ohio, so that GM's afterthought as expressed in the postscript provided boundaries that would have given the company lands out of Pennsylvania's jurisdiction—the strip of land now comprising the West Virginia panhandle. Actually, all these calculations were for naught. There is no indication that Shelburne intended to make retribution to the company, and only a few weeks after GM wrote this letter Pres. John Blair of the Virginia Council sounded a warning in the House of Burgesses that could not have improved matters. Blair reported that illegal settlements on Redstone Creek and the Cheat River had been made in violation of the Proclamation of 1763, and that "These Banditti . . . [will] open afresh those Sluices of Blood" unless the colonial government enacted "some prudent Law." The Treaty of Fort Stanwix in 1768 broke down the Proclamation Line concept but did not advance Ohio Company claims. John Mercer died on 14 Oct. 1768, severing George Mercer's closest link with the company and leaving GM even more burdened with company affairs. George Mercer carried on his lobbying activities in London and published the *Case of the Ohio Company* (*ca.* 1768) in support of company claims, but he was no match for Benjamin Franklin and other backers of the Grand Ohio Company, which had overlapping claims with the original Ohio Company. Acting on his own authority, Mercer finally merged company claims with the Grand Ohio enterprise in May 1770. See James Mercer to GM, 9 Jan. 1772.

The bracketed words *of* and *leave* are conjectures made because the right margin of the Ms is frayed.

From William Fitzhugh

[DEAR SIR   Rousby Hall July 12th 1768
    I have] the Pleasure to Send for your Accep[tance a] Ram & Ewe Lamb by Mr. Heward [and later I] intend on Old Ewe with [her spring lambs will] be sent [. You may make u]se of their Dam that [they may be] Sort [*short?*] Shorn with any Certain [results. If these] are taken proper Care of you [can hope] for no Better.
    [Mrs. Fitzhug]h Brot. me a Son two Days [ago and joins] in Complts to you & your [lady. Yo]ur Obed[t. &] Huml Ser[vt]
                                                    [WILLIAM FITZHUGH]

[The ewes] are Slit in Both Ears & [the Ram] on the Right Side.

RC (Mason Papers, DLC). The letter has been partly burned, and is preserved in three scorched separate fragments.

ROUSBY HALL was a manor located near the mouth of the Patuxent River in Calvert County, Md. Fitzhugh was GM's nephew.

The portions in brackets are conjectures.

To the Public

                                                    [12 December 1768]
    Whereas the Subscriber, did, in the Year One Thousand Seven Hundred and Sixty-seven, give under his Hand, a Note, promising

to pay unto John Bond, senr. of *Baltimore-Town*, a Sum of Money, upwards of Thirty Pounds Currency, Twenty Pounds of which Sum is paid, and a Receipt thereof entered on the said Note, the Remainder was agreed to be left unpaid, until I was satisfied by the Judgment of Men, concerning some just Demands, I have against said John Bond. I therefore desire that no Person will take an Assignment of the aforesaid Note, as I will not pay the Remainder, until I am fully satisfied it is justly due. As Witness my Hand, this Twelfth Day of Twelfth Month, called *December*, One Thousand Seven Hundred and Sixty-eight.

GEORGE MASON

Printed from Annapolis *Md. Gaz.*, 5 Jan. 1769.

To John Posey

[[*ca. Jan. 1769.* Washington signed a security bond for a debt Posey owed GM, and, when the note was due, Posey failed to settle the matter. Washington wrote Posey on 11 June 1769 (Fitzpatrick, ed., *Writings of Washington*, II, 507) that "Colo. Mason hath several times spoke to me on Acct. of your Bond . . . since he wrote to you himself; and I should presume, must now have greater Calls for the money than he himself apprehended, inasmuch as he has been disappointed of receiving £350 of the Publick for his executed Negroes. . . ." In a second letter to Posey of 26 July, Washington reminded their neighbor that GM "had premptorily demanded payment of the Money by the 10th. of April last," reproached Posey for "delaying the matter from January till this time" (*ibid.*, II, 518), and added that GM "gave you and me both Notice so long ago as January, that he should expect the Cash in April. . . ."]]

The Nonimportation Association of 1769

[5 April to 18 May 1769]

I. From George Washington, 5 April 1769
II. To George Washington, 5 April 1769
III. Agreement of Philadelphia Merchants, 10 March 1769
IV. Memorandum of Agreement with George Washington, 21 April 1769
V. To George Washington, 23 April 1769
VI. The Nonimportation Association as Corrected by Mason, 23 April 1769
VII. The Letter of "Atticus," 11 May
VIII. The Nonimportation Resolutions of 1769, 18 May 1769

EDITORIAL NOTE

The colonists' relief over repeal of the Stamp Act in 1766 was short lived. Desperately searching for new sources of revenue, the determined Chancellor of the Exchequer, Charles Townshend, had calculated that £40,000 might be raised annually by taxing certain British exports to the colonies. The colonists in 1765 had insisted that Parliament could not pass an internal tax, so it was reasoned that a duty on exports was external—and therefore acceptable. Parliament approved the plan during one of Lord Chatham's lapses.

Alarmed over news of the Townshend Acts, the Virginia Assembly in 1768 petitioned Parliament to repeal the measures. "*That the Parliament may make Laws for regulating the Trade of the Colonies has been granted,*" the Assembly conceded. "But," despite Townshend's distinction, "*a Tax imposed upon such of the British Exports, as are the necessaries of Life . . . [we] conceive to be a Tax internal to all Intents and Purposes*" (JHB, 1766–1769, 166–168).

George Mason was a spectator to these events and was sympathetic to the remedy recommended at northern meetings called by political leaders and angry merchants. In Boston, New York, and Philadelphia outspoken tradesmen had urged their colleagues to retaliate against the new taxes with an economic boycott, a successful device in the Stamp Act crisis. In forming nonimportation associations, groups of citizens pledged themselves not to purchase British goods until grievances were redressed. Word of their efforts reached Mount Vernon and Gunston Hall as the news of colonial resistance fanned out across Virginia.

Washington served in the House of Burgesses as a Fairfax County delegate. In 1768 he had observed the tenor of the House as its first protest was fashioned and directed toward London. When another session of the Burgesses was less than two months away, both Washington and Mason received packets containing copies of the Agreement of Philadelphia merchants (6 Feb. 1769), the Philadelphia Merchants' Association (10 March 1769), the covering letter of Philadelphia merchants to Annapolis merchants (15 March 1769), the Annapolis merchants' reply (March 1769), and another Annapolis merchants' letter (25 March 1769). Upon receiving this intelligence from their mutual friend, Dr. David Ross, Washington wrote Mason and plainly sought advice on how to proceed (5 April 1769). Mason answered that same day, saying he had started to write "something of the Sort" but discontinued his labor because of illness. Then, about three weeks later, Mason wrote Washington (23 April 1769) saying that "in looking over" the proposed Association, a copy of which Washington had already seen, he had "made some few Alterations in it," which Mason proceeded to write on the back of his letter. Washington's endorsed copy of the Association bears all but one of Mason's recommended changes, interlined in Washington's handwriting. This document is in the hand of an unidentified writer. Clearly, Mason was not the primary author. Indeed, the document is obviously modeled on the Philadelphia Merchants' Association of 10 Mar. 1769.

The long-standing error of historians in attributing the Association to Mason can be traced back through the biography of Mason by his distant kinswoman, Kate Mason Rowland, to the early 19th-century historian, Jared Sparks. Citing Sparks as her sole authority (Rowland, I, 138), she asserted that the resolutions "in the handwriting of George Mason, were found among Washington's papers by the latter's biographer." Elsewhere, Miss Rowland wrote that the draft of the 18 May 1769 resolves "corresponds exactly with the one written by George Mason, except that two short articles were added and one of Mason's omitted." The resolutions in the appendix to Miss Rowland's first volume were copied from John Daly Burk's *History of Virginia . . .* (Petersburg, Va., 1804–1816), III, 345–349. She also attributes a rejected article as one "of George Mason's left out by the Burgesses."

Incautiously Sparks assumed the Association draft in the Washington Papers was in Mason's handwriting and in 1834 wrote: "On comparing it [the printed Association in Burk's *History*] with Mr. Mason's manuscript draft, retained by Washington, I find it precisely the same, except the addition of two short articles, and the omission of another. . . . As Mr. Mason was not then a member of the House of Burgesses, and as Washington left home for Williamsburg shortly after receiving the draft, he [Washington] must have taken it with him to the Assembly, and of course have been a principal agent in procuring its adoption." (See Jared Sparks, ed., *Writings of George Washington* [Boston, 1834–1837], II, 356*n*).

Obviously Miss Rowland accepted Jared Sparks' judgment. "Washington took the paper with him to the Assembly," she wrote, "and the burgesses . . . apparently adopted its principles with one accord." (See Rowland, I, 138, 389–393.) No closer to the primary source was John Fiske. The burgesses went to the Apollo Room of Raleigh's Tavern, Fiske wrote, and "adopted a series of resolutions prepared by Washington" (John Fiske, *The American Revolution* [Boston, 1919], I, 75).

The list of historians misled by Sparks, Rowland, Fiske, *et al.*, is long, but in more recent times critical scholars have sensed a fallacy. When John C. Fitzpatrick edited Washington's papers, he would have recognized GM's hand but assumed the draft was a duplicate of the resolves sent along with the merchants' correspondence. A glance at Mason's letter of 5 April disproves this assumption. Fitzpatrick simply concluded that "Washington evidently was unaware at that time of Mason's authorship of the nonimportation association" (*Writings of Washington*, II, 500*n*). Since neither Sparks nor Fitzpatrick had bothered to compare the 10 March Association with the Virginia Association, the error was not Washington's. More recently, in *The Papers of Thomas Jefferson*, editor-historian Julian Boyd (I, 31*n*) accepts Mason's authorship although he points out that Arthur Lee's "Monitor" letters appearing in the *Virginia Gazette* that spring "anticipated at many points Mason's Nonimportation Resolutions."

On circumstantial evidence, a case could be made for Richard Henry Lee as the probable Association author. Richard Henry Lee was a burgess from Westmoreland County, the first county to protest the Townshend Acts to the House in 1768. The draft endorsed by Washington, which is the only extant draft, is by an unknown hand. Lee was present in Williamsburg for the meetings between 16–18 May, and Lee was the fifth signer of the Association. Mason never claimed authorship and indeed said a few weeks earlier that he had been too ill to carry out such an undertaking. Burk's *History of Virginia*, published only thirteen years after Mason's death, never assigned authorship to a single individual. Jared Sparks assumed that Mason was the author because of circumstances, and since 1834 his assertion has been unchallenged.

The original compiler of the Virginia Nonimportation Resolutions borrowed heavily from the Philadelphia Merchants' Association of 10 March 1769. Certainly Mason proposed a few changes, and there must have been other suggestions before the committee made its final report on 18 May. In the circumstances, it seems possible that Richard Henry Lee drafted the Virginia Resolves of 1769.

From George Washington

DEAR SIR: Mount Vernon 5th, April 1769.

Herewith you will receive a letter and sundry papers which were forwarded to me a day or two ago by Doctor Ross of Bladensburg. I transmit them with the greater pleasure, as my own desire of knowing your sentiments upon a matter of this importance exactly coincides with the Doctrs. inclinations.

At a time when our lordly Masters in Great Britain will be satisfied with nothing less than the deprivation of American freedom, it seems highly necessary that some thing shou'd be done to avert the stroke and maintain the liberty which we have derived from our Ancestors; but the manner of doing it to answer the purpose effectually is the point in question.

That no man shou'd scruple, or hesitate a moment to use a——ms in defence of so valuable a blessing, on which all the good and evil of life depends; is clearly my opinion; yet A——ms I wou'd beg leave to add, should be the last resource; the denier resort. Addresses to the Throne, and remonstrances to Parliament, we have already, it is said, proved the inefficacy of; how far then their attention to our rights & priviledges is to be awakened or alarmed by starving their Trade & manufactures, remains to be tryed.

The northern Colonies, it appears, are endeavouring to adopt this scheme. In my opinion it is a good one; & must be attended with salutary effects, provided it can be carried pretty generally into execution; but how far it is practicable to do so, I will not take upon me to determine. That there will be difficulties attending the execution of it every where, from clashing interests, & selfish designing men (ever attentive to their own gain, & watchful of every turn that can assist their lucrative views, in preference to any other consideration) cannot be denied; but in the Tobacco Colonies where the Trade is so diffused, and in a manner wholly conducted by Factors for their principals at home, these difficulties are certainly enhanced, but I think not insurmountably increased, if the Gentlemen in their several Counties wou'd be at some pains to explain matters to the people, & stimulate them to a cordial agreement to purchase none but certain innumerated Articles out of any of the Stores after such a period, nor import nor purchase any themselves. This, if it did not effectually withdraw the Factors from their Importations, wou'd at least make them extremely cautious in doing it, as the prohibited Goods could be vended to none but the non-associater, or those who wou'd pay no regard to their association; both of whom ought to be stigmatized, and made the objects of publick reproach.

The more I consider a Scheme of this sort, the more ardently I wish success to it, because I think there are private, as well as public advantages to result from it. The former [is] certain, however precarious the other may prove; for in respect to the latter I have always thought that by virtue of the same power (for here alone the authority derives) which assumes the right of Taxation, they may attempt at least to restrain our manufactories; especially those of a public nature; the same equity & justice prevailing in the one case as the other, it being no greater hardship to forbid my manufacturing, than it is to order me to buy Goods of them loaded with Duties, for the express purpose of raising a revenue. But as a measure of this sort will be an additional exertion of arbitrary power, we cannot be worsted I think in putting it to the Test. On the other hand, that the Colonies are considerably indebted to Great Britain, is a truth universally acknowledged. That many families are reduced, almost, if not quite, to penury & want, from the low ebb of their fortunes, and Estates daily selling for the discharge of Debts, the public papers furnish but too many melancholy proofs of. And that a Scheme of this Sort will contribute more effectually than any other I can devise to immerge the Country from the distress it at present labours under, I do most firmly believe, if it can be generally adopted. And I can see but one Set of people (the Merchants excepted) who will not, or ought not, to wish well to the Scheme; and that is those who live genteely & hospitably, on clear Estates. Such as these were they, not to consider the valuable object in view,

[97]

& the good of others, might think it hard to be curtail'd in their living & enjoyments; for as to the penurious Man, he saves his money, & he saves his credit; having the best Plea for doing that, which before perhaps he had the most violent struggles to refrain from doing. The extravagant & expensive man has the same good plea to retrench his Expences. He is thereby furnished with a pretext to live within bounds, and embraces it.—Prudence dictated economy to him before, but his resolution was too weak to put it in practice; for how can I, *says he*, who have lived in such a manner change my method? I am ashamed to do it: and besides, such an alteration in the System of my living, will create suspicions of a decay in my fortune, & such a thought the World must not harbour; I will e'en continue my course: till at last the course discontinues the Estate, a sale of it being the consequence of his perseverance in error. This I am satisfied is the way that many who have set out in the wrong track, have reasoned, till ruin stares them in the face. And in respect to the poor & needy man, he is only left in the same situation he was found; better I might say, because as he judges from comparison, his condition is amended in Proportion as it approaches nearer to those above him.

Upon the whole therefore, I think the Scheme a good one, and that it ought to be tryed here, with such alterations as the exigency of our circumstances render absolutely necessary; but how, & in what manner to begin the work, is a matter worthy of consideration; and whether it can be attempted with Propriety, or efficacy (further than a communication of sentiments to one another) before May, when the Court & Assembly will meet together in Williamsburg, and a uniform plan can be concerted, and sent into the different Counties to operate at the same time, & in the same manner every where, is a thing I am somewhat in doubt upon, & shou'd be glad to know your opinion of. I am Dr. Sir Your most obdt. hble Servant

G. Washington

FC (GW Papers, DLC). From Washington's letterbook, entered: "To George Mason Esqr." and endorsed "Mount Vernon 5th. April 1769."

Washington enclosed with this letter copies of messages which passed between Annapolis and Philadelphia merchants dated 6 Feb. 1769, 15 Mar. 1769, ? Mar. 1769, and 25 Mar. 1769, and the Philadelphia Merchants Association of 10 Mar. 1769. These are reprinted in Hamilton, ed., *Letters to Washington*, III, 349–354. Hamilton also erroneously attributed the Virginia Resolves of 1769 to GM when his work was published in 1901, halfway between Kate M. Rowland's renewed claim and Edward Channing's acceptance of it in 1912. The 10 Mar. 1769 Agreement, which was also sent to GM by Dr. Ross, is printed below.

To George Washington

DEAR SIR   Gunston-Hall 5th. April 1769.
 I have yr. Favour of this Day, inclosing the Resolves of the
Merchts. in Philadelphia &c. which I return by the Bearer, as I had
before recd. Duplicates of them from our Friend the Doctor.
 I entirely agree with you that no regular Plan of the Sort pro-
posed can be entered into here before the Meeting of the Genl.
Court at least, if not that of the Assembly; when a Number of
Gentlemen, from the different Parts of the Country, will have an
Opportunity of conferring together, & acting in Concert; in the
mean Time it may be necessary to publish something preparatory to
it in our Gazettes, to warn the People at least of the impending
Danger, & induce them the more readily & chearfully to concur in
the proper Measures to avert it; & something of this Sort I had
begun; but am unluckily stop'd by a Disorder which affects my
Head & Eyes in such a Manner, that I am totally incapable of
Business, proceeding from a slight Cold's checking an Attack of an
Arisipelas or St. Anthony's-Fire (a Complaint I am very subject to)
so soon as I am able, I shall resume it, & shall then write you more
fully, or endeavour to see you: in the mean Time pray commit to
Writing such Hints as may occur.
 Our All is at Stake, & the little Conveniencys & Comforts of Life,
when set in Competition with our Liberty, ought to be rejected not
with Reluctance but with Pleasure: Yet it is plain that in the Tobo.
Colonys we can't at present confine our Importations within such
narrow Bounds as the Northern Colonys, a Plan of this kind, to be
practicable, must be adapted to our Circumstances; for not steadily
executed, it had better have remained unattempted. We may retrench all Manner of Superfluitys, Finery of all Denominations, &
confine ourselves to Linnens Woolens &c, not exceeding a certain
Price: it is amazing how much this (if adopted in all the Colonys)
wou'd lessen the American Imports, and distress the various Traders
& Manufacturers in Great Britain—This wou'd quickly awaken
their Attention—they wou'd see, they wou'd feel the Oppressions we
groan under, & exert themselves to procure us Redress: this once
obtain'd, we shou'd no longer discontinue our Importations, confining ourselves still never to import any Article that shou'd hereafter
be taxed by Act of Parliament for raising a Revennue in America;
for however singular I may be in my Opinion, I am thoroughly

convinced that (Justice & Harmony happily restored) it is not the Interest of these Colonys to refuse British Manufactures: our supplying our Mother-Country with gross Materials, & taking her Manufactures in Return is the true Chain of Connection between us; these are the Bands, which, if not broken by Oppressions, must long hold us together, by maintain[in]g a constant Reciprocation of Interest: proper Caution shou'd therefore be used in drawing up the proposed Plan of Association. It may not be amiss to let the Ministry understand that untill we obtain a Redress of Grievances, we will with hold from them our Commoditys, particularly refrain from making Tobacco, by which the Revennue wou'd lose fifty times more than all their Oppressions cou'd raise here.

Had the Hint I have given with Regard to the Taxation of Goods imported into America been thought of by our Merchants before the Repeal of the Stamp Act, the late american Revennue Acts wou'd probably never have been attempted.

I am wth. Mrs. Mason's Comps. & my own to Your Lady & Family. Dr. Sir Yr. most obdt. Servt.

G. MASON

P.S.—
Next Friday is the Day appointed
for the Meeting of the Vestry—

[enclosure]

The Following Agreement Was Entered into by the Merchants of Philadelphia the 10th. March 1769.

The Merchants and Traders of the City of Philadelphia having taken into their serious consideration the present State of the Trade of this Province and of the American Commerce in general observe with Anxiety That the Debt due to Great Britain for Goods imported from thence is very great and the means of paying this Debt in the present situation of Affairs likely to become more and more precarious. That the difficulties under which they now labour as a Trading People are owing to the Restrictions, Prohibitions and ill advised Regulations in several late Acts of the Parliament of Great Britain in particular that the last unconstitutional Acts imposing Duties on Tea, Paper, Glass &c for the Sole purpose of raising a Revenue being injurious to Property and destructive to Liberty have a necessary Tendency to prevent the payment of old Debts or the contracting of New; & are of consequence ruinous to Trade. That notwithstanding the many earnest Applications already made there is little reason to expect a Redress of these Grievances. Therefore in Justice to themselves and their Posterity as well as to the Traders of Great Britain concerned in the American Commerce they have Voluntarily and Unanimously entered into the following Resolutions in hopes that their Example will Stimulate the Good People of this Province to be frugal in the Use & Consumption of British Manufacture and that their Brethren the Merchants and Manufacturers of Great Britain may from Motives of Friendship and Interest be engaged to exert themselves to obtain Redress of those Grievances under which the Trade and Inhabitants of America at present labour.

First Confirming the Agreement entered into the Sixth of February last it is unanimously Resolved and Agreed. That the Subscribers will neither directly nor indirectly import from Great Britain nor any other part of Europe (except Linens & Provisions from Ireland immediately) any kind of Goods Ship'd after the first of April next except the following Articles, Tin Plates, Wire, Powder, Shot, Lead, Sail Cloth, Wool Combs, Wool & Tow Cards, Sheerman Sheers Drugs Medicines, Dye Stuff, Salt, Coal, Brimstone, School Books, Sugar Moulds, Chalk and Whiting untill the late Acts imposing Duties on Tea, Glass &c for the purpose of raising a Revenue are repealed.

Secondly That in all Orders which any of the Subscribers may send to Great Britain (after the ninth instant for other Articles than those above enumerated) they shall and will direct their Correspondents not to Ship them untill the above Acts are repealed.

Thirdly That if any Person, Strangers or others shall Contrary to the Tenor of this Agreement import any Goods the Subscribers will by all lawfull & prudent Measures discountinance such Persons and will not purchase any Goods so imported.

Fourthly That these Resolves shall be binding on all and each of the Subscribers who do hereby each and every Person for himself upon his Word & Honour agree that he will Strictly and firmly adhere to and abide by every Article of this Agreement from this time for and during the Continuance of the above mentioned Acts or untill a General Meeting of the Subscribers after three Days Public Notice shall determine otherwise.

RC (Washington Papers, DLC). Addressed to Washington and endorsed. The enclosure is among the papers which Washington endorsed: "*Old Papers Respecting the Non-importation of British Goods/*1767/&/1774."
OUR FRIEND THE DOCTOR was David Ross of Maryland, who had sent similar

packets to both GM and Washington. The extraordinary role of the few newspapers in spreading dissent is evident when GM writes of publishing SOMETHING PREPARATORY [to a legislative protest] IN OUR GAZETTES. Except for a few Philadelphia newspapers, their reliance was upon only the newspapers printed in Annapolis, Baltimore, and Williamsburg. The allusions to his illness which caused an interruption of SOMETHING OF THIS SORT make it evident that GM gave his attention to amending another person's work rather than preparation of an original plan. Since the Virginia Nonimportation Association of 1769 presumably was prepared by another Virginian, it is clear that that person also had access to the enclosed agreement from the Philadelphia merchants. A comparison between the 10 Mar. document and the Association as corrected by GM on 23 Apr. (*q.v.*) shows that the writer borrowed liberally from the introductory statement and from the second, third, and fourth articles.

The enclosure is in an unidentified handwriting.

Memorandum of Agreement with George Washington

[*21 Apr. 1769.* A memorandum in GM's handwriting, dated and endorsed by Washington, concerning a parcel of land on Little Hunting Creek. The original was in the hands of a private collector in 1967. A photostat is owned by the Mount Vernon Ladies' Association. See *Henkel's Sale Catalogue* No. 663 (Philadelphia, 1891).]

To George Washington

DR SIR   Gunston Hall 23rd: April 1769.

Upon looking over the Association, of which I sent you a Copy, I have made some few Alterations in it, as per Memdm. on the other Side.

I beg your Care of the inclosed Letters; & heartily wishing you (what I fear you will not have) an agreeable Session, I am Dr Sr Yr. most obedt. Sert.

G MASON

PS

I shall take it as a particular Favour if you'll be kind enough to get me two pr. Gold snaps made at Wms.burg for my little Girls; they are small rings with a joint in them, to wear in the Ears, instead of Earrings: also a pr. of Toupee Tongs.

Among the enumerated Goods after the Articles Oyl & Fruit is added—Sugars—after Millenary of all Sorts is added—*Lace of all Sorts*—after the Article of Gauze is added (*except Boulting Cloaths*)—

In the fifth Resolve the Word—*Slaves*—in the second Line is struck out, & the word—*hereafter*—is added between the Word, any, & the word, imported,—At the End of the Sixth Resolve after Tobacco-Debts, are added the Words—*due to them*

NB. the Reason of making this last Alteration is that at a time when the Government endeavours to call everything Seditious, it might be urged that the Subscribers took upon them a Sort of legislative Authority, in declaring they wou'd make Regulations relative to Tobo. Debts, now they have an undoubted Right to make what Regulations they please in Debts due to themselves as the Option will still remain in the Debtors

RC (Washington Papers, DLC). Addressed: "To George Washington Esqr." and endorsed by Washington: "From G. Mason./ Aprl. 28th. 1769."

Washington wrote in all of GM's recommendations except the last one on tobacco debts. Apparently GM had already sent Washington a copy of the Association, then decided several additions were necessary. Since the copy is in an unidentified hand, the assumption is that the author himself had broadcast several copies and this one fell in GM's hands.

The Nonimportation Association as Corrected by Mason

[23 April 1769]

The Merchants, Traders, Gentlemen, and other principal Inhabitants of the Colony of Virginia in general & of the County of in particular, deeply affected with the Grievances and Distresses with which his Majesty's American Subjects are oppressed, and dreading the evils which threaten the Ruin of themselves and their posterity, by reducing them from a free and happy people to a Wretched & miserable State of Slavery, having taken into their Serious Consideration the present State of the Trade of this Colony, and of the American Commerce in general, observe with anxiety that the Debt due to Great Britain for Goods imported from thence is very great, and the means of paying this Debt in the present Situation of affairs likely to become more and more precarious—that the Difficulties under which they now labour as a Trading people are owing to the Restrictions prohibitions, & ill advised Regulations in several late Acts of parliament in Great Britain; in particular that the last unconstitutional Acts imposing Duties on Tea, Paper, Glass &c. for the sole purpose of raising a Revenue in America, being injurious to property, & destructive to Liberty, have a necessary Tendency to prevent the payment of Old Debts or the Contracting of New, and are of Consequence ruinous to Trade—

That notwithstanding the many earnest applications already made there is little reason to expect a Redress of these Grievances. Therefore in justice to themselves & their posterity, as well as to the Traders of Great Britain concern'd in the American Commerce, the Subscribers have Voluntarily & Unanimously entered into the following Resolutions, in Hopes that their Example will Stimulate the good people of the Colony to be frugal in the Use & Consumption of British Manufacture, and that their Brethern the Merchants & Manufacturers of Great Britain may from motives of Interest justice, & Friendship be engaged to exert themselves to obtain Redress of those Grievances under which the Trade & inhabitants of America at present Labour.

First It is unanimously agreed on & resolved this Day of 1769. That the Subscribers as well by their own Example as by all other legal ways & means in their power, will promote & encourage Industry & Frugality & discourage all manner of Luxury & Extravigance.

Secondly That they will not at any time hereafter directly or indirectly import or cause to be imported any Manner of Goods Merchandize or Manufactures which are or shall hereafter be taxed by Act of Parliament for the purpose of raising a Revenue in America (except such only as orders have been already sent for) nor purchase any such after the first Day of September next of any person Whatsoever—But that they will always consider such Taxation in every Respect as an absolute prohibition, and in all future Orders direct their correspondents to ship them no Goods whatever taxed as aforesaid.

Thirdly That the Subscribers will not hereafter directly or indirectly import or cause to be imported from Great Britain or any part of Europe (except such Articles of the produce or manufacture of Ireland as are brought hither imediately from thence, & Fruit & Oyl imediatly from the Mediteranean & except also such Goods as orders have been already sent for) any of the Goods hereinafter enumerated vizt. Spirits, Wine, Cyder, perry, Beer, Ale, Malt, Barley, peas, Beef, Pork, Fish, Butter, Cheese, Tallow, Candles, Oyl, Fruit, ⟨Sugar⟩ pickles, Confectionry, Pewter, Hoes, Axes, Watches, Clocks, Tables, Chairs, Looking-glasses, Carriages, Jointers & Cabinet Work of all Sorts, & Upholstery of all Sorts, Trinkets & Jewellery, plate, & Gold & Silver Smiths Work of all Sorts, Ribbons & Millenary of all sorts, ⟨Lace of all sorts⟩ India Goods of all Sorts (except Spices) Silks of all Sorts (except Sewing Silk) Cambricks, Lawn, Muslin, Gauze ⟨except Boulting Cloths⟩ Callico or Cotton Stuffs of more than 2/ pr. yd. Linnens at more than 2/ pr. yr. Wollen Worsted & Mix'd Stuffs of all sorts at more the 1/6 pr. yd. Broad Cloaths of all kinds at more than 8/ pr. yd. Narrow Cloaths of all kinds at more than 3/ pr. yd. Nets, Stockings, Shoes, & Boots, Saddles, & all Manufacturers of Leather & Skins of all kinds until the late Acts of parliament imposing Duties on Tea, paper, Glass &c. for the purpose of raising a Revenue in America are repealed; and that they will not after the first of September next purchase any of the above enumerated goods of any person whatever, unless the above mentioned Acts of parliament are repealed.

Fourthly   That in all orders which any of the Subscribers may hereafter send to Great Britain they shall & will expressly direct their correspondents not to Ship them any of the above enumerated goods, untill the before mentioned Acts of parliament are repealed; and if any Goods are ship'd them contrary to the tenor of this Agreement, they will refuse to take the same, or make themselves chargible therewith.

Fifthly   That they will not import any Slaves, or purchase any ⟨hereafter⟩ imported untill the said Acts of parliament are repeale'd.

Sixthly   That if the Measures already entered into should prove ineffectual, & our Grievances & oppressions shoud notwithstanding be continue'd; then & in that case, the Subscribers will put a stop to their exports to Europe of Tar, pitch, Turpentine, Timber, & Lumber, & Skins and Furs of all sorts, and will endeavour to find some other Employment for their Slaves and other Hands than cultivating Tobacco, which they will entirely leave off making, & will enter into such Regulations as may be necessary with Regard to Rents & other Tobacco Debts ⟨due to them⟩.

Seventhly & Lastly   That these Resolves shall be binding on all & each of the Subscribers, who do hereby each and every person for himself upon his Word & Honour agree, that he will strictly & firmly adhere to & abide by every Article of this Agreement from the time of his signing the same for & during the continuance of the before mentioned Acts of parliament; or untill a general Meeting of the Subscribers, after one Months public Notice, shall determine otherwise; the second Article of this Agreement still, & forever continuing in full power & Force.

MS (Washington Papers, DLC). In an unidentified hand, with the angle-bracketed portions added by Washington, at GM's suggestion.

After the first seven lines of the preamble, the author borrowed almost verbatim from the introduction to the Philadelphia Merchants' Association of 10 Mar. 1769 (*q.v.*). Portions of the second, third, and fourth articles were also extracted from the Philadelphia agreement. The first article reiterates the frugality concept that was the foremost in the first Boston protests (see Charles M. Andrews, "The Boston Merchants and the Non-Importation Movement," Colonial Society of Massachusetts, *Transactions, 1916–1917*, XIX [Boston, 1918], 159–259.) The fifth article rebukes the slavery traffic, a complaint GM and Richard Henry Lee shared. The sixth article hinted at an embargo on naval stores, furs, and tobacco, the chief colonial exports to Britain; and may have been inserted to bolster prices. The seventh article is virtually word for word from the Philadelphia agreement, except the final clause relating to the second article.

Washington kept this copy with the Annapolis-Philadelphia merchants' correspondence, later added a letter from 25 burgesses to their colleagues dated 31 May 1774, and attached a slip of paper to the lot which he endorsed: "*Old Papers Respecting the Non-importation of British Goods*/1767/&/1774." In making GM's suggested correction of the fifth article, Washington crossed through the word "Slaves" after the words "any imported."

The Letter of "Atticus"

NUMBER II.   [11 May 1769]
Æquam memento rebas in arduis
Servare mentem;   HOR.

It is of the utmost Consequence, in our present Difficulties, equally to avoid Rashness and Despair. Violent Counsels have seldom been productive of good, either in private or public affairs: Despondence is the proper Companion of Guilt, but not of Innocence; and wou'd be even more fatal than Violence itself.

As no Measures shou'd be attempted, until their Justice, Practicability, and Efficacy, have been duly weigh'd; so they shou'd be exerted with Unanimity and Resolution worthy their Importance.

It is the Opinion of the best Judges, that the Trade of *Great-Britain* with other Nations, has been for some Years upon the Decline: That her Merchants, are undersold at foreign Markets, is a general Complaint, and a natural Consequence of the Luxury diffused thro' all Ranks of People; whereby the Price of Labour and Manufactures is raised above the Value in other Countries. The *Spanish* Trade, once so lucrative, is, by the Conduct of our own Ministry, and the Family Compact of the House of *Bourbon*, almost reduced to nothing. The Trade with *Portugal*, is lessening every Year. The Balance of Trade with *France*, has long been against them; and, but for the Article of Tobacco, wou'd be immensely so. Numberless Instances, of the same Sort, might be given: Yet, under all these Disadvantages, it is acknowledged, that upon the whole, the Wealth, the Trade, the Shipping, and the maritime Power of *Great-Britain*, have increased beyond the Idea of former Times.

This she owes to her *American* Colonies: They have made her ample Amends for the Decay of all her other Commerce: Here is her Grand-Market for all her various Manufactures, and hence is she principally supplied with gross Materials.

This is the only Trade in which she cannot be rivalled; and which nothing but her own Tyranny and Folly can ever deprive her of. Had she suffered her *American* Subjects to continue in the Enjoyment of a mild and equitable Government, and given proper Encouragement to our Trade, the Benefits she derives from us wou'd have been continually increasing; as all our Gain wou'd have center'd in *Great-Britain* in return for her Manufactures. But, since a contrary, and unaccountable System of Politics, has been adopted, and we are not allowed to purchase the Manufactures of our Mother-Country, unless loaded with Taxes to raise a Revenue from us, without our Consent; since all our Complaints have been disregarded, and nothing but a total Deprivation of our Liberty, and entailing Slavery upon us, and our Posterity, can satiate the Malice of our Cruel Enemies; is it not high Time to endeavour to convince the Inhabitants of *Great-Britain,* that our Enemies are equally theirs; and, by refusing to take their Manufactures, and withholding from them our Commodities, until our Grievances are redressed, demonstrate to them that we cannot be wounded but thro' their Sides?

These are the proper Means to use upon the present interesting Occasion. These are the Arms with which GOD and Nature have furnished us for our Defence; a prudent and resolute Exertion of which, will soon obtain what has been refused to our most ardent Supplications.

Some People may think such a Plan impracticable in the Tobacco Colonies: First, because most of our Merchants, being only Factors, cannot enter into an Association for restraining their Imports, without the Consent of their Principals; and, Secondly, because we have so few Manufactures of our own, that we shall still be under a Necessity of importing them from *Great-Britain.* To the first, it may be answered; that we will, in Justice to these Gentlemen, and their Owners, acquaint them with our Intentions, leaving it entirely to themselves, to import just what they shall think proper: We will not attempt to lay them under any Restrictions, or use any Manner of Violence: We will only cease to import any, but certain enumerated Goods, ourselves, and refuse to purchase them of others, who do import them after a limited Time.

The second Objection is indeed a more weighty one: It is acknowledged that there are some Articles which we must still import; but far the greater Part we can do without: The Necessaries of Life lie within a narrow Compass, and many of these, our own Country will supply. The little Luxuries and Conveniencies of Life, we may chearfully part with, when we reflect that we are thereby securing the Liberty and Happiness of our Posterity.

We have certainly no Occasion to send to *Great-Britain* for any Thing that we eat or drink. Finery, from thence, of all Denominations may be rejected, and most Sorts of Household-Furniture; we may confine ourselves to the cheapest Kind of Goods, to Linens and Woollens, &c. not exceeding a certain Price.

A Man may be as warm in a Coat that costs but Ten Shillings, as in one that cost Ten Pounds: Habit and Custom will reconcile us to many Things that are irksome at first, and soon make that reputable, which was before thought mean and scandalous. Let the principal Gentlemen but set the Example, they will be quickly followed by the Bulk of the People.

What will not the Love of Liberty inspire!

This Measure, which has been so often recommended, and is now only repeated, has this peculiar Advantage; that it cannot easily be counteracted: No ministerial Mandates nor circular Letters: No Instructions to Governors, nor Orders to Generals, can oblige us to buy Goods, which we do not choose to buy.

If we were to desist purchasing Slaves, and making Tobacco, we shou'd have a Number of Spare Hands to employ in Manufactures, and other Improvements; every private Family wou'd soon be able to make whatever they wanted, for their own Use: Many of the Manufactures of *Great-Britain*, finding no longer the usual Encouragement at Home, wou'd remove hither for Employment, a general Spirit of Frugality and Industry wou'd prevail, and our Difficulties daily decrease. It wou'd moreover be attended with another happy Effect; It wou'd convince the British Government, that the Revenue must lose fifty Times more by the late iniquitous ministerial Projects than can ever be raised in *America*; even if the Nation was to incur no extraordinary Expence by attempting to carry them into Execution.

Our Fellow-Subjects in *Great-Britain*, wou'd no longer be imposed upon, by that popular, but fallacitous Argument, that their own Burdens will be lessened, in Proportion as ours are increased. Their own Interest wou'd quickly awaken their Attention: They wou'd see, They wou'd feel the Oppressions we groan under, and exert themselves effectually on our Behalf: A candid and a thorough

Examination wou'd be brought on, and the Conduct of the Ministry exposed in its proper Light.

Our Complaints wou'd be heard, our just Demands granted, and the mutual Confidence and Harmony, which is so much the Interest both of *Great-Britain* and *America,* wou'd be happily restored.

ATTICUS.

Printed from *Md. Gaz.,* 11 May 1769. The essay also appeared in the 11 May editions of both Purdie & Dixon's and Rind's *Va. Gaz.*

Arthur M. Schlesinger, *Prelude to Independence* (New York, 1958), 125–126, indicates that GM was "Atticus"—a belief shared by William Van Schreeven. These careful scholars based their assumption on GM's 5 April 1769 letter to Washington which has several sentences that appear almost verbatim in Atticus' second essay. The first essay was also printed in both the Annapolis and Williamsburg newspapers. The *Md. Gaz.* prefaced its initial article: "A GENTLEMAN having favoured us with this, and a succeeding NUMBER, we shall with Pleasure insert them. . . ." The present editor believes the likelihood that GM was that gentleman is too circumstantial for an outright assertion of his authorship. The style of Atticus "Number I" is most unlike GM's—the sentences and paragraphs are short, the argument mainly abstract, and more or less imitative of similar articles in the Philadelphia press. The second essay was unquestionably written by either GM or someone who had access to his 5 April letter. But it is beyond doubt that GM and Washington were sharing their thoughts on this topic with Dr. David Ross of Md., and probably also with Richard Henry Lee. Inasmuch as GM professed himself too ill to do the writing early in April, is it reasonable to assume that he recovered rapidly and wrote the articles, copied them twice, and dispatched them to printers by late April? It seems more likely that he was still ill late in April and thus only bothered to write suggestions on the draft sent to Washington of the Non-importation Association. On the other hand, one could interpret the 23 April letter to mean that the "inclosed letters" he forwarded to Washington were not personal ones, but the "Atticus" articles. However, the editor thinks that Washington relayed copies of GM's 5 April letter to other interested parties, possibly to Dr. Ross and Lee, and thus GM's expressions found their way into the newspaper articles as borrowed ideas rather than the brain-child of "Atticus," whose identity remains a mystery.

The Virginia Nonimportation Resolutions of 1769

[18 May 1769]

We his Majesty's most dutiful Subjects, the late Representatives of all the Freeholders of the Colony of Virginia, avowing our inviolable and unshaken Fidelity and Loyalty to our most gracious Sovereign, our Affection for all our Fellow Subjects of Great-Britain; protesting against every Act or Thing, which may have the most distant Tendency to interrupt, or in any wise disturb his Majesty's Peace, and the good Order of his Government in this

Colony, which we are resolved, at the Risque of our Lives and Fortune, to maintain and defend; but, at the same Time, being deeply affected with the Grievances and Distresses, with which his Majesty's American Subjects are oppressed, and dreading the Evils which threaten the Ruin of ourselves and our Posterity, by reducing us from a free and happy People to a wretched and miserable State of Slavery; and having taken into our most serious Consideration the present State of the Trade of this Colony, and of the American Commerce in general, observe with Anxiety, that the Debt due to Great-Britain for Goods imported from thence is very great, and that the Means of paying this Debt, in the present Situation of Affairs, are likely to become more and more precarious; that the Difficulties, under which we now labour, are owing to the Restriction, Prohibitions, and ill advised Regulations, in several late Acts of Parliament of Great-Britain, in particular, that the late unconstitutional Act, imposing Duties on Tea, Paper, Glass, &c. for the sole Purpose of raising a Revenue in America, is injurious to Property, and destructive to Liberty, hath a necessary Tendency to prevent the Payment of the Debt due from this Colony to Great-Britain, and is, of Consequence, ruinous to Trade; that, notwithstanding the many earnest Applications already made, there is little Reason to expect a Redress of those Grievances; Therefore, in Justice to ourselves and our Posterity, as well as to the Traders of Great-Britain concerned in the American Commerce, we, the Subscribers, have voluntarily and unanimously entered into the following Resolutions, in Hopes that our Example will induce the good People of this Colony to be frugal in the Use and Consumption of British Manufactures, and that the Merchants and Manufacturers of Great-Britain may, from Motives of Interest, Friendship, and Justice, be engaged to exert themselves to obtain for us a Redress of those Grievances, under which the Trade and Inhabitants of America at present labour; We do therefore most earnestly recommend this our Association to the serious Attention of all Gentlemen, Merchants, Traders, and other Inhabitants of this Colony, in Hopes, that they will vary readily and cordially accede thereto.

First, It is UNANIMOUSLY agreed on and resolved this 18th Day of May, 1769, that the Subscribers, as well as their own Example, as all other legal Ways and Means in their Power, will promote and encourage Industry and Frugality, and discourage all Manner of Luxury and Extravagance.

Secondly, That they will not at any Time hereafter, directly or indirectly import, or cause to be imported, any Manner of Goods,

Merchandize, or Manufactures, which are, or shall hereafter be taxed by Act of Parliament, for the Purpose of raising a Revenue in America (except Paper, not exceeding Eight Shillings Sterling per Ream, and except such Articles only, as Orders have been already sent for) nor purchase any such after the First Day of September next, of any Person whatsoever, but that they will always consider such Taxation, in every Respect, as an absolute Prohibition, and in all future Orders, direct their Correspondents to ship them no Goods whatever, taxed as aforesaid, except as is above excepted.

Thirdly, That the Subscribers will not hereafter, directly or indirectly, import or cause to be imported from Great-Britain, or any Part of Europe (except such Artlices of the Produce or Manufacture of Ireland as may be immediately and legally brought from thence, and of the Goods herein after enumerated, viz. Spirits, Wine, Cyder, Perry, Beer, Ale, Malt, Barley, Pease, Beef, Pork, Fish, Butter, Cheese, Tallow, Candles, Oil, Fruit, Sugar, Pickles, Confectionary, Pewter, Hoes, Axes, Watches, Clocks, Tables, Chairs, Looking Glasses, Carriages, Joiner's and Cabinet Work of all Sorts, Upholstery of all Sorts, Trinkets and Jewellery, Plate and Gold, and Silversmith's Work of all Sorts, Ribbon and Millinery of all Sorts, Lace of all Sorts, India Goods of all Sorts, except Spices, Silks of all Sorts, except Sewing Silk, Cambrick, Lawn, Muslin, Gauze, except Boulting Cloths, Callico or Cotton Stuffs of more than Two Shillings per Yard, Linens of more than Two Shillings per Yard, Woollens, Worsted Stuffs of all Sorts of more than One Shilling and Six Pence per Yard, Broad Cloths of all Kinds at more than Eight Shillings per Yard, Narrow Cloths of all Kinds at more than Three Shillings per Yard, Hats, Stockings (Plaid and Irish Hose excepted) Shoes and Boots, Saddles, and all Manufactures of Leather and Skins of all Kinds, until the late Acts of Parliament imposing Duties on Tea, Paper, Glass, &c. for the Purpose of raising a Revenue in America, are repealed, and that they will not, after the First of September next, purchase any of the above enumerated Goods of any Person whatsoever, unless the above mentioned Acts of Parliament are repealed.

Fourthly, That in all Orders, which any of the Subscribers may hereafter send to Great-Britain, they shall, and will expressly direct their Correspondents not to ship them any of the before enumerated Goods, until the before mentioned Acts of Parliament are repealed; and if any Goods are shipped to them contrary to the Tenor of this Agreement, they will refuse to take the same, or make themselves chargeable therewith.

Fifthly, That they will not import any Slaves, or purchase any imported, after the First Day of November next, until the said Acts of Parliament are repealed.

Sixthly, That they will not import any Wines of any Kind whatever, or purchase the same from any Person whatever, after the First Day of September next, except such Wines as are already ordered, until the Acts of Parliament imposing Duties thereon are repealed.

Seventhly, For the better Preservation of the Breed of Sheep, That they will not kill, suffer to be killed, any Lambs, that shall be yeaned before the First Day of May, in any Year, nor dispose of such to any Butcher or other Person, whom they may have Reason to expect, intends to kill the same.

Eighthly and Lastly, That these Resolves shall be binding on all and each of the Subscribers, who do hereby each and every Person for himself, upon his Word and Honour, agree that he will strictly and firmly adhere to and abide by every Article in this Agreement, from the Time of his signing the same, for and during the Continuance of the before mentioned Acts of Parliament, or until a general Meeting of the Subscribers, after one Month's public Notice, shall determine otherwise, the second Article of this Agreement still and for ever continuing in full Power and Force.

[Signed by eighty-eight burgesses and Richard Starke, Clerk to the Association.]

Printed copy (Vi). Names of the signing burgesses are printed, followed by a list of toasts drunk before "the Gentlemen retired." Nineteen other subscribers approved a concluding promise to observe the Association. The entire document appears in Boyd, I, 27–31, where GM is identified as the author.

Circumstances explained in the preceding editorial note mistakenly brought GM credit for a major role in the preparation of this document. It is more likely that Richard Henry Lee prepared the Ms with liberal borrowing from the Philadelphia Merchants' Agreement of 10 Mar. 1769 (q.v.).

On 16 May the Virginia House of Burgesses passed a series of resolutions claiming "the sole Right of imposing Taxes on the Inhabitants of . . . *Virginia*," affirming the right of petition, and protesting the removal of accused "Persons, to Places beyond the Sea, to be tried" (JHB, 1766–1769, 212–218). The royal governor reacted by dissolving the session, whereupon the burgesses moved to a private dwelling and chose a committee to draft a non-importation association that would allow Virginians to protest British policy peaceably but in unmistakable terms. The committee which drafted the resolves may have included Lee and Washington, who were among the first signers. Since GM was not a burgess, he could only applaud their action from afar—although several of GM's suggestions in the drafting stage had been retained in the final version. The committee in Williamsburg lengthened the preamble by avowing loyalty to the king, changed the tenses, altered the pronouns, and then followed much of the draft Washington had brought from Mount Vernon, beginning with the words "deeply affected." The earlier allusions to merchants were broadened by an additional clause ending the first paragraph. The third article was slightly altered but GM's recommendations stood, exceptions were allowed for PLAID AND IRISH HOSE, and the earlier the exemption for FRUIT & OYL IMEDIATLY FROM THE MEDITERANEAN was dropped. In the fifth article, GM's added "hereafter" was dropped and a specific date added. The sixth and seventh articles (on importing wines and butchering sheep) were original in this document, while an article from the 23 Apr. draft threatening an embargo was expunged. Copies of the Association were then printed for circulation in the burgesses' home counties. The Association was featured in the *Va. Gaz.* (Purdie & Dixon) on 25 May 1769, which carried a news item that indicated the situation was not particularly tense for on 19 May Gov. Botetourt had entertained "a very numerous and polite company" at the Palace honoring the queen's birthday. Later Botetourt made common cause with the burgesses over repeal of the Townshend Acts and threatened to resign if they were not revoked. Charles M. Andrews (Col. Soc. of Mass., *Trans.*, *1916–1917*, XIX [1918], 249) implies that southern planters stood to gain from strict enforcement of the nonimportation resolves because they would force prices for agricultural products higher. Andrews also maintains (214–215) that "in the case of the tobacco colonies [the Associators] defined nonimportation in terms that were much less restrictive" than in Boston or Philadelphia, "and they limited the operation of the agreement to the time when the repeal of the acts should take place." J. Franklin Jameson traced the idea of an Association in English history to 1584 ("The Association," American Historical Association, *Annual Report for 1917*, 305–312). Jameson cited the Association of 1688 where the signers pledged a united front until their grievances were redressed. Certainly the colonists saw themselves treading upon the same constitutional ground that Englishmen had crossed about a century earlier, as the words "Association" and later "Convention" indicate. The Associations had their effect, for on 5 Mar. 1770 Lord North moved for repeal of the Townshend duties (East Indian tea excepted). However, on that same day British troops fired into a Boston mob. Thus the Association of 1769 was renewed and its reinforcement tightened as GM bestirred himself and became a more active participant in public affairs. See the Association of 22 June 1770.

To George Washington

[[*14 Oct. 1769*. Washington and Mason were concluding a land sale, probably the 300-acre Hunting Creek tract, and exchanged notes over the weekend of 14–15 Oct. In his letter of 17 Oct. GM mentions Washington's letter, probably of 15 or 16 Oct., which indicates they were executing the deed as part of the sale. The *Henkel's Sale Catalogue* No. 663 of 1891 lists this letter as sold to a Mr. Honeyman, who also bought GM's letter to Washington of 17 Oct. The latter is now owned by the Regents of Gunston Hall. Not found.]]

To George Washington

DEAR SIR   Gunston Hall Octor. 17th. 1769.
    I have your Favour, returning the Deed I sent you, which I have not had an Opportunity of executing before Witnesses that cou'd be at this Court; I shall therefore endeavour to wait on you with it at

Posey's Sale, or sooner, if I am able to ride. It is certain that there is no Warranty contain'd in the Deed, nor did I apprehend you expected one, or I shou'd have objected to it at the Time, as I have not an Acre of Land in the World for with which I would give a general Warranty. The Destruction of Records, the Loss of Papers, & the Negligence of the Hands thro' which in process of Time the Lands may pass, are with the unanswerable Objections to general Warrantys; let the Title be ever so good at the Time of the Sale; but in this particular Case, I lookd upon a Warranty as totally out of the Question. I candidly told you all I knew about Hooper's Survey, or the mark'd line, when I left the Matter to yr own Choice. You know in what manner the Agreement was made, & had there turn'd out less Land within the Line than the Quantity sold (in which Case I was to have paid you by the Acre for the Deficiency) I shou'd have required Nothing more from you than a Relinquishment of your own Title for the Difference, in such a Manner as to bar any Persons hereafter claiming under you; which is always the Case of a Release, & in this Light only I understood, & still do understand our Agreement; tho' I take it to be a Matter of very little Importance; because I verily believe the Land contain'd in Thompson's Patent to be as safe as any Tract of Land in the County. I have all the original Papers relative to it bye me, which I shou'd be glad you wou'd examine, if you have any Doubt about it; & the rather, because it gives me Concern that there shou'd have arisen any, the least Misapprehension between us. I have examined the Deed over again, & I think it contains as full a Confirmation of yr Title, & Release of mine, as Words can express; if not, I am willing to add anything to it for that Purpose, which you can desire.

I must again trouble you with an Ordr. to the Treasurer for the Money due to me from the Country; it's to be hoped there is by this Time Cash in the Treasury, & that the House will be permitted next Session to go thro' the public Business. I have some Thoughts of petitioning Your Honours for an Allowance of Interest.

Mrs. Mason offers her Comps. to Mrs. Washington, & Miss Custis; to whom Please to Present those of Dr Sir Yr. most Obt. Sert

G Mason

RC (Gunston Hall).

THE DEED I SENT YOU is probably the conveyance of 300 acres on Hunting Creek which GM had sold to Washington. (The deed, dated 24 Oct. 1769, was listed in the *Henkel's Sale Catalogue* No. 663 in 1891.) POSEY'S SALE was the three-day auction of Capt. John Posey's assets. Posey was a neighbor of GM's and Washington's who was forced into bankruptcy. On 23 Oct. 1769 Washington noted in his Diary (Fitzpatrick, ed., *Diaries of Washington*, I, 349–350) that

he attended the sale "with Colo. Mason . . . and Colo. Mason's Son George."
THE MONEY DUE TO ME FROM THE COUNTRY was probably a treasury warrant
issued to GM by the colony of Virginia for some public debt. A shortage of
more than £100,000 in the colony's treasury was revealed after the death of
Treas. John Robinson in 1766, and left the public accounts in an impecunious
state. See Mays, *Pendleton*, I, 174–223.

Colons used by GM to break sentences in the first and second paragraphs
have been changed to periods, and the next word capitalized.

To William Brent, Daniel Carroll, and Others

[[*17 Nov. 1769.* A two-page letter which relates terms of an offer to buy
certain lands from Brent. GM wrote that he would wait for their
arrival at Dumfries to conclude the bargain. The last owner of public
record, the State Historical Society of Wisconsin, reports that this
letter disappeared from its Ms collection about 1945. Not found.]]

From George Mercer

[[*2 Jan. 1770.* GM acknowledges this letter in his reply to George
Brent [?] of 6 Dec. 1770. Mercer was in desperate straits and had
presented a petition to the Board of Trade dated 18 Dec. 1769 in an
effort to block the Vandalia Company plans. Perhaps Mercer was
reporting this action to GM and he may have enclosed the pamphlet
Case of the Ohio Company, which was probably printed about this
time. In the memorial Mercer begged for an opportunity to appear
before the Board "to justify the company's pretensions. . . ." (*Case of
the Ohio Company*, 35–36). Not found.]]

To Charles and Landon Carter

GENTLEMEN   Gunston-Hall 14th. May 17[70?]
I intended to have waited on you at Nevill[e's] but am prevented
by a Cold & Fever, which confines me to the House. On the other
Side is a Copy of a Letter I wrote some Time ago to Mr. Chs. Carter
of Corotoman; as I have never recd. any Answer, I did not know but
it might have misca[r]ryed, which occasions my giving you the
Trouble of this, in Confirmation of what I then wrote. If you accept
of my Offer, I can pay you thirtee[n] or [fo]urteen [hun]dred
pounds Sterling upon the E[xe]cution of the Deeds, or by the June
Oyer Cou[rt] the Remainder as soon as I sell my Tobacco: 'tis true
I have a much more considerable Sum th[an] this out at Interest, but
I can't relye upon getting [it?] so soon as you may want the

Money: & I w[ill] by no m[eans co]ntract for any thing but what [I] am sure of being able to perform. My Reaso[n] for offering Bills of Exchange is that my Dealings f[or] some Years past having been in Maryland f[or?] Bills, I have not any Cash bye me, nor cou'd I venture at any Rate to engage for more than two or three hundred pounds in Virga. Currency.

Your dispatching my Man as soon as you conveniently can will oblige. Gentm. Yr most Hbl Sert.

G MASON

RC (Carter Papers, VIU).
NEVILLE'S Ordinary was a tavern on the old Dumfries Road about 40 miles west of Gunston Hall (Harrison, 491–492). A LETTER I WROTE SOME TIME AGO has not been found, but appears to have been on the same engrossing subject—land. The property GM was seeking apparently was Broad Run Tract in Loudoun County. Bracketed portions of the text represent missing words or parts of words in the Ms, which has several tears on the folds and margins.

From Richard Henry Lee

[[*26 May 1770.* Mentioned in GM's letter of 7 June 1770. Apparently concerned strengthening the Nonimportation Association in Virginia and may have commented on the unfavorable effect of Parliament's mercantilistic policies towards the colonies. Not found.]]

To Richard Henry Lee

DEAR SIR   Gunston-Hall June 7th. 1770.
Your favor of the 26th May did not come to Hand till the 5th Instant, or I should have answered sooner. I now enclose you the Abstract f[rom the] Act of Parliament in the 4th. Year of his present Majesty's Reign, with some Remarks thereon; to which I beg to refer you, & think you will find them worthy of Consideration, as the sd. Act of Parliament has never been totally repealed.

I am glad to hear that the Members below intend to establish some further Regulations to render the Association effectual, & I know of none that will answer the End proposed, but preventing by all legal & peaceable Means in our Power (for we must avoid even the Appearance of Violence) the Importation of the enumerated goods; Experience having too fully proved that when the Goods are here, many of our People will purchase, even some who affect to be called Gentlemen. For this Purpose, the Sense of Shame & the Fear of

Reproach must be inculcated, & enforced in the strongest Manner; and if that can be done properly, it has a much greater Influence upon the Actions of Mankind than is generally imagined. Nature has impress'd this useful Principle upon every Breast: it is a just observation that if Shame was banished out of the World, she wou'd carry away with her what little Virtue is left in it. The Names of such Persons as purchase or import Goods contrary to the Association should be published, & themselves stigmatized as Enemys to their Country. We shou'd resolve not to associate or keep Company with them in public Places, & they should be loaded with every Mark of Infamy and Reproach. The Interest, too of the Importer may be made subservient to our Purpose; for if the principal People renounce all Connection & Commerce for ever with such Merchants, their Agents & Factors, who shall import Goods contrary to the Tenor of the Association [?] They will hardly venture to supply their worst Customers with such Articles, at the Hazard of losing their best; but I don't see how these Regulations can be effected by any other Means than appointing Committees in the Countys, to examine from Time to Time into the Imports, & to convey an Account of any Violation of the Association to the Moderator, to be by him publish'd, or by a Committee appointed for that purpose in Wmsburg, or in such other Manner as shall be judged best; for without such Committees in the Country, I am convinced we shall once more fail of carrying the Plans into Execution; as it is of great Consequence to have these committees composed of the most respectable men pos[sible]. It will be best that one Committee be appointed from two or more countys, as the Circumstances of particular Parts of the Country may require; & such of the Merchants as are Members of the Association, ought by all Means to be of [on?] these Committees. It is true in Maryland there is a Committee in every county; but their countys are generally larger than two of ours. The Committees, whenever there is an importation of Goods within their respective Districts, shou'd convene themselves, & in a civil Manner apply to the Merchants or Importers concern'd, & desire to see the Invoyces & Papers respecting such Importation, & if they find any Goods therein contrary to the Associati[on] let the Importers know that it is the Opinion & Request of the Country that such Goods shall not be opened or stored, but reship'd to the Place from whence they came; and in Case of Refusal, without any Manner of Violence, inform them of the Consequences, & proceed to publish an Account of their conduct. I am persuaded there are few Importers who wou'd persist in refusing to comply with such a

Request, & proper Resolution in the Association, with one or two public Examples, wou'd quickly put an End to it. The Objection that this wou'd be infringing the Rights of others, while we are contending for Liberty ourselves, is ill founded. Every Member of Society is in Duty bound to contribute to the Safety & Good of the Whole; and when the Subject is of such Importance as the Liberty & Happiness of a Country, every inferior Consideration, as well as the Inconvenience to a few Individuals, must give place to it; nor is this any Hardship upon them; as themselves & their Posterity are to partake of the Benefits resulting from it. Objections of the same kind might be made to the most useful civil institutions.

It may perhaps be proposed to have such Goods as are imported contrary to the Association, stored here unopened, instead of reshiping them; but, besides the Risque of having such Goods privately sold, storeing them wou'd by no Means answer the same Purposes as reshiping them; for if the Goods are reship'd, they will most of them be returned to the wholesale Dealers, & Shop keepers, & occasion an imediate Stagnation of Business between them & the Manufacturers. This wou'd be Practice, not Theory; & beyond anything else, [convince the people] of Great [Britain that we are *in earnest* by an appeal to their own senses. I am at a loss to determine, even in my own mind, whether these proposed regulations ought to have retrospect, so as to require the reshiping of goods that were already imported before the 14th of this month. Not that I think there is any injustice in it, because all such persons as have imported goods contrary to the Association, have done it with their eyes open, and at their own peril, with a view to private gain, which deserves no countenance from the public; & those merchants who have conformed themselves to the opinion and interest of the country have some right to expect that *violators* of the Association shou'd *suffer*] upon the Occasion. The principal Objection, is the seeming Impracticability of such a Measure, which wou'd put the Committees upon very minute & difficult Inquirys. On the other Hand there are some strong Reasons for such Retrospect. There is great cause to believe that most of the Cargoes refused to be received in the other Colonies have been sent to this. I will mention some recent Instances; particularly a Ship a few Weeks ago from Baltimore in Maryland, with a Cargoe of about £3000—and a Committee which sat a few Days ago in Port Tobacco, after examining a Merchants Imports there, & finding nothing contrary to Association, at last accidentally stumbled upon an Invoyce of eight or nine hundred pounds of anti Association Goods—the Nest was there, but the Birds were flown— no such goods cou'd be found—they had been privately sent to

Virginia. Unless these Machinations can be counteracted, and their Contrivers effectually disappointed, Virginia will become the Receptacle of all the Goods refused by the other Colonies, & from hence they will be sent again privately, in small Quantitys at a time, to frustrate the Associations of the other Parts of the Continent, to our everlasting Scandal, and to the weakening of that mutual Confidence, which in these oppressive and dangerous Times shou'd be so carefully cherished and preserved.

Suppose (to observe a Sort of Medium) that all Goods imported contrary to the Association which now remain unopened, or uncut, shou'd be directed to be reship'd; or if this is thought too much the Retrospect may be limitted to a certain Time; so as to include [the goods that shall come fro]m the neighbou[ring] Colonies, which I [believe is but a late practice. I have had some conversation with the neighboring merchants upon the subject; they profess themselves ready to acquiesce in whatever shall be thought the interest of the country. Mr. Henderson, in particular, declares that he will cheerfully order to be packed up such goods as are contrary to the Association in any of the stores he has the direction of (and you know he is concerned for one of the greatest houses in the tobacco trade), and either store them until our grievances are redressed, or reship them if the gentlemen of the Association shall require it. In his own store he says there are no goods contrary to the Association. In this I think he *means*] well; it is not the Interest of his Owners to forfeit the Esteem and Good-will of People of this Colony. To do the Merchants in this neighbourhood Justice, they have, so far as I have been able to observe, behaved in a very becoming Manner, & have all along testified their Willingness to accede to any Measures that shall be judged conducive to the Public Good.

Whoever looks over with attention the Proceedings & arguments of the ministerial Party in the H——e of C——ns will be convinced that the late Vote for a partial, instead of a total Repeal of the Revenue Act complained of, was founded upon an Opinion that the Americans cou'd not persevere in their Associations; the Custom-House Books shew'd that the Exports to Virginia in particular were very little, if at all, lessened; and that the Exports to this Colony are of greater Importance to Great Britain than any other on this Continent, will not be denied by any Man acquainted with the Subject, This shews the Necessity of our exerting ourselves effectually upon the present Occasion; our Sister Colonies all expect it from us, our Interest, our own Liberty & Happiness, as well as that of our Posterity, everything that is near & dear to us in this World requires it. The. . . .

RC (ViHi). Kate Mason Rowland saw the four-page Ms before it was partially destroyed; and she may have also seen the covering address, for she described the letter as "written to Richard Henry Lee" (Rowland, I, 144).

The ABSTRACT from a parliamentary act probably was from the Sugar Act of 1764 (4 George III, c. 15) which not only taxed certain products but also strengthened customs regulations, gave admiralty courts jurisdiction, and left crown agents and informers virtually free from fear of damage suits (Curtis P. Nettels, *The Roots of American Civilization; A History of Colonial Life* [New York, 1947], 615). The act had been slightly altered in 1766. THE LATE VOTE FOR A PARTIAL . . . REPEAL of the Townshend Acts dropped the duties on paper, paint, and glass but left East Indian tea a taxable item. The CUSTOM-HOUSE BOOKS did indeed show that Virginia was Great Britain's best American customer. For the year ending 24 Dec. 1770, Britain exported goods worth £717,782 to Virginia-Maryland out of a £1,925,571 sold to the 13 colonies. Moreover, this was an increase of £229,420 over 1769, convincing proof that the Nonimportation Association of May 1769 had not achieved its purposes. See U.S. Bureau of the Census, *Historical Statistics of the U.S., Colonial Times to 1957* (Washington, 1960), 757.

A case for Lee's authorship of the Virginia Nonimportation Association of 1770 would be strengthened by citing this letter, since GM alludes to THE MEMBERS BELOW, names now missing because part of the document is lost. But GM's deep involvement in the Nonimportation crisis is apparent, and the tightened regulations he favored for the county enforcement committees may have affected Lee's thinking. Otherwise, the similarity of language in GM's second paragraph and the second paragraph of the 1770 Resolutions is indeed remarkable. A number of colons have been changed to periods. On pages three and four of the manuscript, parts of which are now lost, the longer sections in brackets are taken from Rowland, I, 146–147. The italicized words within these brackets are the editor's conjectures for words that were also missing when Miss Rowland made her copy *ca.* 1890. At least one more page is missing from the original Ms.

Commission as Fairfax County
Justice of the Peace

13 June 1770, Williamsburg. John West, GM, Daniel McCarty, John Carlyle, William Ramsay, Charles Broadwater, John West, Jr., Bryan Fairfax, Sampson Darrell, Henry Gunnell, Robert Adam, William Payne, William Adams, Hector Ross, Alexander Henderson, George Washington, and Edward Payne are appointed Justices of the Peace for Fairfax County by Governor Botetourt.

Printed document (Emmet Collection, NN). A single sheet, with the names of the appointees filled in, and signed "Botetourt."

Virginia Nonimportation Association

[22 June 1770]

The ASSOCIATION *entered into last Friday, the 22d instant, by the Gentlemen of the House of Burgesses, and the Body of Merchants, assembled in this city.*

We his Majesty's most dutiful and loyal subjects of *Virginia*, declaring our inviolable and unshaken fidelity and attachment to our gracious sovereign, our affection for all our fellow subjects of *Great Britain*, and our firm determination to support, at the hazard of our lives and fortunes, the laws, the peace, and good order of government in this colony; but at the same time affected with great and just apprehensions of the fatal consequences certainly to follow from the arbitrary imposition of taxes on the people of *America*, for the purpose of raising a revenue from them, without the consent of their representatives; and as we consider it to be the indispensable duty of every virtuous member of society to prevent the ruin, and promote the happiness, of his country, by every lawful means, although in the prosecution of such a laudable and necessary design some unhappy consequences may be derived to many innocent fellow subjects, whom we wish not to injure, and who we hope will impute our conduct to the real necessity of our affairs: Influenced by these reasons, we do most earnestly recommend this our association to the serious attention of all Gentlemen merchants, traders, and other inhabitants of this colony, not doubting but they will readily and cordially accede thereto. And at the same time we, and every of us, do most solemnly oblige ourselves, upon our word and honour, to promote the welfare and commerical interests of all those truly worthy merchants, traders, and others, inhabitants of this colony, who shall hereafter conform to the spirit of this [associ]ation; but that we will upon all occasions, and at all times [hereaft]er, avoid purchasing any commodity or article of goods whatsoever from any importer or seller of *British* merchandise or *European* goods, whom we may know or believe, in violation of the essential interests of this colony, to have preferred their own private emolument, by importing or selling articles prohibited by this association, to the destruction of the dearest rights of the people of this colony. And for the more effectual discovery of such defaulters, it is resolved,

That a committee of five be chosen in every county, by the majority of associators in each county, who, or any three of them, are hereby authorized to publish the names of such signers of the association as shall violate their agreement; and when there shall be an importation of goods into any county, such committee, or any three of them, are empowered to convene themselves, and in a civil manner apply to the merchant or importers concerned and desire to see the invoices and papers respecting such importation, and if they find any goods therein contrary to the association to let the importers know that it is the opinion and request of the country that such goods shall not be opened or stored, but reshipped to the place from whence they came: And in case of refusal, without any manner of violence, inform them of the consequences, and proceed to publish an account of their conduct.

Secondly. That we the subscribers, as well as our own example as all other legal ways and means in our power, will promote and encourage industry and frugality, and discourage all manner of luxury and extravangance.

Thirdly. That we will not hereafter, directly or indirectly, import, or cause to be imported, from *Great Britain,* any of the goods hereafter enumerated, either for sale or for our own use; to wit, spirits, cider, perry, beer, ale, porter, malt, pease, beef, fish, butter, cheese, tallow, candles, fruit, pickles, confectionary, chairs, tables, looking glasses, carriages, joiners work, and cabinet work of all sorts, riband, *India* goods of all sorts, except spices and calico of more than 3s. sterling per yard, upholstery (by which is meant paper hangings, beds ready made, furniture for beds, and carpetting) watches, clocks, silversmiths work of all sorts, silks of all sorts (except womens bonnets and ha[ts,] sewing silk, and netting silk) cotton stuffs of more than 3s. sterli[ng] per yard, linens of more than 2s. sterling per yard (except *Ir*[*ish*] linens) gauze, lawns, cambrick of more than 6s. sterling per yar[d,] woollen and worsted stuffs of all sorts of more than 2s. sterling per yard, broadcloths of more than 8s. sterling per yard, narrow cloths of all kinds of more than 4s. sterling per yard, not less than 7–8ths yard wide, hats of greater value than 10s. sterling, stockings of more than 36s. sterling per dozen, shoes of more than 5s. sterling per pair, boots, saddles, mens exceeding 25s. and womens exceeding 40s. sterling, exclusive of bridles, which are allowed, portmanteaus, saddle bags, and all other manufactured leather, neither oil or painters colours, if both, or either of them, be subject to any duty after the 1st of *December* next. And that we will not import, or cause to be imported, any horses, nor purchase those which may be imported by others after the 1st of *November* next.

Fourthly. That we will not import or bring into the colony, or cause to be imported or brought into the colony, either by sea or land, any slaves, or make sale of any upon commission, or purchase any slave or slaves that may be imported by others after the 1st day of *November* next, unless the same have been twelve months upon the continent.

Fifthly. That we will not import any wines, on which a duty is laid by act of Parliament for the purpose of raising a revenue in *America,* or purchase such as may be imported by others, after the 1st day of *September* next.

Sixthly. That no wine be imported by any of the subscribers, or other person, from any of the colonies on this continent, or any other place, from the time of signing this association, contrary to the terms thereof.

Seventhly. That all such goods as may or shall be imported into this colony, in consequence of their having been rejected by the association committees in any of our sister colonies, shall not be purchased by any associator; but that we will exert every lawful means in our power absolutely to prevent the sale of all such goods, and to cause the same to be exported as quickly as possible.

Eightly. That we will not receive from *Great Britain,* or make sale of, upon commission, any of the articles above excepted to, after the first day of *September* next, nor any of those articles which may have been really and *bona fide* ordered by us, after the 25th of *December* next.

Ninthly. That we will not receive into our custody, make sale of, or become chargeable with, any of the articles aforementioned, that may be ordered after the 15th of *June* instant, nor give orders of any from this time; and that in all orders which any of us may hereafter send to *Great Britain* we will expressly direct and request our correspondents not to ship us any of the articles before excepted, and if any such goods are shipped contrary to the tenour of this agreement we will refuse to take the same, or make ourselves chargeable therewith.

Provided nevertheless, that such goods as are already on hand, or may be imported according to the true intent and meaning of this association, may be continued for sale.

Tenthly. That a committee of merchants, to be named by their own body, when called together by their chairman, be appointed to take under their consideration the general state of the trade in this colony, and report to the association, at their next meeting, a list of such other manufactures of *Great Britain,* or commodities of any kind whatever, now imported, as may reasonably, and with benefit to the colony, be excepted to.

Eleventhly. That we do hereby engage ourselves, by those most sacred ties of honour and love to our country, that we will not, either upon the goods which we have already upon hand or may hereafter import within the true meaning of this association, make any advance in price, with a view to profit by the restrictions hereby laid on the trade of this colony.

Twelfthly. That we will not at any time hereafter, directly or indirectly, import, or cause to be imported, or purchase from any person who shall import, any merchandise or manufactures exported from *Great Britain,* which are, or hereafter shall be, taxed by act of Parliament for the purposes of raising a revenue in America.

Resolved, that a meeting of the associators shall be called at the discretion of the Moderator, or at the request of twenty members of the association, signified to him in writing; and in case of the death of the present Moderator, the next person subscribing hereto be considered as Moderator, and act as such until the next general meeting.

Lastly. That these resolves shall be binding on all and each of the subscribers, who do hereby, each and every person for himself, agree that he will strictly and firmly adhere to and abide by every article of this association from the time of his signing the same until the act of Parliament which imposes a duty on tea, paper, glass, and painters colours, be totally repealed, or until a general meeting of one hundred associators, after one month's publick notice, shall determine otherwise, the twelfth article of this agreement still and for ever continuing in force, until the contrary be declared by a general meeting of the members of this association.

Signed in *Williamsburg,* this 22d of *June,* 1770.

[164 printed names follow]

The Subscribers, Inhabitants of the County of Fairfax in the Colony of Virginia having duly considered the above agreement and association and being ever convinced of the Utility and real necessity of the Measures therein recommended, do sincerely and cordially accede thereto; and do hereby voluntarily and faithfully each and every Person for himself upon his Word and Honour Agree and Promise that he will strictly and firmly adhere to and abide by every Article and resolution therein contain'd according to the true Intent and meaning thereof.

JOHN WEST	THOS. KIRKPATRICK
WM. RAMSAY	JONATHAN HALL
JOHN CARLYLE	HENRY MCCABE
JOHN DALTON	GEO. GILPIN
ROBERT ADAM	WILL BALMAIN
JOHN WEST JUNR	RO. HARRISON
HARRY PIPER	JOHN MUIR
JAMES STUART	JAMES KIRK
THOS. CARSON	G MASON
JOHN HITE JUNR	

Printed document with handwritten additions (Washington Papers, DLC). The names of the 164 signers are printed in Boyd, I, 46–47. The Fairfax County subscription is in Washington's handwriting, written below the printed broadside.

Although authorship of the Association resolves is uncertain, Richard Henry Lee was in Williamsburg as a burgess from Westmoreland County and had been working on a revision of the 1769 Association, as GM's letter of 7 June 1770 indicates. The exchange of ideas between GM and Lee which the 1769 Association set in motion is an important facet of their public careers, particularly here and again in 1776 and 1787/1788. This Association follows the tone and spirit of the 1769 resolutions except that the list of enumerated goods was expanded and a committee system devised with powers similar to those outlined in GM's letter to Lee dated 7 June. Washington, as a burgess from Fairfax County, was enjoined to add subscribers. The Association proved to be a disappointment. GM analyzed its weaknesses in his letter of 6 Dec. 1770, and William Nelson reported to Lord Hillsborough on 19 Dec. 1770 that "The Spirit of Association . . . seems to me from the defection of the Northern Provinces, to be cooling every day." See JHB, 1770–1772, xxxi.

Because of slight tears, parts of several words are missing, but have been completed in the bracketed portions.

From [George Brent?]

[[*7 July 1770*. George Brent was a distant relative of GM's. Brent, or the "kinsman" GM was writing, had sent him the *Letters of Junius*, whose pro-American writings found a receptive Virginia audience. GM notes in his letter of 6 Dec. 1770 that this was "the third [letter] you have obliged me with since you left Virginia," but none have been found.]]

From George Mercer

[[*24 July 1770*. Acknowledged in GM's letter of 6 Dec. 1770, which indicates that Mercer may have told a gloomy story about Ohio Company affairs without telling the whole truth. Mercer wrote that he was considering a return voyage to Virginia, but seems to have omitted mention of the 7 May 1770 compromise in which Mercer merged company claims with those of the Grand Ohio or Vandalia Company. In return for withdrawing the conflicting Ohio Company claims, Mercer appears to have received at least one share in the Grand Ohio Company, although Bailey incorrectly says the agreement "gave Mercer personally one seventy-second share of the [Grand Ohio] company's stock." The quoted document Kenneth P. Bailey, *The Ohio Company of Virginia and the Westward Movement* . . . (Glendale, Calif., 1939) 260–264) only mentions two shares awarded to the Ohio Company partners. James also speaks of Mercer's separate share (James, *George Mercer, 64*). Mercer's brother noted on 9 Jan. 1772 (q.v.) that the London-based Virginian personally owned "one share and a half" in the Grand Ohio Company. How did a man in a penurious condition manage to acquire shares which he apparently believed were worth

£ 15,000? Thus the circumstances indicate that Bailey's assumption was right, even though the cited evidence does not. Samuel Wharton's statement of 17 July 1777 (Mulkearn, 326) shows Mercer still possessed a single share which was charged with an assessment of £ 24 17s.1d. Mercer's letter to GM has not been found.]]

To Messrs. McCarty and Barry

GENTM.   Gunston-Hall Sept. 22d. 1770.

Having sold all my Tobacco, I expect to deliver my Notes on Monday next, & have therefore sent the Bearer for a Note for the transfer Hhd. due to me from you, & also a Note for the light Hhd. C M No. 1. which I desired might be reprized about six Weeks ago, & which I make no Doubt has been done accordingly. There will Still be a small Ballance due to me from your Warehouse, as youll perceive by the Acct. below. Please to dispatch the Bearer, & oblige Yr. Hble. Servt.

G MASON

1770 Pohick Inspection_____Dr.   Nett Tobo.
ToBacco from last year's Acct. Nett_____ 399.
May to credt. Isaac Gates, ordr. of Mr. Barry_____ 530.
27th. To a trans. Note, to Mr. McCarty, No. 18. Gross_____ 530.
                                                           1060.
                                    2   Ct. off   −21.
                                                           1039.
Augt. 1st. To a light Hhd. to prize, C M No. 1. Nett 855.
                           Caske 30_____ 885.
To Mr. Hector Ross's ordr. to Wm Bronaugh assign'd
                           to me 250. transfer, 2
                           Ct. off is_____ 245.
                                                          2568.
Augt. 1st. Ct.   By my Ordr. to Chas. Mablahorn trans.
                       103. 2   Ct. off_____ 101.
                                                          2467.

RC (MeHi). Addressed: "To Messrs. McCarty & Barry / Inspectors at Pohick," and noted in the lower left corner "℔ Negroe Bellfast." Presumably the addressees were Daniel McCarty and John Barry.

The TRANSFER HHD. was a hogshead packed from loose tobacco and exchanged for transfer notes totaling the required amount. Transfer tobacco was inferior to a crop tobacco hogshead, which was fully packed from the same grade and marked by the planter. THE LIGHT HHD. C M NO. 1 probably bore the initials of the cooper who made the hogshead, unless time has faded an original G into a C on the Ms (see Philip A. Bruce, *Economic History of Virginia in the Seventeenth Century* . . . , I [New York, 1895], 442). Tobacco was REPRIZED, i.e., repacked, after the hogshead was opened for inspection. POHICK warehouse must have been at the mouth of Pohick Creek, adjacent to Daniel McCarty's estate at "Cedar Grove," about four miles from "Gunston Hall."

To [George Brent?]

DEAR SIR Gunston-Hall 6th. Decemr. 1770.

I have your Favour of the 7th of July, which is the third you have obliged me with since you left Virginia: that I have not answer'd them sooner, I hope you know is not oweing to Want of Friendship; it will always give me pleasure to hear of your Welfare; & a young Fellow of twenty must not stand upon Ceremony with an old one of five & forty.

I am much obliged to you for the Pamphlets you sent me; we have had them in detach'd Peices in the public papers; but there is no judging of such Performances by Scraps. Junius's Letters are certainly superior to anything of the kind that ever appeared in our Language: the two most remarkable periods for Party-writings were about the Change of the Ministry in Queen Ann's Time, & the [latter End] of Sir Robt. Walpoles Ministry, in the late King's Reign; & altho' the ablest Men in the Nation then entered the Lists, their Performances fall far short of Junius. Most of our best Writers have imitated the florid Ciceronian Style, but this Author is really an Original; learned & elegant without the Vanity of seeming so, his Manner of Expression tho' new, & almost peculiar to himself, is yet free from the Affectation of Singularity; bold & nervous, like the Genius of the Nation he writes for.

The non-Importation Associations here are at present in a very languid State, most People seem'd inclined to try what the Parliament will do this winter towards redressing the American Grievances; as they shew'd some Inclination last Session to a Reconciliation. We are not without Hopes that, when Men's Passions have had time to cool & Reason takes Place, this most desireable End may be attain'd, & that happy Harmony restored which for more than a Century produced such mutual Benefits to both Countrys. Perdition seize the Man whose arbitrary Maxims & short-sighted Policy first interrupted it! But shou'd the oppressive System of taxing us without our Consent be continued. The Flame, however smother'd now, will break out with redoubled Ardour, & the Spirit of Opposition

(Self-defence is its' proper Name) wear a more formidable Shape then ever—more formidable, because more natural & practicable.

The Associations, almost from one End of this Continent to the other, were drawn up in a Hurry and form'd upon an erronious Principle; it was imagined that they wou'd occasion such a sudden Stagnation in Trade, & such Murmers among the Manufacturers of Great Britain that the Parliament wou'd not only see but feel the Necessity of immediately repealing the American Revenue Acts. One Year wou'd do the Business; & for one Year or two we cou'd do without importing almost anything from Great Britain. Men sanguine in an interesting Subject easily believe that must happen which they wish to happen, & thus the Americans enter'd into Agreements which few were able to perform even for the Short Time at first thought necessary. Many Circumstances have concurr'd to frustrate such a Scheme, particularly the unusual Demand for British Goods from the northern Parts of Europe & more than anything else the Impracticability of the Scheme itself & the Difference between the Plans adopted in the different Provinces. Time has pointed out our Mistakes, & Errors well known are more than half corrected.

Had the Subject been well digested, & an Association entered into which People wou'd have felt themselves easy under, persevered in, had one general Plan been form'd exactly the same for all the Colonys (so as to have removed all cause of jealousy or Danger of interfering with each other) in the Nature of a sumptuary Law, restraining only Articles of Luxury & Ostentation together with the Goods at any Time taxed, and at the same Time giving all possible Incouragement to American Manufactures & Invitations to Manufacturers from Eurpop to remove hither & settle among us, & as these increased from time to time still decreasing our Europian Imports [such] an Association then form'd upon these Principles wou'd have gather'd strength by Execution, & however slow in its Operation it wou'd have been certain in its Effects. It may perhaps be thought that the Trade of Great Britain wou'd be little affected by such a Restriction, but *Luxury* & *Ostentation* are comprehensive Terms & I wou'd venture to affirm that it wou'd immediatly lessen the Imports to this Continent from great Britain £300,000 ℔ Annum, & the Government wou'd lose more in one Year on two Articles only (manufactured Tobacco & Malt Liquors) than it wou'd gain in ten by the American Revenue Acts. Such a Plan as this is now in Contemplation God grant we may have no cause to carry it into practice. Had the Colonies any Intention of throwing off their Dependance? Was the Sovereignty of great Britain really in Dispute, as the Ministry affect to believe, Administration wou'd be right in asserting the Authority of the Mother Country; it wou'd be highly culpable if it did not do so; but the wildest Chimera that ever disturbed a Madman's Brain has not less Foundation in Truth than this Opinion. The Americans have the warmest Affection for the present Royal Family; the strongest Attachment to the British Government & Constitution; they have experienced it's Blessings & prefer it to any that does or ever did exist; while they are protected in the Injoyment of [its] Advantages they will never wish to change, there are not five Men of Sense in America who wou'd accept of Independance if it was offered. We know our own circumstances too well; we know that our Happiness our very Being depends upon our Connection with our Mother-Country. We have always acknowledged we are always ready to recognize the Sovereignty of Great Britain but we will not submit to have our own Money taken out our Pockets without our Consent; because if any Man or any Set of Men take from us without our Consent or that of our Representatives one shilling in the Pound we have not Security for the remaining nineteen. We owe to our Mother-Country the Duty of Subjects but will not pay her the Submission of Slaves. So long as Great Britain can preserve the Vigour & Spirit of her own free happy Constitution so long may she by a mild & equal Government preserve her Sovereignty over these Colonies. What may be the Effect of Violence & Oppression no Man can answer; but any Man may venture to pronounce that they can never be productive of Good.

In Answer to your Question about the Subscription for Mr. Wilkes, there was a Subscription set on Foot to ship that Gentlemen 45 Hhds. of Tobo. as a small Acknowledgement for his Sufferings in the Cause of Liberty which I believe wou'd have been filled up, but for the very Mr. Miles whom you mention; he very officiously contrived to get the Subscription into his Hands, & after collecting some of the Tobacco & applying it to his own Use; as soon as the Matter took wind, fearing a little American Discipline upon the Occasion, he scamper'd off with the Subscription-Paper, & has never been heard of here since. I do not tell you this of my own Knowledge (for I never saw Miles) but I believe there is no Doubt of the Truth of the Fact.

I received a Letter from my Kinsman Colo. Mercer dated the 24th. of July speaking very doubtfully of the Ohio Company's Affairs in England; this is only the third Letter from him which ever came to my Hands since I saw him in Virginia untill this very Day when I received a small Packet from him containing some interesting Intelligence, but of a very old Date, so long ago as the 2d. of last January from what he says of the many Letters he has wrote me & from what I know of the numbers I have wrote him I am convinced some S——l who knows our Hand-Writing must have intercepted them; tho I can't pretend even to guess at any particular Person. He tells me in his Letter of the 24th of July that he shall leave England in September, otherwise Mr. McPherson's going to London wou'd have afforded me a certain Opportunity of assuring him that a few Years Absence has neither erased him out of my Memory or Affection; as to the Ohio Company's Affairs here I cou'd have given him no Satisfaction or Information. It is absolutely more diffic[l]t to procure a Meeting of our Members than it is to assemble a German Diet—notwithstanding Appointments & Advertisements without number I verily believe there has never been a Meeting of the Company since he went from Virginia.

As your Brother Robert goes to London in the same Ship by which I write, he will inform you fully of the Situation of your Relatives & Friends in Virginia & Maryland; all at Gunston Hall join in wishing you Health & Happiness, with Dear Sir Yr. affection. Kinsman & hble. Sert.

G. MASON

RC (Mason Papers, DLC). The addressee presumably was Robert Brent's brother, George, a distant relative of GM's.

JUNIUS's LETTERS (anon., *The Letters of Junius* [London, 1771]) were popular in the colonies because of their support for the American cause against the British ministry. GM's praise was an echo of the encomiums heaped on their anonymous author, who has been identified as Sir Philip Francis (1740–1818), amongst others. THE SUBSCRIPTION FOR MR. WILKES was part of the American effort to ease John Wilkes's financial embarrassment after he had been committed to prison on 27 Apr. 1768. A London committee of "Supporters of the Bill of Rights" had several American counterparts and the combined groups raised over £ 17,000, though no thanks were due to the unidentified MR. MILES.

The six-page letter gives the appearance of hasty composition. The date seems to have been changed from 5 Dec. to 6 Dec., and there are a number of minor alterations made by crossing through words, none of which changed essential meanings.

To Alexander Henderson

DEAR SIR.   Gunston Hall 17th. Febry. 1771.

There has been such shameful Havock made of the Deer during this Snow, when the poor Creatures cou'd not get out of any Body's

Way, that I hope the Magistrates & Gentlemen of the County will think it their Duty to make an Example of the Offenders; and as I understand many of them intend to avoid half the Penalty by informing against each other I now make [an] Information to you against such Offenders as have come to my Knowledge; a List of which with the Number of Deer kill'd by each Person, you have on the other side; so that if any of them shou'd inform agst. their Comrades, their Scheme will be disappointed by my prior Information.

If the Magistrates will exert themselves properly, I think the Fines to this Parish will be upwards of £200—for if the Informations are made by Gentlemen 'tis probable they will give their Part of the Fines to the Parish after indemnifying themselves for their Expences. I am Dr Sir Yr. most Hble. Sert

G MASON

[on the reverse side]
Information made by George Mason Gentm. 17th. Febry. 1771. to Mr Alexander Henderson one of his Majesty's Justices of the Peace for Fairfax County against the several Persons whose Names are underwritten, Inhabitants of Truro Parish in the sd. County, for hunting & killing Deer in the said Parish since the first Day of January last past, contrary to Law

> vizt. against
> William Reredon for killing_____3. Deer
> John Reredon_____Do._____4. Do.
> Robt. Boggess Senr.__Do._____2. Do.
> Samuel Beach_____Do._____2. Do.
> James Hardwick Lane__Do._____2. Do.
> Thomas Brookbank_____Do.____,__3. Do.
> John West____Do._____[4?] Do.
> Robert Church___Do._____5. Do.
> Joseph Ransom___Do._____7. Do.
> William Western___Do._____5. Do.
> Joseph Bailey_____Do._____4. Do.
> Thomas Molan____Do._____1. Do.

List continued on the other [s]ide
List of Persons inform'd against for hunting & killing Deer contrary to Law, continued from the other Side—
against

[131]

William Douglass, Son of Robt. Douglass	}for killing_____1. Deer	
Thomas Athie, Son of Walter Athie	}Do._____1. Do.	
William Simpson (at Belmont)	Do._____2. Do.	
Walter Athie_____	Do._____6. Do.	

NB. G Mason will wait on Mr. Henderson, as soon as the Weather will permit, in Ordr. to obtain Warrants according to the annex'd Informations, & to give in a List of the Witnesses to be Summoned—

RC (CSmH). The General Assembly in 1734 had outlawed the killing of deer between 1 Jan. and 31 Aug. by a conservation act (Hening, IV, 425). The penalty was a fine of 15 shillings for each deer killed.

To Peyton Randolph

SIR,   [18 July 1771]
We the committee of the associators in Fairfax county, at the request of Mr. Alexander Henderson, merchant in Colchester, and Mr. William Balmain, merchant in Alexandria, on the 16th day of April last, carefully examined the invoices, and other papers, relative to two cargoes of goods just imported in the ship Anne, Captain Huie, from Glasgow, and consigned to the said Henderson and Balmain, respectively; both which cargoes we found perfectly conformable to the association. Mr. Henderson, at the same time, mentioned to us a small package which had been sent him as a compliment from Great Britain, not then come to hand; so that he was not certain of its contents, but believed it contained a case of silver handled knives and forks, and promised, upon his honour, if it proved so, or contained any other articles contrary to association, to deliver them up to be stored. And on the 18th day of June last, at the request of the same Gentlemen, we examined the invoices and papers, relative to two other cargoes of goods, just imported in the ships Janie and Patuxent, consigned as aforesaid, and found these cargoes also in every respect agreeable to the association; except nine mens fine hats in Mr. Henderson's cargo, charged from twelve shillings to sixteen shillings and sixpence each, and three ditto in Mr. Balmain's, charged at eleven shillings each: Upon enquiring into the cause of this, and perusing copies of the letters which had passed upon the occasion between Messr. Glassford and Henderson, mer-

chants of Glasgow (who shipped the goods) and the manufacturers, we were fully convinced that the same was a mistake of the manufacturers, and contrary to the direction and intention of the said Messr. Glassford and Henderson. In justice to these Gentlemen, and their agents here, we think it incumbent on us to declare that they have, in our opinion, hitherto strictly adhered to the spirit and intention of the association, which we heartily wish had been done with the same sincerity and good faith by all other importers; but we fear there has been too much cause given for the public declaration made to us by Mr. Henderson and Mr. Balmain at our last meeting, "that they found so little regard paid to the association by others, and such quantities of goods imported into different parts of the colony diametrically opposite both to the spirit and the letter of the articles entered into, that they should think themselves obliged for the future, in justice to their constituents (however contrary to their own sentiments) to send their orders in the same manner with other importers; restraining themselves only from importing tea, and other taxed articles, which they were still determined to adhere to."

We will not presume to dictate to the members of the association in general how far it may, or may not, be consistent with good policy to attempt keeping up a plan here, which is now dropped by all our sister colonies, except refusing to import tea, and such other articles as are, or may be, taxed for the purpose of raising a revenue in America (which, we trust, will never be departed from until our grievances are redressed) but we must beg leave to represent to your, Sir, the real necessity there is for speedily convening a sufficient number of the associators, to form such regulations as may put all the members upon an equal footing, in practice as well as theory; for, at present, those who faithfully adhere to their engagements have the mortification, not only of seeing their own good intentions frustrated by the negligence, the insincerity, and the mal-practices of others, but many of them find themselves, from the same causes, greatly embarrassed in their business, and their trade daily falling into the hands of men, who have not acted upon the same honourable principles, and who have very little title to the countenance, or even the connivance of the public. We are, with great respect, Sir, Your most obedient humble servants,

G. Mason,
G. Washington,
Peter Wagener,
John West,
John Dalton.

Printed from *Va. Gaz.* (Rind), 18 July 1771. Addressed "To PEYTON RANDOLPH, Esq; Moderator."

Randolph was moderator of the Nonimportation Association formed at Williamsburg on 22 June 1770 (*q.v.*) to boycott British goods in retaliation for the Townshend Acts of 1767, which had not been totally repealed by Parliament. An article of the association (which GM and others subscribed to in Fairfax County) permitted merchants to clear their names by submitting invoices or inventories of cargoes to the county committee.

From George Mercer

MY DEAR SIR   Holles Street London August the 8th: 1771

I have so often troubled you on the Subject of the Ohio Company's Affairs that I am afraid even you will think I give myself and you unnecessary Employment—but as there are at least half of the numbers who compose that *Extraordinary Company* whom I really do not esteem half as much as I do you, I mean as Gentlemen if they can be so called and abstracted from the Affinity you used formerly to claim with me. I have made the matter extremely plain to them in the enclosed Letter which though short I assure you fully contains my Resolutions as to their Concerns: And I should hope if there is a Power of thinking left in the Majority of the Members, I know many of them always think right, they will not, I am sure (Judgment however would be given against them in a court of Equity and good Conscience) Condemn me for demanding *one* clear answer to all the Letters I have wrote for eight years past to my Friends, my Relatives, my Acquaintances, the Committee of the Company, and the Company at large, concerning the Agentcy the Company appointed me to, on the 3d. of July 1763. giving me full Power and Authority to act for them as Seemed best to me, and I would appeal to themselves and the world for the Uprightness of my conduct towards them: And I may at the same time venture to say that I can prove I might have gained as good Terms for myself as I have for the Ohio Company at large, as their grant seemed rather an object of Contempt in their opponents, than a matter which merited serious Attention. And [that was] the only time I could ever prevail on the English members to go one yard to assist me, because they found my American Constituents treated me with so little respect. It was publicly declared by the opposite party in their presence, that they did not value the Claim of the Ohio Company at Six Pence, tho' they would all wish to serve me, and as I before hinted to you in my general letter, I could have procured the same Terms for myself, and should have been moreover amply rewarded for my Assistance, and discoveries of what I know of the Country and I can assure you that no step has been taken with out my Privity since the Agreement I entered into on Behalf of the Company. I have frequently represented to the Members of the Company in America, the trouble and fatigue and Expence and opposition I have encountered—and have notwithstanding never been honored with a Line of their Orders—they entered into a Resolution the 3d. July 1763. that they would repay me any Expence not exceeding £2000 I should subject myself to in Consequence of that appointment. I have wrote them Several Times, that Resolution would not procure me here 2000 Farthings on their Credits and I am obliged again to repeat that I have wrote them too, that I had expended for them near £1000 raised on my own private Credit. And I had wrote them that I had strained my Credit for them as far as it would stretch—but not one word of answer to all this—no Money, no Credit, no Approbation of my past Conduct, or orders for my future. Is this Sir treatment for an Agent, for one whom the Company reposed such a Confidence in? You give in Virginia your Negro Agents whom you call Gang Leaders Approbation, and sometimes an additional allowance of Meat or Cloath at Christmas, and yet the Ohio Company, out of their great Generosity and politeness, have never said to me well done good and faithful Slave, nor have they ever troubled themselves about repaying me the money I have put out of my pocket for them. I believe if I recollect, some of the Company know that if Money does lie in the Streets to be picked up here, that they have not been able to find out the man who would or could do it for them, and I fancy the Company *in general* know that their Partner H——y is not very alert in giving them Credit and I can assure them he is as Costive of his Cash to me as any man in England is, and that he has assured me a thousand times, he never will again trust them for a Shilling—how then do the Company gues I am to raise the £2000 they are to repay me on the *very first* notice, after I have given them Notice at least twenty times that I was half that sum in Advance, and have never been able to get 12d. in Return, or even an Answer to one of my Letters? The curse of dancing attendance on the Ministers and public Boards I have frequently mentioned though with less than a thousandth Part of the humiliating Circumstances that are forced upon the poor Wretch who is obliged to cringe and ask a Favor of them. Let the Company too, if ever they will trouble themselves to think of the Agreeable State they have put, and endeavour, nay appear, to resolve to keep me in, remember they will see an Article in my account (if they ever mean to peruse it) of

£125 charged as so much paid for House Rent, Expenses for Clerks, Coach Hire pr year, and two Guineas pr Day for Extra Charges [which are] allowed by the English Members to their Agent here who has besides an allowance of £1000 pr Annum from them for his Trouble. And the members in America allow the same person £2000 pr Annum more, in which we are not concerned.

[GEORGE MERCER]

Tr (ViHi). In a copyist's handwriting, with no signature, but endorsed at the bottom of the last page: "Copy of a letter to Col Mason Treasurer of the Ohio Company dated Augst. the 8th. 1771 complaining of want of Instructions and Remittances." The reverse side carries a similar endorsement, including "Col George Mercer to Col George Mason."

Mercer's frustrating career as the Ohio Company agent in London is summed up in this letter, which details the Virginian's trials without telling the whole truth. When Mercer says I MIGHT HAVE GAINED AS GOOD TERMS FOR MYSELF he makes it appear that he came off badly from his negotiations with the Vandalia Company on 7 May 1770, when he merged the Ohio Company claims with the Vandalia (or Grand Ohio) group. The truth was that Mercer received a full share out of this arrangement while the twenty Ohio Company partners were left to divide two shares. GM's letter of 13 Jan. 1772 makes it clear that even then Mercer's duplicity was not known to the Virginia members. In fact, Mercer seems to have turned into a London coxcomb, though his biographer (James, *George Mercer*, 66) is loathe to admit it. THE COMPANY . . . PARTNER H——Y is Osgood Hanbury, who fell heir to his brother John's share. By THE ENGLISH MEMBERS TO THEIR AGENT HERE Mercer must mean the Vandalia Company agents, but his unfortunate use of pronouns was only one of Mercer's faults.

Mercer's letters have a tendency to be disjointed, replete with dangling antecedents and obfuscating pronouns. For clarity's sake the editor has added parentheses and several words in brackets.

From Robert Carter

[[*24 Oct. 1771.* Apparently concerned Ohio Company affairs. George Mercer alluded to the letter in his note to Carter of 6 Aug. 1774 (Emmet Collection, NN). Not found.]]

From James Mercer

SIR   [9 January 1772]

At the last General Court I reced a Letr. from my Brother addressed to the Ohio Company, left open for my perusal, in which he greatly complains of the Silence & neglect of the Company, ever since he went to England contrary to their Ingagements at parting. The consequence of their Silence he says has left him in an State of uneasy suspense as he cou'd not say whether they were bound to abide by a Compromise he had made on behalf of the Ohio Company with a Company formed by Mr. Walpole & others, stiled the Grand Company, who having petitioned for a Tract of Country including the Lands desired by the Ohio Compy and being united with such of the Nobility & Ministry as promised Success, left little hopes of the Ohio Company's succeeding in their claim upon so slight an Interest as theirs.—The consequence of this Silence he adds leaves him in this further disagreeable State as to oblige him to advance Moneys agreeable to the Terms of the Grand Company without any certainty of ever being reimbursed by the Ohio Company, as if the Grand Company shou'd fail in obtaining their Grant the Ohio Company might then say they disapproved of the union, & thereby leave him to bear the Loss whereas, shou'd the Grand Compy succeed, whereby the Union wou'd prove very advantageous, the Ohio Company might then claim the benefit of it without ever having ever advanced or even risqued one shilling. Things being thus circumstanced (very unequally as every Body must allow) my Brother adds that at that time (the 15th of Augt.) he had incurred a Forfeiture of the Ohio Compy Share in the Grand Company by failing to pay 450 £ Sterl a Sum that that share was chargeable with; by which, agreeable to the Terms of the Gd. Compy the share was sold, but my Brother writes he prevailed on a Friend to purchase it for his Use, in order to endemnify himself, for the advances he had been at & was likely to be at on that acct., but that he will consider himself as a Trustee holding for the Ohio Company or such Members of it as shall shew they intend to act fairly and who shall, while the Fate of the Grand Company's Grant is in suspence, agree to be bound by his Acts, & shall directly remit him their proportion of the Money he was then actually in advance together with a reasonable Sum for the expences he must necessarily be in advance for expences incurred on the Ohio Company's Business. The Sum then in advance exclusive of these expences he sets at 1350 £ Sterl besides the 450 £ pd. after the Forfeiture—observing however that more must be furnished at the Completion of the Grand Company's Grant which was finally to be determined on the 25th Day of Oct: then following. This Letr. I delivered to Colos. Lee Tayloe & Carter, they being on the Spot as Members of the Court, the second readily consented to abide by any Measure my Brother had taken or shou'd pursue for the Compy. The others had their scruples, & all agreed a meeting shou'd be called, promising themselves to appoint & advertize it so soon as they shou'd know when it might be, not to interfere with the coming Elections; as they neglected to do so, & as I feared the Resolutions of the 21[25?]th of Oct: on the Subject of the Grand Company, might soon be expected to arrive here, when it wou'd be too late for the Companys agreeing or disagreeing to abide by my Brothers Proceedings, I took upon me to request & advertize a meeting on the 15th of Decr. at the Stafford Court House the usual place of meeting, strengthening my Request with an assurance that it was with the advice of three of the Compy who were members of the Genl. Court, who being well known to be equally Interested with any of the Compy I well hoped a meeting might be had, but to my Surprize not a Soul (Colo. Ths Lee excepted) attended, nor was a single Letr. of my Brothers forwarded by those who had them, tho they cou'd not know but the rest of the Members wou'd have met & wanted a Sight of them. Under these Circumstances I am obliged to ask the determinations of the Members of the Compy seperately at the expence of an express, the Bearer; each Member can bend himself singly as much to his benefit in this Case as if in Company at a legal Meeting; for, for such as do assent to do Justice, my Brother agrees to hold such a share as that number wou'd have been entitled to had the Ohio Company's Interest in the Grand Company never been fortified as already mentioned. What my Brother defines to be Justice in this Case, is, that while the members of the Compy are ignorant of the Fate of the Grand Company's Grant, they shall say, will they, aye or nay, be bound by his transactions for the Company, and accept of the benefit of his Compromise with the Grand Company in Lieu of their Claim as Members of the Ohio Company besides this he expects that each Member who agrees to his Measures will immediately remit his proportion of the expence of such Measures which he set out 150 £ Sterl at the least for each Share. How far the Company are bound in Law & Honor to abide by my Brothers Conduct, and to remit him his advances will appear from the Orders of that Company enter'd on their Journals at a meeting held the 4th July 1763 purposely to form his Rule of Conduct when they parted with him—true Copy's of which are inclosed. It is to observed that Mr. Charleton Palmer never expended a Shilling for the Ohio Compy since my Brothers arrival in England so that my Brother might well advance 2000 £ on the Credit of the Company's order. How far his Powers will authorize the compromise he has made must be the subject of a future Question shou'd it ever grow into a dispute, but at present I think I may observe that If his known integrity will not acquit him of every species of disingenuity on this

Occasion, that I may safely appeal to what any Member who suspects the force of the obligation just mentioned (if any such there be) will readily admit, that is, his Interest which is greater than any Member of the Ohio Company being proprietor of one share & a half in that Company. What he has accepted in lieu of his & the other members Claims I can't say—but I understand he has long ago & very fully mentioned the particulars in Letrs. to the Compy which as there has been no meeting I presume are in the knowledge of but few of the members. Therefore for the Information of those who are Stangers to these Letrs It may not be superfluous to add that in his Letrs to me he says it is a 36th part of the Grand Company's Grant which will equall if not exceed the Quantity the Ohio Company expected, that as there is to be a distinct Government the shares in this Grant may reap advantages which they cou'd not have done had the Ohio Company succeeded in their own Grant, in fine, that he esteemed their share to be worth 20,000 £ Sterl.

Having thus fully stated all that I can suggest for your forming a true Judgt. on the Subject proposed for yr. determination, I am to request that you will by the Bearer let me know that determination, if in the affirmative I hope you will send me by the same Hand a Bill for at least 250 £ Sterl. that I may remit it to my Brother before he leaves London, when I dare say he will stand in great need, if only to pay off Scores made for the use of the Ohio Company. As the Bearer is hired by the Day, dispatch will save money to the Ohio Company or my Brother. I am Sir Yr. humble Servant

Js. Mercer

FC (Mercer Papers, PPiU). The date is apparent from GM's reply of 13 Jan. 1772. A notation on the Ms indicates copies were made and sent to GM, James Scott, "Mr or Mrs Chapman," Lunsford Lomax, and Richard Lee.

A COMPROMISE . . . ON BEHALF OF THE OHIO COMPANY was George Mercer's arrangement of 7 May 1770 wherein the company's conflicting land claims were merged with the Grand Ohio or Vandalia Company in return for two shares, or a one-thirty-sixth interest. George Mercer had failed to mention the compromise, or what was probably his personal fee of at least one share, when he wrote GM on 24 July 1770 (*q.v.*). The Grand Ohio or Vandalia Company (also known as the Walpole Company) had been organized in 1769 to purchase 2,400,000 acres from the crown in the Ohio Valley and establish a 14th colony there. The most recent and accurate scholarship detailing the plan is set forth in Sosin, *Whitehall and the Wilderness*, 181–210, 223–224, 227–228. It is impossible to determine whether Mercer was overwhelmed by the political connections of the Walpole group or was simply bribed into surrendering the Ohio Company claims. AS THERE IS TO BE A DISTINCT GOVERNMENT was another of the fantasies that touched the hapless Virginia expatriate, who apparently was led to believe he might receive a royal appointment as governor of the Ohio Valley colony. In fashionable London circles there was talk of retreating to a sylvan paradise on the banks of the Ohio, and George Mercer was the one of the few persons in London who had actually seen that country. GM's reaction was to repudiate Mercer's compromise in his reply of 13 Jan. 1772 (*q.v.*).

The Mercer family, father and sons, were not noted for the clarity of their letters. In this Ms periods have been substituted for many dashes, several parentheses and commas added, and one dangling question mark (or perhaps it is an exclamation point) have been deleted. The letter gives the appearance of hasty draftsmanship, but the version printed in Mulkearn, 312–315 compounds some of the original flaws in communication.

To James Mercer

DEAR SIR.   Gunston-Hall Janry. 13th. 1772.

I last night received your Favour of the 9th. Instant by Express; the Subject of which is of such Importance to the Ohio Company that I think a Meeting of the Company absolutely necessary; and have therefore appointed one at Stafford Court House on Teusday the 11th. of Febry next; which is as soon as the Members in Virginia & Maryland can have Notice of it by the public Papers; at which Time & Place I hope to have the Pleasure of seeing you; & must beg the Favour of you to bring with you the Ohio Company's Order Book; which was left many Years ago in the Hands of your Father, & has never been in my Possession since. I shou'd have attended the Meeting last Month advertized by you; but did not see the Advertisement, or know any thing of the Matter, until the Night before the Day you had appointed; altho' any thing that cou'd have been done then, wou'd have been too late for the Determination of the new Company's Grant; which you say was fixed to the 25th. of October last.

If Colo. Mercer has Cause to complain of the Ohio Company's Neglect or Silence, it is not my Fault. I imediatly ordered such Money to be paid as the Company directed; and your Father was, I think upon the Terms proposed by himself, appointed to correspond with Mr. Palmer & Colo. Mercer. Since your Father's Death, I have not received any Letter[s] from Colo. Mercer, till last Winter; when I received two or three; some of them was a year after their Dates, and all of them some Time after Colo. Mercer had assured me he shou'd take Ship for Virginia; otherwise I shou'd imediately have answer'd them; and that I have not done it since, is oweing to the same Cause—Colo. Mercer being constantly expected here. The last Time I saw you (I think in February last at Colchester, since which I have not had a Line from Colo. Mercer) you told me he had been detain'd only on a particular Occasion, & was expected here early in the Spring; and you wrote me from the last General Court, that he had taken his Passage in Capt. Anderson, & his Arrival expected every Day.

The Sentiments of the Ohio Company in general upon the Subject of your Letter, I am not acquainted with; but as you desire to know the Opinion of each particular Member imediatly, whilst the Success or Fate of the Grand Company (as it is called) is still unknown to us; I think myself obliged to give you mine, in the most explicit & candid Manner, as well on Account of my Interest in the Ohio Company, as on the Score of private Friendship. I can by no Means approve the Bargain Colo. Mercer has made with the Grand Company; nor do I think his Instructions or Power from the Ohio Company authorized him to make such a One: and making all due Allowances for the superior Interest of the Grand Company, I had much rather have trusted to the Faith of Government, upon his late Majesty's Instructions, than have withdrawn our Caveat against the Grand Company's Grant, upon the Terms Colo. Mercer did. It appears to me, from what Colo. Mercer wrote, that he might have had our first 200,000 Acres guaranteed to us, upon the Terms of the royal Instructions, to Sir William Gooch—that is in as many Surveys and within what Limits we chose; this wou'd have been ten thousand Acres to each of us, and cou'd we have been permitted Entrys & Deeds for that Quantity paying the usual Quit-Rents of Virginia, with the Indulgence of ten Years Exemption, without any further Charge or Trouble, I shou'd have prefer'd it infinitely to what is now done: altho' we shou'd then have lost more than one half the Land we had a Right to expect from the Royal Promise; upon the Faith of which we had expended so large a Sum of Money. One thirty sixth Part of the Grand Company's Grant may be an Object of Consequence to one or two Men; but that divided again into twenty Parts, wou'd reduce each of our Shares to a seven hundred & twentieth Part of the said Grant, & render it so trifling as not to be worth our Regard; at least I can not think it worth mine: and rather than advance the Sum of one hundred & fifty Pounds Sterling (the Quota now required by Colo. Mercer from each Member) or even half of it, upon so distant, and (to me) inconsiderable a Prospect, I wou'd submit to lose every Shilling I have already advanced. In such a Case, I shou'd think (with the old Proverb) the first Loss the best, and avoid involving my Family in a Scheme, which might give them much Trouble & Vexation, & even if it succeeded, cou'd never product them much Profit. These Sir are my real Sentiments, upon the most mature Deliberation I am capable of; and I am sure you will pardon the Freedom with which I have given them.

What Expences the Ohio Company may have incurr'd in England I know not; having never seen any Acct. of them; except Mr. Charlton Palmer's Bill for about fifty Guineas; but as nothing has been obtain'd from Government for us, I can have no Idea of their being very considerable.

As you will have a speedier & safer Conveyance to Wmsburg, than I can have from hence, I take the Liberty of inclosing you two advertizements, for Rind's & Purdie's & Dixon's Papers; which please to order them to insert imediatly; having no small Money just now bye me, I must beg the Favour of you to pay the Printers for publishing the Advertisements, & charge the same to me; I will repay you the first Time I see you. I have also troubled you with a Letter to Mr. Waller, desiring him to transmit me, under Cover directed to your Care, a Copy of Mr. Hanbury's Acct. as setled by Colo. Mercer in London; that it may be laid before the Company; who, I hope will take proper Measures to discharge it: when you receive it, you will be so kind to forward it to me by some safe Hand. I must also intreat you to bring with you to the Meeting a Copy of your Father's Acct. with the Ohio Company; for as it is so very difficult to procure a Meeting of the Company; whenever there is one, these things shou'd be finally setled. I am Dr Sir Your affecte. Kinsman & Hble Sert

G Mason

P.S.

Upon looking into the Virginia Gazette, I find the Assembly is to meet on the 6th. of February; which wou'd prevent a Meeting of the Ohio Company at the Time proposed: I have therefore altered it, & fixed the Meeting of the Company on Monday the 30th. of March; and as I shall have Time enough to send the advertisements myself, I have not troubled you with them.

G M.

RC (Mercer Papers, PPiU). Addressed: "To James Mercer Esqr./in Fredericksburg," and noted, "⅌ his Express."
By this time the outcries against delayed letters probably were wearing thin, although GM had suspected something other than poor mail service was at fault (see his letter of 6 Dec. 1770). John Mercer died in Oct. 1768 and GM reported receiving a packet from George Mercer in Dec. 1770. THE BARGAIN COLO. MERCER HAS MADE was the agreement of 7 May 1770 whereby George

Mercer merged Ohio Company claims with the Grand Ohio Company for two fractional shares in the latter enterprise. OUR CAVEAT AGAINST THE GRAND COMPANY'S GRANT was George Mercer's request to the Board of Trade on 18 Dec. 1769 "not to make any grant, within the limits prescribed by the royal instruction to the [Ohio] company." Mercer's petition (reprinted in *Case of the Ohio Company*, 35–36) came as the Grand Ohio Company was seeking approval of its overlapping claim, but Mercer did not mention the rival company by name. The other Virginia partners agreed with GM, for Richard Lee sought approval of the Virginia Council later in 1772 for their 200,000-acre grant, a move evidently calculated to forestall the Grand Ohio claims. As GM saw it, each Ohio Company partner was losing the difference between the 10,000 acres they expected through their original grant, and the 3,030 acres they might receive if the Grand Ohio scheme worked. GM's letter along with replies from other company partners are reprinted in Mulkearn, 315–323.

Ohio Company Advertisement

[5 March 1772]

A MEETING OF THE OHIO COMPANY, upon Business of the utmost Importance, at Stafford Courthouse, on *Monday* the 30th of this Instant (March) is desired by

G. MASON, Treasurer.

Printed from *Va. Gaz.* (Purdie & Dixon), 5 March 1772.

Ohio Company Advertisement

[14 May 1772]

THE EXPECTED MEETING OF THE OHIO COMPANY, on the 30th of *March* last, being prevented by the Sitting of the Assembly, a Meeting of the said Company, at Stafford Courthouse, on Monday the 25th of *May* next, on Business of the utmost Importance, is desired by

G. MASON, Treasurer.

Printed from *Va. Gaz.* (Purdie & Dixon), 14 May 1772.
When GM scheduled the meeting for late Mar. he had not expected an unusually long session of the General Assembly. The House of Burgesses began its sessions on 10 Feb. and did not adjourn until 11 Apr. The company partners finally met, scorned George Mercer's deal with the Grand Ohio Company, and petitioned the Virginia Council for confirmation of their 1749 grant. Richard Lee sent a covering letter with the petition, which the Council read on 27 July 1772. The petition is missing, but the Council noted that the signers complained of "their Agent Col George Mercer's having undertaken without their Consent or Authority to make an Agreement of Copartnership" with the Walpole

group. James, *Ohio Company*, 265–266, reprints the council minutes. The Council's clerk was ordered to inform Lee that since the company already had "an Order in their Favour, it does not appear necessary for the Board to do any Thing farther." James considers this an ambiguous answer, but GM must have thought otherwise. In all likelihood GM and the partners now believed they had a clear signal from the Council to proceed to make their surveys.

Account of Lawrence Washington with the Ohio Company, 1750–1772

		[19 May 1772]	
		Dr.	Virga.
1750.	Lawrence Washington Esqr.	Sterling	Curry.
	To his Proportion of the first Remittance made by the Company to John Hanbury	125.0. 0.	
	To Do. of the Money paid the Treasurer here		41.1. 6.
Decr. 3d.	To Do. of the second Remittance ord[ere]d. by the Committee	30.0. 0.	
10th.	To Hugh Parker		0.11. 0.
1751 May 23d.	To his Proportion of the Money ordered by the Compy. to be paid the Treasurer		15.0. 0.
1752 Novr. 22d.	To Do. of the Remittance to Mr. Hanbury	50.0. 0.	
	To Do. of the Money ord[ere]d. to be pd. the Treasurer		15.0. 0.
	NB. There is a pr. of Strouds charg'd to the Compy. (in Mr. Hanbury's Acct.) deliver'd Mr. Washington for which he never accounted wth. the Company	£205.0. 0.	£71.12. 6.
1752.	The Executors of Lawrence Washington Esqr. decd. Dr.		
	To Ballance of above Acct. due from the Deceased	50.0. 0.	15.11. 0.
1753 Novr. 22d.	To one Year's Interest thereon	2.10. 0.	0.15. 6½

1763. Novr.   To ten Year's Interest on
               Do.   25.0. 0.   7.15. 5.
           *   To an over credit of 21/6 Cash
               pd. Mr. Chapman when he was ⎫
               Treasurer; for Mr. Washington ⎪
               is credited £11. .1. .6, & it ap- ⎬   1.1. 6.
               pears by Mr. Chapman's Acct. ⎪
               that he paid only one Pistole & ⎪
               £8. .18. .6   ⎭
                                              _____
                                               £77.10. 0.   £25.3. 5½

               To Contra Ballance   17.10. 0.   25.3. 5½
1764 Novr.   To one Year's Interest on the ⎫
               sd. Sterling Ballc. & on the ⎬ 0.17. 6   0.15. 6½
               original Curry. Debt of   ⎪
               £15.11. 0.   ⎭
1771. Novr.   To seven Years Interest on   6.2. 6.   5.8. 9½
               Do.
1772 May 8th. To Interest to this Date,
               5 & ½ Months   0.8. 0.   0.7. 1½
                                              _____
                                               £24.18. 0.   £31.14.11.

                Errors Excepted for the Ohio Company

                        ₰ G MASON

to the Ohio Company   Cr.

                                                       [Va.
                                              Sterling   Currency]
               By his Bill on Osgood Gee
               Esqr. & Co. Mercht in
               London   125.0. 0.   [11. 1. 0.]
               By Cash paid Mr. Chapman (NB.
               over credit of 21/6)*
March 29th.   By Cash paid G. Mason, the
               Compy's. Treasurer,   30.0. 6.
               By his Order on John
               Hanbury Esqr   30.0. 0.
1751. July 16th By Geo Mason (on Acct of
               Lotts in Alexandria)   15.0. 0.
               By Ballance charged to the
               Acct. of his Executors   50.0. 0.   15.11. 0.
                                              _____
                                               £205.0. 0. £71.12. 6.

	Contra	Cr.	
1763. Novr.	By a Bill of Exchange paid by Colo. John Carlyle to Mr. James Mercer on the Compy's Acct.	60.0. 0	
	By Ballance recharged	17.10. 0.	25.3. 5½
		£77.10. 0.	£25.3. 5½

Fairfax County sct.

Colo. George Mason made Oath before me that the above Acct. is to the best of his Knowledge just & true Given under my Hand this 19th. of May 1772

A. HENDERSON

Ms (Mount Vernon Ladies Assoc., Mount Vernon, Va.). Entirely in GM's handwriting (except for Henderson's signature) and endorsed by him: "The Estate of Lawrence Washington Esqr. decd. with the Ohio Compy. May 8th: 1772."

After Lawrence Washington's death on 26 July 1752 John Carlyle became the active executor of the estate (Freeman, *Washington*, I, 264–267). Lunsford Lomax had purchased Washington's Ohio Company share and was admitted as a full partner in Nov. 1752. A final settlement on the unpaid balance was probably in the offing.

Missing words from the torn second page are in brackets.

To John Craig

SIR   Mr. Eilbeck's Septemr. 29th: 1772.

I have about £150 or £200 Maryd. Curry. (great Part of it in Gold & Silver) for which I want Bills of Exchange Pble at 60 Days Sight: I have therefore sent the Bearer to know if you want Cash for Bills at the present Current Exchange; which I am told is 52½ ⅌ Ct. at Annapolis. Your Answer by the Bearer will oblige Sir Yr. most Hble Sert.

G MASON

RC (Morristown National Historical Park, N.J.). Addressed: "To Mr. John Craig Mercht. in Port Tobacco."

Eulogy for Ann Eilbeck Mason

9 March 1773. Ann Mason died after a long illness at "about three O'Clock in the morning"—a detail noted by the bereaved GM when he wrote a eulogy for his thirty-nine-year-old wife in the family Bible. In

1966 the Bible was returned to Gunston Hall. All of GM's entries are carried in Appendix C of this volume. His son, John, later noted that after Ann Mason's death GM "for some days, paced the rooms, or [walked] from the house to the grave (it was not far) alone." See Rowland, I, 161–162.

Last Will and Testament

[20 March 1773]

I, George Mason of Gunston Hall in the Parish of Truro and County of Fairfax, being of perfect and sound mind and Memory and in good health, but mindful of the uncertainty of human Life, and the imprudence of a man's leaving his Affairs to be setled upon a death bed, do make and Appoint this my last Will and Testament. My soul I resign into the hands of my Almighty Creator, whose tender mercy's are all over his works, who hateth nothing that he hath made, and to the Justice and Wisdom of whose Dispensations I willingly and chearfully submit humbly hopeing from his unbounded mercy and benevolence, thro the Merits of my blessed Savior, a remission of my sins. My body I desire may be decently buried at the Descretion of my Exors. herein after named, close by the side of my Dear and ever lamented wife—and as for all the worldly Estate with which it has pleased God to bless me, I dispose of it in manner and form following.

Impremis It is my will and Desire, and I hereby direct and order that all my lands, Slaves with their increase, Stocks, rents, Crops, Tobacco, and Money And Debts due to me, with the yearly interest arising thereon, with all my other Estate of what nature soever in Virginia Maryland or else where, be kept together and considered as one common stock, for the payment of my Debts and Legacies and the Maintenance and Education of my children, and the payment of their fortunes, untill my said Children respectively come of age or Marry; when and not before each of them is to receive his or her part of the same as herein respectively devised or bequeathed to each of them; and when any one of my Children shall come of age or Marry and receive his or her part of the same Accordingly, the residue still to Continue and remain in the said common Stock untill another of my children shall come of Age or Marry, and so on in the same manner, until the youngest of my Children shall come of Age or Marry, and receive his or her part of the same as Aforesaid; It being my intention that my Exors shall not have the trouble and Perplexity of keeping different Accts. with all my children, but only one general Account for the whole. Item, I give and bequeath unto each of my four Daughters, Ann Mason, Sarah Mason, Mary Mason, and Elizabeth Mason, and to each of their heirs for ever, when they respectively arrive to the Age of Twenty One Years, or Marry which ever shall first happen the following Slaves with their Increase respectively from the date of this my Will. To my eldest Daughter Ann the four Following Slaves and their increase. To wit, Bess (the Daughter of Cloe) and her child Frank, mulatto Priss (the Daughter of Jenny) and Nell (the Daughter of Occoquan Nell) To my Daughter Sarah the three following slaves with their increase, to wit, Hannah and Venus (the Daughter of Beck) and Mulatto Mima (the Daughter of Jenny) to my Daughter Mary the following Slaves with their Increase To Wit, Ann and Nell, the Daughter of House Nell, and little Jenny (the Daughter of Jenny) To my Daughter Elizabeth the three following Slaves with their Increase to wit, Vicky the Daughter of Occoquan Nell, Sarah (the Daughter of great Sue) and Rachel (the Daughter of Beck) and I confirm unto my three eldest Daughters, Ann Sarah, and Mary their right and title respectively to a Negro Girl given to each of them by their Grand Father Mr. William Eilbeck Dec'd. to wit, a Negro Girl named Penny to my Daughter Ann— a Negro Girl named Priss to my Daughter Sarah and a Negro Girl named Nan to my Daughter Mary. But in the mean time, that is untill my Daughters respectively come of Age or Marry, the Profits of all such the above mentioned Slaves as shall not be employ'd in waiting upon any of my said Daughters, or for their use in the House, are to remain in and be considered as part of the Common Stock for the purpose herein before mentioned and if any one or more of my said Daughters should happen to die under Age and unmarried then and in that case it is my will and desire and I hereby Direct and Order that all the Slaves with their Increase herein before bequeath'd to such Daughter or Daughters shall go to and be equally divided between my other Daughters, or to the Survivor of them, to be delivered them or her, as herein before directed. I also give to each of my sd. four Daughters One Bed and Furniture, to be delivered them at the time and in the manner aforesaid. Item, I give and bequeath unto each of my sd. four Daughters Ann, Sarah, Mary and Elizabeth (except such of them as may happen to marry and have actually received their fortune in my lifetime) the sum of six hundred Pounds Sterling, out of my money, Debts due to me, & the Profits of the Common Stock of my Estate, the sd. sum of Six hundred Pounds, Sterling to be paid to each of them, without Defalcation or Diminution, when then they respectively arrive at the Age of Twenty one years, or Marry, which ever shall first happen; exclusive of any sum or sums given or to be given to any of them by their Grand Mother Mrs. Eilbeck, or for which I have taken or may take bonds for their use or in any of their respective Names. And if any one of my said Daughters should die under age and unmarried it is my will and Desire, and I hereby direct and order that the Money herein bequeath'd to such Daughter shall go to and be equally divided between all my other surviving Daughters; Such of them as may happen to be of Age or Married at the time, to receive their part of the same and the residue to remain in the common stock, until my other surviving Daughters respectively come of Age or Marry. But if two or more of my Daughters should happen to die under Age and unmarried, then and in that case it is my will and desire, and I hereby direct and order that so much of their money only shall go to my surviving Daughters or Daughters as will increase the fortune of each or either of them to the sum of one Thousand Pounds Sterling exclusive of their Slaves (or of any money given them by their Grand Mother Mrs. Eilbeck as aforesaid) to be paid them or her in the manner above directed, and that the residue shall remain in the common Stock, for the benefit of my four youngest Sons in the Manner herein after directed. Item— I give and devise unto my eldest son George Mason and his heirs forever, when he arrives to the Age of Twenty one years or marry's which ever shall first happen, my Mansion house and Seat at Gunston Hall, with all my lands thereto belonging or Adjoining being between five and Six Thousand Acres; Also a small Tract of Land Adjoining to the Land of the Revd. Mr. Lee Massey, Purchased by my Father of Giles and Benoni Tillett; and in General all my Lands between Potomack River, Occoquan River and Pohick Creek in Fairfax County, excepting and reserving unto my Exors. the right and Previlidge of keeping three Quarters upon the said Land, to be considered as part of the common Stock of my Estate, for the Benefit of my Younger Children, and of working the same number of hands as are work'd at the said three Quarters respectively at the time of my Death, with the right and Previlidge of getting timber for the proper use of the said three Quarters or Plantations on any part of the said Lands. That is to say one Quarter in the bottom of Dogues Neck (commonly call'd the Occoquan Quarter) untill all my sons come of Age, with all the Land which I have usually tended and made use of at the said Quarter, and such other convenient and adjoining Land as is necessary for the use of the same, and the benefit of suffering all the

Stock properly belonging to the said Quarter to range and run at large in the said Neck. And the two other Quarters at Hallowing Point, and upon the Land I bought of William Courts, until all my sons except the Youngest come of Age; with all the Land between the upper line of the said Tract Bought of William Courts, the river and the great Marsh; and the benefit of All the Stocks properly belonging to the said two Quarters ranging and running at large within the New neck fence; my Executors keeping the said Quarters and Plantations in good order, and repair and delivering up the same accordingly at the respective expiration of the times aforesaid or when the Crops then growing threon are finished, unto my said Son George Mason or his heirs, But if my said Son George Mason should die under Age and unmarried, it is my will and Desire, and I hereby direct and order that all the lands herein devised unto him shall go and descend unto his heir at Law and his Heirs for ever, in the same manner as if my said Son George had been in the Actual Possession of the same before his death, and shall not be devided among my residuary Legaties herein after named. Item, I give and bequeath unto my Son George Mason and his heirs for ever when he arrives to the Age of twenty one years, or Marrys, which ever shall first happen, the seven following Slaves, to wit, Alice, Bob Dunk, yellow Dick, Bob (the son of Occoquan Nell) Peter (the son of Great Sue) Judy and Lucy; together with all the Slaves which shall properly belong to and reside at my two upper Quarters in Dogues Neck Adjoining to the Great Marsh at the time of my Death (Except such of them as may happen to be any of the Slaves by name specifically bequeath'd to some of my other children) also all my Stock of horses, Cattle, Sheep & hogs shall properly belong to and be wintered at my said two upper Quarters in Dogues Neck at the time of my Death, with all the Plantation Utensils and Impliments of Husbandry thereto belonging, also one fifth part of all my Books, and household furniture in and about my Dwelling house. But if my said Son George Mason shou'd die before he comes of Age, and unmarried, then and in that case it is my Will and desire; and I hereby direct and Order that all Slaves as well as all the personal Estate herein before bequeath'd him shall be equally divided between my other surviving sons, and for that purpose shall remain in the common Stock until my other sons respectively come of Age or Marry.

Item, I give and bequeath unto my said Son George Mason & his heirs for ever all my stock in the Ohio Company as a member thereof, together with my share and part of all the said Company's

Lands; but whatever Ballance (if any at the time of my Death) appears by my Books of Acct. to be due from me to the said Ohio Company is to be paid out of the Common Stock of my Estate, in the same manner as any other debts. I also give and bequeath unto my said Son George Mason my Gold Watch, which I Commonly wear, also a large Silver Salver, which being an old peice of family plate, I desire may remain unaltered. And I confirm unto him his right and title to a negro man named Dick, given him by his Grand father Mr. Eilbeck; and likewise his right and title to two Negroe men named Tom and Liberty, exchanged with him by me for two other negroe men given him by his Grand Mother Mrs. Eilbeck; also to a large silver Bowl given him by my Mother, in which all my children have been christened, and which I desire may remain in the family unaltered for that purpose. And whereas my Son George will soon be of Age, and if I shou'd happen to die during the minority of my other children, they will probably live with him, and he may not chuse to charge his Brothers and Sisters with their Board, Altho' it must put him to a considerable trouble and Expence, Then and in that case therefore I give unto my said Son George, whilst my children live with him as aforesaid, the right and previlege of taking in any Year from any of my Quarters, whilst they remain in the Common Stock, such Quan[ti]ty of provisions for his family's use; and also of employing such and so many of my house servants in his family, as he and my other Executor shall judge reasonable and necessary for the above mentioned purpose, and adequate to the Expence and trouble thereby occasioned; without being accountable for the same.

Item, I give and devise unto my son William Mason and his heirs for ever, when he arrives at the Age of twenty one years or Marry's, which ever shall first happen, all my lands upon Chickamuxson and Mattawoman Creeks in Charles County in the province of Maryland, that is to say all my land in christian Temple Mannor, and my Tract of land called Stump Neck (formerly called Dogues Neck) with two hundred Acres of land thereto adjoining, and included in the same original Patent; Excepting and reserving to my Exors. the right and previlege of retaining and keeping in their hands, as part of the common Stock of my Estate, for the benefit of my Younger children, until all my sons come of Age, the last mentioned Tract of Land called Stump Neck, with the said two hundred Acres of Land thereto adjoining, and of keeping a Quarter thereon, and working the same number of hands for the purpose aforesaid as are worked on the same at the time of my Death. I also give and devise unto my said son William Mason and his heirs for ever, in like manner, a Tract of one hundred and fifty Acres of Land (whereon George Adams now lives) near Port Tobacco in the said County and Province, the same being one moiety of a Tract of Land called Partnership; And if my sd. son William shou'd die before he comes of Age and unmarried, then and in that case I give and devise all the above mentioned Lands upon Chickamuxon and mattawoman Creeks unto my Youngest Son Thomas Mason and his heirs for ever; And the above mentioned Tract of Land near Port Tobacco (upon which George Adams lives) I give and devise unto my son Thomas Mason and his heirs for ever.

Item, I give and devise unto my said son William Mason and his heirs for ever, when he arrives at the Age of twenty one years or Marry's, which ever shall first happen, the two following slaves, to-wit, Milly (the Daughter of Kate) and Sampson (the son of Mrs. Eilbeck's Bess) Also one fifth part of all my Books, and household furniture in or about my Dwelling house. I also give and bequeath unto my said son William my silver Watch, which I formerly used to wear, and I confirm unto him his right and title to a Negro lad named Cato given him by his Grandfather Mr. Eilbeck.

Item. I give and devise unto my son Thomson Mason and his heirs for ever, when he arrives at the Age of twenty one years, or marry's, which ever shall first happen, all my Lands in Thompson's Patent (repatented in my own name) Between Dogues run and the South Branch of Little hunting Creek; excepting and reserving to my Executors the right and previlege of setling two Quarters with eight working hands at each upon such parts thereof as they shall think fit, unless the said Quarters shall be setled thereon by me in my life time, and of retaining and keeping in their hands one of the said quarters So settle[d] by me or them with land thereto adjoining sufficient to work the hands belonging to the same, as part of the common stock untill all my sons come of Age. I also give and devise unto my said son Thomson Mason and his heirs for ever, in like manner all my Lands upon both sides the North Bra[n]ch of little Hunting Creek, contained in Thomas Stafford's Patent, Thomas Sandifords Patent (repatented in my own Name) George Brent's Sale to William Bourne, and part of Ball's Patent which I bought of Mr. Sampson Darrell; Also all my lands in Mason's and Heryford's Patent upon the Branches of Dogues run and Accotinck, being one moiety of the Land devised by my Grandfather Colo. George Mason Dec'd. to his Daughters Elizabeth and Rosanna; also a small Tract of Land contiguous thereto, originally Patented by one William Williams, and Purchased by my Father of Winifred Ball Daughter and heir at Law to the said Williams, it being the land whereon Edward Violett lived, also a Tract of about four hundred Acres of Land Patented by my Father upon the upper side of Dogues Run, adjoining the Mathew's Patent, and in general I give and devise unto my said son Thomson Mason and his heirs for ever, when he arrives at the Age of Twenty one Years or Marry's, which ever shall first happen (except as before excepted) all my lands upon the Branches and Waters of Dogue run and little hunting Creek in Fairfax County being in the whole about three Thousand three hundred Acres. And if my said son Thomson Mason shou'd die under age and unmarried then and in that case, I give and devise all the above mentioned Lands in Thompson's Patent, between Dogues run and the South Branch of little hunting Creek (being about thirteen hundred Acres) and also all the above mentioned Lands in Stafford's and Sandiford's Patent's in George Brent's Sale to William Bourne, and part of Balls patent which I Bought of Mr. Sampson Darrell, (being about seven hundred Acres upon both sides the North Branch of little hunting Creek) unto my youngest son Thomas Mason & his heirs forever. But it is my will and desire, and I hereby direct and order that all the other lands herein before devised unto my son Thomson Mason shall, if he die under Age and unmarried as aforesaid, go and descend unto my eldest son and heir George Mason and his heirs for ever, in the same manner as if my said son Thomson had been in the actual possession of the same before his death.

Item. I give and devise unto my said son Thomson Mason and his heirs forever, when he arrives at the age of twenty one years, or marry's which ever shall first happen, the two following Slaves, to wit. Sally (the Daughter of Lucy) and Joe (the son of Mrs. Eilbeck's Bess) also one fifth part of all my Books and household furniture in and about my Dwelling house. And I confirm unto my said son Thomson Mason his right and Title to a Negro lad named Cupid, given him by his Grand father Mr. Eilbeck.

Item. I give and devise unto my son John Mason and his heirs for ever, when he arrives at the Age of twenty one years or marry's, which ever shall first happen, all my lands adjoining to and near rock Creek Ferry upon Potomack River; that is to say the lands contained in Thomas Ousley's, Thomas Gowing's, and my Father's Patents (all repatented in my own Name) with the lands I purchased of Ellis and Bradie, and of Daniel Jennings, and a small Tract of Land I took up as vacant Land between my other Tracts; and in general all my Lands between four mile run and the lower falls of Potomack river, in the Parish and County of Fairfax, being about two thousand Acres. I also give and devise unto my said son John Mason and his heirs forever, in like manner, my Island in Potomack river, opposite the mo[u]th of rock Creek, which I hold under a patent from the lord proprietor of Maryland by the name of Barbadoes, I also give and devise unto my said son John Mason and his heirs forever in like manner, all my Lands upon and between the main south run of Accotinck and the branches of Difficult run, in the upper end of Truro Parish in Fairfax County, Patented by my Father, with a small Tract of Land thereto adjoining, patented in my own name, being together about two Thousand Acres. And if my said son John Mason shou'd die under Age, and unmarried, then and in that case I give and devise all the above mentioned Lands between four Mile run and lower falls of Potomack river, together with my before mentioned Island of Barbadoes, unto my youngest son Thomas Mason and his heirs for ever. But it is my Will and Desire, and I hereby direct and Order, that all the other Lands herein before devised unto my said son John Mason, upon and between the main south Branch of Accotinck and the branches of Difficult run shall if he die under Age and unmarried as aforesaid, go and descend unto my Eldest Son and heir George Mason and his heirs for ever, in the same manner as if my said son John Mason had been in the Actual Possession of the same before his Death.

Item, I give and bequeath unto my said son John Mason and his heirs for ever when he arrive at the Age of twenty one years or marry's which ever shall first happen, the following Slaves, to wit, Harry (the son of house Poll) and Peg (the Daughter of Chloe) also one fifth part of all my Books and household furniture in and about my Dwelling house.

Item. I give and Devise unto my youngest son Thomas Mason and his heirs for ever, when he arrives at the Age of Twenty one Years, or marry's which ever shall first happen, all my land upon the lower side of Occoquan River, Patented by my Father and Colo. Robinson, together with the right and benefit of keeping the Ferry over Occoquan from both sides of the river; which has been vested in me and my ancestors from the first Settlement of this part of the Country and long before the Land there was taken up or patented; also all my lands upon the branches of Neabscoe, purchased by my Father of Mrs. Ann West; also all my land upon Potomack River in Cock Pit Point Neck; also all my Land upon the upper side of Chappawamsic Creek: and in general all my Lands in the County of

Prince William. I also give and devise unto my said Son Thomas Mason and his heirs forever, when he arrives at the age of Twenty one years or marrys, which ever shall first happen, all my Lands adjoining to each other upon Goose Bay and Potomack river in Charles County in the Province of Maryland, being four different Tracts; the lower most called St. Benedicts, Originally granted to Bennett Marchegay, the next called Mason's fields Patented by my Mother Mrs. Ann Mason; the next (interfearing with Masons fields) a Tract of one hundred and fifty Acres, without any particular name, whereon Henry Fletcher formerly lived, who purchased the same of Henry Aspinall, to whom it was Originally granted; and the upper called Fletchers Addition, Originally granted to the said Henry Fletcher; and in general all my Lands between Chickamuxon Creek and Goose Bay in the said County and province. And if my said son Thomas Mason shou'd die under age and unmarried: then and in that case I give and devise all the above mentioned Lands between Chickamuxon Creek and Goose Bay in Charles County in the Province of Maryland unto my son William Mason and his heirs forever. But it is my Will and desire, and I hereby, direct and Order that all the other Lands herein before devised unto my said son Thomas Mason in the County of Prince William and Colony of Virginia, together with the right and benefit of keeping Occoquan Ferry shall if he die under age and unmarried as aforesaid, go and descend unto my eldest son and heir George Mason and his heirs for ever, in the same manner as if my said son Thomas had been in the actual Possession of the same before his Death.

Item, I give and bequeath unto my said son Thomas Mason and his heirs forever, when he arrives at the age of Twenty one years or Marrys which ever shall first happen, the two following slaves, to-wit, Kack (the son of House Nell) and Daphne (the Daughter of Dinah) also one fifth part of all my Books and household furniture in and about my Dwelling house.

Item. I give and bequeath unto my said son Thomas Mason the sum of six hundred pounds Sterling to be paid him when he arrives at the age of twenty one years or Marrys, which ever shall first happen out of my money and debts due to me, and the profits of my Estate; if so much remain in the common Stock after the payment of my Debts, and Legacies, the maintenances and education of my children, and the payment of my Daughters fortunes, and if there is not so much as the said sum of six hundred pounds Sterling, then whatever lesser sum there is remaining in the said common Stock. And least the manner in which I have limitted and directed the descent of some of my Lands shou'd occasion any dispute or induce any openion that I intended to entail them; I hereby declare that it is not my intention to entail any part of my Estate upon any of my Children; but to give all and each of my sons, when they respectively come of Age or Marry, an absolute fee simple Estate in all the Lands respectively devised them, and in all such Lands also as any of them may happen to take by the death of any of their brothers, the common legal descent of some of my Lands being herein before altered, only in case any of my sons to whom such Lands are respectively devised shou'd die under Age and unmarried, while their Lands remain'd in the common Stock of my Estate, and had not yet come into their actual possession. And whereas I hold sundry Tracts of Land in the County of Hampshire in Virginia, and in the County of Frederick in the province of Maryland, near Fort Cumberland, patented in my name in Trust for the Ohio Company, I authorize and direct my Executors to convey the same by such Deeds as Cou[n]sel learned in the law shall advise (with special warranty only against my heirs, and all claiming under me) unto the said Ohio Company, upon their paying the ballance of my bond with the Interest thereon, due to Mr. Bladen, or to Mr. Tasker's Executors for the purchase of part of the said Lands, so that the said bond may be taken up and cancelled, and my Estate indemnified therefrom; excepting and reserving unto my eldest son George Mason and his heirs for ever my part and share of and in the said Lands as a member of the said Ohio Company.

Item. All the remaining part of my slaves, with their increase, Stocks of all kinds, and Money, and debts due to me, Crops, profits and all other personal Estate whatsoever in the common Stock not herein otherwise disposed of—I give and bequeath unto my four youngest sons, William, Thomson, John and Thomas, (whom I make my residuary Legatees) and their heirs for ever, to be equally divided between them, when and as they respectively arrive at the Age of twenty one Years or marry, which ever shall first happen. And if one or more of my said four youngest sons shou'd die under age and unmarried, then and in that case it is my will and desire and I hereby direct and order, that all the Slaves, together with all the Stocks, Money or other personal Estate whatsoever bequeathed to such son or sons, or which he or they wou'd have been entitled to upon comeing of age or marrying, shall be equally divided between the survivors of all my five sons, George, William, Thomson, John and Thomas; such of them as may happen to be of age or married at the time to receive their part of the same, and the residue to remain in

the common Stock untill the others respectively come of Age, or
marry; or shall go to the Survivor of my five sons, if only one of
them shou'd live to come of age or marry. And if any of my sons or
Daughters shou'd happen to marry and die, during the minority of
theirs Brothers or Sisters, leaving a child or children behind them, it
is my will and desire and I hereby direct and order that such child
or children shall receive the same part or portion of the Estate
which the parent or parents wou'd have been entitled to upon the
death of any of my sons or Daughters respectively, under age and
unmarried as aforesaid. And whereas there is in my hands as Executor to Mr. William Eilbeck Decd. a considerable sum (as will appear
by my Account with his Estate) which by his will is bequeathed to
and divided among his Grand Children, my children, which I am
answerable to them for and have a Power of laying out for their
benefit; and as I have herein not only given much more to each of
my said children than their respective shares of his Estate in my
hands amounts to but have disposed of both that and my own Estate
among them all, in order to make the best provision in my power for
them all, and if any of my children were notwithstanding to claim
after my death theirs parts of their said Grand Fathers Estate in my
hands, over and above what I have given them, it wou'd occasion
much confusion, and alter the disposition which I have herein before
made, to the prejudice and injury of some of my children; I do
therefore declare that what I have herein before given unto all and
each of my said children is inclusive of, and in satisfaction for what
was due to them from me as Mr. Eilbeck's Executor, And that the
several Devises Requests and Legacys herein devised bequeath'd or
given to each of my said children are upon express condition of each
of them respectively releasing and discharging my Estate and Executors from any claim or demand on Account of the ballance due from
me to the said Mr. Eilbeck's Estate   Accounts already setled or to
be setled with the Commissary in Maryland; and if any one or more
of my said children, when they respectively come of Age, shou'd
refuse to release and discharge my Executors accordingly; then and
in that case it is my Will and desire, and I hereby direct and Order
that all the Estate herein by me given to such child or children shall
be forfeited, and shall go to and be equally divided among my other
children, and their heirs for ever. And as their are Debts due to me
to a considerable amount by Bond, the Yearly Interest of which will
be a great advantage to the common Stock of my Estate, I desire and
direct my Executors to continue the said debts upon Interest, either
in such hands as they shall be in at the time of my Death, or in such

other hands, and upon such other Security as they, in their discretion, shall judge best, untill the money shall be wanting from time to time for any of the purposes by me directed; and likewise to be let out upon Interest such Money as can at any time be spared out of the Profits of my Estate. I also authorize and direct my Executors to settle a Quarter or Quarters upon my Land between Dogues run and the south branch of little hunting Creek as herein before mentioned (unless the same shall have been setled by me before my death) when they shall think it most for the Interest of my Estate so to do; as also upon any of the other Lands herein devised to either of my three youngest sons, Thomson, John, or Thomas, either with any slaves that can be spared from my other Quarters or Plantations, or with Slaves to be purchased by them for that purpose, with any Money that can be spared out of the common Stock of my Estate, with out interfering with my Daughter's fortunes, or with the money bequeath'd unto my youngest son Thomas; all which Quarters and Slaves are to be considered as part of the common Stock for the purpose before expressed. I likewise empower and direct my Executors to erect Marble Tomb Stones over the Graves of my honoured Father and Mother, and my Dear wife; if the same is not done by me in my life time. And that no dispute or difficulty may arise to my Executors or my children about the manner in which that part of my Estate given to my residuary Legatees is to be divided among them, I hereby declare it to be my will and intention that when each or either of them comes of Age or Marrys, he is to receive his part or portion thereof, as it stands at such time respectively (always having regard to and reserving a Sufficient sum of my Money and debts still in the common Stock to pay the Money that may thereafter be due to any of my Daughters for their fortunes, as well as the Money bequeath'd to my youngest son Thomas Mason) so that any of them after having received and withdrawn their parts from the common Stock, are not to be entitled to any share of the subsequent increase or profits thereof and consequently not to any of the Slaves that may afterwards be born or purchased, nor liable to any loss that may happen therein; except such part of the common Stock as may happen afterwards to fall to them by the death of some of their Brothers or Sisters. Yet the fortunes herein given to my Daughters in Money are to be secured to them notwithstanding at all events; and in case of any deficiency in their said fortunes by failure of Securitys, or any other inevitable Accident, the same is to be made good, in equal Proportion by all my residuary Legatees, as well those who had before, as those who had not received their parts out of the common Stock. And I appoint my good friends the Revd. Mr. James Scott, the Revd. Mr. Lee Massey, Mr. John West Junr. Colo. George Washington and Mr. Alexander Henderson, (when ever it shall be necessary) to make such estimation division and Alotment to and among my several residuary Legatees; and it is my Will and desire, and I hereby direct and Order that such Estimation Devision and Alotment as they or any three of them, shall from time to time make, and give under their hands and Seals shall to all intents and purposes whatsoever be conclusive and binding upon my said residuary Legatees and their heirs. I hope they will be so charitable as not to refuse undertaking this trouble for the sake of a friend who when living wou'd chearfully have done them any good office in his Power. I recommend it to my sons, from my own Experience in Life, to prefer the happiness of independance & a private Station to the troubles and Vexations of Public Business; but if either their own inclination or the Necessaty of the times shou'd engage them in Public Affairs, I charge them, on a Fathers Blessing, never to let the motives of private Interest or ambition to induce them to betray, nor the terrors of Poverty and disgrace, or the fear of danger or of death deter them from Asserting the liberty of their Country, and endeavouring to transmit to their posterity those Sacred rights to which themselves were born.

I release and remit unto my Brother Thomson Mason and his heirs for ever, a certain debt of three hundred & ten pounds four shillings and five pence ¾ Sterling and nine pounds twelve Shillings and four pence Currency due to me on Account of Money advanced for him many years ago, while he was in England, for which it was never my intention to make him Answerable, as will appear by an entry to that purpose in my own hand writing annexed to the Account in my Book. And whereas my brother is indebted to me a further considerable Sum on Account of a Protested Bill of Exchange drawn by him and of a Bond I paid for him to Mrs. Bronaugh's Estate, I desire and direct my Executors not to bring any suit against him for the recovery of the said Debt, but to wait untill he can conveniently pay the same.

I give and bequeath unto Mrs. Heath, the wife of Thomas Heath of Stafford County the Sum of forty Shillings Sterling, in first Cost of Goods, a Year, during her life to be laid out for her in necessarys for her own particular use. And if her son Mr. Richard Hewitt, my old school fellow and Acquaintance from my childhood, Shou'd unfortunately be reduced to necessitous Circumstances, I desire and direct my Executors to Supply him with necessarys for his support and maintenance out of my Estate: And I particularly recommend this care to my children if it shou'd be necessary after they come of Age. I give to Mr. John Moncure a Mourning ring of three Guineas Value, which I desire him to wear in memory of my Esteem for my much lamented friend his Deceased Father. I desire my old and long tried friends the Revd. Mr. James Scott and Mr. John West Junr. each of them to accept of a mourning ring of the same Value.

I leave to my friend and relation the Revd. Mr. Lee Massey a Mourning ring of the same Value; and I intreat the favor of him to advise and assist my Executors in the direction and management of my Affairs; I am encouraged to request this of him from the experience I have had myself of his good Offices that way; and I am satisfied that both he and my worthey friend Mr. Cockburn will excuse the trouble I now give them, when they reflect upon the Necessaty that dying men are under of thus imploying the care and kindness of the living; which must also one day be their own case; and as the most acceptable acknowledgment I can make them, I desire them to receive out of the common Stock of my Estate the sum of ten pounds a year, to be laid out by them in private charitys, upon such as they shall Judge worthey objects.

I also give to my cousin Mrs. Cockburn a mourning ring of the same Value; And I desire her and my cousin Miss Bronaugh and Mr. Cockburn to accept of a Suit of Mourning each.

Lastly I appoint my eldest son George Mason and my good friend Mr. Martin Cockburn Executors of this my last Will and Testament, and Guardians to my children, untill they respectively come of Age. And it is my Will and desire, and I hereby direct and order that no Securitys shall be required of them by the Court, but only their own Bonds taken for the performance. In Witness whereof I have to this my said last Will and Testament all in my own hand writing, and contained in fifteen Pages, set my hand and affixed my seal this 20th day of March in the year of our Lord One Thousand Seven Hundred and Seventy three.—

Signed & Sealed & Published & declared to be the last Will and Testament of   G. Mason   (SEAL)
Mr. George Mason, in our presence &
Subscribed by us in his presence.
Gusts. Scott, Elizabeth Bronaugh,
Ann Cockburn, John West Junr. Robt.
Graham, John Davidson.

Tr (Will Book "F" No. 1, Fairfax County, Va., Clerk's Office). In a copyist's handwriting.

The death of Ann Eilbeck Mason on 9 Mar. 1773 caused GM to consider his own mortality. For many days after his wife's death GM occupied his time with preparation of this will, which he never amended before he died in 1792. By a separate agreement with Sarah Brent, whom GM married in 1780, she did not participate in the distribution of his estate. GM's provision that all his property be held in ONE GENERAL ACCOUNT to avoid THE TROUBLE AND PERPLEXITY OF KEEPING DIFFERENT ACCTS. was successful partly because the children had all reached the age of legal responsibility or had married, so a partial distribution of his property had already taken place. In 1773, George Mason, Jr., was 20 and the eldest child, while three-year-old Thomas was the youngest. Although estates were usually inventoried by the executors and recorded, no such itemized statement of GM's estate exists, perhaps because of the care GM exercised in drafting this will with its specific details and many contingencies. GM continued to add to his real estate holdings after 1773, and certain lands in Virginia and Maryland (patented through headright claims or as Ohio Company property) were eventually deeded to George Mason, Jr., and his heirs. Additional minor land holdings acquired after 1773 were distributed by the executors without a surviving record. MY ISLAND IN POTOMACK RIVER was known as Barbadoes Island, and later as Mason's Island or Analostan Island. When possible such place names are identified in the glossary. The privilege of operating OCCOQUAN FERRY was first granted to GM's grandfather in 1684 by the Virginia General Assembly. The allusion to RICHARD HEWITT, MY OLD SCHOOL FELLOW, is one of the few surviving clues that GM was formally educated (his uncle wrote of GM's tutor in Mulkearn, 200–201). The provisions directed to Thomson Mason (GM's brother), James Scott, and John West, Jr., were for nought, as all preceded GM in death. This will was presented for probate on 16 Oct. 1792 (q.v.).

When copied in the Will Book GM's fifteen-page document required 24 pages. The original will has not been located. The clerk's copy (with modernized spellings) was reprinted in Rowland, II, 457–472, with a commentary on the distribution of GM's lands to his heirs.

Headright Purchase from Harry Piper

22 June 1773. A certificate claiming headrights (i.e., warrants for fifty acres of land) for each of 377 persons, with their names, from Harry Piper; a clerk's attestation that Piper made the claim under oath, and that the certificate was the first "issued from any Office"; and Piper's conveyance of the claim to GM "in consideration of the sum of Forty-seven pounds two shillings & six pence Current Money." Signing of the three-page document was witnessed by Bryan Fairfax, Philip Alexander, and William Grayson. This appears to be the first of many transactions GM made in acquiring headright purchases. Further entries are listed in Appendix B. GM's memorandum which he wrote in support of these claims was probably written about this time and is printed as "Extracts from the Virginia Charters," *ca.* July 1773 (q.v.).

Tr (CSmH).

Mercantile Advertisement

FAIRFAX, July 13, 1773.
The subscriber has a neat assortment of EUROPEAN and INDIA GOODS, which he will lump off cheap for ready money, tobacco, credit, or bond, with interest from the date, and approved security.

GEORGE MASON.

Printed from *Va. Gaz.* (Rind), 15 July 1773.
It is not absolutely certain that the advertiser was GM of Gunston Hall.

Ohio Company Advertisement

[22 July 1773]

A MEETING OF THE
OHIO COMPANY
IS DESIRED
At *Stafford* Courthouse, on *Tuesday* the 27th of *August,*
On Business of the utmost Importance.

G. MASON, Treasurer.

Printed from *Va. Gaz.* (Purdie & Dixon), 22 July 1773. A similar advertisement was published in the *Va. Gaz.* (Rind) of the same date.

The urgent business was probably a consideration of the Privy Council order to the Board of Trade of 7 Apr. 1773, which forbade the issuance of warrants or patents for land grants beyond the proclamation line of 1763 without special orders. The order had arrived in America by June 1773, and was discomforting to Virginians who held claims in the Ohio Valley. News of the order may have caused Washington to publish his call for leaseholds in the Ohio country, which appeared in the same newspaper. A discussion of the shifting British policy is found in St. George Sioussat, "The Breakdown of the Royal Management of Lands in the Southern Provinces, 1773–1775," *Agricultural History,* III (1929), 67–98.

Ohio Company Advertisement

[29 July 1773]

A MEETING OF THE
OHIO COMPANY
IS DESIRED
At *Stafford* Courthouse, on *Friday* the 27th of August,
On Business of the utmost Importance.

G. MASON, Treasurer

N.B. In the first Publication of this Advertisement a Mistake was made in the Day of the Week appointed for the above Meeting:

Friday (being the 27th of *August*) ought to have been inserted instead of *Tuesday*.

Printed from the *Va. Gaz.* (Purdie & Dixon), 29 July 1773.

Ohio Company Advertisement

[5 August 1773]

A MEETING OF THE OHIO COMPANY is desired at Stafford courthouse on Friday the 27th of August next, on business of the utmost importance.

GEORGE MASON, Treasurer.

In the first publication of this advertisement the meeting is said to be on TUESDAY the 27th of August; but as the 27th of that month happens on a FRIDAY, I hope those concerned will be aware of the mistake. G.M.

Printed from the *Va. Gaz.* (Rind), 5 Aug. 1773.

Extracts from the Virginia Charters

(Annotated by Mason) [*ca.* July 1773]

       In 1676 K. Ch. 2nd gave a Charter 'To the Colony of Virginia' confirming the antient importation right of 50 acres for every person imported into the Colony. This seems to acknowledge and confirm the Company's right to the Charter to be in the Colony after the dissolution of the former.

       See Sect. 4th of the 3d Charter of James 1st. by which harbors, fisheries, &c.&c. &c. are granted to the Company which being of a public nature must plainly inure to the people of the Colony, after the dissolution of the Company if this dissolution had been legal. Sed Quere.

Anno 1606 April 10th.

       Charter, or Letters Patent first granted by King James the First to the two Companys, commonly called the London Company & the Plymouth Company, for two several Colonies to be made in Virginia, & other Parts and Territories of America, along the Sea Coasts, between 34 Degrees & 45 Degrees of North Latitude.

Sect: IV.

       Vizt. To Sir Thomas Gates, Sir George Somers, & others, called the first or London Company, to begin to settle & plant the first Colony any where upon the said Coast of

Virginia or America between 34 Degrees and 41 Degrees of North Latitude; and granting them all the Country &c from the said first seat of their settlement or plantation for the space of fifty English Miles all along the said Coast, towards the West & South West, as the Coast lieth; and for the like space of fifty miles all along the said Coast, towards the East & North East or towards the North, as the coast lieth; with all the Islands within one hundred Miles directly over against the said sea Coast; and also all the Country from the said fifty Miles every way on the Sea Coast, directly into the Main Land, for the space of one hundred English Miles, and that none other of his Majesty's subjects shall plant or inhabit behind, or on the back side of them, towards the main Land, without the express Licence or Consent of the Council of that Colony thereunto in writing first had & obtained.

Sect: V.   And to Sir Thomas Hanham, Raleigh Gilbert & others, called the second or Plymouth Company, to begin to settle & plant the second Colony, anywhere upon the Coast of Virginia and America between 38 Degrees and 45 Degrees of North Latitude; and granting them all the Country &c. from the said first seat of their settlement or plantation, for the like space of fifty Miles all along the said Coast, towards the West & South West, or towards the South, as the Coast lieth, and for the like space of fifty Miles all along the said Coast, towards the East & North East, or towards the North, as the Coast lieth; with all the Islands within one hundred Miles directly over against the said Sea Coast; and also all the Country from the said fifty Miles every way on the Sea Coast, directly into the Main Land for the space of one hundred Miles. And that none other of his Majesty's subjects shall plant or inhabit behind, or on the back of them, towards the Main Land, without the express Licence of the Council of that Colony in writing thereunto first had and obtained.

Sect. VI.   Provided that the Plantation or Habitation of such of the said Colonies as shall last plant themselves as aforesaid, shall not be made within one hundred miles of the other of them, that first began to make their plantation as aforesaid.

Sect. VII.   Granting & ordaining that each of said Colonies shall have a Council which shall govern & direct all Matters & Causes which shall arise or happen within the same several Colonies &c. with many privileges & immunities; among others;

Sect. XV. That all & every the persons being his Majesty's subjects, which shall dwell & inhabit within every or any of the said Colonies or Plantations & every of their Children which shall happen to be born within any of the Limits & precincts of the said several Colonies & plantations, shall have & enjoy all Liberties, Franchises & Immunities, to all Intents and Purposes, as if they had been abiding & born within the Realm of England, or any other of his Majesty's Dominions.

Sect. XVIII. And finally that his Majesty, his Heirs & Successors, upon petition for that purpose, shall & will by Letters patent, under the Great Seal of England give & grant unto such persons, their Heirs & assigns, as the respective Councils for the said two Colonies, or the most part of them shall for that purpose nominate & assign, all the Lands, Tenements &

XIX. Hereditaments, which shall be within the precincts limited for the said Colonies respectively, as aforesaid, to be holden

XX. of his Majesty, his heirs & successors, as of their Manor of East Greenwich in the County of Kent, in free & common Soccage only, and not in Capite.

With a Clause declaring the full & perfect Efficacy of such Letters patent, so to be granted as aforesaid. &c.[1]

Anno

1609 The Company for the said first or Southern Colony (to this Day called the Colony & Dominion of Virginia) having been joined by a great Number of the Nobility & principal Gentry in England, a second and more extensive Charter was granted them by King James the first, incorporating them by the Name of the Treasurer & Company of Adven-

Sect. VI. turers and Planters of the City of London for the first Colony in Virginia; reciting, confirming, explaining & enlarging the former Charter, and granting them all those Lands, Countries and Territories situate, lying and being in that part of America called Virginia, from the Point of

1. In Consequence of this Charter, the first or Southern Colony, which still retains the Name of Virginia, was undertaken & begun by several Persons, in and about London, who fitted out two or three Ships under the Command of Captn. Christopher Newport, which sailed from England to America. The first Land they discovered on this Coast was the Southern point or Cape of Chesapeake Bay which they called Cape Henry (the name it still retains) here they first landed and after spending some days in examining the Country, and looking for a proper place for their Settlement, they fixed upon a peninsula about forty Miles up Powhatan River (since called James river) & on the North side of it, which they called James Town, in compliment to the King; the name it has ever since retained. At this place the Seat of Government remained for a great many Years. And from this beginning proceeded the Colony of Virginia.

Land called Cape or point Comfort, all along the Sea Coast, to the Northward, two hundred Miles; and from the said point of Cape Comfort, all along the Sea Coast, to the Southward, two hundred Miles, and all that space or Circuit of Land, lying from the Sea Coast of the precinct aforesaid, up into the land, throughout from Sea to Sea, West & North West; and also all the Islands lying within one hundred Miles, along the Coast of both Seas of the precinct aforesaid; with all the Soils, Grounds &c. for ever; to be holden of his Majesty, his Heirs and Successors, as of their Manor of East Greenwich; in free and common soccage, and not in Capite.

Sect. VII.   Nevertheless charging, commanding, warranting & authorising the said Treasurer & Company, to convey, assign & set over such particular portions of Lands, Tenements & Hereditaments unto such his Majesty's subjects, naturally born, or Denizens, or others, as well Adventurers as planters, as by the said Company shall be nominated, appointed & allowed; wherein Respect to be had, as well of the proportion of the Adventure, as to the Special Service, Hazard, Exploit or Merit of any person, so to be recompensed, advanced or rewarded.[2]

2. Pursuant to the above last recited Clause, Sect. VII., the said Company in the Year 1616 (Sir George Yeardly being then their Governor in Virginia) ordained & ordered that 50 Acres of Land should be assign'd and granted to every person removing himself into the said Colony from Great Britain or Ireland; and to every person who should import others, 50 Acres for each person so imported. This was the first Rise of the ancient Custom of granting Lands upon Importation Rights; which is now no less than 158 years old; it appears to have been interwoven with the Constitution of the Colony from its first settlement & constantly practiced afterwards. In the Year 1621, two remarkable Instances occur. 50,000 Acres were granted to one Captn. Newce, for the importation of 1,000 persons. And sixty *Young Maids* being brought over by private Adventurers to make wives for the Planters. 50 Acres of Land for each was granted to the persons who imported them. After the Government was taken into the Hands of the Crown, upon the Dissolution of the Virginia Company, the same right & Custom was always continued, as appears from the old patents & Records in the Secretary's office. In the Year 1662, an Act of Assembly was made, prescribing the manner of proving such Importation Rights to Lands, and obtaining Certificates thereof, to entitle the Claimers to Surveys and patents. And in the Year 1676 the said Custom & Right was solemnly confirmed and continued, according to the ancient usage & practice, by Charter from King Charles the Second to the Colony of Virginia, under the Great Seal of England: which Charter was recognized by Act of Assembly in the year 1677, prescribing the Form of Patents for the future; in which Form is recited the Continuance & Confirmation of the said Ancient Right & Privilege, which hath been enjoyed by the Subjects of this Colony ever since, and great quantities of Lands from time to time granted accordingly, so that Mr. Stith, in his History of Virginia (which is chiefly extracted from ancient Records),

Sect.
VIII.
Appointing & ordaining that the said Company shall have a perpetual Council residing in England; which Council shall have a seal for the better Government and administration of the said plantation, besides the legal Seal of the Company or Corporation.

Sect.
IX & X
Nominating the particular Members of the said Council, & also the Treasurer for the Time being.

Sect.
XI.
And granting & declaring that the said Council or Treasurer, or any of them shall from thenceforth be nominated, chosen, continued, displaced, changed, altered & supplied, as Death or other several occasions shall require, out of the Company of the said Adventurers by the Voice of the greater part of the said Company & Adventurers in their Assembly for that purpose. Provided always that every Counsellor, so newly elected, shall be presented to the Lord Chancellor of England, or to the Lord High Treasurer of England, or the Lord Chamberlain of the Household of his Majesty, his Heirs & Successors for the Time being, to take his Oath of a Counsellor to His Majesty, his Heirs & Successors for the said Company of Adventurers & Colony in Virginia.

Sect.
XIII.
Giving granting for his Majesty, his Heirs & Successors, full power & Authority to the said Council, as well at the present Time as hereafter from time to time, to nominate, make, constitute, ordain & confirm, by such Name or Names, Stile or Stiles, as to them shall seem good, and likewise to revoke, discharge, change & alter, as well all & singular Governors, officers & Ministers, which already have been made, as also which hereafter shall be by them thought fit & needful to be made or used, for the Government of the said Colony & Plantation.

Sect.
XIV.
And also to make, ordain & establish all manners of Orders, Laws, Directions, Instructions, Forms and Ceremonies of Government & Magistracy, fit & necessary for & concerning the Government of the said Colony and Plantation; and the same to abrogate, revoke, or change, not only within the precincts of said Colony, but also upon the seas in going & coming to & from the said Colony, as they in their good Discretion, shall think to be fittest for the good of the Adventurers & Inhabitants there.

mentioning this right & Custom, had good reason for his remark; That "this is the ancient, legal, & a most indubitable Method of granting Lands in Virginia."

Sect.   Declaring also for his Majesty, his Heirs & Successors,
XXII.   That all & every the persons, being the subjects of his Majesty, his Heirs & Successors, which shall go & inhabit within the said Colony & Plantation & every of their Children and posterity which shall happen to be born within any of the Limits thereof, shall have & enjoy all Liberties, Franchises, & Immunities of free Denizens & natural Subjects, within any of their other Dominions, to all Intents & purposes, as if they had been abiding & born within the Realm of England, or any other of the Dominions of his Majesty, his Heirs & Successors.[3]

3. There can be no Doubt but this & every Clause relating to the People & inhabitants in general (not to the particular property of the Company) under the Faith of which our Ancestors left their Native land, and adventured to settle an unknown Country, operates & inures to the Benefit of their Posterity for ever; notwithstanding the Dissolution of the Virginia Company, had such Dissolution been ever so legal. But a new doctrine has been lately broach'd by the Writers against America "That the Charters granted to the Colonies were originally illegal, as containing Powers & Rights which the Crown, being only one Branch of the Legislature, could not grant, and having never been confirm'd by Act of Parliament, that they are of Course void & of no effect." The first Assertion happens to be false; and if it was true, the Consequences deduced from it are erroneous.—When America was discover'd, the sending abroad Colonies had been unknown in Europe from the times of the ancient Greeks and Romans (for the Irruptions of the Goths and other barbarous Northern Nations can't be regarded in that Light). To the People of Great Britain the Scene then opening was entirely new; and altho' the People removing from thence to settle Colonies in America, under the Auspices & protection, & for the Benefit of Great Britain, would by the Laws of Nature & Nations have carried with them the Constitution of the Country they came from, & consequently been entitled to all its advantages: Yet not caring to trust altogether to general principles applied to a new subject, and anxious to secure to themselves, & their posterity, by every means in their power, the Rights & privileges of their beloved Laws & Constitution, they entered into solemn Compacts with the Crown for that purpose. Under the Faith of these Compacts, at their own private Expence & Hazard, amidst a thousand Difficulties & Dangers, our Ancestors explored & settled a New world; their posterity have enjoyed these Rights & privileges from Time immemorial; and have thereby (even if the Charters had been originally defective) acquired a legal Title. It ought to wear well; for it has been dearly earned. King, Lords and Commons compose the British Legislature, but the Constitution has lodged the executive power in the Crown. The Disposition of foreign or newly acquired Territory hath ever belonged to the Executive. This power has been constantly exercised by our Kings in numberless instances. At the Conclusion of the last War, Martinico, Guadaloupe &c. (tho' acquired at the national Expense) were disposed of by the Crown; and however the policy may have been censured, the King's right was never disputed. —If the Crown can make an absolute & unlimited Alienation to Foreigners; a fortiori, can it make a modulated Grant to Subjects. The American Charters, therefore are legal ab origine. —Equally false and absured is the Idea of Great Britain's Right to govern these Colonies as conquered Provinces, for we are the Descendants, not of the Conquered, but of the Conquerors.

Sect.
XXIII.
Giving and granting also unto the said Treasurer & Company & their Successors, & to such Governors, Officers & Ministers, as shall be by the aforesaid Council constituted & appointed, according to the Nature & Limits of their Offices & places respectively, that they shall & may from time to time for ever hereafter, within the said precincts of Virginia, or in the way by sea thither & from thence, have full and absolute power & Authority to correct, punish, pardon, govern, & rule all such subjects of his Majesty, his Heirs & Successors, as shall from time to time Adventure themselves in any Voyage thither, or that shall at any time hereafter, inhabit in the Precints & Territories of the said Colony as aforesaid, according to such Orders, Ordinances, Constitutions, Directions & Instructions, as by the said Council as aforesaid, shall be established. So always as the said Statutes, Ordinances & proceedings, as near as conveniently may be agreeable to the Laws, Statutes Government & policy of the Realm of England.

Sect.
XXVI.
Declaring his Majesty's Royal Will & Pleasure, that in all questions and Doubts that shall arise, upon any difficulty of Construction or interpretation of any thing contained either in this or in other former Letters patent, the same shall be taken & interpreted, in the most ample & beneficial Manner for the said Treasurer & Company & their Successors and every Member thereof. And concluding with the following clause.

Sect.
XXIX.
Any Act, Statute, Ordinance, Provision, Proclamation or Restraint, to the contrary hereof, had, made, ordained or provided, or any other Thing, Cause or Matter whatsoever, in any Wise notwithstanding.

Anno.
1612
Sect.
I.
II.
III.
A third Charter was granted by King James the First to the same Virginia Company, reciting & confirming their former Charter, and setting forth that the said Company had petitioned for an Enlargement of their former Letters Patent, as well for a more ample extent of their Limits & Territories into the Seas adjoining to, & upon the Coast of Virginia, as also for some other Matters & Articles, concerning the better Government of the said Company & Colony, in which point the former Letters patent do not extend so far, as Time and Experience hath found to be needful & convenient.

Sect.
IV.
Giving, granting & confirming unto the said Treasurer & Company, & to their Heirs & Successors for ever all &

singular those Islands whatsoever situate, lying & being in any part of the Ocean or Seas bordering upon the Coast of the said first Colony of Virginia, & being within three hundred Leagues of any the parts heretofore granted to the said Treasurer & Company in the former Letters patent, and being within or between the one & fortieth & thirtieth Degrees of a Northern Latitude; together with all & singular the Soils, Lands, Grounds, Havens, Ports, Rivers, Waters, Fishings, Mines & Minerals &c. and all & singular other Commodities, Jurisdictions, Royalties, Privileges, Franchises and Preheminences, both within the said Tract of Land upon the Main, and also within the said Islands & Seas adjoining, whatsoever & thereunto or thereabouts, both by sea & Land, being or situate—To be holden as of the Manor of East Greenwich &c.[4]

Sect. VII   Ordaining & granting that the said Company once every week or oftener at their pleasure, might hold a Court & Assembly, for the better Order & Government of the said Plantation, to consist of the Treasurer or his Deputy, & at least five of the Council, and fifteen other Members of the Company; which should be a sufficient Court for the ordering & dispatching all such casual & particular Occurrences, & Matters of less Consequence & weight, as shall from time to time happen, concerning the said plantation.

Sect. VIII.   But that for the ordering & disposing of Matters, & Affairs of greater weight & Importance, & such as concern the

---

4. This Clause, Sect. IV. of this Charter, respecting the ports, rivers, waters, & Fishings, and a Clause of the same nature in Sect. VI. of the Second Charter (not particularly recited in these Extracts) being of a publick Nature in which the People & Inhabitants were interested as well as the Company, it is presumed could not be destroyed or avoided by the Dissolution of the Virginia Company, & may avail us if the Proprietor of Maryland should ever disturb the peace or possessions of any of the People of this Colony, by an attempt to exercise the Rights he pretends to claim on the South side of the Potomack river, of which he hath never been in possession: for upon an attentive examination of the Virginia Charters, perhaps it may appear that the said Proprietor hath little Title, except Length of Possession, to many of the Powers he holds. How far these Charters can be urged against the Claim he is now setting up to that Tract of Country, between the great North and South Branches of Potomack river, the Inhabitants of which have been long settled there as a part of this Colony, under the Faith of its Laws, & are represented in our Legislature; & who if the said proprietor's claim was to be established (besides the risque of their present Titles to the Lands) would be forced from under the immediate protection of the Crown & subjected to a proprietary Government; whereby their Lives and Fortunes might be at the Mercy, not of their Sovereign, but of a fellow subject, may soon become a Question of Importance.

publick weal, particularly, the manner of Government, from time to time to be used, the ordering & disposing of the Lands, & the settling & establishing a Trade, there should be held upon four different certain Days (therein named) one great & general Assembly; which four Assemblies to be stiled & called the four Great & General Courts of the Council & Company of Adventurers for Virginia; & should have full Power & Authority from time to time & at all times hereafter, to elect & chuse Discreet Persons to be of the said Council for the said Council, and to nominate & appoint such officers as they shall think fit & requisite for the Government, managing, ordering & dispatching the Affairs of the said Company; & shall likewise have full power & Authority to ordain and make such Laws & Ordinances for the Good & Welfare of the said Plantation, as to them, from time to time shall be thought requisite and meet: So always, as the same be not contrary to the Laws & Statutes of the Realm of England.

Sect. XVI to Sect. XIX.
Giving & granting to the said Treasurer & Company full power & Authority, Liberty & Licence, to erect & publish, open & hold one or more Lottery or Lotteries, within the City of London, or within any other City or Town in England; with divers Orders for the Regulation and Encouragement of such Lottery or Lotteries.

Sect. XX.
Declaring that in all Questions & Doubts that shall arise upon any Difficulty of Construction or Interpretation, of any thing contained in these or any other of the former Letters patent, the same shall be taken & interpreted in most ample & beneficial Manner for the said Treasurer and Company, & their Successors, & every Member thereof.

Sect. XXI.
And lastly ratifying & confirming unto the said Treasurer & Company, & their Successors for ever, all & all manner of Privileges, Franchises, Liberties, Immunities Profits and Commodities whatsoever granted unto them in any of the former Letters patent, & not in these presents revoked, altered, changed or abridged Any Statute, Act, Ordinance, provision proclamation or Restraint, to the Contrary thereof &c. notwithstanding.[5]

5. The principal Design of this third Charter, besides making some new regulations in the Government of the Company & Colony, and empowering them to raise Money by Lotteries in England, seems to be to grant to the said Company the Islands of Bermudas, otherwise called the Somer Islands; which

Anno 1621 July 24th.	The Treasurer Council & Company in England passed & established an Ordinance under the common Seal of the said Company, for settling the Constitution & Form of Government in Virginia.[6]

Sect.
I.
II.
Declaring their Motives & Authority for the same, & ordaining & declaring, that from thenceforward there should be two supreme Councils in Virginia, for the better Government of the said Colony.

Sect.
III.
The one of which Councils to be called the Council of the State (whose Office shall chiefly be Assisting with their Care, Advice & Circumspection, to the Governor) shall be nominated, placed, & displaced, from time to time by them the said Treasurer, Council & Company, & their successors: nominating for the present, the Members of the said Council of State, vizt.: Sir Francis Wyatt the then Governor, & nineteen other Gentlemen therein named; earnestly praying & desiring, & strictly charging & commanding the said Counsellors & Council, to lend their Care & Endeavour to assist the Governor; first & principally in the Advancement of the Honour & service of God, & the Enlargement of his Kingdom amongst the Heathen people; and next in erecting of the said Colony in due Obedience to his Majesty, & all lawful Authority from his Majesty's directions; and lastly in Maintaining the people in Justice and Christian Conversation amongst themselves, and in strength & ability to with-

---

the said Virginia Company, within a few years, sold to Sir George Somers and others, called the Somer Island Company; which was afterwards dissolved, much about the same time, & in the same manner, with the Virginia Company.

6. This Ordinance was brought over, the October following, by Sir Francis Wyatt (who succeeded Sir George Yeardly in the Government here) and is generally presumed to have been the Original plan, & first Draught of our Constitution, from which the Assembly of Virginia took its rise; but it was in fact rather a Confirmation of that Form of Government, which the people here, in imitation of their Mother Country, had before adopted: for it appears from ancient records, that two Years before this, vizt. in June, 1619, Sir George Yeardly held an assembly of the Representatives of the people. Counties were not yet laid off; but the several Townships, settlements or Hundreds elected their Representatives; from whence the said Assembly was first called the House of Burgesses, a name proper to the Representatives of Burroughs or Towns (but conveying a diminutive and inadequate Idea of an Assembly representing the whole Body of the People) which Custom hath very improperly continued to this Day; altho' all our Representatives, four Members only expected, have for a great Length of Time, been chosen by the Shires or Counties.

stand their Enemies. And this Council to be always, or for the most part residing about or near the Governor.[7]

Sect. IV. The other Council more generally to be called by the Governor, once Yearly & no oftener, but for very extraordinary & important Occasions, shall consist, for the present,

7. The Powers by this Clause vested in members of the first Virginia Council properly belong to a Council of State. But to what an alarming & enormous height hath the Jurisdiction of their Successors increased? In whose hands are lodged the Executive, the Legislature, and the Judicative powers of the State: & consequently the Life, Liberty, & property of the Subject? That this hath not yet produced much Evil or Opposition is candidly acknowledged because the Council has generally been composed of Men, whose Character, Interest, & Connections here, have restrained them within the Bounds of Moderation; because the Emoluments of the Office are not a sufficient Temptation to mercenary Strangers to sollicit the appointment; And because Luxury, Venality, and a general Corruption of Manners have not yet thoroughly taken Root among us. But when it is considered that this Board is entirely dependant upon the Crown; that the Authority of its Members is not hereditary, & if it was, that it could descend to but one of their children; that no Man's Rank or Fortune, how great soever can exempt him from the common Course of human affairs; and that their own posterity must quickly be distributed among the different Classes of Mankind, and blended with the Mass of the people; there cannot be a more striking proof of the prevalence of the Lust of power in the Mind of Man, than that these Gentlemen should be tenacious of Jurisdictions as unsafe & dangerous to their own Families as to the Community. Not only mean & sordid, but extremely short sighted & foolish, is that species of self Interest, which, in political questions, opposeth itself to the publick good; for a little cool Reflection must convince a Wise man, that he can no other way so effectually consult the permanent Welfare of his own Family & posterity, as by securing the Just Rights and Privileges of that Society to which they belong. But it is easier to describe a disease in the Body-politic, than to point out a proper Physician. Perhaps the lenient hand of a wise & patriotic Prince. Perhaps some noble & publick spirited Governor, who would then indeed deserve a Statue.

Perhaps the Constitution may by Degrees work itself clear, by its own innate strength, the virtue & Resolution of the Community, as hath often been the Case in our Mother Country. This last is the natural Remedy; if not counteracted by that slow Poison, which is daily contaminating the Minds & Morals of our People. Every Gentlemen here is born a petty Tyrant. Practiced in Acts of Despotism & Cruelty, we become callous to the Dictates of Humanity, & all the finer feelings of the Soul. Taught to regard a part of our own Species in the most abject & contemptible Degree below us, we lose that Idea of the Dignity of Man, which the Hand of Nature had implanted in us, for great & useful purposes. Habituated from our Infancy to trample upon the Rights of Human Nature, every generous, every liberal Sentiment, if not extinguished, is enfeebled in our Minds. And in such an infernal School are to be educated our future Legislators & Rulers. The Laws of impartial Providence may even by such Means as these, avenge upon our Posterity the Injury done a set of Wretches, whom our Injustice hath debased almost to a Level with the Brute Creation. These Remarks may be thought Foreign to the design of the annexed Extracts—They were extorted by a kind of irresistible, perhaps an Enthusiastick Impulse; and the author of them conscious of his own good Intentions, cares not whom they please or offend.

of the said Council of State, & of two Burgesses out of every Town, Hundred, or other particular Plantation, to be respectively chosen by the Inhabitants: which Council shall be called the General Assembly, wherein (as also in the said Council of State) all Matters shall be decided, determined, & ordered by the greater part of the Voices then present; reserving to the Governor always a negative Voice. And this General Assembly shall have free power to treat, consult & conclude, as well of all emergent Occasions concerning the publick Weal of the said Colony & every part thereof, as also to make, ordain, & enact such general Laws & Orders, for the Behoof of the said Colony & the good government thereof, as shall from time to time appear necessary or requisite.[8]

8. It is plain from this Clause that the Gentlemen of the Council were originally no more than so many Constant Members of the Assembly without being elected by the People; that they sat, with the Governor, in the same House, & had a common Vote in all Matters, with the Representatives of the People; that a Negative was lodged in the Governor alone; and that the House, thus constituted, was called the General Assembly; the stile yet retained in all our legislative proceedings; tho' great Alterations have been since made in the original Constitution. In this situation the Council continued long after the Virginia Company was dissolved, & the Government of the Colony was vested in the Crown. In those early Times when the number of the People's Representatives was small, the Influence of the Council was very considerable in the General Assembly; at first, indeed, they made a Majority; but in process of Time as the Country became more inhabited, Counties were laid off, & the number of our Representatives greatly increased, the Vote of the Members of the Council was in a manner sunk in such a numerous Assembly; & the democratical part of our Constitution had no other check here than the Governor's negative: this might be productive of Inconvenience; to remedy which, the Gentlemen of the Council, of their own mere Motion, thought proper to Walk up stairs & formed in Imitation of the English House of Peers, a separate & distinct Branch of the Legislature. That such a separate Branch, such an intermediate Power between the People and the Crown, is really necessary, no candid Man, well inform'd in the principles of the British Constitution, & acquainted with the tumultuary Nature of Publick Assemblies, will deny; but he may with great propriety urge, that the Members of this Intermediate Branch of the Legislature should have no precarious Tenure, that it should at least be for Life, and whether their Authority was hereditary or not, that they should be equally independent of the Crown and of the People; and that neither the Administration nor the common Judicative powers of the State can be safely lodged in their hands. As some Amendments in our Judicial proceedings have been lately proposed, it may not be amiss to mark here a Capital Error in the Constitution of our supreme Courts. When any man thinks himself injured by the Judgement of a Court of Law, or a Decree of Chancery, the British Constitution hath given him an Appeal; this is an inherent Right in the Subject, of which he can't be deprived without being robb'd of a valuable part of his Birth right, & the most effectual means that human Wisdom could devise to secure the property of Individuals. A Court of Appeals therefore, or

Sect. V.   Whereas in all other things requiring the said General Assembly, as also the said Council of State, to imitate & follow the policy of the Form of Government, Laws, Customs, & Manner of Trial, & other Administration of Justice, used in the Realm of England, as near as may be, even as the said Treasurer & Company themselves, by His Majesty's Letters Patent, are required.

Sect. VI.   Provided that no Law or Ordinance made in the said General Assembly, shall be or continue in Force or Validity, unless the same shall be solemnly ratified & confirmed in a General Quarter Court of the said Company in England, and so ratified be returned to them under the said Company's seal; It being their Intent to afford the like measure also unto the said Colony, that after the Government of the said Colony shall once have been well framed & settled accordingly; which is to be done by the said Treasurer & Company, as by Authority derived from his Majesty, and the same shall have been so by them declared, no Orders of Court afterwards shall bind the said Colony unless they be ratified in like manner, in the General Assemblys.[9]

---

that Court which is the dernier Resort, should be so constituted as that no Suit cou'd originate there; for otherwise, when the Subject is aggrieved, he is left without Redress. Their useful Distinction seems hitherto to have been totally neglected in this Colony.

9. This Ordinance or Charter for settling a Form of Government in Virginia, was made by the Treasurer, Council & Company in England, by virtue of the powers vested in them, for that purpose by the 14th & 23d Sections of King James's second Charter, & the 8th section of his third Charter to the said Company; and being made while the said powers were in full Force and Efficacy, & the Authority of the Company unquestionable, there can be little Doubt of its Validity; and that it gave the People of Virginia as good a Title to chuse their own Representatives to enact laws, as if it had been made & granted by the King himself; but this does not now seem to be a subject much worth our Enquiry; for if this Ordinance was annihilated, our Rights as British Subjects, & particularly that invaluable one of chusing our own Representatives in a Virginia Parliament, which we have uniformly enjoyed & exercised for more than one hundred & fifty years, could be shaken only by Violence & Injustice, aided by our own Folly, or by Force of Arms.

Some parties and Factions having arisen in the Virginia Company, & several Disputes having happened with the King & his Ministry, King James the First by Proclamation dated July 24th 1624 forbid & suppressed the Courts of the said Company at their usual place of Meeting in the City of London; and soon after the Lords of his Majesty's privy Council appointed a new Governor of the said Company, which being expressly contrary to their Charters, they refused to acquiesce in such Appointment; and thus rejecting the Officers nominated by the Ministry, and forbid to act under their own, their Courts & Meetings were discontinued, & their Business & Proceedings stopp'd: for though there had been a Quo Warranto brought in the King's Bench, & the process serv'd upon several of the Members, who entered their Defence, the same was never brought to any Decision or Hearing: but the Company chagrined with the Discouragements & Opposition lately received from the King & Ministry, disgusted with the Schisms & Factions in their own Body, & wearied with so great & constant Expence, after some faint struggles submitted & quietly gave up, or rather forbore any further Exercise of their Rights; and the Government of the Colony was taken into the King's Hands. An Event (however illegally & arbitrarily brought about) very happy for the People of Virginia; who were thereby taken from under a Proprietary Government, and placed under the immediate Government & Protection of the British Crown.

The Bounds of the Colony (as well as the Form of Government) remained unaltered until King Charles the First in the Year 1632, by Charter to Cecilius Calvert Lord Baron of Baltimore, established the Proprietary & Province of Maryland. That Country being then uninhabited, the Importance of it little known or attended to, and the scene of Confusion introduced by the Civil War in England prevented the people of Virginia making any Opposition. In the succeeding Reign (with equal Inattention in the Virginians) the Provinces of Pensylvania and Carolina were erected; the Southern Part of the first & the Northern part of the latter, being within the ancient Limits of Virginia. The Dutch & Swedes having possessed themselves of the Country on the Sea Coast, between New England and Maryland; King Charles the Second in the year 1664, granted all the Country so usurped, to his Brother the Duke of York, and an English Fleet having reduced the Dutch and Swedish settlements, the Duke of York parcelled out that Country to under proprietors, one of whom was William Penn, the Son of Admiral Penn. All these Proprietors except William Penn, afterwards sold or surrendered their Charters to the Crown. Mr. Penn retained his part, and had it increased & confirmed to him in consideration of a Debt due from the King to his Father; & from thence arose the Province of Pensilvania. There being few or no Settlements on the Southern Parts of this Coast, a grant was made in the Year 1663, by King Charles the Second, to several of his Courtiers, vizt. the Earl of Clarendon, the Duke of Albemarle, the Lord Craven, the Lord Berkely, the Lord Ashley Cooper, Sir George Carteret, & Sir William Colleton, for the Country called Carolina; the greatest part of which (the Earl of Granville only retaining his ancestor's, Sir George Carteret's part) was sold by the Heirs of these Proprietors to the Crown; and out of it were form'd the Provinces of North Carolina, South Carolina & Georgia. And by these Means have the ancient & original Boundaries been contracted; & the Colony and Dominion of Virginia reduced to its present Limits.

In the Year 1669 a Grant was made by King Charles the second to Henry Earl of Saint Albans, John Lord Berkley, Sir William Moreton and John Tretheway Esqr. of all that Tract of Land or Territory lying between Rappahannock & Potomack Rivers, commonly called the Northern Neck (now in the possession of the right honble. the Lord Fairfax) and altho' there was a proviso that the same should not infringe or prejudice any Contract or Grant whatsoever before made or granted by the Governor & Council of Virginia; and that the said Patentees, their Heirs & Assigns, & all the Inhabitants of the said Tract of Land or Territory, should be in all things subject & obedient to such Laws & Constitutions, as were or should be made by the Governor, Council & Assembly of Virginia; yet some Royalties & considerable Powers being thereby vested in the said Patentees, it roused the Attention of the General Assembly; who apprehensive that the People might be injured or oppressed by Men of such powerful Interest, in the year 1674 passed an Act of Address & Supplication, asserting the Rights & Privileges granted to this Colony by his Majesty's Ancestors, representing the Dangers & ill Conse-

1676 ⎤ Charter, under the great Seal of England, granted by
Octr. ⎬King Charles the Second to the Colony of Virginia.
10th. ⎦ Declaring & granting for his Majesty, his Heirs & Successors, from time to time, inhabiting within the Colony &
Plantation of Virginia, shall have their immediate Dependance upon the Crown of England, under the Rule & Government of such Governor or Governors as his Majesty his
Heirs or Successors, shall from time to time appoint in that
Behalf; & of or upon no other person or persons whatsoever.[10]

That the Governor for the time being, shall be resident in that
Country, except his Majesty, his Heirs or Successors shall at any
time command his attendance in England or elsewhere; in which
case a Deputy shall be chosen, to continue during the absence of
such Governor, in manner as hath been formerly used; unless his
Majesty, his Heirs or Successors shall think fit to nominate such
Deputy. And if any Governor shall happen to die, then another
Governor shall and may be chosen, as hath been formerly used, to
continue until his Majesty, his Heirs & Successors, shall appoint a
new Governor.[11]

Confirming & establishing all Lands possessed by the several &
respective planters & Inhabitants of Virginia to them & their Heirs
for ever, where the property of any particular Man's interest, in any
Lands there, shall not be altered or prejudiced by Reason thereof.

Declaring & granting that there shall be assigned, out of the Lands
not already appropriated for each of such of the Subjects of his
Majesty, his Heirs & Successors, as shall from time to time go to

---

quences of such Grants to Lords & others, & praying that his Majesty would be
graciously pleased to revoke the said Grant, and for securing them from Fears
in time to come, of being removed from his Majesty's immediate protection, to
confirm their Liberties, Privileges, Immunities, Rights & Properties, as aforesaid,
by his Majesty's Royal Charter. Certain Gentlemen were appointed to present
this Act; which procured the last Charter ever granted to this Colony: vizt.
that from King Charles the Second, bearing date the 10th Day of October in
the 28th Year of his Reign, An. Dom: 1676, as on the other side.

10. This first Clause expressly operates against the Establishment of any new
Government or Propreietary in any part of Virginia. For the King is as much
bound by the Act of his Predecessors, as any private Subject holding an Estate
from his Ancestor, is bound by the Act of such Ancestor. And accordingly,
this Charter effectually put a stop to all further Applications of that Nature.

11. The Rule established by his present Majesty, requiring the Governor to
reside here, is exactly conformable to this Clause of the Charter; and considering how fully it is expressed; especially when construed in the manner required
by the last Clause, (which applies to every part of the Charter) it is strange
that it remained so long unattended to.

dwell in the said Plantation, fifty Acres of Land, as according as hath been used, & allowed, since the first Plantation, to be held of his Majesty, his Heirs & Successors, as of their Manor of East Greenwich in their County of Kent in free & common Soccage.[12]

And that all Lands possessed by any Subject inhabiting in Virginia, which is Escheated or shall Escheat to his Majesty, his Heirs & Successors, shall & may enjoyed by such Inhabitant or Possessor, his Heirs & Assigns for ever, paying two Pounds of Tobacco Composition for every Acre; which is the Rate set by his Majesty's Governor, according to his Majesty's Instruction to him in that Behalf.

And that the Governor and Council of Virginia for the time being, and in the absence of the Governor, the Deputy Governor & Council, or any five or more of them, whereof the Governor or his Deputy to be always one, shall & thereby have full power & Authority to hear & determine all Treasons, Murders, Felonies, & other Offences committed or done, within the said Government, so as they proceed therein, as near as may be to the Laws & Statues of the Kingdom of England.[13]

And lastly of his Royal Goodness, graciously to continue to favour the subjects of his Majesty, his Heirs & Successors, which then did or thereafter should inhabit in the said Country of Virginia, & to give the more liberal & ample Encouragement to plantations there, declaring his Royal Will & pleasure to be, that all & every Clause, Article, & Sentence in these his said letters Patent, contained,

12. By this Clause, the old Custom first introduced about Sixty Years before by the Virginia Company, of granting Lands for the Importation of People, which had been constantly continued & exercised after the Dissolution of the said Company, is clearly & authentically confirmed & established, according to the ancient usage & practice; and being thereby made a part of the Constitution of Virginia, cannot be avoided or invalidated by any Proclamation, Instruction or other Act of Government (vid. Not[es] 2d & 10th) This & the following Clause granting all Escheat Lands to the Possessor upon a fixed moderate Composition, are certainly Articles of great Importance, and will be still more so, if by any new Regulations of Government, the Quit Rent of the Crowns Lands here should hereafter be raised; as all lands coming under the Description of either of those Clauses, would be exempt from such new Regulations.

13. This Clause investing the Governor & Council with full power & Authority to hear & determine all Treasons & other offences committed within this Government, expounded, (as required by the last Clause) in the most beneficial & available Sense for the advantage of his Majesty's Subjects here, is very inconsistent with the extraordinary Measure lately adopted by the British Ministry. A plan so contrary to the first principles of Liberty & Justice, as would much better become the Divan at Constantinople, than the Cabinet of London.

shall be from time to time, for ever thereafter, as often as any Ambiguity, Doubt or Question shall or may happen to arise thereupon, expounded, construed, deemed & taken, to be meant & intended; and shall inure & take Effect, in the most beneficial & available Sense, to all intents & Purposes, for the Profit & Advantage of the Subjects of his Majesty, his Heirs & Successors, of Virginia aforesaid, as well against his Majesty, his Heirs & Successors, as against all & every other person & persons whatsoever; any Law, Statute, Custom or Usage to the Contrary thereof in anywise Notwithstanding.[14]

14. By this Charter the subjects of Virginia are for ever to remain under the immediate protection of the British Crown, & be subject only to its Government here. The Governor is to reside in this Country. The Titles of their Lands are confirmed to the Inhabitants. Any vacant Lands are from time to Time to be granted for the Importation of People into the Colony, according to antient Custom; and all the Lands which shall at any time Escheat, are confirmed to the Possessors upon certain moderate Terms.

The Governor and Council have full Power & Authority to try all Treasons & other Offences committed here. And the Design of the Charter is declared to be, to continue to favour the Subjects which then did, or afterwards should inhabit the said County of Virginia, and for the more liberal & ample Encouragement to plantations there (that is to encourage the increase and Extension of the Settlements there) every part of the Charter is to be construed & take Effect in the most advantageous & available Sense for the Benefit of the Subjects of the said Country of Virginia.

The Country of Virginia is only mentioned at large & in general Terms in this Charter, & not described or ascertained by any particular Limits or Boundaries. It can't be confined to the Country then settled, which would be totally inconsistent with the Design of giving Encouragement "to Plantations there" and would exclude more than nine tenths of the present Inhabitants. It can't mean the Country at that time purchased from or ceded by the Indians; for this would also exclude the greatest part of the present Inhabitants. Nor can posterior purchases of Lands from the Indians be used as arguments against the Extent of this Charter, without impeaching the Crown's Right to those Lands at the time of making the Charter. A Doctrine of a dangerous Nature, & diametrically opposite to the Claims of Great Britain in her Negotiations & Treaties with other Nations, as well as the Reasons for which the King entered into the late war, one of which was the Incroachments made by the French upon the territory of Virginia. If such purchases could operate against the extent of the Virginia Charter, they would have operated against the Grant of the Northern Neck; far the greater part of which was possessed by the Indians, when the said grant was made, & not purchased from them for many years after. So late as Queen Anne's Reign the Blue ridge of mountains separated the possessions of the British subjects here from those of the Indians: Yet in the last reign the King and Council gave Lord Fairfax a Judgement for the Lands to the Fountain Head of Potomack River, near fourscore miles beyond the Blue Ridge. As our Settlements were extended & the wild Game destroyed, the Indians have been forced to remove further for the Convenience of Hunting. As they retired, purchase after purchase hath been made of them, and temporary lines or Boundaries from time to time accordingly settled between them & the English Inhabitants here. It is not above fifty years since the People of Virginia settled beyond the Blue Ridge: it is near thirty Years since they first begun to settle on the West side of the Alleghany or Appalatian Mountains, and at this time there are several thousand families settled to the Westward of the said Mountains, on the Branches & waters of the Ohio river. When the Colony of Virginia was settled the Lands first purchased of the Indians were only upon & near the Mouths & larger parts of the Rivers, then to the Falls of the said Rivers, then to the Blue Ridge of Mountains; afterwards to the Alleghany Mountains, and lately to the River Ohio. Many of these purchases have been made since the Charter of Charles the second. If the said Charter was not affected by the former purchases from the Indians, neither is it by the last; nor can it be by any purchase made hereafter. For (not to mention the liberal & beneficial Manner of Construction which we have a right to) the plain, natural, & obvious meaning of the Charter is, to grant & confirm certain Rights, privileges & Immunities to all his Majesty's Subjects, who then did or ever should inhabit that Tract of Country in America, usually called Virginia, according to the Description and Boundaries of the original Charters, not before otherwise appropriated or disposed of by his Majesty's Ancestors. In this situation hath it remained from the time of this last Charter; and in this Manner hath Virginia been constantly laid down ever since, in all the English maps, as well those published by publick Authority as others, to wit, Bounded on the North by Maryland & Pennsilvania; on the East by the Atlantic Ocean; on the South by Carolina; and on the West by the great South Sea, or by the Western Limits of the British Dominions, which were never clearly ascertained until the last Treaty of Peace, in the Year 1763, fixed then by a Line drawn along the Middle of the River Mississippi. Several Acts of the British Crown & Government, as well as many Laws of this Colony (which receiving the Royal Assent are also Acts of the British Crown & Government) have from time to time corresponded with and confirm'd these Bounds of Virginia. It will be sufficient to mention a few Instances, as there are none which contradict them. In the 4th Year of the Reign of Queen Anne, An: Dom: 1705, an Act of Assembly was made here, empowering the Governor for the Time being, with the Consent of the Council, by Charter or Grant, under the seal of th's Colony, to grant to any such person or persons, their Heirs, Executors, Administrators or Assigns, as should at his or their own Charge, make Discovery of any Town or Nation of Indians, situate or inhabiting to the Westward of, or between the Appalatian Mountains, the sole liberty & Right of trading to & with all & every such Town or Towns, Nation or Nations of Indians, so discovered as aforesaid, for the space of fourteen Years, then next ensuing, with such Clauses or Articles of Restraint, or Prohibition of all other persons from the said Trade, & under such penalities & Forfeitures as shall be thought convenient. In an additional Instruction from his late Majesty, King George the second, to Sir William Gooch Bart. Lieut. Governor & Commander in Chief of the Colony and Dominion of Virginia, or to the Commander in Chief of the said Colony for the time being, Given at the Court of St. James's the 16th Day of March 1748/9 in the 22d Year of his Reign, reciting a petition which had been presented to his Majesty by the Ohio Company, the said Governor is directed & required forthwith to make the petitioners & their Associates, a Grant or Grants of two hundred thousand Acres of Land betwixt Romanettoe's & Buffaloe Creek, on the South side of the River Alleghany, otherwise Ohio, and betwixt the two Creeks & the Yellow Creek on the North side of the said River, or in such other parts of the West of the Alleghany Mountains as shall be adjudged most proper by the said Petitioners, for making Settlements thereon, within his Majesty's Colony of Virginia &c.

In the Year 1753 An Act of Assembly was made here "For further encouraging persons to settle on the Waters of the Mississippi" Declaring that

it would be a means of cultivating a better Correspondence with the neighbouring Indians, if a further Encouragement be given to Persons who have
settled or shall settle upon the waters of the Mississippi, in the County of
Augusta (which was then the Frontier County quite across this Colony) and
that a considerable number of persons, as well his Majesty's natural born
subjects, as foreign protestants were willing to come in to this Colony with
their Families & Effects, & settle upon the Lands near the said Waters, in Case
they can have Encouragement for so doing; that settling that part of the
Country will add to the Strength & Security of the Colony in general, & be a
Means of augmenting his Majesty's Revenue of Quit Rents. And enacting
"That all persons being Protestants who have already settled, or shall hereafter
settle & reside upon any Lands situate to the Westward of the Ridge of
Mountains, that divides the Rivers Roanoke, James & Potomack from the
Mississippi, in the County of Augusta, shall be & are exempted & discharged
from the payment of all publick, County, & parish Levies, for the Term of
fifteen Years next following."

And in the Year 1754, another Act of Assembly was made here "For the
Encouragement & protection of the settlers upon the waters of the Mississippi"
Declaring that many of his Majesty's faithful subjects had been encouraged by
the Acts of the general Assembly heretofore made, to settle & inhabit on his
Lands in this Colony, on & near the Waters of the River Mississippi; & that it
hath been represented to the General Assembly that the Subjects of the French
King, & by their Instigation, the Indians in alliance with them, had encroached
on his Majesty's said Lands, murdered some of his Subjects, & taken others
Captive, and spoiled them of their Goods and Effects; impowering the
Treasurer of this Colony to borrow a sum of Money upon Interest, nominating
certain Directors (Members of both Houses of Assembly) and impowering
them from time to time, with the consent & approbation of the Governor, or
Commander in Chief for the time being, to direct & appoint how the said
Money shall be applied, towards protecting & defending his Majesty's subjects,
who then were settled, or thereafter should settle on the waters of the River
Mississippi. And laying sundry Duties & Taxes on the inhabitants of this
Colony, for raising a Fund to repay the Money to be so borrowed. And for
the same purposes were several hundred thousand pounds granted by the
General Assembly, & levied upon the people of Virginia, during the Course of
the late War. And soon after the Conclusion of the War, to wit in the Year
[1769] it being thought expedient, in order to conciliate the Minds of the
Indians, then but lately withdrawn from the French Interest, to extend a
temporary Line or Boundary between the Inhabitants of this Colony & the
Southern Indians, across the Alleghany Mountains to the Ohio River; the sum
of [not more than £2500] was granted by the General Assembly, & levied
upon the people of Virginia, [to the] Charge thereof, upon a formal Requisition made by the Crown for that purpose.

These Quotations & Examples are sufficient to shew in what sense the
Charter of King Charles the second, respecting the Bounds of this Colony, hath
been always understood; and to demonstrate that the Country to the Westward of the Alleghany Mountains, on both sides the Ohio River, is part of
Virginia. And consequently that no new Government or proprietary can
legally be established there. Nor hath any attempt of that sort ever been made
from the time of the said Charter, until the late extraordinary application of
Mr. Walpole & his Associates to the Crown, to grant a Proprietary Charter, &
create a new Government between the Alleghany Mountains & the River Ohio
(in direct Violation [torn] Virginia Charters) which would not only have
taken away great part of the Territory of this Colony; but would have
removed from under the immediate protection of the Crown, & the Govern-

ment of Virginia, several thousand Inhabitants, Settled there under the Faith of the said Charters, as well as many subsequent Acts of Government, and the Encouragement of the Publick Laws. It would also have greatly injured the only regular Seminary of Learning in Virginia, by reducing one of the principal Branches of its Revenue, the profits arising from a Grant of the Office of Surveyor General of Virginia, made by their Majesties King William & Queen Mary, to the President & Professors of William & Mary College. And have introduced a precedent of a very alarming & dangerous Nature to the Liberties, Rights, & privileges of his Majesty's Subjects of this Colony.

To this illegal & injurious attempt several Gentlemen in Virginia, the Ohio Company, were made in some Measure accessary, without their Knowledge & very contrary to their inclination; but at their first general Meeting, after having received Notice of it, they unanimously declared their Disapprobation of the Measure, & their absolute Refusal of having any Concern in it; which Resolution they not only entered in their own Books, & communicated to the Members of their Company in England; but for their Justification to posterity, sent a Copy thereof to the Governor & Council, to be entered, if they thought fit, on their Journals.

This project of Mr. Walpole's was fabricated by the same fertile [torn] who first suggested it to the Earl of [Rochford] to apply to [the Lords of Trade] for a Grant of the Islands in Delaware Bay, which probably would have taken effect, to the ruin of many reputable families, if his Lordship, after a Day's debate before the Lords of the Council, had not had Grace enough to be ashamed of it, & drop his pretensions. And tho' the Scheme for a new Government on the Ohio at present seems to be rejected or suspended; yet considering how favorably it was entertained by some of the publick Boards in England, it may be proper for the General Assembly of Virginia, at this Time to assert our Rights by a Dutiful Remonstrance & Petition to the Crown.

Which is humbly submitted to their Consideration

[N.] B. The first Charter for Carolina, the orders to the Commissioners for running a dividing Line between North Carolina & Virginia, with their proceedings & report thereon, the Articles of the Peace of Utrecht, & Aix la Chapelle, with the proceedings of the Commissaries of the two Nations respecting the Boundaries of the English and French colonies, the Royal Instructions from time to time to the Governors of Virginia, the several Orders of the Council relative to the Back Lands, the Judgement of the King & Council upon the Patent Fee in Govr. Dinwiddie's Time, & several other publick Documents, may throw much light upon this interesting Subject.

Memorandum

According to the best late Maps, Virginia as at present bounded extending to the River Mississippi, contains about 141,000 square miles, or 90,240,000 Acres.

49,452 square miles in England according to Geography of Engld. pubd. in 1746 or 42,196,700 acres.

Tr (Bancroft Collection, NN). In a copyist's handwriting, with the title: "Extracts from the Virginia Charters with some Remarks on them made in the year 1773." A note in the copybook indicates the transcript was made from the original in GM's handwriting, then possessed by James Murray Mason and later lost or destroyed.

This treatise covered two subjects of vital concern to GM—headrights and the territorial limits of Virginia. It was probably written for the perusal of certain members of the General Assembly in the hope that a Petition would be sent to the Crown based on GM's chief arguments. The timing of the document was determined partly by circumstances and also by a personal decision. In Apr. 1773 the Privy Council curtailed a colonial governor's power to grant lands. Despite this, and shortly after Ann Mason's death, GM began accumulating headright certificates. His inventory of 12 July 1779 indicates that by the late summer of 1773, GM owned certificates which entitled him to warrants for 24,850 acres. To buttress the legality of these claims, it seemed necessary to prove both the validity of such headrights and of Virginia's jurisdiction over lands in the Ohio watershed. Certainly the lands GM hoped to gain through these warrants would have to be patented in the western counties, not in the Northern Neck (Harrison, 120n). Renewed interest in western land speculation was evident. Amidst vague rumors of a 14th colony in the West, Washington pressed for the long-promised military grants along the Ohio. GM's neighbor wrote a prospectus on 15 July 1773 offering 20,000 acres along the Ohio and Great Kanawha rivers where settlers might "enjoy the lands in peace and safety, notwithstanding the unsettled counsels respecting a new colony on the *Ohio* . . . [and] if the scheme for establishing a new government on the *Ohio* . . . should ever be effected, these must be among the most valuable lands in it. . . ." (Fitzpatrick, *Writings of Washington*, III, 144-146). While the Ohio Company's plans faltered, GM may have reasoned that headrights would give him some personal advantage in acquiring western tracts. GM also hoped to discredit the Vandalia or Walpole Company claims by proving that Virginia's title to the western lands antedated the Treaty of Fort Stanwix (1768). Much of GM's treatise is borrowed from William Stith's *History of the First Discovery and Settlement of Virginia*, which was first printed in Williamsburg in 1747. The acknowledged use of MR. STITH in FOOTNOTE TWO is a carefully copied quotation (see page 139 of the 1865 Sabin reprint), but GM relied most heavily on Stith's appendices for the several Virginia charters (1606, 1609, 1612, and 1621) and his marked sections are copied from Stith. In FOOTNOTE THREE GM went beyond Stith to comment on the assertion of British writers (particularly after 1765) that colonial legislatures had usurped their function by claiming the sole right to levy taxes. The phrase "liberty of an Englishman," wrote Soame Jenyns in 1765, implied no exemption from parliamentary taxation overseas, ". . . nor is there any charter that ever pretended to grant such a privilege to any colony in America; and had they granted it, it could have had no force; their charters being derived from the Crown, and no charter from the Crown can possibly supersede the right of the whole legislature." (See "The Objections to the Taxation of our American Colonies . . . ," in S. E. Morison, ed., *Sources and Documents Illustrating the American Revolution 1764-1788* [Oxford, 1948], 20). GM's FOOTNOTE FOUR concerned boundary problems between Maryland and Virginia that surveys of 1736 and 1746 presumably had settled. But in 1753, the sixth and last Lord Baltimore claimed that the Maryland border encompassed all territory between the north and south branches of the Potomac. In 1771 Maryland surveyors marked a line northward from the source of the south branch, but this proved to be an empty gesture, for the Fairfax Stone planted on the north branch in 1746 became the basis for the final boundary (Charles O. Paullin, *Atlas of the Historical Geography of the United States*, ed. John K. Wright [Washington and New York, 1932], 77-78, and plate 98). GM's peevish obiter dictum in FOOTNOTE SEVEN indicates his distrust of the powerful Council and his recurring fear that slavery was corrosive to the spirit of liberty. In later years GM repeated the same sentiments at the Federal Convention and recalled one sentence almost verbatim on 22 Aug. 1787. GM's plea for SOME AMENDMENTS IN OUR JUDICIAL PROCEEDINGS IN FOOTNOTE EIGHT stemmed from the fact that the Council was "by Custom . . . the supreme Judges . . . in all Causes, *viz.* in Chancery, King's Bench, Common-Pleas, Exchequer, Admiralty, and Spirituality, and there lyes no Appeal from them but to the King in Council. . . ." (Henry Hartwell, James Blair, and Edward Chilton, *The Present State of*

Virginia and the College, ed. Hunter D. Farish [Williamsburg, 1940], 34). Three years later GM wrote his own solution into a draft of the proposed Virginia constitution which provided for life tenure for judges, a supreme court of appeals, chancery court, and admiralty court (see draft of 8–10 June 1776). Jefferson drafted a similar proposal (Boyd, I, 361). In committee GM's 1776 plan was altered by adding the words "general court"—the body became a five-man court of both appeals and original jurisdiction on civil and criminal cases. Their operation in 1785 is explained in Thomas Jefferson, *Notes on the State of Virginia,* ed. William Peden (Chapel Hill, 1955), 131–132. The first part of FOOTNOTE NINE is paraphrased from Stith's final pages (329–331), which concluded with the "illegal Dissolution" of the Virginia Company in 1624. Thereafter, GM probably was guided by the *Acts of the Assembly . . . ,* which were printed in Williamsburg in 1733, 1752, and 1769. Uneasiness over the NORTHERN NECK grant of 1669 led to passage in 1674 of an ACT OF ADDRESS & SUPPLICATION (Hening, II, 311–314). The CERTAIN GENTLEMEN appointed to present the colony's case were Francis Morryson, Thomas Ludwell, and Robert Smith. They petitioned the crown for a new charter in Nov. 1675. In FOOTNOTE ELEVEN, GM's complaint over a long procession of nonresident governors was muted by the consecutive appointments of Lords Botetourt and Dunmore as governors-in-residence. Praise for the 1676 charter in FOOTNOTE THIRTEEN allowed GM to contrast the older trial procedure with the Parliamentary acts of 1764 and 1767, which gave vice-admiralty courts broad powers, including the conduct of trials beyond the defendant's neighborhood. In FOOTNOTE FOURTEEN GM argued from experience as well as history, for in his boyhood the fringe of Virginia settlements was little more than 80 miles due West of Dogue's Neck. GM quoted parts of Sec. XIV of the 1705 ACT OF ASSEMBLY *"for prevention of misunderstanding between the tributary* Indians . . ." (Hening, III, 464–469); all of the 1753 ACT OF ASSEMBLY, except that the printed act (Hening, VI, 258) exempted Protestants from taxes "for the term of ten years"; and portions of the 1754 ACT OF ASSEMBLY (Hening, VI, 416–420). He seems to have relied upon memory for the 1769 act (Hening, VIII, 342–343) which empowered the treasurer to spend up to £2,500 "to defray the expences of negociation, and running" of the Indian boundary line. GM took pains to undermine any pretensions MR. WALPOLE & HIS ASSOCIATES had to a conflicting title for the Ohio Valley lands, since he probably now knew that the Privy Council had approved the Walpole Grant in July 1772 (Sosin, *Whitehall and the Wilderness,* 205). GM and the Va. shareholders in the Ohio Company had repudiated an unauthorized merger of their claim with the Walpole partners (see GM to James Mercer, 13 Jan. 1772, and Ohio Company Advertisement, 14 May 1772). Possibly GM had seen one of the few extant copies of a 1772 pamphlet, written by Benjamin Franklin and/or Samuel Wharton, which supported the Walpole-Vandalia scheme (Sosin, *Whitehall and the Wilderness,* 202–203n) while dismissing Va.'s rights. At about the time GM wrote this memorandum, the Vandalia grant was mired in a British bureaucratic bog but the idea persisted to trouble him after the Revolution (see GM to Samuel Purviance, 20 May 1782). THE EARL OF ROCHFORD (1717–1781) was a partner in the Walpole Company and had also applied for a royal grant in Delaware Bay (*Journal of the Commissioners for Trade and Plantations* [London, 1920–1938], XIII, 278, 288–291). Though Rochford was a royal favorite, his plan foundered during the ensuing crisis of 1773–1775. GM's addenda on THE FIRST CHARTER FOR CAROLINA . . . & SEVERAL OTHER PUBLICK DOCUMENTS listed materials supportive of Va.'s claims and jurisdiction over territory as far north as Hudson's Bay. His memorandum on THE BEST LATE MAPS may have been based on John Mitchell's map of British North America, first published in London in 1755. Whatever map GM used, he modestly calculated the outer limits for Virginia's claim. The territory Virginia claimed until its cession of 1784 was closer to 340,000 square miles, but this was later scaled down to 121,525 square miles (see Jefferson's *Notes on Virginia,* ed. Peden, 3–4). In June 1774 GM condensed the EXTRACTS into a petition for the governor and Council of Virginia (*q.v.*).

The Bancroft copy is headed: "Note by James M. Mason," with "G.M. handwriting" in brackets. The 50-page text was reprinted in Rowland, I, 393–414, with this notation: "A draft of the above in George Mason's handwriting was preserved by Richard Henry Lee, and was formerly to be found at the University of Virginia, among the Lee Papers. A copy was made from it in 1842 for Genl. John Mason, from which this is transcribed. The original draft is now missing." The Rowland text contains spelling, punctuation, and capitalization alterations and unmarked conjectures for missing words. In the final paragraph the transcription noted that the original document was torn and that several words were therefore omitted. Conjectures for those missing words are bracketed herein.

To George Washington

DEAR SIR.   Gunston-Hall   Decemr. 21st: 1773.

The embarrass'd Situation of my Friend Mr. Jas. Mercer's Affairs gives me much more Concern than Surprize. I always feared that his Aversion to selling the Lands & Slaves, in expectation of paying the Debts with the Crops & Profits of the Estate, whilst a heavy Interest was still accumulating, wou'd be attended with bad Consequences, independant of his Brother's Difficultys in England; having never, in a single Instance, seen these sort of Delays answer the Hopes of the Debtor. When Colo. Mercer was first married, & thought in affluent Circumstances by his Friends here, considerable Purchases of Slaves were made for him at high prices (& I believe mostly upon Credit) which must now be sold at much less than they cost: He was originally burthened wth: a proportionable Part of his Father's Debts; most of which, as well as the old Gentleman's other Debts, are not only still unpaid, but must be greatly increased by Interest; so that even if Colo. Mercer had not incurr'd a large Debt in England, He wou'd have found his Affairs here in a disagreeable Situation. I have bye me Mr. Mercer's Title-Papers for his Lands on Pohick Run, & on Four-Mile Run, in this County; which I have hitherto endeavour'd to sell for him in Vain; for as he left the Price entirely to me, I cou'd not take less for them than if they had been my own; this Difficulty will not be lessened, but the Contrary, by your becoming the Purchaser: Had I sold them to an indifferent Purchaser, I shou'd, in the common Way of Business, have stretch'd my Demand as far as it wou'd bear; but between you & Mr. Mercer I wou'd fain consider myself as a mutual Friend & Arbiter; & from any Connections with him, I know he wou'd wish me to act in that

Manner; which renders it an Affair of some Delicacy, & takes it out of the common Mode of Business. I have had some Applications from Maryland, to only one of which I paid much Regard; this was from a Gentleman whose Circumstances I was well acquainted with & knew his payments cou'd be relyed on; I expected, in answer to what I said to him, that he wou'd have appointed a Day to meet me on the Lands & examine them; but have heard nothing from him lately; which I ascribe merely to an Indolence of Temper, for which he is pretty remarkable. The Tract upon four-Mile Run is contain'd in two Patents, one granted to Stephen Grey for 378. Acres, the other to Gabriel Adams for 790. Acres they appear by the Platt to over measure considerably, & contain, clear of Strutfield's elder Patent, (with which they interfere) 1225 Acres. I have formerly been upon this Land; but it's so many Years ago, that I now know very little of it, from my own Knowledge; but from the best Information I have had that Part of it upon Four-Mile Run (in Stephen Grey's Patent) is tollerable good, & the other mean; but from it's Vicinity to Alexandria; which now bids fair to be a very a considerable Town, I think it must be worth £1000—Curry. Colo. Carlyle (whose Lands adjoin) told Mr. Mercer that it was worth 20/ an Acre, & that if he had the Money, he wou'd give that Price for it; perhaps this might be only one of the Colonel's ———; yet it has raised Mr. Mercer's Expectations. Upon the Whole Sir, if you will appoint any Day after Christmass, I will wait on you, & we will ride over the Land together; when we shall both be better able to judge of it's Value. There was some little Difficulty in the Title from Stephen Grey; which Mr. Mercer has been very candid in laying open to me, & which Mr. Pendleton (whose Opinion I have) has I think clear'd up in a very satisfactory Manner.

I am much obliged to you for yr. Information concerning the Lands upon the Western Waters. I long to have a little chat with you upon the Subject; & if Doctr. Connelly, who has promised to spend a Day or two with me as he returns from Wmsburg, is as good as his Word, I will do myself the Pleasure of taking a Ride with him to Mount-Vernon.

I heartily wish Mrs. Washington & you a merry Christmass, & many, very many, happy New-Years; and am, very sincerely, Dr Sir yr. affecte. & obdt. Sert.

G. MASON

P.S. Mr. Lund Washington was so kind to promise my Son He wou'd have some corn I bought of yr. overseer Cleveland, waggoned to my Quarter on little Hunting Creek; I beg the favour of you to remind him of it.

RC (Washington Papers, DLC). Addressed and endorsed by Washington "Upon the Sale of Mr Mercer's Land. M."

James and George Mercer's financial woes became general knowledge in the summer of 1773 as the Mercer's family debts finally came to a reckoning. In June 1773 Mercer had offered the Pohick and Four-Mile tracts for sale (8 July 1773, *Md. Gaz.*). His notice declared that GM was empowered to sell the tracts as Mercer's agent. As one holder of a Mercer note, on 19 July 1773 Washington had asked Mercer if he had either slaves or "any Land unincumbered that you could give a Mortgage on?" The original £446 debt seems to have been contracted by John Mercer, and was one of many outstanding obligations against the estate. James Mercer had complicated matters by selling other lands on his brother's behalf, while George Mercer had himself mortgaged the same property (James, *George Mercer*, 70–72). George Mercer, sinking into debt in London, had signed a power of attorney on 1 May 1773 authorizing GM, Washington, and John Tayloe to sell his property in Frederick and Loudoun counties (*Va. Gaz.* [Rind], 30 June 1773). GM negotiated this sale for the Four-Mile Run tract with Washington, and on 12 Dec. 1774 Washington wrote James Mercer a summary of the various transactions. Washington mentioned his purchase of "the four Mile run Land" for cancellation of the £446 debt and an additional £450, which indicates Washington paid close to GM's appraisal (Fitzpatrick, ed., *Writings of Washington*, III, 249–250 and 255*n*). MR. PENDLETON was Edmund Pendleton, the learned Caroline County lawyer. THE LANDS UPON THE WESTERN WATERS were a topic of much concern because of uncertain British policy toward transmontane land grants in which both GM and Washington had invested heavily. DOCTR. CONNELLY was John Connolly, the western adventurer whose friendship turned sour and who was later arrested as a British agent (see GM to the Maryland Council of Safety, 29 Nov. 1775).

Bill of Sale for Pohick Church Pew

[24 February 1774]

THIS INDENTURE made this 24th Day of February in the Year of our Lord one Thousand Seven Hundred Seventy four Between the Vestry of Truro Parish in the County of Fairfax of the one part & John Manley Son & Heir of Harrison Manley Decd. late of the Said Parish & County of the Other part; WHEREAS the Said Vestry did on the 5th. Day of June—in the Year 1772 Order Sundry Pews in the New Church on the upper Side of Pohick to be Sold at the laying of the Next parish Levy, to the Highest bidder; for the benefett of the Parish; Persuent to which order the Said Pews were Sold Accordingly by the Vestry at the Laying of the Said Next parish levy On the 20th Day of November in the Same Year and the Said Harrison Manley decd. then purchased one certain Pew in the Said Church for the price of fifteen pounds Ten Shillings Current Money to Wit the Pew Number'd 30 Situate between the Two

Long Isles and Adjoining the North Isle & the Cross Isle as by the proceedings and records of the Said Vestry reference being thereunto had; May more fully and at large appear; AND WHEREAS the Said Harrison Manley hath Sence Departed this life without haveing made any disposition of the Said Pew. NOW THIS INDENTURE WITNESSETH that the Said Vestry for and in consideration of the Said Sum of fifteen pounds Ten Shillings Current Money to them in hand paid for the Use of the Said parish by the Said John Manley Son & Heir to the Said Harrison Manley before the Sealing and Delivery of these presents, the Receipt whereof is hereby confessed and Acknowledged have granted, Bargained and Sold Alien'd and confirmed and by these presents do grant Bargain and Sell Alien and confirm unto the Said John Manley Son & Heir of Harrison Manley decd. the Said Pew in the Said New Church lately Built on the Upper Side of Pohick in the Said parish of Truro & County Afsd. Numbered and Setuated as above Mentioned TO HAVE AND TO HOLD the Said Pew above discribed unto the Said John Manley Son & Heir of Harrison Manley Decd. his Heirs & Assigns to the Only proper use and behoof of him, the Said John Manley Son & Heir of Harrison Manley Decd. his Heirs and Assigns for ever. AND the Said Vestry for themselves and their successors (Vestry Men of Truro Parish) do covenant and grant to & with the Said John Manley Son & Heir of Harrison Manley Decd. his Heirs and Assigns that he the Said John Manley Son & Heir of Harrison Manley Decd. his Heirs and Assigns Shall and May for ever hereafter peaceably & quietly have hold and enjoy the Said Pew above Mentioned and described without the Law full Let Henderence Interuption or Molestation of any Person or Persons whatsoever. IN WITNESS Whereof the Vestry Now present (being a Majority of the Members) have hereunto Set Their hands and affixed their Seals the Day & Year first above Written—

G MASON	T. ELLZEY
G WASHINGTON	THOS. WITHERS COFFER
DANIEL McCARTY	THOS. FORD
ALEX. HENDERSON	PET. WAGENER
	MARTIN COCKBURN

SIGNED SEALED & DELIVERED⎱
  in presence of   ⎰
  THOS. TRIPLETT
  JOHN GUNNELL
  JOHN BARRY
  WM. TRIPLETT

Ms (Fairfax County, Va., Clerk's Office). Possibly in the handwriting of the vestry clerk, John Barry, but signed by each vestry man.

On 20 Nov. 1772 GM had purchased pews three and four "adjoining the South Wall of the Church . . . at the price of fourteen Pounds eleven shillings and eight pence each, being the Average price, at which the Six pews first set up between the two long Isles and above the Cross Isle sold." Washington paid £16 for his pew "next [to] the Communion Table" (Truro Parish Vestry Book, DLC). After the death in 1771 of Daniel French, the original contractor of Pohick Church, GM became responsible for its completion as executor of the French estate. The church was in use for several years before the vestry officially accepted GM's accounting at their 24 Feb. 1774 meeting. This made it legally possible to finally execute deeds for this pew and others sold in 1772.

Truro Parish Advertisement

[31 March 1774]

To be LET *on* Friday *the 22d of* April, *at the new Church near* Pohick, *in* Truro *Parish,* Fairfax *County, to the lowest Bidder, by the Vestry of the said Parish.*

THE building of a Brick Vestry House 24 Feet long and 18 Feet wide, the enclosing of the said Churchyard 158 Feet square, with Posts and Rails, the Posts to be of sawed Cedar, and the Rails yellow Pine, clear of Sap, with three han[d]some Palisade Gates, the Whole to be done in the neatest and most substantial Manner.

G. MASON,
THOMAZIN ELLZEY, }Churchwardens.

Printed from the *Va. Gaz.* (Rind), 31 Mar. 1774. Also appeared in Annapolis *Md. Gaz.*, 31 Mar. 1774.

GM and Ellzey were charged by the vestry on 24 Feb. 1774 with "having failed to let the Building of a Vestry House at the new Church pursuant to a former Order" and directed to place advertisements for bids (Truro Parish Vestry Book, DLC). The original order was for a brick enclosed churchyard, but on 25 Feb. the vestry "reconsidered their order of Yesterday . . . and considering that the Expence thereof will be too burthensome to the Parish . . . have changed their Opinions, and do accordingly order that (instead of a Brick Wall) the said Church Yard be inclosed with a Post and Rail Fence. . . ." Apparently there was no successful bidder, for the vestry minutes of 28 Nov. 1774 directed GM and Ellzey to "agree with Workmen to build a Vestry House," but the outbreak of war brought further delays.

Proposal to Form an Agricultural Company Under Mr. Mazzei's Direction

[*March–April?*] *1774.* An undated subscription to raise funds by the sale of £50 shares in a company "for the Purpose of raising and making

Wine, Oyl, agruminous Plants and Silk" bore thirty-eight names, including GM's as the holder of one share. The money was to be used by Philip Mazzei, who was to direct the project. The entire text is printed in Boyd, I, 156–159, where the date is fixed from entries in Jefferson's Fee Book.

Ms (Virginia Miscellany, DLC). In an unidentified hand. The original has not been found.

To Martin Cockburn

DEAR SIR   Williamsburg, May 26th, 1774.

I arrived here on Sunday morning last, but found every body's attention so entirely engrossed by the Boston affair, that I have as yet done nothing respecting my charter-rights and, I am afraid, shall not this week.

A dissolution of the House of Burgesses is generally expected; but I think will not happen before the House has gone through the public business, which will be late in June.

Whatever resolves or measures are intended for the perservation of our rights and liberties, will be reserved for the conclusion of the session. Matters of that sort here are conducted and prepared with a great deal of privacy, and by very few members; of whom Patrick Henry is the principal.

At the request of the gentlemen concerned, I have spent an evening with them upon the subject, where I had an opportunity of conversing with Mr. Henry, and knowing his sentiments; as well as hearing him speak in the house since, on different occasions. He is by far the most powerful speaker I ever heard. Every word he says not only engages but commands the attention; and your passions are no longer your own when he addresses them. But his eloquence is the smallest part of his merit. He is in my opinion the first man upon this continent, as well in abilities as public virtues, and had he lived in Rome about the time of the first Punic war, when the Roman people had arrived at their meridian glory, and their virtue not tarnished, Mr. Henry's talents must have put him at the head of that glorious Commonwealth.

Inclosed you have the Boston Trade Act, and a resolve of our House of Burgesses. You will observe it is confined to the members of their own House: but they would wish to see the example followed through the country; for which purpose the members at their own private expense, are sending expresses with the resolve to their respective counties. Mr. Massey will receive a copy of the resolve from Col. Washington; and should a day of prayer and fasting be appointed in our county, please to tell my dear little family that I charge them to pay strict attention to it, and that I desire my three eldest sons, and my two eldest daughters, may attend church in mourning, if they have it, as I believe they have.

I begin to grow heartily tired of this town and hope to be able to leave it some time next week, but of this, I can't yet be certain. I beg to be tenderly remembered to my children, and am, with my compliments to my cousins and yourself, Dear Sir, Your affectionate and obedient servant,

G MASON.

Printed from William Maxwell, ed., *The Virginia Historical Register and Literary Notebook,* III (Richmond, 1850), 27–29. The original reportedly was destroyed when the Alexandria Museum burned in 1850. Addressed: "To Mr. Cockburn."
News of THE BOSTON AFFAIR (Boston Port Bill) had reached Williamsburg by 19 May when its passage was reported in the *Va. Gaz.* (Purdie and Dixon) that day. The newspaper carried an abstract of the bill's provisions, which GM probably sent as an enclosure with the House of Burgesses resolution of 24 May which set 1 June (the day the bill became operative in Boston harbor) as "a day of Fasting, Humiliation, and Prayer. . . ." (JHB, 1773–1776, 124). GM's guess that the House would continue in session until late June was incorrect, for Lord Dunmore dissolved the House on the same day GM was writing his letter. Dunmore stopped the session because the 24 May resolution was "conceived in such Terms as reflect highly upon his Majesty and the Parliament of Great Britain." Copies of the resolution were ordered printed for distribution in their home counties by each burgess. Rev. Lee Massey of Pohick church would have been expected to prepare "a Sermon, suitable to the Occasion." The resolution and other documents which sprang from private caucuses, where GM was a spectator if not participant, are printed in Boyd, I, 105–112.

Prince William County Resolves

[6 June 1774]

At a Meeting of the Freeholders, Merchants, and other Inhabitants of the County of *Prince William,* and town of *Dumfries,* in the Colony of *Virginia,* at the Court House of the said County on *Monday,* the 6th day *June,* in the year of our Lord 1774.

Resolved, And it is the unanimous opinion of this meeting, that no person ought to be taxed but by his own consent, expressed either by himself or his Representatives; and that, therefore, any Act of Parliament levying a tax to be collected in *America,* depriving the people of their property or prohibiting them from trading with one another, is subversive of our natural rights, and contrary to the first principles of the Constitution.

Resolved, That the city of *Boston,* in the *Massachusetts Bay,* is now suffering in the common cause of *American* liberty, and on account of its opposition to an Act of the *British* Legislature, for imposing a duty upon tea, to be collected in *America.*

Resolved, That as our late Representatives have not fallen upon means sufficiently efficacious to secure to us the enjoyment of our civil rights and liberties, that it is the undoubted privilege of each respective county, (as the fountain of power from whence their delegation arises,) to take such proper and salutary measures as will essentially conduce to a repeal of those Acts, which the general sense of mankind, and the greatest characters in the nation, have pronounced to be unjust.

Resolved, And it is the opinion of this meeting, that until the said Acts are repealed, all importation to, and exportation from, this Colony ought to be stopped, except with such Colonies or Islands in *North America* as shall adopt this measure.

Resolved, And it is the opinion of this meeting, that the courts of justice in this Colony ought to decline trying any civil causes until said Acts are repealed.

Resolved, That the Clerk of this Committee transmit copies of these Resolves to both the printers in Annapolis and Philadelphia, to be published in their Gazettes.

Per order,   EVAN WILLIAMS, *Clerk Com'tee.*

Printed from Force, *American Archives,* I, 388. It was first printed in the *Va. Gaz.* (Rind), 9 June 1774.

GM has hitherto not been considered the author of these resolutions. The editor's case rests on the proximity of Dumfries to Gunston Hall (about 14 miles), GM's known interest in both the nonimportation movement and the Boston Port Bill, and the stylistic evidence which is mentioned in the textual note below. That GM was involved in Prince William affairs is certain, as his petition of 10 Dec. 1781 written for the county's citizens proves. GM owned property along the Occoquan Creek in Prince William County and was well known in Dumfries. His commitment to nonimportation as a weapon in the struggle with England was of long standing. He had recently returned from Williamsburg and must have either volunteered or sought to help Prince William County freeholders express their concern and make a plea for nonexportation as well as nonimportation of goods.

A comparison of the Prince William and Fairfax resolves reveals stylistic similarities that establish GM as author of both documents beyond all reasonable doubt. In both documents there are common phrases: CONTRARY TO THE FIRST PRINCIPLES OF THE CONSTITUTION (1PW and 5F); the citizens of Boston NOW SUFFERING IN THE COMMON CAUSE OF AMERICAN LIBERTY (2PW and 10F); IT IS THE OPINION OF THIS MEETING (4PW and 16, 17, 19, 20, 21F); COURTS . . . OUGHT TO DECLINE TRYING ANY CIVIL CAUSES (5PW and 19F). Such phrases, particularly the one relating to "the first principles of the Constitution," recur in GM's private and public papers throughout the Revolutionary period (e.g., Art. 13, Va. Dec. of Rights, 1776). Herbert L. Ganter's article, "The Machiavellianism of George Mason," *WMQ*, 2d Ser., XVII (1937), 239–264, suggests that GM absorbed much of his political philosophy from the *Discourses on Livy*. Certainly GM had access to *Cato's Letters* and could have read in No. 16: "*Machiavel* tells us, that no Government can long subsist, but by recurring often to its first Principles. . . ." (John Trenchard and Thomas Gordon, *Cato's Letter's* [London, 1755], I, 108). The brevity of "this measure" suggests that the Prince William resolutions were written hurriedly, with little previous consultation. By mid-July, when the Fairfax resolutions were introduced, GM had digested his thoughts and other opinions to fashion a more comprehensive plan. The Westmoreland resolves of 22 June 1774 (Force, *American Archives*, I, 437–438) probably prepared by Richard Henry Lee, show striking similarities. Cooperation between Lee and GM from 1769 onward is well established.

Petition for Warrants for Lands in Fincastle County

[17 June 1774]

To his Excellency the Governor and the Honble the Councill of Virginia—The Memorial & Petition of George Mason of the County of Fairfax

Humbly Sheweth

That ⟨in⟩ the Charter granted by King James the first to the Virginia Company in the year 1609 [there] is Among Others a Clause declaring "That it is his Royal Will & Pleasure, & Charging, comanding warranting & authorising the Treasurer & the said Company, & their Successors, to Convey asign & sett Over, Such particular portions of lands, Tenaments & Heridtaments, unto such his Majestys loving Subjects, Naturally born, Denizens, or Others, as well adventurers as planters, as by the said Company shall be nominated, appointed & Allowed, Where in Respect to be had as well of the proportion of the Adventure, as of the special Service, Hazard, Exploit, or Meritt of any Person, so to be recompence[d], Advanced or rewarded" PURSUANT to which, within a few years after, fifty Acres of Land were ordered to be asigned & granted to every Person importing himself into this Collony; & to every person who should import others, fifty Acres for each person so imported. This, as your Memorialist Conceives, was the Original, or first Rise of the Antient Custom of granting Lands in Virginia, Upon Importation-Rights; which ⟨is⟩ now more than an hundred & fifty years Old, & Appears to have been interwoven with the Constitution of the Colony, from its first settlement, That the same was Constantly practised during the said Company's Government here & after the

[193]

Government was taken into the Hands of the Crown, upon the Dissolution of the Virginia Company, the same Custom & Right was always Allowed & Continued, as Appears by the Patents, & Records in the Secretarys Office; the Titles to great Part of the Lands in this Colony being founded upon importation-Rights; & the Constant Stile of the Old Patents is "the said Lands being due by & for the transportation, or by & for the Importation of . . . . . . Persons into this Colony." That in the Year 1662, and Act of Genral Assembly was made, prescribing the Manner of proving Rights to Lands due for the Importation of Servants, & obtaining Certificates thereon, to intitle the Importers to Surveys & Patents; & giving such proofs & Certificates the preference to Actual Surveys without them & in the same Year, another Act of Assembly was made, reciting that the former ⟨laws⟩ concerning deserted Lands, reserved to the first Taker-up his Rights to take up Lands in Another Place, & enacting that for the future, in Care of deserted Lands, the Rights, as well as the Lands shall be forfeited, & the grantee made incapable of useing any of them afterwards: from which Law it is Clear, that Importation-Rights are Always good, until they have been Applyed to Patents for Land, and the Said Land forfeited, by Want of Seating & Planting. That in the Year 1676, the said custom & Right to Lands was solemnly confirmed & continued, by Charter & Letters patent from King Charles the Second, to the Colony of Virginia, under the Great Seal of England "*As According as hath been used & Allowed from the first plantation;* to ⟨be⟩ held of his Majesty his Heirs & Successors, as of their Manor of East Greenwich in their County of Kent, in free & common Soccage" and declaring "That all & Every Clause, Article and Sentence, in the said Letters patent contained, shall be from time to time for ever hereafter, as often as any Ambiguity Doubt or Question, Shall or may happen to Arise thereupon, expounded, construed, deemed & taken to be meant & intended, & Shall enure & take Effect, in the *Most beneficial and available Sense,* to All intents & purposes, for the *proffit & Advantage of the Subjects of Virginia,* as well against *his Majesty his Heirs and Successors,* as against all & Every other Person or Persons whatsoever" which Charter was recognised by an Act of Assembly in the year 1677, ⟨prescribing⟩ a perticular form of *all Patents* for the future, in which form is recited "That his Majesty had been graciously pleased by his said Letters Patent, to Continue & Confirm the Ancient Right & priviledge of granting fifty Acres of Land *for every Person imported* into his Majesty's Colony of Virginia" & it Appears from the Patent Record books, that all Lands in this Colony, ex[c]ept escheat Lands, were Granted upon importation-Rights Only; until in or about the year 1710, when Treasury-Rights, or paying a certain Consideration in Money to ⟨the⟩ Crown for Lands, was first Introduced here; but that the same never affected Lands claimed under the Royal Charter; for the Ancient Rights to Lands due for the importation of People Still Continued upon the same footing as before, & hath ever been held Sacred & inviolable and Subject to ⟨no⟩ new Charge or Imposition Whatever; & great Quan⟨ti⟩tys of Land, from time to time granted Acordingly. That from the Earliest times of this Colony, there hath been Alowed to the secretary, & ⟨the⟩ Clerks of Countys by Law, a certain fee for Certificates of Rights to Land; and upon the Last Regulation of the Fee Bill in Virginia, Within thess few years, the Legislature Alowed to the County Court Clerks "For proving Rights for lands, produced at one time, belonging to one person, & Certificates thereof, a Fee of thirteen Pounds of Tobacco" & to the Secretary "for ⟨recording⟩ a Certificate ⟨of rights⟩ fifteen Pounds of Tobacco" & by An Act of Assembly made in the year 1710, when Treasury Rights were first introduced it was (among other things) enacted "That upon the passing of any patent for Land Thereafter; the Secretary of this Colony & Dominion, for the time being, should cause such patent to be truly Entred upon the Records of his office, together With ⟨the⟩ Certificate of Rights, *either by importation*, or by Money paid the receiver-Genral of this Colony" Which Your Memorialist is well informed hath Continued to be the practice ever Since; and that thess two modes of Granting Lands, Since the year 1710, as before mentiond have never in ⟨the⟩ Least interfered with Each Other; as the Crown Could only Alter the Terms, or fix a New Price upon the Lands, to which there was no Legal Right. So that Mr. Stith, in his History of Virginia (which is Chiefly extracted from Records) mentioning the Custom ⟨of⟩ granting lands for the importations of People, had good reason for his remark; that "this is the Antient, Legal, and a most indubitable Method of granting Lands in Virginia." And your Memorialist, with All due submission, begs Leave to Observe, that the King being as much bound by the Act of his Royal Predecessors, as any Private Subject, holding an Estate from his Ancestor, is bound by the Act of ⟨that⟩ Ancestor; & the before mentioned Ancient Right to Any Vacant or ungranted Lands in this Colony, having been Solemnly continued & Confirmed, by the Said Charter from King Charles the Second, in Manner herein before mentioned, the same was thereby made part of the Law & Constitution of this Country, and hath remained so ever since; & there fore can not be Avoided, injured, invalidated, or in any manner affected, by any Proclamation, Instruction, or other Act of Gover[n]ment; ⟨nor⟩ subjected to any new Charge, Expence, Burthen, or Imposition whatsoever. For which reasons, your Memorialist most Humbly Conceives that any ⟨instruction⟩, or Later Regulations, respecting the ungranted Lands in this Colony, from ⟨our⟩ present most gracious Sovering, ever Obse[r]vant of the Laws, & atentive to the just Rights of his People, were never Meant, or intended to affect Lands due as aforesaid, under the Royal Charter. That your Petitioner confiding in, & upon the faith of the before mentioned Royal Charter, Laws & Custom hath been at great trouble & Expence, & hath Laid out Considerable Sums of Money, in purchasing from the Importers, legal Certificates of Rights to Large Quantitys of Land, due for the Importation of People from great Britain and Ir[e]land into this Colony & Prays that he may be admited to Entrys for the said Lands, upon the Western Waters, in the County of Fincastle; upon his producing the usual Certificates & Assignment, [or] that his Excellency the Governor, will be Pleased to Gr[ant your] petition[er his] Warrants for Surveying the same, which Ever his Excellency and ⟨this⟩ Honble board Shall Judge most Proper. And your Petitioner will Ever pray.

G MASON

Ms (Jefferson Papers, DLC). In a copyist's handwriting, endorsed: "Copy of the petition presented to the Governor & Council June 1774 by George Mason, praying Entrys, or Warrants, for Lands Due for the importation of People, According to the Royal Charter."

FINCASTLE COUNTY was created in 1772 beyond the Blue Ridge Mountains in a division of Botetourt County (Hening, VIII, 600). From John Blair's copy of the Council minutes for 17 June 1774, which GM kept and later endorsed (Ms collection, CSmH), it is clear that GM appeared before the Council to press his headright claims. Blair's minutes record that the Council members were "of Opinion that the Rights to the Lands prayed for in the Memorial is founded upon the Charters, Laws and Custom of Virginia. . . . But his Excellency being restrained by his Majesty's Instruction from granting Lands on any Western Waters, the Council advised his Excellency to represent the whole Matter to his Majesty, for farther Directions thereupon." The petition is a shortened version of GM's "Extracts from the Virginia Charters" which had probably been prepared in July 1773 (q.v.). This petition eventually came into Thomas Jefferson's possession and is reprinted in Boyd, I, 112–116, with annotations. Dunmore's anomalous position vis-à-vis the western lands deserves further study by historians. Supposedly in sympathy with Virginia speculators, he had helped bring on Dunmore's War with the Shawnees which cleared the way for Virginia excursions in the Kentucky district. The Privy Council order of 3 Feb. 1774 forbade royal governors from making land grants while a new auction system of surveyed parcels was created. Faced with this order Dunmore procrastinated, and then news of the Quebec Act arrived in Aug. 1774 which indicated British western policy was taking a harder line. Part of

Dunmore's problem must have stemmed from his shifted position after he left the governorship of New York to serve in Virginia, for in 1770 he had urged Lord Hillsborough to prevent settlements in the Ohio valley (Berthold Fernow, *The Ohio Valley in Colonial Days* [Albany, 1890], 276–277). But on the same day the Virginia Council had listened to GM's plea for a relaxed land grant system, the Quebec Act passed the House of Lords despite Pitt's insistence that it struck down "barriers against the return of Popery and of Popish influence" (*Parliamentary History of England from the Earliest Period to the Year 1803* . . . [London, 1806–1820], XVII, 1403–1404). Prof. Sioussat considered GM's action "a test case" of the 3 Feb. 1774 order. By this interpretation, GM questioned the legality of an ex post facto order (Sioussat, "Breakdown of Royal Management," *Ag. Hist.*, III [1929], 82). The Virginia Convention of 1775 appointed a committee to determine "whether the King may of right advance the terms of granting Lands in this Colony." GM and Jefferson were on the committee when it recommended on 15 Aug. 1775 a suspension of western land sales and surveys (Force, *American Archives*, III, 382).

The words in angle brackets were interlined, or substituted for other words, by Jefferson.

Certification of Importation Rights

[*ca.* June 1774]

Certificates granted by Fairfax County Court

1773. June 22d. to Harry Piper for Importation of 377. Persons			
1773. July 20. to Robert Adam for		87.	
1773. July 20. to George Mason		5.	469.

Do. by PrinceWilliam County Court

1773. Augt 2d. _____ to John Smith _____		28.	
1774. March 11th _____ to CumberlandWillson	40.		
Do. _____ Do. _____	20.	77.	
Do. _____ Do. _____	17.		
Do. _____ to Alexander Campbell—	41.		
Do. _____ Do. _____	28.	69.	
1773. Decr. 6 _____ to John Graham _____	132.		
Do. _____ Do. _____	85.	217.	391.

Do. by Henrico County Court

1774. May Court to Thomas Smith _____	137.
Land claimed by G Mason for _____	997.

Do. by Prince William County Court

1773. June 5th. James Scott Clk_____	59.

I have examined the Certificates of the Proof of the above Importation rights, and find them to be in the most usual form of those returned to the Secretary's Office, on which Patents have issued, and that these would be received into the Office, with Surveys returned there, in order to obtain new Patents. I do further certify that such Rights always have been, and still are received into the Office of course.

BEN: WALLER CL:

Ms (CSmH). A single page, with the dated entries in GM's handwriting and the certification in a clerk's hand. Endorsed by GM: "No. 3. Certificate from Mr. Waller that the Proofs & Certificates in the County Courts, being by him examined, are in due form."

On 17 June 1774 GM petitioned the governor and Council of Virginia for warrants to lands in Fincastle County to the amount of his headright or importation right certificates. The British Privy Council had suspended the granting of lands while a new revenue-producing system of auctions was under study. The Virginia Council delayed action on GM's claim and then the Quebec Act of 1774 arrived, with its prohibition on western land grants. The numbered endorsement indicates that GM used the document as evidence in pressing his claims, though the outcome for GM was less than satisfactory. He preserved the record and presented his claim again in July 1779, with more success.

Waller wrote several illegible abbreviations after "Cl[erk]:".

Receipt for Daniel McCarty

[ca. 8 July 1774]

Capt. Daniel McCarty

Dt.		Contra	
To ferry at Occoquan ⎱ for the year 1772 ⎰	0.12.6.	1773. By Mr. French's ⎱ Estate for four	
To Do. for the yr. 1773	12.6.	Days Waggoning ⎰	£2.10.0.
To Cash in full	1. 5.0.	at 12/6	
	£2.10.0.		

E. E.🜚
G MASON

RC (Location unknown, 1969). A reproduction of this small document was in a collection of Mason items sent by a private collector to the editorial offices in 1964. The collector attributed the original Ms to the Boston Public Library. The Boston Public Library disclaims any knowledge of the document, and further research on its whereabouts has been unsuccessful.

DANIEL MC CARTY was GM's neighbor and probably a frequent user of the Occoquan ferry, an income-producing property GM inherited from his father (Rowland, I, 50–51). The town of Colchester was built by the ferry site, at the mouth of Occoquan Creek. E. E. abbreviated the precautionary "Errors Excepted" on 18th-century business documents.

GM's marginal date is only partially legible.

Fairfax County Committee

EDITORIAL NOTE

The Boston Port Bill was the catalytic agent which brought colonial resistance to a critical stage. Mason had been in Williamsburg when news of the bill's passage reached the General Assembly and soon became more than a spectator to events that would ultimately bring mounting tension, civil commotion, war, and independence to the thirteen united colonies. It all seemed a fulfillment of the prediction in *Cato's Letter* LXVII, printed in December 1722, that the colonies "must, by the natural course of human Affairs . . . at last grow too powerful and unruly to be governed by our [British] Interest only." After a decade of crisis marked by the Stamp Act, Declaratory Act, Sugar Act, and the confused twistings and turnings of administrative boards, the Port Bill came as the *coup d'grace* to further compromise. Mason's own dramatic conversion from a passive planter to a militant patriot is chronicled from his 1766 letter denouncing the Stamp Act through the Nonimportation Associations of 1769. However, the next step would be some form of armed resistance, and his experiences at Williamsburg, Gunston Hall, and Mount Vernon had converted Mason into a Virginian-American. Mason had advocated the use of county committees during the economic boycott that followed the Townshend Acts. Now the county committees vied with each other in Virginia in their eagerness to subscribe money and food for the relief of Boston. Mason may have been in Alexandria on 5 July 1774 when £273, 38 barrels of flour, and 150 bushels of wheat had been pledged from Fairfax County for "the industrious poor of the town of Boston" (Force, *American Archives*, I, 517). Freeholders were meeting in every county to choose representatives for the special August meeting of the House of Burgesses after thay had "an Opportunity of collecting the Sense of their respective Counties" on "the alarming Crisis" (Boyd, I, 111–112). The next Fairfax County meeting on 14 July chose Washington and Charles Broadwater as burgesses, and apparently adjourned until 18 July to consider ways and means of forcing Great Britain to redress American grievances. Meanwhile, Washington met Mason at Mount Vernon the following Sunday afternoon. Their conversations must have centered around instructions for the burgesses, for Mason stayed at Mount Vernon that night and the two rode into Alexandria the next day, after "the two men whipped into shape a paper containing twenty-four resolves" (Curtis P. Nettels, *George Washington and American Independence* [Boston, 1951], 90). The copy now in the Washington Papers is in Mason's handwriting and may have been the one which Washington carried to Williamsburg in August. The style of the resolves is Mason's, but as is often the case, the resolves represent a consensus rather than an individual opinion. It is likely that Mason had already helped prepare a hurried manifesto for the Prince William County meeting on 6 July. Eleven days later his ideas and Washington's crystallized into a historical account of mounting abuse from "the British Ministry" in what seemed a conspiracy to oppress the colonists. Almost simultaneously, Jefferson was preparing his indictment of British policy with the observation that occasional "acts of tyranny" might be accidental, "but a series of oppressions, begun at a distinguished period, and pursued unalterably thro' every change of ministers, too plainly prove a deliberate, systematical plan of reducing us to slavery" (Boyd, I, 125). The Williamsburg Association of 27 May had suggested a general congress to consider unified action, a proposal which the county committees endorsed. However, the Fairfax Resolves went further than most committee actions by recommending that a continental congress devise "a general and uniform Plan for the Defence and Preservation of our common Rights. . . ." Though the primary device in such a plan was economic boycotts similar to those Mason and Richard Henry Lee had concocted in 1769-1770, its expansion and enforcement procedures represented a sharp turn in British-American relations. Washington carried the Resolves to Williamsburg in early August, and from there to the First Continental Congress in Philadelphia. In a matter of weeks—breath-taking speed when the circumstances are considered—the Resolves had been revised and reappeared as the Continental Association of 20 October 1774. The emergence of an idea is discernible in comparing Mason's letter to Richard Henry Lee of 7 June 1770 with the Virginia Nonimportation Resolves of 22 June 1770 and the Fairfax Resolves, for in these documents the plan of searching out and publicly castigating violators of the boycott was set forth through a kind of vigilance committee. When the Continental Congress adopted this same approach, as Professor Nettels observes, "it ceased to be a recommending body and became a legislature" (Nettels, *Washington and American Independence*, 91-92). Thus portions of the Fairfax Resolves, in language Mason had used four years earlier, provided a means for enforcing the nonimportation associations. The verbal behavior of the colonists seemed to verge on treason, as the twenty-third Fairfax Resolve proved, for though it asked for a conciliatory petition to George III, it ended with a blunt warning that if their monarch ignored American pleas "there can be but one Appeal" —force. Petitions had been tried before and would be tried again, but Mason and his neighbors in Fairfax County acted skeptically when they met in September 1774. The resulting militia agreement was ostensibly aimed at hostile Indians, but the "present alarming Situation of all the

British Colonies" spelled out the cause plainly. Colonel Mason never knew, so far as the evidence admits, the rigors of a campaign; but he knew what a militiaman ought to have handy in defense of "the just Rights & Privileges of our Country, our Posterity & ourselves, upon the Principles of the British Constitution." The new year brought faint hopes of a reconciliation, so Mason stayed in the thick of the resistance movement by drafting a specific plan to create a substantial armed force in Fairfax County. Mason's plan indicates that the Virginians were as willing to fight as the men of Massachusetts. Americans everywhere were caching gunpowder and promising to perfect themselves "in the military exercise and discipline. . . ." The combustible materials were collected that spring in Fairfax County, ready for that first spark struck on 19 April 1775 near Boston.

Fairfax County Resolves

[18 July 1774]

At a general Meeting of the Freeholders and Inhabitants of the County of Fairfax on Monday the 18th day of July 1774, at the Court House, George Washington Esquire Chairman, and Robert Harrison Gent. Clerk of the said Meeting—

1. RESOLVED that this Colony and Dominion of Virginia can not be considered as a conquered Country; and if it was, that the present Inhabitants are the Descendants not of the Conquered, but of the Conquerors.

   That the same was not setled at the national Expence of England, but at the private Expence of the Adventurers, our Ancestors, by solemn Compact with, and under the Auspices and Protection of the British Crown; upon which we are in every Respect as dependant, as the People of Great Britain, and in the same Manner subject to all his Majesty's just, legal, and constitutional Prerogatives. That our Ancestors, when they left their native Land, and setled in America, brought with them (even if the same had not been confirmed by Charters) the Civil-Constitution and Form of Government of the Country they came from; and were by the Laws of Nature and Nations, entitiled to all it's Privileges, Immunities and Advantages; which have descended to us their Posterity, and ought of Right to be as fully enjoyed, as if we had still continued within the Realm of England.

2. RESOLVED that the most important and valuable Part of the British Constitution, upon which it's very Existence depends, is the fundamental Principle of the People's being governed by no

Laws, to which they have not given their Consent, by Representatives freely chosen by themselves; who are affected by the Laws they enact equally with their Constituents; to whom they are accountable, and whose Burthens they share; in which consists the Safety and Happiness of the Community: for if this Part of the Constitution was taken away, or materially altered, the Government must degenerate either into an absolute and despotic Monarchy, or a tyrannical Aristocracy, and the Freedom of the People be annihilated.

3. RESOLVED therefore, as the Inhabitants of the american Colonies are not, and from their Situation can not be represented in the British Parliament, that the legislative Power here can of Right be exercised only by ⟨our⟩ own Provincial Assemblys or Parliaments, subject to the Assent or Negative of the British Crown, to be declared within some proper limited Time. But as it was thought just and reasonable that the People of Great Britain shou'd reap Advantages from these Colonies adequate to the Protection they afforded them, the British Parliament have claimed and exercised the Power of regulating our Trade and Commerce, so as to restrain our importing from foreign Countrys, such Articles as they cou'd furnish us with, of their own Growth or Manufacture, or exporting to foreign Countrys such Articles and Portions of our Produce, as Great Britain stood in Need of, for her own Consumption or Manufactures. Such a Power directed with Wisdom and Moderation, seems necessary for the general Good of that great Body-politic of which we are a Part; altho' in some Degree repugnant to the Principles of the Constitution. Under this Idea our Ancestors submitted to *it:* the Experience of more than a Century, during the Government of his Majesty's Royal Predecessors, hath proved it's Utility, and the reciprocal Benefits flowing from it produced mutual uninterrupted Harmony and Good-Will, between the Inhabitants of Great Britain and her Colonies; who during that long Period, always considered themselves as one and the same People: and tho' such a Power is capable of Abuse, and in some Instances hath been stretched beyond the original Design and Institution. Yet to avoid Strife and Contention with our fellow-Subjects, and strongly impressed with the Experience of mutual Benefits, we always Chearfully acquiesced in it, while the entire Regulation of our internal Policy, and giving and granting our own Money were preserved to our own provincial Legislatures.

4. RESOLVED that it is the Duty of these Colonies, on all Emergencies, to contribute, in Proportion to their Abilities, Situation and Circumstances, to the necessary Charge of supporting and defending the British Empire, of which they are Part; that while we are treated upon an equal Footing with our fellow Subjects, the Motives of Self-Interest and Preservation will be a sufficient Obligation; as was evident thro' the Course of the last War; and that no Argument can be fairly applyed to the British Parliament's taxing us, upon a Presumption that we shou'd refuse a just and reasonable Contribution, but will equally operate in Justification of the Executive-Power taxing the People of England, upon a Supposition of their Representatives refusing to grant the necessary Supplies.

5. RESOLVED that the Claim lately assumed and exercised by the British Parliament, of making all such Laws as they think fit, to govern the People of these Colonies, and to extort from us our Money with out our Consent, is not only diametrically contrary to the first Principles of the Constitution, and the original Compacts by which we are dependant upon the British Crown and Government; but is totally incompatible with the Privileges of a free People, and the natural Rights of Mankind; will render our own Legislatures merely nominal and nugatory, and is calculated to reduce us from a State of Freedom and Happiness to Slavery and Misery.

6. RESOLVED that Taxation and Representation are in their Nature inseperable; that the Right of withholding, or of giving and granting their own Money is the only effectual Security to a free People, against the Incroachments of Despotism and Tyranny; and that whenever they yield the One, they must quickly fall a Prey to the other.

7. RESOLVED that the Powers over the People of America now claimed by the British House of Commons, in whose Election we have no Share, on whose Determinations we can have no Influence, whose Information must be always defective and often false, who in many Instances may have a seperate, and in some an opposite Interest to ours, and who are removed from those Impressions of tenderness and compassion arising from personal Intercourse and Connections, which soften the Rigours of the most despotic Governments, must if continued, establish the most grievous and intollerable Species of Tyranny and Oppression, that ever was inflicted upon Mankind.

8. Resolved that it is our greatest Wish and Inclination, as well as Interest, to continue our Connection with, and Dependance upon the British Government; but tho' we are it's Subjects, we will use every Means which Heaven hath given us to prevent our becoming it's Slaves.

9. Resolved that there is a premeditated Design and System, formed and pursued by the British Ministry, to introduce an arbitrary Government into his Majesty's American Diminions; to which End they are artfully prejudicing our Sovereign, and inflaming the Minds of our fellow-Subjects in Great Britain, by propagating the most malevolent Falsehoods; particularly that there is an Intention in the American Colonies to set up for independant States; endeavouring at the same Time, by various Acts of Violence and Oppression, by sudden and repeated Dissolutions of our Assemblies, whenever they presume to examine the Illegality of ministerial Mandates, or deliberate on the violated Rights of their Constituents, and by breaking in upon the American Charters, to reduce us to a State of Desperation, and dissolve the original Compacts by which our Ancestors bound themselves and their Posterity to remain dependant upon the British Crown: which Measures, unless effectually counteracted, will end in the Ruin both of Great Britain and her Colonies.

10. Resolved that the several Acts of Parliament for raising a Revenue upon the People of America without their Consent, the creating new and dangerous Jurisdictions here, the taking away our Trials by Jurys, the ordering Persons upon Criminal Accusations, to be tried in another Country than that in which the Fact is charged to have been committed, the Act inflicting ministerial Vengeance upon the Town of Boston, and the two Bills lately brought into Parliament for abrogating the Charter of the Province of Massachusetts Bay, and for the Protection and Encouragement of Murderers in the said Province, are Part of the above mentioned iniquitous System. That the Inhabitants of the Town of Boston are now suffering in the common Cause of all British America, and are justly entitled to it's Support and Assistance; and therefore that a Subscription ought imediatly to be opened, and proper Persons appointed, in every County of this Colony to purchase Provisions, and consign them to some Gentleman of Character in Boston, to be distributed among the poorer Sort of People there.

11. Resolved that we will cordially join with our Friends and Brethren of this and the other Colonies, in such Measures as shall

be judged most effectual for procuring Redress of our Grievances, and that upon obtaining such Redress if the Destruction of the Tea at Boston be regarded as an Invasion of private Property, we shall be willing to contribute towards paying the East India Company the Value: but as we consider the said Company as the Tools and Instrument of Oppression in the Hands of Government and the Cause of our present Distress, it is the Opinion of this Meeting that the People of these Colonies shou'd forbear all further Dealings with them, by refusing to purchase their Merchandize, until that Peace Safety and Goodorder, which they have disturbed, be perfectly restored. And that all Tea now in this Colony, or which shall be imported into it shiped before the first Day of September next, shou'd be deposited in some Store-house to be appointed by the respective Committees of each County, until a sufficient Sum of Money be raised by Subscription to reimburse the Owners the Value, and then to be publickly burn'd and destroyed; and if the same is not paid for and destroyed as aforesaid, that it remain in the Custody of the said Committees, at the Risque of the Owners, until the Act of Parliament imposing a Duty upon Tea for raising a Revenue in America be repealed; and imediatly afterwards be delivered unto the several Proprietors thereof, their Agents or Attorneys.

12. RESOLVED that Nothing will so much contribute to defeat the pernicious Designs of the common Enemies of Great Britain and her Colonies as a firm Union of the latter; who ought to regard every Act of Violence or Oppression inflicted upon any One of them, as aimed at all; and to effect this desireable Purpose, that a Congress shou'd be appointed, to consist of Deputies from all the Colonies, to concert a general and uniform Plan for the Defence and Preservation of our common Rights, and continueing the Connection and Dependance of the said Colonies upon Great Britain under a just, lenient, permanent, and constitutional Form of Government.

13. RESOLVED that our most sincere and cordial Thanks be given to the Patrons and Friends of Liberty in Great Britain, for their spirited and patriotick Conduct in Support of our constitutional Rights and Privileges, and their generous Efforts to prevent the present Distress and Calamity of America.

14. RESOLVED that every little jarring Interest and Dispute, which has ever happened between these Colonies, shou'd be buried in eternal Oblivion; that all Manner of Luxury and Extravagance

ought imediatly to be laid aside, as totally inconsistent with the threatning and gloomy Prospect before us; that it is the indispensable Duty of all the Gentlemen and Men of Fortune to set Examples of Temperance, Fortitude, Frugality and Industry; and give every Encouragement in their Power, particularly by Subscriptions and Premiums, to the Improvement of Arts and Manufactures in America; that great Care and Attention shou'd be had to the Cultivation of Flax, Cotton, and other Materials for Manufactures; and we recommend it to such of the Inhabitants who have large Stocks of Sheep, to sell to their Neighbors at a moderate Price, as the most certain Means of speedily increasing our Breed of Sheep, and Quantity of Wool.

15. RESOLVED that until American Grievances be redressed, by Restoration of our just Rights and Privileges, no Goods or Merchandize whatsoever ought to be imported into this Colony, which shall be shiped from Great Britain or Ireland after the first Day of September next, except Linnens not exceeding fifteen Pence ⅌ yard, ⟨German Oznabrigs⟩ coarse woolen Cloth, not exceeding two Shillings sterling ⅌ Yard, Nails Wire, and Wire-Cards, Needles & Pins, Paper, Salt Petre, and Medecines; which may ⟨which three Articles only may⟩ be imported until the first Day of September, one thousand seven hundred and seventy six; and if any Goods or Merchandize, othe[r] than those hereby excepted, shou'd be ship'd from Great Britain, ⟨or Ireland⟩ after the time aforesaid, to this Colony, that the same, immediately upon their Arrival, shou'd either be sent back again, by the Owners their Agents or Attorn[ey]s, or stored and deposited in some Ware-house, to be appointed by the Committee for each respective County, and there kept, at the Risque and Charge of the Owners, to be delivered to them, when a free Importation of Goods hither shall again take Place. And that the Merchants and Venders of Goods and Merchandize within this Colony ought not to take Advantage of our present Distress, b[u]t continue to sell the Goods and Merchandize which they now have, or which may be shiped to them before the first Day of September next, at the same Rates and Prices they have been accustomed to do, within one Year last past; and if any Person shall sell such Goods on any other Terms than above expressed, that no Inhabitant of this Colony shou'd at any time, for ever thereafter, deal with him, his Agent, Factor, or Store keepers for any Commodity whatsoever.

16.   RESOLVED that it is the Opinion of this Meeting, that the Merchants and Venders of Goods and Merchandize within this Colony shou'd take an Oath, not to sell or dispose of any Goods or Merchandize whatsoever, which may be shiped from Great Britain ⟨or Ireland⟩ after the first Day of September next as aforesaid, except the ⟨three⟩ Articles before excepted, and that they will, upon Receipt of such prohibited Goods, either send the same back again by the first Opportunity, or deliver them to the Committees in the respective Countys, to be deposited in some Warehouse, at the Risque and Charge of the Owners, until they, their Agents or Factors be permitted to take them away by the said Committees: the Names of those who refuse to take such Oath to be advertized by the respective Committees in the Countys wherein they reside. And to the End that the Inhabitants of this Colony may know what Merchants, and Venders of Goods and Merchandize have taken such Oath, that the respective Committees shou'd grant a Certificate thereof to every such Person who shall take the same.

17.   RESOLVED that it is the Opinion of this Meeting, that during our present Difficulties and Distress, no Slaves ought to be imported into any of the British Colonies on this Continent; and we take this Opportunity of declaring our most earnest Wishes to see an entire Stop for ever put to such a wicked cruel and unnatural Trade.

18.   RESOLVED that no kind of Lumber shou'd be exported from this Colony to the West Indies, until America be restored to her constitutional Rights and Liberties if the other Colonies will accede to a like Resolution; and that it be recommended to the general Congress to appoint as early a Day as possible for stopping such Export.

19.   RESOLVED that it is the Opinion of this Meeting, if American Grievances be not redressed before the first Day of November one thousand seven hundred and seventy five, that all Exports of Produce from the several Colonies to Great Britain ⟨or Ireland⟩ shou'd cease; and to carry the said Resolution more effectually into Execution, that we will not plant or cultivate any Tobacco, after the Crop now growing; provided the same Measure shall be adopted by the other Colonies on this Continent, as well those who have heretofore made Tobacco, as those who have n[o]t. And it is our Opinion also, if the Congress of Deputies from the several Colonies shall adopt the Measure of Non-ex-

[207]

portation to Great Britain, as the People will be thereby disabled from paying their Debts, that no Judgements shou'd be rendered by the Courts in the said Colonies for any Debt, after Information of the said Measure's being determined upon.

20. RESOLVED that it is the Opinion of this Meeting that a solemn Covenant and Association shou'd be entered into by the Inhabitants of all the Colonies upon Oath, that they will not, after the Times which shall be respectively agreed on at the general Congress, export any Manner of Lumber to the West Indies, nor any of their Produce to Great Britain ⟨or Ireland⟩, or sell or dispose of the same to any Person who shall not have entered into the said Covenant and Association; and also that they will not import or receive any Goods or Merchandize which shall be ship'd from Great Britain ⟨or Ireland⟩ after the first Day of September next, other than the before enumerated Articles, nor buy or purchase any Goods, except as before excepted, of any Person whatsoever, who shall not have taken the Oath herein before recommended to be taken by the Merchants and Venders of Goods nor buy or purchase any Slaves hereafter imported into any Part of this Continent until a free Exportation and Importation be again resolved on by a Majority of the Representatives or Deputies of the Colonies. And that the respective Committees of the Countys, in each Colony so soon as the Covenant and Association becomes general, publish by Advertisements in their several Counties ⟨and Gazettes of their Colonies⟩, a List of the Names of those (if any such there be) who will not accede thereto; that such Traitors to their Country may be publickly known and detested.

21. RESOLVED that it is the Opinion of this Meeting, that this and the other associating Colonies shou'd break off all Trade, Intercourse, and Dealings, with that Colony Province or Town which shall decline or refuse to agree to the Plan which shall be adopted by the general Congress.

22. RESOLVED that shou'd the Town of Boston be forced to submit to the late cruel and oppressive Measures of Government, that we shall not hold the same to be binding upon us, but will, notwithstanding, religiously maintain, and inviolably adhere to such Measures as shall be concerted by the general Congress, for the preservation of our Lives Liberties and Fortunes.

23. RESOLVED that it be recommended to the Deputies of the general Congress to draw up and transmit an humble and dutiful Petition and Remonstrance to his Majesty, asserting with decent

Firmness our just and constitutional Rights and Privileg[es,] lamenting the fatal Necessity of being compelled to enter into Measur[es] disgusting to his Majesty and his Parliament, or injurious to our fellow Subjects in Great Britain; declaring, in the strongest Terms, ou[r] Duty and Affection to his Majesty's Person, Family, [an]d Government, and our Desire to continue our Dependance upon Great Bri[tai]n; and most humbly conjuring and besecching his Majesty, not to reduce his faithful Subjects of America to a State of desperation, and to reflect, that from our Sovereign there can be but one Appeal.

And it is the Opinion of this Meeting, that after such Petition and Remonstrance shall have been presented to his Majesty, the same shou'd be printed in the public Papers, in all the principal Towns in Great Britain.

24. RESOLVED that George Washington Esquire, and George Broadwater Gent. lately elected our Representatives to serve in the general Assembly, be appointed to attend the Convention at Williamsburg on the first Day of August next, and present these Resolves, as the Sense of the People of this County, upon the Measures proper to be taken in the present alarming and dangerous Situation of America.

Ms (Washington Papers, DLC). Endorsed in an unknown hand: "Resolves at a Meeting held at Fairfax C.H. July 18th 1774. Geo. Washington was president of the meeting."

GM's use of the expression FIRST PRINCIPLES OF THE CONSTITUTION in his public papers, as a postulate of the British Constitution, is defined here as "the People's being governed by no Laws, to which they have not given their Consent." The phrase is used in the Prince William Resolves and remained with GM throughout his life as a shibboleth in state papers and public debate. GM had also accepted the prevailing idea of many patriot writers that A PREMEDITATED DESIGN AND SYSTEM, FORMED . . . BY THE BRITISH MINISTRY, accounted for American woes. By 1774 the assumption of a ministerial conspiracy against American liberty was a fixed article of faith among patriots (Bernard Bailyn, ed., *Pamphlets of the American Revolution, 1750–1776* [Cambridge, Mass., 1965], I, 74–83). THE TWO BILLS LATELY BROUGHT INTO PARLIAMENT which GM charged with violating the Massachusetts charter were the Administration of Justice Act and Massachusetts Government Act, legislative companions of the Boston Port Bill. The former offered a change of venue for Britons charged with crimes during the Boston riots or when enforcing British laws, and Lord North insisted its purpose was "to give every man a fair and impartial trial" (*Parliamentary History*, XVII, 1200). The act "regulating the Government of Massachusetts Bay" broadened the governor's powers, altered the method of selecting juries, and forbade town meetings without the governor's consent (Nettels, *Roots of American Civilization*, 642; see also Jack Sosin, "The Massachusetts Acts of 1774: Coercive or Preventive?" *Huntington Library Quarterly*, XXVI [1963], 235–252). The idea of PAYING THE EAST INDIA COMPANY £15,000 for the tea destroyed at Boston had been proposed by Benjamin Franklin in Feb. 1774, and was written into the Port Bill as a condition for a reopened Boston. However, reparations were rejected by Bostonians after the Port Bill arrived as "a ransom for the restoration of the harbor privileges" (Benjamin Woods Labaree, *The Boston Tea Party* [New York, 1964], 221–222). There was some discussion of reparations to the East India Company in Virginia (see *Va. Gaz.* [Rind], 1 July, 1 Sept. 1774) as well as rumors the Continental Congress would make restitution, but nothing came of the scheme. GM must have known that Parliament had refused on 19 Apr. 1774 to repeal A DUTY UPON TEA by a vote of 49 yeas to 182 nays (*Parliamentary History*, XVII, 1273). Washington took these resolves to Williamsburg where they became the framework for the Virginia Association of 1774, and furnished a model for the Continental Association approved by Congress on 20 Oct. 1774 at Philadelphia. Two additional resolutions were passed on 18 July by the Fairfax County meeting. One named Washington, GM, and 23 others to serve on the County committee with emergency powers, and the second ordered their proceedings transmitted "to the printers at Williamsburg" (Ms coll., Vi).

A careful scholar who studied the eight-page Ms states (Nettels, *Washington and American Independence*, 92): "It is not known whether Washington or Mason originated the Fairfax Resolves." Less cautious was Freeman (*Washington*, III, 362–363), who indicates that GM was chosen to draft the Resolves at the 5 July meeting and prepared them prior to 17 July. The editor believes circumstantial and stylistic evidence is sufficient to make clear GM's dominant role in drafting the Resolves. Washington's willingness to introduce them at the Williamsburg meeting in Aug. and to work for the Continental Association is obvious, but the phraseology and the selection of both grievances and remedies must have been left to GM's judgment. Except for the word "our" in angle brackets (third resolution), the document is entirely in GM's handwriting. The italicized words in angle brackets in the 16th, 19th, and 20th resolutions were crossed through by GM. The portions in regular brackets were inserted either for clarity's sake or to remedy gaps caused by tears in the sixth and seventh pages of the Ms.

The full text of two resolutions (25 and 26) added at the 18 July meeting, along with GM's Resolves, was printed in Rowland, I, 418–427.

Fairfax County Militia Association

[21 September 1774]

At a Meeting of a Number of Gentlemen & Freeholders of Fairfax County in the Colony of Virginia, on Wednesday the 21st: Day of September 1774, George Mason Esqr. in the Chair, the following Association was formed & entered into.

In this Time of extreme Danger, with the Indian Enemy in our Country, and threat'ned with the Destruction of our Civil-rights, & Liberty, and all that is dear to British Subjects & Freemen; we the Subscribers, taking into our serious consideration the present alarming Situation of all the British Colonies upon this Continent as well as our own, being sensible of the Expediency of putting the Militia of this Colony upon a more respectable Footing, & hoping to excite others by our Example, have voluntarily freely & cordially entered into the following Association; which we, each of us for ourselves respectively, solemnly promise, & pledge our Honours to each other, and to our Country to perform.

That we will form ourselves into a Company, not exceeding one hundred Men, by the Name of The Fairfax independant Company of Voluntiers, making Choice of our own Officers; to whom, for the Sake of Good-order & Regularity, we will pay due submission. That we will meet at such Times & Places in this County as our said Officers (to be chosen by a Majority of the Members, so soon as fifty have subscribed) shall appoint & direct, for the Purpose of learning & practising the military Exercise & Discipline; dress'd in a regular Uniform of Blue, turn'd up with Buff; with plain yellow metal Buttons, Buff Waist Coat & Breeches, & white Stockings; and furnished with a good Fire-lock & Bayonet, Sling Cartouch-Box, and Tomahawk. And that we will, each of us, constantly keep by us a Stock of six pounds of Gunpowder, twenty pounds of Lead, and fifty Gun-flints, at the least.

That we will use our utmost Endeavours, as well at the Musters of the said Company, as by all other Means in our Power, to make ourselves Masters of the Military Exercise. And that we will always hold ourselves in Readiness, in Case of Necessity, hostile Invasion, or real Danger of the Community of which we are Members, to defend to the utmost of our Power, the legal prerogatives of our Sovereign King George the third, and the just Rights & Privileges of our Country, our Posterity & ourselves upon the Principles of the British Constitution.

Agreed that all the Subscribers to this Association do meet on Monday the 17th. Day of October next, at eleven o'Clock in the Fore-noon, at the Court House in Alexandria

MS (Washington Papers, DLC). Most of an endorsement in GM's hand has been torn away.

The Virginia Convention of 1774 had authorized each company to establish an independent militia company. This device permitted the formation of a militia "Independent, that is, of the royal governor, who commanded the regular militia organization" (Nettels, *Washington and American Independence*, 92). On 30 Aug. 1774 GM journeyed to Mount Vernon and met with Washington, Pendleton, Henry and Thomas Triplett, and possibly at this meeting GM was encouraged to act as chairman of the Fairfax Committee during Washington's absence (to serve on the Virginia delegation at the Continental Congress). THE INDIAN ENEMY was making war on the frontier, some several hundred miles to the west, and this furnished a partial excuse for creating a military arm that could also help enforce the nonimportation associations. Commissions in the colonial militia came from the governor, but GM's plan provided a more democratic method. The committee usually deferred to Washington's judgment on matters of detail and must have consulted him about the uniform and accoutrements.

The two-page Ms, in GM's handwriting, may have been copied for Washington's use. The version printed in Rowland, I, 181–182 is attributed to the "Mason Papers" without provenance.

Fairfax County Committee of Safety Proceedings

[17 January 1775]

Resolved, That the defenceless state of this County renders it indispensably necessary that a quantity of Ammunition should be immediately provided; and as the same will be for the common benefit, protection, and defence of the inhabitants thereof, it is but just and reasonable that the expenses incurred in procuring the same should be defrayed by a general and equal contribution. It is therefore recommended that the sum of three Shillings per poll, for the purpose aforesaid, be paid by, and for every tithable person in this County, to the Sheriff, or such other Collector as may be appointed, who is to render the same to this Committee, with a list of the names of such persons as shall refuse to pay the same, if any such there be.

Resolved, That this Committee do concur in opinion with the Provincial Committee of the Province of *Maryland,* that a well regulated Militia, composed of gentlemen freeholders, and other freemen, is the natural strength and only stable security of a free Government, and that such Militia will relieve our mother country from any expense in our protection and defence, will obviate the pretence of a necessity for taxing us on that account, and render it unnecessary to keep Standing Armies among us—ever dangerous to liberty; and therefore it is recommended to such of the inhabitants of this County as are from sixteen to fifty years of age, to choose a Captain, two Lieutenants, an Ensign, four Sergeants, four Corporals, and one Drummer, for each Company; that they provide themselves with good Firelocks, and use their utmost endeavours to make themselves masters of the Military Exercise, published by order of his Majesty in 1764, and recommended by the Provincial Congress of the *Massachusetts Bay,* on the 29th of *October* last.

Printed from Force, *American Archives,* I, 1145. The resolves first appeared in the *Va. Gaz.* (Pinkney), 2 Feb. 1775.

Washington had returned from Philadelphia and was chairman of the meeting which approved both resolutions. On 15 Jan. 1775, Washington entertained "Colo. Mason and son, Mr. Dulany and Mr. Cockburn" as guests at Mount Vernon and probably planned these resolutions then (John C. Fitzpatrick, ed., *The Diaries of George Washington, 1748–1799* [Boston, 1925], II, 182). The two following days were spent, Washington recorded, drilling the Fairfax Company at Alexandria, where the need for better arms and quantities of ammunition became apparent. Because of the emergency, Washington and GM advanced funds to purchase the powder (GM to Washington, 17 Feb. 1775). Much of the Maryland resolution forming militia companies in Dec. 1774 (in Force, *American Archives*, I, 1032) contains stylistic mannerisms later identified with GM (such as "A Plan for Embodying the People" and Art. XIII, Va. Dec. of Rights), so that the editor must resist the temptation of claiming GM's authorship. It is certain GM was visiting Maryland frequently in this period because of his mother-in-law's grave illness. Lacking positive evidence, however, it is sufficient to note the similarities which were catch-phrases well known to public men of that day. The specifications for the militia by age and rank are identical to those of the Maryland resolution. The MILITARY EXERCISE was *The Manual Exercise, as Ordered by His Majesty, in the Year 1764, Together with Plans and Explanations of the Method Generally Practised at Reviews and Field-Days . . .* (Boston, 1774).

The original Ms is missing. The state archivist of Virginia, W. J. Van Schreeven, has collected Ms copies of all county committee proceedings for the Revolutionary period. He reported that a Ms of the Fairfax County proceedings has never been found. Freeman (*Washington*, III, 399) speculates that the author was "almost certainly George Mason" and credits GM with "a sense of humor" for the ironic comment "that such militia will relieve our mother country." Rowland, I, 427–430, erroneously assumed that these resolutions and the plan "for embodying the People of this County" were both approved by the 17 Jan. 1775 meeting. In this instance Miss Rowland may have followed the lead of Force, who placed GM's undated militia plan immediately below the 17 Jan. proceedings.

To George Washington

DEAR SIR.   Gunston-Hall February 6th. 1775.

My Friend Colo. Harrison (who is now at yr. House) promised to spend a Day or two with me on his Way Down. I beg the Favour of you to present my Compliments to him; & excuse my being under the disagreeable Necessity of being from Home, until the latter End of this Week; when if he is not gone down, I shall be very glad to see him here. Poor Mrs. Eilbeck has had a Cancer on her Breast for several Months, which has increased so much lately as to affect the whole Breast; upon which the Doctors have determined that there is a Necessity for extirpating it imediatly, by amputation of the Breast, before any of the Roots or Fibres of the Cancer affect the Vital Parts; & when I came Home Yester[day] from Alexandria, I found a Messenger here, desiring me to go over to-day upon this Occasion, wth. my Daughter Nancy. I apprehend such an Opperation must be a very dangerous one, & therefore shall not care to leave Mrs. Eilbeck for two or three Days after it is perform'd.

[213]

Inclosed you have a Copy of the Plan I drew for embodying the People of this County; in which you'll be pleased to make such Alterations as you think necessary. You will observe I have made it as general as I well cou'd; this I thought better at first, than to descend to particulars of Uniform &c. which perhaps may be more easily done, when the Companys are made up.

I suppose you have seen the King's Speech, & the Addresses of both Houses in the last Maryland Paper; from the Style in which they speak of the Americans, I think we have little Hopes of a speedy Redress of Grievances; but on the Contrary we may expe[c]t to see coercive & vindictive Measures still pursued. It seems as if the King either had not receiv'd or was determined to take no Notice of the Proceedings of the Congress.

I beg my Comps. to Mrs. Washington & the Family at Mount-Vernon, and am

Dear. Sir yr. affect. & obdt. Sert.

G MASON

vid: postscript on ⎫
—another paper ⎭

P.S. I beg Pardon for having almost forgot to say any thing in Answer to yr. favr. respecting the Choice of Delegates from this County to attend the Convention at Richmond. It appears to me that the Burgesses for the County are our proper Representatives upon this Occasion; and that the best method to remove all Doubt or Objection, as well as to save Trouble, will be for the County Committee to meet & make an Entry & Declaration of this, as their Opinion.

Wou'd it not be proper for the Committee of Correspondence to write to the two Mr. Fitzhughs, Mr. Turberville, & such other Gentlemen as live out of this County & have Quarters in it, acquainting them wth. the ordr. of the Committee relative to the Payment of 3/ for each Tytheable, & desiring them to give their Overseers, or Agents here Orders accordingly?

GM

RC (Washington Papers, DLC). Enclosure: Fairfax County Militia Plan, in an unidentified hand, printed below.

COLO. HARRISON was Nathaniel Harrison of Prince George County, a family friend. MRS. EILBECK was Sarah Edgar Eilbeck, GM's mother-in-law. The enclosed PLAN . . . FOR EMBODYING THE PEOPLE, also known as the Fairfax County Association, was an expansion of the resolution passed by the County Committee of Safety on 17 Jan. 1775. THE KING'S SPEECH and the responses of Parliament were printed in the Annapolis Md. Gaz., 2 Feb. 1775. Apparently Washington had written GM regarding the 20 Feb. 1775 election for selecting county representatives to the scheduled Mar. meeting of the Virginia Convention at Richmond. THE TWO MR. FITZHUGHS, and MR. TURBERVILLE were probably Hugh Fitzhugh of "Eagle's Nest," William Fitzhugh of "Marmion," and John Turberville (Hamilton, ed., *Letters to Washington*, V, 96*n*). THE PAYMENT OF 3/ was the levy of 17 Jan. 1775 to furnish arms and ammunition for the Fairfax Independent Company.

Either because the personal note was not germane to political affairs, or because of Victorian squeamishness, Rowland (I, 184) omits all mention of Mrs. Eilbeck's breast cancer.

Fairfax County Militia Plan "for Embodying the People"

[Enclosure of 6 February 1775]

Threatened with the Destruction of our antient Laws & Liberty, and the Loss of all that is dear to British Subjects & Freemen, justly alarmed with the Prospect of impending Ruin,—firmly determined, at the hazard of our Lives, to transmit to our Children & Posterity those sacred Rights to which ourselves were born; and thoroughly convinced that a well regulated Militia, composed of the Gentlemen, Freeholders, and other Freemen, is the natural Strength and only safe & stable security of a free Government, & that such Militia will relieve our Mother Country from any Expense in our Protection and Defence, will obviate the Pretence of a necessity for taxing us on that account, and render it unnecessary to keep any standing Army (ever dangerous to liberty) in this Colony, WE the Subscribers, Inhabitants of Fairfax County, have freely & voluntarily agreed, & hereby do agree & solemnly promise, to enroll & embody ourselves into a Militia for this County, intended to consist of all the able-bodied Freemen from eighteen to fifty Years of Age, under Officers of their own Choice; & for that Purpose to form ourselves into distinct Companies of Sixty-eight Men each; and so soon as the said Companies, or any of them in convenient neighbourhoods & Districts are completed, to chuse from among our Friends and acquaintaince, upon whose Justice, Humanity & Bravery we can relie, a Captain, two Lieutenants, an Ensign & four Serjeants for Each Company; every Captain respectively to appoint four Corporals & a Drummer for his Company, which Election of officers is to be annual in any Company, if the Majority of the Company think fit; & whenever a sufficient Number of Companies shall be made up, all the said Companies are to be formed into a Regiment, under the Command

of a Colonel, Lieutenant-Colonel, & Major, to be chosen by the
Captains, Lieutenants & Ensigns of the said Companies; which Elec-
tion of Field-officers is to be annual also, if the Majority of the
Officers think fit. And such of us have, or can procure Riphel Guns,
& understand the use of them, will be ready to form a Company of
Marksmen or Light-Infantry for the said Regiment, chusing our
own Officers as aforesaid, & distinguishing our Dress, when we are
upon Duty, from that of the other Companies, by painted Hunting-
Shirts and Indian Boots, or Caps, as shall be found most convenient,
—Which Regulation & Establishment is to be preserved & continued, until a regular and proper Militia Law for the Defence of the
Country shall be enacted by the Legislature of this Colony. And we
do Each of us, for ourselves respectively, promise and engage to
keep a good Fire-lock in proper Order, & to furnish Ourselves as
soon as possible with, & always keep by us, one Pound of Gunpowder, four Pounds of Lead, one Dozen Gun-Flints, & a pair of
Bullet-Moulds, with a Cartouch Box, or powder-horn, and Bag for
Balls. That we will use our best Endeavours to perfect ourselves in
the Military Exercise & Discipline, & therefore will pay due Obedience to our officers, & regularly attend such private and general
Musters as they shall appoint. And that we will always hold ourselves in Readiness, in Case of Necessity, Hostile-Invasion, or real
Danger, to defend & preserve to the utmost of our Power, our
Religion, the Laws of our Country, & the just Rights & Privileges of
our fellow-Subjects, our Posterity, & ourselves, upon the Principles
of the English Constitution.

Ms(Washington Papers, DLC). Written in an unidentified handwriting.
GM intended that this plan or association should be circulated and signed to
implement the 17 Jan. 1775 resolution of the Committee of Safety. Much of the
language is copied from that resolution, which in turn had the stylistic flavor
and some provisions of the Dec. resolution of the Maryland Provincial
Congress (Force, *American Archives*, I, 1032). It is not known whether GM
was instrumental in shaping the original resolve or simply approved of it so
thoroughly that he borrowed the most apt phrases. Obviously, he was reading
the Annapolis *Md. Gaz.*, which had printed the Maryland resolve on 15 Dec.
1774. Washington or R. H. Lee may have taken this plan to the Richmond
convention, for verbatim portions appear in the Convention resolution of 23
Mar., and the general outlines are evident in Jefferson's "Report of Committee
to Prepare a Plan for a Militia," which was presented 25 Mar. 1775 (Boyd, I,
160–161). The Convention agreed to the report, thus giving ex post facto
support to the Fairfax and other county committees that had already started a
collection from "every titheable person in their county." The Fairfax County
levies were collected by GM's son and accounted for on 17 Apr. 1775.
The modernized text printed in Rowland, I, 428–430, gives the erroneous
impression that this plan had been presented to the Committee of Safety
meeting on 17 Jan. 1775. In his accompanying letter, GM calls this two-page

Ms "a Copy of the Plan" he had drafted. The original, which may have been
sent to a printer, is now missing. A literal text was printed in Hamilton, ed.,
Letters to Washington, V, 94–95.

Memorandums for Mr. Lawson

AS TO THE RE-SURVEY ON THE COVE

[1774?]

From what Colo. Cresap has told him; perhaps Col. Cresap (to
whom I have wrote often upon the Subject, but never received any
answer) may have had the Resurvey made, & a proper Certificate
return'd to the Land Office; in that Case, Mr. Lawson has Nothing
more to do than to carry the Certificate from the Office to his
Lordship's Agent, & pay Him the Caution Money, at the Rate of
five pounds Sterling hund. Acres, for the vacant Land included
therein, taking his Rect. & upon his Indorsation on the Certificate,
that the Ld. proprietor's Dues are paid, a Patent will issue from the
Land Office, which is to be granted, in the common Form, to
George Mason his Heirs & Assigns—and there will be no Occasion
to trouble either the present or the late governor with my letters
etc. NB. The Patent must be signed by the Governor—the Certificate shou'd pass thro the Hands of the Examiner General before a
Patent can issue; but I believe this is usually done imediatly after the
Return to the Office. If the Certificate of Re-survey has been
return'd more than two Years to the Office, & any Person, taking
Advantage of the non-payment of the Caution Money, has lodged
Information, or made Application for the Land, a Caveat must be
entered in my Name agst. such Person's having a Patent, if you find
it necessary; but as it will clearly appear from the Deputy Survey-
or's Letter to me wth. the Warrant return'd to me unexecuted, that
I have been guilty of no Omission; for being inform'd that no
Certificate had been returned, or Re-survey made, I had no Founda-
tion for paying, or tendering the Caution Money. Under these
Circumstances, I apprehend a Patent will be granted me, notwithstanding any other Person's Application. If no Certificate of Re-survey has been return'd (which I believe will turn out to be the Case)
then Mr. Lawson will apply to the present Governor, & Colo.
Sharpe, & endeavour to get his Excellency Mr. Eden's order to the
Land Office to renew the Warrant of Resurvey, or take such other
Steps as shall appear best.

AS TO THE RE-SURVEY ON THE
LIMESTONE ROCK

A Certificate of Re-survey has no Doubt been return'd to the Office, but how long I know not, as I never cou'd get a Copy of it from Surveyor until April 1769, as will appear by his Deputy's Letter to me, enclosing the Certificate of Limestone Rock, & the Warrant on the Cove; altho' I had often applyed for it; & when I did receive it, I found it was return'd in the name of Daniel Cresap; so that I was, & still am at a Loss [as to] what Application to make to the Office, or how to act with Regard to paying the Caution Money for the Vacant Land; which I shou'd not care to do, unless I can obtain the Patent in my own name. This I wrote to Col. Cresap about, & desired him to get a proper Assignment from his Son; & by what he has said to Colo. Mercer, perhaps he may have done so, & lodged it with the Certificate in the Land Office; if so, Mr. Lawson has nothing more to do but to pay the Caution Money, & take out the Patent in my Name, as before directed, in the Re surveys, on the Cove; unless some Person has already made Application for the non-payment of the Caution Money; in which Case it may be necessary to enter a Caveat in my Name agst. a Patent &c. but as the Surveyor has return'd the Resurvey in the Name of a Person in fact no Way concer'd or interested in it, I shou'd apprehend no such Advantage cou'd be taken of me, who am the Person really interested, & that under such Circumstances a Patent wou'd be granted to me, notwithstanding such an application.* Indeed I am apt to believe that there has been a Mistake made either by the Surveyor, or some of the Clerks in the Land Office; for to the best of my Remembrance, the Warrant was actually renewed in my own Name, & if so, the Warrant ought to have issued in my Name, & the Certificate shou'd have been return'd accordingly; this the Office Books will shew, & if it shou'd prove so, I suppose the Surveyor must alter the Certificate. At all Events it will be proper to tender the Caution Money to his Lordship's Agent, & get him to indorse upon the Certificate that the Money has been tendered. Or perhaps it will be found necessary to lay what they call a Proclamation Warrant upon it:—Tho' upon the Whole, as these, & all the adjacent Lands are now included within the Bounds of his Lordship's new Mannor, I apprehend no Person can have made any Application on Account of the non-payment of the Caution Money, & that they still remain in the Power of the Government; & I make no Doubt, upon being truly inform'd of the Circumstances, the Judges of the Land Office will grant the Patents upon the Payment of the Lord Proprietor's Dues. *Qn. if the two Years allowed for the Payment of the Caution Money shou'd not be computed from the time the Surveyor furnishes the Person with a Copy of the Certificate? I have not been furnished with a Copy of the Certificate more than one year.

NB. any Tobo. charges attending the Patents &c. may be sent against me into Charles County as usual, where I have an Estate, & to the Sherif of that County [where] all Officer's fees agst. me have been sent for many Years

G MASON

NB. Neither of these Warrants [in] any way concern my Dispute with Doctr. Ross, being quite different Tracts of Land

G MASON

Ms (CSmH). Endorsed in an unidentified hand: "Memdm to Mr Lawson Respecting the Cove & Limestone Rock Lands &c."

MR. LAWSON appears to have been an Annapolis lawyer charged with clearing GM's title to lands acquired in the course of Ohio Company business. THE COVE, a tract of 510 acres, had been patented by GM on 24 June 1763. LIMESTONE ROCK was a 63-acre tract, acquired at about the same time. Resurveys may have been necessary because of faults in the original documents or as a precaution, as by the fall of 1763 GM was involved in "a bitter struggle" for clear titles to some Maryland lands with Dr. David Ross of Blandensburg (James, *Ohio Company*, 125). COLO. THOMAS CRESAP was the original patentee of Limestone Rock (10 Aug. 1753) and probably of the Cove also. Protracted litigation bridged the war years, and in the spring of 1783 Dr. Ross's case came before the Maryland courts, and on 2 May 1783 GM appears to have bought a quit-claim deed from Cresap's heirs to Limestone Rock. On the next day, GM sold the land to Thomas Beall (*ibid.*, 177). GM's notation that neither tract was involved in MY DISPUTE WITH DOCTR. ROSS was an afterthought that took on meaning with the years, for Ross pursued GM through the courts in litigation that did not end until 1821 over a tract known as Pleasant Valley (*ibid.*, 179–183).

The allusions to Apr. 1769 as somewhat remote, and the obvious concern over the L[OR]D PROPRIETOR's DUES, indicate the document was written prior to 1775. The document, except for the endorsement, is in GM's hand.

From George Washington

[[*14* (?) *Feb. 1775.* Washington and GM were charged with procuring gunpowder for the Fairfax Independent Militia Company, and a mistake had been made in filling their order with Alexandria merchant John Harper. Apparently Washington wanted GM's advice on whether to take all the powder or only that part which they needed. Thomas Johnson of Maryland had been working on a bill to improve navigation on the Potomac, and Washington appears to have discussed and perhaps encouraged GM to draft similar legislation for Virginia. Washington's letter is mentioned in GM to Washington, 17 Feb. 1775. Not found.]]

To George Washington

Dear Sir.   Gunston-Hall Febry. 17th. 1775.

I return'd from Maryland but last Night, not being able to leave Mrs. Eilbeck sooner, & don't know how quickly I may be called there again, as I think she is far from being out of Danger, & the Doctor has some Apprehensions of a Mortification. I will if I can, be at Alexandria on Monday; but it is uncertain, as well for the Reason above mentioned, as that I am at this time unwell with a bad Cold & a little Pain in my Breast.

I can't conceive how Mr. Harper cou'd make such a Mistake as to buy double the Quantity of Powder wanted for this County, when he had the Order in Writing sign'd by you & me: if there is any Ambiguity in the said Writing (for I don't now recollect the Words) by which Mr. Harper might be led into such a Mistake, I think we are in Honour bound to take the whole off his Hands; otherwise it does not appear to me that he can reasonably expect it; tho' I am exceedingly concern'd that any kind of Misunderstanding shou'd happen in an Affair, which must have given Mr. Harper a good deal of Trouble, & which I am convinced was undertaken by him merely from public Motives, & a Desire to oblige the Committee. I remember your mentioning, in Conversation, to Mr. Harper, an Application made to you from Loudoun County to procure a Quantity of Powder for their Committee, upon six Months credit, & telling him if it cou'd be purchased in Philadelphia upon such Credit, you wou'd see the Money paid when it became due; to which he answered that powder was generally a ready-Money Article there, & at this time in particular, he did not imagine it cou'd be got upon Credit. I speak from Recollection (having had no Concern in the Affair) but as nearly as I can remember, this is the Substance of what passed between you & him respecting the Loudoun Committee, & may possibly have occasioned the Mistake; at least I can account for it no other Way.

I have already paid Messrs. Mc Crea & Maise half their Acct. and my half the Money due to Mr. Harper for the articles ordered for Fairfax County, is at any Minute ready, having kept a Sum in Gold by me for that Purpose, that Mr. Harper shou'd not be disappointed in the Payment; but if it will be attended wth. no Inconvenience to him, it will suit me better to make the Payment ten Days hence than now; because I think in that time I can collect [a] good Part of the Money from the People, and as the Collection will be partly in Paper Dollars & Pensilvania Money, which from Mr. Harper's Connections to the Northward, may suit him as well, or perhaps better than Gold, yet it will not replace the Gold wth. equal Convenience to me; I mention this only as Matter of mutual conven-ience, at the same time making a Point not to disappoint Mr. Harper; & I must beg the favour of you Sir to communicate this to him, that I may send up the Money whenever he wants it, without giving him any Trouble on the Subject.

I shall send my Son George out imediatly to make what Collec-tion he can, being furnish'd with a List of Tytheables for that Purpose: if you incline to do any thing of that kind, you shall have a Copy of the List, distinguishing those who have paid to him. I think this Method will reimburse us sooner, & save Commissions & Trou-ble to the Sherif.

I had gone a good Way thro' the Bill for improving the Naviga-tion of Potomack, before I went to Maryland, & am happy in finding that I had fallen into many of Mr. Johnston's Sentiments, tho' I was a Stranger to them, 'til I recd. yr. Letter upon my Return last Night. I wish it was in my Power to spend a Day wth. him on the Subject. Some of his Remarks are not so intelligible to me as they wou'd be, if I had all the Queries which he seems to answer. When he mentions of some kind of Jealosy least the Virginians shou'd have some Advantage, & that there shou'd be some Equality between the Maryland & Virga. Subscriptions, I can have no Idea of. What Matter is it whether the Majority of the Subscribers are Marylanders or Virginians if their Property is put upon an equal Footing & the Work is of general advantage to both Provinces? Nor can I think his Notion of proportioning the Tolls to the average Profits can well be reduced to Practice. A sufficient Sum can't be raised by those only who are locally interested; men who are not, will not advance their Money, upon so great a Risque but wth. Veiws of great & increasing Profit, not to depend upon future Alterations: the Tolls, to be sure, must be moderate, such as the Commodities will bear, with advantage to the Makers; it is probable for some Years they will yield very little Profit to the Undertakers, perhaps none; they must run the Risque of this, as well as of the ultimate Failure of the Undertaking, & surely if they succeed they

[221]

have a just Right to the increased Profits; tho' in process of Time they may become very great. If I am not misinform'd, this is the Principle upon which everything of this Nature has been successfully executed in other Countrys.—My Paper will not permit me to add more at present, than that I am Dr. Sir Yr. affecte. & obdt. Servt.

G. Mason

RC (Washington Papers, DLC).

MRS. EILBECK, GM's mother-in-law, had been operated on for breast cancer and recovered from the effects, as she lived until Dec. 1780. The meeting AT ALEXANDRIA ON MONDAY was held on 20 Feb. to select delegates to the Richmond Convention of 1775. MR. HARPER was the Quaker merchant who had ordered gunpowder for the Fairfax Independent Militia Company, on the personal credit of both Washington and GM. MESSRS. MCCREA and MAISE (actually, Mease), were Alexandria merchants. GM did send his son out to collect the weapons levy and gave an accounting on 17 Apr. (q.v.). THE BILL FOR IMPROVING THE NAVIGATION OF POTOMACK was a project to cut a canal from the tidewater to Fort Cumberland. A plan already approved by the Virginia General Assembly (Hening, VIII, 570–579) had been written by GM's brother, Thomson Mason, in 1772 which would have created a private corporation to build and maintain the canal. Washington had served on the House of Burgesses committee with Thomson Mason and took an active interest in promoting the canal scheme. Speculators in western lands—which included Washington, Johnson, and GM—expected a rise in land values if a cheaper mode of transportation could be devised. Johnson had written Washington on 21 Feb. 1774 (Washington Papers, DLC) that he helped push a £3,000 appropriation for western road-building through the Maryland General Assembly and "made a shew of pushing for a further Sum for improving the River with a View to secure more certainly the £3,000 for the Road." Meanwhile, John Ballendine publicly announced a scheme to build a canal and announced (Va. Gaz. [Purdie & Dixon], 3 Nov. 1774) the appointment of 21 Virginians and 22 Marylanders as trustees of the plan. The Virginians included GM, Thomson Mason, and Washington, while Johnson was listed as a Maryland trustee. A meeting of the trustees, scheduled at Georgetown on 12 Nov. 1774, drew scant attention and was rescheduled for 26 Jan. 1775 with no more success (Fitzpatrick, ed., Diaries of Washington, II, 170, 183). Ballendine continued to promote his scheme and announced in the Annapolis Md. Gaz., 16 Feb. 1775, that he was hiring 50 slaves to start work on a canal. On 24 Jan. 1775 Johnson had written Washington saying "you may depend on my best Endeavours to get a Bill passed here similar to yours . . . I really believe if I had not a foot of Land above the falls I should be as warm a friend to the Scheme . . ." (Hamilton, ed., Letters to Washington, V, 85). GM apparently had access to a later letter of Johnson's addressed to Washington, which is now lost. Thomson Mason's earlier bill provided for a public lottery, an elaborate system of tolls, and a deadline (1 Nov. 1773) which was not met, and the plan was thus stillborn. GM continued to work on a draft and reported his labors finished on 9 March 1775. GM's bill may have been the one passed by the Virginia General Assembly in June 1775 (JHB, 1772–1776, 274) which never became operative as the military crisis mounted. However, GM's participation in matters involving the Potomac continued to 1785.

As in the printed version of GM's 6 Feb. 1775 letter to Washington, Rowland (I, 185) again omitted details of Mrs. Eilbeck's illness.

To George Washington

DEAR SIR.   Gunston-Hall   Febry. 18th. 1775.

I shall always think my self obliged to any Friend to communicate wth. Freedom & Candour whatever Doubts he may have of my Conduct towards him, as the most effectual Means of preventing Misrepresentation; and I hope you will believe me when I assure you that you have greatly misconstrued my Intentions in making the Collection I mentioned. Was either of us to take the advantage of receiving what he wou'd from those who are most able & willing to pay, leaving the other to scuffle as he wou'd wth. the rest, it wou'd not only be unequal & ungenerous, but absolutely dishonest: the thing is self-evident, & needs no Proof.

I thought that the Collection wou'd not be made by the Sherif 'til late in the Summer, & that therefore collecting as much as we cou'd ourselves wou'd not only save Commissions, but expedite the Business, & reimburse us so much the sooner. I had also another Reason, not finding that simular Measures were adopted in the other Countys, I was, & still am of Opinion that the Collection may be more easily made now than some time hence. I hinted your taking the same Measures, & offer'd a Copy of the List of Tytheables, distinguishing such as had paid to me: by these Means I imagined we cou'd, between us, collect the greatest Part of the Money in two or three Weeks, when a Dividend of what we had both received cou'd be easily made; leaving the rest to be collected by the Sherif or by any other Person (if the Sherif refused) at his Leisure; & as I expected a good deal might be paid in Pensilvania Curry. & paper Dollars, I thought, if Mr. Harper wou'd wait a few Days, I shou'd get such Money off my Hands (instead of being obliged to keep it upon my own Acct.) without Injury to any one; for otherwise the advancing or not advancing the Money just at this time, makes not a farthing odds to me, having kept a Sum bye me on Purpose; and nothing cou'd be further from my Mind than the Idea of making a partial Collection for my own seperate Benefit; it can not but give me Concern that I shou'd be thought capable of such disingenuous Conduct. I may perhaps be blameable for not explaining myself fully before; but in a Matter so palpable, I had no Conception that it was necessary.

It has not been in my Power to do any thing, since I came from

Maryland, towards the Potomack River Bill; but I will apply to it as soon as I can, & when finish'd forward it to you.

By a Letter from Maryland Yesterday I am inform'd that his Majesty has ordered his Embassadors at the different Courts in Europe to declare his American Subjects in a State of Rebellion.

I am, wth. my Comps. to Mrs. Washington & the Family at Mount Vernon, Dr Sir Yr. affecte. & obdt. Servt.

G MASON

RC (Washington Papers, DLC). Addressed and endorsed.

Washington obviously had informed GM, probably in a letter since destroyed, that he was displeased with the collecting procedures outlined in GM's letter of 17 Feb. 1775. GM recorded the weapon levy accounts and gave a full statement on 17 Apr. 1775. The LETTER FROM MARYLAND YESTERDAY (now lost) must have contained rumors rather than facts, for although George III had said privately that America was in a state of rebellion, a formal proclamation was not issued until 23 Aug. 1775 (Force, comp., *American Archives*, III, 240).

To George Washington

DEAR SIR.   Gunston-Hall   March [8] 9th. 1775.

I have at last finished the Potomack River Bill; which I now send you, together with some very long Remarks thereon, & a Letter to Mr. Johnston; into which you'll be pleased to put a Wafer, when you forward the other Papers to him. I also return the Acts of Assembly, & Mr. Johnston's Notes, which you sent me. This Affair has taken me five times as long as I expected; and I do assure you I never ingaged in any thing which puzled me more; there were such a Number of Contingencys to provide for, & drawing up Laws a thing so much out of my Way I shall be well pleased if the Pains I have bestowed upon the Subject prove of any Service to so great an Undertaking; but by what I can understand, there will be so strong an Opposition from Baltemore, & the Head of the Bay, as will go near to prevent it's passage thro' the Maryland Assembly, in any Shape it can be offered.

I suppose you have heard of the late Purchase made by some North Carolina Gentlemen from the Cherokee Indians, of all the Country between the Great Conhaway & the Tennissee Rivers. I think, considering this Colony has just expended abt. £100,000, upon the Defence of that Country, that this is a pretty bold Stroke of the Gentlemen. It is suspected some of our Virga. Gentlemen are privately concern'd in it.

I have always expected that the new fangled Doctrine lately

broach'd, of the Crown's having no Title beyond the Alleghany Mountains 'til after the Purchase at Fort Stanwix,—wou'd produce a thousand other Absurdities & Squabbles. However, if I am not mistaken, the Crown, at that Treaty, purchased of the Six Nations all the Lands as low as the Tenissee River. So now I suppose, we must have a formal Tryal whether the six Nations or the Cherokees had the legal Right; but whether this is to be done by Ejectment, Writ of Enquiry,—Writ of Partition, or what other Process, let those who invented this curious Distinction determine. The Inattention of our Assembly to so grand an Object, as the Right of this Colony to the western Lands, is inexcusable, & the Confusion it will introduce endless.

If I knew when you set off for the Convention at Richmond, I wou'd trouble you wth. two or three Virga. Curry. Bills, to make my second Payment to Mr. Mezzay, as I may not perhaps have an Opportunity of sending it in April.

We make but a poor Hand of collecting; very few pay, tho' every body promises, except Mr. Hartshorn, of Alexandria; who flatly refused: his Conscience I suppose wou'd not suffer him to be concern'd in paying for the Instruments of Death. George has been very unwell for some Days past; as soon as he gets well he intends up into the Forrest, where he has not yet been.

The Family here join in their Compliments to Mrs. Washington, & the Family at Mount Vernon, with Dr Sir Your affecte. Hble Servt.

G MASON

RC (Washington Papers, DLC). Addressed, and two of the four pages numbered (60, 61), probably by a clerk or curator.

THE POTOMACK RIVER BILL, which had been on GM's mind for some weeks, was meant as a joint effort that would have evoked similar aid from Maryland in the construction of canals enabling ocean-going vessels to ascend the Potomac as far as Fort Cumberland. The idea appealed to western land speculators and GM, Thomson Mason, Washington, Thomas Johnson and others with trans-Allegheny interests had been enlisted by John Ballendine in a scheme that appeared to be on the verge of activity (see GM to Washington, 17 Feb. 1775, and notes). The bill may have been the basis for a measure introduced in the House of Burgesses by James Mercer, who certainly owed GM and Washington a favor, on 5 June 1775 (JHB, 1772–1776, 191). Neither the bill enclosed here nor that Mercer introduced has been found. The latter bill, calling for a company capitalized at £40,000 to extend "Navigation of the River *Potomack*," passed the Virginia General Assembly but never became operative because the war intervened. Similarly, Ballendine's venture faltered and was abandoned, but the idea implanted was revived after the war. JOHNSTON'S NOTES and GM's letter to Johnson are lost. The Marylander's involvement is related in Edward S. Delaplaine, *The Life of Thomas Johnson* . . . (New York, 1927), 59–84. The Maryland General Assembly eventually acted on the proposal in 1784, and GM became a Virginia commissioner in the interstate negotiations of 1785. THE LATE PURCHASE . . . FROM THE CHEROKEE INDIANS was Richard Henderson's purchase of some 20,000,000 acres between the Kentucky River and the Cumberland River watershed, in Mar. 1775. GM probably had heard of Henderson's broadside issued in Dec. 1774, which announced the sale of land before the negotiations at Sycamore Shoals were held (Jack Sosin, *The Revolutionary Frontier, 1763-1783* [New York, 1967], 75-77). William Byrd and other Virginians were also dickering for these lands; and settlers in the area shifted their allegiance to Virginia so that in 1776 it was created as Kentucky County (Frederic L. Paxson, *History of the American Frontier 1763-1893* [Boston, 1924], 29-30). This prevented a long legal quarrel to establish Virginia jurisdiction over the region, although GM's memory was correct about the lower limits of THE PURCHASE AT FORT STANWIX, which went down the Ohio left bank "to the Country as far South as that [Tennessee] River . . ." (E. B. O'Callaghan, *The Documentary History of the State of New-York,* I [Albany, 1849], 589). MR. MEZZAY was Philip Mazzei, the Italian promoter, who had persuaded GM, Washington, Jefferson, and other Virginians to underwrite a company "for the Purpose of raising and making Wine, Oil, agruminous Plants and Silk" (see Boyd, I, 156-158). A POOR HAND OF COL-LECTING the weapons levy for the Fairfax militia eventually improved (see account of 17 Apr. 1775). MR. HARTSHORN was a Quaker merchant who served on the Fairfax Committee of Safety. George Mason, Jr., was making the collection. UP INTO THE FORREST may have been the current expression for the interior woodlands in Fairfax County.

GM predated this letter on 8 Mar., as his comment in the 9 Mar. message indicated.

From George Washington

[[*9 Mar. 1775.* Washington's message was acknowledged in GM's answer of this day. The letter from Mount Vernon must have mentioned Washington's continuing concern over collections of the weapons levy for the Fairfax County militia company. Washington's correspondence with Thomas Johnson relating to the Potomac River navigation bill may also have been reported. Washington was about to depart for the Richmond Convention, and may have also volunteered to carry on some personal business for GM while there. Not found.]]

To George Washington

DEAR SIR   Guns[ton] Hall   March 9th. 1775.

I had wrote the inclosed Letter last Night, & was just sending my Man off with it, & the other Papers, when your Messenger came; by whom you will now receive them, made up within the Cover of the Acts of Assembly.

I beg you to inform Mr. Johnston that the Bill I have drawn is intended only as a Ground-work, & that I desire every part of it may be submitted to his Correction.

My Son George has been unwell some time. He went Yesterday wth. his Sister to Mrs. Eilbeck's, as soon as he returns, & has a little Leisure, he will make out a Copy of the List of Tytheables. You will be pleased to leave Directions wth. Mr. Lund Washington about the Collection. We have had an Opportunity of speaking to most of the Gentlemen out of the County, who have Titheables in it, & they have promised to give Directions for the Payment; I don't now recollect any whom it will be necessary to write to, but Colo. Henry Fitzhugh of Stafford, & Mr. John Turberville of Westmoreland.

I take the Liberty of inclosing you £ 18.. Virga. Curry., out of which I must beg the favour of you to pay to Mr. Nicholas, or Mr. Mezzay, £ 12..10.. Ster: for my second payment in the Wine Compy. due the 1st. of May next, & take a Rect. accordingly: I had not Bills to come nearer the Sum; but the Balce. you can repay me when you return. I send you the Cherry-Graffs you desire, but am afraid they are rather too forward: the bundle wth. the white Stick in it is May-Dukes; the other the large black May Cherrys. I am Dr Sir Yr. affecte. & obdt. Sert

G MASON

RC (Washington Papers, DLC). Addressed and endorsed.

Some information in GM's predated letter of 9 Mar. is repeated. Washington was concerned about ways and means of collecting a weapons levy for the Fairfax County militia. GM's letter of 18 Feb. 1775 must have quieted some of Washington's earlier fears. LUND WASHINGTON tended to business matters during his cousin's absence. The enclosed cash directed to Robert Carter Nicholas or MR. MEZZAY was GM's subscription for Philip Mazzei's vineyard promotion which was popularly called "the Wine company" (Boyd, I, 159). Washington was preparing for a journey to Richmond, where he could perform some personal business while serving in the Virginia Convention for the last time.

[From George Washington]

[[5 Apr. 1775. John C. Fitzpatrick's List of the Washington Manuscripts . . . carries an item for this date as a "contemporary copy" of a letter from Washington to GM. The entry was supposed to be in Vol. XVI, item 1973 of the Washington Papers, and an investigation of the Washington Papers in 1968 showed the item so numbered to be a 3 Aug. 1775 enclosure in a report from L. Baldwin to Washington. No such Ms is mentioned in the Index to the George Washington Papers (Washington, 1964). The editor therefore concludes that Fitzpatrick's entry is an error.]]

1775

Account of Fairfax County
Weapons Levy

[17 April 1775]

Virga.
Curry.

1775 March, Cash Collected by G Mason
Junr. in both Parishes, for 509.
Tytheables at 3/ as per List & } 76..7..0.
Acct. given into the Committee
From which deduct, for so much lost
in change, _____0..9..6. 1..14..0.
Do. Charges of Collection, ⅌
Bill, 12/, & 12/6_____1..4..6. } 74..13..0.
G Mason's own & his Son's Tythe-
ables in both Parishes_____64 @ 3/_____ 9..12..0.

84.. 5..0.

April 17th. Cash Paid by G Mason to Colo.
Washington (for his part) deducted_____ 31..17..0.
The Sum reimbursed G Mason in Part Pay-
ment for Powder &c. is_____£52.. 8..0.

1775 Colo. Washington's Tythe-
ables in both Parishes_____137. at 3/_____ 20..11..0.
Apl. 17th. Cash paid him by G Mason (Part of
his Collection)_____ 31..17..0.

The Sum reimbursed Colo. Washington in Part
Payment for Powder &c. is_____£52.. 8..0.

E. E. ⅌ G Mason

Ms (Marietta College Library, Marietta, Ohio). In receipt form, written and
endorsed by GM.
The Fairfax County Committee of Safety had ordered the collection of a
three-shilling fee from every titheable person to provide arms and ammunition
for the Fairfax Independent Militia Company then forming. Washington and
GM had proceeded to order gunpowder and pledged their credit for its
payment. Washington appears to have misunderstood GM's collecting methods, as the letter of 18 Feb. 1775 indicates. This account would have settled
matters before Washington left for his place in the Continental Congress. For a
further accounting of GM's activities in the procurement and distribution of
war materiel, see Appendix B.

[228]

Remarks on Annual Elections for the Fairfax Independent Company

[*ca.* 17–26 April 1775]

A moment's reflection upon the principles on which this company was first instituted, and the purposes for which it was formed, will evince the propriety of the gentleman's motion; for it has been wisely observed by the deepest politician who ever put pen to paper, that no institution can be long preserved, but by frequent recurrence to those maxims on which it was formed.

This company is essentially different from a common collection of mercenary soldiers. It was formed upon the liberal sentiments of public good, for the great and useful purposes of defending our country, and preserving those inestimable rights which we inherit from our ancestors; it was intended in these times of extreme danger, when we are threatened with the ruin of that constitution under which we were born, and the destruction of all that is dear to us, to rouse the attention of the public, to introduce the use of arms and discipline, to infuse a martial spirit of emulation, and to provide a fund of officers; that in case of absolute necessity, the people might be the better enabled to act in defence of their invaded liberty. Upon this generous and public-spirited plan, gentlemen of the first fortune and character among us have become members of the Fairfax Independent Company, have submitted to stand in the ranks as common soldiers, and to pay due obedience to the officers of their own choice. This part of the country has the glory of setting so laudable an example: let us not tarnish it by any little dirty views of party, of mean self-interest or of low ambition.

We came equals into this world, and equals shall we go out of it. All men are by nature born equally free and independent. To protect the weaker from the injuries and insults of the stronger were societies first formed; when men entered into compacts to give up some of their natural rights, that by union and mutual assistance they might secure the rest; but they gave up no more than the nature of the thing required. Every society, all government, and every kind of civil compact therefore, is or ought to be, calculated for the general good and safety of the community. Every power, every authority vested in particular men is, or ought to be, ultimately directed to this sole end; and whenever any power or authority whatever extends further, or is of longer duration than is in its nature necessary for these purposes, it may be called government, but it is in fact oppression.

Upon these natural just and simple positions were civil laws and obligations framed, and from this source do even the most arbitrary and despotic powers this day upon earth derive their origin. Strange indeed that such superstructures should be raised upon such a foundation! But when we reflect upon the insidious arts of wicked and designing men, the various and plausible pretences for continuing and increasing authority, the incautious nature of the many, and the inordinate lust of power in the few, we shall no longer be surprised that free-born man hath been enslaved, and that those very means which were contrived for his preservation have been perverted to his ruin; or, to borrow a metaphor from Holy Writ, that the kid hath been seethed in his mother's milk.

To prevent these fatal effects, and to restore mankind to its native rights hath been the study of some of the best men that this world ever produced; and the most effectual means that human wisdom hath ever been able to devise, is frequently appealing to the body of the people, to those constituent members from whom authority originated, for their approbation or dissent. Whenever this is neglected or evaded, or the free voice of the people is suppressed or corrupted; or whenever any military establishment or authority is not, by some certain mode of rotation, dissolved into and blended with that mass from which it was taken, inevitable destruction to the state follows.

> "Then down the precipice of time it goes,
> And sinks in moments, which in ages rose."

The history of all nations who have had liberty and lost it, puts these facts beyond doubt. We have great cause to fear that this crisis is approaching in our mother country. Her constitution has strong symptoms of decay. It is our duty by every means in our power to prevent the like here.

If it be objected to the intended regulation that there may be inconvenience in changing officers who, by having served as such, have acquired a superior degree of military knowledge, the example and experience of the most warlike and victorious people that ever existed is directly against such a suggestion.

While the Roman Commonwealth preserved its vigour, new consuls were annually elected, new levies made, and new officers appointed; a general was often recalled from the head of a victorious army, in the midst of a dangerous and important war, and a successor sent to finish the expedition which he had begun. A long and almost constant series of success proved the wisdom and utility of measures which carried victory through the world, and at the same time secured the public safety and liberty at home; for by these means the people had always an inexhaustible fund of experienced officers, upon every emergency, untainted with the dangerous impressions which continued command naturally makes. But when by degrees these essential maxims of the state were undermined, and pretences were found to continue commanders beyond the stated times, their army no longer considered themselves the soldiers of the Republic, but as the troops of Marius or of Sylla, of Pompey or of Ceasar, of Marc Antony or of Octavius. The dissolution of that once glorious and happy commonwealth was the natural consequence, and has afforded a useful lesson to succeeding generations.

It has been lately observed by a learned and revered writer, that North America is the only great nursery of freemen now left upon the face of the earth. Let us cherish the sacred deposit. Let us strive to merit this greatest encomium that ever was bestowed upon any country. In all our associations; in all our agreements let us never lose sight of this fundamental maxim—that all power was originally lodged in, and consequently is derived from, the people. We should wear it as a breastplate, and buckle it on as our armour.

The application of these general principles to the subject before us is too obvious to need a minute illustration. By investing our officers with a power for life, or for an unlimited time, we are acting diametrically contrary to the principles of that liberty for which we profess to contend, and establishing a precedent which may prove fatal. By the purport of the proposed regulation every objection is obviated, every inconvenience removed; and the design of the institution strictly adhered to. It is calculated to prevent the abuse of authority, and the insolence of office on the one hand, and create a proper spirit of emulation on the other; and by an annual rotation, will in a few years breed a number of officers. The proposed interval of a year will defeat undue influence or cabals; and the capacity of being rechosen afterwards, opens a door to the return of officers of approved merit, and will always be a means of excluding unworthy men, whom an absolute rotation would of necessity introduce. The exception made in favor of the gentleman who by the unanimous voice of the company now commands it, is a very proper one, justly due to his public merit and experience; it is peculiarly suited to our circumstances, and was dictated, not by compliment, but conviction.

In a company thus constituted, no young man will think himself degraded by doing duty in the ranks, which he may in his turn command, or has commanded. For these reasons I very cordially give my assent to the gentleman's motion, and hope it will have the unanimous approbation of this company. If any of the members continue to think that the choice of the officers ought to be confined to this town, they can introduce it by way of amendment to the motion, and the merits of the proposition may be freely discussed.

Printed from Rowland, I, 430–433.

The conjectural date is based on indications in the text that the militia company had already organized on a loose basis in Jan.–Feb. 1775, as GM's 6 Feb. 1775 plan "for Embodying the People" demonstrates. GM was also crossing the Potomac frequently to visit Mrs. Eilbeck in Feb. 1775, and would not have attended conflicting militia meetings. By 17 Apr. an accounting of the weapons levy had been made, and on 26 Apr. the militia company met at Alexandria (Fitzpatrick, ed., *Diaries of Washington*, II, 193). Obviously, GM's remarks were based on a motion that related to rank and length of service, and were meant to counteract those "little dirty views of party" discernible in Alexandria. The occasion gave GM an opportunity to spell out his political philosophy of the Revolution that was about to commence in earnest. Certainly, by favoring the annual election of officers, GM helped initiate a democratic process which was regarded in nearby Maryland as an assault upon the established order (David Curtis Skaggs, "Maryland's Impluse Toward Social Revolution: 1750–1776," *Journal of American History*, LIV [1968], 782). These remarks reveal GM's effort to base the Revolution on what he regarded as some established universal truths. The declaration that ALL MEN ARE BY NATURE BORN EQUALLY FREE AND INDEPENDENT was used again by GM in his first draft of the Virginia Declaration of Rights (18 May–12 June 1776), as was much of the remainder of the second paragraph. Because of the exactness of language used, it could be argued (but not proved) that GM had a copy of these remarks before him while drafting the 1776 document. The borrowed METAPHOR FROM HOLY WRIT is from *Exodus 23:19*. The two-line quotation, "Then down the precipice of time . . . ," was a family favorite for Thomson Mason used the same lines in his essay by "British American, No. V," in the *Va. Gaz.* (Rind), 30 June 1774. The author may have been Lucretius, who wrote in *De Rerum Natura*: ". . . una dies dabit exitio, multosque per annos sustentata ruet moles it machina mundi" (Cyril Bailey, ed., [Oxford, 1947], III, 1335). A LEARNED AND REVERED WRITER may have been "Junius," the contemporary Whig partisan who contrasted British corruption with American virtue. Perhaps GM paraphrased from Letter L: "The spirit of the Americans may be a useful example to us. . . . Patriotism, it seems, may be improved by transplanting" (*Genuine Letters of Junius* [London, 1771], 363). The allusion to Washington's selection as the company commander as A VERY PROPER ONE would seem to fix the debate prior to Washington's departure on 4 May 1775 for Philadelphia and a larger military role.

Miss Rowland probably copied the remarks from a Ms in a private collection around 1890. Her provenance statement—"Mason Papers, MS. copy"—creates doubt as to whether she copied from the original Ms or from a copy, but the internal evidence in favor of GM's authorship is overwhelming. She modernized the text and undoubtedly made alterations in spelling, punctuation, and sentence structure. The editor assumes that the word "revered" in the ninth paragraph was not written "reverend" by GM as appears in Rowland, I, 432. The location of the original is a mystery.

From George Washington to the
Fairfax County Committee

GENTN: Philadelphia, May 16, 1775.

If I could have communicated any thing by the last Post certain and satisfactory, I should most assuredly have done it agreeable to my promise, but the only articles of Intelligence which came to my hands were containd in the Gazetees, and went regularly to you. This is pretty much the case at present, and leaves me little to add, as the Congress are again under the Tye of Secrecy in respect to their proceedings till the business is finished, or particular parts of it published by order; the principal design therefore of my writing to you at this time, and under these circumstances is, to recommend strongly, in case a Convention of the Virga. Delegates should be called (as the Treasurer has been advis'd to do) in my absence, that some other person may be chosen Pro: tem to serve in my Room; in order that, the County may, at this important Crisis, be fully represented; the necessity of a full, and able Representation at such a juncture as this, must be too obvious to need a Comment, or words to enforce the recommendation.

We have a very full Congress, and I flatter myself that great unanimity will prevail among the Members of it. The Colony of New York is said, not only to be hearty, but zealous in the cause. I wish, and I hope it may be so, but, as I never entertaind a very high opinion of your sudden repentances, I will suspend my opinion till the arrival of the Troops there.

The Provencial Congress of the Massachusetts bay have voted 13,600 Men, the other Governments of New Engd. have followed their example in proportionate numbers, and the Troops at Boston are confind within the Neck by about 9000 of them, Intrenchd, by which means all Communication between the Town and Country is cut off, and the Army and Inhabitants of Boston, it is said, somewhat distressed for Provisions. We have no late Accts. from thence; but it is supposed Genl. Gage will keep close till he receives his reinforcemt., to consist, our Accts. says of abt. 2000 Men and to be expected the last of this month. What he will then do, time only can tell. The Depositions taken after the Action at Lexington I inclose you, when oppy. offers please to forwd. a Copy or two into the back Counties.

As Mr. Milnor has just given notice that he shall set out at One clock this day instead of tomorrow (as I expected) I am obligd to write in more haste than I otherwise should have done, I am etc.

G. WASHINGTON

Printed from Fitzpatrick, *Writings of Washington*, XXXVII, 510–512.

A CONVENTION . . . CALLD . . . IN MY ABSENCE by the TREASURER—Robert Carter Nicholas—was to thrust GM into the center of Virginia Revolutionary politics. GM was named as Washington's replacement and was a Fairfax delegate to the Richmond convention of 1775, beginning a term of service that stretched until May 1780. He was later elected although he did not serve for several terms (Oct. 1780; May 1781; Oct. 1786; May 1787) but finished his public career as a Fairfax delegate in the Oct. 1787 session. MR. MILNOR was a Philadelphia merchant who was forwarding supplies to the Fairfax Committee.

To William Lee

DEAR SIR,   Virginia, Gunston-Hall May 20th: 1775

I shall ship you, ⅌ your Ship The Adventure Capt. Brown, one hundred Hogsheads of Virginia Potomack River Tobacco (most of which is now on board the Ship's Craft) on which I must desire you imediatly to make a safe Insurance on my Account, to receive eleven pounds Sterling per Hogshead, in Case of Loss.

I expect the Certainty of the Exports being stop'd here on the 10th. of September next, if not much sooner, will raise what Tobacco gets to Market to an amazing Price: indeed was there not this extraordinary Cause, I think Tobacco must be high; which is my Reason for shipping so largely. People in general have not prepared this year for Crops of Tobo. as usual; and even those who have will be able to make very little, from the uncommon Scarcity of Plants, greater than in the noted Year 1758, or perhaps than ever was known within Memory of Man, and the Season now too far advanced to raise more. You may depend upon this Information as a certain Fact, in all the upper Parts of Virginia & Maryland; what is the Case in the lower Parts, I do not certainly know; but from the Weather, I have no Doubt but that this Scarcity of Plants is general, thro' the two Colonies. I shall write you more fully by Capt. Browne; and am Dr Sir, Yr. most Hble Sert.

G MASON

RC (PHC). In GM's hand, marked "Copy," and addressed to Lee "⅌ the Shipwright Captn. Brooke." Endorsed with a notation that it was "Recd 18 July 1775" and answered. The endorsement includes: "Entd P B pa[ge] 90 Depos 2," which indicates it was used in the lengthy litigation that followed.

William Lee was Richard Henry Lee's brother. He had established himself as a London merchant specializing in the tobacco trade, and was elected an alderman of the city as a mark of public esteem. This innocent letter introduced a vexing transaction that strained relations between GM and the Lee family, brought a charge of outright dishonesty against William Lee, and was still troubling GM 17 years later. After the open rupture between America and Great Britain, planters with tobacco hogsheads readied them for shipment prior to the nonexportation deadline (10 Sept. 1775) set by Article IV of the Continental Association of 1774. GM's expectation was that prices might exceed those of THE NOTED YEAR 1758, when they ranged between 25 and 50 shillings per cwt. The enormous quantity involved, which may have totaled over 50,000 pounds, was on the other hand a dumping operation that worked against the kind of short supply condition extant in 1757–1759 (J. B. Killebrew and Herbert Myrick, *Tobacco Leaf* . . . [New York, 1923], 7; Hamilton, ed., *Letters to Washington*, II, 379). Nonetheless, GM had reason to suspect that Lee was not attentive to his best interests. At least 11 ensuing letters passed between GM and Lee, and the matter finally was settled by the Virginia courts in GM's favor, but for far less than the bonanza prices GM hoped for when this letter was written. CAPTAIN BROWNE was Edward Browne, Lee's business partner.

To Richard Henry Lee

DEAR SIR.   Gunston-Hall   May 31st: 1775

My Son George has a Mind to spend some Days in Philadelphia, while the Congress is sitting; and as he has been yet very little in the World, & young Fellows are too apt to fall into bad Company, in a place where they have no Acquaintance, I must presume so far on your Friendship as to recommend him to your Notice and Advice, for which I am sure he will be thankful.

We hear Nothing here from the Congress; I presume their Deliberations are (as they ought to be) a profound Secret. I hope the procuring Arms & Amunition next Winter, when the Ships of War can't cruise upon our Coasts, as well as the Means of laying in good Magazines of Provisions &c to the northward, will be properly attended to.

I cou'd almost wish that we paid the Ministry the Compliment of stopping our Exports to Great Britain & the West Indies at the same time their restraining Bills takes place; that our Operations might have a fair Start with theirs, & our Measures have the Appearance of Reprizal. I think you are happy in having Doctr. Franklin at the Congress; as I imagine no Man better knows the Intentions of the Ministry, the Temper of the Nation, & the Interest of the Minority.

The Ship you expected from your Brother into York River, has been arrived about a Fortnight; the Adventure, I believe, will sail next week; she has been delayed a good deal by the Scarcity of Craft. My hundred Hhds. (ninety of them in one Warehouse) were all ready before the Ship came out of Rappahannock, and in order to give her all the Dispatch in my Power (hearing the Capt. cou'd not engage sufficient Craft) I employ'd a Craft myself to carry sixty Hhds. on board. I have wrote by two or three different Vessels for Insurance at £11. Ster: ℔ Hhd. but if you have an Opportunity of writing to yr. Brother from Philadelphia, I shou'd be glad to have the Order repeated.

I most sincerely wish you Health & Happiness, and am, Dr Sir, Your affecte. & obdt. Servt.

G MASON

RC (Lee Papers, ViU). Addressed and apparently placed by Lee into a 1775 file as "No. 286."

Obviously GM expected little good to come from conciliatory gestures by the Congress and was more interested in long-range preparations, as his own involvement in procuring weapons indicated. GM's wish that Great Britain would extend the Restraining Bill to the southern colonies was already a fact. The New England Restraining Bill affected commercial relations between the northern colonies and the maritime world by limiting their trade to Great Britain, Ireland, and the British West Indies, "thus rebuking the Association agreement made by the Continental Congress to ban such trade" (Lawrence Henry Gipson, *The Triumphant Empire* . . . [New York, 1965], 300). Meant to punish New England as the arch-offenders, the plan was extended to the southern colonies when their contumacious conduct was reported in London, and a bill to restrain the trade of Virginia, Maryland, Pennsylvania, New Jersey, and South Carolina received George III's approval on 13 Apr. 1775. (The two bills are printed in Force, comp., *American Archives*, I, 1691-1696 and 1716-1720.) Thus, GM's hope that OUR MEASURES HAVE THE APPEARANCE OF REPRIZAL was realized, though Prof. Gipson asserts that the Continental Association failed to bring irresistible pressure on Parliament. Rather, Gipson reports, there was an active upturn in the British economy during 1775. The presence of DOCTR. FRANKLIN AT THE CONGRESS was a result of Franklin's return to Pennsylvania in the late winter months of 1775 and his immediate appointment as a congressional delegate. MY HUNDRED H[OGSHEA]DS of tobacco had been loaded on the *Adventure* and consigned to William Lee in London for sale, hopefully for skyrocketing prices. See GM's letter to William Lee, 20 May 1775. Although GM was unusually anxious about this huge shipment, it was routine procedure to send many copies of a commercial order to London, to make certain that at least one finally reached its destination.

To William Lee

DEAR SIR   Virginia   Gunston-Hall, June 1st. 1775.

I wrote you the 20th of last Month, informing you that I shou'd ship you one hundred Hhds. of Tobo. ℔ the Adventure Capt. Brown &c. (and sent Duplicates ℔ different Ships) to which I beg Leave to refer. As I don't expect the Bills of Lading will come to my Hands before the Adventure sails, I have desired the Favour of Mr. Edwd.

[236]

Brown to inclose you one of the Bills of Lading ℗ the Ship; and least any Mistake shou'd be made in the Bills of Lading, or the Ship's Books, I think it proper to send you an exact List of the Sd. Hund. Hhds. Seventy Hhds. thereof mark'd G. M._G.^{H}M._G.^{O}M. and G.^{D}M are my own Crops at different Quarters; the thirty Hhds. mark'd G.◊.M. are Rent Tobo. but mostly good Planter's Crops: they were originally in the Planter's Marks; but I order'd them to be remark'd & number'd, as mentioned in the inclosed List. I hope they will come to an excellent Market, and don't doubt your making the most of them: indeed I shou'd imagine, in the present Situation of Affairs, Tobo. must rise to a Price not known before in the present Century; but I think it not improbable that the Parliament may stop the Export from Great Britain, & prolong the Time for Payment of the Duties, in order to keep a Stock for the Home Consumption; shou'd you find this likely to happen, I must desire that my Tobacco may be sold before the next Meeting of Parliament; as such a Measure wou'd greatly reduce the Price: and I am apprehensive that more than ordinary Caution will be necessary in selling to safe Hands; as few Houses can stand such a Shock as the Stopage of the American Trade will give. These are Suggestions of my own; I think they are not ill founded, and submit them to your Consideration.

You may, with the greatest Certainty relye upon the Stopage of our Exports on the 10th of Septemr. next, if not sooner; I am inclined to think they will cease in July; that the operations here may have a fair start with your Fishery & restraining Bills; which instead of dissolving or weakening the American Associations, will only serve to rivet them, by convincing all Ranks of People what they have to expect from the present Ministry. The Americans were pretty unanimous before, but the Acts of the present Session of Parliament, and the Blood lately shed at Boston have fix'd every wavering Mind; and there are no Difficulties or Hardships which they are not determined to encounter with Firmness & Perseverance. God only knows the Event; and in his Hands, confiding in the Justice of our Cause, we chearfully trust it!

The Junto, before this reaches you, will find how egregiously they have been misinform'd & mistaken in the Defection they expected in New-Yorkers no longer hesitate to join with the other colonies in all their Measures for obtaining Redress, the Quakers, to the surprize of every body, are arming, & learning the military-Discipline, thirty two companys, of the Citizens of Philadelphia, appear regularly every morning at Sun rise upon the public Parade, and as a sample of the Defection of North Carolina, I send you Governor Martin's Speech to his Assembly, and their Address.

The provincials have possess'd themselves of Triconderoga and Crown Point, and we have a Report here that a Deputation of eight Indian Chiefs, from the six Nations is arrived at Philadelphia, to offer the Assistance of their People in the common Cause of America; but this wants Confirmation.

There is a full Meeting of the Members of the Congress; but Nothing from it has as yet transpired, except their advice to the People of New-York, respecting their Conduct, in Case of the arrival of Troops there; which no Doubt you will have transmitted in the Northern Papers.

I beg my Compliments to your Lady, with whom I formerly had the Honour of being acquainted at Green Spring; and desire to be remembered to your Brother; of whose Welfare & yours it will always give me pleasure to hear. I am Dear Sir   Your most obdt. Servt.

G MASON

RC (Lee Papers, ViHi). Addressed to Lee "⅌ the Adventure Capt. Brown."

GM had insured this large shipment of tobacco at £11 per hogshead, which meant he valued the cargo at 44 shillings per cwt. or a premium price. Since other planters had similar expectations of unloading their tobacco before the 10 Sept. 1775 deadline imposed by the Continental Association, the London market absorbed a normal inflow of Virginia-Maryland leaf without significant price rises. GM was anxious to show that most of his shipment was in the superior graded planter's tobacco, which bore his special mark burned on the cask. RENT TOBACCO was an inferior grade, gathered in lots of less than 500 pounds and repacked. GM expected that Parliament would alter the system of bonding tobacco for export, so that a shortage in England would not occur. The FISHERY RESTRAINING BILLS were passed by Parliament in the spring of 1775, greatly restricting American commerce and shipping after July 1775 until "the Trade and Commerce of his Majesty's subjects may be carried on without interruption within the said Colonies" (Force, *American Archives*, I, 1719). They were enacted before news of Lexington-Concord reached London, which of course placed colonial resistance in a new light. By THE JUNTO, GM meant the British ministry headed by Lord North, which many Americans considered a conspiratorial body intent upon enslaving the colonies. THE DEFECTION THEY EXPECTED IN NEW-YORKERS and OF NORTH CAROLINA alludes to the tender attitude of Parliament in Feb. and March 1775, when New York and North Carolina were excluded from provisions of the Restraining Bills on the assumption that those two colonies were not implicated in resistance measures. GOVERNOR MARTIN'S SPEECH warned members of the North Carolina General Assembly not to participate in the "illegal" Provincial convention. The North Carolinians ignored Martin's warning, cast their lot with the Continental Congress, and pledged resistance to "a variety of oppressive and unconstitutional proceedings" by Parliament (Force, *American Archives*, II, 264). TRICONDEROGA fell to Ethan Allen's command on 10 May 1775, the same day Seth Warner's forces took CROWN POINT. GM probably saw both events fully reported in the

Annapolis *Md. Gaz.* 25 May 1775. That same newspaper reported Congress's ADVICE TO THE PEOPLE OF NEW-YORK, which was to allow British troops to land in New York but to permit no building of fortifications and to "repel force by force." "GREEN SPRING" was William Lee's home on the James-York peninsula, a palatial establishment Lee acquired by his marriage to Hannah Phillippa Ludwell, WITH WHOM I FORMERLY HAD THE HONOUR OF BEING ACQUAINTED. The brother TO BE REMEMBERED was Arthur Lee.

From Lee Massey

[[*10 July 1775.* GM acknowledged a letter from the Rev. Lee Massey which contained a notice of the Fairfax County freeholders meeting, and also a note from William Ramsay. The meeting was called to pick delegates for the Richmond Convention, and Massey and Ramsay seem to have urged GM to permit his nomination. Not found.]]

To William Ramsay

DEAR SIR: Gunston Hall, July 11, 1775

My friend Mr. Massey sent me yesterday the advertisement for a meeting of the freeholders to-morrow, with a letter from you on the subject; which was the first notice of the county having any intention of requiring my attending the Convention at Richmond next week as one of its representatives. And though ambition has no longer charms for me I am extremely sensible of the obligation I am under to you and the other gentlemen of Alexandria for your favorable opinion. I have considered the matter with the best judgment I am capable of, and am sincerely concerned that my situation in life will not permit me to accept the appointment.

I entreat you, Sir, to reflect on the duty I owe to a poor little helpless family of orphans to whom I now must act the part of father and mother both, and how incompatible such an office would be with the daily attention they require. This I will not enlarge on. Your own feelings will best explain it; and I rely on your friendship to excuse me to the gentlemen of the committee and my other friends. I am dear Sir, &c.,

G. MASON

Printed from Rowland, I, 198. The original Ms was probably in a descendant's hands when Miss Rowland copied it. Her provenance (in 1892) was: "Mason Papers."

Washington had been appointed commander-in-chief of the American army on 15 June, but he had already suggested in a letter of 16 May 1775 that his replacement be selected from Fairfax County to serve in the Virginia Convention. GM's entreaties were for naught, as his fellow citizens chose him to replace Washington at the forthcoming meeting in Richmond.

From William Lee

DEAR SIR! London 13 July 1775
I have just recd. yr. favor of May 20 & am greatly obliged by yr. consignmt. per the Adventure. In consequence of orders from my Br. RH Lee I have insured for you £1000 in the Adventure but on Rect: of yr. £145 more was added mak: on the whole £1145 wch: in case of loss will cover abt. £1100 nett. Unless yr. Tobo: is of a very good quality I cannot flatter you with the prospect of gaining as much by its safe arrival for notwithstanding the very alarmg: prospect of public affairs, the price of Tobo. is just as it was some months ago nor do I think it will rise till after Xtmas and then it will depend a good deal on the quantity that is actually made this year, for the buyers will never believe you are in earnest about not shipg:, if you make it, untill they experience yr. resolution by their want of the commodity; However you maybe assured of my exerting myself to return you a pleasing Acct: of Sales. We every day expect to hear of the Spaniards besieging Gibraltar. Shd. this be the case a Genl. European War will take place in 12 Mos. I am &c.

[WILLIAM LEE]

FC (Lee Letterbook, ViHi). In a copyist's hand, with a margin note indicating that it was carried "℔ Capt. Falconer."

One of GM's letters probably (dated 20 May 1775) had arrived before the cargo came to port. Lee's report of stabilized London tobacco prices was accurate. As was the case with southerners at a later time, GM and his fellow planters believed their staple crop was necessary for British prosperity. What seems to have happened in 1775 and 1776 was that the British decided to look elsewhere for tobacco, since the Navigation laws that had long protected the American market were no longer operative. Thus the great profit GM had hoped to gain proved chimerical, as Lee was suggesting in this letter. On the other hand, Lee's subsequent actions indicate a duplicity on his part that led to lengthy but eventually successful litigation carried on by GM.

To George Washington

[[*ca. 14 July 1775.* GM congratulated Washington upon his appointment as commander of the Continental troops and probably explained his reluctant acceptance of Washington's former place as the Fairfax County delegate to the Richmond Convention. GM noted on 14 Oct. 1775 that he had written this letter "a little before my being ordered to the Convention", where GM was recorded as present on 17 July. The letter is now missing.]]

To Martin Cockburn

DEAR SIR: Richmond, July 24th, 1775

Having an opportunity pr. Edw'd Blackburn (who promises to
drop this at Colchester) I snatch a moment to let you know that I
am well, and to desire to be kindly remembered to my dear children,
and the family at "Springfield." I have not since I came to this place,
except the fast-day and Sunday, had an hour which I could call my
own. The committee (of which I am a member) appointed to
prepare an ordinance for raising an armed force for the defence and
protection of this colony, meet every morning at seven o'clock, sit
till the Convention meets, which seldom rises before five in the
afternoon, and immediately after dinner and a little refreshment sits
again till nine or ten at night. This is hard duty, and yet we have
hitherto made but little progress, and I think shall not be able to
bring in the ordinance till late next week, if then. This will not be
wondered at when the extent and importance of the business before
us is reflected on—to raise forces for immediate service—to new-
model the whole militia—to render about one-fifth of it fit for the
field at the shortest warning—to melt down all the volunteer and
independent companies into this great establishment—to provide
arms, ammunition, &c.,—and to point out ways and means of raising
money, these are difficulties indeed! Besides tempering the powers
of a Committee of Safety to superintend the execution. Such are the
great outlines of the plans in contemplation. I think I may venture to
assert (though nothing is yet fixed on) that in whatever way the
troops are raised, or the militia regulated, the staff officers only will
be appointed by Convention, and the appointment of all the others
devolve upon the county committees. If the colony is parcelled into
different districts for raising a battalion in each, I have proposed that
the committees of each county in the district appoint deputies of
their own members for the purpose; so that every county may have
an equal share in the choice of officers for the battalion, which seems
to be generally approved.

On Wednesday last I gave notice in Convention, that on Monday
I should offer the inclosed resolve; which was accordingly done this
day, and after a long debate, carried by a great majority. The
Convention will to-morrow appoint a delegate to the Congress in
the room of General Washington, when I believe Mr. Wythe will
be almost unanimously chosen. As there will be other vacancies, I
have been a good deal pressed by some of my friends to serve at the

Congress, but shall firmly persist in a refusal, and thereby I hope prevent their making any such proposal in the Convention.

I enclose a letter for my son George (though I suppose he is before this time set off for the Springs) which by some strange mistake came to me from Alexandria per post. We have no news but what is contained in the public papers, which you generally get sooner than we can here. I am, Dr. Sir, your affectionate Friend and Servant,

G. MASON

FC (ViHi). Copied by James Murray Mason, GM's grandson, and sent to the Virginia Historical Society in 1848. Mason wrote William Maxwell in Jan. 1848 that he had made copies of five letters written by GM and "the originals are in possession of my father [John Mason]." The original has long been lost.

Despite his efforts to renounce a more active political role, GM was manuevered into accepting Washington's vacated seat at the Virginia Convention of 1775. On 11 July GM begged to be excused from the chore, yet a week later he was in Richmond and appointed to the select committee to prepare an ordinance to raise and embody "a sufficient Armed Force" (Force, *American Archives*, III, 368). The ordinance was debated at length, amended, and finally read to the Convention on 18 Aug. 1775. GM's role in shaping this major piece of legislation is undefined, but his previous experience on the Fairfax Committee of Safety would have been useful. The ordinance is printed in Force, *American Archives*, III, 397-411. Meanwhile, GM had been appointed to the colony's Committee of Safety which would SUPERINTEND THE EXECUTION of the bill, including the granting of commissions. GM's suggestion that county committees participate in the selection of district battalion officers was part of the ordinance. On 19 July GM had served notice that he would bring in a nonexportation resolution, probably motivated by the British Restraining Act, for it moved the deadline on exports forward from 10 Sept. to 5 Aug. 1775. This was the INCLOSED RESOLVE, printed below, which soon brought wails of protest from Norfolk merchants. GM appears to have been ill when their petition was heard on 1 Aug., but the Convention considered the remonstrance "highly reflecting" on its honor, and absolved GM of the merchants' charge of undue haste. GEORGE WYTHE was appointed as Washington's replacement at the Continental Congress, and GM correctly predicted his own name would soon be thrust forward for a similar post, which he would decline. George Mason, Jr., was unwell and had been advised to spend some time at a medicinal bath, but it is not clear whether THE SPRINGS was one of the hot watering places in old Augusta (now Bath) County, or the sulphur springs in Berkeley County. Young Mason visited both in a vain search for health (see GM to Washington, 8 Mar. 1779; GM to George Mason, Jr., 8 Jan. 1783).

Nonexportation Resolution
Virginia Convention of 1775

Resolved [24 July 1775]

That no Flour, Wheat or other Grain, or Provisions of any kind be exported from this Colony to any Part of the World, from and after the fifth Day of August next, until the Convention or Assembly of this Colony, or the honourable the continental Congress shall order otherwise; that no Quantitys of the said Articles, more than are necessary for the Use of the Inhabitants, be brought to, collected, or stored in the Towns, or other Places upon or near the navigable Waters; that the respective County-Committees be directed to take Care that this Resolve be effectually carried into Execution; and that all Contracts made for the Sale and Delivery of any such Articles for Exportation between this Time and the tenth Day of September next be considered as null and void.

Resolved also, that it be recommended to the Inhabitants of this Colony, with five Miles of Tide-Water, not to thresh out more of their Wheat than may from Time to Time be wanted for Home-Consumption; unless the same be imediatly removed at leas[t] five Miles from any Landing.

Ms (Vi). In GM's handwriting. A copy was enclosed in GM's letter to Martin Cockburn, 24 July 1775.

Concern over a food shortage seems to have promoted the convention to move the 10 Sept. deadline on exportations forward to 5 Aug. GM probably was unaware that on 17 July the Continental Congress had opened a loophole in the nonexportation agreement. In a desperate measure to encourage the importation of arms and ammunition, the Congress voted to exempt vessels importing munitions from the Continental Association "within nine months from the date of this Resolution, [and they] shall be permitted to load and export the produce of these Colonies, to the value of such Powder and Stores . . . the Non-Exportation Agreement notwithstanding." (Force, *American Archives*, II, 1883). Norfolk merchants reacted quickly to GM's resolution, and on 1 Aug. complained of the "great hardships and inconveniences" it would impose upon them (Force, *American Archives*, III, 372). Three days later the convention rejected their protest as "directly tending to destroy that necessary confidence reposed by the good people of this Colony in their Representatives." GM's resolution "was not adopted with great haste, as unjustly insinuated" in the Norfolk petition, but "was done on the maturest deliberation, a Member of the convention having given previous notice that, at a future day, he intended to move for such a Resolution. . . ." The delegates acknowledged the risk of damage to stored wheat, and conceded that the previous year's crop of maize should be exempted from the provision upon "proper proofs" that "they had actually provided or chartered vessels" prior to the 24 July resolution. The merchants also had to give county committees of safety assurances that the corn would not be shipped to any "of the Northern Colonies" where it might fall into enemy hands. However, on 8 Aug., a letter from the Maryland Convention delegates indicated to Peyton Randolph that they would not pass a similar resolution. The Richmond Convention then decided to repeal GM's resolve because "the good purposes intended by the said Resolution cannot be effected without a general agreement of the neighbouring Provinces" (Force, *American Archives*, III, 376).

From William Lee

DEAR SIR!   London, 29 July 1775

The Adventure Capt. Brown is arrived & brot. me yr. very obliging favr. of June 1st wth: 100 hhds of yr. Tobo. wch: I before wrote you via Phila. were insured according to yr. orders. You may be assured of my best endeavors to return you satisfactory Sales, but the situation of things here is so perplexed & alarming that it is impossible to judge with precision whether it will be best to sell now or wait the Winter market; for my own part I am inclined to think the prices are now as high as they will be for 6 Mos: to come & if the event of parliamtry: interposition wch: you apprehend, & not without reason, shd: interfere things will not mend. When we consider the great loss of weight, especially when Tobo: is landed at this season of the year it is perhaps most advantageous to sell as soon as possible, however as I am fortunately not in distress for money, you may rely on my acting as appears to me most beneficial for you. The present prices, tho' no great demand, are for export 3¼ to 4⅌ lb. for the best stout, waxy & black Jas. River Tobo:. The home consumption price not better, unless for the finest York river & clean good stemd Tobo:. it is clear to me that the American trade to G.B. can never be restored to its former channel. I have more at stake in this business than most people, however the love I have for my Country, as well as an ardent affection for universal Liberty makes me submit with patience to the decrees of Providence which I am convinced over rules in this unhappy contest between G.B. & the Colonies;—therefore I am sure, as *Justice* is the most amiable attribute of an almighty direction, that you must in the end be successful. We have only the Ministl.: Acct.: of the Bloody engagemt: on the 17 June at Charles Town near Boston, wch: from thence appears greatly to the disadvantage of the Regulars. The Ministers still have no thought of relentg: & fresh supplies of Arms & Ammunition are preparing to be sent to Boston. All I can say is, Quem Deus vult perdere, prius dementat—America must now be a great Empire or a sink for Slaves. Mrs: Lee & my Br. are much obliged by yr. kind Remembrance & I am &c

[WILLIAM LEE]

FC (Lee Letterbook, ViHi). In a clerk's hand; partially quoted in Worthington Chauncey Ford, ed., *Letters of William Lee* . . . (Brooklyn, 1891), I, 167–168.
Price discrepancies for tobacco sold in the last half of 1775 by London agents caused bitterness and court action that lingered long beyond the Revolution. GM's buoyant hopes of May 1775 led him to expect premium prices for his large shipment, a hope based on a presumed shortage resulting from nonexportation policies after 10 Sept. 1775. But other planters reasoned the same way, and apparently the London market absorbed some dumping by planters until the winter months arrived, when it was clear that the colonies were in earnest about the two-way boycott. Lee eventually reported to GM that he sold the 100 hogsheads for £1053 in 1775, or slightly more than £10 per hogshead. By 5

Sept. 1775 tobacco prices had slipped to 11–12 shillings per cwt. (John Norton to Nathaniel Littleton Savage, 2 Feb. 1776, in Francis Norton Mason, *John Norton & Sons Merchants of London and Virginia* . . . [Richmond, 1937], 395). GM had insured the cargo for £1,100 and might have been content except that prices rose dramatically later in the year (*ibid.*, 464–465). Raw statistics tell the story of skyrocketing prices on the London tobacco market after 1775, when British warehouses took 101,337,361 lbs. of American tobacco against 14,698,400 lbs. in 1776 and 361,394 lbs. in 1777 (David Macpherson, comp., *Annals of Commerce* [London, 1805], IV, 37). THE BLOODY ENGAGEM[EN]T ON 17 JUNE was the Battle of Bunker Hill. The Latin version of a Greek quotation is translated: "Whom God wishes to destroy, he first deprives of reason," and was attributed to Euripides by James Boswell in his *Life of Johnson* (1783 ed.).

To Martin Cockburn

DEAR SIR. Richmond Augt. 5th. 1775.

Capt. Grayson informing me that he shall set out on his Return Home to-morrow, I take the Opportunity of writing to you, tho' I have Nothing very agreeable to communicate. We are getting into great Confusion here, & I fear running the Country to an Expence it will not be able to bear—3,000 Men are voted as a Body of standing Troops, to be forthwith raise, & form'd into three Regiments, the first to be commanded by Mr. Patrick Henry, the second by Colo. Thos. Nelson, & the third by Mr. Wm. Woodford. A great push was made for Colo. Mercer of Fredericksburg to the 1st. Regiment; but he lost it by a few Votes, upon the Question between him and Mr. Henry; tho' he had a majority upon the Ballot.

The Expence of the last Indian war will be near £150,000, our Share of the Expence of the continental Army £150,000 more, the Charge of the Troops now raising, & the Minute-Men with their Arms &c. £350,000; these added together will make an enormous Sum, & there are several Charges still behind; such as the Voluntier Compys at Williamsburg, the Payment of the Members of the Convention &c. However nothing is yet absolutely conclusive, & some Abridgement may yet perhaps be made; tho' at present there is little Prospect of it.

As it is proposed that a Company of fifty Men for the standing Army shall be raised in each County, my Son George may perhaps have a Mind to enter into the Service; in which Case, pray tell him that it will be very contrary to my Inclination, & that I advise him by all Means against it. When the Plan for the Minute-Men is compleated, if he has a Mind to enter into that I shall have no Objection: as I look upon it to be the true natural, and safest

[245]

Defence of this, or any other free Country; & as such, wish to see it encouraged to the utmost. I shou'd have wrote to him but that it was uncertain whether he was at Home, or at the Springs.

I have been very unwell, & unable to attend the Convention for two or three Days, but am now getting better, & attended again to Day, & am going out to morrow to visit a Friend in the Country. God knows when I shall get home again. Remember me kindly to my dear children—the family at Springfield; & all Friends; and believe me Dr. Sir, Yr. affect. Friend and Servt.

G. MASON

RC (Mason Papers, DLC). Addressed and endorsed as received on 9 Aug. GM's appears to have given the letter to William Grayson, who forwarded it to Alexander Henderson at Colchester.

GM had an adversion to standing armies and was not convinced that three Virginia regiments were needed to be in readiness for any projected British invasion. Hugh Mercer had 41 votes and Henry 40 on the first ballot when the 1st Regt. colonelcy was being determined, but on the second count Henry was selected (Force, *American Archives*, III, 375).

The modernized version printed in Rowland, I, 203–204, is incorrectly dated 25 Aug. 1775.

To George Washington

[[*ca. 6 Aug. 1775*. GM wrote Washington on 14 Oct. that he had previously written to the general "in August from Richmond" with hints of "the Partys & Factions which prevail'd" at the Convention. GM found the experience painful and was at times ill, a fact he may have relayed to Washington while giving the current state of vital legislation. Not found.]]

An Ordinance for Establishing a General Test Oath

[19 August 1775]

WHEREAS the long premeditated and now avowed Design of the British Ministry to force Loyal Colonists into an abject surrender of their Rights and Priveleges as Freemen, are still persisted in by the British Government and have been lately attempted to be carried into execution in this Colony by Lord Dunmore as Chief Majestrate, by an unexampled & wanton suspension of the Law of the Land & Institution of that horrid Supporter of Tyranny, Law Martial, by seising, and imprisoning and transporting the persons of our peaceable Citizens, by declaring our Servants and Slaves free and inviting & arming them to assassinate their Masters, our innocent Wifes and

[246]

helpless Children, which cruel and horrid Measures have been countenanced & supported by some wicked Persons among ourselves in wanton violation of their plighted Faith voluntarily offered in support of our late happy Constitution: It is now become indispensably necessary, by an Appeal to Heaven, to enter into a more firm Union for our common defence, and to distinguish those deserving our Protection from such as are Enemies to our just Cause.

Be it therefore ordained by the Delegates and Representatives of the several Counties and Corporations within this Colony and Dominion of Virginia now assembled in General Convention And it is hereby Ordained by the authority of the same, that the Committees of the several Counties & Corporations within this Colony, having themselves first taken & subscribed [th]e following Oath in Committee, shall and they are hereby authorized and required to appoint such of their Members as they may think proper, to render the same to be taken & subscribed by each & every Freeman within their Counties above the age of sixteen years Vizt. "I ——— ——— of the Parish of ——— in the County of ——— in the Colony of Virginia do solemnly & sincerely promise & declare that I will not directly or indirectly violate the Association now in force in this Colony but that I will conform thereto so long as the same shall continue in force; that I will not take up Arms against the good People Freemen Inhabitants of this Colony or any other part of America acting under & in support of the Ordinances of general Convention during the unhappy differences now subsisting between Great Britain and America, nor will I directly or indirectly by correspondence, Signs or Tokens or by any ways or means aid, assist, or support any Power that shall or may be emploied against the good People of America: And I do declare that I will defend and support this Colony against all Invasions & Insurrections whatsoever that shall or may be made against the Rights & Liberties of America according to my abilities & pursuant to ordinances of General Convention—So help me God—

Provided always that the people called Quakers shall affirm to the same effect & also subscribe the same.

And be it farther Ordained by the authority aforesaid that the Members of the Committee appointed as aforesaid & each & every [one] of them be and they are hereby authorized & required to tender the said Declaration to be made sworn to, affirmed & subscribed as aforesaid to the several persons, within such districts as shall be described by the said Committees and to return to their respective Committees the names of the persons taking and subscribing the same, also a List of those who shall refuse so to do, within three months after their appointment, to be carefully filed & preserved by the said Committees, and every person so appointed & neglecting to return such List shall be subject to a fine to be inflicted by the respective Committees not exceeding——Pounds.

And be it farther Ordained that the respective Committees shall and may and they are hereby required to summon all persons so refusing to take the Oath or make the Affirmation aforesaid to appear before them in Committee, where the said Oath shall be again tendered to such persons to be taken and subscribed and upon their refusing so to do, the said Committee shall enter such refusal in their Minutes describing the persons so refusing, their place of Nativity, Residence and occupation & thereupon order every person so refusing to be disarmed & not to depart above five Miles from their place of Residence 'til the further order of the said Committee, without a special Licence in writing from them. And in case such Persons shall fail to appear before the said Committee when duly summon'd the said Committee shall order them to be summoned again & in case of a second failure to attend, upon proof on Oath of such Summons being served, the said Committee shall proceed against them in the same manner as is directed against persons appearing & refusing as aforementioned.

And be it farther ordained that all & every person so refusing or failing to attend the Committees as aforesaid & being entered on their Minutes as Delinquents shall & they are hereby declared to be subject to the payment of treble Taxes as imposed by Ordinance of last Convention during the Continuance therof; to commence & be payable by or before the tenth Day of June next, to be levied & collected by such persons as the Committee of the several Countys shall appoint, who shall account for the same with the Treasurer of this Colony for the time being in the same manner and under the like Penalties as are directed by the last mentioned Ordinance respecting the collection of the other Taxes imposed thereby. And to the end that such persons may be distinguished from the worthy Members of the Community, the County Committees aforesaid shall publish the names of such Delinquents in the Virginia Gazette—Provided always and be it further Ordained that if any such Delinquent shall at any time within six months after his refusal being enter[ed] as aforesaid, be willing & shall make Oath (or being one of the People called Quakers shall make affirmation) as aforesaid before the Committee of the County wherein his default was entered, such Committee shall admit him so to do & grant Certificate thereof and in such case, such Delinquent shall thence forward be exempt from all Penalties and Restrictions imposed by this Ordinance, in the same manner as if he had originally conformed to the Regulations thereof.

Tr (Vi). In a clerk's handwriting, with interlineations in an unidentified hand. Endorsed: "An Ordinance for establishing a general Test" and dated.

On 16 Aug. 1775 GM and Josiah Parker of Isle of Wight County were instructed by the Convention to draft this ordinance. In a letter of 22 Aug. GM said he "drew the ordinance for a general Test" and the Richmond merchants were "well pleased with it." The Convention postponed action on the ordinance on 25 Aug. (Force, *American Archives*, III, 390), but approved GM's resolution that same day which made the British merchants rest easier (*q.v.*). The language of the preamble reflects the Virginians' shocked reaction to Lord Dunmore's practice of offering slaves freedom in return for service to the British cause. The NOW AVOWED DESIGN OF THE BRITISH MINISTRY related to the conspiracy charges which GM and other colonists believed true (see Bailyn, ed. *Pamphlets of the American Revolution*, I, 88–89). GM's thinking was attuned to the prevailing practice of justifying revolutionary actions by citing British misdeeds (Gordon S. Wood, "Rhetoric and Reality in the American Revolution," *WMQ*, 3rd Ser., XXIII [1966], 26–32). As an architect of the committee of safety system, GM was inclined to keep as much power as possible in local hands. Bearing in mind the 18th-century belief in the efficacy of oaths, GM was creating a surveillance system for the county committees that would have eased enforcement of the Nonimportation or Continental Associations. GM was also sensitive to the merchants' distress, as they wished to escape the onus of their birthplace and could have taken this oath without being disloyal subjects. By its inaction, however, the Convention allowed the matter to rest with GM's 25 Aug. resolution recommending "lenity and friendship" toward well-disposed Britons. In 1777, a regular oath of allegiance for all males over 16 was passed by the Virginia legislature (Hening, IX, 281–283) when GM was absent because of illness.

Several additions have not been set apart, since none of the handwriting is GM's. The four-page Ms may have been prepared by the convention clerk, John Tazewell.

From George Washington

[[*20 Aug. 1775*. GM acknowledged a letter of this date from Washington which must have been a reply to GM's earlier note congratulating the new commander-in-chief upon his appointment. As Washington had moved into a larger sphere of action and influence, GM assured his neighbor that "I shall always think myself honour'd by your Correspondence & Friendship" (GM to Washington, 14 Oct. 1775). Washington's letter has not been found.]]

To Martin Cockburn

DEAR SIR   Richmond   Augt 22d 1775.

Colo. Blackburn telling me he shall set out for Pr. Wm. [Prince William County] to-day, I take the opportunity of informing you that I am now pretty well, tho' I was exceedingly indisposed for several Days, some of which I was confined to my Bed, but a little fresh Air, good Water, & exceeding kind & hospitable Treatment from a neighbouring Country Gentleman has recover'd me. I have found my Apprehensions in being sent to this Convention but too well verified. Before the Choice of Delegates for the ensueing Congress, I was personally applied to by more than two thirds of the Members, insisting upon my serving at the Congress, but by assuring them that I cou'd not possibly attend, I prevailed on them not to name me, except abt. twenty who wou'd take no Excuse. A Day or two after, upon Colo. Bland's Resignation, a strong Party was form'd at the Head of which were Colo. Henry, Mr. Jefferson, & Colo. Carrington, for sending me to the Congress at all Events, laying it down as a Rule that I wou'd not refuse if ordered by my Country: in Consequence of this, just before the Ballot, I was publickly called upon in Convention, & obliged to make a public Excuse, & give my Reasons for refusal, in doing which I felt myself more distress'd than ever I was in my Life, especially when I saw Tears run down the President's cheeks. I took Occasion, at the same time, to recommend Colo. Francis Lee; who was accordingly chosen in the room of Colo. Bland. But my getting clear of this Appointment has avail'd me little, as I have been since, in Spite of every thing I cou'd do to the Contrary, put upon the Committee of Safety; which is even more inconvenient & disagreeable to me than going to the Congress. I endeavour'd to excuse myself, & beg'd the Convention wou'd permit me to resign; but was answer'd by an universal NO. The 3,000 regular Troops (exclusive of the western frontier Garrisons) first proposed to be raised are reduced to 1,000 to be form'd into two regiments, one of eight the other of seven Compys. These 15 Compys are to be raised in the 15 western Shoar Districts, the Captains & subaltern Officers to be appointed by the Committee of the respective District, form'd by a Deputation of three Members from the Committee of each County in the District. The first Regiment is commanded by Colo. Henry, Lieut. Colo. Christian, & Majr. Eppes, the second Regiment by Colo. Wm. Woodford, Lieut. Colo. Chs. Scott & Majr. Spotswood. A Regiment of Minute-Men of 680 rank & file, is to be raised in the Eastern Shoar District, & a regiment of 500 rank & File in each of the fifteen Districts on the Western Shoar with the same Field & Staff Officers, Chaplain, Surgeon &c. as the regiments of regulars, & wth. the same Pay, when upon Duty in the District, or drawn into actual Service—the officers

[250]

to be appointed by the District Committees, & commissioned by the Committee of Safety—the militia Officers are all to give up their present Commissions, & be nominated by the respective Committees of the Counties, the militia Companys to be exercised once a Fortnight, except the three winter Months, & general County Musters twice a Year. Arms Tents &c. to be provided for the Minute-Men at the public Charge. These are the great out-lines of our Plan of Defence which I think a good, tho' a very expensive one; the particulars wou'd take up too much room for a common Letter; paricular rules are drawn up for the better regulation & Government of the Army; to which both the Minute-Men and Militia are subjected when drawn out into actual Service. The volunteer Companys are all discharged & melted down in the plan for the Regiments of Minute-Men. These Informations you may rely on, as the Ordinance Yesterday received it's final fiat.

There are several ordinances under the Consideration of the Committee of the whole House & nearly compleated, vizt. one for the raising of Money & imposing Taxes, one for furnishing Arms & encouraging the making Salt-petre, Sulphur, Powder & Lead, one for appointing a Committee of safety & defining it's Powers, which are very extensive, one for regulating the Elections of Delegates & County Committees, & one for establishing a general Test. The Maryland Convention not concurring in the Resolve for imediatly stoping the Export of Provision[s], it became necessary to rescind ours; that our ports, as well [as] theirs, might be kept open til the 10th of Sept.

A very sensible petition from the merchants who are Natives of great Britain has been put into my Hands, & will be presented to-day or to-morrow praying that some certain Line of Conduct may be prescribed to them, & a recommendation to the people from the Convention, respecting them. As I drew the ordinance for a general Test, I have endeavour'd to make it such as no good Man wou'd object to: the Merchants here declare themselves well pleased with it. Pray excuse me to Mr. Massey, Mr. McCarty, Mr. Henderson, & all enquiring Friends for not writing to them, & tell them I consider all public news wrote to you, as to be communicated to them, & such of my Constitutents as desire Information.

I expect the Convention will rise abt. the End of this or the Begining of next week. The Members of the Committee of safety (of which I send you a List) meet next Friday; how long I shall be detain'd on that Business God only knows. My kind Regards to my

dear Family, & to the Family at Spring-field conclude me. Dr
Sir   Yr. affectn. Friend & Sert.

G MASON

P.S.   Every Ordinance goes thro all the Formalities
of a Bill in the House of Burgesses has three
readings &c. before it is passed, & in every
respect wears the Face of Law. Resolves or
Recommendations being no longer trusted to in
Matters of Importance.

RC (Mason Papers, DLC). Addressed and overwritten with fragmentary
notes.

COLO. BLACKBURN was Thomas Blackburn, the Prince William County convention delegate. GM's fear of becoming heavily involved in revolutionary
politics were confirmed when A STRONG PARTY WAS FORM'D . . . FOR SENDING ME
TO THE CONGRESS. GM was not nominated on 11 Aug. when the annual election
for the Continental Congress delegation was held, but when Richard Bland
declined his appointment on 15 Aug. GM was nominated as Bland's replacement. He then served on the committee "to examine the ballot-box," which
reported one vote for GM, one for John Banister, 37 for Francis Lightfoot Lee,
and 36 for Carter Braxton (Force, *American Archives*, III, 382). The tearful
convention PRESIDENT was Peyton Randolph. On 17 Aug. GM was chosen to
the Committee of Safety, running second in a field of 11 candidates behind
Edmund Pendleton. GM was a member of the committee which drafted "An
Ordinance for raising and embodying a sufficient Force for the defence and
protection of this Colony" which passed on 21 Aug. 1775 (Hening, IX, 9–35).
This was the first revolutionary legislation GM contributed to which required
vast knowledge and much committee work, and its enactment was de facto
proof that Virginia intended to wage a full scale war. The army thus raised
was to be under the direct control of the Committee of Safety. GM and Josiah
Parker were appointed to the committee FOR ESTABLISHING A GENERAL TEST oath
on 16 Aug. and GM reported to the convention with a proposal on 19 Aug.
The convention postponed final action on the oath bill on 25 Aug. A VERY
SENSIBLE PETITION FROM THE MERCHANTS was presented to the convention on 25
Aug., (Force, *American Archives*, III, 391–392). The petitioners declared
themselves ready to share the civilian's burdens of resistance against their
"Parent State," but asked for guidelines so that "they may move as useful
members of the community, without being held to the necessity of shedding
the blood of their countrymen. . . ." GM seems to have written the convention
resolution (*q.v.*), which was unanimously adopted, that held the merchants'
petition was reasonable and urged the county committees of safety and the
citizenry in general "to treat all natives of *Great Britain*, resident here, as do
not show themselves enemies to the common cause of America, with lenity
and friendship." The convention adjourned on 26 Aug. 1775. The Virginia
Committee of Safety named included GM, Pendleton, John Page, Richard
Bland, Thomas Ludwell Lee, Paul Carrington, Dudley Digges, William Cabell,
Carter Braxton, James Mercer, and John Tabb. GM's candid thoughts upon the
convention's proceedings and his colleagues were expressed in a letter to
Washington on 14 Oct. 1775.

The last of the four pages has been used for some monetary calculations and
is overwritten in a handwriting other than GM's: "L Massey/for Colchester/&
to be kept in appropriate paper/for the Use of the Family." A modernized text
of this letter is printed in Rowland, I, 206–208.

Resolution concerning Peaceable British Subjects Resident in Virginia

[25 August 1775]

Resolved, unanimously, That the said Petition is reasonable, and it is recommended to the Committees of the several Counties and Corporations, and others the good people of this Colony, to treat all natives of *Great Britain*, resident here, as do not show themselves enemies to the common cause of *America*, with lenity and friendship; to protect all persons whatsoever in the just enjoyment of their civil rights and liberty; to discountenance all national reflections; to preserve, to the utmost of their power, internal peace and good order; and to promote union, harmony, and mutual good-will, among all ranks of people.

Resolved, also, That the said Petition, together with this Resolve, be forthwith published in the *Virginia Gazettes*.

Printed from the journal of the convention in Force, *American Archives*, III, 392.

This resolution is printed in the convention journal below the petition of British merchants seeking guidance "in this dangerous crisis." GM noted on 22 Aug. that "A very sensible petition from the merchants who are Natives of great Britain has been put into my Hands. . . ." The "Ordinance for a general test" which GM drafted had been postponed by the Convention earlier in the day, but this resolution carried its own message to the county committees of safety and seems to have achieved its goal, for a general test oath was not passed by the Virginia legislature until 1777. That the matter was more real than theoretical is proved by the concurrent incident in Maryland, where a Harford County merchant was declared "an enemy to America" and banished (Robert Purviance, *A Narrative of Events . . . During the Revolutionary War* [Baltimore, 1849], 37–39). The merchant was James Christie of the firm of Wilson & Christie, almost certainly a Scotsman.

From William Aylett

[[*29 Sept. 1775*. Aylett was acting as commissary for the Virginia troops authorized by the Richmond convention, and his colonel's commission probably was authorized by the Committee of Safety meeting at Hanover between 18 and 21 Sept. (Edmund Pendleton to Commissary of Purchases, 1 Sept. 1775, in David John Mays, ed., *The Letters and Papers of Edmund Pendleton, 1734–1803* [Charlottesville, 1967], I, 118). He apparently asked GM for details about supplies that might have been available in Fairfax County (GM to Aylett, 2 Oct. 1775). Not found.]]

To William Aylett

DEAR SIR.   Gunston-Hall Octer. 2d. 1775

Your Favour of the 29th. ulto. from Dumfries, did not come to Hand 'til last night. I had upon the Committee of Safety's first Meeting at Hanover Town, transmitted to the President an Acct. of such Articles for the Use of the Troops, as cou'd be procured in this Part of the Country, wth. the Terms of Sale &c. and desired to know whether the Committee wou'd have any, & what Part of them purchased; but have not Yet recd. any Answer. I imagine the Gentn were at a Loss what Directions to give respecting them, until they cou'd have an Acct. of the Articles you had previously contracted for; as soon as they are inform'd of those, I presume they will give Orders for purchasing such Articles as may still be wanted in the Invoyce I sent them. I observe you mention among the Articles not yet procured, coarse white Linnens; I am afraid it will be very difficult to get them, as I know of none to be had upon any Terms in this Part of the Country, except about fifteen or sixteen pr. of 7/8 Garlia, imported by the Ohio Compy several Years ago, which I forgot to mention to the Committee; they have always been kept dry, & close pack'd up in a Chest; so that I believe they are not damaged: They cost from 30/ to 44/-Ster: ℔ pr. & I think might answer for Soldier's Shirts. Every thing else which I have been able to find out fit for the Troops, to be purchased in this Neighbourhood, the Comm[ittee] have been already fully inform'd of. I am Dr. Sir Your most Hble. Sert.

G MASON

P.S.

I have been very ill lately, & am now barely able to walk about the House.

RC (Vi). Addressed to King William County, to be carried by Lt. Col. William Christian of the 1st Virginia Regiment. Endorsed, with the covering side bearing practice lines from an unknown writer's pen [William Armistead?].

Aylett was a convention delegate from King William County and became the Virginia Regiment commissary. The Committee of Safety was scheduled to meet at Hanover on 18 Sept. to provide for contracts, military stores, deliver commissions, "administer the Oaths to the Field-Officers of the Regulars chosen by the Convention" as well as the district subalterns in attendance, and receive the recruiting levies (Force, *American Archives*, III, 435). The 7/8 GARLIA obviously refers to a textile and may have been GM's spelling of "Gaelic" or "garland," although neither the *Oxford English Dictionary* nor

Bailey's *English Dictionary* (1755 ed.) indicate such usage. Apparently GM had access to Ohio Company goods that must have been stored in the Northern Neck, and possibly at Gunston Hall.

To George Washington

DEAR SIR.   Virginia, Gunston-Hall, Octor. 14th. 1775.

I wrote you in July, a little before my being ordered to the Convention, congratulating you upon an Appointment, which gives so much Satisfaction to all America; and afterwards in August from Richmond: since which I have to acknowledge your Favour of the 20th. of Augt. which nothing but want of Health shou'd have prevented my doing sooner, as I shall always think myself honour'd by your Correspondence & Friendship. I hinted to you in my last the Partys & Factions which prevail'd at Richmond: I never was in so disagreeable a Situation, and almost despaired of a Cause which I saw so ill conducted. Mere Vexation & Disgust threw me into such an ill State of Health that before the Convention rose, I was sometimes near fainting in the House: since my Return Home I have had a severe Fit of Sickness, from which I am now recovering; but am still very weak & low.

During the first Part of the Convention Partys run so high, that we had frequently no other Way of preventing improper Measures but by Procrastination, urging the previous Question, & giving Men time to reflect: however after some Weeks, the Bablers were pretty well silenced, a few weighty Members began to take the Lead, several wholsome Regulations were made, and if the Convention had continued to sit a few Days longer, I think the public Safety wou'd have been as well provided for as our present Circumstances permit. The Convention, not thinking this a time to relye upon Resolves & Recommendations only, and to give obligatory Force to their Proceedings, adopted the Style & Form of Legislation, changing the Word enact into *ordain:* their Ordinances were all introduced in the Form of Bills, were regularly referred to a Committee of the whole House, and underwent three Readings before they were passed. I inclose you the Ordinance for raising an arm'd Force for the Defence & protection of this Colony: it is a little defaced by being handled at our District Committee, but it is the only Copy I had at present bye me. You will find some little Inaccuracies in it; but upon the whole, I hope it will merit your Approbation. The Minute-Plan I think is a wise one, & will in a short time furnish 8,000 good Troops, ready for Action, & composed of men in whose Hands the

Sword may be safely trusted: to defray the Expence of the Provisions made by this Ordinance, & to pay the Charge of the last Year's Indian War, we are now emitting the Sum of 350,000 £ in paper Curry. I have great Apprehensions that the large Sums in Bills of Credit now issueing all over the Continent may have fatal Effects in depreciating the Value, and therefore opposed any Suspension of Taxation, and urged the necessity of imediatly laying such Taxes as the People cou'd bear, to sink the Sum emitted as soon as possible; but was able only to reduce the proposed Suspension from three Years to one. The Land & poll-Tax (the Collection of which is to commence in June 1777) will sink 50,000 £ per Year; & instead of the usual Commissions for emitting & receiving, the Treasurer is allowed an annual Sallery of 625 £. Our Friend the Treasurer was the warmest Man in the Convention for imediatly raising a standing Army of not less than 4000 men, upon constant Pay: they stood a considerable time at 3000, exclusive of the Troops upon the western Frontiers; but at the last reading (as you will see by the ordinance) were reduced to 1020 rank & file. In my Opinion a well judged Reduction, not only from our inability to furnish at present such a number with Arms & Ammunition, but I think it extreamly imprudent to exhaust ourselves before we know when we are to be attack'd: the Part we have to act at present seems to require our laying in good Magazines, training our people, & having a good Number of them ready for action. An ordinance is passed for regulating an annual Election of Members to the Convention, & County-Committees—for encouraging the making Salt petre, sulphur & gunpowder—for establishing a Manufactory of Arms, under the Direction of Commissioners; and for appointing a Committee of Safety, consisting of eleven members, for carrying the Ordinances of the Convention into Execution, directing the Stations of the Troops, & calling the Minute Battalions, & Draughts from the Militia into Service, if necessary, &c.

There is also an Ordinance establishing Articles for the Government of the Troops, principally taken from those drawn up by the Congress, except that a Court Martial upon Life & Death is more cautiously constituted, & brought nearer to the Principles of the common Law.

Many of the principal Familys are removing from Norfolk, Hampton, York & Williamsburg, occasioned by the Behaviour of Lord Dunmore; & the Commanders of the King's Ships & Tenders upon this Station.

Whenever Your Leisure will permit, it will always give me the greatest Pleasure to be inform'd of your Welfare, & to hear what is doing on the great American Theatre.

I most sincerely wish You Health, and Success equal to the Justice of our Cause; and am, with great respect, Dear Sir Your affecte. & obdt. Servt.

G. MASON

P.S.

I beg the favour of you to remember me kindly to General Lee, & present him my respectful Compliments.

RC (Washington Papers, DLC). Addressed: "His Excellency General Washington."

GM's letters to Washington written in July and Aug. are missing, as is YOUR FAVOUR OF THE 20TH. OF AUGT. The PARTYS & FACTIONS . . . AT RICHMOND which disgusted GM were common to most colonial assemblies in 1775, and as Edmund Pendleton described the three contending groups: "The Sanguine are for rash Measures without consideration, the Flegmatic to avoid that extreme are afraid to move at all, while a third Class take the middle way and endeavor by tempering the first sort and bringing the latter into action to draw all together to a Steddy, tho' Active Point of defense . . . ," (Pendleton to Joseph Chew, 15 June 1775, in Mays, ed., *Pendleton Papers*, I, 110). GM was probably working in the moderate unit—the "third Class"—by the middle of Aug. Several delegates had come to Richmond after serving at Philadelphia and their presence may account for GM's distinction between THE FIRST PART OF THE CONVENTION and the business after 9 Aug. when the congressional delegation (including Jefferson, Henry, and Pendleton) arrived. THE ORDINANCE FOR RAISING AN ARM'D FORCE was a committee production, but GM seems to have been a prime mover in the business (Force, *American Archives*, III, 397–418). OUR FRIEND THE TREASURER was Robert Carter Nicholas, ordinarily a moderate rather than THE WARMEST MAN on money and military matters. The legislation mentioned by GM is printed in Hening, IX, 35–74. The Virginia military code WAS BROUGHT NEARER TO THE PRINCIPLES OF THE COMMON LAW by providing that a death sentence "shall not be pronounced unless twelve [out of fifteen members] of the Court-Martial concur in such sentence." THE BEHAVIOUR OF LORD DUNMORE threatened landings by British troops between Norfolk and Williamsburg, and later fear spread to the Potomac and Chesapeake Bay region. GENERAL LEE was Charles Lee, then Washington's second-in-command, whom GM probably had met at Mount Vernon in Dec. 1774.

The paragraph beginning "There is also an Ordinance . . ." was written in the left margin of the fourth (and last) Ms page. A modernized text is printed in Rowland, I, 210–212.

To John Hancock

SIR   Virginia, Fairfax County Novemr. 23rd. 1775.

The Committee of this County inform'd of the present Scarcity of Salt in this Colony in general, & in this Part of it in particular, sensible of the Difficulty, perhaps Impracticability of procuring it, if not done this Winter, and apprehensive of the great Distress and Discontent that the Want of this necessary Article may occasion among the People, as well as the Impossibility of furnishing proper provisions for the Regiments of Minute-Men & Draughts from our Militia which may be call'd into Service next Spring, have directed us to apply to the honble the Continental Congress, praying them to encourage the Importation of Salt, either by permitting the Exportation of Country-Produce in Return, in such Manner as is allowed upon the Importation of Military-Stores, or in such other Manner as that honble Board shall judge best. We beg Leave Sir, thro' you, to lay the Request, as a Matter of the utmost Importance to the good People of this Colony, & the public Service, before the Gentlemen of the Congress, and are, with the greatest Respect, Sir

Your most obdt. Servts.

G MASON
JOHN DALTON
WM. RAMSEY
JOHN CARLYLE
JOHN MUIR
JAMES KIRK

} Committee of Correspondence for Fairfa[x] County

RC (Papers of Continental Congress, DNA). Addressed and endorsed. Both pages are in GM's handwriting (except the signatures).

The nonexportation ban was in effect after 10 Sept. 1775, so that the permission of Congress was needed to lift the embargo on produce. The committee's petition and similar entreaties probably went to the Virginia delegation, and in any event produced results, for on 15 Dec. Congress passed a resolution permitting George Meade & Co., Philadelphia merchants, "to export from the Colony of *Virginia* so much of the produce of that country as shall be equal in value to any quantity of Salt, not exceeding six thousand bushels, which they shall carry and safely deliver there to the Committee of Safety or their order . . ." (Force, *American Archives*, III, 1952). The critical need for salt, which was a preservative as well as condiment, brought a lifting of the nonexportation and nonimportation bans by a 29 Dec. resolution that exempted Virginia, Maryland, and North Carolina from the agreement. The conventions or committees of safety were to superintend the relaxed regulations solely to procure salt "for the use of the inhabitants . . . now suffering great distress by the scarcity of that necessary article . . ." (*ibid.*, 1963).

To the Maryland Council of Safety

GENTLEMEN.   Virginia Gunston-Hall, Novr. 29th. 1775.

Having just received the following important intelligence, and not knowing whether you were apprized of the Character & dangerous designs of Majr. Connelly, I thought it proper *imediatly* to transmit it to your board, together with a copy of a letter & Intelligence, respecting him, recd. sometime ago from his excellency General Washington. This appeared to me the more necessary as the prisoners being taken up in your province, we could give no orders here for their safe Custody. Majr. Connelly was taken above Frederick Town in Maryland, in his way to the Indian Country and with him a Doctr. Smith from Charles County & one Cameron, they are all now fast by the heels in the goal of Fredrick Town. Connelly, we are told, had with him a Commission from Genl. Gage to raise a number of Indians, & with them to penetrate, thro' the Country, towards Alexandria in the spring, where He wou'd be met by Lord Dunmore. Commissions for the other two were to be furnished hereafter.

Who this Doctr. Smith is I know not, Cameron I take to be the deputy Indian agent to the southward, from whom a letter was intercepted last July, advising the Government to raise a number of the Creek & Cherokee nations, to fall upon the back Inhabitants, offering his service upon the occasion, & boasting of his Interest with these Indians. I make no doubt but your Board will take proper measures to prevent the escape of such dangerous men, and am, with the greatest Respect. Gentn. Your Most Obdt. Servt.

G Mason

FC (MdAA). From the copybook kept for the Maryland Council of Safety. The original Ms has been lost.

Maj. John Connolly was a loyalist with a knowledge of frontier conditions along the Ohio. Connolly and the two other tories were turned over to the jurisdiction of the Continental Congress and jailed in Philadelphia (Force, *American Archives*, III, 1946). Connolly, Dr. John D. F. Smyth, and Alan Cameron sought their release on parole from Congress early in 1776. By 1777 Smyth had either been released or escaped, but Cameron, who had served as an Indian agent in S.C. before the war, was injured in a jailbreak attempt and remained in prison until 1778 (Harold Hancock, "John Ferdinand Dalziel Smyth—Loyalist," *Maryland History Magazine*, LV [1960], 346–358). Connolly was being held as a spy rather than as a British prisoner-of-war late in 1778, a circumstance that provoked a curt exchange of notes between the Continental Congress and the British (Worthington C. Ford, *et al.*, eds., . . . *Journals of the Continental Congress, 1774–1789* [Washington, 1904–1937], XII, 1125–1129). The letter addressed to GENERAL WASHINGTON (reprinted in William H. Browne, *et al.*, eds., *Archives of Maryland* [Baltimore, 1883–19—], XI, 93–94) was from a William Cowley. Cowley told of Connolly's relationship with the British and his orders to capture Fort Pitt with the aid of pro-British Indians. A contemporary account of the so-called "Connolly's Plot" is found in Reuben Gold Thwaites and Louise Phelps Kellogg, eds., *The Revolution on the Upper Ohio, 1775–1777* . . . (Madison, 1908), 136–142.

Instructions of Fairfax County Committee to Their Convention Delegates

GENTLEMEN   Alexandria, 9th. Decem. 1775.

When ministerial Tools are employing every wicked Machination to accomplish their unjust Purposes, 'tis high time every virtuous

Citizen shou'd be on the Watch guarding those Liberties, which the Tyrants have mark'd out for Destruction; Actuated by these Motives, and wishing to contribute to the Protection of this Colony & the common Cause; we the Committee of Correspondence for the County of Fairfax beg leave to present you our Representatives in Genel Convention w'th: a few such Observations, as we think maybe usefull at this Period of imminent Danger.

By late accounts from the Southward it appears that Lord Dunmore is daily increasing in Force & Garrison; we hoped that the two Regiments of Regulars wou'd e'er this have circumscrib'd his Career and prevented his insulting this Colony in Proclamations & Plunder; it seems he still continues to pester us, and numbers on the Minute Establishment are call'd into actual Service. Shou'd there still be a Necessity for augmenting the Army, for the more effectual Defence of this Colony; we wou'd recommend the raising of Regulars for the Purpose; daily Experience evinces, that the Minute System is very inadequate to the Design; wherever the Colony is expos'd and vulnerable, there we wou'd recommend Regular Forces to be station'd; an Arrangement might be made so as to contribute alternately to each others Assistance on the Shortest Notice of an Attack—we wou'd likewise advise, your promoting the fitting out a few Vessells of War, to protect the Bay & Rivers, from Lord Dunmore's Pirates, we beg leave to assure you such Vessells are attainable, can be man'd & equipp'd.

We allso request that you will encourage, some effectual Plan, for supplying the Colony with Arms & Ammunition, as we do apprehend, the calling a Number of Men to the lower Parts of the Colony, unaccoutred is incurring an Expence to little purpose & exhibiting to the World the Shadow of an Army.

The Ordinance for arming the Militia we think ineffectual & dependant on a Contingency, we wish not to happen, *the Default of the People*. The Sword is drawn, the Bayonet is allready at our Breasts, therefore some immediate Effort is necessary to ward off the meditated Blow, let the County Lieutenants be supply'd with Arms from the Armory at Fredericksburg, or have Liberty to buy them any where at the Country's Expence, and the Fines go into the common Fund—it seems that a considerable Force hath been employ'd to guard the little Money in the Treasury; let us observe that an interior Part of the Colony, seems best calculated for preserving the public Money & Military Stores, there, less liable to Depradation, consequently, an inconsiderable Guard necessary. Be pleas'd to acquaint the Convention, that there are at Winchester, fourteen Cannon, at Cressaps two, at Fort Cumberland six in good order and belonging to the Colony, these might be useful on Navigation, at their present Situation not wanted, the Committee of Safety have been wrote to on this Subject, but no answer given to the Letter.

From the present System adopted by those at the Head of Affairs, it wou'd appear that the upper parts of the Colony were to be left destitute of Defence, and totally neglected. Companies on the Minute Service call'd out of the Northern District e'er those in the Southern one, more contiguous to the Place for Action have repair'd to it. Why is this part of the Country to be left unguarded? when it appears, not only from the public Papers, but Lord Dunmore's Assignation with *Conoly* that Alexanderia was to be their place of rendezvous in the Month of April next, a place well known to the Officers who were out on Genl. Braddock's Expedition, a safe Harbour for Ships of War & commanding a most material part of the Colony.

If we are to be govern'd by a Council of Safety, we do recommend, that you give your Voice for a full and equitable Representation, as the only means to unite us & produce the most salutary Effects; to sum up the whole of our requests, we beg you will use your utmost Endeavours, that Men may be rais'd on the Regular Establishment, & Vessells arm'd, both to be stationed at such Places as will contribute to the Safety of the Colony at large, that you be not sparing in the raising of Money for the good of the Colony, but be cautious in the distribution of it for be the Taxes in future what they may we shall cheerfully retrench every other Luxury to secure that of being free, and are with much Regard & Esteem Gentlemen Your obt huble Serv'ts,

> JOHN DALTON
> WILLIAM RAMSAY
> JOHN MUIR
> JOHN CARLYLE
> JAMES KIRK
> GEO. GILPIN
> RICHD. CONWAY

RC (Vi). Addressed to GM and Charles Broadwater, the Fairfax County delegates. Endorsed: "Retd. to Comtee. on State of the Colony." The letter was read to the Convention on 18 Dec. 1775.

The hasty call for a Dec. convention session was perhaps too fast for GM. At any rate, GM did not serve. (The "Mr. Mason" mentioned in the convention minutes is David Mason of Sussex County). GM knew of Dunmore's activities and was doubtless aware of the governor's 7 Nov. 1775 proclamation (Force, *American Archives*, III, 1385) which declared martial law in effect and labelled as a traitor "every person capable of bearing arms" who did not "resort to His Majesty's standard." Most alarming to Virginians was the section which offered freedom to slaves and indentured servants who would join the British army. Dunmore was aboard a British man-of-war lying off Norfolk and expected to carry the war inland, possibly with aid from Maj. John Connolly directed toward Alexandria as a rendezvous. See the Cowley letter in Browne, ed., *Archives of Maryland*, XI, 93–94.

To the Maryland Council of Safety

Fairfax County Jany 31st. 1776.

SIR.

Being empowered & directed, by the Committee of Safety for this Colony, to build two row gallies, one to carry a 24, & the other an 18 pounder, & provide three arm'd cutters for the protection of Potomac River, we think it proper to inform your board that this measure will be carryed into execution with all possible expedition, & that we hope to have your co-operation, in adopting some similar plan, for the same purpose, we beg the favour of an answer by the first opportunity; and am, with the greatest respect, Sir Yr. most obdt. Hble Serts.

G. MASON.

JOHN DALTON

FC (MdAA). The copyist misread Dalton's name and it appears as "Galton," an error repeated in Browne, ed., *Archives of Maryland*, XI, 127.

The threat of depredations by Lord Dunmore and the general military situation had alarmed many Fairfax County citizens, as their instructions of 9 Dec. 1775 (*q.v.*) indicated. Dalton, an Alexandria merchant, seems to have been a prime mover in the business and with GM's help had started purchasing saltpeter and sulphur in large quantities (*Account Book, Committee of Safety, 21 Oct. 1775 to 5 July 1776,* Vi). This letter followed a similar plea for cooperation from the Virginia Committee of Safety made on 27 Jan. 1776, which the Maryland group acknowledged (Browne, ed., *Archives of Maryland*, XI, 143). The Maryland Council replied that the ship *Defence* was scheduled to start cruising in Chesapeake waters on 1 Mar. 1776, but that "Our Inexperience in naval preparations, prevents us at present from either approving or disapproving your plan of Row Gallies for the protection of Potowmack river." The Council was also pessimistic about increased naval operations until its land forces had been supplied with weapons and powder. GM and Dalton proceeded to act independently, under instructions from the Virginia Committee of Safety, for creating a Potomac fleet (see GM and Dalton to the Maryland Council, 15 Mar. 1776).

To the Virginia Committee of Safety

[[*3 Feb. 1776.* GM was a member of the colony's first committee of safety as well as the Fairfax County committee, and had been active in creating a naval force to patrol the Potomac. The Virginia Committee of Safety records have been lost, but Rowland, I, 219*n*, indicates that a calendar of correspondence acknowledged GM's letter of this date. "I continue to correspond constantly with that Board," he told Washington on 2 Apr. 1776, even though GM had asked to be excused from reappointment at the Jan. meeting of the Richmond convention (Force, *American Archives*, IV, 87). GM's letter has not been found.]]

From the Virginia Committee of Safety

[[*10 Feb. 1776*. GM and John Dalton were busily engaged in assembling a small fleet to protect towns and estates along the lower Potomac. This letter, which is now missing, appears to have concerned the Potomac project from the circumstances. Rowland, I, 219*n*, mentions a calendared entry of this date in the committee journal, "A letter wrote to Col. George Mason in answer to his of the third." The committee's records have been lost.]]

To Robert Carter

SIR   Gunston-Hall March 12th. 1776

Capt. Hancock Lee & one Mr. Leet are return'd from surveying the Ohio Companys 200,000 Acres of Land, & are now here making out their Returns, & setling their Accts. in assisting about which I am closely ingaged; as I wish to have every thing as clear & regular, as possible. They have got it all in one Tract, upon a large Creek, call'd Licking Creek; which falls into the Ohio River, on the South East Side, abt. 150 Miles below the Scioto River, & abt. 80 Miles above the Mouth of the Kentucky River; so that it is clear both of Henderson's & the Vandalia Company's Claim. By all Accounts it is equal to any Land on this Continent, being exceedingly rich & level.

The Charges of the Survey come to about £650 Curcy., & I have never recd. a farthing from the Members towards it except £49.9.9 from Richd. Lee Esqr. & £100 Ster: from Colo. Tayloe (for Mr. Lomax & himself) which wth. my own Quota of £50 Ster: makes £199.9.9 Sterling. It wou'd be unreasonable that I shou'd advance the Remainder, even if I had the Money; but the Fact is I have it not, & the Men are all waiting for their Wages, by which I am extreamly distress'd; having always, thro' Life, made it a Rule of comply punctually wth. my Contracts. On this Occasion, upon the Credit of the Ohio Compy., & the particular Promises of several of the Members to advance £50 Ster: each, I agreed to make myself liable for the Charges of this Survey, & am now like to suffer for it. I ask no Pecuniary favour of any Man, & desire only Justice. I must acknowledge that you was not one of the Members who promised to make the said Advance, & that you told me, when I last conversed wth. you on the Subject, you believed you shou'd not make any further Advances as a Member of the Ohio Compy., & wou'd rather lose what you had already paid then run any further Risque; and it is therefore that I now put it to you, as a Man of Honour, or, what is more intelligible & important, as an honest Man, whether you intend to claim any Benefit from the Survey lately made or not? If you do, surely you ought to indemnifie me from all but my proportional Charge. If you do not, you shou'd let us know it candidly; that yr. Shares may be disposed of, for the Payment, or sunk in the Company; or if you do no[t lik]e to be further concern'd, & will sell out to [me, I] will purchase one, or perhaps both yr Shares. In Case you intend to claim yr. Part of this Survey, I am convinced you will imediatly furnish me wth. yr. Proportion of the Money; and at any Rate, I flatter myself you will pardon the Freedom wth. which I have express'd myself on the Subject; & ascribe it to it's true Cause, the Sincerity, & real Regard, with which I am, Sir, Yr. most Hble Sert.

G MASON

RC (Mount Vernon Ladies' Assn., Mount Vernon, Va.). Addressed: "The Honble Robt. Carter Esqr./Westmoreland County," with the sender's note "to the Care of Richd. Lee Esqr."

Amidst wartime tensions GM still served as treasurer of the Ohio Company. Hancock Lee and Daniel Leet reportedly spent a year or more completing surveys that included most of the present Bourbon County, Ky., as well as portions of adjoining counties between the main and south forks of the Licking River. See the map opposite p. 162 in James, *Ohio Company*, for location. GM ignored George Mercer's merger of 1770 with the Vandalia Company and attempted to stake a prior claim to this fertile region. If a partner's share was SUNK IN THE COMPANY he apparently forfeited his rights, "thereby reducing the net number of outstanding shares or claims on the assets" (Livermore, *Early American Land Companies*, 233).

The bracketed portions are supplied from the edited text in Rowland, I, 215. Miss Rowland must have seen the manuscript before it was damaged. The letter bears an outer endorsement: "Geo: Mason/dated 12 March 1776./ receivd 5th Octr [followg.?]/ Col. R. Lee, delivered the/Letrs to R. McKeldow."

To the Maryland Council of Safety

GENTLEMEN.   Virginia, Fairfax County March 15th 1776.

Being employed by the Committee of Safety for this colony to fit out three armed cruisers, & two row gallies, for the protection of potomack River, we have, in consequence thereof, bought three sloops; the largest of which (called the American Congress) will mount 14 Carriage Guns, 6 & 4 pounders, & be man'ed with about ninety men. We are now raising the company of

Marines, which will be compleated in a few days; she has most of her guns mounted, the shot are now casting, at a Furnace in the Neighbourhood, & if we had powder, she wou'd be very soon fit for action. We wrote to our delegates at the congress to purchase for us in Philadelphia twenty Barrels of powder, & forward it to us by land, to serve 'til we could get a larger supply, which they promised to do; so soon as it could be procured there, but none has yet come to hand, & we are very uneasy, least some of the enemies cutters should come up this river, to destroy our vessels, before they are in a posture of defence. As this equipment will be as beneficial to the inhabitants on the north side of potomack as to those on this side, we doubt not the disposition of your board to promote it, and under these circumstances, we take the liberty to apply to you for the loan of ten bars. of the powder lately imported for yr. province, in Capt. Conway's vessel now in the eastern Branch of potomack, which shall be replaced out of the first powder we receive from the northward, or else where: if ten bars. cant be spared, even five or six bars. wou'd be very serviceable, & might answer our purpose until the supply we expect from Philadelphia arrives. We beg the favour of an imediate answer, & hope that the urgency & importance of the Business will excuse the trouble we have taken the liberty to give you. We are with much Respect Gentn. your most obdt. Serts.

G. MASON
JOHN DALTON.

FC (MdAA).
Throughout the winter of 1775/1776 Virginians expected depredations from Lord Dunmore's flotilla, which was cruising off Norfolk. GM and Dalton had corresponded with the Virginia Committee of Safety concerning a Potomac defense force and were apparently encouraged to proceed, with or without the aid of the Maryland councilors. The Committee of Safety Account Book (Vi) shows that GM and Dalton purchased saltpeter and sulphur in Dec., to prepare for gunpowder manufacture in Fairfax County. The letter TO OUR DELEGATES AT THE CONGRESS has not been found, but by 2 Apr. Dalton could report that a ton of gunpowder had arrived from Philadelphia (Dalton to Daniel St. T. Jenifer, in Browne, ed., *Archives of Maryland*, XI, 306–307). Meanwhile, the Md. Council of Safety cooperated by ordering Col. Joshua Beall to deliver ten barrels of gunpowder to GM and Dalton on 19 Mar. 1776 (q.v.), from the cargo of the sloop *Molly* commanded by Capt. Thomas Conway.

From the Maryland Council of Safety

GENTN: [Annapolis] 19th. March 1776.
    In Answer to your Favor of the 15th. we have directed Colo: Beall to deliver to your Order ten Barrels of Gun-Powder; we shall

do every thing in our Power to promote the general Welfare, and for that Purpose are now encreasing our Marines.

We are &c.

FC (MdAA).

Apparently acting under instructions from the Va. Committee of Safety, GM and Dalton were assembling a defense force to patrol the upper Potomac. They asked for a loan of ten barrels of gunpowder on 15 Mar. from the ship *Molly*, which was at anchor on the Md. side of the Potomac. As Dalton explained on 2 Apr., Capt. Conway's sloop *Molly* turned ten barrels over to GM and Dalton but a ton of gunpowder arrived from Philadelphia, so the loan was repaid immediately. Cooperation between the Fairfax County committeemen and the Council continued throughout the summer (see Browne, ed., *Archives of Maryland*, XI, 293, 294; XII, 78). COLO: BEALL was Joshua Beall of Prince Georges County.

To George Washington

DEAR SIR.   Virginia Gunston-Hall April 2d. 1776

We have just received the welcome News of your having, with so much Address & Success, dislodged the ministerial Troops, and taken Possession of the Town of Boston. I congratulate you, most sincerely, upon this glorious & important Event—An Event which will render General Washington's Name immortal in the Annals of America, endear his Memory to the latest Posterity, and entitle him to those Thanks which Heaven appointed the Reward of public Virtue.

It is the common Opinion here that we shall have a Visit from General Howe, in some of the middle, or Southern Colonies; but it does not seem well founded. I am very unable to judge of military Affairs; but it appears to me that if Genl. Howe acts the Part of a wise Man, & an experienced Officer, he will not venture a sickly, worn out, disgusted, and disgraced Army in a Country where he must meet imediate Opposition, and where any Misfortune might produce Mutiny, or general Desertion. I think it much more probable that he will retire to Hallifax, give his Troops a little time, by Ease & Refreshment, to recover their Spirits, & be in Readiness, as soon as the Season permits, to relieve Quebec; keeping some Ships of War cruising off Boston Harbour, to protect & direct the Transports which may arrive. New York, or any of the northern united Provinces are too near Cambridge; for if he cou'd not maintain the advantageous & strongly fortified Port of Boston, what reasonable Hope has he of gaining & maintaining a new one, in the Face of a superior Army? You will perhaps smile at these speculative & idle suggestions upon a Subject, which will probably be reduced to a Certainty, one Way or other, long before this reaches your Hands; but when I am conversing with you, the many agreeable Hours we have spent together recur upon my Mind; I fancy myself under your hospitable Roof at Mount Vernon, and lay aside Reserve. May God grant us a return of those halcyon Days; when every Man may sit down at his Ease under the Shade of his own Vine, & his own fig-tree, & enjoy the Sweets of domestic Life! Or if this is too much, may He be pleased to inspire us with spirit & resolution, to bear our present & future Sufferings, becoming Men determined to transmit to our Posterity, unimpair'd, the Blessings we have received from our Ancestors!

Colo. Casewell's Victory in N. Carolina, & the military Spirit which it has raised will be an Obstacle to any Attempts in that Quarter. Maryland & Virginia are at present rather unprepared, but their Strength is daily encreasing: the late Levys here have been made with surprizing Rapidity, and the seven new Regiments are already in a Manner compleat except as to Arms, in which they are very deficient; but they are coming in, in small Quantitys, from different Parts of the Country, & a very considerable Manufactory is established at Fredericksburg. Large Ventures have been lately made for military Stores; for which Purpose we are now loading a Ship for Europe, with Tobo. at Alexandria; her Cargoe is all on float, & I hope to have her under sailing orders in a few Days. Notwithstanding the natural plenty of provisions in this Colony, I am very apprehensive of a great Scarcity of Beef & Pork among our Troops this Summer, occasioned by the People's not expecting a Market, until the Slaughter-Season was past: I find it extreamly difficult to lay in a Stock for about 300 men in the Marine Department of this River.

Ill Health, & a certain Listlessness inseperable from it, have prevented my writing to you so often, as I wou'd otherwise have done but I trust to your Friendship to excuse it: the same Cause disabled me from attending the Committee of Safety this Winter, and induced me to intreat the Convention to leave me out of it. I continue to correspond constantly with that Board, & I hope am no less usefully employed; thinking it, in such times as these are, every Man's Duty to contribute his Mite to the public Service. I have in Conjunction with Mr. Dalton, the Charge of providing & equiping arm'd Vessels for the Protection of this River. The thing is new to me; but I must endeavour to improve by Experience. I am much obliged to the Board for joining Mr. Dalton with me: He is a steady diligent Man, & without such Assistance I cou'd not have undertaken it. We are building two Row-Gallies, which are in considerable forwardness; & have purchaed three Sloops for Cruisers, two of them, being only from forty to fifty Tons Burthen, are to mount 8 Carriage Guns each, 3 & 4 Pounders, they are not yet fitted up, & we are exceedingly pu[z]zled to get Cannon for them; the other, the American Congress, is a fine Stout Vessel, of about 110 Tons Burthen, & has such an easy draught of Water, as will enable her to run into most of the Creeks, or small Harbours, if she meets wth a Vessel of superior Force: she mounts 14 Carriage Guns 6 & 4 pounders; tho' we have thoughts of mounting two 9 Pounders upon her main Beam, if we find her able, as we think she is, to bear them: her Guns are mounted, & are to be tryed tomorrow. We have twenty Bars. of Powder, & about a Ton of Shot ready; more is making; Swivels we have not yet been able to procure, but she may make a tollerable Shift without, til they can be furnish'd; we have got some small Arms, & are taking every Method to increase them, & hope to be fully supplyed in about a Week more, her Company of Marines is Raised, & have been for some time exercised to the use of the great Guns; her Compliment of Marines & Sea-Men, is to be 96 Men. We are exerting ourselves to the utmost, & hope to have her on her Station in less than a Fortnight, & that the other Vessels will quickly follow her, and be able to protect the Inhabitants of this River from the piratical Attempts of all the Enemies Cutters' Tenders & small Craft.

Imediatly upon Rect. of yr. former Letters, I applyed to some of the Maryland Committees, as well as those on this Side; in Consequence of which, the several most convenient places on this River were sounded, & thoroughly examined; but effectual Batteries were found, in our present Circumstances, impracticable. Mr. Lund Washington tells me he sent you the Draughts & Soundings taken upon this Occasion. A Regiment, commanded by Colo. Mercer of Fredericksburg, is stationed on this Part of the River, and I hope we shall be tollerably safe, unless a Push is made here with a large Body of Men. I think we have some Reason to hope the Ministry will bungle away another Summer, relying partly upon Force, & partly upon Fraud & Negotiation. The Family here join with me in presenting their best Compliments to yourself & Lady, as well as to Mr. Custis & his. If in any of your Affairs here, I can render you any acceptable Service, I beg you will use that Freedom with which I wish you to command   Dear Sir   Your affecte. & obdt. Servt.

G MASON

RC (Washington Papers, DLC). Addressed to Washington at his "Head Quarters at Boston," and endorsed in Washington's handwriting.

The seige of Boston by Washington's army lasted until 17 Mar. 1776, when Howe's army withdrew aboard British frigates bound for a mysterious destination insofar as Americans were concerned. Howe's whereabouts led to much speculation and, as early as 20 Jan. 1776, readers of the *Va. Gaz.* (Dixon and Hunter) were warned "that the seat of war would be removed to the middle provinces . . . In all probability Virginia is one of the immediate objects . . . and it is necessary we should be prepared." GM's prediction that Howe would move to Halifax, Nova Scotia, made him a better prophet than some newspaper gossips, for the British army did rendezvous at that point before moving to the Hudson River estuary in July. CASEWELL'S VICTORY was the battle at Moore's Creek Bridge, fought in N.C. on 27 Feb., where Col. Richard Caswell was one of the patriot leaders. The victory was reported in the Williamsburg newspaper on 23 Mar. A VERY CONSIDERABLE MANUFACTORY . . . AT FREDERICKSBURG was the arsenal directed by Fielding Lewis. GM had served on the first Virginia Committee of Safety, but was not reappointed on 16 Dec. 1775 by the Richmond convention, which GM did not attend (Force, *American Archives*, IV, 87). Chronic illness was a familiar complaint of GM's, but he was active on the Fairfax County committee, as these details on outfitting the Potomac defense force indicate. Efforts to find cannon and sails for the vessels involved Dalton and GM throughout the spring and summer of 1776. On 2 Apr. Dalton wrote a Maryland councilor "the scarcity of Sail Duck & proper Sized Cannon plague us much" (Browne, ed., *Archives of Maryland*, XI, 306). On 19 July the Maryland Council of Safety "ordered Mr. Hughes to send immediately to Geo. Town two 18 pounders . . . to be delivered to Messrs. Mason and Dalton's order." Washington's FORMER LETTERS to GM, apparently with suggestions for placing shore batteries along the Potomac, have not been found. THE REGIMENT, COMMANDED BY COLO: MERCER, was the 3rd Virginia Regiment, led by Col. Hugh Mercer.

The text printed in Rowland, I, 216–219, is modernized.

From George Washington

DEAR SIR, New York. May 10th. 1776.

The uncertainty of my return, and the justice of surrendering to Mr. Custis, the Bonds which I have taken for the Monies raised from his Estate and lent out upon Interest, As also his Moiety of his deceased Sister's Fortune (consisting of altogether of Bonds &c.), obliges me to have recourse to a friend to see this matter done, and a proper Memorandum of the transaction made. I could think of no person in whose friendship, care and Abilities I could so much confide, to do Mr. Custis and me this favour as yourself; and, therefore, take the liberty of soliciting your Aid.

In Order that you may be enabled to do this with ease and propriety, I have wrote to the Clerk of the Secretary's Office, for attested Copies of my last settled accounts with the General Court in behalf of Mr. Custis and the Estate of his deceased Sister; with which and the Bonds, I have desired him and Mr. Washington to wait upon you for the purpose above mentioned.

The Amount of the Balance due, upon my last settled Accounts, to Mr. Custis, I would also have assigned him out of my moiety of his Sister's Bonds; and, if there is no weight in what I have said, in my Letter to Mr. Lund Washington, concerning the rise of exchange, and which, to avoid repetition, as I am a good deal hurried, I have desired him to shew you, I desire it may meet with no Notice, as I want nothing but what is consistent with the strictest justice, honour, and even generosity; although I have never charged him or his Sister, from the day of my connexion with them to this Hour, one Farthing, for all the trouble I have had in managing their Estates, nor for any expense they have been to me, notwithstanding some hundreds of pounds would not reimburse the monies I have actually paid in attending the public Meetings in Williamsburg to collect their debts, and transact these several matters appertaining to the respective Estates.

A variety of occurrences, and my anxiety and hurry to put this place, as speedily as possible, into a posture of defence, will not, at this time, admit me to add more than that I am, with unfeigned Regard, Dear Sir, Your mo obt. & affectionate humble servant,

G. WASHINGTON.

FC (Washington Papers, DLC). In a copyist's handwriting.

Washington's stepson, John Parke Custis, had inherited a sizeable estate from his father and a share of HIS DECEASED SISTER'S FORTUNE upon the death of Martha Parke (Patsy) Custis in 1773 (Freeman, *Washington*, III, 335-337). Washington hurried to New York from his Cambridge base and complained that he was totally occupied with military affairs "from the time I rise out of my Bed till I go into it again" (Washington to John Augustine Washington, 29 Apr. 1776). Freeman noted that the General also lamented that "the 'badness' of his memory hampered him in managing his affairs at long range" (*Washington*, IV, 412n). Custis and his wife Eleanor, *nèe* Calvert, had recently left New York bound for the South. Washington had also written his cousin LUND WASHINGTON on 10 May (Fitzpatrick, ed., *Writings of Washington*, V, 29-31): "I would have Mr. Custis and you repair to Colonel Mason, and get him, as a common friend to us both, as a Gentlemen well acquainted with business and very capable of drawing up a proper Memorandum of the transaction, to deliver him his own Bonds . . . and at the same time deliver him as many Bonds out of the other parcel, endorsed Miss Custis's Bonds, as will pay him his Moiety of her Fortune, and the Balance which will appear due to him from me, at my last settlement with General Court." Washington also gave details of several investments and concluded, "as I have not wrote fully to Colonel Mason on this subject . . . if necessary, let him have this Letter." Washington's concern over THE RISE OF EXCHANGE related to the balance owed to the Custis estate in British pounds, which had appreciated in the intervening years. "If I was to turn Current Money Bonds into Sterling, I should be a considerable sufferer, when I had not, nor could have, any interest in delaying of it. . . ."

The settlement with Custis took several years, and GM's subsequent role as a disinterested third party is obscure, but see Washington's letter to Bartholomew Dandridge, 20 Apr. 1782 (*ibid.*, XXIV, 141) and Freeman, *Washington*, V, 402*n*.

A misplaced period in the first sentence, retained in Fitzpatrick, ed., *Writings of Washington*, V, 28, has been changed to a comma for clarity's sake.

To Richard Henry Lee

DEAR SIR.   Williamsburg May 18th. 1776.

After a smart fit of the Gout, which detain'd me at Home the first of the Session, I have at last reached this Place, where, to my great Satisfaction, I find the first grand Point has been carried nem: con: The opponents being so few, that they did not think fit to divide, or contradict the general Voyce. Yr. Brother Colo. T. Lee will inclose you the Resolve. The Preamble is tedious, rather timid, & in many Instances exceptionable; but I hope it may answer the Purpose. We are now going upon the most important of all Subjects—Government: The Committee appointed to prepare a plan is, according to Custom, overcharged with useless Members. You know our Conventions. I need only say that it is not mended by the late Elections. We shall, in all probability have a thousand ridiculous and impracticable proposals, & of Course, a Plan form'd of hetrogenious, jarring & unintelligible Ingredients; this can be prevented only by a few Men of Integrity & Abilitys, whose Countrys Interest lies next their Hearts, undertaking this Business, and defending it ably thro' every stage of opposition. I need not tell you how much you will be wanted here on this Occasion. I speak with the Sincerity of a Friend, when I assure you that, in my opinion, your absence can not, must not be dispensed with. We can not do without you— Mr. Nellson is now on his Way to Philadelphia; & will supply your place in Congress, by keeping up the representation of this Colony. It will be some time I presume before that Assembly can be fully possess'd of the Sentiments & Instructions of the different Provinces; which I hope will afford you time to return. Pray confer with some of your ablest Friends at Congress upon the Subject of foreign Alliances; what Terms it will be expedient to offer. Nations, like Individuals, are govern'd by their Interest— Great Britain will bid against us— Whatever European Power takes us [by] the Hand must risque a War with her. We want but two things—a regular Supply of military Stores, and a naval Protection of our Trade & Coasts—for the first we are able & willing to pay the Value in the Produce of our Country—for the second, we must give something adequate—to offer what is not worth accepting will be trifleing with ourselves. Our Exports shou'd not be bound as affected by Treaty; our Right to these shou'd be sacredly retain'd. In our Imports perhaps we may make Concessions as far as to give a Preference to the Manufactures as Produce of a particular Country: this wou'd indeed have the Effect of every other Monopoly: We shou'd be furnished with Goods of worse Quality, & at a higher Price than in an open Market; but this wou'd only force us earlier into Manufactures. It is an important & delicate Subject, & requires thorough Consideration. I know you will excuse my loose Thoughts; which I give you in a Hurry, without Order, but without Reserve. I have not time to copy or correct having only borrowed half an Hour, before I attend the House, which is now meeting. At all Events, my dear Sir, let us see you here as soon as possible. All your Friends anxiously expect you, & none more than

Your Affecte Friend & Sr[t].
G. MASON

P.S. You who know what Business is now before the Congress, & in what Forwardness, as well as how yr. Colleagues stand affected, as to capital Points, will be best able to judge whether, at this great Crisis, you can do most Service there, or here, & I am sure you will act accordingly.

RC (ViHi).
GM appears to have arrived at the Convention on 18 May, for he was named to three committees that day, a good indication of initial attendance. THE FIRST GRAND POINT was Edmund Pendleton's 15 May resolution instructing the Virginia delegates in Congress "to propose to that respectable body to declare the United Colonies free and independent States . . ." (Mays, ed., *Papers of Edmund Pendleton*, I, 178–179). YR BROTHER was Thomas Ludwell Lee, Stafford County delegate and sometime committee colleague of GM's. A committee to draft "a Declaration of Rights, and such a plan of Government as will be most likely to maintain peace and order" was appointed on 15 May and GM was added three days later. Because GM was recovering from the gout, and was also impatient by nature, he immediately plunged into the assignment and prepared a first draft of the Declaration of Rights within a few days, probably before the following weekend. (*q.v.* 20–26 May). MR. NELLSON was Thomas Nelson, who had introduced Pendleton's resolves and was entrusted with carrying them to Philadelphia. THE SUBJECT OF FOREIGN ALLIANCES had been a high topic of conversation at Williamsburg, and GM may have seen Lee's letter of 12 May sent to the capital in which Lee said "it must be evident beyond a doubt that [a] foreign Alliance is indispensable, and should be immediately sought" (Ballagh, *Lee Letters*, I, 191). GM's entreaties may have helped speed Lee to Williamsburg, for Lee reported from the capital on 29 June "I have been in this City a week. . . ."
A modernized and at times faulty text is printed in Rowland, I, 226–227.

Order of the Virginia Convention
regarding the Indiana Company

[20 May 1776]

Ordered that an Advertisement, signed by a certain George Morgan, for setting up a Land-Office, called the Indiana Land-Office, for issueing Warrants for surveying, and containing Proposals for granting Lands within the Limits and Territory of Virginia be referred to the Committee on the State of the Colony.

Ms (Vi). GM wrote this originally as a resolution, but deleted the word "Resolved" before it was presented.

The ADVERTISEMENT was George Morgan's notice, published in the *Pa. Packet* on 15 Apr. 1776, announcing land sales by the Indiana Company from its Pittsburgh office (Thomas Perkins Abernethy, *Western Lands and the American Revolution* [New York, 1937], 147). Morgan was Thomas Wharton's associate but somehow managed a congressional appointment as an Indian agent on 10 Apr. (Max Savelle, *George Morgan Colony Builder* [New York, 1932], 87). On 1 May 1776 the *Pa. Gaz.* carried a public notice dated at Philadelphia on 20 Apr. 1776 indicating that the Indiana Company was offering lands in a western area, possibly in conflict with Pennsylvania claims then on appeal in London. GM probably heard about the advertisement from Richard Henry Lee, who was among the Virginia delegation in Philadelphia that challenged Morgan's right to offer questionable titles. However, Abernethy hints that Benjamin Harrison or Carter Braxton, Virginia delegates to the Continental Congress, might have been personally interested in promoting the rival Indiana claims (Abernathy, *Western Lands*, 147-148). Virginians based their opposition on colonial statutes which forbade private land purchases from Indians (Hening, III, 465), legislation which supported the Ohio Company claims which rested on a royal grant. Meanwhile, the Convention was presented with a petition from Richard Henderson and his associates on 15 June seeking recognition of the Watauga purchase from the Cherokees. On 24 June the Convention passed resolutions, possibly written by GM, recommending that western settlers be granted a preference when "the validity of the titles under such *Indian* deeds and purchases, shall have been considered and determined on by the Legislature . . ." (Force, *American Archives*, VI, 1588). An accompanying resolve made it clear that henceforth, "no purchases of Lands within the chartered limits of *Virginia* shall be made, under any pretence whatever, from any *Indian* Tribe or Nation, without the approbation of the *Virginia* Legislature." GM must have written this warning to the Henderson and Wharton groups that were clinging to hopes of valid titles through tribal purchases. Then, in the Constitution adopted on 29 June, it was explicitly declared that "no purchases of Land shall be made of the *Indian* Natives but on behalf of the Publick, by authority of the General Assembly" (*q.v.*).

The *Journal* text of the order printed in Force, *American Archives*, VI, 1530-1531, is a slight alteration of GM's original statement, which was written on a scrap of paper.

1776

The Virginia Declaration of Rights

[*ca.* 20 May–12 June 1776]

I. First Draft [*ca.* 20–26 May]
II. Committee Draft [27 May]
III. Final Draft [12 June]

EDITORIAL NOTE

Few documents have ever had such a wide impact on society and yet brought so little public recognition for the principal author as the Virginia Declaration of Rights. Mason had barely settled in his place at the Virginia Convention before he was appointed to the special committee formed to draft "a Declaration of Rights, and . . . a plan of Government. . . ." Beginning with the 10 May advice from Congress for each colony to assume sovereign powers, the rapid chain of events in the spring of 1776 had swept away doubts about severing English ties and curbed the hesitant patriots. Within five days the Virginia Convention had passed Edmund Pendleton's forthright resolution calling for a direct act by the Continental Congress to strike for independence. A corollary of the convention action was a resolution creating the drafting committee for a bill of rights and constitution. Four weeks later Mason and the other committeemen had waded through two drafts, debated the propositions from a theoretical standpoint and as practical politicians, and finally adopted the Virginia Declaration of Rights unanimously.

Mason took the lead in drafting the Declaration, perhaps because his skill in collecting ideas on paper was acknowledged and partly because of his impatience. "The Political Cooks are busy in preparing the dish," Pendleton wrote Jefferson on 24 May, "and as Colo. Mason seems to have the Ascendancy in the great work, I have Sanguine hopes it will be framed so as to Answer it's end, Prosperity to the Community and Security to Individuals, but I am yet a stranger to the Plan" (Boyd, I, 296). As Mason revealed his irritation with parliamentary procedures and "useless" committee members in his intimate letter to Richard Henry Lee on 18 May, he was about to plunge into a work that he had been preparing for since 1765. From the "Scheme for Replevying Goods Under Distress for Rent" (23 December 1765), with its strictures on resistance and the evils of slavery, Mason had been called upon periodically to give expression to shared thoughts on colonial rights and the propriety or necessity of colonial resistance. Thus Mason's role as patriot spokesman evolved until a decade of dissension erupted in revolution. Committees need direction, and the twenty-seven member group appointed by the Virginia Convention under chairman Archibald Cary was cumbersome. Edmund Randolph later recalled that "many projects of a bill of rights and constitution" were examined, most of them exhibiting an "ardor for political notice, rather than a ripeness in political wisdom. That proposed by George Mason swallowed up all the rest, by fixing the grounds and plan, which after great

[274]

discussion and correction, were finally ratified" ("Edmund Randolph's Essay on the Revolutionary History of Virginia 1774–1782," *VMHB*, XLIV [1936], 44).

Some time during the week 20–26 May, Mason prepared a list of ten propositions. These, with Thomas Ludwell Lee's additions, are here considered as the original draft which Lee probably sent to his brother, Richard Henry Lee, on 1 June (Hutchinson-Rachal, I, 172). To this core of ideas the committee had added eight propositions, all of which were read to the Convention on 27 May and ordered printed immediately so that a full discussion could be scheduled for 29 May (Force, *American Archives*, VI, 1538). The committee report was printed by either Alexander Purdie or by John Dixon and William Hunter, discussed on 29 May, and published in Dixon and Hunter's *Virginia Gazette* on 1 June 1776. Then came a brief delay, Thomas Ludwell Lee reported on 1 June, caused by the tactics of "a certain set of aristocrats, for we have such monsters here, [who upon] finding that their execrable system cannot be reared on such foundations, have to this time kept us at bay on the first line, which declares all men to be born equally free and independent. . . . The words as they stand are approved by a very great majority, yet by a thousand masterly fetches and stratagems the business has been so delayed that the first clause stands yet unassented to by the Convention" (quoted in Rowland, I, 240). Edmund Randolph recalled that Robert Carter Nicholas led the cavilling over the first line with its frightening phrase—"born equally free." The conservatives balked, concerned that such an expression in a slave-holding society might be an open invitation to a slave insurrection.

Mason's anxiety, not to mention his irritation, over such a turn of events can only be guessed. Randolph's recollection was that the liberal delegates replied "that with arms in our hands, asserting the general rights of man, we ought not to be too nice and too much restricted in the declaration of them; but that slaves not being constituent members of our society could never pretend to any benefit from such a maxim" ("Randolph's Essay," *VHMB*, XLIV [1936], 45). This was no time for Mason to answer the implicit challenge in the conservative argument and go the whole distance by suggesting that slavery was indeed a malignant element that needed drastic surgery. Perhaps, as in 1765, Mason's instincts told him this was not the time "to expose our weakness by examining this subject too freely." So the alarm bell of slavery was hardly sounded as the Virginia Convention warmly considered whether human rights were above property rights, but chose finally to sidestep an ultimate choice.

After another day of debate on 3 June, the Convention turned to other matters and did not consider the Declaration of Rights again until 10 June. Sometime during the two sessions, Patrick Henry withered supporters of the ban on ex post facto laws with a hypothetical example of how a public enemy might escape justice, and so that provision was dropped. Meanwhile, James Madison had importuned the delegates to broaden the article on religious toleration. Textual notes below relate these matters in more detail. By 11 June the debating ceased and only one more session was required to have the Declaration of Rights transcribed and passed unanimously.

As the legal scholar R. Carter Pittman has noted ("Jasper Yeates's Notes on the Pennsylvania Ratifying Convention, 1787," *WMQ*, 3d Ser., XXII [1965], 304n), the widespread and almost immediate influence of the Virginia Declaration of Rights on other nascent states was attributable to newspaper reprints of the committee draft of 27 May. The *Virginia Gazette* (Dixon & Hunter) of 1 June first placed the draft in general circulation. Almost certainly one of the Virginia delegates at the Continental Congress allowed his copy of this draft to reach printers of the *Pennsylvania Evening Post*, where it appeared on 6 June, incorrectly dated "May 24." On 8 and 12 June Philadelphians again saw the committee draft in the widely circulated *Pennsylvania Ledger* and *Pennsylvanian Gazette* columns. The next day, in Annapolis, the misdated reprint of the committee draft appeared in the *Maryland Gazette*. Other newspapers quickly followed suit, spreading the 27 May draft up and down the seaboard. Thus the expanded version of Mason's first draft had a profound impact on other Americans whose task it was to create new governments.

Starting in Pennsylvania later in 1776, and sweeping through seven other states, the Virginia Declaration became a model for similar documents as it became the Revolutionary fashion to affix a preamble to state constitutions until Massachusetts finally ratified its plan of government in 1780. Clinton Rossiter has called the Virginia Declaration of Rights and the Massachusetts Constitution (mainly written by John Adams) as "among the world's most memorable triumphs in applied political theory" (*The Political Thought of the American Revolution* [New York, 1963], 231). The French intellectual, Brissot, was soon hailing "l'immortelle declaration de l'Etat de Virginie sur la liberte des cultes," and his countryman Condorcet asserted that the author of the Virginia Declaration had earned "the eternal gratitude of mankind" (Lucy M. Gidney, *L'Influence des États-Unis d'Amérique sur Brissot, Condorcet et Mme. Roland* [Paris, 1930], 42; J. Salwyn Schapiro, *Condorcet and the Rise of Liberalism* [New York, 1934], 221).

Thus Mason moved into the circle of the Revolutionary literati, a place where few other than lawyers ever ventured. The Virginia Convention had anticipated the moral requirements of 1776, and announced to the world what the Americans believed to be significant in human affairs—life, liberty, property, and the pursuit of happiness and safety. More than a legal document, the Virginia Declaration of Rights set forth what may be an unattainable national goal. Mason's generation was by turns hardheaded and given to dreaming. They expected that "unborn generations" of Americans would build on their legacy. It was only a start.

First Draft of the Virginia Declaration of Rights

[*ca.* 20–26 May 1776]

A Declaration of Rights, made by the Representatives of the good People of Virginia, assembled in full Convention; and recommended to Posterity as the Basis and Foundation of Government.

That all Men are born equally free and independant, and have certain inherent natural Rights, of which they can not by any Compact, deprive or divest their Posterity; among which are the Enjoyment of Life and Liberty, with the Means of acquiring and possessing Property, and pursueing and obtaining Happiness and Safety.

That Power is, by God and Nature, vested in, and consequently derived from the People; that Magistrates are their Trustees and Servants, and at all times amenable to them.

That Government is, or ought to be, instituted for the common Benefit and Security of the People, Nation, or Community. Of all the various Modes and Forms of Government, that is best, which is capable of producing the greatest Degree of Happiness and Safety, and is most effectually secured against the Danger of mal-adminis-tration. And that whenever any Government shall be found inade-quate, or contrary to these Purposes, a Majority of the Community had an indubitable, inalianable and indefeasible Right to reform, alter or abolish it, in such Manner as shall be judged most conducive to the Public Weal.

That no Man, or Set of Men are entitled to exclusive or seperate Emoluments or Privileges from the Community, but in Considera-tion of public Services; which not being descendible, or hereditary, the Idea of a Man born a Magistrate, a Legislator, or a Judge is unnatural and absurd.

That the legislative and executive Powers of the State shoud be seperate and distinct from the judicative; and that the Members of the two first may be restraind from Oppression, by feeling and participating the Burthens they may lay upon the People; they should, at fixed Periods be reduced to a private Station, and re-turned, by frequent, certain and regular Elections, into that Body from which they were taken.

That no part of a Man's Property can be taken from him, or applied to public uses, without the Consent of himself, or his legal Representatives; nor are the People bound by any Laws, but such as they have in like Manner assented to for their common Good.

That in all capital or criminal Prosecutions, a Man hath a right to demand the Cause and Nature of his Accusation, to be confronted with the Accusers or Witnesses, to call for Evidence in his favour, and to a speedy Tryal by a Jury of his Vicinage; without whose unanimous Consent, he can not be found guilty; nor can he be compelled to give Evidence against himself. And that no Man, except in times of actual Invasion or Insurrection, can be imprisoned upon Suspicion of Crimes against the State, unsupported by Legal Evidence.

That no free Government, or the Blessings of Liberty can be preserved to any People, but by a firm adherence to Justice, Moderation, Temperance, Frugality, and Virtue and by frequent Recurrence to fundamental Principles.

That as Religion, or the Duty which we owe to our divine and omnipotent Creator, and the Manner of discharging it, can be governed only by Reason and Conviction, not by Force or Violence; and therefore that all Men shou'd enjoy the fullest Toleration in the Exercise of Religion, according to the Dictates of Conscience, unpunished and unrestrained by the Magistrate, unless, under Colour of Religion, any Man disturb the Peace, the Happiness, or Safety of Society, or of Individuals. And that it is the mutual Duty of all, to practice Christian Forbearance, Love and Charity towards Each other.

That in all controversies respecting Property, and in Suits between Man and Man, the ancient Tryal by Jury is preferable to any other, and ought to be held sacred.

(That the freedom of the press, being the great bulwark of Liberty, can never be restrained but in a despotic government.

That laws having a restrospect to crimes, & punishing offences committed before the existence of such laws, are generally dangerous, and ought to be avoided.

N. B. It is proposed to make some alteration in this last article when reported to the house. Perhaps somewhat like the following

That all laws having a retrospect to crimes, & punishing offences committed before the existence of such laws are dangerous, and ought to be avoided, except in cases of great, & evident necessity, when safety of the state absolutely requires them. This is thought to state with more precision the doctrine respecting ex post facto laws & to signify to posterity that it is considered not so much as a law of right, as the great law of necessity, which by the well known maxim is—allowed to supersede all human institutions.

Another is agreed to in committee condemning the use of general warrants; & one other to prevent the suspension of laws, or the execution of them.

The above clauses, with some small alterations, & the addition of one, or two more, have already been agreed to in the Committee appointed to prepare a declarition of rights; when this business is finished in the house, the committee will proceed to the ordinance of government.

T. L. Lee)

Ms (Mason Papers, DLC). Entirely in GM's handwriting, except for the portions of the last two pages in Thomas Ludwell Lee's hand beginning "That the freedom of the press. . . ." The Ms in the Madison Papers, DLC, marked "first Draught" of the "Virginia Declaration of Rights" is a copy which was greatly altered at Madison's direction (see textual note below).

Although conjectures have been made regarding the place and time of GM's authorship of the 10 articles in his handwriting (the text above through the sentence ending ". . . and ought to be held sacred"), it is probable that he turned his thoughts to the draft only after he arrived in Williamsburg and was appointed to the drafting committee. In all likelihood, GM wrote his 10 original articles between 20 and 24 May. The committee then probably discussed them and made their additions on GM's own Ms, which Thomas Ludwell Lee then borrowed and sent to his brother, Richard Henry Lee. T. L. Lee wrote his kinsman on 1 June that he had "enclosed you by last post a copy of our declaration of rights nearly as it came through Committee" (quoted in Irving Brant, *James Madison* [Indianapolis, 1941–1961], I, 428). Brant observes that the last post before 1 June leaving Williamsburg had been on 25 May. Brant speculates that R. H. Lee brought the manuscript back to Williamsburg later in June and returned it to GM, hence "its presence among his [i.e., GM's] papers" in the Library of Congress. The portions in angle brackets are in Lee's hand. In his textual criticism of the three major drafts (Mason-Lee, committee, and final), Brant first pointed out that GM probably later added four more articles. "The authorship of two—the tenth and fourteenth—is unknown. . . . With one article defeated and two combined, the eighteen reported by the committee were cut to the sixteen adopted" (Brant, *Madison*, I, 237). For precedent in preparing a bill of rights the Convention had a variety of documents ranging from the English Bill of Rights of 1689 to the Declaration of Rights passed by the Continental Congress in Oct. 1774. The latter echoed John Locke's *Second Treatise on Civil Government* by recalling that all men are equally entitled to life, liberty, and property; and specific resolutions spoke of the rights of assembly and petition, of legislative consent, and of freedom from standing armies (Robert Allen Rutland, *The Birth of the Bill of Rights* [Chapel Hill, 1955], 26–27). Besides familiarity with the strictures of Locke, Montesquieu, Machiavelli, Montagu, Sidney and the ancient writers on polity, GM and his colleagues were also acutely aware of the warnings in Plutarch, the classical commentaries from antiquity, and the more recent observations from *Cato's Letters* (by Trenchard and Gordon) or the mysterious *Junius*. Well might GM have joined Jefferson in declaring that his singular achievement was not in the "originality of principles or sentiments . . . [but rather] it was intended to be an expression of the American mind" with its authority resting on "the harmonizing sentiments of the day. . . ." Beyond the brief preamble, GM barely rephrased Locke's dictum "That all men by nature are equal." "All Men are born free; Liberty is a Gift which they receive from God himself," *Cato's Letters* (II, 216) had proclaimed in 1720, and it seems almost certain that GM was familiar with these lines. Similarly, he knew by heart "Locke's trinity of natural rights—his 'life, liberty, and property'" (Helen Hill [Miller], *George Mason, Constitutionalist* [Cambridge, Mass., 1938], 141); and from *Cato's Letters* came the admonition that "Happiness is the chief End of Man" (II, 300). American antecedents for the first article are mentioned in Arthur M. Schlesinger, Sr., "The Lost Meaning of 'The Pursuit of Happiness,'" *WMQ*, 3d Ser., XXI (1964), 325–327, and Herbert Lawrence Ganter, "Jefferson's 'Pursuit of Happiness' and Some Forgotten Men," *WMQ*, 2d Ser., XVI (1936), 422–434, 558–585. In a real sense, however, GM had simply recalled his own material from his "Remarks on Annual Elections for the Fairfax Independent Company" of 1775, wherein he spoke in almost identical language of natural rights, and of the Fairfax Resolves with their concern for "the Safety and Happiness of the Community" (18 July 1774). Similarly, GM's second proposition is a rewording of a favorite principle appearing in the Prince William County Resolves and both of the Fairfax County addresses. The third paragraph espousing the INDEFEASIBLE RIGHT TO REFORM was whiggish doctrine carried forward by the American patriots as they asserted "a natural right to relieve ourselves" (Carl Becker, *The Declaration of Independence* . . . [New York, 1922], v). GM was thoroughly familiar with the Bible, and he must have been impressed with Algernon Sidney's documented justification of rebellion from the Scriptures (*Discourse Concerning Government* [Philadelphia, 1805], II, 18, 21, 22). Sidney also quoted Grotius to prove that when a monarch entered "a devilish conspiracy against the people" a good man's nature compelled him to revolt. *Cato's Letters* reminded Englishmen and British-Americans that "Every Man in the State of Nature, had a Right to repel Injuries, and to revenge them" (I, 67). The idea is also implicit in Locke's *Second Treatise*, when he criticizes the maxim *"that all Men being born under Government . . . it is impossible any of them should even be free, and at liberty to unite together, and begin a new one . . ."* (John Locke, *Two Treatises of Government*, ed. Peter Laslett [Cambridge, Eng., 1960], 362). Elsewhere, Locke warned that whenever "legislators endeavor to take away, and destroy the property of the people," this misuse of power justified a revolt so the people might "resume their original liberty." GM's fourth proposition enunciates his personal opinion on THE IDEA OF A MAN BORN A MAGISTRATE, based on the prevailing concept of natural man and natural abilities as contrasted with corrupting systems based on heredity. In his earlier "Remarks on Annual Elections" GM set forth his guiding political principle of natural merit recognized by "frequently appealing to the body of the people." Frequent elections created a system by which "the Roman Commonwealth preserved its vigour," and the abandonment of which brought the "dissolution of that once glorious and happy commonwealth . . . a useful lesson to succeeding generations." This statement led to GM's next (fifth) provision, calling for a separation of powers as delineated by Montesquieu, and his predilection for annual elections as gleaned both from historical treatises on ancient Greece and Rome as well as eighteenth-century admonitions. "I can see no Means in human Policy to preserve the publick Liberty," *Cato's Letters* cautioned, ". . . but by the frequent fresh Elections of the People's Deputies . . . the only Way to put them in mind of their former Condition . . . is often to reduce them to it" (II, 239–240). Lockean theory comes to the foreground in the assertion THAT NO PART OF A MAN'S PROPERTY CAN BE TAKEN FROM HIM without his consent, and indeed the "great and *chief end* . . . of Men's uniting into Commonwealths . . . *is the Preservation of their Property"* (Locke, *Two Treatises*, ed. Laslett, 368–369). One suspects that GM was so heavily committed to the Lockean concept of a propertied society that in the Fairfax Resolves he could denounce "a wicked, cruel, and unnatural trade" in slaves without suggesting that laws be enacted to end slavery. Since slaves were not considered as men but as property in GM's society, it was no inconsistency to maintain that all men were born equal. The nettlesome point would surface during the Convention debates after 29 May. The seventh proposition became a landmark in American criminal trial procedure and indicates that GM's service as a justice of the peace led him to study more than charters and land laws. Safeguards for accused persons IN ALL CAPITAL OR CRIMINAL PROSECUTIONS were gleaned from the Magna Carta, the Petition of Right, John Lilburne's celebrated defense, and the English common law (Helen H. Miller, *The Case for Liberty* [Chapel Hill, 1965], 146–148, 164–166). While praising GM's ideas for reflecting "stylistic elegance, a philosophic cast of mind," and a widespread acquaintanceship with Anglo-American law that was "genuinely creative," Leonard Levy assesses the criminal trial procedures GM staked out as marked with "a certain carelessness" (*Origins of the Fifth Amendment: The Right Against Self-Incrimination*

[New York, 1968], 406–407). Levy points out that since 1677 Virginia had a law which held that a person charged with a felony was guarded against self-incrimination (Hening, II, 442), and he is critical of GM's "bad draftsmanship, which is not easily explained," in this proposed article. The convention remedied some of these faults, Levy adds, but left untouched GM's "superfluousness" in ALL CAPITAL OR CRIMINAL PROSECUTIONS and "the inadequate statement" that A MAN HATH A RIGHT TO DEMAND THE CAUSE AND NATURE OF HIS ACCUSATION instead of positive knowledge of the charges. "Compulsory process should have been guaranteed," Levy concludes. "Thoughtlessness, rather than indifference or a purposeful narrowing, seems to be the best explanation for the self-incrimination clause" (*Origins of the Fifth Amendment*, 408). In fairness to GM, it should be remembered that he hurriedly assembled a legal beacon which has stood the ravages of nearly two storm-tossed centuries. Levy recognizes this fact when he says that GM's "handiwork has been more praised, and justly praised, than critically analyzed." Despite its flaws, Levy concedes that GM's safeguards for persons accused of crimes "became a model for other states" and for the federal Bill of Rights. GM's call in the eighth paragraph for a FREQUENT RECURRENCE TO FUNDAMENTAL PRINCIPLES "sounds today like a mere jumble of virtuous words but carried the impact of social revolution to educated men of the eighteenth century" (Brant, *Madison*, I, 242). Again, GM was recalling language he had used in both the Fairfax Resolves and his "Remarks on Annual Elections" as the revolutionary crisis worsened. Brant may be going too far when he reads into the phrase a "redistribution of wealth to a point that would allow no man to be idle and yet retain a fortune" (*ibid.*). Instead, GM must have meant a return to a lifelong personal commitment to moderation and frugality as well as a conviction that a contrary course evidenced "strong symptoms of decay." Significantly, this sentence met general approval at every stage of the debate and still was untouched in the final draft. GM's experience as an Anglican vestryman and county justice of the peace was joined to a philosophical approach toward THE EXERCISE OF RELIGION that probably found its best expression in Locke's *Essay on Toleration*. Perceptive delegates, and particularly James Madison, enlarged the concept by textual emendations and deletions after 27 May. The ANCIENT TRYAL BY JURY in civil suits was also related to GM's judicial experience in Fairfax County, although Englishmen and British-Americans had long been conditioned to speak of "this great Jewel of Liberty, Trials by Juries" (Henry Care [William Penn?], comp., *English Liberties, or the Free-born Subject's Inheritance* [Boston, 1721], 203). The 11th and 12th propositions are in Thomas Ludwell Lee's handwriting, but since they were added after committee discussion, it is hazardous to say categorically that they originated either with Lee or GM. On 18 May the *Va. Gaz.* (Dixon & Hunter) carried a brief essay extolling "LIBERTY *of the* PRESS . . . the palladium of our LIBERTIES," and insisting that "liberty of speech is a natural right." "Freedom of Speech," said *Cato's Letters* (I, 100), "is the great Bulwark of Liberty." All this lip-service provided background for what became the first explicit legal sanction for a free press. The tendency has been to assume that GM originated this proposition (Brant, *Madison*, I, 237). The ban on LAWS HAVING A RETROSPECT TO CRIMES provided quarrelsome debate as Art. IX in the committee draft of 27 May (*q.v.*). Stylistic evidence indicates that GM had a hand in the alteration of this proposal, particularly the paraphrased statement on THE GREAT LAW OF NECESSITY . . . THE WELL KNOWN MAXIM which GM was fond of quoting (see GM to the Merchants of London, 6 June 1766). Of course, ex post facto laws must have originated in expediency, which is often opposed to the slower processes of law. Coke somewhat implies that ex post facto laws were passed to punish witchcraft and sorcery in civil rather than ecclesiastical courts (Edward Coke, *The Third Part of the Institutes of the Laws of England* . . . , 4th ed. [London, 1669], 44). The influential Blackstone, writing in the 1760s, denounced ex post facto laws. Punishment for actions "converted to guilt by a subsequent law . . . must of consequence be cruel and unjust" (William Blackstone, *Commentaries on the Laws of England* . . . [New York, 1858], I, 45). Before the draft was presented to the Convention, each article was numbered, articles VI, VIII, XI, XII, XV, and XVI were added, and the entire list was printed for the delegates' perusal.

GM's 1778 copy of the Declaration of Rights, which he labelled "Copy of the first D[r]aught by GM."—was "a composite of the original, the committee draft and the final draft, with one word transplanted from the Declaration of Independence" (Brant, *Madison*, I, 236). GM's claim threw scholars off the track by his remark that the 1778 copy presented the declaration "just as it was drawn and presented by me to the Virginia Convention" (GM to [Mr. Brent?], 2 Oct. 1778). Brant, in his researches on Madison's involvement with the drafting process at the convention, came across another "first draft" in the Madison Papers (DLC) and proceeded to unravel the mystery of how so many purportedly original manuscripts could exist. Comparing the texts of various manuscripts, Brant correctly determined the Mason-Lee document was in fact the first draft, that it was altered in the committee, and amended by the committee of the whole prior to the final passage on 12 June. Brant also determined that Madison had confused matters "in his old age" by revising notes on his printed copy of the committee report and incorrectly labeling it the "original text . . . as it was drawn by Geo. Mason" (Brant, *Madison*, I, 239). This misinterpretation was accepted by Madison's biographer, John C. Rives, who accepted Madison's restored text uncritically. Rowland, I, 433–438, reprints both the 1778 copy in GM's handwriting and the Mason-Lee draft without explaining the circumstances, so that both are mentioned as the "original" draft. A facsimile of the 1778 copy is also inserted between pages 240 and 241 of Rowland, I. Miss Rowland was anxious to defend GM against claims on behalf of purported co-authors (Meriwether Smith and Patrick Henry) of the Declaration. Thus she accepted the 1778 copy uncritically, affirming "with almost absolute certainty" that it "was prepared by him [GM] before he appeared in Convention." The first draft prepared by GM and Lee she viewed "as showing the appearance of the paper in one of its stages, as it was passing through the committee, and it indicates the order in which the articles were taken up for consideration" (Rowland, I, 239). In short, Miss Rowland assumed that GM wrote 16 articles, took them to the Convention, saw them expanded and then returned to the original form GM had proposed. This was the mistake an aged Madison had also made, as Brant demonstrated in 1941. The matter would now seem settled beyond further argument: GM wrote out 10 propositions and probably helped compose two more in this original working draft. His further role is explained in the notes following the committee and final drafts.

Committee Draft of the Virginia Declaration of Rights

[27 May 1776]

A DECLARATION *of* RIGHTS *made by the representatives of the good people of* Virginia, *assembled in full and free Convention;* ⟨*which rights do pertain to us, and our*⟩ *posterity, as the basis and foundation of government.*

[282]

1. THAT all men are born equally free and independent, and have certain inherent natural rights, of which they cannot, by any compact, deprive or divest their posterity; among which are, the enjoyment of life and liberty, with the means of acquiring and possessing property, and pursuing and obtaining happiness and safety.

2. That ⟨all⟩ power is vested in, and consequently derived from, the people; that magistrates are their trustees and servants, and at all times amenable to them.

3. That government is, or ought to be, instituted for the common benefit, ⟨protection,⟩ and security, of the people, nation, or community, of all the various modes and forms of government that is best, which is capable of producing the greatest degree of happiness and safety, and is most effectually secured against the danger of mal-administration; and that whenever any government shall be found inadequate or contrary to these purposes, a majority of the community hath an indubitable, unalienable, indefeasible right, to reform, alter, or abolish it, in such manner as shall be judged most conductive to the publick Weal.

4. That no man, or set of men, are entitled to exclusive or separate emoluments or privileges from the community, but in consideration of publick services; which, not being descendible, or hereditary, the idea of a man born a magistrate, a legislator, or a judge, is unnatural and absurd.

5. That the legislative and executive powers of the state should be separate and distinct from the judicative; and that the members of the two first may be restrained from oppression, by feeling and participating the burthens of the people, they should, at fixed periods, be reduced to a private station, return into that body from which they were ⟨originally⟩ taken, ⟨and the vacancies be supplied⟩ by frequent, certain, and regular elections.

6. ⟨That elections of members to serve as representatives of the people, in assembly, ought to be free; and that all men, having sufficient evidence of permanent common interest with, and attachment to, the community, have the right of suffrage.⟩

7. That no part of a man's property can be taken from him, or applied to publick uses, without his own consent, or that of his legal representatives; nor are the people bound by any laws but such as they have, in like manner, assented to, for their common good.

8. ⟨That all power of suspending laws, or the execution of laws, by any authority without consent of the representatives of the people, is injurious to their rights, and ought not to be exercised.⟩

9. That laws having retrospect to crimes, and punishing offences, committed before the existence of such laws, are generally ⟨oppressive,⟩ and ought to be avoided.

10. That in all capital or criminal prosecutions a man hath a right to demand the cause and nature of his accusation, to be confronted with the accusers or witnesses, to call for evidence in his favour, and to a speedy trial by an impartial jury of his vicinage, without whose unanimous consent he cannot be found guilty, ⟨nor⟩ can he be compelled to give evidence against himself; that ⟨no man be deprived of his liberty except by the law of the land, or the judgment of his peers⟩.

11. ⟨That excessive bail ought not to be required, nor excessive fines imposed, nor cruel and unusual punishments inflicted.⟩

12. ⟨That warrants unsupported by evidence, whereby any officer or messenger may be commanded or required to search suspected places, or to seize any person or persons, his or their property, not particularly described, are grievous and oppressive, and ought not to be granted.⟩

13. That in controversies respecting property, and in suits between man and man, the ancient trial by jury is preferable to any other, and ought to be held sacred.

14. That the freedom of the press is one of the great bulwarks of liberty, and can never be restrained but by despotick governments.

15. ⟨That a well regulated militia, composed of the body of the people, trained to arms, is the proper, natural, and safe defence of a free state; that standing armies, in time of peace, should be avoided, as dangerous to liberty; and that, in all cases, the military should be under strict subordination to, and governed by, the civil power.⟩

16. ⟨That the people have a right to uniform government; and therefore, that no government separate from, or independent of, the government of Virginia, ought, of right, to be erected or established within the limits thereof.⟩

17. That no free government, or the blessing of liberty, can be preserved to any people but by a firm adherence to justice, moderation, temperance, frugality, and virtue, and by frequent recurrence to fundamental principles.

18. That religion, or the duty which we owe to our CREATOR, and the manner of discharging it, can be ⟨directed⟩ only by reason and conviction, not by force or violence; and therefore, that all men should enjoy the fullest toleration in the exercise of religion, according to the dictates of conscience, unpunished and unrestrained by the magistrate, unless, under colour of religion, any man disturb the

peace, the happiness, or safety of society. And that it is the mutual duty of all to practice Christian forbearance, love, and charity, towards each other.

Printed report (ViHi). This two-page document was probably printed by Alexander Purdie, although he appears to have permitted his rivals Dixon and Hunter to become the first to make its contents public (in their *Va. Gaz.* of 1 June 1776). The type styles are virtually identical in these versions, but Purdie was inclined to spell "publick" in the archaic way, while the 1 June *Va. Gaz.* carried a modernized "public" along with the older form of "despotick." In short, printer-editor Purdie appears to have been about two weeks behind his competitors, for he did not print the Declaration until 14 June, after the final version had been approved.

From the time GM's first draft was studied until the committee report went to the printer, six propositions were added and certain changes made in the original. The words enclosed in angle brackets were added by the committee, possibly at a Saturday session on 25 May. Alterations in punctuation have not been noted. Brant alludes to a copy of this report which does not have the words "deprive or" in the first article (*Madison*, I, 428), so he may have seen still another uncorrected version of the committee report. In the original third article GM wrote "inalianable" which was changed here precisely as Jefferson's "inalienable" in the Declaration of Independence became improperly "unalienable." The final word—unalienable—was then considered as meaning that which "may not be altered," while the proper "inalienable" meant that "which cannot be alienated or transferred to another *by Law*" (editor's italics, see Bailey's 1755 *English Dictionary*). Dumas Malone hints that a printer's error may have changed the Jefferson MS, and this would explain the inappropriate word here as well (*The Story of the Declaration of Independence* [New York, 1954], 72). In ARTICLE FIVE GM's word "returned" was changed to the present tense and the final clauses transposed. ARTICLE SIX on the ELECTION OF MEMBERS bears GM's stylistic imprint and expresses a fundamental part of his political philosophy. Locke, who preferred to call a political community a commonwealth, insisted in his *Second Treatise on Government* that the "great and chief end . . . of men's uniting into commonwealths" was to preserve property; and here GM aligns property rights with suffrage as indispensible partners in a just society. GM later amended this proposition slightly and included parents, even propertyless parents, as qualified by a PERMANENT COMMON INTEREST in a commonwealth (see 1787 Convention debates, 7 Aug. entry). Thus GM revised his 1776 judgment that only a freeholder should be entitled to vote. The POWER OF SUSPENDING LAWS was denied the king in the 1689 English Bill of Rights and GM or a committeeman thought it should be explicitly set forth. GM later (1778) claimed authorship of ARTICLE EIGHT. LAWS HAVING RETROSPECT TO CRIMES had been mentioned in the first draft, where this proposition appeared in T. L. Lee's handwriting. The word "dangerous" in the original draft was later changed to "oppressive," and the entire ARTICLE NINE may have been a committee suggestion shaped in words by GM and Lee. GM's original provision on the rights of accused persons and criminal trial procedure was left intact, but his earlier exceptions allowed "in times of actual Invasion or Insurrection" were dropped in committee and the bracketed portion added. Sedition and treason were heinous crimes in the tory histories of GM's day, but the rebellious Virginians in the Convention preferred to skip all mention of "Crimes against the State" in the tenth article. ARTICLE ELEVEN stressed the growing American resentment against a medieval heritage of ear-slitting, stake-burning, branding, and other capital punishments repulsive to a society that increasingly sought proof of man's virtues instead of his wickedness. A committee addition, this article may have been given its persuasive brevity by GM. Moreover, this is the only article in the Revolutionary declarations of rights which was accepted almost verbatim for the federal Bill of Rights in 1789–1791. GM claimed its authorship but rejected an association with ARTICLE TWELVE, which in 1778 he lumped with ARTICLE SIXTEEN as "2 more articles . . . added . . . not of fundamental nature." Perhaps his attitude toward general warrants was linked with the deleted section of his provisions for accused persons, which countenanced stringency in time of war. GM recognized expediency as the handmaiden of political action and foresaw the relative position of civil liberties to particular circumstances. Since he valued equally the annual election of officials, it followed in his political catechism that an arbitrary misuse of power would be redressed in due course. The wording of ARTICLE FIFTEEN is characteristically GM's, similar to his admonition in the "Plan for Embodying the People" of 6 Feb. 1775 regarding A WELL REGULATED MILITIA. Standing armies were decried in the English Bill of Rights and throughout the 18th century by British and American writers who denounced permanent military establishments. "No despotick government can ever subsist without the support of that instrument of tyranny and oppression, a standing army" was the typical judgment (Edward Wortley Montagu, *Reflections on the Rise and Fall of the Antient Republicks. Adapted to the Present State of Great Britain* [London, 1759], 153). The 16th article, which GM disavowed, was a device to keep western counties within Virginia's jurisdiction. FREQUENT RECURRENCE TO FUNDAMENTAL PRINCIPLES was another of GM's catch phrases which has an ambiguous ring in the 20th century but apparently had a clear meaning in 18th-century America. As drafted in ARTICLE SEVENTEEN it is an enlargement of GM's introductory "Remarks on Annual Elections for the Fairfax Independent Company" (Apr. 1775). GM's first draft of the proposition on THE FULLEST TOLERATION may have been hurriedly considered, for there was little change in the committee prior to 27 May but a fundamental alteration came when James Madison gave ARTICLE EIGHTEEN more thought (Brant, *Madison*, I, 244–250). The important changes occurred in the committee of the whole and are noted in the final draft (*q.v.*). The 20th-century tendency to question the omission of certain civil rights is an academic speculation that makes "the great Virginia Declaration of Rights appear to be an erratic document compiled in shipshod fashion" (Levy, *Origins of the Fifth Amendment*, 408). By 1791, a total of 90 topics had been included in the various state and federal versions of bills of rights (see Edward Dumbauld, *The Bill of Rights and What It Means Today* [Norman, Okla., 1957], 161–166). Levy points out that the Declaration "did not alter Virginia's system of criminal procedure nor express the totality of rights which actually flourished." Despite historical hindsight that finds flaws, at the time it was visible evidence of American revolutionary idealism writ large. Thomas Ludwell Lee sent this printed draft to his brother in Philadelphia, where Congressman Richard Henry Lee probably circulated it and gave printer John Dunlap a copy. R. Carter Pittman's researches showed that it was this committee draft which was first printed in the *Pa. Evening Post* on 6 June 1776, whence it spread up and down the seaboard and across the Atlantic (see "Book Review," *VMHB*, LXVIII [1960], 110–111). The effect of its publication in England (in *Almon's Remembrancer*, 1776, Pt. 2, 221–222) can only be surmised, but the committee's Declaration was the model that had considerable impact in France and subsequently in western thought (see Schapiro, *Condorcet*, 221, 223–228; Georg Jellinek, *The Declaration of the Rights of Man and of Citizens* . . . , trans. Max Farrand [New York, 1901], *passim*).

Angle brackets enclose committee additions to the first draft. Changed prepositions, minor alterations in punctuation, and the transposition of words have not been noted.

Final Draft of the Virginia Declaration of Rights

[12 June 1776]

A DECLARATION OF RIGHTS made by the Representatives of the good people of VIRGINIA, assembled in full and free Convention; which rights do pertain to ⟨them and their⟩ posterity, as the basis and foundation of Government.

1. That all men are ⟨by nature⟩ equally free and independent, and have certain inherent rights, of which, ⟨when they enter into a state of society,⟩ they cannot, by any compact, deprive or divest their posterity; ⟨namely,⟩ the enjoyment of life and liberty, with the means of acquiring and possessing property, and pursuing and obtaining happiness and safety.

2. That all power is vested in, and consequently derived from, the People; that magistrates are their trustees and servants, and at all times amenable to them.

3. That Government is, or ought to be, instituted for the common benefit, protection, and security of the people, nation, or community;—of all the various modes and forms of Government that is best which is capable of producing the greatest degree of happiness and safety, and is most effectually secured against the danger of mal-administration;—and that, whenever any Government shall be found inadequate or contrary to these purposes, a majority of the community hath an indubitable, unalienable, and indefeasible right, to reform, alter, or abolish it, in such manner as shall be judged most conducive to the publick weal.

4. That no man, or set of men, are entitled to exclusive or separate emoluments and privileges from the community, but in consideration of publick services; which, not being descendible, ⟨neither ought the offices⟩ of Magistrate, Legislator, or Judge, ⟨to be hereditary⟩.

5. That the Legislative and Executive powers of the State should be separate and distinct from the Judicative; and, that the members of the two first may be restrained from oppression, by feeling and participating the burdens of the people, they should, at fixed periods, be reduced to a private station, return into that body from which they were originally taken, and the vacancies be supplied by frequent, certain, and regular elections, ⟨in which all, or any part of the former members, to be again eligible, or ineligible, as the law shall direct⟩.

6. That elections of members to serve as Representatives of the people, in Assembly, ought to be free; and that all men, having sufficient evidence of permanent common interest with, and attachment to, the community, have the right of suffrage, ⟨and cannot be taxed or deprived of their property for⟩ publick uses without their own consent or that of their Representative ⟨so elected,⟩ nor bound by any law to which they have not, in like manner, assented, for the publick good.

7. That all power of suspending laws, or the execution of laws, by any authority, without consent of the Representatives of the people, is injurious to their rights, and ought not to be exercised.

8. That in all capital or criminal prosecutions a man hath a right to demand the cause and nature of his accusation, to be confronted with the accusers and witnesses, to call for evidence in his favour, and to a speedy trial by an impartial jury of his vicinage, without whose unanimous consent he cannot be found guilty, nor can he be compelled to give evidence against himself; that no man be deprived of his liberty except by the law of the land, or the judgment of his peers.

9. That excessive bail ought not to be required, nor excessive fines imposed, nor cruel and unusual punishments inflicted.

10. That ⟨general⟩ warrants, whereby any officer or messenger may be commanded to search suspected places ⟨without evidence of a fact committed,⟩ or to seize any person or persons ⟨not named, or whose offence is⟩ not particularly described ⟨and supported by evidence,⟩ are grievous and oppressive, and ought not to be granted.

11. That in controversies respecting property, and in suits between man and man, the ancient trial by Jury is preferable to any other, and ought to be held sacred.

12. That the freedom of the Press is one of the greatest bulwarks of liberty, and can never be restrained but by despotick Governments.

13. That a well-regulated Militia, composed of the body of the people, trained to arms, is the proper, natural, and safe defence of a free State; that Standing Armies, in time of peace, should be avoided as dangerous to liberty; and that, in all cases, the military should be under strict subordination to, and governed by, the civil power.

14. That the people have a right to uniform Government; and, therefore, that no Government separate from, or independent of, the Government of *Virginia*, ought to be erected or established within the limits thereof.

15. That no free Government, or the blessing of liberty, can be preserved to any people but by a firm adherence to justice, moderation, temperance, frugality, and virtue, and by frequent recurrence to fundamental principles.

16. That Religion, or the duty which we owe to our *Creator*, and the manner of discharging it, can be directed only by reason and conviction, not by force or violence; and, therefore, all men ⟨are equally entitled to the free⟩ exercise of religion, according to the dictates of conscience; and that it is the mutual duty of all to practise Christian forbearance, love, and charity, towards each other.

Printed from Force, *American Archives*, VI, 1561–1562. Contemporary copies appeared in the *Va. Gaz.* (Purdie) on 14 June 1776 and in the Dixon and Hunter *Va. Gaz.* of 15 June 1776. A Ms of the final draft as approved by the Convention has not been found.

The committee report was ordered printed after two readings at the 27 May convention session. With the committee report in hand, debate resumed on 29 May but immediately struck a snag. "A certain set of Aristocrats, for we have such monsters here, finding that their execrable system cannot be reared on such foundations, have to this time kept us at bay on the first line, which declares all men to be born equally free and independent," Thomas Ludwell Lee complained on 1 June (letter to R. H. Lee, Rowland, I, 240). Edmund Randolph recalled that Robert Carter Nicholas based his opposition to the "born equally free" phrase on its latent dangers in a slaveholding society. To Nicholas's charge that the phrase might be "the forerunner of . . . civil convulsion," the liberals present rejoined "that with arms in our hands, asserting the general rights of man, we ought not be too nice and too much retricted in delineation of them; but that slaves not being constituent members of our society could never pretend to any benefit from such a maxim" ("Randolph's Essay," *VMHB*, XLIV [1936], 44). Parliamentary manuevering appalled GM, so it is likely that he joined the petulant Lee in condemning haggling over the first clause. The words "by nature" were then substituted for "born" as a preface to the opening phrase on man's pristine condition; and "natural" was dropped to make it read "certain inherent rights" as a further indication of the slaveholder's sophistry and discomfort. More pressing business intervened so that further debate by the committee of the whole was postponed until 3 June. At this point Edmund Pendleton apparently suggested that a qualifying phrase be added—WHEN THEY ENTER INTO A STATE OF SOCIETY (Mays, *Pendleton*, II, 121-122). This clause was meant to uphold the abstract idea of freedom while accomodating the realities of slavery, a compromise made "perhaps with too great an indifference to futurity, and not without inconsistency" ("Randolph's Essay," *VMHB*, XLIV [1936], 45). On 4 and 5 June the debate continued, wedged between other urgent business, and then on 10 June John Blair read "several amendments" to the Declaration made by the whole house. At this point all the arguments had been used and the final report was ready. In the intervening debates ARTICLE FOUR, which Randolph said "explodes an inheritance in office," was rephrased by dropping GM's "the idea of a man being born a Magistrate . . . is unnatural and absurd" in favor of a simple directive against hereditary positions. A provision was tacked on to ARTICLE FIVE directing the legislature to deal with any prohibitions on reelection of either legislators or the governor. ARTICLE SIX was a merger of the committee's sixth and seventh articles, with GM's clause on property shortened and taxation mentioned explicitly. Randolph's recollection was that ARTICLE SEVEN "was suggested by an arbitrary practice of the king of England before the revolution of 1688" ("Randolph's Essay," *VMHB*, XLIV [1936], 46). Along with the consolidation, the Convention approved Patrick Henry's request to drop the article forbidding ex post facto laws. At least that was Randolph's recollection, but since he also attributed incorrectly the articles on religion and FUNDAMENTAL PRINCIPLES to Henry there is room to admit his memory could have garbled three points as easily as two. For what it is worth, Randolph said that Henry defeated the ex post facto provision on the Convention floor by drawing "a terrifying picture of some towering public offender, against whom ordinary laws would be impotent . . ." ("Randolph's Essay," *VMHB*, XLIV [1936], 47). By 1778 Henry and Jefferson were both convinced of the need for a conditional attainder aimed at the renegade Josiah Philips (Hening, IX, 463–464), legislation that clearly would have violated the committee's deleted ninth article. The article on CAPITAL OR CRIMINAL PROSECUTIONS stood intact as a summary of an accused person's rights in 18th-century America, although a modern historian has noted its omissions and indicates the self-incrimination clause was "a sonorous declamation of the common-law right of long standing" (Levy, *Origins of the Fifth Amendment*, 409). Levy contends that ARTICLE EIGHT neither altered the current practice of "criminal procedure nor express the totality of rights which actually flourished" in GM's Virginia. Additions to ARTICLE TEN spelled out the nature of obnoxious general warrants, which were purposefully vague. The crown's use of general warrants during the 1770's, particularly in seaports, had heightened tension between America and England, but Randolph said the article "was dictated by the remembrance of the seisure of Wilkes' paper under a warrant from a Secretary of State" ("Randolph's Essay," *VMHB*, XLIV [1936], 46). John Wilkes's problems after the 1763 publication of *North Briton* No. 45 were well known in America, where great sympathy was created by the arrest of Wilkes and 48 others under general warrants signed by the secretaries of state, Lords Halifax and Egremont. GM disassociated himself from authorship of the article, however, by omitting it from his 1778 copy with the comment that articles 10 and 14 were "not of fundamental nature." Apparently little debate was occasioned by other provisions until the final article on religious freedom. Randolph mentioned, however, that ARTICLE FOURTEEN "proceeded partly from local circumstances; when the charter boundaries of Virginia, were abridged by royal fiats in favor of Lord Baltimore and Lord Fairfax, much to the discontent of the people: and partly from recent commotions in the west" ("Randolph's Essay," *VMHB*, XLIV [1936], 46–47). Of course the boundary line between Pennsylvania and Virginia was not settled in 1776, nor was there agreement on where the western Maryland boundary stood. Conflicting claims by speculative land companies based in other colonies were made more precarious by this article, and thus GM had a vested interest in it because of his Ohio Company activities. Nevertheless, he repudiated any claim of authorship for this article in his commentary written on the 1778 copy (see his letter to [Mr. Brent?], 2 Oct. 1778). The slight change between GM's original article on religious toleration and the final ARTICLE SIXTEEN hardly indicates the powerful forces that surged around this explosive issue. In its final form as accepted by the Convention, GM's phrase "that all men should enjoy the fullest toleration" was expanded by James Madison's salient substitute phrase, "that all men are equally entitled to enjoy the free exercise of religion." The whole committee dropped the word "enjoy" and approved Madison's change, after it had rejected his first substitute which eschewed "violence or compulsion," and declared "that no man or class of men ought, on account of religion to be invested with peculiar emoluments or privileges" (Brant, *Madison*, I, 242–245). Randolph's imperfect memory may have actually jumbled the circumstances involved in the revisions of ARTICLE SIXTEEN, for Madison's suggestion would have "knocked out the established Anglican church" and would also have blocked Henry's efforts in the 1780s to subsidize dissenting ministers (*ibid.*, 246). It seems clear now that Madison, as a young and inexperienced delegate, successfully urged Edmund Pendleton to bring in his second substitute article. Henry may have supported the change, but Randolph called the proposition Henry's and only remembered that in the floor debate Henry was asked "whether it was designed as a prelude to an attack on the established church, and he disclaimed such an object." Brant believes Pendleton was persuaded to offer the Madison substitute although he "never would have sponsored such an amendment on his own initiative . . . [yet] he no doubt welcomed it as a means of getting rid of Madison's first proposal, which would have disestablished the church" (*ibid.*, 247). Taken as a whole, Randolph's early summation of the Convention's aims seemed judicious. "In the formation of this bill of rights two objects were contemplated: one, that the legislature should not in their acts violate any of those cannons [*sic*]; the other, that in all the revolutions of time, of human opinion, and of government, a perpetual standard should be erected, around which the people might rally, and by a notorious record be forever admonished to be watchful, firm and virtuous" ("Randolph's Essay," *XMHB*, XLIV [1936], 47). Yet in 1788, in the midst of angry debate, Randolph told the Virginia ratifying convention that the Declaration of Rights "is of no validity, because, I conceive, it is not formed on due authority . . . it has never secured us against any danger: it has been repeatedly disregarded and violated" (Robertson, 60). Randolph's harsh commentary sprang from Henry's verbal veneration of the Declaration in 1788, when, as an Antifederalist, Henry insisted the proposed federal Constitution would obliterate state bills of rights. In less passionate circumstances the Declaration has been acclaimed as an intellectual guidepost of the American Revolution. Certainly John Adams's expectations had been answered in full measure, for only a few days earlier Adams had written Henry that "that we all look up to Virginia for examples" (letter of 3 June 1776, Charles Francis Adams, ed., *The Works of John Adams* . . . [Boston, 1850–1856], IX, 387). In a matter of weeks printed copies of the Declaration draft were broadcast throughout the new nation and reached Europe to find fresh root there. Because the committee draft contained GM's original rather than Madison's amended article on religious freedom, the expansiveness of the final draft was unnoticed for decades. Indeed, one scholar stated that GM's ideas concerning individual liberty "cannot be understood without reference to the principles of the Protestant Reformation," while GM's notions on statecraft reflected "the liberal political theory of the seventeenth century" (Miller, *George Mason*, 139). In GM, Mrs. Miller added, "Both the principles and the theory came to him focused by the clarifying glass of 18th-century rationalism." GM soon realized the Declaration would have a profound effect on the ideological foundations of the emerging Republic. Thus he wrote in 1778 of how Americans had been "treading upon enchanted Ground" as they moved toward freedom and independence (letter of 2 Oct. 1778). Rarely given to claims of authorship, GM even became boastful as he reviewed his Convention role of May–June 1776, and acknowledged that he wrote "This Declaration of Rights [which] was the first in America; it received few Alterations or Additions in the Virginia Convention (some of them not for the better) and was afterwards closely imitated by the other United States."

Major changes from the committee draft are enclosed in angle brackets. Minor alterations of words or punctuation have not been noted.

Resolution concerning Dispatches for Martinique

[29 May 1776]

Resolved that the Committee of Safety be ⟨directed⟩ to transmit to the Island of Martinico in the West Indies, by a Packet-Boat, with the greatest Expedition, the following Resolutions of the General Congress, vizt. that of the 23d. of March for making Reprisals on British Property; that of the 6th. of April for open Ports and a free Trade in all the united Colonies, and that of the 15th. of May for a Recommendation to the respective Assemblies and Conventions concerning Government; together with the Resolve of this Convention of the 15th. of May, containing Instructions to the Virginia Delegates in the said General Congress. That the said Resolutions, and also a Copy of this Resolve, be enclosed under cover directed to ⟨Richard Harrison⟩ Esquire; who is hereby authorised and desired to deliver them imediatly to the Governor of the said Island.

Ms (Vi). A clerk has written "In Convention May 29. 1776" at the top of this one-page document.

The printed Convention *Journal* does not indicate that the resolution was either debated or passed, but the Ms Journal (Vi) indicates that it was rescinded. The Continental Congress resolution of 15 May urged each of the United Colonies to establish an independent government. On the same day, the Virginia Convention had instructed its Philadelphia delegation to propose "in General Congress" that they jointly "declare the United Colonies free and independent States. . . ." Martinique, as a French Caribbean colony, was destined to become an important trading center for American ships that could elude the British naval blockade. RICHARD HARRISON became the Virginia commercial agent for St. Pierre and Martinique. This resolution possibly did not need legislative implementation because the Committee of Safety was perfectly free to send Harrison, under the broad mandate granted by both the 1775 and 1776 Conventions.

The words enclosed in angle brackets were added by a clerk.

To the People of the Thirteen United Colonies

31 May 1776. The newspaper essay thus addressed as a letter appeared in the *Va. Gaz.* (Purdie) on 31 May bearing many of GM's stylistic mannerisms. It is a plea for an immediate declaration of independence from Great Britain, with rhetorical questions and a syntax similar to GM's letter of 2 Oct. 1778, with even some verbatim parallels. The essay, reprinted in Force, *American Archives*, VI, 629, is less than a column in length. It states that the writer had been a loyalist until "Nine months ago"—about the time George III rejected the Olive Branch Petition. Elsewhere, GM dated his conversion to militant separatism from that time. The writer also makes much of the necessity for independence—a point GM repeatedly admits in his correspondence (e.g., see his letter to the London Merchants prepared for the London *Public Ledger*, 6 June 1766; and the letter of 2 Oct. 1778). Is it possible that GM had enough spare time from his Convention chores in Williamsburg to write this plea and sign it "ARISTIDES?"

Resolution Denying Governor Eden a Safe-Conduct Pass

[31 May 1776]

Sundry proceedings of the Convention of the Province of Maryland, respecting the Letters from Lord George Germain to Governour Eden, which had been intercepted in Virginia, and transmitted to the Maryland Council of Safety, to give them timely Notice of the Duplicity and dangerous Designs of the said Governour[,] And Resolutions containing a Request and Permission to the said Governour to depart the said Province unmolested, with all his effects, with a Passport for that Purpose, under colour of his being obliged, whilst he remains, to obey the Mandates of the British Ministry, altho the President of their Council of State, upon whom the said Resolutions declare the Government devolves, in the Absence of the Governour, will be equally under the same Obligation which proves the necessity of changing their present Government, instead of continueing it, contrary to the Resolves and Recommendations of the General Continental Congress; together with the Copy of an Address to the said Governour, and a Letter from the President of the said Convention to the President of the Committee of Safety here, desiring a like Passport from Virginia, being laid before this Committee,

Resolved, as the opinion of this Committee, that the said Proceedings, Resolutions, and Address, have been obtained thro the undue Influence of the proprietary Interest and present Government in the said Province of Maryland; that they tend to dissolve the Union upon which alone the Salvation of American Liberty depends; and therefore, that this Convention will not in any Manner be accessory to the same, nor grant any permission or passport to the said Governour Eden, or his Retinue, to pass through Virginia.

Resolved also, that a Copy of the said Proceedings, Resolutions, and Address, of the Maryland Convention, together with this Resolve, be forthwith printed in the Virginia Gazette.

Ms (Vi).

The acrimony touched off by the intercepted Germain-Eden letters indicates that Maryland and Virginia were separated by more than rivers and bays. Early in Apr. 1776 Capt. James Barron, commander of a patriot vessel roving in Chesapeake Bay, captured letters from the British secretary of state, Lord George Germain, addressed to the Maryland royal governor, Robert Eden. Germain's letters, among other things, intimated that Eden had been in secret communication with disaffected Americans, and reported a task force was ready to proceed to the southern colonies and restore "legal government in that part of America" (quoted in Bernard C. Steiner, *Life and Administration of Robert Eden* [Johns Hopkins University Studies in Historical and Political Science, XVI, Baltimore, 1898], 106). Eden had not been molested because he was considered "a harmless neutral" and the ruling gentry allowed the royal governor his freedom, yet their exposed seaboard position made them wary of overt actions that might provoke the British fleet (Nettels, *Washington and American Independence,* 278). Germain's message could have been interpreted as instructions for Eden to cooperate with the detested Lord Dunmore in reasserting British dominion over Maryland and Virginia. This seems to have been the cause for alarm raised when Barron turned the letters over to Maj. Gen. Charles Lee, who had come to Williamsburg as the newly appointed commander of the Southern Department of the Continental army. Lee consulted with the Virginia Committee of Safety and on 6 Apr. ordered the Baltimore Committee of Observation "immediately to seize the person of Governor Eden: the sin and blame be on my head. I will answer for all to the congress" (Purviance, *Narrative of Events,* 50–51; Steiner, *Life of Eden,* 108–109). The Virginia Committee of Safety was agreeable to this maneuver, which reflected a distrust of the Maryland Council of Safety, perhaps because of a private conversation Lee had held with Samuel Purviance, chairman of the Baltimore committee, that cast doubt on the Annapolis committee's vigor. On 14 Apr. Purviance dispatched troops under orders to arrest Eden and deliver him to Baltimore. At the same time, Purviance wrote the president of the Continental Congress, John Hancock, a letter which through some ineptness was read to the whole assembly—though obviously the letter had a confidential tone—for it repeated the assertion that the Maryland Council was "timorous and inactive." Hancock read the letter but did not reveal its author. Two days later, Hancock wrote both the Baltimore committee and the Maryland Council of Safety with orders from Congress to arrest Eden and seize his papers. Meanwhile, the Council took affront at these complicated proceedings and clearly believed they had been insulted by roundabout efforts to arrest Eden. Instead of ordering Eden's arrest, the Council treated him with the utmost deference (Browne, ed., *Archives of Maryland,* XI, 338–339). The Council was satisfied, for the moment, of Eden's honorable conduct, but was indignant at the actions of Purviance. Complaint was soon made of the "Indignity offered our Board by the Committee of Safety of Virginia, and the want of Confidence in the Balt. Committee." Thomas Johnson, a Maryland delegate in Philadelphia, complicated matters by pointing to Purviance's letter as the root of many evil reports (*ibid.,* 347). The question of Eden's custody seemed of little moment as the Council and congressmen appeared more zealous in punishing the anonymous letter-writer than in confining Eden. While spending much effort to fix blame on Purviance, the governor was allowed his freedom; but despite Gen. Lee's official explanation of the circumstances (David Ridgely, *Annals of Annapolis* . . . [Baltimore, 1841], 251–252), Purviance was soon censured and reprimanded by the Maryland Convention (24 May). Concurrently, the Annapolis Convention reviewed the Germain-Eden letters and concluded that Eden's conduct did not merit his arrest. Indeed, the delegates went on record as seeking "to preserve, as far as may be, the ostensible form of Government, in hopes it may have some influence towards a reunion with *Great Britain*" (Force, *American Archives*, VI, 736–737). The Maryland Convention then approved a resolution (really, a recommendation) informing Eden that the "publick quiet and safety" made his peaceable departure necessary. The fawning tone of the Maryland resolution, the implicit rebuff to Congress, and the request for a safe conduct pass for Eden from the Virginia Committee of Safety all had their effect in Williamsburg. On 29 May the Virginia Convention reacted with a resolution that was not printed in the proceedings, probably for security reasons. GM's angry resolution was more candid than diplomatic. Virginia Archivist W. J. Van Schreeven has noted that the Ms Convention journal entry for 3 June 1776 read: "Order of Friday to be expunged & other Resoln. inserted in its Room resp[ectin]g. Maryland." This meant that GM's original resolution was dropped for another version which was then inserted in the printed proceedings (Force, *American Archives*, VI, 1544–1545). Apparently after studying the matter over the weekend, the delegates decided to explain in some detail their refusal to cooperate with a sister state and scold the Maryland Convention for "a vote of fatal tendency to the common cause." The Ms copy of the resolution (as finally approved) is in a clerk's handwriting. It was printed in the *Va. Gaz.* (Purdie) on 7 June 1776. Coolness between the two conventions remained, even after Eden departed on 24 June aboard the *Fowey*.

The Ms is headed: "In Convention May 31 1776." (in a clerk's hand). GM originally wrote as though the report came from "this Convention," but he later crossed this through and changed the wording to indicate this was a "Committee" report. His abbreviated "altho" and "thro" were expanded by the clerk, who also added a "u" to GM's "Governor."

Virginia Constitution of 1776

[8 June–29 June 1776]

I. Mason's Plan [8–10 June]
II. Final Draft [29 June]

EDITORIAL NOTE

While Mason eventually took credit for authorship of the Virginia Declaration of Rights, he never listed the Constitution adopted by the 1776 Convention among his achievements. This modesty stemmed both from Mason's tendency to avoid boastfulness and the common knowledge among Convention delegates that Mason was the principal architect of both the state papers which signaled a new era in American history. Mason, always impatient with cumbersome legislative bodies, took his service on the unwieldy committee to prepare a declaration of rights and a constitution more seriously than any other member. Even before the Declaration of Rights was finally adopted, Mason had turned his mind to shaping a constitution based on those fundamental principles he was so fond of quoting.

In all likelihood, Mason tried to steer a middle course between the conservative faction and the outspoken radicals. Carter Braxton's pamphlet, *Address to the Convention of the Colony and Ancient Dominion*

*of Virginia; on the subject of Government in general and recommend-
ing a particular form to their consideration,* was a high-toned performance that would have cooled revolutionary ardor had it kindled any
support. But the "Contemptible little Tract," as Richard Henry Lee
called it, "betrays the little Knot or Junto from whence it proceeded."
(letter [to Edmund Pendleton?], 12 May 1776, Ballagh, *Lee Letters,* I,
190). Possibly a second plan had been drafted by Meriwether Smith,
though the evidence here is more traditional than substantial. It is
possible that Richard Henry Lee wrote "A GOVERNMENT SCHEME" for the
10 May 1776 issue of Purdie's *Virginia Gazette.* This piece must have
caused a stir among the delegates in Williamsburg, and in its simplicity
it was the seedling for Mason's plan. The "Scheme" called for a
bicameral legislature with a governor chosen jointly by the two houses
for a one-year term. A Council of State with twelve members would
"be promiscuously chosen" from the legislature annually. Most of the
power resided in the legislature, which could appoint judges for life
"during good behaviour," and a cluster of secondary officials (such as
the solicitor general and attorney general) who would serve seven-year
terms. The details were not spelled out.

Still another plan of government which had been circulated in
Virginia was that drafted by John Adams and printed as *Thoughts on
Government: Applicable to the Present State of the American Colonies.*
Richard Henry Lee admired the democratic tone of this work, and may
have written "A GOVERNMENT SCHEME" with Adams's ideas in mind
(Boyd, I, 334, 337).

Whatever models Mason chose, he injected some original ideas of his
own and had the plan ready when the special committee began to
deliberate. William Fleming wrote Jefferson on 15 June that the proposed Constitution "is yet in embryo," and then on 22 June he again
repeated that Mason's proposed constitution "has already taken up about
a fortnights time" (Boyd, I, 386, 406). What Edmund Randolph recalled
of the incident—that Mason's proposals "swallowed up all the rest, by
fixing the grounds and plan, which after great discussion and correction, were finally ratified," is confirmed on all sides ("Randolph's
Essay," *VHMB,* XLIV [1936], 44). Jefferson, who had prepared several
drafts because he considered carefully drafted constitutions at this
critical point as "the whole object" of the Revolution, also reviewed the
scene with magnanimity later and gave Mason the full credit (Boyd, I,
329). "The fact is unquestionable, that the Bill of Rights and the
Constitution of Virginia were drawn originally by George Mason, one
of our really great men, and of the first order of greatness" (Jefferson to
A. B. Woodward, 3 April 1825, quoted in Miller, *George Mason,* 144).
This generosity from Jefferson overlooked the lengthy preamble to the
1776 Constitution which Jefferson himself wrote. Madison also recalled
the circumstances and with more detail. The 1776 Constitution of
Virginia, Madison wrote, originated "with George Mason, who laid
before the Committee appointed to prepare a plan a very broad outline,
which was printed by the Com[mitt]e for consideration, & after being
varied on some points & filled up, was reported to the Convention where

a few further alterations gave it the form in which it now stands" (letter to A. B. Woodward, 11 September 1824, quoted in *ibid.*, 144).

The meticulous scholarship of Julian Boyd, editor of *The Papers of Thomas Jefferson,* has already traced the constitution through seven stages and integrated the various texts with extensive annotation (Boyd, I, 329–386). This material is readily available and therefore only those drafts directly related to Mason's activity are published here. Jefferson and Mason were on fundamental agreement on the main point: the citizen-voter was the source of all governmental authority. This was the bedrock of their political philosophy. Jefferson would have moved farther and faster than Mason, however, in altering the old system. As Boyd shows, Jefferson's various drafts struck at the established Anglican church, worked to correct the unequal representation in the legislature, and liberalized land distribution. His work on the Constitution also prepared him for the task as draftsman of the Declaration of Independence and was in no manner wasted effort.

No manuscript of Mason's proposed constitution has been found. What probably happened was that his original copy was used as a working plan, altered in the committee, and sent about 19 or 20 June to the Williamsburg printer who prepared copies for the entire Convention to peruse. Fleming sent one of these copies to Jefferson. Madison also saved his, and from these two printed committee reports the essence of Mason's plan is clear. Stylistically, he followed the "scheme" of 10 May with the prefatory "Let the legislative, executive, and judicative departments . . ." in all but the last article. The legislature would consist of two branches, known as the General Assembly, and would be elected and meet annually. Lower house legislators would be selected from the counties, towns, and the College of William and Mary by freeholders "qualified according to law and ancient usage." The upper house would be selected from twenty-four senatorial districts by a unique method. Twelve electors holding property worth five hundred pounds would be chosen by the voters, who would in turn pick a senator. All laws would originate in the lower house but could be amended in the Senate except appropriations, which went to the Senate to be "wholly approved or rejected." The governor was to be elected by the General Assembly for an annual term, with no veto power or right to dissolve their sessions. An eight-member Council of State would be chosen by the General Assembly from its membership "to assist in the administration of government." The Council membership would rotate and the governor would serve as president of the Council. Judgeships and major state offices would be filled by legislative appointments, while minor state and county officials would be named by the governor. The General Assembly would choose delegates for the Continental Congress, but militia appointments were left to the governor. Legislative rules were established, the government was to be known as the Commonwealth of Virginia, and a final article implemented the entire proposal by providing for an interim government until the spring of 1777.

Mason's choice of the word "commonwealth" was no happenstance.

Mason knew passages of John Locke's *Second Treatise on Government* verbatim. None struck Mason more forcefully than Locke's notion that a commonwealth was a form of government wherein the legislature was supreme. A written constitution in itself was salutary because "whoever has the Legislative or Supream Power of any Common-Wealth, is bound to govern by establish'd *standing Laws,* promulgated and known to the People, and not by Extemporary Decrees . . ." (Locke, *Two Treatises,* ed. Laslett, 371). Thus Mason was reflecting the consensus of Virginia patriots who favored a separation of powers, but not an equality of powers, in the branches of government somewhat as the English Whigs of a century earlier had turned on the crown. And as the crown's prerogatives suffered in 1688, so the executive office in Mason's constitution was mostly substance with little form. The recent memory of the detested Lord Dunmore, along with hundreds of jarring experiences under royal appointees, confirmed Locke's message concerning legislative supremacy.

Mason's ability to summarize prevailing opinion on the functions and role of government in an agrarian society speeded up the Convention's business. A lost letter Mason wrote to his friend, the Rev. Lee Massey, probably would tell us much of his personal thoughts on how the main business was carried off with such dispatch. At any rate, by 23 June Mason reported the delegates believed their work was nearly over.

And so it was, for on 24 June the printed copies of Mason's draft were distributed to the Convention. Minor changes came from the special committee, while others arose from the general debate as the clerk read through the draft, and then labored through a second reading. Mason's (and perhaps Lee's) subjunctive form was changed to the imperative. Words were inserted, to be struck out later, and some of Mason's clauses were lined through and then restored. (Boyd, I, 369–377, indicates the alterations and emendations that took place in both the small and larger committee sessions.) A good deal of the final revision simply ordered "Strike out the Word Let." After more debate on 26 and 27 June, the Convention heard the revised Constitution read for a third time. A significant addition came with the inclusion of an article (portions of it taken from Jefferson's draft) which was meant to squelch the claims of land speculators by reaffirming Virginia's boundaries under the 1609 charter. From Mason's viewpoint, Jefferson's proposition was well timed, for it gave support to the Ohio Company claims and could have been assigned to selfish motives had the thought come from him.

On 28 June the delegates made immediate plans to implement the new form of government by choosing "Governour, Privy Council, and Attorney-General, for this country" on the next day. Unanimous adoption of the Constitution on 29 June was a formality (Force, *American Archives,* VI, 1598). The Convention stayed in session, gathering up loose legislative ends, electing Patrick Henry as the first governor, and preparing the ways and means of carrying on the war. For the weary Mason, however, it was time to return to his neglected plantation, his beloved jut of land along the Potomac. The new form of government would work, Mason knew, if only there was "a firm adherence to justice, moderation, temperance, frugality, and virtue, and . . . frequent recurrence to fundamental principles."

Mason's Plan for the Virginia Constitution of 1776

[8–10 June 1776]

A PLAN OF GOVERNMENT

Laid before the committee of the House, which they have ordered to be printed for the perusal of
the members.

1. Let the legislative, executive, and judicative departments, be separate and distinct, so that neither exercise the powers properly belonging to the other.

2. Let the legislative be formed of two distinct branches, who, together, shall be a complete legislature. They shall meet once, or oftener, every year, and shall be called the GENERAL ASSEMBLY OF VIRGINIA.

3. Let one of these be called the Lower House of Assembly, and consist of two delegates, or representatives, chosen for each county, annually; of such men as have resided in the same for one year last past, are freeholders of the county, possess an estate of inheritance of land, in Virginia, of at least one thousand pounds value, and are upwards of twenty four years of age.

4. Let the other be called the Upper House of Assembly, and consist of twenty four members; for whose election, let the different counties be divided into twenty four districts, and each county of the respective district, at the time of the election of its delegates for the Lower House, choose twelve deputies, or sub-electors, being freeholders residing therein, and having an estate of inheritance of lands within the district of at least five hundred pounds value. In case of dispute, the qualifications to be determined by the majority of the said deputies. Let these deputies choose, by ballot, one member for the Upper House of Assembly, who is a freeholder of the district, hath been a resident therein for one year last past, possesses an estate of inheritance of lands in Virginia of at least two thousand pounds value, and is upwards of twenty eight years of age. To keep up this assembly, by rotation, let the districts be equally divided into four classes, and numbered, at the end of one year after the general election. Let the six members elected by the first division be dis-

placed, rendered ineligible for four years, and the vacancies be supplied in the manner aforesaid. Let this rotation be applied to each division according to its number, and continued in due order annually.

5. Let each House settle its own rules of proceeding direct writs of election for supplying intermediate vacancies; and let the right of suffrage, both in the election of members for the Lower House, and of deputies for the districts, be extended to those having leases for land, in which there is an unexpired term of seven years, and to every housekeeper who hath resided for one year last past in the county, and hath been the father of three children in this country.

6. Let all laws originate in the lower House, to be approved, or rejected, by the Upper House, or to be amended with the consent of the Lower House, except money bills, which in no instance shall be altered by the Upper House, but wholly approved or rejected.

7. Let a Governour, or chief magistrate, be chosen annually, by joint ballot of both Houses; who shall not continue in that office longer than three years successively, and then be ineligible for the next three years. Let an adequate, but moderate salary, be settled on him, during his continuance in office; and let him, with the advice of a Council of State, exercise the executive powers of government, and the power of proroguing or adjourning the General Assembly, or of calling it upon emergencies, and of granting reprieves or pardons, except in cases where the prosecution shall have been carried on by the Lower House of Assembly.

8. Let a Privy Council, or Council of State, consisting of eight members, be chosen by joint ballot of both Houses of Assembly, promiscuously from their members, or the people at large, to assist in the administration of government. Let the Governour be President of this Council; but let them annually choose one of their own members, as Vice-President, who, in case of the death of absence of the Governour, shall act as Lieutenant-Governour. Let three members be sufficient to act, and their advice be entered of record in their proceedings. Let them appoint their own clerk, who shall have a salary settled by law, and take an oath of secrecy, in such matters as he shall be directed by the Board to conceal, unless called upon by the Lower House of Assembly for information. Let a sum of money, appropriated to that purpose, be divided annually among the members, in proportion to their attendance; and let them be incapable, during their continuance of office, of sitting in either House of Assembly. Let two members be removed, by ballot of their own Board, at the end of every three years, and be ineligible for the three

next years. Let this be regularly continued, by rotation, so as that no member be removed before he hath been three years in the Council; and let these vacancies, as well as those occasioned by death or incapacity, be supplied by new elections, in the same manner as the first.

9. Let the Governour, with the advice of the Privy Council, have the appointment of the militia officers, and the government of the militia, under the laws of the country.

10. Let the two Houses of Assembly, by joint ballot, appoint judges of the supreme court, judges in chancery, judges of admirality, and the attorney-general, to be commissioned by the Governour, and continue in office during good behaviour. In case of death or incapacity, let the Governour, with the advice of the Privy Council, appoint persons to succeed in office pro tempore, to be approved or displaced by both Houses. Let these officers have fixed and adequate salaries, and be incapable of having a seat in either House of Assembly, or in the Privy Council, except the attorney-general and the treasurer, who may be permitted to a seat in the Lower House of Assembly.

11. Let the Governour, and Privy Council, appoint justices of the peace for the counties. Let the clerks of all the courts, the sheriffs, and coroners, be nominated by the respective courts, approved by the Governour and Privy Council, and commissioned by the Governour. Let the clerks be continued during good behaviour, and all fees be regulated by law. Let the justices appoint constables.

12. Let the Governour, any of the Privy Counsellors, judges of the supreme court, and all other officers of government, for mal-administration, or corruption, be prosecuted by the Lower House of Assembly (to be carried on by the attorney-general, or such other person as the House may appoint) in the supreme court of common law. If found guilty, let him, or them, be either removed from office, or for ever disabled to hold any office under the government, or subjected to such pains or penalties as the laws shall direct.

13. Let all commissions run in the name of the Commonwealth of Virginia, and be tested by the Governour, with the seal of the commonwealth annexed. Let writs run in the same manner, and be tested by the clerks of the several courts. Let indictments conclude, Against the peace and dignity of the commonwealth.

14. Let a treasurer be appointed annually, by joint ballot of both houses.

15. In order to introduce this government, let the representatives of the people, now met in Convention, choose twenty four members

to be an upper House; and let both Houses, by joint ballot, choose a Governour and Privy Council; the Upper House to continue until the last day of March next, and the other officers until the end of the succeeding session of Assembly. In case of vacancies, the President to issue writs for new elections.

Printed document (Jefferson Papers, DLC). This two-page committee report is all that survives of GM's original plan. Perhaps GM's handwritten copy was transmitted to the printers to prepare the report and never returned to the Convention clerk. The other known copy is in the Madison Papers, DLC.

As Helen Hill Miller has noted, "the absence of a first draft in his [GM's] handwriting makes impossible exact comparision between his plan the form finally adopted" (*George Mason,* 143). However, the printed report of the special committee which William Fleming sent to Jefferson on 22 June corroborates numerous statements that GM was the principal author (Boyd, I, 368–369, 386, 406). While the intellectual sources of GM's plan range from John Locke's pronouncements to American experience in statecraft, he sought to bring together the essential ideas current in revolutionary Virginia on what constituted a workable framework. It is possible that GM had seen John Adams's letter to R. H. Lee of 15 Nov. 1775, which outlined a constitution and added that "In this way, a single month is sufficient, without the least convulsion, or even animosity, to accomplish a total revolution in the government of a colony" (Adams, *Works,* IV, 186). Certainly, there was much kinship between the ideas of Adams, Lee, and GM—all wanted brief plans that would implement the revolutionary ideas concerning "life, liberty, and the pursuing and obtaining of happiness and safety." Basic to this philosophy was the supremacy of the legislature, a principle impressed by Locke on the whole generation. Another postulate was the separation of powers under a bicameral legislature. Jefferson's attention to the problem produced three drafts, proof that the construction of free governments was much on the young Virginian's mind. The three Jefferson drafts, printed in Boyd, I, 337–365, show more attention to specific details of government, include a list of personal liberties, and provide a broader base for both representation and suffrage than GM conceived proper. Jefferson also wanted the constitution ratified by voters in two-thirds of the counties before it became operative. Though some 20th-century historians have found Jefferson's plans too hastily conceived, so that "by comparison Mason's work was a model of completeness" (Levy, *Origins of Fifth Amendment,* 408), both Jefferson and GM accomplished their aims. Jefferson's long preamble and several important additions were finally added by 29 June, and GM's essential plan permitted the newly proclaimed Commonwealth of Virginia to go into operation, anticipating the Declaration of Independence by a few weeks. There was an urgency in the Williamsburg air, and GM responded by drafting this plan which was not vastly altered in the special drafting body or in the committee of the whole. GM probably consulted the "GOVERNMENT SCHEME" from the 10 May *Va. Gaz.* (Purdie), which Richard Henry Lee may have written, for a basic framework. GM's plan codified much of the old practices of colonial Virginia government, explicitly limited the powers of the separate branches, and did nothing to disturb the colonial statutes already in force. "Free government is the protecting the People in their Liberties by stated Rules" was a maxim of GM's day (*Cato's Letters,* II, 249). To this sound principle GM seemed to reflect also Pufendorf's charge that "Human Lawgivers are not us'd to cut every Thing to the quick" (*Law of Nature and Nations* [London, 1729], 23). The details which Jefferson included were missing in GM's draft, probably because GM's intellectual bent was toward brevity (he was not, after all, a lawyer) and the exigencies of the situation called for an interim government that would allow the details to be filled in later. In drafting the Declaration of Rights, GM believed he was enunciating timeless principles of human conduct for a good and happy society. The old form of government, deriving its powers from the crown, had not outlived its usefulness so much as it needed a new source of authority, i.e., the people. This explains the residue of power in a legislature composed of FREEHOLDERS OF THE COUNTY, who owned AN ESTATE . . . OF LAND . . . OF AT LEAST ONE THOUSAND POUNDS VALUE. This qualification continued the landed gentry in office, not because there was a threat from city-dwelling holders of capital, but because this was the confirmed system from previous Virginia experience. The unique plan of electors to choose the upper house "has the appearance of being an original scheme, probably one that Mason conceived" (Boyd, I, 369n). These legislators, with LANDS IN VIRGINIA OF AT LEAST TWO THOUSAND POUNDS VALUE, would give a conservative check on the lower house but both would be representative of the landed class. GM was convinced that if a man had either property or children, he had a stake in society and should be a participant in its decisions. Hence a leaseholder or one who WAS THE FATHER OF THREE CHILDREN would qualify as a voter, though technically propertyless. MONEY BILLS, acts for collecting taxes or dispensing public money, had been an exclusive power of the House of Burgesses since 1689 (Jack P. Greene, The Quest for Power . . . [Chapel Hill, 1963], 66–67). Wording of the article creating a COUNCIL OF STATE . . . CHOSEN . . . PROMISCUOUSLY from the General Assembly membership may indicate that GM was attentive to the "GOVERNMENT SCHEME" of 10 May, since the language and ideas are nearly identical (Boyd, I, 369n). John Adams's pamphlet, Thoughts on Government, which was circulated in Williamsburg in May-June of 1776, strongly advocated the "rotation of all offices" (Adams, Works, IV, 197). GM's provision for rotation of councilors would have effectively ended the older system of long tenure that oftentimes made a councilor's seat seem hereditary. By granting the weakened executive power APPOINTMENT OF THE MILITIA OFFICERS, GM's plan (perhaps borrowed for Adams's pamphlet) preserved the vaunted civilian control of the military power. For the 10th article on the judiciary, GM must have consulted his lawyer colleagues in establishing a system compatible to a landed society that looked to the ocean for its commerce and communications with the rest of the world. The appointment of minor functionaries confirmed the working arrangement already in practice but substituted the elected governor for the king's appointee. Henceforth all commissions would be IN THE NAME OF THE COMMONWEALTH OF VIRGINIA, explicit recognition—as Locke averred—that the form of government was based on the supremacy of the legislature. The 13th article also shows more influence by Adams's pamphlet, wherein the similarity of phrases and ideas is pronounced. The implementation, or 15th, article would seem to indicate that GM and the special committee members did not conceive that the plan would be perpetually effective. Its spirit is rather that of a tentative offering, a way to keep the country moving and the war prosecuted until a happier day and some experience would afford leisure for the adoption of a more precise system. No man present, least of all GM, would have been so rash as to predict that the plan was going to provide the people with a constitution that would last until 1830 or furnish a model for other emerging states. Although Jefferson saw "very capital defects" in the Constitution a decade later (Notes on the State of Virginia, ed. William Peden [Chapel Hill, 1955], 118), this was the wisdom of hindsight and a judgment based on his unfortunate term as governor. As Edmund Randolph remembered the situation, some of the radical delegates were so anti-British they were eager to dump rather than salvage the vestiges of English constitutionalism. The demand that the governor be stripped of the veto power was a case in point. Randolph recalled that Patrick Henry was the lone delegate with enough popularity to risk an attack on this idea as creating a governor who "would be a mere phantom" at the mercy of the legislature "unless he could interpose" a check on the legislature ("Randolph's Essay," *VMHB*, XLIV [1936], 48). The unequal legislative apportionment that favored tidewater counties, Randolph added, was approved "without a murmur, and even without a proposition to the contrary." Land ownership as a requisite for voting rights was also so acceptable that Randolph could not recollect a single voice that spoke against this restriction. Looking back on the 1776, Randolph saw in the Convention and Constitution proof "that the most expanded mind, as that of George Mason's was, who sketched the constitution, cannot secure itself from oversights and negligencies, in the tumult of heterogeneous and indistinct ideas of government, circulating in a popular body, unaccustomed to much abstraction" (*ibid.*, 105). With the retrospective wisdom of a former governor, Randolph said the council rather than an aid became a clog, with the councilors courting legislative favor because of "the triennial ostracism of two of them." Disenchanted by 1784, Madison's jaundiced view was that the Constitution had been enacted "from impulse of necessity." Madison catalogued a list of 11 defects and agreed with Jefferson that a "Power from the people is no where pretended." In short, the Convention delegates had taken extraordinary powers in launching a wartime emergency government which should either be altered or ratified by the people (Brant, *Madison*, I, 251–252).

Final Draft of the Virginia Constitution of 1776

[29 June 1776]

[A preamble written by Jefferson was added to the revised draft, which is printed in Boyd, I, 377–379. This statement is similar in tone and content to portions of the Declaration of Independence. George III is blamed for a long train of abuses, ranging from "putting his negative on laws the most wholesome and necessary for the publick good"; to "declaring us out of his Allegiance and Protection. . . ."]

By which several acts of misrule, the government of this country, as formerly exercised under the crown of *Great Britain*, is TOTALLY DISSOLVED.

We therefore, the delegates and representatives of the good people of VIRGINIA, having maturely considered the premises, and viewing with great concern the deplorable condition to which this once happy country must be reduced, unless some regular adequate mode of civil polity is speedily adopted, and in compliance with a recommendation of the General Congress, do ordain and declare the future form of Government of *Virginia* to be as followeth:

The legislative, executive, and judiciary departments, shall be separate and distinct, so that neither exercise the powers properly belonging to the other; nor shall any person exercise the powers of more than one of them at the same time, except that the Justices of the county courts shall be eligible to either House of Assembly.

The legislative shall be formed of two distinct branches, who, together, shall be a complete legislature. They shall meet once, or oftener, every year, and shall be called the GENERAL ASSEMBLY OF VIRGINIA.

One of these shall be called the HOUSE OF DELEGATES, and consist of two representatives to be chosen for each county, and for the District of *West Augusta*, annually, of such men as actually reside in and are freeholders of the same, or duly qualified according to law, and also of one delegate or representative to be chosen annually for the city of *Williamsburg*, and one for the borough of *Norfolk*, and a representative for each of such other cities and boroughs, as many hereafter be allowed particular representation by the legislature; but when any city or borough shall so decrease as that the number of persons having right of suffrage therein shall have been for the space of seven years successively less than half the number of voters in some one county in *Virginia*, such city or borough thenceforward shall cease to send a delegate or representative to the Assembly.

The other shall be called the SENATE, and consist of twenty four members, of whom thirteen shall constitute a House to proceed on business, for whose election the different counties shall be divided into twenty four districts, and each county of the respective district, at the time of the election of its delegates, shall vote for one Senator, who is actually a resident and freeholder within the district, or duly qualified according to law, and is upwards of twenty five years of age; and the sheriffs of each county, within five days at farthest after the last county election in the district, shall meet at some convenient place, and from the poll so taken in their respective counties return as a Senator ⟨to the House of Senators⟩ the man who shall have the greatest number of votes in the whole district. To keep up this Assembly by rotation, the districts shall be equally divided into four classes, and numbered by lot. At the end of one year after the general election, the six members elected by the first division shall be displaced, and the vacancies thereby occasioned supplied from such class or division, by new election, in the manner aforesaid. This rotation shall be applied to each division, according to its number, and continued in due order annually.

The right of suffrage in the election of members for both Houses shall remain as exercised at present, and each House shall choose its own speaker, appoint its own officers, settle its own rules of proceeding, and direct writs of election for supplying intermediate vacancies.

All laws shall originate in the House of Delegates, to be approved or rejected by the Senate, or to be amended with the consent of the House of Delegates; except money bills, which in no instance shall be altered by the Senate, but wholly approved or rejected.

A Governour, or chief magistrate, shall be chosen annually, by joint ballot of both Houses, to be taken in each House respectively, deposited in the conference room, the boxes examined jointly by a committee of each House, and the numbers severally reported to them, that the appointments may be entered, (which shall be the mode of taking the joint ballot of both Houses in all cases) who shall not continue in that office longer than three years successively, nor be eligible until the expiration of four years after he shall have been out of that office. An adequate, but moderate salary, shall be settled on him during his continuance in office; and he shall, with the advice of a Council of State, exercise the executive powers of government according to the laws of this commonwealth; and shall not, under any pretence, exercise any power or prerogative by virtue of any law, statute, or custom, of *England:* But he shall, with the advice of the Council of State, have the power of granting reprieves or pardons, except where the prosecution shall have been carried on by the House of Delegates, or the law shall otherwise particularly direct; in which cases, no reprieve or Pardon shall be granted but by resolve of the House of Delegates.

Either House of the General Assembly may adjourn themselves respectively. The Governour shall not prorogue or adjourn the Assembly during their sitting, nor dissolve them at any time; but he shall, if necessary, either by advice of the Council of State, or on application of a majority of the House of Delegates, call them before the time to which they shall stand prorogued or adjourned.

A Privy Council, or Council of State, consisting of eight members, shall be chosen by joint ballot of both Houses of Assembly, either from their own members or the people at large, to assist in the administration of government. They shall annually choose out of their own members a president, who, in case of the death, inability, or necessary absence of the Governour from the government, shall act as Lieutenant Governour. Four members shall be sufficient to act, and their advice and proceedings shall be entered of record, and signed by the members present (to any part whereof any member may enter his dissent) to be laid before the General Assembly, when called for by them. This Council may appoint their own clerk, who shall have a salary settled by law, and take an oath of secrecy in such matters as he shall be directed by the board to conceal. A sum of money appropriated to that purpose shall be divided annually among the members, in proportion to their attendance; and they shall be incapable, during their continuance in office, of sitting in either House of Assembly. Two Members shall be removed, by joint Ballot of both Houses of Assembly at the end of every three years, and be ineligible for the three next years. These vacancies, as well as those occasioned by death or incapacity, shall be supplied by new elections, in the same manner.

The Delegates for *Virginia* to the Continental Congress shall be chosen annually, or superseded in the mean time by joint ballot of both Houses of Assembly.

The present militia officers shall be continued, and vacancies supplied by appointment of the Governour, with the advice of the Privy Council, on recommendations from the respective county courts; but the Governour and Council shall have a power of suspending any officer, and ordering a court-martial on complaint of misbehaviour or inability, or to supply vacancies of officers happening when in actual service. The Governour may embody the militia, with the advice of the Privy Council; and, when embodied, shall alone have the direction of the militia under the laws of the country.

The two Houses of Assembly shall, by joint ballot, appoint Judges of the Supreme Court of Appeals, and General Court, Judges in Chancery, Judges of Admiralty, Secretary, and the Attorney-General, to be commissioned by the Governour, and continue in office during good behaviour. In case of death, incapacity, or resignation, the Governour, with the advice of the Privy Council, shall appoint persons to succeed in office, to be approved or displaced by both Houses. These Officers shall have fixed and adequate salaries, and together with all others holding lucrative offices, and all ministers of the Gospel of every denomination, be incapable of being elected members of either House of Assembly, or the Privy Council.

The Governour, with the advice of the Privy Council, shall appoint Justices of the Peace for the counties; and in case of vacancies, or a necessity of increasing the number hereafter, such appointments to be made upon the recommendation of the respective county courts. The present acting Secretary in *Virginia*, and Clerks of all the County Courts, shall continue in Office. In case of vacancies, either by death, incapacity, or resignation, a Secretary shall be appointed as before directed, and the Clerks by the respective courts. The present and future Clerks shall hold their offices during good behaviour, to be judged of and determined in the General Court. The Sheriffs and Coroners shall be nominated by the respective courts, approved by the Governour with the advice of the Privy Council, and commissioned by the Governour. The Justices shall appoint Constables, and all fees of the aforesaid Officers be regulated by law.

The Governour, when he is out of office, and others offending against the state, either by mal-administration, corruption, or other means by which the safety of the state may be endangered, shall be impeachable by the House of Delegates. Such impeachment to be prosecuted by the Attorney-General, or such other person or persons as the House may appoint in the General Court, according to the laws of the land. If found guilty, he or they shall be either for ever disabled to hold any office under Government, or removed from such office *pro tempore*, or subjected to such pains or penalties as the laws shall direct.

If all, or any of the Judges of the General Court, should, on good grounds (to be judged of by the House of Delegates) be accused of any of the crimes or offences before-mentioned, such House of Delegates may, in like manner, impeach the Judge or Judges so accused, to be prosecuted in the Court of Appeals; and he or they, if found guilty, shall be punished in the same manner as is prescribed in the preceding clause.

Commissions and Grants shall run, *In the Name of the* COMMONWEALTH *of* VIRGINIA, and bear test⟨e⟩ by the Governour with the Seal of the Common wealth annexed. Writs shall run in the same manner, and bear test⟨e⟩ by the clerks of the several courts. Indictments shall conclude, *Against the peace and dignity of the commonwealth.*

A Treasurer shall be appointed annually, by joint ballot of both Houses.

All escheats, penalties, and forfeitures, heretofore going to the King, shall go to the commonwealth, save only such, as the legislature may abolish, or otherwise provide for.

The territories contained within the Charters erecting the Colonies of *Maryland, Pennsylvania, North* and *South Carolina,* are hereby ceded, released, and forever confirmed to the people of those colonies respectively, with all the rights of property, jurisdiction, and government, and all other rights whatsoever which might at any time heretofore have been claimed by *Virginia,* except the free navigation and use of the rivers *Potowmack* and *Pohomoke,* with the property of the *Virginia* shores or strands bordering on either of the said rivers, and all improvements which have been or shall be made thereon. The western and northern extent of *Virginia* shall in all other respects stand as fixed by the charter of king James the first, in the year one thousand six hundred and nine, and by the publick treaty of peace between the courts of *Great Britain* and *France* in the year one thousand seven hundred and sixty three; unless by act of ⟨this⟩ legislature, one or more territories shall hereafter be laid off, and governments established westward of the *Allegheny* mountains. And no purchase⟨s⟩ of land shall be made of the *Indian* natives but on behalf of the publick, by authority of the General Assembly.

In order to introduce this government, the representatives of the people met in Convention shall choose a Governour and Privy Council, also such other officers directed to be chosen by both Houses as may be judged necessary to be immediately appointed. The Senate to be first chosen by the people, to continue until the last day of *March* next, and the other officers until the end of the succeeding session of Assembly. In case of Vacancies, the speaker of either House shall issue writs for new elections.

Printed from the 5 July 1776 supplement of the *Va. Gaz.* (Purdie). A clerk's copy (Vi) seems to have been used by the printer, judging from the directions interlined on the Ms (Boyd, I, 383n).

GM's role at the Convention seems to have been that of a draftsman and expediter. From a variety of pamphlets and newspapers suggestions, he drew together and articulated the chief aims of the progressive faction of the Convention. Jefferson later listed "the bolder spirits of Henry, the Lees, Pages, Mason, &c., with whom I went in all points" (letter to P. H. Wirt, 14 Aug. 1814). Their goal was a smooth, rapid transition from a royal colony to a republican form of government, and the 15 May resolution from the Continental Congress urging states to speed this change was a sufficient challenge to their ingenuity. Although the sources of the resulting Virginia Constitution may have harked back to the Cromwellian Commonwealth (Miller, *George Mason*, 142-143), the immediate problem was solved by infusing Lockean doctrines with colonial experience in self-government. In the debates of 26-28 June the Convention approved the addition of Jefferson's indictment of George III as a preamble, delineated the lines of power (often using or paraphrasing parts of Jefferson's previous drafts, as Boyd, I, 384n-386n, notes), and completed the transition from a royal to a republican government. Out of the debate there also came approval of Jefferson's proposition to reaffirm the state boundaries along lines established by the 1609 royal charter. Lacking a journal of the Convention debates, it is fruitless to speculate on what changes GM approved or indeed wrote himself between 22 and 28 June. His lost letter to Rev. Lee Massey of 23 June might have explained such matters, for GM mentions that he has reported there "what we are doing in Convention." The relatively brief debate on the constitution indicates that GM's original plan formed the basis for a compromise between the progressive and conservative factions. Edmund Pendleton deplored the rising "Spirit of Party, that bane of all public Councils" in Williamsburg (Boyd, I, 472). Thus for the sake of accommodation "few or no changes were made where the existing governmental framework had not been subject to great strain" (Miller, *George Mason*, 147). The major alterations in GM's plan were in the composition and selection of the General Assembly. The ban on ALL MEMBERS OF THE GOSPEL as legislators probably reflected the unhappy debates on the Parson's Cause that shook the colony in 1763. Other important changes (1) prohibited a breach of the separated powers concept, (2) provided for ESCHEATS, PENALTIES, AND FORFEITURES, and (3) defined the Virginia boundaries as fixed by the 1609 royal charter—all originally proposed by Jefferson and added by his friends during the floor debate. The provision permitting the impeachment when THE GOVERNOUR . . . IS OUT OF OFFICE is traceable to the Athenian code which held officials accountable after their tenure expired (Gummere, *American Colonial Mind*, 186). The overall goal was to provide a bridge between the crown colony and independency with a minimum of overt change. Contrasted with more modern instruments (the 1907 Oklahoma Constitution filled sixty-four printed pages) it was a model of simplicity. The full text was soon reprinted in other states (Annapolis *Md. Gaz.* on 18 and 25 July, and the Boston *Continental Journal* on 2 Aug. 1776). R. H. Lee immediately hailed the instrument as "very much of the democratic kind . . . [a] political machine, which I hope is sufficiently guarded against the Monster Tyranny" (Ballagh, I, 203). Nonetheless, certain flaws appeared after a decade of experience. Madison called the council "a grave of useful talents" and sounded GM out on a revising convention in 1783. Madison then reported to Jefferson that GM *"was sound and ripe and I think would not decline a participation in the work. His heterodoxy lay chiefly in being too little impressed with* either the *necessity* or the *proper means of preserving* the confederacy" (Boyd, VI, 377). Jefferson was concerned lest GM was "determined to sleep on" instead of joining the reform forces (Boyd, VI, 381). By 1785, Jefferson was openly critical of the Constitution, although he recalled that it was the first "formed in the whole United States. No wonder then that time and trial have discovered very capital defects in it" (*Notes on Virginia*, 118). Chief among the critics' concerns were the inequality of legislative representation (favoring the tidewater counties and penalizing the piedmont ones) and the property qualification for voting rights. Jefferson also objected to the seemingly high-handed way in which the 1776 Convention enacted a permanent constitution. "So far as a temporary organization of government was necessary to render our opposition energetic, so far their organization was valid" (*ibid.*, 122). With the coming of peace, Jefferson thought a sober second look at the 1776 constitution would bring the necessary reforms. Meanwhile, GM showed no disposition to rush toward change and in 1783 favored a delay in constitutional revision "until the present ferment . . . has subsided, and men's minds have had time to cool" (letter to William Cabell, 11 May 1783). The reform forces failed to gain the initiative as Jefferson proceeded to France and Madison became more involved in national affairs. Despite constant criticism, the 1776 constitution continued to serve the Commonwealth until a revisioning convention met in 1829/1830. The new constitution was submitted to the people and ratified in 1830, although some of its opponents were sympathetic to John Randolph's remark that there had been little improvement "by an Assembly in which every man thought himself a George Mason."

Slight variations in punctuation and prepositions from the clerk's copy (Vi) are the essential difference between Purdie's version and that printed in Boyd, I, 377–383. The portions in angle brackets appear on the clerk's copy. It was Purdie's version which was widely reprinted and established as a model elsewhere.

From Martin Cockburn

[[*ca.* 18 June 1776. GM acknowledged this letter, which has not been found, in his reply of 23 June from Williamsburg. It appears to have contained queries for the Steptoe family—possibly James or John—of Northumberland County. Cockburn seems to have also mentioned GM's family, and particularly George Mason, Jr., who was left in nominal charge of Gunston Hall during his father's absence.]]

To Martin Cockburn

Dear Sir.   Williamsburg June 23d. 1776.

I recd. yr. obliging favour yesterday ♍ post, wch. not having time to answer then, I take the Opportunity of doing it to-day, ♍ Capt. Westcot. The Business you mention shall be attended to, so far as Richd. Lee Esqr. can inform me; for neither of the Mr. Steptoes have been here. Having just wrote a long Letter to our Friend Mr. Massey, I must beg Leave to refer you to him for what we are doing in Convention. Public News we have none, more than you'll see in the Papers, except that one of that infernal Crew the Gutridge's has just taken a french West India Man, coming to trade with us, & carried her up to Dunmore's Fleet, at Gwinn's Island. On Friday arrived here from James Town, taken by Capts. Barron, 217 highland Soldiers (very likely Fellows) of the 42d. & 71st Regiments. I only mention this, because from Purdy's acct. one might be puzled to know whether they were Soldiers or Emigrants: the Cadets, which are only two, will have their Parolle, & the common Soldiers will be distributed in the middle Counties, & permitted to contract for Wages with such as will employ them. The Convention have determined to adjourn next Saturday; but I hardly think they will be able to do it so soon. I am rejoiced to hear of my dear Children's Health, as well of your Family's, to all whom please to remember me kindly. Tell George his recruiting Expences are not allowed, nor any of the Minute Officers. I have got a Warrant for £3..5 for the two Guns, chd. in his Acct. furnished the Detachment of his Compy. wch. march'd with Ensign Cofer. I have spoken to Capt. Lee about the two Guns, his Compy. carried from Dumfries; but he says he knows nothing about them, & unless George can make some other Proof, they will be lost, & no Satisfaction recd. for them;

especially as Capt. Lee's Company, wth. the rest of the third Regiment is ordered to march imediatly to Carolina. He shou'd also get a
Certificate from Ensign Cofer for the Musket he took of mine from
John Tillet's Shop; tho' I had much rather have the Musket return'd; for as we have a Bayonet for her, she wou'd now sell at
£5..10. As I don't think I can be up in time, George must do the
best he can wth. our Harvest, & must be as saving as he can of Rum
& Provisions. Rum now sells here from 10/ to 12/ P. Gallon. He
shou'd have all the Scythes & Cradles & Rakes got in order. Pray
excuse Haste, & believe me Dear Sir Your sincerely affecte.

G M[ASON]

RC (Mason Papers, DLC). Addressed to Cockburn at "Spring-field . . . to
the Care of Mr. Henderson." Endorsed: "Recd. 30th June 1776."
  Cockburn's letter has not been found. Also missing is the LONG LETTER TO . . .
MR. MASSEY with its account of the Convention business. THAT INFERNAL CREW
THE GUTRIDGE'S was the John Goodrich family, turncoats who became tory
privateers after taking a £5,000 advance from the Committee of Safety for
gunpowder (Grigsby, II, 46n) and after defying the Convention. Gwynn
or GWINN'S ISLAND, at the mouth of the Piankatank River, was used by Lord
Dunmore for a tory base until its destruction by patriots in midsummer 1776.
The ambiguous PURDY'S ACCT. was in printer Alexander Purdie's Va. Gaz. of 21
June 1776 and dated 22 June (either a misprint or the paper was published
casually): "This morning capt. James Barron came to town from Jamestown,
with the agreeable news that he and his brother, in two small armed vessels,
were safe arrived . . . [and had captured] the Oxford transport from Glasgow,
having on board 217 Scotch Highlanders, with a uumber [sic] of women and
children, which they took last Wednesday evening, on her way up to Gwyn's
island, to join lord Dnnmore [sic]." Warrants from the Committee of Safety
authorized purchases of weapons for use by minutemen and Virginia regiments. GM furnished accounts for the Committee's approval, sometimes with
more success (see receipt of 28 Dec. 1777). ENSIGN COFER was John Cof(f)er, an
officer in George Mason, Jr.'s company of minutemen. Virginia troops were
ordered to join Gen. Charles Lee as he hurried to thwart the anticipated
landing of Sir Henry Clinton's forces at Charleston, S.C. However, the Va.
Gaz. (Purdie) of 21 June 1776 reported that it was not THE THIRD REGIMENT but
the 8th (under Col. Muhlenberg) that was moving southward.
  Most of GM's signature has been torn away.

To Reverend Lee Massey

[[23 June 1776. GM wrote Martin Cockburn on this day: "Having just
wrote a long Letter to our Friend Mr. Massey, I must beg Leave to refer
you to him for what we are doing in Convention." This lost letter
probably would have filled in many gaps concerning GM's involvement
in drafting the Virginia Constitution of 1776. The special committee
had used his plan as the basis for their work and by 22 June the major
business had been completed when delegate William Fleming sent a

printed copy "drawn by Colo. G. Mason and by him laid before the committee" to Jefferson in Philadelphia (Boyd, I, 406).]]

Resolutions on Western Land Titles and the Private Purchases of Land from Indian Tribes

[[*24 June 1776.* In response to a petition from "the Inhabitants on the Western frontiers . . . complaining of exorbitant demands made on them for Lands claimed by persons pretending to derive titles from Indian deeds and purchases," the Virginia Convention passed two resolutions. The first recognized the preemptive rights of bona fide settlers until the status of all western land claims could be settled. The second resolution declared: "That no purchase of Lands within the chartered limits of *Virginia* shall be made, under any pretence whatever, from any *Indian* Tribe or Nation, without the approbation of the *Virginia* Legislature." No Ms of these resolutions has been found, nor does the *Journal* (as reprinted in Force, *American Archives*, VI, 1588) give a clue on authorship. GM's heavy involvement in the western land problem and his continuing concern over the so-called "unappropriated and waste lands" (i.e., land still in the public domain belonging to Virginia) make it highly probable that he either wrote or helped write both resolutions. Certainly they were a prelude to the bills on western lands (13 Dec. 1777 and 14 Jan. 1778, *q.v.*), drafted by Jefferson and GM, which finally clarified the status of the commonwealth's public lands.]]

Report of the Committee Appointed to Devise a Great Seal for the Commonwealth of Virginia

[5 July 1776]

To Be Engraved on the Great Seal.

Virtus, the genius of the commonwealth, dressed like an *Amazon*, resting on a spear with one hand, and holding a sword in the other, and treading on TYRANNY, represented by a man prostrate, a crown fallen from his head, a broken chain in his left hand, and a scourge in his right.

In the exergon, the word VIRGINIA over the head of VIRTUS: and underneath the words *Sic semper tyrannis.*

On the reverse, a groupe.

LIBERTAS, with her wand and *pileus.*

On one side of her CERES, with the *cornucopia* in one hand, and an ear of wheat in the other.

On the other side ÆTERNITAS, with the globe and phoenix.
In the exergon, these words:
DEUS NOBIS HAEC OTIA FECIT.

Printed from the *Proceedings of Convention*, 5 July 1776 entry (page 76 is erroneously numbered 86).

A great seal for the new commonwealth seemed to be urgent business, because it was unthinkable in the 18th century to proceed on public business without one. The resolution was read three times and approved in the space of one day, but there were long delays in its execution. (See William Lee's letters of 17 and 18 Aug. 1779, Lee Letterbooks [ViHi] on the search for an engraver.) GM was appointed to the design committee and apparently acted as chairman, since he brought the committee report before the Convention. This was a courtesy usually accorded the author of a bill or resolution, and Grigsby assumed GM was the principal designer (Hugh Blair Grigsby, *The Virginia Convention of 1776* [Richmond, 1855], 167). R. H. Lee also served on the committee, and as he was often GM's most intimate collaborator, Lee may have been instrumental in the design (letter to Samuel Adams, 6 July 1776, Ballagh, *Lee Letters*, I, 207). Probably because of remarks in Burk, *History of Virginia*, IV, Appendix 14, an apocryphal story gained credence that George Wythe designed the seal. Both Wythe and R. C. Nicholas also served on the design committee. A popular schoolbook used in the 19th century (Mary Tucker Magill, *A History of Virginia for the Use of Schools* [Lynchburg, 1890], 207) probably helped spread the claim of Wythe's design. Kate Mason Rowland denied Wythe's role as the chief designer, however, and countered with citations from secondary sources vouching for GM's originality. Miss Rowland also dropped a veiled hint that Jefferson had promoted what she chose to regard as the Wythe myth (Rowland, I, 264–265). In 1952 W. E. Hemphill, in "The Symbolism of Our Seal," *Virginia Cavalcade*, II, 27–34, and in William Edwin Hemphill, *et al.*, *Cavalier Commonwealth* . . . , 2d ed. (New York, 1963), 159, suggested that the seal was "conceived chiefly by George Wythe." The Virginia state archivist, Dr. W. J. Van Schreeven, a keen scholar of the various Virginia conventions, believes the design was "a composite affair, with Mason having the predominant part in drafting the report" (letter to editor, 5 May 1966). Certainly any member of the committee was familiar with the classics and could have drawn upon his knowledge of historical and legendary characters for symbols appropriate to the political climate of 1776. American patriots were still smarting from George III's rebuff of the Olive Branch petition, and it was not difficult to imagine a symbolic Virginia, DRESSED LIKE AN AMAZON, triumphant over a tyrant such as the British monarch was conceived to be in July 1776. SIC SEMPER TYRANNIS carried important connotations for patriots who exalted Brutus and Cato as ancient heroes. The motto DEUS NOBIS HAEC OTIA FECIT (God bestowed upon us this leisure) may have been inspired by Virgil's *Eclogues* as Gummere suggests (*American Colonial Mind*, 14n). Jefferson, pleased by the main design, had a different reaction to this inscription. "But for god's sake what is the 'Deus nobis haec *otia* fecit," he asked John Page (letter of 30 July 1776, Boyd, I, 482). "It puzzles everybody here [in Philadelphia]; if my country really enjoys that *otium* [leisure], it is singular, as every other colony seems to be hard struggling. . . . This device is too ænigmatical, since if it puzzles now, it will be absolutely insoluble fifty years hence." Jefferson's distaste seems to have been shared elsewhere, for on 18 Oct. 1779 GM introduced a bill providing for a great seal with the bewildering motto dropped for a single word: *Perseverando*. Seal designing was indeed a protracted affair. A committee to devise a great seal for the U.S. was appointed on 4 July 1776, but the final design was not approved until 20 June 1782.

[To George Washington?]

[[*July–Aug., 1776.* B. J. Lossing, *Mary and Martha Washington* (New York, 1886), 137, contained this purported extract of a letter from GM to Washington:

> Dunmore has come and gone, and left us untouched except by some alarm. I sent my family many miles back in the country, and advised Mrs. Washington to do likewise, as a prudential movement. At first she said "No; I will not desert my post;" but she finally did so with reluctance, rode only a few miles, and plucky little woman as she is, stayed away only one night.

Rowland, I, 213, reprinted this material, noting that it was extracted "from an old newspaper." Dunmore's forces were marauding as close to Gunston Hall as Aquia Creek in late July (*Va. Gaz.* [Purdie], 26 July 1776), and it was reported that Dunmore "took leave of the capes of Virginia" on 7 Aug. (*ibid.,* 9 Aug. 1776). Lossing's tendency to accept historical materials uncritically is well known. Freeman, *Washington,* II, 405–406, illustrates the inconsistencies in Lossing on another letter allegedly in the Washington correspondence. The editor believes the same test of truth is applicable here, and that the Lossing quotation lacks authenticity. Whatever the original basis for the statement, it is now unsupported.]]

Thomson Mason to Thomas Jefferson and Others

23 August 1776. Nicholas Cresswell (1750–1803), an English adventurer who was eager to obtain a safe-conduct pass, solicited aid from Thomson Mason of Raspberry Plain, Loudoun County. In his journal Cresswell noted that on 21 August he "Called at Mr. Mason's" and was promised "a letter of recommendation to some of the members of the Congress." Cresswell recorded that on 23 Aug. GM's brother "gave me letter[s] to Messrs. Francis Lightfoot Lee, Thos. Stone, Thos. Jefferson, and John Rogers Esq. all members of the Congress" (*The Journal of Nicholas Cresswell 1774–1777* [London, 1925], 151). In an epilogue, Cresswell makes it clear that his benefactor was GM's brother (*ibid.,* 226–229). Boyd, XV, 582–583, mistakenly identifies the letter-writing "Mr. Mason" as GM.

To the Privy Council of Virginia

[[*ca. 10 Oct. 1776.* The minutes in H. R. McIlwaine, ed., *Journals of the Council of State of Virginia . . .* (Richmond, 1931–1953), I, 199, indicate that a letter from GM had been "lately received complaining of the

Order made by this Board the twentieth of last Month directing the
Brigantine Adventure to proceed to Cape Nichola Mole instead of to
Dunkirk as first intended and the same having been referred to the
Consideration of the Navy Board." The *Journal* continues: "They now
report their Opinion to be in favour of the former destination of the
said Brigantine. Ordered therefore that the order of the twentieth of
last Month be rescinded." The order of 20 Sept. (*ibid.*, 168) which
brought GM's complaint directed the *Adventure* "now lying at York,
with tobacco" and considered unfit, to proceed to Portsmouth and
"there to unload and refit, and after relading, that she proceed to Cape
Nichola Mola, instead of Dunkirk, as the more desirable mart in the
present Circumstances of things. . . ." The letter has not been found.]]

To John Hancock

SIR   Virginia, Fairfax County, Octor. 19th: 1776.
    At the Request of the Inhabitants of the Town of Alexandria, I
take the Liberty to trouble you with the inclosed Order of the
Virginia Council. Understanding that Messrs. Hughes's of Frederick
County Maryland (who are the only Persons on this Part of the
Continent to be depended on for Cannon) are under Contract with
the Congress for all the Cannon their Works can possibly make in a
Year, and having no other Means of carrying the above mentioned
order of Council into Execution, the Inhabitants of the said Town
humbly beg Leave, thro' you Sir, to represent their Case to the
honble the Congress, & pray for an order to Messrs. Hughes's to
furnish them with the Cannon wanted, out of those ingaged for
Continental Service: they are unacquainted with the Terms of
Messrs. Hughes's Contract; but if the Price is more than £ 35. Virga.
Curry ℔ Ton (the rate our Council have prescribed) they will pay
the Difference themselves. If the Congress is pleased to indulge them
with such an order, the sooner it can be granted the better; as the
fortifieing the said Town will be very advantageous to the Trade of
great Part of Virginia & Maryland, and give considerable Encouragement to foreign Adventurers, by affording them Protection at a
good Port, where they can speedily procure Cargoes of Country-
Produce. I beg the favour of an Answer, as soon as Convenience will
permit, and am, with much Respect Sir Yr. most obdt. Hble Servt.
                G MASON Chairman of Fairfax County Committee

RC (Papers of Continental Congress, DNA). Addressed to Hancock: "Post
on public Service." A clerk's endorsement reads: "NO. 11 19 Oct. 1776 Letter
from J. Maison Chairman of the Committee for Fairfax County Virginia
Requesting in behalf of the Committee & Inhabitants of Alexandria, to be

permitted to purchase of Messrs. Hughes the Continental Contractor for Cannon several Pieces to Defend the Town of Alexandria[.] Inclos'd A Resolve of the Council ordering the Inhabit[an]ts. to purchase Cannon &c. at the public Expence."

Alexandria citizens had petitioned the Virginia Council for permission to buy sixteen cannon and two forges "at the Public Expence" for defense of the town. The summer raids along the Potomac by Lord Dunmore's forces, including the burning of William Brent's home in Stafford County, alarmed tidewater Virginians and caused the town of Alexandria to build two shore batteries and form an artillery company to man them. GM sent the Council Order of 7 Sept. 1776 authorizing the weapons purchase as an enclosure. The MESSRS. HUGHES were Daniel and Samuel Hughes, operators of an iron works that was an important source of heavy weapons with a reputation for expeditious manufacturing upon reasonable terms (Fitzpatrick, ed., *Writings of Washington*, XIV, 329). The Council was carrying on functions of the superseded Virginia Committee of Safety, which had been empowered to collect and dispense all public arms and ammunition (Hening, IX, 53). When he reached Williamsburg, GM offered the petition to the House of Delegates (JHD, 1828 ed., 13 Nov. entry), where it was referred to a committee studying "the state of the country." On 6 Dec. the House ordered a committee to prepare a bill defraying the expenses of erecting fortifications that would include a clause empowering the governor, with the advice of the privy council, "to form out of the two militia companies in the town of *Alexandria* . . . one artillery company" that would drill twice a week, mount guard, and be paid "only when upon duty." GM was named as chairman of this committee and apparently wrote the clause which was part of a bill passed on 18 Dec. (*q.v.*).

The text in Rowland, I, 267, is mistakenly dated "Oct. 17, 1776."

Resolution Directing the Governor to Send Cavalry Forces to General Washington

[5 December 1776]

Resolved, That the Governour be desired to give proper orders for the immediate march of the troops of horse raised in this Commonwealth, with their officers, to join general *Washington,* agreeable to the requisition of the War Office in *Philadelphia,* and to transmit to the said office a list of such articles as the said troops may stand in need of.

Printed in JHD, 1828 ed., 5 Dec. entry. The Ms has not been found.

GM was directed to carry this resolution to the Senate, the usual procedure when the author or sponsor of a bill or resolution was present. Washington's army was retreating across New Jersey, and needed reinforcements desperately. Gov. Henry had sent to the House earlier in the day a requisition from the Continental War Office in Philadelphia urging that "the light horse" troops maintained by Virginia be "marched with all possible expedition to join general *Washington*." In such circumstances, when the sense of the House was well known, a member would be charged with drafting a resolution on the spot. GM appears to have been chosen on this occasion.

Amendment to the Bill Exempting Dissenters from Contributing to the Established Church

[5 December 1776]

[To stand before the preamble.]

WHEREAS several oppressive Acts of Parliament respecting Religion have been formerly enacted, and Doubts have arisen and may hereafter arise whether the same are in Force within this Common-Wealth or not, for Prevention whereof Be it enacted by the General Assembly of the Common-Wealth of Virginia, and it is hereby enacted by the Authority of the same, That all and every Act ⟨or Statute either⟩ of ⟨the⟩ Parliament ⟨of England, or of Great Britain⟩, by whatsoever Title known or distinguished, which renders criminal the maintaining of any Opinions in Matters of Religion, forbearing to repair to Church, or the exercising any Mode of worship whatsoever, or which prescribes punishments for the same, shall henceforth be of no Validity or Force within this Common-Wealth.

[agreed]

Ms (Vi). A single sheet in GM's hand, with clerk John Tazewell's bracketed additions.

Following the adoption on 12 June 1776 of the Virginia Declaration of Rights with its proclamation that all men were "equally entitled to the free exercise of religion, according to the dictates of conscience," the days of an established church in Virginia seemed numbered. To hasten that end, many dissenting congregations contributed to a deluge of petitions praying for relief from a variety of harassments. Such petitions had been almost routine before 1776, but their number and relevance heralded a new era by the autumn of 1776, when the dissenters could hail the 16th article "as the rising sun of Religious liberty" in the new commonwealth. Thus, said the Prince Edward County dissenters, the legislature could and should "relieve them from a long night of Ecclesiastical bondage" by completing the disestablishment of the Anglican church (quoted in Mays, *Pendleton*, II, 133). From Culpeper, Prince William, Albemarle, Amherst and other counties came a torrent of demands that "every religious denomination . . . be put upon an equal footing, independent of [one] another" (JHD, 1828 ed., 22 Oct. entry; see also William Taylor Thom, . . . *The Struggle for Religious Freedom in Virginia: The Baptists*, Johns Hopkins Studies in Historical and Political Science, XVII [Baltimore, 1900], 55–58). Anglican churchmen fought back with their own claims that great injustices would result if tax-supported parishes were stripped of their privileges (JHD, 1828 ed., 8 Nov. entry), and their Methodist cousins were allies in maintaining that Christianity needed sanctions from the state. GM had been elected by the Fairfax County freeholders as one of their delegates to the new General Assembly and by 11 Nov. 1776 he had taken his place beside Madison and Jefferson in the battle raging over the religious issue. GM's younger colleagues had already served on Carter Braxton's committee on religion, which had been charged with studying the petitions and providing legislative recommendations. Jefferson recalled that the in-fighting occasioned by the dissenter's petitions "brought on the severest contests in which I have ever been engaged" (Ford, *Writings of Jefferson*, I, 53). GM left no memoirs relating the quarrels as the liberal delegates strained with the Nicholas-Braxton-Pendleton faction for a relaxation of the special privileges allowed the Anglican church, but he must have been briefed by Jefferson and Madison after six middle-ground resolutions were introduced on 19 Nov. (JHD, 1828 ed., 63). These resolves called for a repeal of ancient harsh acts aimed at squelching dissenters and viewed the dissenters' petitions as "reasonable," but went on to uphold the concept of legislative regulation for "publick assemblies of societies for divine worship." GM, Jefferson, and Madison were appointed to the special commit-tee charged with bringing in a bill that would implement recommendations implicit in the resolutions. Much of the burden must have fallen on Jefferson, who had devoted much time to studying the legal questions involved and whose ideas had formed the core of the earlier resolves (Boyd, I, 527–530). Temporarily overmatched by the conservatives, GM and his liberal friends lost ground and on 30 Nov. the liberal tide of 19 Nov. seemed reversed. Jefferson, who had been on a special leave, hurried back to the House of Delegates and probably worked with Madison and GM to salvage this amendment. GM's version, which retains verbatim some parts of Jefferson's earlier draft, was written on a scrap of paper and accepted by the committee of the whole house when the bill was finally passed on 5 Dec. 1776. The bill, with the Mason-Jef-ferson amendment, repealed all laws requiring church attendance and exempted dissenters from direct tax support for the Anglican church, but left untouched the Act of 1705 which maintained the symbolic established church (Hening, IX, 164–167). The way for further change was left open, however, by a clause which recognized "a great variety of opinion" existed that challenged the general assessment (tax-support) law. "This difference of sentiments cannot now be well accommodated, so that it is thought most prudent to defer this matter to the discussion and final determination of a future assembly when the opinions of the country in general may be known." The conservatives thus gained a postponement of the forthright action that GM, who favored persuasion rather than compulsion in religious matters, hoped would implement the Declaration of Rights. But as Jefferson noted, "Although the majority of our citizens were dissenters . . . a majority of the legislature were churchmen" (Ford, *Writings of Jefferson*, I, 54). The drumfire of dissenting petitions continued. Almost a decade passed before Jefferson's bill calling for a total disestablishment was enacted, and it was Madison abetted by GM who mustered the necessary votes in 1785/1786 to end the last vestige of an established church in Virginia.

The portions in angle brackets are omitted in Hening, IX, 164.

Resolutions on the Virginia-Pennsylvania Boundary Settlement

[17 December 1776]

The Committee to whom the Answer of the Committee of the Convention of the State of Pensilvania to the Proposals formerly made by the Virginia Convention, for the Settlement of a temporary Boundaries between the two Countries & sundrie other Papers con-cerning the same, were referred, have had the same under their

Consideration, & have come to the following Resolutions thereon—

Resolved, that it is the mutual Interest of the Common-Wealths of Virginia and Pensilvania that the Bounderies between them be speedily setled & ascertained, in the most amicable & indisputable Manner, by the joint Agreement and Concurrence of both; but that this desirable End being unattainable by Diffidence or Reserve [or Evasion], your Committee are concerned to find that the Committee of the Pensilvania Convention have confined themselves to general Observations on the Cession and Release made by the Common-Wealth of Virginia, without attempting to shew that the temporary-Bounderie proposed was really inconsistent with the same, or offering any thing with Certainty, on the Part of Pensilvania in it's Stead, until the true Limits of their Charter cou'd be authenticly ascertained & setled.

Resolved, that as the Bounderies expressed in the Pensilvania Charter may admit of great Doubt, & Variety of Opinion may arise on the Construction, and it is expedient & wise to remove, as much as possible, all Cause of future Controversy (the great Principle upon which the Virginia Convention acted in making the aforesaid Cession & Release) to quiet the Minds of the People who may be affected thereby, & to take from our common Enemies an Opportunity of fomenting mutual Distrust & Jealousy, this Common-Wealth ought to offer such reasonable terms of Accommodation (even if the Loss of some Territory is incurred thereby) as may be cordially accepted by our Sister-State, & an End put to all future Dispute, by a firm & permanent Agreement & Settlement.

Resolved therefore, that the Virginia Delegates in Congress be empowered & instructed to propose to the Common-Wealth of Pensilvania a final Accommodation of our disputed Bounderies, in the following Manner.

That the meredian Line drawn from the Fountain or Head of Potomack River shall be extended, from the Intersection of the Line run between the Proprietors of Maryland & Pensilvania (commonly called Mason & Dixon's Line) due North, until it intersects the Latitude of forty Degrees, & from thence the Southern Bounderie of Pensilvania shall be extended, on the said fortieth Degree of Latitude, until the Distance of five Degrees of west Longitude, from Delaware River, shall be compleated thereon; the same to be ascertained by proper astronomical Observations; that from the Completion of the said five Degrees of Longitude, upon the said fortieth Degree of Latitude, the Western Bounderie of Pensilvania shall be fixed at five Degrees of Longitude from it's Eastern, either in every

Point thereof, according to the Meanders of Delaware River, or (which is perhaps easier & better for both) from proper Points or Angles on the said Delaware River, with intermediate streight Lines between; and whenever the said western Bounderie shall be run, that the Degrees of Longitude be also fixed by astronomical Observations, at proper Points and Angles, on the said western Bounderie, answering to the Points or Angles on the said River Delaware, and from these, that there be streight Lines run, corresponding as near as may be, with the beforementioned streight Lines, or reduced Courses of the said River. For which Purpose, if the Common-Wealth of Pensilvania shall accept this Offer, and whensoever they shall have signified their Agreement to the Bounderies herein proposed, the Governour & Council are empowered & desired to appoint Commissioners, to proceed with a proper Mathematical Apparatus, & in Conjunction with Commissioners to be appointed on the Part of the Common-Wealth of Pensilvania, to ascertain & run the said Southern, or Southern & Western Bounderie, until the same shall strike the Ohio or Alleghany River; which it is apprehended is as far as they can yet be extended, with Safety, on account of the Indians. Saving their private Property & Rights to all Persons who may have acquired Titles under either Country respectively, previous to the ascertaining & running such Bounderie; altho' they shou'd be found to fall within the other.

Ms (Vi). Three pages in GM's handwriting, with dated endorsements by John Tazewell (clerk, House of Delegates) and John Pendleton (clerk, Senate).

Clashes between rival factions of settlers in western Pennsylvania early in 1775 stemmed from the vagueness of the Virginia-Pennsylvania boundaries. It was bad enough for Virginians to worry about Lord Dunmore and the British on their eastern flank, but the idea of a civil commotion on the western fringes was intolerable. Accordingly, the Virginia Convention on 15 June 1776 proposed that a temporary boundary line should be accepted "until we have leisure [sic] to refer the final decision to some Arbitrating Power between us . . . and would be most likely to give general Satisfaction" (Boyd, I, 388). Jefferson became a key figure in the negotiations, which the Virginia delegates in Philadelphia were instructed to carry on, and with his usual thoroughness he approached the matter from a legal-historical viewpoint. The Virginia Convention had favored a line from the headwaters of the Potomac along Braddock's Road to the Youghiogheny River, and down that stream or the old road in rough fashion until the Allegheny River was reached. Jefferson was not on the Virginia delegation at the Continental Congress which conferred with a Pennsylvania committee, but nothing was resolved except to place a Pennsylvania counterproposal before the Virginia General Assembly (ibid., 466). Almost a week before GM arrived in Williamsburg this problem had been turned over to a special committee that included Jefferson. Obviously Jefferson and GM discussed the matter, and GM must have seen the notes Jefferson had accumulated in his study of the various charters, maps, and military roads.

Jefferson appears to have concluded that the line Virginia recommended was the fairest because it would discommode the least number of settlers. Because of extensive land speculations by groups in Pennsylvania and Virginia, the contest defied an easy or speedy solution; and indeed GM's long connection with the Ohio Company gave him a vested interest in preserving the area south of the Ohio River under Virginia jurisdiction. "Our pretensions are not merely founded on a Whim of Ld. Dunmore," Edmund Pendleton had cautioned Jefferson, "as they almost made me beleive [sic] when at Philad[elphia] but on solid grounds, which however we shall be ready to submit to the Judgment of Impartial Judges as soon as our common Enemy will afford us leisure" (Boyd, I, 463). Such a day was far off, however, and Jefferson left Williamsburg on 14 Dec., leaving the business in GM's hands. The boundary conceived in GM's resolution gave the disputed area around Fort Pitt to Pennsylvania, but raised the southern Pennsylvania boundary somewhat above an extension of the Mason & Dixon line, and was to be "a final Accomodation" rather than a wartime expedient. (The proposed line is detailed in Paullin, *Historical Atlas of U.S.*, plate 97G). Haggling over the line continued. GM reported for a House committee again on 12 Dec. 1778 (*q.v.*), when agreement seemed no nearer. In the autumn of 1779, however, accord was finally reached, although a final survey of the line was delayed until 1784/1785.

GM wrote the bracketed words "or Evasion" but later crossed through them.

Addition to the Act Providing for the Internal Defenses of Virginia

[18 December 1776]

And be it farther enacted, That the governour, by and with the advice of the privy council, may, and he is hereby authorised and empowered to form out of the two militia companies in the town of Alexandria, in the county of Fairfax, one artillery company, to consist of fifty matrosses, with proper officers, to be duly exercised at the batteries in the said town twice in every week, and to mount proper guards at the same; and the officers and matrosses of the said company, when on duty, shall receive the same pay and provisions, and be subject to the like rules and regulations, as the other artillery companies in the service of this state receive and are subject to.

Printed from Hening, IX, 198. No Ms of the clause has been found.

GM helped his constituents in Alexandria who had taken the initiative in preparing defenses for the town. On 19 Oct. 1776 he had written to the Continental Congress, seeking permission for the town's priority in buying sixteen cannon (after the Virginia Council approved the request, as GM guided the Alexandrians through the channels of authority). In its 7 Sept. 1776 order the Council approved the public expenditure of money for the weapons but referred the matter of raising and paying an artillery company to the General Assembly. Accustomed to red tape, GM dutifully submitted the Alexandria petition to the House of Delegates (JHD, 1828 ed., 13 Nov. entry), praying that the commonwealth would pay the troops manning the batteries, when they were on duty, the equivalent pay of artillerymen on state or continental service. On 6 Dec. the House resolved that the Alexandria petition was "reasonable," i.e., would be granted, and a committee headed by GM was appointed and charged with attending to the matter in a pending bill "defraying the expenses of erecting fortifications." Somehow it became more convenient to slip the clause into *"An Act for making a farther provision for the internal security and defence of this country"* (Hening, IX, 192–198), so Alexandria had its batteries and its defenders, and the commonwealth had promised to pay all the bills.

Resolution Proposing an Exchange of Row-Gallies

[18 December 1776]

Whereas a Requisition from the honble the Continental Congress for building six Row-Gallies, for the Protection of the continental Troops in their transportation over the different Rivers in Virginia, was laid before the last Convention: And, as several row-Gallies, of the same Construction and Size with those in Delaware River, have been lately built here, very proper for such Purpose, but unfit for Sea Service. Resolved that it be an Instruction to the Delegates from this Common-Wealth to make an Offer of six of the said Gallies, ready built & equip'd, to the Congress, for the aforesaid Purpose of protecting & transporting their Troops; and that the Commissioners for naval affairs furnish the said six row-Gallies accordingly, and settle the Price of them, as nearly as possible, at what they cost this Common-Wealth.

Ms (Vi). In GM's handwriting, with dated endorsements signed by house clerk John Tazewell and Senate clerk John Pendleton.

Circumstances make it likely that GM was helping the Fairfax County Committee of Safety unload several small vessels that had been ordered and built under near-panic conditions almost a year earlier. On 9 Dec. 1775 the Fairfax committee had beseeched GM and his colleague Charles Broadwater (the county's delegates to the Virginia Convention) to expedite the building and equipping of vessels to patrol the Potomac. The immediate cause for their alarm was rumors drifting northward from Lord Dunmore's tiny flotilla off Norfolk, so that GM and John Dalton proceeded to outfit three cruisers and two row galleys as a Potomac defense force (see letter to Maryland Council of Safety, 15 Mar. 1776). Dunmore's marauders never came as far as Alexandria during the following summer, but the town meanwhile had built two shore batteries and apparently no longer needed the row galleys. A companion resolution (for defending Chesapeake Bay) by GM, reinforces the likelihood that from a condition of great scarcity, the Virginia naval force was soon to have an oversupply of row galleys unless the Continental Congress and the Maryland Council of Safety cooperated.

Resolution for the Defense of Chesapeake Bay

[18 December 1776]

Resolved that the Governor be desired to write to the Maryland Council of Safety, to inform them that four Gallies, of eighty odd feet Keel, intended for the Protection of Chesapeake Bay & the adjacent Cape Coasts, are now building in Virginia, & in great forwardness, & that the General Assembly have directed four more Gallies, much larger than the former, to be imediately built and equip'd for the same Purpose, and conceiving that the Inhabitants of Maryland are equally interested in a Measure calculated for the mutual Defence & advantage of both Countries, have no Doubt of the hearty Concurrence & Assistance of this Sister-State, in supplying their proper Quota of Gallies to aid in Concert with those belonging to this Common-Wealth.

Ms (Vi). In GM's handwriting, with dated endorsements signed by house clerk John Tazewell and Senate clerk John Pendleton.

This resolution, introduced as a companion to the resolve offering six row gallies to the Continental naval office, may have been a genuine request for cooperation from the Maryland Council of Safety or it might have been an implicit offer of row gallies for Maryland cash. Since the embroglio over the Eden correspondence in the spring of 1776, with the Virginia Convention scolding the neighboring state for its dalliance, cooperation between the two Potomac overseers had been less than notable. By Dec. 1776 the threat posed by Lord Dunmore had been erased with the destruction of his base at Gwinn's Island, and the town of Alexandria had turned its energy toward the construction of two shore battiers (see GM to John Hancock and enclosure, 19 Oct. 1776). It is possible that Virginia naval forces were considered more than adequate, and that the Maryland Council would have found a ready seller if its "Quota of Gallies" was deficient.

Resolution Allowing Georgia Recruiting Officers to Seek Enlistments in Virginia

[18 December 1776]

Resolved, as it is essential to the safety of the American cause that the southern states should be speedily put on such a respectable footing as may enable them to resist the attempts of the common enemy, that therefore the Georgia officers be permitted to raise as many men in this commonwealth as shall be sufficient to complete the quota of continental troops required from that state, under the like restrictions as were heretofore imposed on the officers from South Carolina who have been permitted to recruit men in this state.

Printed from *JHD*, 1828 ed., 18 Dec. entry.

This resolution was the last of a three matters bundled together in a hurry, from all appearances, and left to GM's care. He carried all three to the senate, the courtesy ordinarily extended to the author of a bill or resolution. It was also an efficient way to smooth legislative channels, for the author could confer directly with the members of the other house and often reach an immediate agreement on any necessary alterations. The other resolutions dealt with the sale of row galleys and joint launching of defense vessels in the Potomac, but this resolve must have related to an act of courtesy toward the Georgia recruiters. Washington's army had been reeling southward since 28 Oct. 1776 and the Battle of White Plains. Virginia had five companies of riflemen attached to the Continental army and was preparing to send more infantry and cavalry to aid Washington, but still the house thought it proper to allow sparsely populated sister states to recruit Virginians for their quotas. "No Carolina gives 50 dollars bounty, and one dollar pr: day, by means of which they have recruited a number of Men out of our companies," Arthur Campbell reported to Patrick Henry on 15 Mar. 1779 (William P. Palmer, ed., *Calendar of Virginia State Papers* . . . [Richmond, 1875–1893], I 317.)

Resolution concerning the Scarcity of Beef and Pork

[19 December 1776]

Whereas it is apprehended that there will be a great Scarcity of Beef & Pork, and that the Contractors & Commissarys for the American Armies will be unable to provide sufficient Magazines for the great Number of Troops now raising for the next Campaign, unless a timely Stop is put to the Exportation; and as an Embargoe in this Common-Wealth (unless simular Measures are adopted by the other united States) will be inadequate to the Purpose.

Resolved that it be an Instruction to the Virginia Delegates to apply to the honble the American Congress, & use their utmost endeavours to procure that the Exportation of Beef Pork & Bacon may be imediately prohibited, throughout the united American States, for such limited time, and under such Regulations as shall be judged proper; And that the Governour be desired to transmit to the said Delegates a Copy of this Resolve by the next Post, or by the first safe Conveyance.

Ms (Vi). In GM's handwriting, with dated endorsements signed by house clerk John Tazewell and Senate clerk John Pendleton.

Resolutions Urging Recruitment and Conferring Emergency Powers on the Governor and Council

[21 December 1776]

It being of the utmost Importance that the nine Battalions heretofore raised within this Common Wealth, & now in Continental Service, shou'd be compleated, & the six new Battalions for the same Service, as well as the three Battalions on the Pay of This Common-Wealth, raised with all possible Expedition.

Resolved *that* it be earnestly recommended to ⟨the Justices⟩ the Members of the County-Committees, ⟨the Militia Officers⟩ & the other good People of this Common-Wealth, to use their best Endeavours to forward & encourage the recruiting Service; upon which the Safety & Happiness of their Country so much depends.

And whereas the present imminent Danger of America, & the Ruin & Misery which threatens the good People of this Common-Wealth and their Posterity, calls for the utmost Exertion of our Strength, & it is become necessary, for the Preservation of the State, that the usual forms of Government shou'd be suspended, during a limitted time, for the more speedy Execution of the most vigorous & effectual Measures, to repel the Invasion of the Enemie.

Resolved therefore, that the Governor is hereby fully authorized & empowered ⟨by & with the advice & consent of the Privy Council⟩ from henceforward, until ten Days next after the first Meeting of the General Assembly, to carry into Execution Such Requisitions as may be made to this Common-Wealth by the American Congress, for the Purpose of encountering or repelling the Enemie, to order the three Battalions on the Pay of this Common-Wealth to march (if necessary) to join the Continental Army, or the Assistance of any of our Sister-States, to call forth any, & such greater Military-force as ⟨they⟩ shall judge requisite, either by embodieing or arraying Companies or Regiments of Voluntiers, or by raising additional Battalions, ⟨appointing & commissioning their proper⟩ Officers and to direct their Operations within this Common-Wealth ⟨under the Command of the Continental Generals or other Officers according to their respective Ranks⟩ or order them to March to join & act in Concert with the Continental Army, or the Troops of any of the united American States, and to provide for their Pay, Supply of Provisions, Arms & other Necessaries, at the Charge of this Common-Wealth ⟨By drawing on the Treasurer for the Money which may be necessary from Time to Time. And the said Treasurer is authorized to pay such Warrant out of any Public Money which may be in his Hands, and the Genl. Assembly will at their next Session make ample Provision for any Deficiency which may happen⟩. But that this Departure from the Constitution of Government, being in this Instance founded only on the most evident & urgent Necessity ought not hereafter to be drawn into Precedent.

Resolved also that the Governor be desired to transmit, by Express, Copys of these Resolves to the American Congress, & to the neighboring States of Maryland and North Carolina, to satisfie them that we are exerting ourselves in defending the Libertys of America

⟨Resolved that our Delegates be instructed to recommend to the Consideration of Congress whether it may not be necessary and expedient in the present Dangerous and critical Situation of America, in order to give Vigour, Expedition and Secrecy to our Military Measures, to invest the Commander in Chief of the American Forces with more ample and extensive Powers for conducting the Operations of the War, and that they will earnestly exhort the different Legislatures of the united American States to adopt the most speedy & effectual Methods for calling their Military Force into Action, & co-operating with the Generals of the American Armies⟩

Ms (Vi). Four pages in GM's handwriting, with endorsements dated by house clerk John Tazewell and senate clerk John Pendleton.

This was the last piece of legislative business transacted by the General Assembly in 1776. The House of Delegates, serving as a committee of the whole on "the state of *America*," discussed for several days the exigencies created by threats from British forces and the pleas of the Continental War Office for more troops. It is apparent that the house accepted GM's omnibus solution: the temporary transfer of its legislative function to the executive branch during the emergency. Proof of this comes from the 21 Dec. entry (JHD, 1828 ed., 107–108) where Henry Lee returned from the senate with an amendment: "Page 2d, line 5th, leave out the words *the usual forms of government should be suspended,* and insert *additional powers be given the Governour and Council.*" The Ms thus used had to be GM's, which corresponds precisely with Lee's description. The change was approved, GM carried the House's assent to the Senate, and Gov. Patrick Henry thereby was free to exercise broad powers in conducting state business until the following Mar.

Several changes in various hands, and the final paragraph in Joseph Prentis's handwriting, are within angle brackets.

Plan for the Committee to Revise the Laws

[13 January 1777]

The Common Law not to be medled with, except where Alterations are necessary.

The Statutes to be revised & digested, alterations proper for us to be made; the Diction, where obsolete or redundant, to be reformed; but otherwise to undergo as few Changes as possible.

The Acts of the English Commonwealth to be examined.

The Statutes to be divided into Periods: the Acts of Assembly, made on the same Subject, to be incorporated into them.

The Laws of the other Colonies to be examined, & any good ones to be adopted.

General Rules in Drawing	Provisoes &c. which wou'd do only what the Law wou'd do without them, to be omitted.
	Bills to be short; not to include Matters of different Natures; not to insert an unnesessary Word, not omit a useful one.
	Laws to be made on the Spur of the present Occasion, and all innovating Laws, to be limited in their Duration

Criminal Law.	Treason & Murder (& no other Crime) to be punished with Death, by hanging, and Forfeiture; saving Dower.
	Petty-treason, Parricide, Saticide; the Body to be delivered over to Surgeons to be anatomized.
	Manslaughter to be punished by Forfeiture & Labour.
	Suicide not to incur Forfeiture, but considered as a Disease.
	Justifiable Homicide not to be punished at all.
	Rape, Sodomy, Bestiality to be punished by Castration.
	Other Crimes punishable by Forfeiture, Fine, Labour in public works, such as Mines, Gallies, Saltworks, Dock-Yards, Founderies, and public Manufactories.
	The Benefit of Clergy & the actual Cautery to be abolished.
	Protection, Comfort &c. by a Parent, Child, or Wife not to be deemed Misprision of Treason.
	Corruption of Blood to be abolished in all Cases.
	Standing mute on Trial to amount to plea of not guilty, & the Court to proceed to Trial, and punishment (if guilty) or Acquittal (if innocent) in same Manner as if the Criminal had pleaded not guilty.
	The Act which makes Concealment by the Mother of the Death of her bastard Child amount to Evidence of her having murdered it to be repealed.
	New Trials to be allowed in Criminal Cases (in favour of the Criminal) during the Term or Session, for good cause shewn to the Judges.
	Whether Pardons shall be allowed or not, in any Instance, the Committee, having not yet determined, defer to be consider'd at the next Meeting.

De-   The Lands to which an Intestate had Title in fee to descend
scents. in Parcernary to Males & Females, in equal portions.

       The Course of Descent to be as follows.

            First to the Children or their Descendants.

If there be no Children or their Descendts. to the Father.

If no father, then_____to the Mother, Brothers & Sisters
                    equally, or the Descendants of
                    Brothers & Sisters.

If neither Father nor Mother,

then_____to Brothers & Sisters, & their
                    Descendants.

If there be neither Father, Mother, Brothers nor Sisters, then
to divide the Lands into Moieties, one of them for the Paternal, the other for the Maternal Relations, to go to each in the
following order.

            First__to the Grandfather

If no Grandfather then_____to Gr:mother, Uncles &
                    Aunts, & Descendants of
                    Uncles & Aunts.

If neither Gr:father nor Gr:

mother then_____to Uncles and Aunts, &
                    their Descendants.

If no Uncles nor Aunts, nor

their Dests., then_____to Great Grandfather.

If no Great Grand Father, then—to Gr:Grd..Mother, wth
                    Gr:Uncles & Aunts &
                  their Descendants.

If neither Gr: Grd fathers nor

mother _____to Gr: Uncles & Aunts &
                    their Descendants.

             And so of the Rest.

Relations of the half Blood to have half a Share with those
in equal Degree of the whole Blood; but to take the whole,
when nearest in Degree to the Deceased.

Representation to be admitted to any Degree of Descendants.

The Person last entitled (i.e. the Decedent) to be considered
as if he had been the Purchaser, without Regard to Seisin, or
the Rule "Paterna paternis, materna maternis."

To share per Stirpes, in every Instance, and not per Capita.

Advancement from the same Ancestor, in his Life-time, to be brought into Hotchpot.

Conveyance by Deed or Will to a Person, without Words of Limitation shewing a less Estate intended, to carry a fee simple.

Dower. Widows to have Dower as heretofore.

Distri- The Distribution of personal Estate to be made conformable
bution. to the Division of Lands, except the Widow's Part; which is to be as heretofore.

Execu- Executions to be first levied on personal Chattels; if the
tions. Sherif can find none, then on Slaves; if he can find no Slaves, then on Lands; if the Sherif levies on Lands or Slaves, for want of personal Chattels, & the Party before Sale produces to him such Chattels sufficient, he shall release the Lands or Slaves: so also where Slaves alone are seised &c.

Debt Execution not to be against the Body, unless Estate concealed; & agst. Estate made more easy.

In Suit for the Debt of a Testator or Intestate, the Heir & Execr. or Admr. shall be join'd.

Sure- Sureties (except for Guardians Exrs. or Admrs.) if not sued
ties within seven years, to be discharged of the Suretyship.

Land The Tenure of Lands to be of the Common Wealth by
Law. Fealty.

Quit-rents to be abolished.

Survivorship among Joint tenants not to take Place.

New Unappropriated Lands to be entered for with Surveyor.
Grants. No man allowed to enter for more than 400 Acres in any one County.

The Breadth of Surveys to be at least one third its length, unless hindered by adjacent Lines, Watercourses or impassable Swamps.

Entries to be surveyed as formerly, & works return'd to Land-Office.

No orders of Governor & Council for Land.

Grants to be signed by Governor, to express the Conditions of Fedelity, & Improvement. No Right Money for Lands to be required.

Lands irregularly obtained to be liable to Caveat.

Caveats to be Entered in Land-Office, but tried before Genl Court: the Facts by a Jury.

Improvements to be the same as by Acts of 1713. C.3. & 1720. C.3.

Lands not improved to be lapsed on Petition.

Petitions for lapsed Lands triable before Gen'l. Court by Jury.

Real Ac-tions. Lands to be recovered by one uniform rational Action.
New Trial to be allowed, at Discretion of Judges.
As many Coparceners as will may join in Action: so the Demandant man join as many as he will Defendants.

The first Period in the Division of the Statutes, to end with 25th. H. 8th.

The Second to end at the Revolution.

The third to come down to the present Day.

A fourth Part to consist of the residuary Part of the Virginia Laws, not taken up in either of the three first Parts; to which is added the criminal Law, and Land-Law.

The fifth Part to be the Regulation of Property in Slaves, & their Condition, and also the Examination of the Laws of the other Colonies.

Alotment of the Parts, to each Member, on the other Side.

T. Jefferson to undertake the first Part, with the Law of Descents.

E. Pendleton the second.

G. Wythe the third.

G Mason the fourth; but if he finds it too much, the other Gentlemen will take off his Hands any part he pleases.

T. Lee the fifth Part.

Ms (Vi). Four pages in GM's handwriting, with an endorsement at the fold: "Plan setled by the Committee of Revisors, in Fredericksburg January 1777."

After passage of Jefferson's bill for a revision of the laws in Oct. 1776, a five-man committee was selected as provided by the law ("by joint ballot of both houses"). The joint ballot resulted in the appointment of Jefferson, Edmund Pendleton, George Wythe, Thomas Ludwell Lee, and GM (JHD, 1828 ed., 5 Nov. entry). The selection of Lee and GM, who were planters and not lawyers, testifies to their standing amongst colleagues as men of considerable intellectual breadth. In an exhaustive editorial note, Boyd (II, 305–324) points out Jefferson's major concern that the committee assume the posture of reformers rather than compilers of the laws. Jefferson regarded legal reform as one of the primary objects of the Revolution, and to that end he left the Continental Congress to work for an "urgently required reformation" of the Virginia code (Ford, *Writings of Jefferson*, I, 48). Thus motivated, Jefferson wrote and introduced some legislation and worked through the revisor's committee for a general overhaul that was reported in June 1779. By that time, Lee and GM had long since parted company with the committee on the grounds that they were not qualified. Lee died in 1778, but GM did not let his interest in the committee's work flag despite his resignation. By mutual agreement the committee convened in Fredericksburg less than four weeks after the General Assembly adjourned. Boyd is undoubtedly correct in saying this document "should be regarded as an aide-memoire representing conclusions arrived at through deliberations of the Committee, rather than as a plan written in whole or in part by any one person. Each of the members of the Committee probably kept a copy . . . but none seems to have survived except that in Mason's handwriting" (Boyd, II, 328). Lacking other documents, it is impossible to determine each committeeman's part in drafting this outline. However, GM's well-known preoccupation with land matters makes it likely that he guided the committee on the sections relating to land grants, leases, survey entries, and related items. Hence the notation that GM will undertake THE FOURTH . . . PART gave him the opportunity to weld his practical experience into the commonwealth law. Apparently, GM's familiar lament of ill health was voiced and led to the stipulation that he might withdraw from the project IF HE FINDS IT TOO MUCH. A smallpox inoculation in the spring of 1777 confined GM to Gunston Hall so that he was unable to attend the House of Delegates session and was on his sickbed when informed that in his absence the General Assembly had chosen him as a delegate to the Continental Congress. GM declined the appointment but returned to Williamsburg in the fall, where he worked closely with Jefferson in the preparation of much legislation, including two notable bills on land matters. These important bills probably had their genesis in the Fredericksburg meeting, for they dealt with fundamental questions related to western land policy. The first bill established a land office (8 Jan. 1778) and the second provided a means of settling "the various and vague claims to unpatented Lands under the former Government" (14 Jan. 1778). Both Jefferson and Mason believed the western lands should be sold to settlers and the funds raised from such sales used to pay off the public debt. A house resolution was accordingly offered by GM on 24 Jan. 1778 to delay disposition of Virginia lands "upon the Western Waters" until the Land Office was established. This was necessary because the bills had been read and committed to a second reading, by which action they were postponed and languished until the spring of 1779 (Boyd, II, 133–138, 162). These measures were the principle contributions GM made to the overall revision, although Jefferson later saw GM's effort as mainly "to remove out of the way the great and numerous orders of council to the Ohio co. Loyal co. Missisipi co. Vandalia co. Indiana co. &c. and the thousands of entries for lands with surveyors of counties, which covered the whole Western country. . . ." (Boyd, II, 138). The 400-acre limitation upon land entries IN ANY ONE COUNTY was retained in the 14 Jan. 1778 bill. NO ORDERS OF GOVERNOR & COUNCIL FOR LAND signalled the end of the royal system with its corruption, favoritism, and greed—although these vices were not legislated out of existence. Despite the provision that caveats (legal proceedings to suspend final confirmation of a title) were to be TRIED BEFORE GENL. COURT: THE FACTS BY A JURY, the bill as passed gave commissioners the power "to hear and determine all Titles to Lands"—a feature that was much criticized as too arbitrary. The law provided that caveats entered prior to the Revolution would be "determined according to the laws in force at the time they were entered" (Hening, X, 50). In 1784, when Jefferson reviewed the process, he listed neither of these bills as major accomplishments, although he considered the bill ending primogeniture and entail as one of the revision's four major achievements (*Notes on Virginia*, ed. Peden, 137). As Rowland mentioned (I, 278), GM's own feelings about this ancient device had already been expressed in his will of 1773, wherein he explicitly announced that each of his sons would receive estates when they reached 21 or married, thereby dispelling "an opinion that I intended to entail any part. . . ." Of the bills catalogued by the revision committee (Boyd, II, 329–333) GM made contributions on four (No. 2, 31 Oct. 1785, concerning general assembly elections; No. 34, 15 June 1779, relating to bills of credit; No. 55, May 1779, delineating citizenship; and No. 89, 29 Dec. 1777, enacted to prevent forestalling). In addition, GM wrote a "Bill Declaring When Laws Shall Be in Force"—probably in May of 1779—which was never enacted, but was made unnecessary by the last sentence of Bill No. 2 as finally enacted. Those bills written by GM are printed in these volumes according to their chronology.

The statement in Rowland, I, 277, that the document "bears in some places the marks of his [GM's] workmanship" is safe enough, but is overlooked in the same paragraph when by implication GM is connected with the laws Jefferson wrote on religious freedom and general education (parts of the latter became law in 1796, four years after GM's death). GM did serve on committees appointed to bring these bills before the House of Delegates. However, Jefferson's authorship of both is established by substantial evidence (Boyd, II, 535*n*, 547*n*–553*n*).

From Richard Henry Lee

[[*12 Feb. 1777*. GM alludes to this letter in his reply to Lee of 4 Mar. Lee appears to have been disturbed by the report from Virginia of his refusal to take depreciated currency for rent from tenants. See the commentary following GM's answer of 4 Mar. for an explanation of the charges against Lee and the outcome.]]

To Richard Henry Lee

DEAR SIR.   Gunston-Hall March 4th. 1777.

I never heard a word of the Report you mention, until the Day before I received yr. Favour of the 12th Ulto. when hearing it accidentally from a second or third Hand, I took upon me immediatly to contradict it; and thought I had good Authority from the

Letters I saw, during the sitting of the Assembly, from you & yr. Brother, Colo. F. Lee, mentioning the Retreat thro' the Jerseys, to affirm that it was an infamous Falsehood. I beleive it has gained no Manner of Credit, & don't think it's worth giving you a Moment's Uneasiness.

The Gallies now building I hope will be able to afford sufficient Protection to our Bay. I am sure they are as many as can possibly be built and man'd, before the next Meeting of the Assembly. I shou'd be glad to be inform'd if the Governor & Council have proposed to the Congress to furnish them our small Gallies, in Lieu of those they ordered to be built here, for the Protection & Transportation of their Troops over our Rivers; & the Result.

We have a very extraordinary Peice of Intelligence (I suppose it's a tory Invention to delay the raising our Army) in Goddart's Baltemore Paper of the 25th. of Febry. If there is any Truth in it, the British Ministry must be hard push'd, & see that a french War is inevitable. Surely Congress will be cautious how they are drawn into a fruitless Negotiation, or commit any Breach of Faith with foreign Nations: they best know the Powers & Instructions given Dr. Franklin. At any Rate, let us do nothing to cramp our Exports to any Part of the World; they are the only Means by which we can expect to discharge the enormous Debt this War has created. —I really think such a Publication ought not to have been suffered, & that the author shou'd be inquired after.

I beg to be kindly remembered to your Brother Colo. F. Lee, & Mr. Page, and am Dr Sir Yr. affecte. Friend & Sert.

G MASON

RC (ViU). Addressed to Lee at the "honble Continental Congress in Balte-more Town ℔ favr of Mr. Thompson." GM also added on the cover: "N.B. this was intended to have been put [on] last Post, but was held [back?]." Endorsed.

THE REPORT YOU MENTION must have been Lee's difficulty that stemmed from a letter written to one of his tenants. According to rumors, Lee had insisted that his rents be paid in produce rather than depreciated paper money. Lee's detractors "insinuated, that he was, in heart, a *tory*, and was, in reality, an *enemy* to the cause of America; that he had refused to take the money of the state . . . [which] embarrass[ed] the public efforts to maintain the war" (R. H. Lee, *Memoir of the Life of Richard Henry Lee* [Philadelphia, 1825], I, 192). The gossip had repercussions, for Lee was dropped from the Continental Congress delegation. However, he was later exonerated by the House, and when GM declined to take a proferred place on the congressional delegation, it was offered to Lee (JHD, 1827 ed., 20 June, 24 June 1777 entries). Inevitably, the rumor-mill twisted the story—the way Edmund Pendleton heard it, Lee had insisted on hard cash from his tenants (Mays, *Papers of Edmund Pendleton*, I, 213). Months later, Lee was still trying to explain the matter away. "Let the date of my letter to Scott be attended to, the State of paper money at the time, the reasons and principles upon which my proposal was founded; and my conduct will appear not only innocent but laudable" (letter to George Wythe, 19 Oct. 1777, Ballagh, *Lee Letters*, I, 335). The VERY EXTRAORDINARY PEICE OF INTELLIGENCE in the Baltimore *Md. Journal* for 25 Feb. 1777 was probably a report, signed by "TOM TELL-TRUTH," which asserted that Gen. Howe had offered American peace terms "and [was], in return, to require *only* our friendship, and a preference in our trade and commerce. . . . My soul overflows with gratitude to the patriotic virtuous King, the august incorruptible Parliament, and wise disinterested Ministry of Britain." The writer accused the Continental Congress of "concealing . . . these glad tidings," but insisted the report was "literally true." In fact, the negotiations authorized by Parliament had proved fruitless, for their basis had to be "renunciation of the Declaration of Independence, whereupon the American delegation broke up the rather amiable conference by taking a firm stand in favor of separation" (Nettels, *Roots of American Civilization*, 718).

Spelling errors have been corrected and the text modernized in the version appearing in Rowland, I, 279–280.

From William Aylett

[[(*Mar.–Apr.?*), *1777*. Col. Aylett, the deputy commissary-general for Virginia, was ordered to purchase large quantities of flour for delivery to the Continental army. He sent this letter, which is now missing, to GM via a Capt. Rigg and it is acknowledged in GM's reply of 19 Apr. 1777. Aylett appears to have informed GM of a flour purchase from Martin Pickett of Fauquier County, which presumably was ready for delivery.]]

To William Carr

[[(*Mar.–Apr.?*), *1777*. Apparently GM received word from the Virginia deputy commissary-general, Col. William Aylett, that flour for the Continental army's use was ready for loading at Dumfries. GM wrote Carr, a Dumfries merchant, "desiring him to dispatch . . . the Flour" which Aylett had bought from a Fauquier County planter-miller "or any other which Mr. Carr himself might have purchased." GM's letter has not been found, but see his report to Aylett of 19 Apr. 1777.]]

From John Muir

[[*ca. 4 Apr. 1777*. Muir was an Alexandria merchant and wheat inspector, sometimes given to overindulgence in strong drink, who was involved in the purchase of flour for Continental troops. GM mentions this missing letter in his 6 Apr. memorandum to Gov. Patrick Henry, and comments upon Muir's social habits in a letter to Col. William Aylett dated 19 Apr. 1777.]]

From William Carr

[[*ca. 4-5 Apr. 1777.* Carr was a Dumfries merchant charged with procuring provisions for troops. This letter is missing, but was alluded to in GM's report to Col. William Aylett concerning flour for the Continental commissary on 19 Apr. 1777.]]

To Patrick Henry

SIR   Gunston Hall April 6th. 1777.

The express who went from here last (Mr. Chew) not being yet returned, and therefore not knowing what orders are given about lading the vessels at Alexandria upon Continental Account, I enclose you the three letters brought by the last three vessels, together with one from Mr. Muir to me mentioning the state of that business, and the quantity of flour required for the vessels already arrived. The whole towns of Dumfries and Alexandria are under innoculation for the small pox, in the latter about 600 persons, which I fear will prevent the flour waggons coming in.

I should like to know how the sale cloth manufactory goes on, and whether Mr. Matthews has got any person acquainted with the new Machines introduced a few years ago from Russia for spinning the thread; which it is said perform the work better, and vastly more expeditiously than common wheels. My reason for this enquiry is, that I think I can engage a workman who served an apprenticeship in one of the great sail cloth Manufactories at Hull, and is master of every part of the business, from breaking the hemp to finishing the sail cloth. He is also acquainted with the clasp harness, and the beforementioned Machines, which by his account are simple and extremely advantageous, and thinks he can instruct a workman to make them. He served his time with a friend of mine in Maryland, who gives him a good Character for honesty and diligence; but knows nothing of his proficiency in his trade, further than his being a complete hemp and flax dresser. Upon his coming over here to enter on board a privateer at Alexandria, I stopt him; and thinking a man so useful to the public ought not to be lost, I prevailed on him, by promising him good wages, and making him hope for some fu[r]ther reward, in case his Machines answered, to lay aside his privateering Scheme for the present, and keep himself unengaged until I could lay this information before the Councilboard.

There are in this County two young Scotch gentlemen, Laughlan McLean and Adam McGlashan, in the list of those ordered by the Court to depart the Commonwealth: having engaged their passage in the ship Albion, and advanced (as was required) half their passage money, they imagined their Names were, of course, inserted in the list of those who intended to go out in the same ship, and had petitioned for further time; but Since they have seen the late Proclamation, they are very uneasy lest through any mistake or omission, they may be thought to have neglected the proper requisites, and subject themselves to Confinement; which might be fatal to one of them, who is in a bad state of health; and have therefore desired me to apply to your Excellency and the Board on their behalf; and if they are not already included in the indulgence granted to the rest of the ship Albion's passengers, to pray the favor of being indulged with such further time as may be necessary until the said ship is ready to sail. These young men have been my neighbors a considerable time, and I know their Conduct has been so inoffensive and unexceptionable, that had they called upon Some witnesses in this neighborhood, of undoubted credit, I think they would have avoided the judgment, which hath been passed upon them; otherwise I should not take the liberty to trouble the Board in their favor. I am very respectfully Sir Yr most ob'd't Serv't

G Mason

Tr (Henry Papers, DLC). A two-page copy, said to have been written by William Wirt Henry, who may have seen the original when he was preparing his *Life, Correspondence and Speeches of Patrick Henry* (New York, 1891).

As a member of the Fairfax County Committee of Safety, GM apparently tried to expedite the purchase of flour UPON CONTINENTAL ACCOUNT, as he explained in a letter to the commissary-general, Col. William Aylett, on 19 Apr. Smallpox outbreaks of epidemic proportions appear to have struck Dumfries and Alexandria about this time and led to mass inoculations, as well as a complaint from Fairfax County free-holders that their elections were barely tended to because of the disease (JHD, 1827 ed., 31 May entry). GM probably saw to it that his whole family was inoculated at this time, and he was to excuse himself from attendance at the House of Delegates because of his own inoculation and its aftermath. MR. MATTHEWS, the sailcloth maker, is not otherwise identified. THE TWO YOUNG SCOTCH GENTLEMEN were in difficulty because the General Assembly on 18 Dec. 1776 (JHD, 1828 ed.) passed a resolution that was aimed at "merchants and others, subjects of" George III ". . . who while they remain here, have frequent opportunities of reducing and corrupting the minds of the people and are suspected of holding correspondence with and giving intelligence to the enemy." The governor and council were directed to deport all Britons who "were partners with, agents, storekeepers, assistant storekeepers, or clerks here, for any merchant of *Great Britain* . . . except only those . . . [who] manifested a friendly disposition to the *American* cause, or are attached to this country by having wives or children here." Gov. Henry duly issued THE LATE PROCLAMATION which led McLean and

McGlashan to book passage on the *Albion,* which the state had chartered, but before the unwelcome Britons embarked the vessel was captured by the British. Henry and the council notified the House of Delegates of the predicament on 27 May 1777 and suggested that it was "impracticable to send them out in any vessel belonging to this State" (JHD, 1827 ed.). GM's fears may have been quieted by the house's action of 10 June, when it was decided to give the governor and council full discretion in the deportations. The suspected Britons who had booked places on the *Albion* were allowed "to go on board any other vessel, or either of the British ships of war in the bay, as shall be most convenient to them . . . under the same regulation on which they were to have embarked on board the ship Albion."

William Wirt Henry and Kate Mason Rowland were preparing their works on distinguished ancestors at about the same time (1889–1900) and exchanged notes (Rowland corres., MiD). Miss Rowland transcribed a copy of the letter for her work, but misread the ship's name, and thus the *Albion* appears as the *Allison* in her modernized version (Rowland, I, 280–282).

From William Aylett

[[*11 Apr. 1777.* This missing letter is alluded to in GM's report of 19 Apr. on the progress of flour purchases made for Continental troops. Aylett was the deputy commissary-general for Virginia and was charged with procuring and forwarding supplies to Washington's army. He was also involved in the purchase of tobacco for the Caribbean and European trade that secured financial credits for purchases to sustain the war effort.]]

From the Privy Council of Virginia

[[*18 Apr. 1777.* An entry in the council journal reports: "A Letter was written to Colo: George Mason requesting him to take charge of two hundred Barrels of Powder imported by Messieurs Norton and Beale for the State." The brief account appears in McIlwaine, ed., *Journals of the Council of State,* I, 393. The gunpowder was probably consigned to GM as a member of the Fairfax County Committee of Safety. The letter has not been found.]]

To William Aylett

DEAR SIR.   Gunston-Hall April 19th. 1777.

As there were five Vessels loading upon Continental Acct. at Alexandria; upon Rect. of yours ℔ Capt. Rigg, I send him, with his Vessel, to the Mouth of Quantico Creek, wth. a Letter to Mr. Carr of Dumfries, desiring him to dispatch him with the Flour you wrote me you had bought of Mr. Pickett, or any other which Mr. Carr himself might have purchased. I have since had a Letter from Mr. Carr, informing [me] that very little of Mr. Picke[t]t's Flour had yet come down, that he had sent an Express to hasten it; but was apprehensive it wou'd be difficult to get Wageners to bring it to Dumfries, on Acct. of the Small Pox there. In the mean time, the Vessel is taking in two or three hund[red]. Barr[e]ls. from Colchester, & will have all the Dispatch, which under these Circumstances, can be given her.

Yesterday Mr. Muir brought me yr. favour of the 11th. Inst. I had before put the flour-Business, at Alexandria, into the Hands of Mr. Wm. Herbert, a Gentleman in whom I think the Public may safely confide. He will correspond with you on the Subject, & transmit you Copys of the Invoyce Bills of Loading &c. I found Mr. Muir so much addicted to Liquor, tho' otherwise very diligent, that I was afraid to leave so important an Affair in his Hands. Very little flour comes down from Colo. Peyton or Mr. Tayler; so that Mr. Herbert must depend chiefly upon purchasing, & for want of Cash, is upon very unequal Terms with the ready Money purchasers, of which there are several in Alexandria; the Farmers & Millers here have been accustomed to receive ready Money, & will not part with their Commoditys without it, except a few particular People, who make a point of prefering the Public, so that the Purchase (which at any Rate will be much impeded by the small pox in Alexandria) will go heavily on; unless Mr. Herbert's Hands are speedily strength'ned.

Colo Peyton & Mr. Tayloe never send any Accts of the Price of their Flour; which renders it impossible to make out the Invoyce of the Vessel's Cargoes with precision.

Mr. Muir has loaded two Vessels, Capt. Doane & Capt Perkins: I have desired him to transmit the Invoyces &c. to you ⅌ Post. He complains much of being considerably in advance for their Cargoes; which sets the heavier upon him, as the Business is now taken out of his Hands. He will send you a Copy of his Acct. & I must beg that the Bal[an]ce. due to him may be imediatly paid; as I think my Credit, in some Measure, engaged therein. I shall always be extreamly ready to do everything in my Power to expedite the Public Business; but it never was my Intention to take a farthing for any Trouble I have been about the Continental flour Vessels.

The small Pox being at almost every one of our public Warehouses renders a Tobo. purchase here, at this time, very difficult, but no Pains that can be taken, shall be spared; the Price has risen, the Buyers lately given 25/ & some of them privately 27/; Yet I hope to make the public Purchase at 25/ & 5/ for Caske. It can't be expected that a Planter who sells a few Hhds. will take an Ord[e]r. for his Money on Wmsburg; & those who live at a Distance will not come down here a second time, when by selling to private Purchasers, they can take this Money Home with them. Those who hold large Quantitys still keep their Tobo. up, upon mere Speculation. These Circumstances render ready Money absolutely necessary in this Purchase.

I am Dr Sir Yr. most obdt. Sert.

G MASON

RC (Vi). Addressed and endorsed.

William CARR and William HERBERT were Alexandria merchants, and Herbert was soon to succeed John MUIR as the port flour inspector. MR. PICKETT'S FLOUR was probably that ground by Martin Pickett in Fauquier County. Col. Henry PEYTON of Prince William County and John TAYLOE of "Mount Airy" were prominent Northern Neck planters (and GM's interchange of Tayler and Tayloe was a commonplace of the day). It is likely that Aylett suggested GM might take a commission on the flour purchases, but as a member of the Fairfax County Committee of Safety he seems to have considered that he acted in an official, patriotic capacity that did not permit him TO TAKE A FARTHING. THE PUBLIC PURCHASE of tobacco was made on behalf of the Commonwealth, and the hogsheads then shipped to St. Eustatia, Martinique, or another Caribbean port en route to European markets—a principle means of financing the war (Nettels, *Roots of American Civilization*, 694–695). As deputy commissary-general for Virginia, Col. Aylett was a principal agent in the traffic. From GM's remarks in his letter to Aylett of 8 June 1777 it would seem that he had been inoculated against the ravages of smallpox, which made him a particular authority for the bill of 12 Jan. 1778 (*q.v.*).

From William Lee

[DEAR SIR]   London 22d May 1777.

I have before sent you Acct Sales for yr 100 hhds of Tobo you sent to my address in 1775, but being apprehensive they must have miscarried, you have duplicates of them. Nett proceeds for the whole £1053:11.10. say One thousand fifty three pounds 11/10 to yr credit, wh[i]ch when compared with others of the same date I think you will be pleased with. Deducting from this Sum £29:1:5 for the insureance leaves £1024:10:9 due to you; But as it is not in my power to pay you here since the unfortunate contest between G. Britain and America has cut us off, not only from all remittances for our debts, but even from the common resources for our subsistance wch we ought to expect from our property with you I take the only method left me of reimbursing you, wch is by the inclosed drafts on those indebted to me with you; saving only £190 which I mean to pay a Bill with for that sum, wch I am advised you have drawn to

Messrs Jenefer & Hooe, tho' the same is not yet come to hand. The drafts inclosed are on Mr John Mills yr Neighbour for £388:17:5 which he owes me on the Ballance of his Acct and £445:12:[...] on Messrs Triplet & Thornton of Fredericksburg who owes me three times the Sum. These orders I hope you will get readily paid wch with the 190 will make the sum of £1024–10–9 the Bal. due to you. I shall always esteem myself happy when It is in my power to be in any manner useful to you, being with very great Esteem & Regard, &c.

[WILLIAM LEE]

FC (Lee Letterbooks, ViHi). In a copyist's hand, headed: "Virginia. Geo. Mason." GM noted (8 Oct. 1778) the letter was actually posted from Nantes in Oct. 1777. The placement of this copy circumstantially indicates the letter was one of about a dozen written from Nantes in late Sept. 1777 but all dated "London, May 22."

Foreseeing the end of British-American trade after the clash at Lexington and Concord, GM had dispatched 100 hogsheads of tobacco to William Lee on 20 May 1775. GM was convinced that the American shift from paper protests to outright battle would bring higher tobacco prices in Europe. Beyond Lee's acknowledgement of the cargo, the subsequent facts of the transaction become obscure. Lee's claim that he had sent an earlier accounting is unsupported by his letterbook entries, and the reported price was an extreme disappointment to GM. In his reply of 8 Oct. 1778, GM implies that Lee has been less than candid in his handling of the transaction and suggests that Lee dumped the tobacco for less than it could have brought in Virginia. GM also infers that Lee tried to convert a sterling debt into an advantageous arrangement by offering GM the balance in depreciated paper currency worth only "one fifth of the [real] Value." GM wanted European goods instead of cash or currency, but Lee seems to have ignored his protests and explicit orders, and instead tried to pay off this debt in Virginia paper money as late as Feb. 1782 (William Lee to Francis L. Lee, 12 Feb. 1782, Lee Letterbooks, ViHi). GM's reaction, after much threatening, was a lawsuit; and in the last months of his life he remained convinced that Lee had "rendered me fictitious Accounts of Sales," mendaciously reporting the tobacco as already sold when in fact it was held back until "the great rise in the price, the Summer following . . ." (GM to John Mason, 5 July 1792). GM's distress was compounded by the fact that William Lee was Richard Henry Lee's brother, and the lawsuit was an embarrassment to their friendship (see R. H. Lee to Charles Lee, 24 June 1789, Ballagh, *Lee Letters*, II, 492–494).

Brackets enclose the missing final figure of the draft on Triplet & Thornton, but the arithmetic appears faulty. For all the mentioned sums to total £1024.10.9, the draft should have been for £445.13.4.

From William Aylett

[[*31 May 1777*. Col. Aylett, the Virginia deputy commissary-general, had instructed GM to buy tobacco on behalf of the state (for reshipment and sale abroad). On 19 Apr. GM explained the local market conditions, and told Aylett that "These Circumstances render ready

Money absolutely necessary. . . .” Aylett, after some delay, sent GM £1,500 in Virginia currency and this letter, which has not been found.]]

From Daniel Carroll

[[*ca. 5–6 June 1777*. GM was acting on behalf of the Virginia deputy commissary-general, Col. William Aylett, in the purchase of tobacco which was being sent to Europe to finance wartime requirements of munitions. Carroll, a versatile Maryland planter, was also acting as an agent for a Philadelphia merchant with European connections. Carroll had agreed to deliver a large quantity of tobacco for the commonwealth's account at a Potomac port. But shortly thereafter, in this missing letter, Carroll wrote that “he was apprehensive of being disappointed in 100 Hhds. [of tobacco consigned] from one of the Philadelphia Gentlemen's Agents on Rappahannock,” and wanted GM to buy extra tobacco as a hedge against nondelivery. Any breakdown in the delivery would have jeopardized a quick loading of the commonwealth's ship. GM also feared that higher prices would have to be paid if he bought the tobacco in piecemeal fashion, but both anxieties were needless as GM found the cargo requirements and the ship's departure was instead delayed by the British naval blockade of Chesapeake Bay. GM explained Carroll's message in his letter to Col. Aylett of 8 June 1777.]]

To Daniel Carroll

[[*7 June 1777*. Carroll, an affluent Maryland planter and Potomac agent for an European mercantile house, contracted to sell GM a large quantity of tobacco which was being bought on the commonwealth's account. Before the tobacco was delivered, however, Carroll expressed doubts to GM that a large portion would be included. Carroll advised GM, because of this uncertainty, to seek the needed one-hundred hogsheads elsewhere. Upon receiving Carroll's message, GM replied that he “cou'd not undertake it, unless a Quantity cou'd at once be bought of two or three people; which I had little prospect of . . . except of some of the Merch[an]ts. at a very high Price, I believe not under 40/. . . .” GM related the whole matter to Col. William Aylett, the Va. deputy commissary-general, so “that the Board may see there has been no neglect in me.” GM's letter is lost, but see his account of the transaction in a letter to Aylett, 8 June 1777. As it developed, GM's anxiety was unwarranted, for he found more tobacco and the cargo was ready to sail some weeks before it could be moved through the temporarily lifted British blockade of Chesapeake Bay, in Aug.]]

To William Aylett

DEAR SIR.   Gunston-Hall   June 8th. 1777

Your favour of the 31st May, with the Sum of fifteen hundred pounds Virga. Money, on Acct. of the Tobo. Purchase, came safe to Hand per Mr. Payne, to whom I gave a rect. for the same: The sd. Purchase is now compleated, & great Part of the Tobo. on board: that is I have purchased the Quantity Daniel Carroll Esqr. (Mr. Pliarne's Agent here) inform'd me wou'd be wanting to fill up the Ship; Mr. Pliarne having previously ingaged to take in a good deal of Tobo. upon Freight for some Gentm. at Philadelphia: He afterwards wrote to Mr. Carroll from Wmsburg, that he was desirous of taking in about 400 Hhds. for this Commonwealth, & leaving out 200 Hhds. of that he had ingaged for in Philadelphia; but Mr. Carroll told me he understood these Gentm. had ordered Insurance, & that he cou'd not avoid the Contracts made with them; upon which we made a Calculation of what I shou'd purchase to fill up the Ship; which I have done accordingly, at the Price of 25/ to 32/ P[er] hund. besides paying 5/ for Caske & 3/ for Inspection, the greater part at 25/.

Yesterday I recd. a letter from Mr. Carroll, advising me that he was apprehensive of being disappointed in 100 Hhds. from one of the Philadelphia Gentlemen's Agents on Rappahannock; which he cou'd not be certain about 'til next Wednesday's Post, & desiring, in that Event, to know if it wou'd be convenient to me to purchase so much more for the Ship on the Commonwealth's Acct. Had I known this sooner, I wou'd chearfully have done it; but being now recovered from the Small pox, I think myself obliged to attend my Public Duty, & my eldest Son being just setting off out for the Augusta Springs, on Acct. of his Health; I wrote Mr. Carroll I cou'd not undertake it, unless a Quantity cou'd be at once bought of two or three people; which I had little prospect of, & even if I had Leisure to attend to it, I am of Opinion that Quantity cou'd not speedily be purchased now, except of some of the Merchts. at a very high Price, I believe not under 40/; but that I shou'd in the meantime endeavour to pick up what I cou'd, least he shou'd be disappointed in the above mentioned 100 Hhds. from Rappahannock. You will do me the favour to lay this matter before the Governor & Council, & if they think fit to order me (in case of Mr. Carroll's

Disappointment) to purchase the Quantity wanted at the before mentioned high Price, it shall be done; but my orders should be expeditious, & Money sent for the Purpose. I have been so particular in mentioning this matter, that the Board may see there has been no neglect in me. The Tobo. I have purchased will be all on board before the private Freighter's Tobo. so that the ships will not be delayed an hour on the Public Acct. I was once thinking (if Mr. Carroll is disappointed) the Ship might run down to York or James River for the Tobo. wanted; but on considering that she is a large Ship, & can't go into shallow Water, this seems to be attended with nearly as great Risque as getting out of the Capes.

Mr. Herbert is much at a Loss in the Execution of yr. last Instructions of the 30th of May, & sent down one of the New England Capts. to me today about it. Capt. Sparkes, in a small Schooner, is just arrived, & his Men upon coming up to Alexandria, & hearing there was a number of Soldiers there in the Small pox, threaten'd instantly to leave the Vessel unless they were imediatly inoculated, as all the rest of their Country-men, who arrived lately, had been; these Fellows follow one another like Sheep, & the Capt. & all his Crew were of course inoculated on Friday Evening last; in this Situation it wou'd [*entire line illegible*] I have therefore ventured to direct Mr. H[erbert] to detain [his] Vessel, 'til he hears further from [you], & promised to advise you of it by this Day's Post. There [are] two continental Vessels now here[, Capt. Barnes,] Capt. Sparkes; I find them both exceedingly averse to going into York or James River, they think the Risque greater than getting out of the Capes, & say they [should be ruined], if then they are [taken,] having [consi]derable property of their ow[n] in the Vessels. The New England men are so cautious, so well used to playing at Hide & Seek with the Enem[y] & so well acquainted with every Shoal & Swash, that if they are permitted to take their own Way, they will probably get out clear. They seem very positive of being able to get thro' Cape Charles in the night. I told them I wou'd lay the matter before you, & desire yr. directions to Mr. Herbert by the next post. I am Dr Sir Yr. most obdt. Sert.

G Mason

P.S. If it is thought proper Capt. Sparkes can easily be loaded at Alexandria. I shou'd be glad to know if the Commonwealth wants any [fur]ther fine Barl. flour. I have 275 barls. of my own, for which I wou'd take 20/ ℔ hund. I have also abt. 14 or 15 Hd. pds. Ship Bread.

[344]

RC (Vi). Addressed and endorsed.

Col. Aylett, the Virginia deputy commissary-general, had authorized GM to purchase tobacco for the state's account as part of a scheme to finance the purchase of munitions abroad. MR. PAYNE may have been William Payne, onetime member of the Fairfax County Committee of Safety. DANIEL CARROLL, the Maryland planter and sometime business agent, was encouraging GM to hedge against nondelivery of some contracted tobacco purchases, but inflation began to force prices up. GM, who considered himself a truly free agent acting only from patriotic motives, was anxious to have Aylett relay the circumstances to the governor and council in Willamsburg. MR. HERBERT was an Alexandria merchant involved in buying flour for the Continental army. The provisions were being loaded at Northern Neck ports, but roving British vessels in Chesapeake Bay made their movements hazardous once they left port. In this case, GM finally bought enough tobacco, but the ship was still in a safe harbor on 22 Aug. (letter to Patrick Henry, 22 Aug. 1777).

A crease and heavy smearing on the fourth page resulted in an illegible line and some missing words, which have been conjecturally added and placed in brackets. The postscript was written on the left margin of the fourth page.

To George Wythe

SIR: Gunston Hall, June 14th, 1777.

I hoped to have attended my duty in the House before this time, or I should not so long have delayed writing on the subject with which I now take the liberty to trouble you; but though I am otherwise thoroughly recovered from the small pox, my arm which has been so much ulcerated where the inoculation was made, still continues so bad, that my being able to attend this session remains doubtful. I must therefore entreat the favor of you sir, to return my thanks to the Assembly for the honor they have been pleased to do me, in appointing me one of their delegates to Congress, and at the same time to inform them that I cannot by any means accept the appointment. My own domestic affairs are so circumstanced as not to admit of my continued absence from home, where a numerous family of children calls for my constant attention; nor do I think I have a right to vacate my seat in the house of delegates, without the consent of my constituents; and such of them as I have had the opportunity of consulting are adverse to it. Was this not the case, I must acknowledge I have other reasons for declining the appointment; which to avoid offence, I forbear giving.

I beg you will excuse this trouble, and believe me, with the greatest respect, Sir, your most obd't Serv't.

G. MASON

Printed from Rowland, I, 283. In 1892, the original Ms., according to Miss Rowland, was in the Virginia State Library; but a search there in 1968 was unavailing. Addressed to Wythe as "Speaker of the House of Delegates."

Sufficient evidence exists to justify the assumption that jealousies and bickering were part of legislative life in Williamsburg despite the almost universally voiced hope that American lawmakers might avoid the factionalism of older republics. GM was identified with the Jefferson-Wythe-Richard Henry Lee group of liberals, but his inoculation spared him from the battle to elect Wythe or to punish Lee. Wythe won in a three-man race for the speakership that normally would have been Edmund Pendleton's for the asking. But Pendleton, the speaker who succeeded Peyton Randolph, had been injured in a riding accident. Despite fundamental differences on the course of revolution, the public men in Virginia readily acknowledged merit in their midst. Hence Wythe assured Pendleton "he considered his appointment as *Vicarious* only, and that he was to restore it to me as soon as I was able to Attend" (Pendleton to William Woodford, 15 May 1777, in Mays, ed., *Papers of Edmund Pendleton*, I, 209). GM had declined a seat in the Continental Congress in Aug. 1775, but a vacancy created by Thomas Nelson's resignation showed that the delegates had short memories. Nelson's resignation came at a time when Richard Henry Lee was accused of unpatriotically demanding "that his tenants covenant to pay their rent in Specie, which was considered as depreciating American paper" (Pendleton to William Woodford, 29 May 1777, *ibid.*, 213). GM had assured Lee in March that the rumor was not "worth giving you a Moment's Uneasiness" (letter to Lee, 4 March 1777), but GM had underestimated the strength of Lee's enemies, who were numerous and of long standing. GM had been re-elected by the Fairfax County freeholders in Apr., although the election was unsuccessfully challenged because of the smallpox epidemic (JHD, 1827 ed., 29, 31 May). It is almost certain, however, that GM never attended the May–June sessions for a variety of reasons; and the "Mr. Mason" mentioned in the house journal must be his brother and Loudoun County delegate, Thomson Mason. Nonetheless, GM was chosen in absentia to fill Nelson's unexpired term, and was then elected to a full term (JHD, 1827 ed., 22 May entry) before this letter had reached the speaker's chair. The delegation thus chosen had been selected with an obvious snub for Lee. Lee's exclusion, an unfriendly but fair-minded rival admitted, was "a most flagrant act of injustice" (J. Banister to Theodorick Bland, Jr., 10 [c. 22] June 1777, in Charles Campbell, ed., *Bland Papers* [Petersburg, 1840], I, 57–58). Lee's reaction was to demand a hearing, and meanwhile GM's unwillingness to serve was made known. Lee vindicated himself at a joint session of the General Assembly and on 20 June an about-face resolution offered him thanks for his patriotic services (Boyd, II, 17; JHD, 1827 ed., 20 June entry). In the earlier balloting, GM had received 77 votes and Lee 2, but in the new situation Lee was offered GM's vacant place and the tempest seemed quieted. Though some constituents approved GM's course of action, one absent neighbor gently reprimanded him for his continued evasion of a larger public role (see Washington to GM, 27 Mar. 1779).

From the Voters of Fairfax County

[20 August 1777]

To GEORGE MASON AND PHILIP ALEXANDER *Esquires.*

GENTLEMEN,

We your constituents of the county of Fairfax, and town of Alexandria, are greatly alarmed at the HIGH PRICE of every

COMMODITY now exposed to sale, and at the distant prospect of their being cheaper, unless some method can be fallen on to lessen the immense quantity of money now in circulation. This done, we apprehend will be a great means of raising the value of money, lowering the price of goods, workmens wages, and enable the soldier to supply himself with more necessaries, and render his service more easy and cheerful to himself, and indeed more beneficial to his country.

We are of opinion, that OUR MONEY, and money in general, has a proper circulation through the country, which the planter, the farmer, and every person that has had any dealing (and most have in some way) must have experienced, from the very high prices they have received from the purchaser, for every article they have sold, some few excepted.

That a tax be immediately laid and collected, we think, would be one great means of giving a proper value to our money. It would lessen the quantity, and consequently be productive of great good to the community.

We think the people are not only able to pay the tax, but that they will cheerfully submit to it; the people in this quarter appear well disposed for the purpose. Therefore we strongly recommend it to you, and enjoin you, to use your utmost e[n]deavours to obtain a law to pass to tax the people of this state, in such sort as your Honourable House shall judge proper.

We are of the opinion, that a GENERAL ASSESSMENT would be the most equi[t]able, and the only way to raise a sum adequate to the purpose. Lo[n]g experience has taught us, that our mode of taxation hitherto adopted never raised the money intended without many additions, or long continuance of the taxes. Let us endeavour to remedy it.

We are of opinion, that opening the COURTS of JUSTICE would operate for the publick good. The people would then pay their debts, or be legally compelled to it. This would enable the merchant to extend his trade; there would be larger importations; and it would be a great means of stimulating us to industry, and prevent our laying out money in superfluous things, that we can well do without. Another salutary end would be obtained; licentiousness would be restrained, and every thing again returned to its prop[e]r channel.

We desire, that you use your utmost interest that the legislature (at any risk) would fall on ways and means to import A LARGE QUANTITY OF SALT, for the use of the people in this state. The

[347]

introduction of this necessary article would ease their minds, and enable them to support their families much better than they can without. They are willing to pay almost any price, if it could be purchased with money. Some provisions also might be made for those who cannot, at any rate, purchase. Should laws for this purpose (which we judge salutary) take place, the immense quantity of money in circulation would decrease, its credit and value increase; our loan office would greatly experience the benefit; every kind of goods would fall in price; the officer and soldier (who claim your greatest care and attention) that are now, or may be hereafter, in the service of his country, to preserve and to secure to us every thing that is dear and valuable, would procure necessaries cheaper, and be enabled to live upon his pay, which at present he cannot do. We might then expect to keep up an army, and it would increase. In our present situation, its duration may have a short existence. Perhaps this may be the last campaign. Should this be the case, we may at last be obliged to submit to the unconditional terms of a tyrant king, corrupt ministry, a venal parliament, and a cruel banditti. Hard terms! forbid it, Heaven!

We hope you join us in opinion, that these at least are probable means to obtain the desired end. We therefore again enjoin you to use your greatest efforts that such laws do pass, by which means you will secure to yourselves the esteem and confidence (we hope) of the publick in general, and of your constituents in particular.

We request, that particular inquiry may be made how the PUBLICK MONEY HAS BEEN EXPENDED; if proper persons are at the head of several departments in which they are employed, not only those that are in the pay of this state, but those that act in this state in the continental service, because we must not only pay our own expenses, but a large proportion of the general expense. Let inquiry be made into the salary given to each person in the several departments of this commonwealth; let every man in office be well paid, but let none make fortunes at the expense of their country. ASSIZE COURTS, and CIRCUIT JUDGES would be a great ease to the people, less expensive to the country, many villanies would appear that are [n]ow concealed; consequently, many would suffer condign punishment that now escape, for reasons too obvious to mention. This has long been thought highly useful. Why has [n]ot a law already passed to procure so great a good to the publick?

If a STATE ENSURANCE OFFICE was opened (and surely it may be done) at least it is worthy [of] the notice of the legislature, it would be a great means of introducing goods of every kind. In consequence, they would be cheaper; the farmer, indeed every body, would experience the use; and the happiness it would diffuse through all ranks of mankind wou'd make them cheerfully pay any tax that the legislature may think necessary to impose for the good of the country.

As we put the greatest confidence in your attachment and attention to the good of your coun[t]ry, we expect that you will pay a proper regard to our opinion and requests in the matters to you recommended. We are, gentlemen, with esteem, your humble servants,

YOUR CONSTITUENTS.

Printed from 26 Sept. 1777 *Va. Gaz.* (Purdie). There was no Alexandria newspaper at this time, so this is not a local reprint but appears to be a Ms. forwarded to the printer with the dateline: "FAIRFAX county, *August* 20, 1777."

GM and Alexander had been elected to the House of Delegates in Apr. The unknown author (or authors) of this public letter probably was a merchant vexed by the problems of rampant inflation induced by the various effusions of paper money from both the Continental treasury and Williamsburg. An imperfect system of taxation, lax collection practices, and a strong prodebtor faction in the legislature combined to make paper money continue its downward spiral. However, GM was sympathetic to efforts to bolster the sagging state credit and was soon to introduce legislation meant to stabilize Virginia currency through A GENERAL ASSESSMENT of 10 shillings upon every £100 of property (Hening, IX, 349–368). The Virginia courts were in a desultory state, a situation partly remedied by legislation early in 1778 which fixed the time and place for sessions of the High Court of Chancery and General Court (Hening, IX, 434). The age-old preservative for meat, A LARGE QUANTITY OF SALT, was in short supply and becoming scarcer by the day. A blow to Virginia demands for this staple came in July, when British men-of-war blocking Chesapeake Bay seized and burned "6 or 7 Salt Vessels" ladened with the precious cargo (Pendleton to William Woodford, 19 July 1777, in Mays, ed., *Papers of Edmund Pendleton*, I, 218). GM was acutely aware of this problem and he probably wrote the bill authorizing military provisioners to seize the vital commodity (JHD, 1827 ed., 14 Jan. entry). The laws of supply and demand worked viciously as salt supplies diminished and prices rose in 1778 and 1779. GM appears to have been instrumental in securing passage of "An act to encourage the importation of salt" (Hening, X, 150–151) in 1779. A STATE ENSURANCE OFFICE as proposed by the Fairfax freeholders would have given a stability to commercial transactions that had been lacking since the rupture with England. Marine insurance rates were high in London, but the assurance of indemnity against losses at sea helped create a maritime trade that fostered English prosperity in the 18th century. The idea of a state-owned agency for insuring cargoes probably had great merit, but was too advanced for the times, and was also somewhat mitigated by the commonwealth's assumption of risks through tobacco purchases at Virginia ports. GM's willingness to sponsor legislation covering some of the listed grievances indicates that he did indeed PAY A PROPER REGARD to the constituents' opinions.

To Patrick Henry

The Commonwealth's Tobacco purchased here has been a long time on board Mr. Pliarne's Ship; but there being no prospect of getting her out soon, I delayed taking the Bills of Lading 'til this Week; one of which (together with a Manifest Containing the Shipping Marks Nos. & Weights of the Tobo.) I have inclosed, per the Ship, to Messrs. J. Gruell & Compy., and now transmit you the other three, with a Copy of my Letter to them.

Herewith you will also receive a Manifest of the Tobo. distinguishing the Planter's Marks & Nos. with the different Prices at which it was bought, and my Acct. by which you will see there remains in my Hands the Sum of £174..5..6; which I will return by the first safe Opportunity to Wmsburg.

To save the Board the Trouble of a tedious Examination of the Addition and Extension of the Tobo. at the various Prices, I have annexed to the Manifest a seperate Acct. stating the Quantity bought of each Person, & the Price; in which the Arrangement of the Tobo. and the Prices is so different from that in the Manifest, that both agreeing, it is impossible either can be wrong; & by this Means, I believe the Accts. may be thoroughly examined in three Minutes.

The Purchase, upon the whole, I think is a cheap one, and I flatter myself will give Satisfaction.

The Inspectors in this Part of the Country, not having received their Commissions at the time, & not thinking themselves answerable, were careless of the Condition in which they received or delivered Tobacco; which has occasioned some Charge in relanding Part of it, repairing Caskes &c. but I thought it better to incur this Expence, than risque sending the Tobacco to Europe in bad Order.

The Trouble I have had in this Business has been much more than I expected; but it was oweing to an unavoidable Accident, the Small-pox at all our [ware] houses; which not only rendered it extreamly diff[icult] to procure Tobacco, but furnish'd many, upon [prices] rising, with a Pretence for avoiding their Contracts. Shou'd any Quantity of Tobacco be hereafter wanted for public Service, I wou'd beg Leave to recommend it to the Board to give Orders some considerable time before the Tobo. is wanted; which will always make the Purchase easier, and the Commodity cheaper.

I am, with the greatest Respect, Sir Your most obdt. Hble Sert.

G Mason

RC (Vi). A three-page letter, addressed and sent "on public Service." Endorsed.

The Revolution freed American planters from the tobacco-marketing limitations of the English Navigation Acts and opened up a world-wide trade, provided the British naval blockade could be circumvented. The short-distance trade route was from Chesapeake Bay to the Caribbean (St. Eustatia, Martinique, or the Danish West Indies), and the most expeditious sales were being negotiated with French and Dutch mercantile houses. Prices for tobacco delivered in Europe rose dramatically in 1776, which brought on a speculative fervor that seemed to herald benefits for America. The decision to buy and sell tobacco on behalf of the state promised mutual benefits—the commonwealth would run the risk of the blockade because the planter had already sold his tobacco, and the state stood to make a huge profit if the hogsheads ever reached a safe port. MR. PLIARNE'S SHIP was probably a vessel chartered by a Philadelphia agent for an European house that was cooperating with Col. William Aylett, the Virginia deputy commissary-general who was financing the purchases on behalf of the state. GM's guess that there was NO PROSPECT OF GETTING HER OUT SOON was perhaps too gloomy. The long British blockade of Chesapeake Bay was temporarily relaxed when cruising men-of-war were probably diverted to escort duty with the British flotilla from New York carrying Howe's army to the Head of Elk (Pendleton to William Woodford, 15 Aug. 1777, in Mays, ed., *Papers of Edmund Pendleton*, I, 221). The British left "A 64 gun ship and a frigate . . . off the spit of York" (*Va. Gaz.* [Purdie], 22 Aug. 1777), but venturesome American vessels slipped through with more ease until the blockade was resumed in Sept. GM seems to have entered the business as a patriotic gesture and was anxious to have his involvement recognized as such. The French mercantile firm of J. GRUELL & COMPY. had contracted with Virginia to furnish arms and supplies (Boyd, III, 91), apparently with the proceeds from tobacco sales. It is likely that GM's SEPERATE ACCT. STATING THE QUANTITY BOUGHT OF EACH PERSON accompanied the cargo, for it is now missing. The SMALL-POX epidemic in northern Virginia during the spring and summer of 1777 disrupted business and seems to have kept GM from the General Assembly sessions in May–June.

A torn portion of the third page destroyed parts of three lines. The restored portions are in brackets.

Legislation to Aid in Recruiting and Supplying Virginia Troops on Duty with the Continental Army

[26 October 1777–14 January 1778]

I. An Act for Speedily Clothing Troops [26–29 November]
II. A Bill to Prevent Forestalling and Engrossing [29 December]

III. An Act for Enabling the Publick Contractors to Procure Stores for Troops [6 January]
IV. An Act for Speedily Recruiting the Virginia Regiments [ca. 26 October 1777–9 January 1778]
V. An Act for Authorising the Seizure of Salt [14 January 1778]

EDITORIAL NOTE

A full assessment of Mason's role in the General Assembly session of 1777–1778 is not possible, but by using scattered primary evidence and a comparison of the several legislative journals a fairly complete idea of Mason's involvement emerges. The session was scheduled to begin in Williamsburg on 4 October 1777, but no quorum was present until the thirteenth. The problem of attendance was a continual one. Mason himself intended to leave for the capital on 26 October, but inclement weather kept him at Gunston Hall for more than a week, so that he did not report to the House of Delegates until 14 November. He arrived at a time of trial and travail for the new state and the infant Republic. The British were attempting to close a military pincers movement, while a long list of internal woes plagued the American war effort. The British threat was turned aside, at least temporarily, by Burgoyne's defeat at Saratoga, but the enormous problem of maintaining both Washington's army and the public credit remained. Yet the handling of weighty public business properly seemed at times to be a matter of low priority. Washington's stepson told the general of Mason's delay and added that Mason's presence in Williamsburg "is of the greatest importance to this State, as I beleive It was never so badly represented as at present" (John Parke Custis to Washington, 26 October 1777, George Bolling Lee Papers [ViHi]). This negative impression of the General Assembly membership in 1777 seems to have been widespread. A friend wrote Madison (who was defeated for re-election) that the Assembly had few members left "who can give a luster to her councils, or authority to her decisions, or even perhaps guide her deliberations with regularity & prudence" (S. S. Smith to Madison, Hutchinson-Rachal, I, 195).

Actually, Mason's colleagues in the Assembly included Jefferson, George Wythe, Edmund Pendleton, Robert Carter Nicholas, Thomas Nelson, Charles Carter, and Benjamin Harrison—a formidable intellectual array when they were all assembled and working. But, as Pendleton was to complain, their work pace "hath been the most tedious I ever experienced, owing to the bad attendance of some Members and the too great refinement of others—insomuch that of the great Subjects before us, we have only finished the Bill for recruiting the Army and that against Forestalling" (letter to William Woodford, 2 January 1777, Mays, ed., Papers of Edmund Pendleton, I, 240). The inclination of the day was to deprecate, and it was indeed a gloomy time as Washington's men huddled around campfires at Whitemarsh and Valley Forge. But the Assembly's efforts to bolster the army's morale and muster-rolls accomplished more than some pessimistic Virginians realized.

After a summer of uncertainty (for a time, Virginians believed Howe's fleet was headed for their shores, rather than his real destination at Head of Elk in Maryland), the reverses at Brandywine and Germantown had sobered Americans to the harsh demands of war. Obviously, the war was going to drag on, despite the rumors and overtures from Parliament. With disaffection rampant in Delaware and New Jersey, there was cause for dire forebodings as some men starved while others sold the British food and fodder for hard cash. But Washington's firmness, coupled with the good news from Saratoga in mid-October, brought both a resolution for Thanksgiving and renewed resolve from the Assembly. Of first importance was Washington's plea for clothing as the mercury dipped along the Schuylkill River. This challenge Mason and his colleagues answered, after Governor Patrick Henry showed them Washington's appeal, with a flurry of legislative activity that helped to hurry blankets and clothing northward. Rumors of hoarding and forestalling (buying goods to corner a market) brought prompt action through an investigation, followed by several bills. These measures were eventually incorporated into one act designed to speed up the provisioning of troops by either the purchase of food at reasonable prices or outright seizure, if the emergency demanded such arbitrary action. Similarly, Washington's warning that enlistments were running out, and that replacements would be needed to keep an army in the field, had to be heeded. In each case, Mason was to serve on a drafting committee, either as a member or as chairman, and though the surviving manuscripts rarely confirm his sole authorship, Mason's leadership in these instances is indicated by drafts, fragmentary notes, journal entries, the letters of his associates, and Mason's own correspondence after the session adjourned. From the revolving chairmanships (usually Charles Carter, Jefferson, Thomas Nelson, or Mason were designated by Speaker Wythe) there are clues but not conclusive evidence of a measure's paternity. More convincing proof, in the absence of a manuscript, is the House's order for a member to carry the approved measure to the Senate, for the author was in the best position to explain a bill, and to negotiate if amendments were needed. Thus as a "floor manager" Mason was probably also the principal author, though not the sole framer, of the bills and acts printed in these volumes even though his handwritten draft cannot be produced as conclusive evidence. Anyone familiar with committee work must understand that a strong-minded leader has a way of persuading his colleagues to a particular point of view; and Mason was both impatient with the committee system and strong willed to the point of being overbearing.

Recruitment was no less urgent than finding blankets and breeches, as Washington had warned repeatedly. Mason had thought the matter through before he left Gunston Hall and told Jacky Custis of his ideas. "What plan Colonel Mason may have in contemplation for filling up the Virginia regiments I know not, but certain I am that this is a measure than [*sic*] can not be dispensed with, nor ought not under any pretext whatsoever" (Washington to Custis, 14 November 1777, Fitzpatrick, ed., *Writings of Washington*, X, 60–61). After Governor Henry wrote Washington that nine wagon-loads of supplies and £15,000 of woolen clothing were headed for his winter camp (*ibid.*, 172n), the problem of expiring enlistments still had to be solved. In desperation, Washington even suggested that the Virginians whose terms were about to expire might laugh at a feeble bounty offer, but would re-enlist if allowed a long Christmas furlough. This would have denied the army any chance for winter action, but the elements and British generalship made such a prospect unlikely anyway. Despite Washington's needs, however, the Virginians at home were skittish about military conscription. Nine regiments were assigned as the Virginia quota for Washington's army by the Congress, which itself lacked authority to draft a single man. If the Virginians already attached to the Continental army refused to re-enlist, they would deprive Washington of the experienced troops he vitally needed. Still, the tendency was to believe that "a well Regulated Militia may be our Salvation and Officers who are not Attentive to their duty ought to be broke like Glass," Jefferson was told after reports from Germantown of drunkness and worse among the commanders of some Virginia troops (letter from John Harvie, 18 October 1777, Boyd, II, 35). Americans had read and said so many good things about the militia that it was hard for them to recognize the militiaman's ineptness. Arbitrary governments in Europe had practiced impressment and conscription for generations while they brutally suppressed opposition to such methods, but in an America of free speech and wide spaces, forced military service was bound to be unpopular. Predictably, the conscription law provoked militant opposition, and in Loudoun County one attempt to draft men for Washington's army "was prevented by the violent & riotous behaviour of the people" (Hutchinson-Rachal, I, 230).

In such circumstances, the roll of deserters was long. Indeed, a colleague of Mason's admitted that the area around Williamsburg was infested with deserters "whose friends Secrete them and the Neighbours connive at it, and what is every one's duty becomes Nobody's" (Pendleton to William Woodford, 29 November 1777, Mays, *Papers of Edmund Pendleton*, I, 238). When Henry suggested to Washington that an amnesty for Eastern Shore deserters might produce salutary results and release recruits for duty elsewhere, Washington conceded that "The Expedient you propose might, and I believe would bring in several [deserters], but I cannot consider myself authorised to adopt it" (letter to Henry, 19 December 1777, Fitzpatrick, ed., *Writings of Washington*, X, 173).

In short, Washington conceived it his duty to train and fight with the army, but it was the lawmaker's obligation to give him that army and keep it fed, clothed, and armed. Certainly since writing the Fairfax Resolves in 1774, Mason had every inclination to agree with Washington's concept of what responsibilities existed and where they lay. Mason's major involvement in helping write and pass laws that would lessen Washington's burden must be understood in that context.

I. An Act for Speedily Clothing the Troops Raised by This Commonwealth Now in Continental Service

[26–29 November 1777]

WHEREAS the probability of a winter campaign hath rendered it indispensably necessary to furnish an immediate supply of clothing for the troops raised in this commonwealth and now in continental service, and the usual methods of supply may prove tedious and inadequate to the present emergency:

For remedy herein, *Be it enacted by the General Assembly*, That the governour, with the advice of the council of state, be, and he is hereby empowered to appoint commissioners, in every part of this commonwealth where he shall think it proper, who shall, and they, or any two of them, are hereby declared to have power and authority respectively to seize all linens, woollens, trimmings, tanned leather, hats, leather breeches, dressed deerskins, shoes, and stockings, proper for the use of the army, which may be found in the possession of any person or persons whatsoever, who hath purchased the same in any of the United States of America for sale; and if any person who may, on good grounds, be suspected by the said commissioners of having concealed any of the said articles in any storehouse, or other place, shall refuse to permit such commissioners to have free access thereto, the said commissioners are hereby empowered, in company with a justice of the peace, and by his order, to break open any locks or doors to enable them to discover whether any such articles are concealed; and where the said justice and commissioners shall meet with resistance in accomplishing this discovery, the said justice is hereby directed to call upon the sheriff, or any constable, for such aid of the county as shall be sufficient to enforce obedience to this act. The said commissioners shall be, and they are hereby required and empowered to appoint four honest and reputable housekeepers of the neighbourhood (of whom any three may act) who, having first taken an oath, to be administered by any one of the commissioners, faithfully and impartially to perform that service, shall appraise such goods in ready money, at a reasonable price.

The commissioners who shall have performed the service shall give a certificate in writing, after such valuation is made, to the holders of such goods respectively, distinguishing the particular species, quantity, and value thereof, with an order to be drawn on the treasurer of this commonwealth to pay the said appraised value to the holder, or his order, within one month after the date thereof, which orders the treasurer is hereby required and directed to pay. And in all cases where such goods shall be applied to the use of the troops in continental service, the same shall be charged to the account of the United American States. And the commissioners, or any two of them, may employ, or if necessary impress, so many workmen as they shall judge sufficient to make up into wearing apparel such clothing and leather. The wages of any workmen impressed, in case of disagreement between the parties, shall be settled in the same manner as the value of the materials seized; and orders for such wages, as well as what shall become due to the persons voluntarily employed, shall be drawn upon the treasurer, paid by him, and charged in manner aforesaid. If any workman impressed shall refuse, or, being a servant, his master shall not permit him to work, the servant or master so offending, upon complaint of the commissioners, or any two of them, may by a justice of the peace, be committed to prison until he shall comply.

The said commissioners shall by some safe conveyance, and in due time, transmit to the treasurer a list of the sums for which they shall have drawn orders, together with the names of the persons in whose favour they were drawn, for his more certain information.

And if any person shall be sued for doing any thing in execution of this act, the defendant may plead the general issue, and give this act in evidence; and if the plaintiff shall be non-suited, or a judgment pass against him upon a verdict or demurrer, the defendant shall recover double costs; and in all such suits the *onus probandi* shall lie upon the plaintiff.

This act shall continue and be in force until the last day of February next.

Printed from Hening, IX, 375–377.

The hurried writing and passage of this bill proves that when Virginians were confronted with problems during the Revolution they acted with what might be called—vis-à-vis 20th-century legislators—blinding speed. After the battle of Germantown (4 Oct. 1777), Washington's army retreated to Valley Forge and prepared for the fateful winter that was only relieved by news of a Franco-American alliance. Distressed by the extreme discomfort of his men, Washington wrote to the governors of several adjoining states with a plea for blankets and clothing. On 13 Nov. Washington wrote Gov. Henry of the critical need for "Cloathing of any kind" and urged Henry to recommend to the General Assembly that they "immediately lay a very moderate Assessment upon the different Counties. . . . But all depends upon its being done speedily, or the Season will be past, before the Supply arrives" (Fitzpatrick, ed., *Writings of Washington*, X, 55–56). Meanwhile, there were reports in Va. of forestalling by avaricious persons who sought to monopolize the supply of cloth, leather, and finished goods which the troops needed. On 25 Nov. the House of Delegates ordered an inquiry into the situation and called for quick action. Henry apparently had made good use of Washington's letter, for the general's recommendation that every county send a complete outfit for each man on active duty with his army was implemented by directions for a bill that would requisition "all proper woollens, linens, shoes and stockings" for that purpose. GM was appointed to the committee charged with framing the act, and on 26 Nov. a bill was brought forward, debated, and passed. The selection of GM as carrier of the bill to the Senate for final approval is circumstantial but rather convincing evidence that he was the principal author of the legislation. Two days after the bill had been mentioned, with its urgency apparent, the Senate returned the bill with its approval (JHD, 1827 ed., 25–27 Nov. entries). Before the week was over it is likely that collections were under way, and meanwhile some good news came from a nearby port. Edmund Pendleton, reporting his concern for the half-naked soldiers, wrote that his anxiety was "much increased by a heavy Snow fallen and Falling. . . . I hope we have taken effectual means to provide for them in point of cloathing and blankets. The Congress, one of our State Ships, is just arrived from France with 1500 blankets, 1200 pair Stockings, a parcel of Cloths and linnens," all of which would be forwarded promptly to Valley Forge (Pendleton to William Woodford, 29 Nov. 1777, in Mays, ed., *Papers of Edmund Pendleton*, I, 238). The *Congress's* arrival may have cut through some of the pessimism that attended passage of the act, although Pendleton admitted his fear that the scarcity of suitable clothing "will prevent much of the beneficial effects of such a measure." The broad powers conferred by the act seem to have been used at once by the governor and council, for by 29 Dec. Virginian John Harvie sent word from Pennsylvania that the "Supply of Cloathing came very Opportunely to Cover the Shivering Limbs of our poor Naked Soldiers" (letter to Jefferson, in Boyd, II, 126). THE PROBABILITY OF A WINTER CAMPAIGN as a preface to the act is a rewording of Washington's admonition that speed was vital, for in his letter to Henry the general's judgment was that "we have the greatest prospect of a Winter Campaign." It is likely that the broad powers authorized for the commissioners were used with some caution, although the temptation for high-handed action seems to dangle from the ONUS PROBANDI ("burden of proof") section. GM doubtless had help in drafting that portion of the act, but the main parts were probably discussed in the House of Delegates on 25 Nov., and the bill drafted that night or early the next day. The companion measure, "A Bill for enabling the public Contractors to procure Stores of Provision[s] necessary for the ensuring Campaign . . . ," was written by GM and first read to the House on 29 Dec. 1777 (*q.v.*). By 19 Dec. Washington learned that nine wagon-loads of supplies had been sent from Virginia and £15,000 spent on woolen clothing that was soon to be shipped to his winter encampment (Fitzpatrick, ed., *Writings of Washington*, X, 172n).

II. A Bill to Prevent Forestalling and Engrossing

[29 December 1777]

Whereas divers persons devoting themselves to Avarice & Extortion, and intending to amass Riches out of the Ruins of their Country, or treacherously to betray it into the Hands of it's Enemies, by forestalling and ingrossing the Provisions necessary for the

Sustenance of it's Armies in the ensuing Campaign, have indus-
triously bought up, and already got into their Possession so great a
Proportion of the Provisions usually brought to Market at this
Season, that there is little Hope of our being able to lay up such
Stores thereof as will be requisite for the Purposes of the succeeding
Year, and some of them refuse to sell the same to the public Agents
Contractors & Commissaries or demand such prices as amount to a
Refusal, because they wou'd endanger a public Bankruptcy; and
others under Pretence of exporting the same for Sale, mean to
Supply our Enemies therewith.

Be it therefore enacted by the General Assembly that from and
after the passing of this Act, no Pork or Beef, living or dead, shall be
exported out of this Commonwealth by Land or by Water by any
Person whatever, except only such as shall be sent thereout for the
Support of the Continental Army by the Agents Contractors or
Commissaries, acting under Appointment from the united States, or
any of them, and except also such Quantity as may be really
necessary for the Crew of any Vessel going out upon a Voyage or
Cruise. And for defeating the Avarice and wicked Intentions of
those who have endeavoured to forestall the Public, and making due
Provision for the American Troops, Be it further enacted that it
shall not be lawful for any Person who hath purchased, or shall
hereafter purchase any Pork or Beef, living or dead, and who shall
have the same on Hand at the time of passing this Act, or at any
time after, during it's Continuance, to sell barter or otherwise dispose of the same, or any Part thereof, unless in the Sustenance of
themselves, their Families, & those in their Employ, or within their
own Houses, to any Person whatever, save only to the Agents
Contractors or Commissaries duly authorised to purchase for the
united American States or any of them; until the Governor &
Council shall by Proclamation declare that the public Wants are
sufficiently provided for.

Every Person offending herein by selling exporting or endeavouring to export Pork or Beef contrary to this Act shall forfeit the
treble Value thereof, one Moiety to the Commonwealth, and the
other Moiety to him who will sue as well for the Commonwealth, as
for himself, or the whole to the Commonwealth, if a Prosecution
shall be first instituted on the public Behalf alone.

This Act shall continue in Force for & during the space of
        months, and from thence to the End of the next
Session of Assembly and no longer.

Ms (Vi). Two pages in GM's handwriting, endorsed by GM as "a Bill for enabling the public Contractors to procure Stores of Provision[s] necessary for the ensuing Campaign & for defeating Practices of those who have attempted to prevent the public herein." A clerk crossed through the words "Practices" and "attempted" to make the last portion read ". . . & for defeating the evil intention of those who have endeavoured to prevent the public herein." A clerk's endorsement below reads: "Decr. 29 1777 Read the first Time. Jan: 2d. 1777 [1778] Read 2d. time & to be engrossed."

Jefferson and GM had been ordered to prepare a bill which would prevent forestalling—cornering of a market, in this case the market in dried or salted beef and pork—shortly after GM arrived at the capital (JHD, 1827 ed., 20 Nov. 1777). However, their work was probably delayed as the House of Delegates had a special committee look into the matter after 25 Nov., and the main business seemed to be the procurement of clothing for Washington's shivering army. Then on 27 Dec. Jefferson and GM were instructed to bring in a bill "for enabling the public contractors to procure stores of provisions necessary for the ensuing campaign. . . ." Two days later, GM's draft was presented to the House with a broader aspect, but it became stalled and finally was grafted onto a companion measure that gave Continental Commissaries and their agents discretionary powers to search for and commandeer the needed beef or pork. This omnibus bill was also titled "An Act for Enabling the Publick Contractors to Procure Stores. . . ."

GM's blank space in this draft was later changed to continue the finally approved measure in force either until the end of the next session or whenever the governor and council proclaimed the emergency ended.

III. An Act "for enabling the publick contractors to procure stores of provisions necessary for the ensuing campaign, and to prohibit the exportation of beef, pork, and bacon, for a limited time."

[6 January 1778]

WHEREAS divers persons, devoting themselves to avarice and extortion, and intending to amass riches out of the ruins of their country, or treacherously to betray it into the hands of its enemies, have industriously bought up, and already got into their possession, so great a proportion of the provisions usually brought to market at this season, that there is little hope of our being able to lay up such stores thereof as will be requisite for the purposes of the ensuing campaign, unless an embargo be laid on the exportation thereof: *Be it therefore enacted by the General Assembly,* That from and after the passing of this act no pork, beef, or bacon, shall be exported out of this commonwealth by land or by water, by any person whatever, except only such as shall be sent thereout for the support of the continental army, or any troops sent out of this commonwealth,

[359]

by the agents, contractors, or commissaries, acting under appointment from the United States, or any of them, or to fulfil contracts already made to supply the owners of certain iron works with a quantity of beef or pork in the state of Maryland in exchange for iron, and except also such quantity as may be really necessary for the crew of a vessel going out upon a voyage or cruise, and such as may be purchased by the agents of the United States as sea stores for any vessels in the continental service going from Maryland or North Carolina on a voyage or cruise. Any person so offending herein, by exporting, or endeavouring to export, pork, beef, or bacon, contrary to this act, shall forfeit the provisions so endeavoured to be exported, which may be seized by any naval officer, where the exportation shall be by water, or by order of any justice of peace, where it happens by land, or happening by water, a naval officer hath not been appointed, or, being appointed, shall not be present at the place where the exportation is intended, and shall also pay the double value thereof, with costs of suit, one moiety to the commonwealth, and the other moiety to him who will sue as well for the commonwealth as for himself, or the whole to the commonwealth, if a prosecution shall be first instituted on the publick behalf alone.

And be if farther enacted, That if any justice of peace, from his own knowledge, or the information of others, shall have cause to suspect that any pork, beef, or bacon, is about to be carried out of this commonwealth contrary to this act, he may issue his warrant for seizing the same; and if the owner shall not give security that he will not carry the same out of the commonwealth, such justice may either retain such provisions for publick use, to be appraised and paid for in manner herein after mentioned, or may cause the same to be sold for the benefit of the owner, and at his or her expense.

And that those who have engrossed, or shall engross, the provisions necessary for the army, and refuse to sell the same for that use at moderate prices, may be disappointed in their wicked designs to distress or ruin their country: *Be it farther enacted,* That if any person who, since the first day of November last, hath purchased, or during the continuance of this act shall purchase, any live stock, or beef, pork, or bacon, more than is sufficient for the consumption of his family, and of those in his employ, shall refuse to sell the same to any agent, commissary, or contractor, acting under appointment of the United States or this commonwealth, for such price as shall be estimated by three freeholders authorised by a justice of the peace by warrant under his hand and seal, and sworn truly and faithfully to ascertain the number and quantity sufficient for the family of the owner and those in his employ, and to appraise the surplus, such agent, commissary, or contractor, by warrant under the hand and seal of a justice of the peace, who is hereby required to issue the same, may, in company with the sheriff or constable, and such assistants as the said justice shall judge necessary, seize such surplus, and for that purpose, in the day time, enter any warehouse or enclosure, paying or tendering to the owner the price so estimated by the appraisers, or in case the seizure be made by an agent, commissary, or contractor of this commonwealth, drawing orders on the treasurer, payable one month after date, and transmitting copies of such orders to the said treasurer in the meantime.

And that any person against whom an action may be commenced for what he shall lawfully do by virtue and in execution of this act may plead the general issue, and give this act in evidence; and if a verdict be found, or a judgment be given for him, he shall recover double costs.

This act shall continue and be in force until the end of the next session of assembly, unless the governour and council shall by proclamation declare that the publick wants are sufficiently provided for, and no longer.

Printed from Hening, IX, 385–387.

Rising prices, a dwindling supply of goods, and marked difficulties in the commissary-general's department occurred in a frightening combination during the Indian summer of 1777. One result was the insistent demand for legislation that would brand forestallers of beef, pork, and other items deemed vital for the army as criminals and prescribe their punishment. Almost a week after his arrival in Williamsburg, GM had been appointed to a committee under Jefferson's chairmanship which was charged with drafting such a bill (JHD, 1827 ed., 20 Nov. 1777 entry). GM was also named to serve on a second committee on 25 Nov. which was to devise a method for clothing troops and incidentally to look into reported forestalling. The clothing emergency was handled with considerable dispatch, but the food problem was temporarily postponed. Then on 27 Dec. both GM and Jefferson were ordered to bring in legislation which would "enable the public contractors to procure stores of provisions" for Washington's dwindling command. Jefferson appears to have turned the business over to GM, for two days later GM presented a bill to prevent forestalling and engrossing. This bill failed to gain final passage on 5 Jan., but GM was appointed to another committee formed to prepare still another bill aimed at blocking the exportation of meat products from the state. On 6 Jan. GM carried a new version of the earlier bill, which now incorporated both the forestalling and nonexportation provisions, to the Senate. As the earlier act had dealt with the problem of blankets and clothing for the army, this became a companion measure which empowered Continental agents or commissaries to commandeer any meat they found while on foraging expeditions, as authorized by this act. Meanwhile, Washington had warned the Continental Congress that "unless some great and capital change suddenly takes place . . . this Army must inevitably be reduced to one or other of these three things. Starve, dissolve, or disperse, in order to obtain subsistence in the best manner they can" (letter to President of Congress, 23 Dec. 1777, Fitzpatrick, *Writing of Washington*, X, 192–193). This grim message reached Williamsburg and on 14 Jan. 1778 the Privy Council advised Gov. Henry "forthwith to send off an active intelligent & proper person to the Northwestern parts of this State in order to buy up all the pork Beef & Bacon that can be procured, & to forward it with all possible Dispatch to Head Quarters" in Valley Forge (Hutchinson-Rachal, I, 216).

IV. An Act for Speedily Recruiting the Virginia Regiments on the Continental Establishment, and for Raising Additional Troops of Volunteers

[*ca.* 26 October 1777–9 January 1778]

WHEREAS it is indispensably necessary that the regiments of infantry raised by the laws of this commonwealth, on continental establishment, be speedily recruited, and such alterations made therein as may assimilate them to the regiments raised by the other United American States for the continental army: *Be it therefore enacted by the General Assembly*, That fourteen of the said regiments be reduced to eight companies each, and be completed by recruits or draughts in manner herein after mentioned; that the officers of the reduced companies be provided for, by appointments, to fill up vacancies in the remaining companies, as they shall happen; and that the battalion on commonwealth establishment, under the command of colonel George Gibson, and now in continental service, be continued in the said service instead of the ninth Virginia regiment, made prisoners by the enemy in the battle of Germantown, until the officers and men of the said regiment shall be exchanged, or the time of service of the men in the said first battalion shall be expired.

And it is farther enacted, That the officers of the said fourteen regiments, as well as those of the said ninth regiment, if they shall be exchanged, shall use their best endeavours to re-enlist all the men therein whose times of service are near expiring, to serve for three years, or during the present war; and each of the men so re-enlisting, as well as those who have already re-enlisted, shall be entitled to a bounty from this commonwealth of twenty dollars, over and above the continental bounty, and the governor and council are desired to take such measures as to them shall seem best for enabling the officers to pay such additional bounty out of the publick money in the hands of the treasurer of this commonwealth.

And as our numbers in continental service, which, according to the proportions heretofore stated by congress, should be eight thousand one hundred and sixty men rank and file, may for some time be deficient: *Be it farther enacted,* That the troops raised for the service of this commonwealth, by an act of assembly passed in the year one thousand seven hundred and seventy six, and intituled "An act for making farther provision for the internal security and defence of this country," shall be forthwith regimented by the governour and council, who, for completing the work as speedily as possible, are hereby authorised to transfer the men enlisted by such officers as procure the smallest proportions of their quotas to such others as come nearest the raising their full quotas; and that a battalion of such troops, to consist of eight companies, if there be sufficient to make such a battalion, and if not, then so many as there are, be marched to join the grand army, there to continue till a sufficient number of recruits may be raised to make good our just proportion, or until the terms of their enlistments shall expire. And the officers and soldiers of the said battalion, under the command of colonel George Gibson, shall be entitled to and receive the same bounty, pay, rations, and clothing, as are allowed to the officers and soldiers in the continental service, so long as they continue therein.

It is farther enacted, That, for securing the completion of the said regiments, a number of men shall be draughted from the single men of the militia of the several counties, and the city of Williamsburg, whether officers or privates, above eighteen years of age, who have no child, in the following proportions, that is to say: From the county of Accomack forty eight, from the county of Albemarle thirty six, from the county of Amelia forty four, from the county of Augusta ninety seven, from the county of Amherst thirty two, from the county of Bedford fifty four, from the county of Berkeley fifty two, from the county of Botetourt sixty, from the county of Brunswick fifty two, from the county of Buckingham twenty six, from the county of Caroline forty one, from the county of Charles City eleven, from the county of Charlotte twenty eight, from the county of Chesterfield thirty, from the county of Culpeper sixty four, from the county of Cumberland sixteen, from the county of Dinwiddie twenty eight, from the county of Dunmore forty, from the county of Elizabeth City five, from the county of Essex twenty two, from the county of Fairfax thirty three, from the county of Fauquier forty eight, from the county of Fluvanna ten, from the county of Frederick forty, from the county of Gloucester thirty two, from the county of Goochland twenty three, from the county of Halifax thirty nine, from the county of Hampshire thirty three, from the county of Hanover thirty nine, from the county of Henrico twenty four, from the county of Henry twenty four, from the county of James City eight, from the county of Isle of Wight twenty four, from the county of King and Queen twenty, from the county of King George fourteen, from the county of King William twenty, from the county of Lancaster eleven, from the county of Loudoun sixty eight, from the county of Louisa twenty four, from the county of Lunenburg twenty two, from the county of Middlesex eight, from the county of Mecklenburg thirty four, from the county of Monongalia forty, from the county of Montgomery thirty, from the county of Nansemond twenty five, from the county of New Kent sixteen, from the county of Norfolk thirty five, from the county of Northampton seventeen, from the county of Northumberland twenty nine, from the county of Orange twenty three, from the county of Pittsylvania thirty six, from the county of Powhatan thirteen, from the county of Prince Edward twenty two, from the county of Prince George twenty, from the county of Princess Anne twenty three, from the county of Prince William thirty two, from the county of Richmond twenty two, from the county of Southampton forty, from the county of Spotsylvania eighteen, from the county of Stafford twenty, from the county of Surry fourteen, from the county of Sussex twenty eight, from the county of Warwick four, from the county of Washington thirty three, from the county of Westmoreland twenty six, from the county of Yohogania forty, from the county of York nine, from the city of Williamsburg eight, and from the counties of Kentucky and Ohio such a number as is equal to one twenty fifth part of their militia. And where any county shall have been divided, during the present session of assembly, the number herein before required from the whole, as it stood undivided, shall be furnished by the counties into which it shall have been divided, in proportion to the numbers of their respective militia; and where two or more counties shall have been formed into a greater number, the numbers herein before required from the said counties, as they stood before such alteration, shall be added together, and each of the counties into which they shall have been formed shall furnish a part of the whole number of men, in proportion to the militia it shall contain, for adjusting which proportions the field officers of the said counties so divided or reformed shall meet together, at such time and place as shall be appointed by the commanding officer of the oldest of the said counties respectively, and each man so draughted shall be entitled to a bounty of fifteen dollars, to be paid by this commonwealth, and be compelled to serve one year, or find an able bodied man to serve in his room in one of the said Virginia regiments on continental establishment. And as well such draughts, as those who enlist under this act, shall after such service be exempted from all other draughts for the regular service, for so long a time after their discharge as they shall have actually served.

And it is farther enacted, That where any county or corporation shall not, either by enlistment or draught, have raised their quota of men for completing the six additional battalions, according to the directions of the act of the former session of assembly, such county or corporation shall respectively proceed to enlist or draught for such deficiency, according to the said act, whether such deficiency arose from the number not having been recruited or draughted at first, or from their having been since discharge as irregularly drawn out, or being unfit for service, at the time of the draught, over and above the number hereby required of such county or corporation.

And to the end that the draughts to be made under this act may be fairly and equally made, *It is farther enacted,* That the county lieutenant or commanding officer of the militia in each county or corporation shall, on or before the second Monday of February next, summon the field officers, captains, and first lieutenants of his militia, to meet at the courthouse, and with them, or such as shall appear, collect from the muster rolls the names of all the officers and men of their militia who have not a wife or child, or who are not exempted by this act, or from militia duty by having a substitute in the army, adding thereto the names of any other such single men as are in the county and not enrolled, and who by the militia law ought to be enrolled, and shall direct all such single men to be summoned to meet at such place and time as the said officers shall appoint, not exceeding ten days thereafter, then and there to determine, by fair and equal lot, which of them shall enter into the service; and at the time and place so appointed, the said field officers and captains, together with two of the four senior magistrates who are not field officers in such county or corporation, having taken an oath to do impartial justice therein, which either of the said justices may administer to the others, shall carefully review the said single men, and examine into their bodily abilities and state of health, and set aside such as shall appear to them to be unfit for service, and shall proceed to draw the lots between the others as followeth, that is to say: They shall cause to be written the word "service" on so many distinct pieces of paper as will amount to the number of men hereby required to be raised in such county or corporation, and shall put the same into a covered hat or vessel; they shall cause also to be written the word "clear" on so many other pieces of paper, of the same form and dimensions, as, with the former, will amount to the number of single men, out of which the draughts are to be made as aforesaid, and put the same into the hat or vessel aforesaid, shaking the same well together, and shall then call the said single men one at a time, as they stand upon the roll, to draw a paper fairly out of the said hat or vessel, the same remaining covered, and being frequently shaken, every [one] of which papers so drawn shall be read aloud, and truly entered on the roll against the name of the person drawing, whether it be "service" or "clear," until the whole papers be drawn out. And if any person liable to the said lot shall fail to appear, or being present shall refuse to draw for himself the said justices, field officers, and captains, shall cause one of the bye-standers to draw for the person so failing or refusing, who shall be bound thereby; and the several persons by or for whom a paper with the word "service" shall be so drawn, shall from thenceforth be deemed soldiers, and compelled to serve or find an able-bodied man to serve in his room as aforesaid. And a list of their names shall be by the commanding officer of such militia transmitted to the governour, or to the commanding officer of the continental troops in this commonwealth, without delay, to whose order they shall be delivered by the said commanding officer of the militia at the courthouse of his county. And in order that the said commanding officer of the militia may be enabled to have the men forthcoming when called for, it shall be lawful for him to restrain them by furlough to such limits as he shall think reasonable; and if any of them shall depart from such limits, or shall fail to appear at any rendezvous by him appointed, they shall be deemed deserters, and treated accordingly.

But as an encouragement to persons to enter voluntarily into the said service, and thereby avoid the necessity of making such draughts, as far as may be done, *It is farther enacted,* That any justice of peace or magistrate, or a commissioned officer of the militia in any county or corporation, as well as such recruiting officers as may be appointed by the governour or the continental commanding officer in this commonwealth, shall have power to enlist any able-bodied men willing to enter into the service, except apprentices and hired servants under written contracts at any iron works, or persons solely employed in the manufacture of fire arms, not having leave in writing from the owner or manager of such works, except also imported servants, and those who are by law obliged to serve to thirty one years of age, and to offer a bounty of ten dollars each from this commonwealth, over and above the continental bounty; to all such as will engage to serve in the said regiments for three years, or during the present war, and to offer a bounty of twenty dollars in the whole to such as will engage to serve therein for one year only; and so many men as can be thereby enlisted into the said regiments, before the time of drawing the lots as aforesaid, in any county, or corporation, shall be deducted from the number of men to be draughted in such county or corporation wherein they shall be listed. And if any single man subject to the draught aforesaid shall procure an able-bodied man so to enlist, such single man shall be thereby exempted from the draught.

It is farther enacted, That if any of the men who shall be draughted into the service shall, after joining the army, enlist to serve therein for three years, or during the present war, every person so enlisting shall be entitled to a bounty of ten dollars, over and above the continental bounty of lands and money; and that the several men to be recruited or draughted pursuant to this act shall have the same pay, rations, and clothing, and be subject to the like rules and regulations, with the other soldiers of the Virginia regiments in the continental army, and shall have the option of entering into such of the companies in the said regiments as they shall choose, in which there shall be room for their admission.

In order to supply the officers and soldiers in the said Virginia regiments with the necessaries of life at moderate prices, and prevent the ruinous exactions they have hitherto been subject to, *It is farther enacted,* That it shall and may be lawful for the governour, with the advice of the council, to appoint an agent, or agents, to import or purchase such necessaries upon the best terms for which they can be had, and cause them to be transported to the encampment of the said regiments, there to be retailed to the officers and soldiers at such prices, to be settled by the governour and council, as articles of the same sort and quality are furnished to other continental troops, either by the continent or their respective states. Or the governour, with the advice of the council, may contract with any person or persons for the delivery of any such necessaries at the camp, at a certain price or prices agreed on, as they shall think most beneficial to the said officers and soldiers. And the governour may from time to time draw on the treasurer of this commonwealth for so much money as shall be necessary for the purposes of this act, taking bond and sufficient security from the agents or contractors, for the faithful performance of their trust, and for their accounting for the money so received, and repaying the same into the treasury, as they shall receive it of the officers and soldiers, by sale of the goods; and the treasurer is hereby required to pay such draughts, out of the publick money in his hands.

And it is farther enacted, That every county or corporation shall be entitled to a deduction from the number of their draughts of one man for every able-bodied deserter from the continental army, enlisted within this commonwealth, who shall be apprehended by any of the inhabitants of such county or corporation, and who shall have one year at least to serve in the said army at the time of his apprehension; and every single man draughted, or subject to the draught, who shall apprehend such deserter and deliver him to the county lieutenant or commanding officer of the militia of his county or corporation, shall be thereby discharged from service, or exempted from the draught; and where more than one of such single men are engaged in such apprehension, they shall settle the matter between themselves by lot or otherwise, so as to entitle one of them to such discharge or exemption, provided the apprehending a deserter the second time shall not be the cause of another exemption. And if any person (except in the case of husband and wife, or of a child concealing a parent, or a widow her son) shall wilfully harbour or conceal any deserter from the army of the United States, or any of them, and be thereof convicted, the offender, if a man capable of military duty, shall be obliged to serve in one of the Virginia regiments on continental establishment during such deserter's time of service, and be entitled to the pay, rations, and clothing, and be subject to the same rules and regulations, as the other troops in the said regiments; and if the offender be a woman, or man incapable of military service, he or she shall pay a fine of fifty pounds, to be recovered by action of debt or information in any court of record, with costs, one moiety thereof to the use of this commonwealth, and the other to the informer, or, in default thereof, suffer three months close imprisonment. All deserters heretofore or hereafter enlisted and draughted in this commonwealth, and not otherwise punished by martial law, shall be compelled to serve double the time of their absence from duty.

And it is farther enacted, That the several county courts be empowered and required to make a reasonable provision at the publick expense for the immediate support of the widows within their respective counties whose husbands shall have died or been slain in the service of the commonwealth, or the United States, if such widows shall have received no support from the general assembly, and for payment thereof may draw orders on the treasurer for the time being, distinguishing therein whether the soldier was in the continental or commonwealth service; and the said treasurer is hereby required to pay the same, out of the publick money in his hands.

And be it enacted, That quakers and menonists who shall be draughted shall be discharged from personal service, and that the field officers and justices who attend the draught shall, and they are hereby empowered, to employ any two or more discreet persons to procure, upon the best terms they can, proper substitutes to serve in their stead, and to adjust and divide the charge thereof among all the members of their respective societies of quakers and menonists in the county, in proportion to the number of tithables in the family of or belonging to each member, and to authorise the sheriff of the county, by warrant under their hands, to levy such charge by distress, in case of any member refusing or neglecting to make payment thereof within ten days after the same shall have been demanded, upon the goods and chattels of the member so refusing or neglecting; and the said commanding officer shall transmit to the governour a list of the names of the substitutes so procured, and a duplicate to the commanding officer of the continental troops in this commonwealth, as aforesaid. Every field officer or magistrate failing to perform any duty herein before imposed on him shall forfeit the sum of one hundred pounds, and every captain or lieutenant for such failure shall forfeit the sum of twenty five pounds, recoverable in any court of record by any person who will sue for the same, as well for himself as for the commonwealth, one moiety thereof to the person so suing, and the other to the commonwealth.

And whereas it is of the greatest importance to the American cause to open the ensuing campaign as early as possible, and to render its operations more decisive and effectual, that the army under the command of his excellency general Washington should be reinforced by an additional number of troops to be raised for that purpose in this commonwealth: *Be it farther enacted,* That every man who shall voluntarily engage to enter into such service, to continue therein for the space of six months from the time of his arrival at the place appointed for the general rendezvous, unless sooner discharged, shall receive a bounty of ten dollars, to be paid in such manner as the governour, with the advice of the council, may direct, so soon as the company to which he belongs shall be complete; and the several officers and privates shall be entitled to the like pay and rations as are allowed to the continental troops. And that each volunteer so serving shall be exempted from any future

[369]

draughts for the regular service for the space of six months after his discharge, provided that no apprentices, or hired servants under written contracts at any iron works, not having leave in writing from the owner or manager of such works, nor any imported servants, shall be admitted as volunteers. The volunteers so engaging shall be formed into companies of sixty eight men each rank and file, under the command of a captain, two lieutenants, one ensign, and four serjeants, and allowed a drummer and fifer. Every eight companies shall compose a regiment, under the commmand of a colonel, lieutenant colonel, and major, and be allowed a chaplain, adjutant, quartermaster, surgeon, two surgeons mates, and a quartermaster serjeant, and the whole shall be under the command of two brigadiers general, if the number of volunteers who may enlist shall make it necessary to appoint them, and shall be subject to the same rules and regulations as are directed for the troops in the continental service. The general and field officers shall be appointed by the governour, having regard in the appointments of the field officers to the situation of the country, making them as diffusive as may be; the chaplain, adjutant, quartermaster, and surgeon, by the commissioned officers of the regiment; and each surgeon and quartermaster shall choose his own mates and serjeant respectively.

And for the greater expedition in raising and collecting the said volunteers, *It is farther enacted,* That the county lieutenant or commanding officer of the militia in each county or corporation shall immediately appoint a general muster or meeting of the several battalions of the militia upon receiving notice of this act, and in the warmest terms represent to them the utility and necessity of strongly reinforcing the continental army, and receive the subscriptions of such as shall be willing to engage in this service in the following terms, to wit: "We do severally enlist to serve in the corps of volunteers now raising to reinforce the continental army, at present under the command of his excellency general Washington, for the time and upon the terms directed by an act of assembly intituled An act for speedily recruiting the Virginia regiments on the continental establishment, and for raising additional troops of volunteers."

Provided, That no person so engaging shall be thereby exempted from the draught to be made for completing the Virginia regiments on continental establishment. And such commanding officer, as well as each other militia officer, or any justice of peace in the county, or corporation, shall continue to receive such engagements at any time afterwards, until the volunteers shall march from such county or corporation; and the names of all persons so engaging shall be by the commanding officer of the county collected, and transmitted monthly to the governour. As soon as a sufficient number of men shall be engaged in any county or corporation to make a company, they shall be called together by the commanding officer of such county or corporation, and shall proceed to the choice of their captain, lieutenants, and ensign, by a majority of votes to be taken by ballot; and when a number sufficient to form a company shall not be enlisted in any county or corporation before the last day of March next, or part of a company shall remain after one or more are completed, in either case they shall be united to the parts of companies in some other county, so as to make up complete companies, who shall then proceed to the choice of their officers as aforesaid, observing to choose a commissioned officer from each part of a company, in rank, according to the[ir] numbers. The several officers so chosen shall be commissioned by the governour, and rank according to their priority of election; and where any elections shall happen on the same day, the priority of rank shall be settled by a general officer, by fair and equal lot between the officers. The governour, with the advice of the council, is desired and empowered to form the several companies into regiments, and appoint the place or places of general rendezvous, and from time to time, as the regiments are completed, to call into duty the field officers for each regiment, from which time their pay, as well as that of the captains, subalterns, and other officers of each regiment, and the privates, shall respectively commence. The general officers shall be entitled to pay from the times they are respectively called into duty, after a sufficient number of regiments shall have been formed to require their superintendence by the governour and council, who have also power to direct at what time the said regiments, or any of them, shall march to join the continental army.

And whereas there are within this commonwealth some religious societies, particularly Baptists and Methodists, the members of which may be averse to serving in the same companies or regiments with others, and under officers of different principles, though they would willingly engage in the defence of their country under the command of officers of their own religion: *Be it enacted,* That the governour, with the advice of the privy council, may, and he is hereby empowered, to appoint proper persons of either of the said religious societies to enlist any members of the same who will engage to enter as volunteers in the manner and upon the terms aforesaid, and such volunteers shall be formed into separate companies, and may choose their own captains, lieutenants, and ensigns; and when a sufficient number of companies shall be raised to form a regiment, the governour, with the advice of the privy council, may appoint proper field officers out of their own societies to such regiment or regiments, who shall be allowed a chaplain, adjutant, quartermaster, surgeon, two surgeons mates, and a quartermaster serjeant, to be appointed in the same manner as herein before directed for the other regiments of volunteers, and as well the officers as privates of such regiments shall be entitled to the same bounty, pay, and rations, and subject to the same rules and regulations, with the other volunteers raised for the same service.

Provided always, That the number of volunteers to be raised pursuant to this act, for six months service, shall not in the whole exceed ten regiments. The governour, with the advice of the council, is hereby authorised to use the most expeditious and effectual means for furnishing the said volunteers with proper tents, arms, and accoutrements, and moreover, to appoint one or more paymasters, commissaries, or contractors, for the more regularly and punctually paying and providing necessaries for the said troops.

Printed from Hening, IX, 337–349.
No problems facing the General Assembly in 1777 demanded more time than those relating to recruiting and keeping an army in the field. GM appears to have seen the crisis as of a dual nature, partly related to the depreciating public credit and in part caused by a faulty and unfair system of raising troops. By 26 Oct. GM had both problems divided into separate categories and was prepared for action. Washington was informed that he had "a remedy against the Depreciation of our Money" and "has likewise a Plan for recruiting an Army, which I think a very good One . . ." (letter from J. P. Custis, 26 Oct. 1777, George Bolling Lee Papers [ViHi]). Upon reaching Williamsburg (some 40 days tardy), GM was soon deep in committee assignments, including a place on one ordered to prepare a bill covering desertions, bounties for enlistments, and a conscript system (JHD, 1827 ed., 4 Dec. entry). The House was more inclined to debate the pending measure to stabilize the state's economy. Meanwhile, nine regiments were still the Virginia troop quota for Washington's army, and their enlistment terms started to expire in Jan. 1778. Washington, no stranger to the feelings of his troops as they paused en route to Valley Forge, told Gov. Henry that he doubted that the Virginians would re-enlist regardless of bounty enticements. The general's counter-suggestion was a Christmas furlough that might extend until Mar., when the spring campaign could begin (letter to Henry, 13 Nov. 1777, Fitzpatrick, ed., *Writings of Washington*, X, 56). Nothing seems to have come of this idea, however, so that the burden on the General Assembly was to devise a method of almost total replacement for the veteran troops before the deadline for their discharge—10 Apr. 1778 (Hening, IX, 81). Indeed, 10 Apr. was the final date for mustering the Virginians out, and those who had enlisted early in 1776 would be clamoring for their discharge as this bill was being written. To meet the emergency this act reduced the size of regiments, relied upon the success of a re-enlistment program, and considered as a last resort the conscription of unmarried militiamen. In short, it was a confession of failure for the 1776 act which had

promised a bounty of twenty dollars and at least one hundred acres of land. While debate on the measure continued, Edmund Pendleton reported the delegates' hopes that more bounties, and stricter enforcement of the laws against desertion would cut down draft quotas. "What recruits are necessary to fill up the Regiments and can't be raised by these methods . . . [will] be made up by drafts from the Militia, but in what manner we have much Variety of Opinion, some say the draft must be from the whole indiscriminately—others by a fair Lot between the Single men and a third Opinion is to take them of Vagabonds. . . . My Sentiments are in favor of the middle way . . ." (letter to William Woodford, 29 Nov. 1777, Mays, ed., *Papers of Edmund Pendleton*, I, 238–239). This compromise on the community's bachelors won out, although its reception went down hard with Virginians and ranged from a Loudoun County riot in Feb. 1778 to unfounded rumors of resistance elsewhere. In Caroline County, Pendleton noted that the "law was generally execrated" but "when the time came, nothing like Opposition appeared" (letter to William Woodford, 15 Feb. 1778, *ibid.*, 250). COLONEL GEORGE GIBSON had reported to Washington before 7 Oct. with a small force "consisting of 226 Effectives," and this understrength regiment was assigned "to supply the place of the 9th Regiment in Muhlenberg's brigade, and do duty there 'till further orders" (General Order, 7 Oct. 1777, Fitzpatrick, ed., *Writings of Washington*, IX, 329). The NINTH VIRGINIA REGIMENT was badly mauled at Germantown, with its field grade and company officers heading a list of casualties (24 Oct. 1777, *Va. Gaz.* [Dixon & Hunter]; Boyd, III, 388–390). Gibson's battalion seems to have been formed as a home guard, then pressed into service in Pennsylvania when Washington appealed for assistance after the Battle of Brandywine. The Continental requisition of 8,160 Virginians was equal to fifteen regiments as conceived by the 1775 Convention (Hening, IX, 9). In actual practice, the various regiments appear to have been far below strength, and only slightly more than 2,000 enlisted men would have been drafted by the provisions of this act. The allowance for apprehension of EVERY ABLE-BODIED DESERTER was an effort to end rampant disaffection. On the eve of the Battle of Germantown there were five advertisements in the 3 Oct. 1777 *Va. Gaz.* (Purdie) seeking aid in rounding up deserters, including sixteen who had disappeared from Fairfax County. Yet the GENERAL MUSTER of the county militia was expected to bring in enough six-month volunteers to complete the state quota. "We are about to send out 5000 Volunteers immediately to reinforce General Washington and assist him in Any Operation the Ice may suggest during the Winter [campaign]" was Edmund Pendleton's hopeful report (letter to William Woodford, 29 Nov. 1777, Mays, ed., *Papers of Edmund Pendleton*, I, 238). Apparently other delegates shared Pendleton's optimism, and this provision as well as the one authorizing the appointment of an agent who would act as a sutler for the Virginia troops were among the former Speaker's pet schemes (*ibid.*). More guarded in his outlook was Richard Henry Lee, who noted passage of this act with its call for five thousand volunteers, "but I am not able to say that many men will be produced by this plan" (letter to Samuel Adams, 1 Mar. 1778, Ballagh, *Lee Letters*, I, 390). Still, to Lee and other Virginians, part of the point was to set an example for the rest of the states. At least 2,500 troops would be raised, Lee added, and he was sure "the virtue and vigor of our eastern brethren will fully equal Virginia on this all important occassion." Despite these cheering words, it was clear to Washington that passing bills was one thing, and raising regiments was another. By late May the act had produced 716 drafted men or their substitutes, while 42 had deserted en route to his camp and another forty-one "had been left on the road" (Fitzpatrick, ed., *Writings of Washington*, XI, 438n). From Valley Forge, Washington wrote Lee "That something has been wrong in conducting the draughts . . . for, out of the 1500 ordered last fall, and the two thousand this spring, we have received only 1242 which is so horrible a deficiency, that I have made a representation thereof to the State" (letter to Lee, 25 May 1778, *ibid.*, 452).

GM's plan for "recruiting an Army," which John Parke Custis must have seen before 26 Oct. 1777 (the date of his letter to Washington in George Bolling Lee Papers [ViHi]), has not been found. It is clear that the main outlines of the bill had been shaped by 29 Nov., but the reported measure was changed by a number of last-minute alterations on the day GM took to it to the Senate (JHD, 1827 ed., 6 Jan. 1778 entry). On 9 Jan. the bill was returned with more suggestions, and after more debate GM then was ordered to carry it back to the Senate with the message that the House "doth recede from their disagreement."

V. An Act "for authorising the seizure of Salt, in the same manner as provisions for the use of the army"

[14 January 1778]

Be it enacted by the General Assembly, That from and after the passing of this act the agents, commissaries, or contractors, acting under appointment of the United States or this commonwealth, shall, and they are hereby authorised and required to seize for the use of the army any salt which they may discover in the possession of any person or persons within this commonwealth imported or purchased for sale, proceeding therein in the same manner as is directed in the case of seizing provisions by an act of assembly passed this session, intituled "An act for enabling the publick contractors to procure stores of provisions necessary for the ensuing campaign, and to prohibit the exportation of beef, pork, and bacon, for a limited time;" save only, that instead of the appraisement by the said act directed the person or persons from whom any salt shall be taken by virtue of this act shall be entitled to five pounds per bushel, together with the charge of carriage from the place of importation, for the same.

This act shall continue and be in force for the space of one month, unless the governour and council shall by proclamation declare that the publick wants are sufficiently provided for, and no longer.

Printed from Hening, IX, 381.

Salt was a necessity of life in a society that lacked refrigeration and so preserved its meat by curing or packing in salt. The naval blockade cut off the supply so that the price advanced rapidly after the summer of 1776. The Alexandria merchants, accustomed to paying 18 cents a bushel in 1774, had mentioned the shortage of salt as a cause for much public distress. "They are willing to pay almost any price," the letter addressed to GM and Philip Alexander continued, "if it could be purchased with money." Yet advertisements in the *Va. Gaz.* (both Dixon & Hunter and Purdie issues) for the late fall and early winter of 1777–1778 indicate salt was available at Williamsburg and Richmond. It is possible that some flagrant conduct by men bent on gouging out enormous profits speeded action on this bill, for it was assigned to a committee with GM as chairman, and was written, passed through three readings, and engrossed—all on 14 Jan. The circumstances indicate an emergency was involved, and that GM wrote the bill although his draft of the measure has not been found (JHD, 1827 ed., 14 Jan. entry). Within a week's time, Gov. Henry implemented the act by ordering "Colonel Simpson to seize two thousand Bushels Salt on the Eastern Shore & send it to . . . the grand Army & to reserve a thousand more to answer further Orders that may become necessary" (letter to Virginia delegates in Congress, 20 Jan. 1778, Hutchinson-Rachal, I, 219).

An Act for Raising a Supply of Money for Publick Exigencies

[26 October 1777–22 January 1778]

I. Mason's Resolutions on Specific Taxes and Unappropriated Lands [13 December]

II. The Act for Raising a Supply of Money [19–22 January 1778]

EDITORIAL NOTE

No military challenge to the struggling United States was more critical than the civilian problems related to changing the former royal colonies into viable, self-supporting, republican communities. Those festering grievances in the colonies after 1763—the specie drainage, western land speculation, corrupt or enfeebled taxing programs, and the suppression of local industry—had not disappeared with the revolution, and indeed a few had become more acute. After more than a year of experience as independent powers, the states learned that the whole structure of revolution would topple unless its financial underpinnings were secured. Britons who had insisted that the Americans were not in favor of any taxation, with or without representation, seemed to have made their point as printing presses provided a temporary solution to a long-range problem. The resulting flood of currency brought on hoarding, led to the disappearance of hard cash, and undermined the confidence of all who bought or sold goods for a living. The plaintive plea from Mason's constituents in Fairfax County (in all probability, the Alexandria merchants were behind it) on 20 August 1777 was doubtless an echo of similar outcries in most seaports and towns where prices were skyrocketing while supplies dwindled. And the whole melancholy scene was played against a backdrop of depreciating currency. "Congress stuffed the maw of the Revolution with paper money" (E. James Ferguson, *The Power of the Purse* [Chapel Hill, 1961], 29).

Mason's acumen as a businessman made him sympathetic with the merchant, while his own plantation holdings gave him needed perspective on public reaction to a stiff tax bill. As a man of means, a creditor, and a believer in reliable contracts, Mason saw in the financial distress a basic weakness that might turn the Revolution into a mockery of freedom. The autumn of 1777 was a critical time, as Thomas Paine's *Crisis Papers* suggested, and the sunshine patriots ran for cover or stayed out-of-doors to bewail the ineptness of men suddenly forced to think and plan in terms of thousands of troops and millions of dollars.

The problem was staggering, but to Mason and his colleagues it was also unavoidable. The commitment to revolution had been made, and so it had to be carried off, otherwise the trinity of "life, liberty, and property" would not be safe. "If our funds fail us not, and our Union continues, no cause was ever safer than ours," Richard Henry Lee wrote at this juncture. "To prevent the former, most extensive and vigorous taxes should immediately take place. The sum in circulation is immense and no corrective can be applied but Taxation, nor was there ever a time when the vast plenty of money rendered that business more easy" (letter to Jefferson, 25 August 1777, Boyd, II, 30). Lee probably dropped the same hint to Mason, and certainly the two men who seemed in harmony on most matters were exchanging ideas often. When Lee, Jefferson, and Mason were agreed upon a given issue, something was bound to happen.

As Washington's army withdrew toward Valley Forge, Mason bestirred himself to the task of pulling Virginia back from the brink of fiscal disaster. Washington kept his ragged army from confronting the enemy, but it was not so certain that the civilian authorities were as gifted in their ability to avoid a financial disaster. Washington's stepson wrote that Mason was "preparing a remedy against the Depreciation of our Money, which I think will do him great Credit." John Parke Custis reported that Mason's plan proposed a withdrawal of £500,000 in depreciating paper money through "a general Assessment [tax] on all Property," and predicted the plan would succeed because Mason's "Valuation of Property is very low, which will render his Plan very agreeable to the People" (letter to Washington, 26 October 1777, George Bolling Lee Papers [ViHi]). The day came when Washington would complain that it took a wagon-load of money to buy a wagon-load of hay. From first-hand experience he knew the evils of depreciated currency. To remedy the problem, Washington wrote, "I know of no person better qualified . . . than Colonel Mason, and shall be very happy to hear that he has taken it in hand. Long have I been persuaded of the indispensable necessity of a tax for the purpose of sinking the paper money, and why it has been delayed better politicians than I must account for" (letter to Custis, 14 November 1777, Fitzpatrick, *Writings of Washington*, X, 60).

In his preparation of a general assessment tax, Mason was on familiar ground, for that system had operated in Virginia for generations under the guise of a levy on tithables. "This term, with us, includes the free males above 16 years of age, and slaves above that age of both sexes" (Jefferson, *Notes on Virginia*, ed., Peden, 82). In colonial Virginia annual levies on tithables had the effect of a general property tax, and the money raised paid the local Anglican minister, supported the poor, and met other parish expenses. Poll taxes, collected in money or tobacco, were used to erect public buildings, repair roads, and build bridges. (See Robert Beverly, *The History and Present State of Vir-*

ginia, ed. Louis B. Wright [Chapel Hill, 1947], 252–254). Set fees on licenses or land patents, and the duty on every hogshead of tobacco, had paid for the functions and functionaries of government, while some of the hardest working officers (such as Justices of the Peace) served for honor but no profit. Moreover, this antiquated system had worked well when the demands placed upon it were light, but a war that required thousands of men under arms and millions of pounds spent in equipping and sustaining them could not be supported in this old-fashioned way. If the people gained their freedom from foreign domination, it was going to cost them something in "blood and treasure."

By the time Mason reached Williamsburg, the general outlines of the remedy he was to propose apparently were known. Edmund Pendleton, still painfully crippled from his riding accident, was also missing when the clerk first called the House roll, but he reported gossip that the delegates were for "changing our mode of taxation into that of a General Assessment" (letter to Richard Henry Lee, 2 November 1777, Mays, ed., *Papers of Edmund Pendleton*, I, 233). By mid-November full debate on the state's financial woes was under way. Other pressing business had to be attended to, however, and the shaping of a tax bill continued while measures were passed to collect clothing for Virginians in the Continental army. By late November the General Assembly reacted to Washington's pleas by appointing a committee to send supplies to Pennsylvania without waste of time, and also enacted a law to punish "engrossing and forestalling"—the euphemism of that day for war-profiteering (JHD, 1827 ed., 25, 26 November entries).

There was a point to all this activity beyond the immediate needs of a starving and threadbare army. Virginia, the most populous and largest state, was also the bellwether commonwealth for the nascent republic. There was more than flattery in the New Englander's remark that "we all look up to Virginia for examples" (Adams, ed., *Works of John Adams*, IX, 387), for this was a time of unparalleled political experimentation. A pragmatic approach met day-to-day problems with solutions born of experience. Some were crude, and nearly all were expedient. The crucial point in November–December of 1777 was: would the paper solution work in practice? "If the late Generous Spirit of Virginia in their Act for Cloathing and Measures for preventing of Forestalling does not Inspire the other States with a Virtuous Emulation the Avarice of Individuals will be more Fatal to the Liberties of America than the sword of the Enemy," a dismayed Virginian in the Continental Congress suggested (John Harvie to Jefferson, 29 December 1777, Boyd, II, 125). Hopefully, exemplary patriotism in Virginia would have its affect in other states that were under seige from "this Monster in Society"—human greed.

The journal entries from the House of Delegates reveal none of the drama enacted each day as the legislators wrestled with a variety of demands that ranged from a widow's petition to the spectre of inflationary chaos. The time involved in discussing the monetary crisis, from 12 November until 20 January, indicates that the House was preoccupied with efforts to find a workable solution. "We have not yet got through the Supply bill, which being on a new plan of assessment," Pendleton wrote, "hath occasioned much Altercation and long debate" (letter to William Woodford, 16 January 1778, Mays, ed., *Papers of Edmund Pendleton*, I, 246). In its final form, the bill gave evidence that as a stopgap measure it still incorporated general reforms. The House's legal revisors' committee program, as Jefferson recalled, had as one aim the enactment of a general assessment bill so that "all public expenses . . . [would be paid] by assessments on the citizens, in proportion to their property" (*Notes on Virginia*, ed., Peden, 137). Thus the emerging act for raising a supply of money was in part a step toward an overhaul of the commonwealth's taxation, and the bill extended the concept of property to include income as well as real estate and chattels. The result was a more sophisticated tax base that would place the heaviest burden on the wealthy, with the beginnings of a modern tax on salaries and profits from business dealings. Clearly, Mason and his colleagues wished to place part of the public burden upon men of commerce who had few or no land holdings, but who had substantial inventories and incomes. The resulting tax on incomes was fixed at the same rate as that on land, slaves, and personal property—one-half of one percent of the evaluation. This seems modest in the twentieth century, but at the time it was to cause problems because of varying evaluations by assessors (Boyd, II, 186). A few years later, Jefferson surveyed the Virginia taxes and noted that the one-percent assessment, "compared with any thing we ever yet paid, would be deemed a very heavy tax" (*ibid.*, 172). The dominant theme in Mason's tax plan was to shift the burden from freeholders to a land office that would sell western lands. Mason considered the public lands beyond the Alleghenies as the best source for long-range public income, and his bill for establishing a land office (8 January 1778), which became a controversial one, was meant as a vehicle for paying off the rising public debt.

Confronted with an unreported legislative debate on a problem of such magnitude, it becomes impossible to discern with any precision the role Mason played in writing and managing the supply bill. The Custis letter to Washington, Mason's own resolutions, his membership on the drafting committee, and his long experience as a county justice and vestryman forced to deal with local levies combine to make a substantial case for the assertion that Mason was probably the chief architect of the revolutionary tax bill of 1778. However, substantial portions must have come from debate during sessions of the committee of the whole, and Nelson's power as chairman during that time must not be overlooked (see Elmer Isaiah Miller, *the Legislature of the Province of Virginia* . . . [New York, 1907], 108, for a description of how the committee of the whole operated).

I. Resolutions on Specific Taxes and Unappropriated Lands

[13 Dec. 1777]

Resolved that it is the Opinion of this Committee that a Duty of   Shillings per Hogshead be imposed upon all Tobacco exported by Land or Water, except such as shall be exported on the Proper Account of this Common-wealth, or of the united American States, or any of them.

Resolved that it is the Opinion of this Committee that part of the unappropriated Lands be disposed of, and the Money arising therefrom applied in Aid of the Funds to be provided for discharging the public Debt; and that a Land-Office be established for granting waste and unappropriated Lands.

Resolved that it is the Opinion of this Committee that a Tax be imposed upon all Horses within this Common-wealth, (except such as belong to the ⟨United States of America⟩ the Common-wealth, or to any College or School) after the rate of ten Shillings for every hundred pounds of the Value of the same.

Ms (Vi). Three separate pieces of paper, all in GM's hand, each with a later notation within brackets: "Dec 13, 1777."

From the 26 Oct. 1777 letter from John Parke Custis to Washington (George Bolling Lee Papers [ViHi]) it is apparent that GM had discussed his ideas for a general assessment bill with others before he left for Williamsburg. Debate on the problems of taxation and currency stabilization began prior to GM's arrival in the House on 14 Nov., but these fragments may have been taken from an earlier draft and brought forward on 13 Dec. 1777, when the committee chairman, Thomas Nelson, made his report on the bill "for raising a supply of money for publick exigencies." The House, acting as a Committee of the Whole, accepted these resolutions and fixed the tax on tobacco at 10 shillings per hogshead (where GM had left the blank space). The House fixed the tax rates to range from three pounds on tavern licenses to five shillings on dogs and every tithable person, but later rescinded the dog tax (JHD, 1827 ed., 13 Dec. entry). For GM, the most important resolution was that concerning the sinking fund to be created from the sale of unappropriated lands. His measure for disposing of the so-called "waste and unappropriated lands" was headed for passage when a motion to postpone it passed (JHD, 1827 ed., 8 Jan. 1778 entry). The entire bill "for raising a supply of money" was passed on 22 Jan. and carried to the Senate by William Fleming.

Portions of the third resolution within angle brackets were added by a clerk.

II. An Act "for raising a supply of money for publick exigencies."

[19–22 January 1778]

I. WHEREAS, the United American States in general, as well as this commonwealth in particular, in the persecution of the present just and necessary war to the defence of our lives, liberties, and property, have been compelled to issue bills of credit for large sums of money, the quantity whereof now in circulation, greatly exceeding the medium of commerce, may occasion a depreciation of its value, to the injury of individuals, and great danger of this and the other

United States, which nothing will so effectually prevent as reducing the quantity, by establishing ample funds for redeeming proportions of it annually, until the whole shall be hereby called in and sunk. It is also necessary that permanent funds should be established to provide for the repayment of the money borrowed or to be borrowed by the United States, as well as by this commonwealth, for carrying on the war, and the interest growing due upon such loans. For making such provision for the just proportion which this commonwealth ought to bear of sinking the said bills of credit of the United States, and of the money borrowed by them, and the interest thereof, as well as to effect the redemption of its own particular bills of credit, and payment of the money borrowed, and interest, in a mode which it is judged will be least burthensome to the people of any which can be adopted, *Be it enacted by the General Assembly,* That a tax or rate of ten shillings for every hundred pounds value, to be ascertained in manner herein after mentioned, shall be paid for all manors, messuages, lands, and tenements, slaves, mulatto servants to thirty one years of age, horses, mules, and plate, on the first day of August one thousand seven hundred and seventy eight; and the like tax or rate shall be paid on the said first day of August in each of the six next succeeding years, by the owner or proprietor of such estates respectively. That the like rate of ten shillings for every hundred pounds shall be paid for all money exceeding five pounds in the possession of one person, by the possessor thereof, on the said first day of August, in each of the said seven years. That a rate of two shillings for every pound be paid for the amount of the annual interest received upon all debts bearing interest, also for the amount of all annuities, including the quitrents payable to the proprietor of the Northern Neck, except such as have been or shall be settled by the general congress, or the assembly or convention of this commonwealth, as a provision for wounded soldiers or their families, to be paid by the creditor or annuitant respectively on the said first day of August, in each of the said seven years. That a tax or duty of ten shillings a wheel upon all riding carriages, fourpence per head on all neat cattle, and five shillings per poll upon all tithables above the age of twenty one years (except soldiers, sailors, parish poor, and such as receive an annual allowance in consideration of wounds or injuries received in the publick service, except also slaves and mulatto servants to thirty one years of age, who, being property, are rated *ad valorem* as aforesaid) shall be paid by the owner or person enlisting such carriages and tithables respectively, on the said first day of August, in each of the said seven years. That a tax of three pounds for every ordinary license, and twenty shillings for every marriage license, shall be paid down to the clerk of the county or corporation court at the time of granting such license, from the time of passing this act until the first day of December one thousand seven hundred and eighty four. That a tax or rate of ten shillings for every hundred pounds of the amount of all salaries, and of the neat income of all offices of profit (those of the military and sea officers in the service of the United States of America, or either of them, in respect of their employments, only excepted) on the said first day of August one thousand seven hundred and seventy eight, and each of the six next succeeding years. That a tax or duty of ten shillings be paid for every hogshead of tobacco exported out of this commonwealth by land or water, by the exporter thereof, from the time of passing this act until the said first day of December one thousand seven hundred and eighty four. That a tax or duty of sixpence per gallon be paid for all spirituous liquors hereafter to be distilled in this common-wealth, to be paid by the distiller, or distilled in any other of the United American States, and imported into this by land or water, at any time before the said first day of December one thousand seven hundred and eighty four. And that every person who hath not taken the oath or affirmation of allegiance to this state required to be taken by an act of the last session of assembly, and shall not take the same before the first day of May next, and who shall fail to produce to the assessors in his hundred a certificate of his having taken such oath or affirmation, shall pay double of the several rates and taxes aforesaid for such property and tithables hereby subject to taxation as he shall be owner of, or shall be in his family.

II. *Provided always*, That nothing herein contained shall be con-strued so as to charge any lands, slaves, stocks, servants, plate, money, debts, or annuities, which shall belong to the United States of America or this commonwealth, or to any county, corporation, parish, town, college, school, or religious society, with any rate or duty hereby imposed, nor to subject to the duty aforesaid any goods, wares, or merchandises, taken from the enemy, brought into this commonwealth, and condemned as lawful prize in the court of admiralty, in the hands of the captors.

III. And for ascertaining the value of the several articles herein before taxed according to such value, *It is farther enacted*, That the freeholders and housekeepers of each county or corporation within this commonwealth shall meet at the courthouse of their respective county, city, or town, on the second Tuesday in March yearly, during the said term of six years, and they, or such of them as shall appear, shall then and there freely elect three able and discreet men of their county or corporation, being landholders having a right to vote for representatives in general assembly, and having visible property therein to the value of eight hundred pounds each, and who is not a member of any of the publick boards, an officer in the navy or army, naval officer, a manager of any publick works, an owner or manager of iron works or manufactory of fire arms, a master or professor in any college or school, a clergyman, sheriff, inspector, or ordinary keeper, to be commissioners of the tax for such county or corporation for the year. The sheriff of the county, and the returning officer of any city or borough, shall cause previous notice of such election to be published in each church and meetinghouse in his county or corporation, at least twenty days before each annual election; and such sheriff or returning officer, together with the two senior justices who shall be present at the election shall proceed to take the poll fairly and impartially, and shall be the final judges of the qualifications of the voters who offer to poll, as well as of the circumstances of the persons voted for, and shall have power to set aside such person who may be voted for as in their judgment hath not visible property to the amount of the sum hereby required, and on the close of the poll shall certify the names of the three persons who have the greatest number of votes, and are so qualified, to the court of their county or corporation, there to be recorded, determining the preference by their own votes, where the number of votes for any two or more persons are equal, and the persons so returned shall be the commissioners of the tax for that year. Each commissioner, before he enters upon the execution of the trust, shall take the following oath (or, being a Quaker or Menonist, shall solemnly affirm and declare to the same effect) before some justice of the peace, to wit: "I A.B. do swear, that as a commissioner of the tax for   county, I will to the best of my skill and judgment, execute the duties of the said office diligently and faithfully, and do equal right and justice to all men in every case wherein I shall act as a commissioner, according to the act of assembly under which I am appointed, to the best of my knowledge, without prejudice, favour, or partiality. So help me God." And shall thereupon meet from time to time, at such place or places as to them shall seem most convenient, and appoint a clerk, at ten shillings per day, to attend them for entering their proceedings, and shall without delay proceed to lay off the county, city, or borough, into so many districts or hundreds as to them shall seem most convenient for making the assessments, bounding the same by water courses, roads,

or other limits of publick notoriety, and having so done, shall choose
two discreet men in each hundred to be assessors or appraisers of
such estate lying therein as is hereby subjected to taxation, each of
whom shall be a landholder having a right to vote for representatives
in the general assembly, which choice shall be certified under the
hands of the commissioners, and delivered to the person first named
in each hundred within twenty days thereafter, together with tran-
scripts of such parts of this act as are necessary for the direction of
the assessors, and such instructions as to the form of their proceedings and return as the commissioners may think proper to give them
for complying with the true intention of this act; and the commissioners in such appointment shall also limit a time, not less than four
weeks, or more than six weeeks, for the assessors to perform their
duty in, and to make return of their proceedings to the commissioners, and shall cause a description of the several hundreds to be
entered on their book, with a list of the names of the persons
appointed assessors in each, and a copy of the instructions given
them as aforesaid. The several persons so named assessors in each
district shall, within five days after receiving notice of their appointment and instructions as aforesaid, go together to one of the said
commissioners, or to a justice of the peace, and there take the
following oath (or, being a Quaker or Menonist, shall affirm and
declare to the same effect) to wit: "I A. B. do swear, that I will well
and truly execute the duty of an assessor, and faithfully, justly, and
impartially assess the pound rate imposed by the act of assembly for
that purpose upon all property within my hundred liable thereto,
according to the best of my skill and judgment, and the directions of
the said act, and therein will spare none for favour or affection, nor
any person aggrieve for hatred, malice, or ill-will. So help me God."
A certificate of which oath shall be endorsed on the appointment of
each set of assessors, and returned therewith to the commissioners,
to be entered on their books. And after being so sworn, the said
assessors shall personally apply to every person within their district
or hundred and require them respectively to give an account upon
oath, which either of the assessors may administer, of all lands,
slaves, mulatto servants to thirty one years of age, horses, mules,
money, silver plate, and interest received which shall become due
after the passing of this act on debts bearing interest, all annuities
(except a publick provision for wounded soldiers and their families)
all riding carriages, neat cattle, and tithable persons above the age of
twenty one years, not being soldiers, sailors, or parish poor, or
persons receiving allowances for wounds received in publick service,

slaves, or servants to thirty one years of age, of which each such person is the owner, or who belong to or reside in his or her family, or which he or she is in possession of as guardian to any orphan, or as executor or administrator of the estate of any person deceased, and also an account of all spirituous liquors distilled or imported by land or by water by any such person from and after the passing of this act for the first year, and afterwards annually from the time of rendering their last preceding account thereof; and every such person shall farther make oath, that he or she hath not shifted or changed the possession of any of the said taxable articles, or used any fraud, covin, or device, in order to evade the assessment thereof. The assessors shall also require all persons in their hundred having publick salaries to render an account of the amount therof, and all persons holding offices of profit (except military and sea officers, in respect of their employments) and residing in their hundred, to render an account upon oath, to the best of their knowledge, of the neat annual income of such office, all and every species of which property so given in, or which the assessors shall by any other ways or means discover, they shall cause to be distinctly entered against the name of the owner or person chargeable with the tax thereon, and proceed to value the lands, slaves, horses, mules, and plate, so given in and discovered, as the same would in their judgment sell for in ready money, having regard to the local situation of lands and other circumstances, taken for such value the middle rate between them, in case the two assessors differ in opinion on the value of any article, extending the value against each species of property, and setting down in a distinct column the amount of the pound rate hereby imposed upon the whole of such property belonging to each person, as well as the taxes of another nature imposed hereby upon such person, and giving such person a memorandum in writing of such pound rate, to enable him or her to provide for payment thereof. And where a tract of land belonging to any person residing or having a plantation with slaves thereon shall lie in two or more hundreds, the same shall be valued by the assessors of that hundred wherein the proprietor lives or hath a plantation, and if the owner doth not reside, or there be no plantation thereon, then the lands shall be assessed in that hundred wherein the greatest quantity thereof shall lie, and in such case the assessors shall enter the county in which the proprietor lives, if they are informed thereof; and when the assessors shall have thus valued all the said taxable property in their hundred, they shall make a fair return of their proceedings to the commissioners, entering the names of the persons assessed in alphabetical order, with the species and value of their property, and the pound rate thereon as aforesaid, and shall therein enter their own names, with each distinct species of taxable property they severally own or possess as aforesaid, and upon such return the commissioners shall examine them severally upon oath, and thereupon extend the value of such property as to the commissioners shall seem just, and the pound rate thereon as aforesaid, and then shall cause all such returns to be entered in their books, to which all persons may have recourse at any seasonable times.

IV. *And it is farther enacted,* That where any person residing within this commonwealth shall receive interest for money from any person residing in any other of the United States, and there shall be a deduction made from the interest due in consequence of a tax imposed in the state where the debtor resides, in such case the creditor, upon producing to the assessors a certificate of such deduction, shall be allowed the amount thereof out of the pound rate hereby imposed on such interest; but no silver plate shall be valued at more than ten shillings per ounce, Troy weight. Which respective rates, or such as shall be hereafter established by the general assembly (as the value of money may rise or fall, or as the necessity of the times require) shall be observed by the several commissioners and assessors as the rule of their conduct in the respective valuations of such property.

V. And whereas great numbers of people have settled on waste and ungranted lands situate on the Western Waters, to which they have not been able to procure legal titles, and the general convention of Virginia, on the twenty fourth day of June one thousand seven hundred and seventy six, did "resolve, that all such settlers upon unappropriated lands, to which there was no prior just claim, should have the pre-emption or preference to grant of such lands," and it is just and reasonable that the lands in their possession thus secured to them should contribute by tax to the common charge, and a mode established for fixing the quantity of their claims, where the same hath not been ascertained, by regular survey, *It is therefore farther enacted,* That all persons who, on or before the said twenty fourth day of June one thousand seven hundred and seventy six, had bona fide settled themselves, or at his or her charge had settled others, upon any waste and ungranted lands on the said Western Waters, and had not by regular entry, survey, or contract, ascertained the quantity of their claim, shall be allowed for every family so settled four hundred acres of land, to include such settlement, or such lesser quantity as the person entitled thereto respectively shall, at the time of the first assessment, declare to the assessors he or she desires to hold; and the assessors of the hundred shall proceed to assess the pound rate upon the proprietor for such lands in manner herein before mentioned, entering in their return the name of every such person, and the quantity of land allotted for or chosen by him or her as aforesaid, and the assessment shall continue to be made from year to year, according to the quantity so fixed, during the term of six years, or until regular surveys shall be made, and grants obtained for the same. But where any such settlers shall have ascertained the quantity of their land by regular survey or contract, in such case, upon their producing the same to the assessors, they shall be assessed for such quantity in the same manner as if a patent had been obtained for the same. But nothing in this act shall be construed in any manner to affect or prejudice the prior claim or title of any person whatsoever in or to any such lands, nor to affect any person residing within the territory northward of the latitude of the line usually called Mason and Dixon's line, and in dispute between this commonwealth and that of Pennsylvania, unless the legislature of the said commonwealth of Pennsylvania shall have imposed taxes on their citizens within the said disputed territory, and then only to such amount as shall have been by them imposed on such their citizens.

VI. And for settling just proportions of the said land tax between landlords and their tenants, to whom the lands were let for terms yet to come, at a time when the value of money was greater, and the price of lands less than at present, *It is farther enacted,* That all lands under lease for an annual rent, and subject to the tax, shall be valued without regard to such rent; but where such valuation shall exceed twenty years purchase, computed upon the annual rent, to be ascertained by the assessors, they shall proceed to assess the landlord the said pound rate upon the amount of twenty years purchase of the rent, and shall assess the tenant the pound rate upon the residue of the value of the land, and distinguish such proportions in their returns; and where such rent shall be reserved in tobacco, or other commodity, the assessors shall value the same in money, in order to adjust such proportion between landlords and tenants. Where any tenant at an annual rent shall be willing to pay the pound rate assessed on his landlord for the lands held by such tenant, it shall be lawful for him or her so to do, and the collector's receipt for the same shall entitle him or her to a deduction for the amount thereof out of the rent; and where the landlord shall reside out of this commonwealth, or have no visible estate whereon to levy the pound rate for the value of his land, in such case the said pound rate shall be paid by or levied upon the tenant or tenants on the said land, not exceeding the annual amount of the rents, and allowed to him or them as aforesaid. If any person shall think him or herself aggrieved by the judgment of the assessors of the hundred, he or she may appeal to the commissioners of the tax in the county or corporation, who shall meet annually on the second Tuesday in July, if fair, if not, the next fair day, at their court-house, for hearing such appeals, and may adjourn from day to day, or to any other place, until they shall have determined all appeals made to them, and upon such hearing may either increase or diminish the assessment made on such person or persons, or let the same remain unaltered, as to them shall seem just, and according to the spirit and intention of this act.

VII. *It is farther enacted,* That the court of each county shall, at their court to be held in the months of April or May one thousand seven hundred and seventy eight, and in each of the six following years, take bond, with sufficient security, of the sheriff, in the penalty of three thousand pounds, payable to the treasurer of this commonwealth for the time being and his successours, for the use of the commonwealth; with condition for the true and faithful collection and accounting for all the duties and taxes hereby imposed within his county, and paying the money for which he shall be accountable according to this act. And if any sheriff shall refuse or fail to give such security, the court shall appoint some other person or persons to collect the said taxes, and take the like bond and security of him or them, which bonds shall be recorded in the courts where they shall respectively be taken, and an attested copy thereof transmitted by the clerk, without delay, to the publick treasurer, which shall be admitted as evidence in any suit or proceeding founded thereon.

VIII. *And it is farther enacted,* That the commissioners of the tax in each county or corporation shall, on or before the first day of August annually, deliver to the sheriff of the county, or to the collector or collectors appointed as aforesaid, a full and perfect list, formed from the returns of the several assessors, of all the persons, in alphabetical order, who reside in the county, and are to pay any rate or tax pursuant to this act, with the amount of what each person is to pay, collecting together what the same person shall be assessed in different hundreds, and distinguishing in what hundred the person chargeable resides or hath effects, taking a receipt from the sheriff or collector for the same, and thereupon such sheriff or collector shall proceed to collect and receive the several taxes and rates according to such list, and to levy the same by distress and sale of the slaves, goods, and chattles, of such persons who shall fail to pay what he or she shall be so assessed on or before the first day of September in any year, the sale of which estate shall be made not less than five days after the distress, for ready money, and notice thereof shall be published at the parish church or most convenient meeting-house, and no security shall be taken, or writ of replevin sued out thereupon; but no sheriff or collector shall seize any slave for such taxes where other sufficient distress shall be shewn him, nor make any unreasonable distress, on pain of being liable to the action of the party grieved, wherein the plaintiff shall recover his full costs, although the damages shall be under forty shillings. And where any lands shall be assessed in a county wherein the proprietor doth not reside, nor hath any effects whereon to levy the said pound rate, and the commissioners shall discover in what other county the proprietor lives or hath effects, they shall transmit the assessment to the commissioners of such other county, to be delivered to the sheriff or collector thereof, and collected, levied, and accounted for, in like manner as the other assessments of such county.

IX. And that lands may not be granted on, or subject to any feudal tenure, and to prevent the danger to a free state from perpetual revenue, *Be it enacted*, That all lands within this common-wealth shall henceforward be exempted and discharged from the payment of all quitrents, except only the lands in that tract of country or territory between Rappahannock and Potowmack rivers, commonly called the Northern Neck; and that the abolition of quitrents may operate to the equal benefit of all the citizens of the commonwealth, the owners of all lands within the said territory, subject to the payment of an annual quitrent of two shillings sterling per hundred acres to the proprietor of the said Northern Neck, shall be allowed the sum of two shillings and six pence current money for every hundred acres, and so in proportion for a greater or lesser quantity, out of the sum which shall be respectively assessed on such lands, so long as their payment of quitrents thereon shall continue, which allowance and discount the commissioners and assessors of the tax are hereby empowered and required to make accordingly, and the commissioners of the tax in each county within the said territory shall make out a list of all such deductions made in their county, and transmit the same to the commissioners of the county of Frederick annually, to be by them delivered to the sheriff of the said county, and such sheriff is hereby required to collect and levy of and upon the proprietor of the said territory for the time being the said pound rate of two shillings for every pound of the amount of the said deductions, and account for and pay the same to the treasurer, in like manner, and subject to the same penalty and proceedings, as is herein before directed for accounting for and paying the other taxes.

X. *And be it farther enacted,* That the late auditor, or deputy auditor general in this commonwealth shall, on or before the twentieth day of March next, transmit to the commissioners of each county, not being within the said territory of the Northern Neck, a certificate at what time the last quitrents were accounted for in such county by the sheriff; and the late receiver, or deputy receiver general, shall within the same time transmit to such commissioners a true copy from his book of the account with each sheriff who hath not fully paid, and a certificate to what time the quitrents have been so fully paid in each county, and upon receiving such accounts and certificates the commissioners in each county shall proceed to call the respective persons who have been sheriffs thereof, within the time the quitrents are unaccounted for, to an account for what they have received thereof in each year, and to move for judgment in the general court or county court against such sheriff, or his deputy or deputies, and his or their securities, or their respective executors or administrators, for the penalty of their respective bonds where they shall fail to account, or for what shall appear due on such account, if they respectively fail to pay the same, and such court shall give judgment accordingly; provided, that ten days previous notice be given of such motion. And having adjusted such accounts with the sheriffs, the commissioners of each county shall make out a list of all arrears of quitrents due from any persons for lands therein to the twenty ninth day of September one thousand seven hundred and seventy four, and deliver the same to the sheriff or collector, to be collected, levied, accounted for, and paid in like manner, and subject to the same penalty and proceedings for neglect, as are provided in the case of the taxes hereby imposed. And the treasurer shall pay to the auditor and receiver general what the auditors of publick accounts shall certify to be reasonable satisfaction for such copies and certificates.

XI. *Provided always,* That no lands situate on the Western Waters shall be subject to the payment of such arrears. And where any quitrents have been paid for such lands, or for other lands to a later period than the said twenty ninth day of September, the sheriff receiving the same shall refund the amount thereof to the person who paid it, his or her executors or administrators; or where the money shall have been paid to the receiver general or treasurer, the amount thereof shall be repaid by the sheriff or collector of the county where the person entitled thereto resides, and be allowed to such sheriff or collector in his account. The said receiver general shall also render an account upon oath of all money now in his hands received for quitrents, or upon the fund formerly appropriated to defray the contingent charges of government, and pay such balance to the treasurer, for the use of this commonwealth, or be compelled thereto by the general court, upon such proceedings as are herein directed for recovering money from the sheriffs or collectors received for taxes. The said receiver shall also render an account of any arrears which may be due to the said contingent fund, which the treasurer shall proceed to receive or recover as aforesaid. The right honourable Thomas lord Fairfax, or the agent or manager of his office, shall also, on or before the said twentieth day of March next, transmit to the commissioners of each county within the territory of the Northern Neck a rent roll of all the lands paying quitrents to the said proprietor in such county, and receive from the treasurer the sum of twenty shillings for each rent roll; and the respective commissioners shall deliver extracts therefrom to the assessors of the several hundreds, for their direction. Every sheriff or collector of the taxes hereby imposed shall, on or before the first day of November yearly, account with the commissioners of the taxes in his county for all the rates, taxes, and duties, put into his hands to collect for such year; and the commissioners shall adjust the said account, allowing for such only as in their judgment could not have been received by a vigilant and faithful collector, and allowing a commission of three per centum for collecting the residue, striking the balance due from such sheriff or collector, and certifying their having examined and passed the account. They shall also at the foot thereof state an account of what shall be due to themselves, their clerk, and the several assessors in the county, for the year's service, and deduct the same from the balance in the hands of the sheriff or collector, who shall pay the amount of such expenses to the commissioners, for the use of themselves and the others; and the account so settled the commissioners shall deliver to the sheriff or collector, after having entered an exact copy thereof in their book, and they shall immediately transmit a copy from their book to the treasurer, to enable him to call upon the sheriff or collector for the money so stated to be due.

XII. *And it is farther enacted,* That every person who shall carry any tobacco out of this commonwealth, by land, shall, before he removes the same from the county where it is made, or from whence it is carried out of this commonwealth, apply to the clerk of the county court, and make oath what number of hogsheads or casks of tobacco he intends to carry out of the commonwealth, and pay the duty of ten shillings per hogshead or cask for the same, taking a certificate of such oath, with the marks and numbers of such hogsheads or casks, and a receipt for the tax, and of which an entry shall be made by the clerk in his books. The master or mate of every ship or vessel, in which tobacco shall be laded or put on board for exportation, shall, at the time of clearing out his ship or vessel, make a true report upon oath of all the tobacco loaden therein, with the marks and numbers of each hogshead thereof, and by whom shipped, and pay down the duty of ten shillings per hogshead for the same to the naval officer, before he is admitted to a clearance. Every naval officer shall half yearly, on the twenty fifth day of April and twenty fifty day of October, render an account upon oath to the publick treasurer of all duties by him received pursuant to this act in the preceding half year, and pay the money for such duties, deducting five per centum for receiving the same. And the clerk of each county or corporation court shall on the same days, half yearly, render an account upon oath to the said treasurer of all the taxes by him received for marriage and ordinary licenses, and for the duty upon tobacco exported by land in the preceding half year, and pay the money for such taxes, deducting five per centum for receiving the same. And every naval officer, or clerk of a court, failing to render such account, shall forfeit and pay the sum of five hundred pounds for every offence; and any naval officer or clerk having accounted, and failing to pay the money stated to be due within one month, shall be proceeded against by the treasurer for the recovery thereof, in manner herein after directed against sheriffs or collectors making default in payment. And every sheriff, or other county collector, who shall fail to settle his account with the commissioners of the taxes in his county annually, on or before the said first day of November, shall forfeit and pay the sum of one hundred pounds for every neglect; and in such case the treasurer may and shall proceed against such sheriff or collector and his securities, his or their heirs, executors, or administrators, as hereafter mentioned, and obtain judgment for the penalty of the bond and costs, to be discharged, except as to the costs, by the payment of what shall be found due for the taxes in such county, in case the sheriff or collector shall, before the levying of the execution, make up an account of the taxes with the commissioners, and obtain their certificate of the just balance.

And if any sheriff or collector of the taxes in any county, having accounted with the commissioners as herein before is directed, shall fail to produce his account so certified to the treasurer of this commonwealth, and pay the balance stated to be due from him on or before the first day of December in any year, the treasurer is hereby empowered and directed, under pain of forfeiting five hundred pounds, to move in the general court, on the tenth day of the next succeeding court, for judgment against such sheriff or collector and his securities, his or their executors or administrators; and the said court, on that day, or so soon afterwards as counsel can be heard, shall proceed to take trial therein by jury, if either party shall desire it without delay, admitting the certificate of the commissioners for proof of the balance found to be due on the account, and such other legal testimony as either party may offer, and to enter judgment for what shall be found due, and costs, and thereon to award execution, upon which the clerk shall endorse that no security of any kind is to be taken, and the officer to whom the same is directed and delivered shall proceed to levy the same by distress and sale of the estate of the defendants, for ready money, taking no security either for replevying of the estate or having the same forthcoming at the day of sale. If any sheriff, or usual returning officer of a county or corporation, shall fail to give notice of the time appointed for the annual election of the commissioners of the tax, or fail to attend at such election (not being hindered by sickness, in which case the under sheriff of the county, or one of the aldermen of the corporation, shall act in his stead) every person so neglecting or failing shall forfeit five hundred pounds. If any person elected a commissioner shall refuse to serve (not having a sufficient excuse, to be judged of by his county or corporation court) he shall forfeit and pay the sum of one hundred pounds, and in case of such refusal, whether the reasons offered be adjudged a good excuse or not, or if any commissioner who undertakes the trust shall die or be disabled to act within the year, the county or corporation court shall appoint another commissioner in the room of him so refusing, dead, or disabled, to act until the next annual election, and so as often as such vacancy shall happen. And if there be no election made of commissioners for any county or corporation, as herein before directed, in such case the court of such county or corporation shall, at their next court, proceed to the choice of commissioners and if there shall happen, from bad weather or other accident, to be no court held for any county or corporation on the court day next after the said second Tuesday in March in any year, in that case the magistrates of such court shall, under the penalty of fivty pounds on each magistrate failing, meet at their courthouse on the next fair day, and then and there judge of the excuses of commissioners elected, and proceed to election of such as may be necessary, either by their having been none elected, or those elected refusing to act as aforesaid. Each commissioner accepting the trust shall be allowed for each day he shall act therein the sum of ten shillings. If any person appointed an assessor shall refuse to serve (not having a sufficient excuse, to be judged of by the commissioners) he shall forfeit and pay the sum of fifty pounds, and all vacancies occasioned by such refusals, or by the death or inability to act of any assessor, shall be supplied, as often as they happen, by the appointment of the commissioners; and each assessor, for performing his duty, shall be allowed what the commissioners shall judge reasonable, not exceed-ing ten pounds per annum. If any person shall refuse to give an account upon oath or affirmation, as herein before directed, of all the articles in his or her possession liable to a pound rate or tax by this act, every person so refusing shall forfeit and pay the sum of one hundred pounds; and the assessors shall proceed to inquire by other means into his or her property, and assess the same according to the best information they can procure. If any person shall carry any tobacco out of this commonwealth by land without paying the duty aforesaid, and obtaining such certificate from the clerk of the county court, as is herein before required, every person so offending shall forfeit ten pounds for every hogshead or cask of tobacco so carried out. And every master or mate of a ship or vessel, on board of which any tobacco shall be loaden for exportation, failing to make a true report of the marks and numbers of such tobacco to the naval officer at the time of clearance, shall forfeit and pay the sum of ten pounds for every hogshead of tobacco exported in such ship or vessel, and not so reported. And if any naval officer shall clear out any ship or vessel, in which tobacco shall be reported to be loaden, without receiving the duty hereby imposed on such tobacco, the naval officer shall be answerable for the duty. All the penalties and forfeitures hereby inflicted shall be recoverable with costs, by action of debt or information, in any court of record, and be appropriated, two thirds to the use of the commonwealth, and paid to the publick treasurer, to assist the purposes of this act, and the other third to the informer, or the whole to the commonwealth, in case a suit for the same shall be first instituted for the common-wealth.

XIII. *And it is farther enacted,* That all waste and unappropriated lands within this commonwealth, as soon as the same shall be granted pursuant to an act of the general assembly, shall be subject to assessment of the said pound rate, in like manner as the lands already granted.

XIV. *And it is farther enacted*, That the land and poll tax, and all other taxes and duties imposed by any former act of assembly or ordinance of convention, and which were payable at any time before the first day of January one thousand seven hundred and eighty four, shall cease; and the said acts and ordinances, so far as they relate to the imposition, collection, and payment of the said taxes or duties, are hereby repealed, except so far as may enforce the collectors of any of the said taxes heretofore due to account for and pay the same.

XV. *And it is farther enacted*, That the treasurer of this commonwealth for the time being shall apply the money which shall come to his hands by virtue of this act, in the first place for and towards the annual payment of the quota of this commonwealth of the principal and interest of money borrowed on treasury notes issued on account of the United American States, supposed by the general congress to be two hundred and forty thousand pounds, for the present year, deducting thereout what is or shall from time to time become due from them to this commonwealth, and the residue for and towards the payment of the interest due or to become due for money borrowed or to be borrowed for the use of this commonwealth, and of the principal money, when due, for the redemption of the treasury notes issued by order of the convention of this commonwealth, redeemable on the first day of January one thousand seven hundred and eighty four, and by virtue of this act, or any former act of general assembly, redeemable on the first day of December one thousand seven hundred and eighty four, and for the annual contingent expenses of this state, and to no other use whatsoever. And the said treasurer shall keep clear and distinct accounts of the said taxes and duties hereby imposed, shewing the neat annual income of each, and lay the same before the general assembly when required; and if there shall be any deficiency in the said taxes and duties to answer the full purposes of this act, the same shall be made good by a farther and adequate tax.

XVI. And whereas it may be necessary to make some farther provision for answering such demands as may be made on the treasury before the said taxes can be collected, *Be it farther enacted*, That George Webb, esq. or the treasurer for the time being, shall, and he is hereby empowered and directed to receive from any person whatever any sum of specie, continental paper dollars, or bills of credit issued by authority of this commonwealth, he or she shall be willing to lend, for any term not exceeding three years, so as such sum be not less than three hundred dollars, or the value thereof in other money lent by any one person, and doth not exceed in the whole five hundred thousand pounds, and to give the lender a receipt for the money lent in the form prescribed in the act of assembly establishing a loan office for the purpose of borrowing money for the use of the commonwealth; and the said treasurer shall keep accounts of the money so borrowed, and conform to all regulations prescribed by the said act.

XVII. *And be it farther enacted,* That the treasurer shall pay the interest of the money due on such certificates annually, and take in discharge the principal thereof at the time or times therein limited for that purpose; or should the lender or bearer of such certificates desire to have the same sooner paid and discharged, the treasurer is hereby authorised to comply therewith, provided the state of the treasury will admit of the same, without prejudice to the publick.

XVIII. *And be it farther enacted,* that if any person within this commonwealth shall forge or counterfeit, alter or erase, any certificate of money lent as aforesaid, or transfer any forged or altered certificate to another, or demand payment at the office of principal or interest thereupon, knowing the same to be forged or counterfeited, altered or erased, every person so offending, being lawfully convicted, shall forfeit his whole estate real and personal; receive on his bare back at the publick whipping post thirty nine lashes, and shall be obliged to serve on board some armed vessel in the service of this state, without wages, not exceeding seven years; provided, that the governour and council for the time being, out of the offender's estate, may make such allowance to his wife and children as to them shall seem just and reasonable.

XIX. And whereas it is altogether uncertain whether the above-mentioned sum of money can be borrowed so soon as the exigencies of government may require, *Be farther enacted,* that the said George Webb, Esquire, or the treasurer for the time being, shall be, and he is hereby empowered to issue treasury notes, in dollars or parts of dollars, for any sum or sums which may be requisite for the purposes of government, and which he may not be able to borrow as aforesaid, so that the money so emitted, with what shall be borrowed by virtue of this act, doth not exceed seventeen hundred thousand dollars; each dollar to be of the value of a Spanish milled dollar, and the parts of a dollar of the same proportionate value. And the said treasurer for the time being may, and he is hereby authorised to cause the said notes to be engraved and printed in such manner as he shall judge most likely to secure the same against counterfeits and forgeries, to appoint proper persons to overlook the press, to number and sign the said notes, upon the best terms on which he can procure them.

XX. *And be it farther enacted*, that all such notes so to be issued shall pass as a lawful tender; and any person attempting to depreciate the value of the same, by any such means or device whatsoever, as is described in several acts of assembly, shall incur the same penalties and forfeitures as are thereby imposed, to be recovered as therein directed. The said notes so to be issued shall be redeemable on the first day of December one thousand seven hundred and eighty four.

XXI. *And be it farther enacted,* that if any person or persons shall forge or counterfeit, alter or erase, any such treasury note, or tender in payment any such, or demand a redemption thereof, knowing the same to be forged or counterfeited, altered or erased, every person so offending, and being thereof lawfully convicted, shall incur the same forfeitures, and suffer the same punishment, as is herein before directed in the case of certificates for money borrowed.

Printed from Hening, IX, 349–368.

It was inevitable that as Virginia moved from a remote crown colony to a self-governing state its creaky fiscal system would require a drastic overhaul. GM apparently tested his ideas on a general assessment bill in conversations and possibly with letters to friends during the autumn of 1777, and by the time he reached Williamsburg on 14 Nov. debate on ways and means of stablizing public credit had already begun. To the committee serving under Chairman Thomas Nelson there is little doubt but that GM rendered considerable service, and it is possible that he already had the general outlines of a bill that the committee of the whole could consider. There seems to have been a general agreement that heavy taxes would curb the depreciating currency (Boyd, II, 30), but the details of such a plan "occasioned much Altercation and long debate" (letter to William Woodford, 16 Jan. 1778, Mays, ed., *Papers of Edmund Pendleton*, I, 246). The BILLS OF CREDIT issued by authority of the Continental Congress after June 1775 were supposed to be retired by states furnishing their quotas of called-in bills collected by taxes. The system broke down almost immediately because of laggard taxing programs in the states. The program enacted here, with its provisions for A TAX OR RATE OF TEN SHILLINGS for £100 of assessed value was a one-half percent assessment. Our knowledge of this and other measures which GM either wrote or helped through the House is incomplete because no letters by GM written during this session have survived. Edmund Pendleton reported that the property tax, "being disgusting where it has been tried . . . was not admitted without much care to make it as Palatable as possible, by confining it to the Capital Articles of Property so as to prevent Rumaging of Houses, and so it stands at 10s. in the £100 value of Lands slaves, money, Horses, Mules and Plate, 4d. a head on Cattle, 2s. in the £ of annuities and Interest of money. . . . Salaries and the nett income of Offices of proffit also pay 10s. in the £100 of their Amount, this however don't extend to the Army or navy" (letter to William Woodford, 31 Jan. 1778, *ibid.*, 246–247). The tax on incomes was an experiment, perhaps in imitation of the Maryland tax reform bill of 1777 which taxed the profits of public officers, professional men, and merchants (Edwin R. A. Seligman, *The Income Tax* . . . [New York, 1911], 379). The task of selecting THREE ABLE AND DISCREET MEN as commissioners became formidable and in time seems to have fallen the lot of the county justices as an appointive rather than elective office (see GM's "Remarks on the proposed Bill for regulating Elections," *ca.* December 1780). In the midst of consideration of the tax bill, the General Assembly had received, read, and approved the Articles of Confederation (JHD, 1827 ed., 9 Dec., 17 Dec. entries). Perhaps this swift stroke on behalf of the Union led to the allowance granted interest payments that might be taxed IN ANY OTHER OF THE UNITED STATES. The provision allowing bona fide settlers on western lands FOUR HUNDRED ACRES was part of GM's resolution of 13 Dec. 1777 (*q.v.*) on WASTE AND UNGRANTED LANDS. The exception granted to settlers NORTHWARD OF . . . MASON AND DIXON'S LINE was needed because the exact boundary between Virginia and Pennsylvania was uncertain and dragged on for nearly a decade before final settlement. It is certain that many Virginians thought themselves AGGRIEVED BY THE JUDGEMENT OF THE ASSESSORS. When John Cropper, Jr., listed reasons for his resignation from the service, one grievance was the "high taxes in Virginia, which fall very heavy on me, being obliged to pay for the present year, four hundred pounds or upwards, for over cultivated lands, that do not yield me one single sixpence profit per annum" (letter to John Jay, 16 Aug. 1777, W. P. Palmer ed., *Calendar of Virginia State Papers and Other Manuscripts* . . . [Richmond, 1875–1893] I, 325). The abolition of all quitrents, EXCEPT ONLY THE LANDS . . . BETWEEN RAPPAHANNOCK AND POTOWMACK RIVERS, left the Fairfax family in possession of that last vestige of royal largesse, in the Northern Neck, although an act for sequestering British property passed during this same session of the General Assembly. The chief reason was the amiable conduct of THE RIGHT HONOURABLE THOMAS LORD FAIRFAX, who was living at "Greenway Court" near Winchester in the quiet enjoyment of his property —more than 5,000,000 acres of it. In the months and years ahead, much complaint was heard over the bill's provisions and it was subject to repeated revision. In less than a year outcries over the "great inequality and injustice . . . from the various opinions of assessors in the same county" brought an amendment that ordered the assessors to meet, "consult together and form some general mode which they shall pursue in rating the several articles of taxation" (Hening, IX, 549). But the general outlines of the bill stood intact for the remainder of the Revolution.

An Act to Prevent Forestalling

[[*20 Nov. 1777–6 Jan. 1778.* Jefferson was appointed chairman of a committee charged with preparation of legislation that would make the activities of wartime profiteers illegal. The bill was brought forward on 29 Nov., read twice, and committed to the committee of the whole. GM, a member of the drafting committee, was ordered to carry the measure to the Senate after its passage (JHD, 1827 ed., 6 Jan. 1778 entry). Any person who bought up food or merchandise for the purpose of "enhancing of the price of any such goods" was declared a forestaller. Regrating and engrossing—purchasing goods for resale—were illegal except in certain cases. Military purchasing agents, iron works operators, persons operating 25 miles beyond the tidewater, citizens using raw materials in the manufacture of goods, and operators of taverns or

inns were exempted from the act. The full title was "An act to prevent
Forestalling Regrating, Engrossing, and Publick Vendues" (Hening, IX,
382–384). Boyd found several drafts in George Wythe's handwriting,
and this may explain why GM carried the bill to the Senate, since
Wythe was the Speaker of the House and could not. The text in Boyd,
II, 561–566, is almost the same as that printed in Hening but has an
additional explanatory note. The legislation was also listed as No. 89 of
the "Catalogue of Bills" for the Committee of Revisors (Boyd, II,
332).]]

An Act to Authorize an Investigation of Disaffection in the Western Counties

[10–22 December 1777]

For more effectually securing the Commonwealth against the designs and attempts of certain evil minded persons now or lately in
the Counties herein after mentioned, who lost to all sentiments of
virtue honour or regard for their country, have been induced to aid
the enemy; be it enacted by the general assembly that Samuel
Washington, Gabriel Jones & Joseph Reed esquires, commissioners
appointed by the united States of America in congress assembled to
repair to Fort Pitt, in Order to investigate the rise progress and
extent of the disaffection in that quarter, or such other persons as
shall be appointed in their room, and shall undertake to execute the
office, be authorised and empowered, and they are hereby authorised and empowered at any time within [six months] after the
passing of this acct to apprehend such Inhabitants of the Counties of
Ohio, Monongolia and Yohogania as shall appear to the said Commissioners to have been concerned in any conspiracy or plot against
the said States, or any or either of them, and to deliver the Offenders
over to the proper civil Officers, to be prosecuted according to Law.
And to provide for the further protection and defense of the
Frontiers, be it further enacted, that the Governor, with advice of
the privy council, may order such part of the militia as may be most
convenient, and as they shall judge necessary, consistently with the
Safety of the commonwealth, to and in conjunction with any
troops, on any expedition which may be undertaken by desire of the
united States of America in congress assembled, against any of our
western Enemies; and also that the Governor with advice of the
privy council at any time within [nine] months after the passing of
this act, may empower a number of volunteers not exceeding [six]
hundred to march against and attack any of our said enemies, and

may appoint the proper officers and give the necessary Orders for the Expedition.

Tr (Vi). A single page in a clerk's handwriting, with the outer endorsement in GM's hand reading: "A Bill for better securing the Commonwealth, and for the further Protection and Defense thereof." That title heads the act as it appears in Hening, IX, 374–375. A clerk's endorsement, below GM's, further reads: "1777. Decr. 19. Read the first Time. Decr. 20th. Read a Second time & to be engrossed."

Wild and vague rumors of disaffection on the western frontier reached the Continental Congress in mid-Nov. 1777. Thomas Wharton, president of Pennsylvania, was sent an account of western depredations and told that "self interest reigns predominant in the Western as well as every other quarter of our Land." A congressional commission was needed, so that commissioners could make "a full inquiry into their discontents and particularly into a hellish design of Conspiracy therefore I beg the State would immediately furnish me with the names of two Gentlemen capable of such a negotiation at Pittsburgh" (Daniel Roberdeau to Wharton, 19 Nov. 1777, Edmund C. Burnett, ed., *Letters of Members of the Continental Congress* [Washington, 1921–1936], II, 561). Congress selected three commissioners and ordered them to proceed to Fort Pitt, but Reed and then Washington declined. Meanwhile, the Virginia House of Delegates heard the reports and on 10 Dec. passed a resolution authorizing the governor and privy council to use troops against "western enemies" and also to investigate the rumored disaffection in OHIO, MONONGOLIA AND YOHOGANIA counties to determine "if any conspiracy or plot against the United States" was afoot (JHD, 1827 ed., 10 Dec. 1777 entry). This bill was returned by the committee on 19 Dec., passed three readings, and was carried to the Senate by GM on 22 Dec. Congress had more difficulty in finding commissioners willing to undertake the business and on 10 Jan. 1778 conferred on Gov. Henry the power to appoint more commissioners (Burnett, ed., *Letters of Continental Congress*, I, 562n). The storm seemed to center around Col. George Morgan, an adversary of the Ohio Company, but in Apr. 1778 the commissioners exonerated him (*ibid.*, 532n). Virginia still claimed the territory around Fort Pitt, hence the state's concern.

In the Ms., Joseph Reed's name is misspelled "Read" but has been corrected here, as it was in the printed version. Blank spaces in the Ms. were filled with the numbers printed within brackets.

A Bill for Establishing a Land Office and Ascertaining the Terms and Manner of Granting Waste and Unappropriated Lands

[13 December 1777–8 January 1778]

WHEREAS there are large Quantities of waste and unappropriated lands within the territorial Limits of this Commonwealth, the granting of which will encourage the migration of Foreigners hither, promote population, increase the Annual Revennue, and create a fund for discharging the Public Debt:

Be it enacted by the General Assembly that an office shall be and is hereby constituted for the purpose of granting Lands within this Commonwealth into which all the Records now in the Secretarys Office of Patents or grants for lands heretofore issued, with all Papers relating thereto, shall be removed, for their safe keeping, and all future grants of lands, shall issue from the said office, in manner and form herein after directed.

A Register of the said Land office shall be appointed from time to time by joint Ballot of both houses of Assembly, who shall give Bond, with sufficient security to the Governor or first Magistrate of this Commonwealth, in the Penalty of   Current Money, shall take an oath for the due and faithfull performance of his Trust, shall hold his office during good behaviour, be entitled to receive such fees as shall hereafter be allowed by Law, and shall have power to appoint a Deputy to assist in executing the business of the said Office. If any vacancy shall happen by the death, resignation, or removal of a Register during the Recess of the General Assembly, the Governor or first Magistrate of the Commonwealth by and with the advice of the privy council, may appoint some other Person, giving Bond and Security and taking an Oath in like manner, to act in the said Office, until the end of the next Session of Assembly.

And for the Encouragement of Foreigners to settle here, and an Inducement to import Inhabitants from Foreign Countries,

Be it enacted that the antient Custom of importation rights shall be continued, and every Person removing from any Foreign Country, or at his charge, importing any Inhabitants, not being Slaves, to settle in this Commonwealth, shall in consideration thereof, be entitled to fifty Acres of Waste or unappropriated lands, for each person so removed or imported, upon certificate from the General Court, or any County Court within the Commonwealth, of due Proof thereof in open Court, by the Oath of the party, or other satisfactory evidence, of the name of every Person so removed or imported, the Country from which he came, the Year of the arrival or importation, that the Person obtaining such certificate had never before proved or claimed his right to land for any of those named therein, and that ⟨such of the Men who are above sixteen Years of Age have⟩ taken the Oath of Fidelity to the Commonwealth.

And for the more equal Distribution of Lands, and to encourage Marriage and Population, by making provision for the natives of the Country, Be it enacted that every Child free born within this Commonwealth, after the establishment thereof, shall upon his or her Marriage and residence for one Year next after such Marriage, within this Commonwealth, be entitled to seventy five Acres of waste or unappropriated land, upon [presenting a] certificate from any court of Record, of due proof having been made of such Nativity, Marriage, and residence, and that the party had never before made proof or obtained Certificate thereof, but the Portion of land so due to the Wife shall, upon such Certificate, be granted to the Husband and his heirs.

And whereas a certain Bounty in lands hath been allowed to Troops, on Continental establishment, raised by the laws of this Commonwealth, and to the Troops upon Virginia Establishment,

Be it enacted that the Officers and Soldiers of the said Troops, as well as the Officers and Soldiers to whom a Bounty in Lands may or shall be hereafter granted by an Law of this Commonwealth, shall be entitled to the Quantity and Portion of Waste or unappropriated Land allowed to them respectively by such Laws; the Commissioned Officers, upon Certificate from the General or Commander in Cheif of the Continental Army, or the Commanding Officer of the Troops on the Virginia Establishment as the case is; and the noncommissioned officers and Soldiers upon Certificate from the Colonel or Commanding Officer of the Regiment or Corps to which they respectively belong, that such Officers or Soldiers have served the time required by Law, distinguishing particularly in what Regiment or Corps such service hath been performed.

And for creating a sinking Fund, in aid of the Annual Taxes, to discharge the Public Debt, Be it enacted that it shall be lawful for any Citizen of this or of any other of the United States, to obtain a Warrant for surveying Waste or unappropriated lands, on paying the consideration of   for every hundred Acres and so in proportion for a greater or smaller quantity, in the following manner, that is to say; if the Quantity required exceed four hundred Acres, such consideration money shall be paid into the hands of the Treasurer, who shall thereupon give to such person a certificate of the payment and of the purpose for which it was made, which, being delivered to the Register of the land office, shall entitle him to a Warrant from the said Register as herein after directed: but if the Quantity required, does not exceed four hundred Acres, such consideration Money shall be paid to the Clerk of the County Court, with whom the Register shall constantly lodge a due number of printed Warrants with Blanks for the name, Quantity and amount of the Consideration, which Warrant shall be filled up and countersigned by such clerk and issued to the Persons paying such consideration money.

And Whereas some of the United American States may not have within their respective Territories waste and unappropriated Lands sufficient to pay the Troops raised within the same, upon Continental establishment, the bounty of Lands Promised them by the American Congress, for which the Public faith is pledged, and it may hereafter become necessary for this Commonwealth to furnish a proportion of such lands for that purpose, on the General account and Charge of the said United States, Be it therefore enacted that for any waste or unappropriated Lands, so to be furnished by this Commonwealth, no greater price or consideration than the Sum of three pounds current money, or Ten Dollars per hundred Acres, shall be charged taken or demanded.

And be it enacted that upon application of any person or persons having Title to waste or unappropriated Lands either by Importation-Rights, Native-Rights, Military-Rights or the larger Treasury-rights, and lodging in the Land Office a proper Certificate thereof, the Register of the said Office shall Grant to such person or persons a printed Warrant specifying the Quantity of Land, and the Rights upon which it is due, authorizing any Surveyor to lay off and Survey the same; and shall regularly enter and Record in the Books of his Office all such Certificates, and the Warrants Issued thereupon; with the names of the persons mentioned in any Importation Certificates.

A Surveyor shall be appointed in every County, to be examined and Certified able by the Professors of William and Mary College and if of good Character commissioned by the Governor with a reservation in such Commission to the said Professors for the use of the College, of one sixth part of the legal Fees which shall be received by such Surveyor: he shall hold his office during good Behaviour, shall reside within his County, and before he shall be capable of entering upon the execution of his office, shall, before the Court of the same County, take an Oath, and give Bond with two sufficient sureties, to the Governor and his Successors, in the Sum of five hundred pounds for the faithful execution of his Office, and shall also take the Oath of fidelity to the Commonwealth. Residence out of the County, or absence therefrom for a longer time than one Month, unless by unavoidable necessity, shall vacate his said Office. So many deputy surveyors, as by the said chief Surveyor shall be certified necessary to do the Business of the County, shall be in like manner examined, Commissioned and Qualified for their Office, who shall be entitled to the whole fees allowed by Law for whatsoever services they shall perform accounting nevertheless for one sixth part thereof to the professors of the College of William & Mary as before directed and one other sixth part to their principal; and if any

Deputy surveyor, or any other on his behalf and with his privity shall pay, or Agree to pay, any greater part of the Profits of his Office, sum of Money in gross, or other valuable Consideration to his principal for his recommendation or interest in procuring the Deputation, such Deputy and principal shall be thereby rendered for ever incapable of serving in such office. No principal Surveyor shall be answerable for any misfeasance in office, by his Deputy. It shall not be necessary for the present chief, or deputy Surveyors of the several Counties, duly examined, Commissioned and Qualified according to the Laws heretofore in force, to be again Commissioned & Qualified under the directions of this Act.

Every person having Importation Rights, Native Rights, military Rights or Treasury rights, and being desireous of Locating the same on any particular waste & unappropriated Land, shall lodge them with the Chief Surveyor of the County wherein the said Lands, or the greater part of them lie, directing the location thereof so specially and precisely as that others may be enabled with certainty to locate other Warrants on the adjacent residuum, which location shall be entered by the Surveyor in a Book to be kept for that purpose. And if on such application at his office, the Surveyor shall refuse to enter such location under pretence of a prior Entry for the same lands made by some other person, he shall have the right to demand of the said Surveyor a view of the Original of such prior entry in his Book, and also an attested Copy of it, paying such Surveyor for the same two shillings and six pence. But it shall not be lawful for any Surveyor to admit the location of any Warrant on Lands within the limits of the Cherokee Indians, nor on any Islands in the Ohio River or lands on the North-west side of the said River; nor on any Lands Westward of the meridian of the mouth of the Cumberland River.

Any chief Surveyor having a Warrant for Lands and desiring to locate the same on Lands within his own County, shall enter such location before the Clerk of the County, who shall return the same to the next Court, there to be Recorded; and the said Surveyor shall proceed to have the Survey made within as short a Time as may be, by some one of his Deputies, or if he hath no Deputy, then by any Surveyor or deputy surveyor of an adjacent County.

Every chief surveyor, shall proceed with all practicable dispatch, to Survey all Lands entered for in his Office, and shall either give to the party concerned personal notice of the Time at which he will attend to make such Survey, or shall publish such notice by affixing an advertisement thereof on the door of the Court-house of the

County, on two several Court days, if the party reside within the said County: and if he reside out of the County, then such publication shall be twice made in the Gazette, the expence of which shall be paid by the Treasurer to the printer, to be repaid as hereafter directed: which time so appointed shall be at least four months after personal notice given or after the second advertisement so published: And if the Surveyor shall accordingly attend and the party, or some one for him, shall fail to appear at the time with proper chain Carriers and a person to mark the lines if necessary, his Entry shall become void, and where the chief Surveyor doth not mean to Survey himself he shall immediately after the entry made direct a Deputy Surveyor to perform the Duty who shall proceed as is before directed in the case of the chief Surveyor.

The persons employed to carry the Chain on any Survey shall be sworn by the Surveyor, whether principal or Deputy, to measure justly and exactly to the best of their Abilities, and to deliver a true account thereof to such Surveyor; and shall be paid for their trouble by the party for whom the Survey is made. The surveyor at the Time of making the Survey shall see the same bounded plainly by marked Trees, except where a Water course or antient marked line shall be the Boundary; and shall make the breadth of such Survey at least one third of it's length in every part, unless where such breadth shall be restrain in both sides by Mountains unfit for Cultivation, by Water Courses, or the Bounds of Lands before appropriated. Within three days after making the Survey, and before he proceeds to make another, he shall deliver to the said party or person so attending a fair and true plat of such Survey, with a Certificate of the Quantity contained, the hundred wherein it lies, the course of the several Boundaries natural and Artificial, antient and new, expressing the proper name of such natural Boundaries where they have any, and the name of every person whose former line is made a Boundary, and also the nature of the warrant on which such Survey was made, and shall at the same time redeliver the said Warrant to the party. The said Plats and Certificates shall be examined and tried by the said principal surveyor whether truly made and legally proportioned as to length and breadth, and shall be entered within two months after the Survey is made, in a Book well bound, to be provided by the Court of his County, at the County charge; and he shall moreover, in the month of July in every Year, return to the professors of William and Mary College and also to the office of his County Court, a true list of all surveys made by him or his deputies in the preceeding twelve Months, there to be Recorded. Any Surveyor, whether principal or Deputy, failing in any of the duties aforesaid, shall be liable to be Indicted before the Judges of the General Court, and punished by fine or by deprivation of his office and incapacity to take it again; and shall moreover be liable to any party injured for all Damages he may sustain by such failure. Every County Court shall have authority at any time to appoint two or more capable persons to examine the Books of Entries and surveys in possession of their chief surveyor and to report in what condition and order the same are kept and, on his Death or removal, to take the same into their possession and deliver them to the succeeding chief Surveyor. Any person holding a land Warrant may have the same executed in one or more surveys; and, in such case, or where the Lands, on which any warrant is located, shall not be sufficient to satisfy such warrant, the party shall be entitled to have the said Warrant exchanged, at the office from which is Issued, for others, of the same amount in the whole, but divided as best may answer the purposes of the party, and entitle Him to so much land elsewhere as will make good the deficiency.

Every person for whom any waste or unappropriated Lands shall be so located and laid off, shall, within twelve months after the survey made, repay to the Treasurer the expence of publishing in the Gazette notice of surveying the said Lands, where such publication shall have been made either for his notification or that of any other who had before entered for the same Lands, which fact the surveyor shall duly note in his Certificate for the information of the Register and shall also return the Plat & Certificate of the said Survey into the Land Office, together with the warrant on which the Lands were surveyed, and may demand of the Register a receipt for the same, and, on failing to make such return or if the breadth of his plat be not one third of it's length as before directed, it shall be lawful for any other person to enter a Caveat in the said Land office against the Issuing of any Grant to him, expressing therein for what cause the Grant should not Issue; or if any person shall obtain a Survey of Lands to which another hath by Law a better right, the person having such better right may in like manner enter a Caveat to prevent his obtaining a Grant till the Title can be determined, such Caveat also expressing the nature of the right on which the Plaintif therein claims the said Land. The person entering any Caveat shall take from the Register a certified Copy thereof, which he shall deliver, on the same day on which he entered his Caveat in the said office, to the Clerk of the General Court; or such entry shall become void; the said Clerk, on receiving the same, shall enter it in a Book, and thereupon Issue a Summons reciting the causes for which such Caveat is entered, and requiring the Defendant to appear on the seventh day of the succeeding Court and defend his Right: and on such Process being returned executed, the Court shall Proceed to determine the right of the cause in a summary way, without pleadings in Writing, impannelling & swearing a Jury for the finding of such facts as are material to the cause, and are not agreed by the parties, and shall thereupon give Judgment on which no Appeal or Writ of Error shall be allowed. A Copy of such Judgment, if in favour of the Def[endan]t, being delivered into the Land Office, shall vacate the said Caveat; and, if not delivered within one Month, a new Caveat may, for that cause be entered against the Grant: And, if the said Judgment be in favour of the Plaintif, upon delivering the same into the Land Office, together with a Plat and Certificate of the Survey, and the rights on which it is claimed, he shall be entitled to a Grant thereof; but, on failing to make such return within six Months after Judgment so rendered, it shall be lawful for any other person to enter a Caveat for that cause against Issuing the Grant: upon which subsequent Caveats, such proceedings shall be had as are before directed in the case of an Original caveat and in any Caveat where Judgment is given for the Defendant, the Court, if they think it reasonable, may also adjudge to him his Costs.

The clerk of every County Court shall, before his said Court, give Bond, paiable to the Governor and his successors, in such sum as the Court in their discretion shall direct, with two sureties to be approved by them, for the faithful discharge of the office of Issuing land-warrants; and shall half-yearly, to wit, in the months of January and July pay into the hands of the Treasurer all monies by him received for such Warrants, deducting for his trouble   per centum therefrom, and shall take from the said Treasurer a certificate thereof which he shall deliver to the Register, together with a true account on Oath of the monies so received, of all Warrants Issued by him, specifying the name of the party and Quantity of Land in each, and of all blank Warrants still remaining on hand: producing moreover to the said Register such Warrants as shall have been taken back from the purchasers in exchange for others & a Certificate from the Court of the said County, signed by the presiding magistrate by order of the Court, that so many blank warrants as are stated in the said Account were by the said Clerk produced to the Court, examined and counted.

The Register shall, before the meeting of every Session of Assembly, return to the Speaker of the house of delegates all Treasury Certificates delivered to him since his last account rendered, together with a list of the same, and the names of the persons from whom they were received, and also an Account of all reimbursements to the public for printed notifications which shall have been certified to him, to be laid before the said house of Delegates and by them referred to the Committee which shall be appointed for settling the Treasurers accounts.

Due returns of the several articles herein before required being made into the Land Office, the Register, within not less than one, nor more than three months, shall make out a Grant by way of Deed Poll to the party having right in the following form. 'A. B. Esqr. Governor of the Commonwealth of Virginia, To all to whom these presents shall come Greeting. Know ye that in Consideration of white Inhabitants imported to settle in this Commonwealth by C.D. [[or in Consideration that C. D. is a native of this Commonwealth, hath married and resided therein for one Year next after such Marriage]] [[or in Consideration that E. D. is a native of this Commonwealth, hath intermarried with C. D. and resided therein for one Year next after such intermarriage;]] [[or in Consideration that C.D. and E. his Wife are natives of this Commonwealth, have intermarried and resided therein for one Year next after such intermarriage]] [[or, in consideration of Military service performed by C. D. to this Commonwealth,]] [[or in Consideration of Military service performed by C. D. to the united States of America,]] [[or in consideration of the Sum of   paid by C. D. into the Treasury of this Commonwealth,]] there is granted by the said Commonwealth unto the said C. D. a certain Tract or parcel of Land containing   Acres lying in the County of   and hundred of &c. with it's appurtenances To have and to hold the said Tract or parcel of Land, with it's appurtenances to the said C. D. and his heirs; to be holden of the said Commonwealth by fealty in free & common soccage. In Witness whereof the said A. B. Governor of the Commonwealth of Virginia hath hereunto caused the Seal of the said Commonwealth to be affixed at   on the   day of   in the Year of our Lord   and of the Commonwealth   A B.'

Upon which Grant the said Register shall endorse that the party hath title to the same, whereupon it shall be signed by the Governor, Sealed with the Seal of the commonwealth and then entered of Record at full length in Books to be provided and kept for that purpose by the Register at the Public expence and being so entered shall be certified to have been registered and then be delivered to the party or his Order. A copy of such Record duly attested by the said Register shall be legal evidence of such Grant in all cases.

So much of all former Acts of Assembly as direct the mode of proceeding in any case provided for by this Act are hereby repealed.

Tr (Vi). 16-page Ms. in a clerk's hand, endorsed by GM: "A Bill for establishing a Land Office & ascertaining the Terms & Manner of granting Waste or Unappropriated Lands." Another copy is in the Jefferson Papers, DLC, from which an annotated text has been printed in Boyd, II, 139–154.

Although GM wrote James Mercer (6 Feb. 1778) that he was the author of this bill, it was in all likelihood the joint product of a subcommittee of two: Jefferson and GM. On 13 Dec. the House of Delegates approved GM's resolution which called for the sale of unappropriated lands to discharge the public debt and for the establishment of a land office. Thomas Nelson was chairman of the committee named to implement the resolution, but all the evidence indicates that it was Jefferson and GM who undertook the burden of drafting a bill. The Jefferson draft probably represents the bill in a more advanced stage, as its text is closer to that of the final act than this clerk's copy, and both bear changes in GM's hand. Dr. Boyd's editorial note prefacing this bill and the companion measure for settling land titles points out the emasculations made during the long legislative battle for enactment of both bills. On 8 Jan. 1778 GM brought the bill onto the floor; it passed two readings and was assigned to the committee of the whole. Other business caused postponements until mid-January, when the measure was rescheduled for consideration "the last day of March next"—in effect tabling the bill for that session, since it was to end within a week's time (JHD, 1827 ed., 17 Jan. 1778 entry). On the final day, GM salvaged what he could with a resolution that delayed the sale of western lands and specified a 400-acre limitation on such sales when they were resumed (JHD, 1827 ed., 24 Jan. entry). This resolution passed, and GM was convinced that the matter would finally be settled that spring. From GM's viewpoint he was concerned both with creating a fund to retire the state's mounting debt, and at the same time protecting the Ohio Company claims to western lands. Hence his additional 24 Jan. resolution, which also passed the House, that declared all claimants to "any unpatented Lands on the said Western Waters by Order of Council" would have a distant deadline for presentation of their claims. This implicit recognition of royal land grants was important to GM, who now left Williamsburg satisfied that both the commonwealth and the Ohio Company (he was still its treasurer and driving force) had been well served. However, GM was to be disappointed, for the May session of the General Assembly postponed action on the western land bill again (JHD, 1827 ed., 25 May entry), and nothing was done until that fall. The bill was re-introduced on 17 Nov. 1778, two days before GM had arrived at the session, and was again shunted aside for reasons that remain obscure. At the spring session of 1779 the measure was again revived, and a committee to draft the bill included GM and Jefferson. On 17 June it finally passed the House. That bill differed somewhat from the original, and some of the unique, liberal features had been lost along the way. Although the 1779 act has been criticized for being restrictive of the small settler and generous to the speculator, the original Jefferson-GM bill was designed to encourage the family unit, even the newly-wedded couple, in the quest for a farm. If the 1779 act was "a colossal mistake" (Abernethy, *Western Lands*, 228), because it favored "absentee speculators," the blame must lay with the many delegates who resisted the liberalizing tendencies of the bill introduced by GM on 8 Jan. 1778. Gone from the act as passed was the ENCOURAGEMENT OF FOREIGNERS and the provision of 75 acres for every native free-born Virginian who took a mate. Missing also was the section recognizing the validity of importation certificates (GM had speculated in these so-called headrights granting 50 acres). Another omission of consequence was the paragraph which recognized that SOME OF THE UNITED AMERICAN STATES MAY NOT HAVE WITHIN THEIR RESPECTIVE TERRITORIES WASTE AND UNAPPROPRIATED LANDS. This generous provision had been written at about the same time the Articles of Confederation had been read and passed by the General Assembly (JHD, 1827 ed., 9, 17 Dec. entries), and this section dealt with the sensitive western land holdings which would keep Maryland out of the Confederation until 1781 (Sosin, *Revolutionary Frontier*, 156). Whereas this bill permitted the county clerk to issue land warrants, the 1779 act granted this authority solely to the Register of the Land Office, "a change which manifestedly gave advantage to the large operator who could afford to keep one or more representatives on hand at such an office" (Boyd, II, 137). Other provisions of the amended act, such as that which allowed an extra five acres in every hundred surveyed "for the variation of instruments," seemed calculated to help the speculator rather than the bona fide settler. As it turned out, GM had more luck in protecting his bill on settling and adjusting land titles from legislative onslaughts, for in its wayward course from 14 Jan. 1778 until final passage in June 1779 it was essentially unimpaired. The 1779 land office act is printed in Hening, X, 50–65.

The portion in angle brackets is in GM's handwriting. The words in double brackets were bracketed in the Ms. Blank portions of the text were filled at some later date. The first, setting the Register's bond, was fixed at £50,000. The second blank was filled with £40 as the cost for 100 acres. The third blank, fixing the percentage of the county clerk's fee for issuing warrants, was deleted in the final act.

Receipt for Commonwealth Funds

28 December 1777. Acknowledgment of receipt of £62 2s.6d. from the Virginia treasury for transmittal to William Weston of £3 "for a Gun furnished Capt. [George] Mason's Minute Comp . . . to William Thompson seven pounds 10/ for pay &c of Militia Compy . . . [to] William Mason eight pounds 11/11 for pay &c. of his Militia Company C. C. Also one pound 8/6 per Ferriages to the Army," presumably for GM's Occoquan Ferry, and £41.12.0 to GM for his "attendance &c. on the Assembly as Delegates from Fairfax." In a clerk's hand but signed by GM.

FC (NNP).

To George Rogers Clark

SIR   Williamsburg Janry. 3d. 1778.

As some Indian Tribes, to the westward of the Mississippi, have lately, without any Provocation, massacred many of the Inhabitants upon the frontiers of this Commonwealth, in the most cruel &

barbarous Manner, & it is intended to revenge the Injury & punish the Aggressors by carrying the War into their own Country

We congratulate you upon your Appointment to conduct so important an Enterprize in which we most heartily wish you Success; and we have no Doubt but some further Reward in Lands, in that Country, will be given to the Volunteers who shall engage in this Service, in addition to the usual Pay: if they are so fortunate [as] to succeed, we think it just & reasonable that each Volunteer entering as a common Soldier in this Expedition, shou'd be allowed three hundred Acres of Land, & the Officers in the usual Proportion, out of the Lands which may be conquered in the Country now in the Possession of the said Indians; so as not to interfere with the Claims of any friendly Indians, or of any People willing to become Subjects of this Commonwealth; and for this we think you may safely confide in the Justice & Generosity of the Virginia Assembly. We are Sir Yr. most Hble Servts.

G: WYTHE
G MASON
TH: JEFFERSON

RC (ICU). Two pages in GM's hand, signed by the three-man legislative committee. Addressed: "To George Rogers Clarke Esqr" and endorsed by Clark with the date, and "abt. Expedition" and "Jeffersons handwriting" in an unknown hand.

Clark talked with Gov. Henry late in 1777 about his plan to conquer the Illinois country and Henry seems to have passed the idea along to Wythe, Jefferson, and GM. Clark appears to have proposed a western expedition that was ostensibly raised TO REVENGE THE INJURY & PUNISH THE AGGRESSORS, but in all likelihood the ulterior motive was the expulsion of the British from the Ohio country north to Canada through seizure of Kaskaskia and Detroit. "Clark's motives for the secret expedition are not clear" (Sosin, *Revolutionary Frontier*, 117), but the strengthened claim of Virginia to the northwest region was bound to result. GM was not disinterested in the outcome, since the Ohio Company claim would be jeopardized in any other circumstance. Henry, empowered by the House to use troops against "western enemies" (JHD, 1827 ed., 10 Dec. entry), ordered Virginia troops under Clark to proceed to the Illinois country. Clark reported on the expedition in considerable detail in a letter to GM dated 19 Nov. 1779 from the Falls of the Ohio (*q.v.*). Details are found in James Alton James, ed., *George Rogers Clark Papers* (Springfield, Ill., 1912–1916), and James's *Life of George Rogers Clark* (Chicago [1928]).

An Act to Prevent Excessive and Deceitful Gaming

[[*6 Jan. 1778.* GM was ordered to carry this act to the Senate, but it was never enacted at this session. It was probably meant as a revision of the 1748 act bearing the same title (HENING, VI, 76–81). Possibly this is the act finally approved by the Oct. 1779 session of the General Assembly

(Hening, X, 205–207), with a variation in the text in Boyd, II, 559–561. Such a measure was listed on the Committee of Revisors' "Catalogue of Bills" and may have been the joint product of Wythe, Jefferson, and GM. There was some public pressure for an antigambling bill in the fall of 1777. An anonymous essayist in the 21 Nov. 1777 *Va. Gaz.* (Dixon & Hunter) suggested that the country's troubles were chargeable to the wicked practice of gambling. The writer urged the General Assembly to pass a law which would call for the arrest of any gambler, who would immediately be "deemed a soldier, to all intents and purposes, and dealt with accordingly." The bill has not been found.]]

A Bill to Regulate Smallpox Inoculations

[12 January 1778]

Whereas the Small-pox, at this time in many parts of the Commonwealth is likely to spread and become general, and it hath been proved by incontestible experience that the late discovery's and Improvements therein have produced great Benefits to Mankind, by rendering a Distemper, which taken in the common way is always dangerous and often fatal, comparatively mild and safe by Inoculation, and the Act for regulating the Inoculation of the small-pox having been found, in many Instances, inconvenient and Injurious ⟨makes it necessary that the same shou'd be amended:⟩ Be it therefore enacted by the General Assembly, that any person ⟨having first obtained in writing to be attested by two Witnesses, the Consent of a Majority of the housekeepers residing within two Miles & not separated by a River or Creek half a Mile wide &⟩ conforming to the following Rules and regulations, may Inoculate or be Inoculated for the small-pox, either in his or her own house, or at any other place. No patient in the small pox shall remove from the House where he or she shall have the Distemper, or shall go abroad into the Company of any person who hath not before had the small-pox or been Inoculated, or go into any Public Road where Travellers usually pass, without retiring out of the same, or giving notice, upon the Approach of any passenger, until such Patient hat recovered from the Distemper, and hath been so well cleansed in his or her person and Cloths as to be perfectly free from Infection, under the Penalty of forty shillings for every offence; to be recovered, if committed by a married Woman from her Husband, if by an Infant from the Parent or Guardian, and if by a Servant or Slave from the Master or Mistress.

Every Physician, Doctor or other person, undertaking Inoculation at any House, shall cause a Written Advertisement to be put up at the nearest public Road, or other most notorious adjacent place, giving information that the small pox is at such House, and shall continue to keep the same set up, so long as the Distemper or any Danger of Infection remains there under the Penalty of forty shillings for every day that the same shall be omitted or neglected; to be paid by the Physician or Doctor, if the offence shall be committed when he is present, or by the Master, Mistress, Manager or principal person of the Family respectively, if the offence is committed in the absence of the Physician or Doctor. Every Physician Doctor or other person, undertaking Inoculation at any Public place or Hospital for the Reception of Patients, shall before he discharges the Patients, or suffers them to be removed from thence, take due care that their persons and Cloths are sufficiently cleansed, and shall give such Patients respectively a Certificate under his hand, that in his Opinion they are free from all Danger of spreading the Infection; under the Penalty of three pounds for every offence; and every person wilfully giving a false Certificate shall be subject to the Penalty of Ten pounds. If any person who hath not had the small-pox, other than those who have been or intended to be inoculated, shall go into any House where the small-pox then is, or intermix with the Patients, and return from thence, any Justice of the Peace of the County, on due proof thereof, may be Warrant cause such person to be conveyed to the next Hospital where the small pox is, there to remain until he or she shall have gone thro' the Distemper, or until the Physician or Manager of the Hospital shall certify that in his Opinion such person can not take the same; And if such person shall not be able to pay the necessary expences, the same shall be paid by the County. Every person wilfully endeavouring to spread or propagate the small pox, without Inoculation, or by Inoculation in any other Manner than is allowed by this Act or by the said recited Act in special Cases shall be subject [to] the Penalty of five hundred pounds, or suffer six Months Imprisonment without Bail or Mainprize. All the Penalties inflicted by this Act may be recovered with Costs by Action of Debt or Information in any Court of Record, where the Sum exceeds five pounds, or where it is under, or amounts to that Sum only by Petition in the Court of the County where the offence shall be committed, and shall be one half to the Informer, and the other half to the Commonwealth, or the whole to the Commonwealth, where prosecution shall be first instituted on the Public behalf alone.

So much of the act of General Assembly intituled "An Act to regulate the Inoculation of the small pox within this Colony" as contains any thing contrary to or within the Purview of this Act, is hereby repealed.

Ms (Vi). Two pages in a clerk's handwriting, endorsed and noted: "1778. Jan: 12. Read the first Time. Jan: 14. Read the 2d time & comm[itte]d to Com[mittee]: of the whole."

GM was chairman of the committee appointed on 27 Dec. 1777 to draft legislation that would amend the harsh 1769 act that levied a £1,000 fine on persons bringing "variolous or infectious matter" into the colony for inoculations but allowed licensed inoculations (Hening, VIII, 371-374). Eight others, including Jefferson, were appointed to the committee but GM's recent experience as an inoculated father of nine gave him unique qualification for fashioning a revision of the antiquated statute. The smallpox epidemic in Virginia during 1777 certainly gave the measure an urgency lacking in more peaceful days. Jefferson's contribution to the bill is uncertain, although Boyd indicates in *The Papers of Thomas Jefferson* (II, 124n) that portions of the preamble "have an indubitable Jeffersonian ring. . . ." GM's emendations on the clerk's copy, along with his carrying of the approved bill to the Senate, makes his major role in the legislation unquestionable (JHD, 1828 ed., 12 Jan. 1778 entry).

The portions in angle brackets are in GM's hand. The bill as finally approved merely changed GM's specification for householders not separated by fresh waters to read "not separated by a river, creek or marsh, a quarter of a mile wide" (Hening, IX, 371-373). It is titled: "An act to amend an act intituled an act to regulate the Inoculation of the Smallpox within this colony."

Resolution Warning British of Retaliation Measures against Prisoners-of-War

[13 January 1778]

Resolved, therefore, nemine contra dicente, That the Speaker of both Houses of Assembly, be empowered and desired to recommend this subject to the immediate attention of the honorable the American Congress, and submit it to their wisdom, whether it is not now become necessary to set apart and reserve a proper number of British prisoners, and to give the enemy due notice that they shall share the same treatment, and suffer whatever punishment shall be inflicted upon the American prisoners in Great Britain; and that in the mean time they will be pleased to direct their agents in Europe to make proper provision for the support of the said Capt. Harris and Capt. Dick, or any other officers, soldiers or sailors, citizens of this Commonwealth, who now are, or hereafter may be, prisoners in Great Britain or Ireland, the charge of which this Commonwealth will make good.

Printed from JHD, 1827 ed., 13 Jan. entry. The Ms resolution has not been found.

The resolution was preceded by a report that Virginia captains John Harris and Alexander Dick were "now under close confinement in Gosport or some other jail in England," had been treated cruelly, and were to be tried as traitors. The preamble further declared that "nothing can restrain our implacable and bloody enemies . . . but a full and firm execution of the laws of retaliation. . . ." Americans were divided in their reaction to the parole granted to British troops under Burgoyne on 17 Oct. 1777, which allowed almost 5,000 enemy soldiers to embark for England "on condition that they would not again participate in the American war" (Nettels, *Roots of American Civilization*, 703). This action seemed all the more foolish to Virginians because the Virginia 9th Regiment attached to Washington's army had been battered at Germantown on 4 Oct. 1777 and many of its ranking officers captured, to be later interned on Long Island (Boyd, III, 388–390). "I hear some Gentleman was Shagreened at Burgoyne and Company being suffered to return on Parole to Britain and not confined here," was Edmund Pendleton's understatement (letter to William Woodford, 8 Nov. 1777, Mays, ed., *Papers of Edmund Pendleton*, I, 235). GM was ordered to carry the resolution to the Senate, hence the presumption that he was its author, although his Ms. has not been located.

A Bill for Settling Land Titles

[14 January 1778]

WHEREAS the various and vague claims to unpattented Lands under the former Government, covering the greater part of the Country on the Western Waters, may produce tedious and infinite Litigation and disputes, and in the mean time Purchasers would be discouraged from taking up Lands upon the Terms lately prescribed by Law, whereby the Fund to be raised in Aid of the Taxes for discharging the Public Debt would be in a great measure, frustrated; And it is just and necessary, as well for the peace of Individuals, as for the Public Weal, that some certain Rules should be Established for setling and determining the Rights to such Lands, and fixing the Principles upon which such Claimers shall be entitled to Patents; to the End that subsequent Purchasers and Adventurers may be enabled to Act with greater Certainty and Safety. Be it enacted by the General Assembly that all Surveys heretofore made by any sworn surveyor, acting under Commission from the Masters of William & Mary College, and founded either upon Charter Importation Rights duly proved and certified according to ancient Usuage, upon Treasury Rights for money paid the late Receiver General, upon Entry's made with the Surveyor of any County for Tracts of Land not exceeding four hundred Acres, according to Act of Assembly upon any Order of Council or regular Entry in the Council Books, or upon any Warrant from the Governor for the time being, for Military Service in Virtue of any Proclamation either from the King of Great Britain or any former Governor of Virginia, shall be good and valid; but that all Surveys for Waste and unpatented Lands made by any other person, or upon any other pretence whatsover, shall be, and are hereby declared null and Void; And that all and every person or persons, his her or their heirs or Assigns, claiming Lands upon any of the before recited Rights & under Surveys made as herein before mentioned, shall upon the Plats and Certificates of such Surveys being returned into the Land Office, together with the Rights, Entry, Order or Warrant upon which they were respectively founded, be entitled to a Patent or Patents for the same; Provided that such Surveys ⟨and Rights⟩ be returned to the said Office within   Months next after the end of this present Session of Assembly: and where two or more persons shall claim the same Land under different Surveys, the person claiming under that Survey which was first actually made shall have the Preference. That all persons their heirs or Assigns claiming Lands under the Charter and ancient Custom of Virginia, upon Importation Rights duly proved and Certified in any Court of Record before the Passing of this Act, as also those claiming under Treasury Rights for money paid the Receiver General   or under Proclamation-Warrants for Military service, and not having located or fixed such Lands by actual Surveys as herein before mentioned, shall be admitted to new Warrants and Entries for the same in the manner directed by the Act intitled an Act for Establishing a Land Office and ascertaining the Terms and manner of granting waste unappropriated Lands upon Producing to the Register of the said Office   the proper Certificates, proofs or Warrants, as the case is, for their respective Rights, within   Months after the End of the present Session of Assembly. [The next four lines of the Ms have been marked to indicate a future entry.] And be it enacted that all Orders of Council or Entries for Land in the Council Books upon the Western Waters except so far as such Orders on entries respectively have been carried into execution by Actual Surveys in manner herein before mentioned, shall be, and they are hereby declared void & of no Effect. And that no claim to Land within this Commonwealth for Military service, founded upon the King of Great Britain's Proclamation in the Year One thousand seven hundred and sixty three, shall hereafter be allowed; except a Warrant for the same shall have been obtained from the Governor of Virginia, during the former Government, or where such service was performed in one of the Virginia Regiments; in which case such Claimant making due Proof thereof in any court of Record shall be admitted to a Warrant & Entry for the same in the manner herein before mentioned.

And whereas great numbers of People have settled in the Country upon the said Western Waters, upon waste and unappropriated Lands, for which they have hitherto been prevented from sueing out Patents, or obtaining legal Titles by the King of Great Britain's Proclamations or Instructions to his Governors, or by the late change of Government; and the present War having delayed, until now, the opening a Land Office, and the Establishment of any certain Terms for Granting Lands, and it is just that those settling under such Circumstances, and Guilty of no neglect or omission on their part, should have some reasonable allowance for the charge and Risque they have incurred, and that the property, so acquired should be secured to them; Be it therefore enacted that all persons, who at any time before the passing of this Act have really and bonafide settled themselves, or at his her or their charge have settled others, upon any waste or unappropriated Lands, to which no other person hath any legal Right or Claim, shall be allowed for every such Family or Settlement the Quantity of four hundred Acres of Land to include such settlement, and to every such Family as for their greater safety have settled themselves in Villages or Townships these shall be allowed their respective Improvements in such Village or Township, together with as much adjacent Land as will make up the like Quantity of four hundred Acres, each Family to have the Preferance in such Land as they have actually occupied, so far as the same can be done; for which Quantity's, to be adjusted ascertained and certified by the Commissioners to be appointed by this Act in manner herein after directed, they shall be respectively entitled ⟨to Warrants, & Entries with the⟩ Surveyor of the County, and upon the due return of the plat and Certificate of Survey, grants may and shall Issue to them & their Heirs according to the Rules & Regulations of the said office. And if any such Setlers shall desire to take up a greater Quantity of Land than is herein allowed them, they shall, on payment of the consideration money required from other purchasers, be entitled to the Preemption, of any greater Quantity of Land, adjoining to such Settlements, not exceeding one thousand Acres, and to which no other person hath any legal right or Claim.

All persons, who before the passing of this Act, ⟨have made regular Entries with the Surveyor of any County, for Lands on the said Western Waters to which no other Person hath a legal Right or Claim, & have not surveyed the same in Manner herein before mentioned, shall be entitled to the Pre-emption, at the State Price, of the Land so entered for; and those who〉 have marked out for themselves any Waste or unappropriated Lands, and made any Improvements theron, shall also be entitled to the pre-emption, upon the like Terms, of any Quantity of Land not exceeding two thousand Acres, to include such Improvements, or so much thereof to which no other person hath any legal Right or Claim: Provided they respectively demand 〈& prove their Claim to〉 such pre-emption, and take out their Warrants of Survey within   Months next after the end of this present session of Assembly, & thereafter duly comply with the Rules & Regulations of the Land Office.

And be it further enacted that all persons claiming Lands on the s[ai]d Western waters and sueing out Patents 〈upon Surveys heretofore made, either under Entries〉 with the Surveyor of any County, or under any Order of Council or Entry in the Council Books 〈& those claiming Tracts of Land not exceeding four hundred Acres hereinallowed〉 them in Consideration of their Settlements, shall be subject to the payment of the usual Composition Money, under the former Government, at the rate of ten shillings Sterling for every hundred Acres, to be discharged in Current Money at thirty three and one third percentum Exchange, and to no other Charge or Imposition whatsoever, save the common office fees.

And Whereas it is represented to this present General Assembly that upon the Lands surveyed for sundry Company's by Virtue of Orders of Council, many people have settled, under the faith of the Terms of Sale Publickly offered by the said Company's or their Agents at the Time of such Settlements, who have made Valuable Improvements thereon, and are now refused Titles to the Lands so Surveyed & Settled, or a much higher price demanded from them: For Remedy whereof, Be it declared & enacted that all persons so settled upon any Lands, except only such Lands as before the Settlement of the same were notoriously reserved by the Company for whom they were respectively surveyed for their own use, shall have their Titles confirmed to them by the Members of such Company's or their Agents, upon Payment of the price at which such Lands were offered for Sale, together with Interest thereon from the time of the respective Settlements.

〈And whereas the Claims of various Persons to the Lands herein allowed to the Inhabitants in Consideration of their Settlements, as well as of those who by this Act are entitled to Pre-emption at the State-Price, may occasion many Disputes, the Determination of which, depending upon Evidence which can not without great Charge & Trouble be collected but in the Neighbourhood of such

Lands, will be most speedily and properly made by Commissioners in the respective Counties.

Be it enacted that the Governor with the Advice of the privy Council may & he is hereby empowered to appoint by Commission under his Hand & Seal four of the most able & discreet Men in each & every County upon the western Waters (any three of whom may act) to continue in office six months from the End of this present Session of Assembly for the purpose of collecting adjusting & determining such claims. Every such Commissioner, before he enters on the Dutys of his Office, shall take the Oath of Fidelity to the Commonwealth, and the following Oath of Office "You shall swear that You will well & truly serve this Commonwealth in the Office of a Commissioner for the County of   for collecting & adjusting & setling the Claims & determining the Titles of such persons as claim Lands in the said County in consideration of having setled thereon, or of Such as claim Pre-emption to any Lands therein, under an Act of General Assembly entitled an Act for adjusting and setling the Titles of Claimers to unpatented Lands under the former Government; and that You will do equal Right to all Manner of People, without Respect of persons; You shall not take by Yourself, nor by any other Person, any Gift Fee or Reward for any Matter done or to be done by Virtue of Your Office, except such Fees or Sallery as the Law shall allow You; and finally in all things belonging to Your said Office, You shall faithfully justly & truly, according to the best of Your Skill & Judgement, do equal & impartial Justice, without Fraud Favour Affection or partiality" which oath shall be administered by any of the said Commissioners to the first of them in Nomination who shall be present, and then by him to the others.

The said Commissioners shall have power to hear & determine all Titles to Lands claimed in Consideration of Settlements made thereon, as also the Rights of all persons claiming Pre-emption to any Lands within their respective Countys, either for Entries made with the County Surveyor, or for the other Considerations mentioned in this Act, and shall imediatly upon Receipt of their Commissions, give at least twenty Days previous Notice by Advertisements at the Churches & Meeting Houses in their County, of the time & place at which they intend to meet, for the Purpose of collecting hearing & determining the said Claims & Titles, requiring all Persons interested therein to attend, & put in their Claims; and may adjourn from Place to Place, & Time to Time, as their business may require; but if they shou'd fail to meet at any time to which they shall have adjourn'd, neither their Commission, nor any matter depending before them shall be thereby discontinued, but they shall proceed to Business when they do meet, as if no such Failure had happened: they shall appoint & administer an Oath of Office to their Clerk, be attended by the Sherif, or one of the under Sherifs of the County, be empowered to administer all Oaths to Witnesses or others necessary for the Discharge of their Office, to punish Contempts in the same Manner as the County Court, & enforce good Behaviour in their presence; they shall have free Access to the County Surveyor's Books, & may order the same to be laid before them at any time or place of their sitting.

In all cases of Dispute, upon claims for settlement, the person who made the first actual Settlement, his or her Heirs or Assigns, shall have the Preferrence; and in all Disputes for the Right of Pre-emption on Entries made with the County Surveyor, the Person, his or her Heirs or Assigns, who made the first Entry.

The Clerk shall keep exact Minutes of all the Proceedings of the Commissioners, and enter the Names of all the Persons to whom either Lands for Settlement, or the right of Pre-emption, as the Case is, shall be adjudged, with their respective Quantitys & Locations. Upon application of any Person claiming a Right to any such Lands, and complaining that another pretends a Right in Opposition thereto, the said Clerk shall issue a Summons, stating the Nature of the Plaintiff's Claim, & calling on the Party opposing the same to appear at a time & place certain, therein to be named, & shew Cause why a Grant of the said Lands may not issue to the said Plaintiff: the said Summons shall be served on the Party by the Sherif of the County, & such Service being return'd thereon, & the Party appearing, or failing to appear, the Commissioners may proceed to Trial, or for good Cause shewn, may refer such Trial to a further Day. The Clerk shall also have Power, at the Request of either Party, to issue Subpaenas for witnesses, to appear at the Time & Place of trial; which shall be had in a summary Way, without pleadings in writing; and the Court, in conducting the said Trial, in all Matters of Evidence relative thereto, & in giving Judgement, shall govern themselves by such Rules & Principles of Law or Equity as are applicable to the Case, or wou'd be the Rule of Trial, of Evidence, or of Decision, were the same before the ordinary Courts of Law or Equity; save only so far as this Act shall otherwise have specially directed. Judgement, when rendered, shall be final, & shall give to the Party, in whose favour it is, a Title against all others who were Partys to the Trial; and if after such Judgement rendered, the Party against whom it is, shall enter the said Lands forcibly, or forcibly detain the same, it shall be lawful for the said Commissioners, or any one of them, or any Justice of the Peace for the County, to remove such Force, in like Manner as if it were committed on Lands holden by Grant actually issued.

The said Commissioners shall deliver to every Person to whom they shall adjudge Lands for Settlement, a Certificate thereof under their Hands, & attested by their Clerk, mentioning the Quantity, & describing as near as may be, the particular Location; noting also therein the Quantity of adjacent Land to which such Person shall have the Right of Pre-emption: and to every other person to whom they shall adjudge the right of Pre-emption to any Lands, they shall in like Manner deliver a Certificate specifying the Quantity & Location of such Land, with the Cause for Pre-emption; for every [delivery] of which Certificates, the Party receiving the same shall pay down to the Commissioners the Sum of ten Shillings, besides a fee of two Shillings & six Pence to the Clerk; And the said Certificates shall entitle the Persons respectively receiving them to an Entry & Survey, or Warrant for the said Lands in such way & such Terms as herein before prescribed upon producing the same to the Surveyor of the County, or to the Register of the Land Office, or to the Treasurer, or County Court Clerk, as the Case may require. The said Commissioners shall transmit to the Register of the Land Office, under their Hands & attested by their Clerk, an exact List or Schedule, in Alphabetical order, of all such Certificates by them granted, & a Duplicate, so signd and attested, to the County Surveyor, for their Information; and in order the more effectually to preserve to such Persons the priority & preferrence of Location, & the Benefit of Pre-emption, for & during the before mentioned Space of   Months from & after the passing of this Act.

The said Commissioners for every Day they shall be actually employed in Discharge of their office shall be allowed the Sum of   Shillings each; they shall be accountable for all the money they shall have received upon issueing Certificates as aforesaid, except the Fee to the Clerk, and shall settle a fair Account with the Treasurer; who is hereby empowered to pay them whatever Ballance may appear due to them thereon, and to receive from them any Ballance which shall be by them due to the Commonwealth.

The Clerk & Sherif shall receive, for their Services, the fees heretofore allowed by Law for the same Services in the County Court, to be paid by the Party, & collected in like Manner as is directed in the ordinary Cases of the same Nature; provided that the

Clerk shall not be allowed any further or other fee for entering and issueing a Certificate than is herein before mentioned.

When the Register of the Land Office shall make out any Grant or Patent to any person or persons for Lands due to him her or them in Virtue of this Act, He shall recite therein the Rights or Cause for which the same became due according to an Act of General Assembly "passed in the Year of our Lord one thousand seven hundred & seventy seven entitled an Act for adjusting and setling the Titles of Claimers to unpatented Lands under the former Government" and if any Part thereof is due in Consideration of purchase Money paid to the Commonwealth, the same shall be distinguished.

And whereas at the time of the late change of Government many caveats against Patents for Lands which had been entered in the Council-Office were depending & undetermined, Be it enacted that all such Caveats, together with the Documents & papers relating thereto, shall be removed into the Clerk's Office of the General Court, there to be proceeded on, tryed & determined in the manner directed by Law for future Caveats.)

Ms (Vi). Eleven pages, the first six in a clerk's handwriting and the remainder in GM's hand. Endorsed: "A Bill for adjusting & settling the Titles of Claimers to unpatented Lands under the former Government. 1778. Jan: 14. Read the first Time."

Although this bill came from the committee appointed 5 Jan. 1778 in the House of Delegates, it covered a range of subjects that had long commanded GM's attention. Jefferson "indubitably worked with Mason on the Bill" (Boyd, II, 137), but unlike the companion measure for establishing a Land Office, most of GM's favorite features in this legislation became law. The bill was read on 14 Jan. and was ready to be engrossed, which meant that it was close to final passage. Something went wrong, however, and on 24 Jan. the committee of the whole voted to table it. The pressures exerted by advocates of Richard Henderson's Transylvania claims or the Philadelphia-based Indiana claim cannot be measured with precision, but they must have been present. Henderson and Wharton had already presented their petitions, and another ostensibly from western settlers asked the General Assembly to set aside "the large Grants of Land formerly made by the King to certain Persons & Companies . . . [such] as the Ohio Company . . . and declare such of them void, as on enquiry and examination you find are . . . and make it known what Lands are grantable by this Commonwealth, and on what Terms . . ." (Miscellaneous petitions, 1776-1777, dated 6 Nov. 1777 [Vi]). Meanwhile, GM's ideas on the use of western land sales as a prop for the state's tottering economy had been accepted by the House, even though his and Jefferson's liberal terms of granting those lands had not (see the Bill for Establishing a Land Office, 13 Dec. 1777). As Jefferson recalled, in this bill for settling claims GM's "great object was to remove out of the way the great and numerous orders of council to the Ohio co. Loyal co. Misissipi co. Vandalia co. Indiana co. &c. and the thousands of entries for lands with surveyors of counties, which covered the whole Western country . . ." (quoted in Boyd, II, 138). At the same time, GM hoped to entrench his own claims for headright certificates, for he had speculated in them heavily after 1773 (22 June 1773, q.v.). As treasurer of the

Ohio Company, GM also wanted a final adjustment to the company's claims that dated back to 1749. Enactment of this bill would mean the eventual possession by GM personally and by the surviving Ohio Company partners generally of between 250,000 and 300,000 acres of western land. Understandably, GM was not inclined to let the legislative maneuver of 24 Jan. block his efforts, and accordingly he presented on that same day a resolution which delayed the issuance of western land titles until a Land Office had been established. A second resolution invited western land claimants to present their credentials (i.e., evidence of grants made by orders from the royal governors and councils) during the ensuing spring. These resolutions passed, and left GM satisfied that at long last the Ohio Company matter could be settled. To that end, GM wrote James Mercer and suggested an early meeting of the company partners (6 Feb. 1778). The bill took care of other land claimants with equal generosity, of course, but the provisions upholding CHARTER IMPORTATION RIGHTS DULY PROVED and admitting NEW WARRANTS AND ENTRIES FOR THE SAME were of direct benefit to GM. On the other hand, the effort to permit bona fide western settlers to claim 400 acres and HAVE THE PREFERRANCE IN SUCH LAND AS THEY HAVE ACTUALLY OCCUPIED was a magnanimous gesture. The STATE-PRICE, OF THE LAND SO ENTERED was fixed at £40 per 100 acres by the Land Office act of 1779. THE USUAL COMPOSITION MONEY was the long-standing royal fee of 10 shillings per 100 acres, paid at the time a royal land title was issued and a primary source of revenue UNDER THE FORMER GOVERNMENT. The exception for settlement of lands NOTORIOUSLY RESERVED BY THE COMPANY would have given strength to any speculators, such as the Ohio or Transylvania companies, that had already surveyed western lands. The section dealing with the appointment and functions of a COMMISSION . . . FOR THE PURPOSE OF COLLECTING ADJUSTING AND DETERMINING SUCH CLAIMS is entirely in GM's handwriting and may have been his sole responsibility. The broad powers granted to the commissioners, including the provision that JUDGEMENT, WHEN RENDERED, SHALL BE FINAL, were somewhat curbed in the act as adopted. Nonetheless, the quasi-judicial body was soon to be criticized in a remark that could have been pointedly directed at GM. "Tryal by Jury is held sacred in their bill of rights," a Pennsylvanian noted, "and is totally taken away by this law" (quoted in Boyd, III, 208). Despite GM's optimism, the bill was not passed in the next session, but again postponed until the fall session of 1778. GM served on the committee charged with bringing in the bill, and an amended version was presented in Mar. 1779. A variety of further amendments, including one which set up districts for hearings by the commissioners, was agreed upon before final passage in June 1779 (JHD, 1827 ed., 17 May, 21 June 1779 entries). The act with its amendments is found in Hening, X, 35–50.

GM's corrections on the first six pages and his full text from page seven onward are enclosed in angle brackets. The corrections by Jefferson and a collation of the draft Ms with the act as adopted will be found in Boyd, II, 155–167. Dr. Boyd believes that the 1777 date in the draft Ms, in GM's hand, is proof that this bill and that for establishing a Land Office "were written at least as early as the Oct. 1777 session, perhaps being drawn before the session was convened" (ibid., 167).

An Act "to prevent private persons from issuing bills of credit in the nature of paper currency"

[22–23 January 1778]

I. WHEREAS divers persons have presumed, upon their own private security, to issue bills of credit, or notes payable to the bearer, in the nature of paper currency, which may tend to the deception and loss of individuals, as well as to the great injury of the publick, by increasing the quantity of money in circulation, already exceeding the present medium of commerce:

II. *Be it therefore enacted by the General Assembly,* That every person who, from and after the passing of this act, shall, without authority from the legislature of this commonwealth, issue, or offer in payment, any bill of credit, or note for any sum of money payable to the bearer, shall forfeit and pay ten time the sum of every such bill of credit, or note payable to the bearer, so issued or offered in payment, to be recovered with costs, by warrant from any justice of the peace where the penalty shall not exceed the sum of twenty five shillings, by petition in the county court where the penalty shall be more than twenty five shillings and shall not exceed the sum of five pounds, or by action of debt or information in any court of record where the penalty shall be above the sum of five pounds; one moiety whereof to the informer, and the other moiety to the use of the county where the offence shall be committed, towards lessening the county levy, or the whole to the use of the county where the prosecution shall be first instituted, on behalf of the county only.

III. *And be it farther enacted,* That any justice of the peace for the county where such offence shall be committed may, and he is hereby empowered and required, either upon his own knowledge or information, and due proof thereof made, to require any person issuing or offering in payment any such bill of credit, or note payable to the bearer, to give bond with sufficient security, in the sum of five hundred pounds, for his good behaviour, and upon refusal or neglect to commit such offender to prison, there to remain until he shall give security accordingly; and if the offender shall thereafter issue or offer in payment any such bill of credit, or note payable to the bearer, the same shall be adjudged a breach of the good behaviour, and forfeiture of the bond.

Printed from Hening, IX, 431–432.

Circumstances make it appear that GM was acknowledged by his House colleagues as their leading authority on financial matters. In the absence of specific evidence, it can only be conjectured that the private BILLS OF CREDIT had been issued by merchants who were exasperated with the depreciating state and continental currency issues and thus resorted to issuing script promissory notes. Certainly such devices have been common in American history during times of financial stress. Whatever the situation, the measure was brought before the House of Delegates in the final rush toward adjournment. GM was appointed chairman of a committee to prepare the bill on 17 Jan., he presented the measure on 22 Jan., and he carried the approved bill to the Senate on the following day (JHD, 1827 ed., 23 Jan. 1778 entry). The other committee members were Edmund Pendleton and Isaac Zane. Private bills of credit are not mentioned in Henry Phillips, Jr., *Historical Sketches of the Paper Currency* . . . (Roxbury, Mass., 1865–1866) although a section treats Virginia emissions (193–210). The state may have feared competition from trustworthy individuals whose pledge of personal credit was more substantial than the meager support for the authorized commonwealth treasury notes. These were "virtually identical with bills of credit, and secured by no real provision for redemption by taxes" (Allan Nevins, *The American States during and After the Revolution, 1775–1789* [New York, 1924], 486). Nevins points out the irresponsible conduct of the General Assembly was evidenced by "the spring of 1777 [when] we find one [emission] for a million dollars; between the fall of 1780 and the spring of 1781 they aggregated £45,000,000." Counterfeiting added to the problem, of course, and although GM and others had faith in the leavening effects of a tax and land-sale program, by late 1781 the House made of paper money collapsed with "a sweeping measure of repudiation" with old bills redeemed at a ratio of 1,000:1 (*ibid.*). As Ferguson observes in *Power of the Purse* (p. 31), it was simpler to issue paper money than to collect taxes. GM, as an advocate of fiscal responsibility, may have become involved on this bill simply because the state's slender financial resources had to be guarded jealously. Had banknotes such as those Robert Morris later issued been in circulation in Virginia, their effect on state currency would have been an undermining of state credit.

Resolutions Declaring the Western Lands Shall Be Sold to Create a Sinking Fund for the Public Debt, After Establishment of a Land Office

[24 January 1778]

Whereas it is of the greatest Importance to this Common Wealth that the waste & unappropriated Lands, to which no Person hath any just Claim, shou'd be disposed of, for the Purpose of creating a sinking Fund, in aid of the Taxes, for discharging the public Debt; and to the End that the Claims to unpatented Lands under the former or present Government may not in the mean time be encreased or strengthened—

Resolved that every Entry with the County Surveyor, or Survey hereafter made in the Country upon the western Waters, under any Pretence or Title whatsoever, until a Land Office shall be established, and the Manner and Terms of granting waste and unappropriated Lands ascertained, shall be voided & of no Effect; and that no Person hereafter setling in the Country upon the said western Waters shall be entitled to any Land, or Pre-emption of Land for such Settlement.

Resolved also that all Persons claiming any unpatented Lands on the said western waters by order of Council shall lay the same before the General Assembly, on or before the 20th. Day of their

next Session, & be at Liberty, in the Mean time, to take the Depositions of any Witnesses they may chuse to examine to [support] such
Claims; giving reasonable Notice thereof to the Person appointed by
the Governor & Council to attend such Examination in the County,
on Behalf of the Common Wealth in Case such Person shall be
appointed.

Ms (Vi). Two pages in GM's hand, with dated endorsements by the clerks
of both House and Senate. In another handwriting the measure has been titled:
"Reso[lutio]n Prohibiting Entries for & Settlement on vacant Lands on the
Western Waters until the establishment of a Land Office/Octo[ber session]
1777."

Shortly before GM introduced these resolutions, he and Jefferson had been
designated as a kind of informal committee-of-two charged with receiving and
presumably reporting on the land claims of Richard Henderson and the
Indiana Company (JHD, 1827 ed., 24 Jan. entry). Earlier in the session (24 Nov.
1777), the House had kept the Henderson claims alive by ordering a hearing
for the indefatigable speculator on the May 1778 calendar. Still earlier, the 1776
Convention appointed 15 commissioners "to take and collect evidence in behalf
of Virginia against persons pretending to have claims for lands within the
territory thereof, under deeds & purchases from the Indians" (Palmer, ed., *Cal.
of Va. State Papers*, I, 272). In contention were Henderson's disputed purchase
from the Cherokees at Fort Watauga in 1775, and a petition from the Indiana
Company of Pennsylvania on 1 Oct. 1776 upholding its claims under the
Treaty of Fort Stanwix. Neither GM nor Jefferson were impartial spectators
to the struggle, for GM was heavily involved in promoting the rival claims of
the Ohio Company against the Indiana Company, while Jefferson "hoped to
befriend the individual settler and to block some of the schemes of the
proprietary interests" (Boyd, II, 64). GM was headed toward a bitter war of
words with the Wharton interests in Philadelphia, but for the moment he was
more concerned with holding back settlement until his plan for paying off the
public debt could be perfected. Both Jefferson and GM had been appointed to
the House committee charged with devising a method of "supporting the credit
of the paper money issued . . . [and] discharging the public debt" through
taxes and western land sales (JHD, 1827 ed., 13 Dec. 1777 entry). GM brought
out a Land Office bill on 8 Jan. 1778 (*q.v.*) that appeared headed for passage
along with a companion measure "for adjusting and setling titles to unpatented
lands," but after passing their first and second readings the two bills were
shelved by a parliamentary stratagem. Defeated on the main proposition, GM
and perhaps Jefferson had enough persuasive power left to bring passage of
these resolutions, and although the session ended that same day (24 Jan. 1778),
GM was optimistic about passage of the main bills at the next session. Possibly
one reason for the delay was that the business of collecting evidence on
Henderson's Transylvania project continued (see Palmer, *Cal. of Va. State
Papers*, I, 273–275, 276–298, 303–311, 315; and Boyd, II, 65–110). Final passage of
the land office and title adjustment bills did not come until the spring of 1779.

The resolutions printed in the JHD, 1827 ed., 24 Jan. 1778 entry, vary slightly
from GM's Ms. In the first resolution, the House deleted the words "County
Surveyor, or" and "ascertained." In the second resolution "also" was deleted. A
clerk had written in the words "with[ou]t. paying for the same such Consideration as shall be hereafter ascertained by the General Assembly, so as no family
be entitled to more than 400 acres" after the end of GM's first resolution and
this was added in the printed version. The use of the ampersand, as well as
GM's spelling and capitalization, were also altered in the printed text.

An Act to Extend the Time for Drafting the Militia

[24 January 1778]

WHEREAS the continuance of this session of assembly, beyond the time it was expected to adjourn, hath made it necessary to enlarge the time in the remote counties appointed for making draughts of the militia, pursuant to the act "For speedily recruiting the Virginia regiments on the continental establishment, and for raising additional troops of volunteers:"

Be it therefore enacted by the General Assembly, That in each county to the westward or north westward of the mountains called the Blue Ridge, the county lieutenant, or commanding officer of the militia thereof, be empowered and required to summon the field officers, captains, and first lieutenants of his militia, to meet at the courthouse, for the purposes of the said act, at any time within fifteen days after he shall have received notice of the said act, although the same be after the second Monday in February next, and thereupon such farther proceedings shall be had, and all persons subjected to the penalties for neglect or breach of duty, as in the said act is directed and prescribed.

Printed from Hening, IX, 433. The full title: "An act to enlarge the time for making draughts of the militia to recruit the Virginia regiments in the continental service."

GM carried this bill to the Senate on 24 Jan. 1778, although it was introduced by Pendleton the preceding day. The Ms of the act is not in GM's hand (Vi), but it was probably a joint effort inasmuch as the point was to aid George Rogers Clark in filling the ranks of a western expedition. Gov. Henry authorized Clark to enroll 350 men, but the detachment which finally embarked for the Ohio country contained only "one hundred & seventy or eighty men" (Hutchinson-Rachal, I, 261, 262*n*).

To James Mercer

Stafford County, Colo. Lee's,
DEAR SIR. Febry. 6th. 1778.

I fully intended to have taken Fredericksburg in my Way from the Assembly, & spent an Evening with you & my Friend Mr. Dick; but was disappointed, by the Accident of my Servant's falling sick on the Road; which detained me four or five Days at Hubbard's & obliged me, at last, to leave him behind me, & hire a Servant to this Place.

I brought in a Bill, this last Session, for establishing a Land-Office,

& ascertaining the Terms & Manner of granting waste & unappropriated Lands, to create a sinking Fund, in Aid of the Taxes, for
discharging the Public Debt; and another for adjusting & setling the
Titles of Claimers to unpatented Land under the former Government: they are both put off for the present; but will undoubtedly be
taken up, & I hope finally setled, in the next Session; & as there will
only be a short time allowed to the previous Claimers, to put in their
respective claims, & sue out Patents, after which they will be bar'd,
it is incumbent upon the Members of the Ohio Company to take the
proper preparatory Steps for making good their Title & obtaining a
Patent for the 200,000 Acres actually surveyed; which is all I have
any Hopes of & that I think is upon such a Foundation, as that
Nothing but our own Negligence can deprive us of it: it is an
Object of sufficient Importance I think to engage our Attention,
being equal, by all Accounts of it, to any Land on this Continent:
there are however some very considerable Difficultys in putting this
Business into a proper Train; which I have not Room to explain in a
common Letter. Your advice & Assistance, both as a Lawyer & a
Friend, will be much wanted, & I flatter myself if you, Colo.
Thomas Lee, & myself cou'd spend two or three Days together on
the Subject, we cou'd reduct it to Order, & we might then call a
Meeting of the Company, which otherwise wou'd answer no good
End. Colo. Lee has promised me to come up to my House, in a few
Days, on this Occasion, & will endeavour to make the time conven-
ient to you; I must intreat you to accompany him, & as this a mere
Matter of Business, & I dare say will prove a troublesome one, I shall
readily pay on the Company's Acct. such charge as you think
reasonable.

I beg to be kindly remembered to Mrs. Mercer & my Young
Relations; [and] am Dr Sir Yr affecte. Kinsman & obdt. Servt.

G MASON

RC (Gunston Hall). Four-page Ms, endorsed [by Mercer?]: "Mason George
Feby. 1778 Abt Ohio Compy Lands
  GM 1½ shares
  JM   estate ½
         2 shares."

The General Assembly session ended on 24 Jan. 1778. GM appears to have
traveled overland from Benjamin HUBBARD's home in Caroline County to
Thomas Ludwell Lee's plantation without skirting Fredericksburg, where MY
FRIEND MR. Charles DICK was one of the managers of a state-operated arsenal.
The bills FOR ESTABLISHING A LAND-OFFICE and for fixing THE TERMS & MANNER OF
GRANTING WASTE & UNAPPROPRIATED LANDS (see JHD, 1827 ed., 13 Dec. 1777 and 14
Jan. 1778 entries) were postponed again at the May 1778 session, and did not
become law until June 1779. Faced by the delay, GM had written a resolution

that was almost certainly fashioned with the Ohio Company in mind. This resolution, which passed the General Assembly on 24 Jan., was a notice to "all Persons claiming any unpatented Lands on the . . . western waters by order of Council" to lay their claims before the General Assembly during its next session. As treasurer of the Ohio Company, GM had already ordered surveys in the Ohio country and believed that these could at long last be validated, a feat made impossible by British land policy after 1763. Mercer had inherited an interest in the Company from his father, John Mercer, which was noted on the endorsement. Whether the projected meeting with COLO. THOMAS LEE was ever held is conjectural, for Thomas Ludwell Lee became ill around 1 Mar. and died on 13 Apr. 1778. Accustomed to misfortune in Ohio Company affairs, GM proceeded to advertise a meeting of the shareholders for 18 May (*Va. Gaz.* [Purdie], 24 Apr. 1778).

GM first wrote "my little Cousins," but crossed it through and settled for MY YOUNG RELATIONS (Mercer and GM were first cousins). The text in Rowland, I, 291–292 is modernized.

From the Privy Council of Virginia

[[*16 Apr. 1778.* The privy council proceedings for this date state that "at the request of Mr. Bowdoin, one of the owners of the Ship Custis it is agreed that the Tobacco belonging to this State on Board the said Ship may be relanded—And the Lieutenant Governor is advised to direct the Public Agent to receive the Tobacco & safely store it in Proper houses till further orders. A Letter was written to Col. George Mason respecting the said Tobacco a Copy of which is filed . . ." (H. R. McIlwaine, ed., *Official Letters of the Governors of the State of Virginia* [Richmond, 1926–1929], I, 265). The letter was probably written on behalf of the Council by Lieut. Gov. John Page, as the body was acting as Board of War and alluded to itself as "the Board." (Actually, the official name as determined by the 1776 Constitution was the Privy Council and it was so called throughout the 18th-century.) GM appears to have been acting as a public agent, empowered to buy, consign, and hold commodities purchased for the commonwealth's account. The letter has not been found.]]

From [——— Brent?]

[[*23 Apr. 1778.* A fragmentary letter from GM dated 2 Oct. 1778 acknowledges receipt of a message "by Mr. Digges." GM's grandson, John Murray Mason, believed the often-quoted letter of 2 Oct. and the earlier correspondence passed between "one of the Mercer family of Virginia, then in England," and his distinguished ancestor. Kate Mason Rowland accepted this version, written on a copy of the fragment, of which many now exist (ViHi, NN, MH). In 1822 the original 2 Oct. letter was still in the possession of GM's son, Gen. John Mason of Georgetown, and the main portions were first printed in H. Niles, *Principles and Acts of the Revolution in America* . . . (Baltimore, 1822), 121–123. 70 years later Miss Rowland accepted the idea that a

Mercer was involved and went a step further, to name the correspondent as GM's "cousin, Col. George Mercer, then in London" (Rowland, I, 237). From internal evidence it is clear that GM wrote to a valued friend, and in the light of George Mercer's machinations as Ohio Company agent in London and GM's reaction to them (see GM to James Mercer, 13 Jan. 1772) it seems improbable that George Mercer was still held in esteem by GM. The editor's opinion is that a Virginian of GM's acquaintance, perhaps sent to England for schooling or caught there by the war, had elicited an account of events since the outbreak of 1775. If this surmise is valid, a member of the numerous, well-traveled Brent family of Stafford County was a more likely correspondent than the discredited George Mercer. Neither letter has been located.]]

Ohio Company Advertisement

[24 April 1778]

A MEETING of all the members of the OHIO COMPANY, residing in *Virginia* and *Maryland*, is desired on *Monday* the 18th day of *May* next, at the house of Mrs. *Jane Vobe*, in *Williamsburg*, on Business, of the greatest importance.   G. MASON, Treasurer.

Printed from the 24 Apr. 1778 *Va. Gaz.* (Purdie).
A resolution written by GM passed the General Assembly on 24 Jan. 1778. It called upon all parties claiming lands under royal grants from the Council to present their case during the May session of the legislature. The 1749 Ohio Company grant of 500,000 acres had never been executed, despite GM's continuing efforts. Now GM was ready to scale the grant down to a more modest 200,000 acres, and he was convinced that the time for final action was at hand (see his letter to James Mercer, 6 Feb. 1778). As it developed, however, the General Assembly was in no mood to implement GM's plan for granting unpatented lands. His bill (Jefferson worked with him on its provisions, but left the main business in GM's hands) permitting distribution of unpatented lands finally passed in June 1779. Meanwhile, conflicting claims from the Philadelphia-based Indiana Company plagued GM's campaign for an ultimate settlement.

To Richard Henry Lee

DEAR SIR: Gunston-Hall July 21st: 1778
I am much obliged to you for the last Papers & the agreeable News they contain. American Prospects brighten every Day; nothing, I think, but the speedy Arrival of a strong British Squadron can save the Enemie's Fleet & Army at N. York; indeed as to their Fleet, I trust the Blow is already struck. We are apt to wish for Peace, I confess I am, altho' I am clearly of Opinion that War is the present

Interest of these United States: The Union is yet incompleat, & will be so, until the Inhabitants of all the Territory from Cape Briton to the Missisippi are included in it; while G. Britain possesses Canada & West Florida, she will continually be setting the Indians upon us, & while she holds the Harbours of Augustine & Hallifax, especially the latter, we shall not be able to protect our Trade or Coasts from her Depredations; at least for many Years to come: the Possession of these two places wou'd save us more than half a Million a Year, & we shou'd then quickly have a Fleet sufficient for the common Protection of our own Coasts; for without some strong-Holds in America, or Naval Magazines in our Neighbourhood, G Britain cou'd seldom, or never keep a Squadron here. If she loses her Army now in America or is obliged to withdraw it, one of which I think must happen, this important Object will probably be obtained in the Course of another Campaign: if the British Ministry act consistently, & in Character, they will not recognise our Independence until this Business is compleated, & until our Prejudices against G. Britain are more firmly rooted, & we become better reconciled to foreign Manners & Manufacturers; it will require no great Length of time to accomplish this, & then the Wisdom of British Counsels will seize the auspicious Moment, & acknowledge our Independence.

Lord Chatham's Death does not seem to be mentioned in the Papers with certainty; but from the weak Condition in which he appeared in the House of lords in April, the account is more than probable.

One can't help being concern'd at the Death of a wise & a good Man; yet it is certainly a favourable Event to America; there was nothing I dreaded so much as his taking the Helm, & nothing I more heartily wish than the Continuance of the present Ministry. After "his most Christian Majesty, & Happiness & Prosperity to the French Nation," my next Toast shall be "long Life & Continuance in Office to the present British Ministry" in the first Bottle of good Claret I get; & I expect some by the first Ships from France.

If Tickets in the second Class of the Lottery are put into the Hands of the Sellers in the former I can very conveniently furnish myself here: I presume the Sellers must be furnished with Lists of the 20 Dollr. Prizes in the first Class, to enable them to make the proper Discounts to the Purchasers in the second.

Your Tobo. is sold at 60/, the highest Price—which has been given here; the Money shall be transmitted, by the first safe Hand, to Mrs. Lee of Belevieu, as you desired.

A very worthy Friend of mine in this County, Capt. Harper, had a partial & unjust Judgement (as he thinks) lately given by a Court of Admiralty in N. Carolina, agst. a Vessel of his (taken by Goodrich in Curratuck Inlet, & recovered by his own Captain's Hands, for Salvage, in favour of some militia Company's, & what was worse, instead of unlading the Vessel, or securing her in a Place of Safety, after they had taken her out of the Possession of Harper's Captain, they only took out some Hhds. of Molasses & Sacks of Salt, & suffered her to remain in the same Spot, with the greatest Part of her Cargoe on Board, until Goodrich return'd from N. York (whither he had carried some other Prizes) & cut the Vessel out from her Moorings; so that Capt. Harper sustains a Loss of the Vessel & the Whole Cargoe, to the amount of several thousand Pounds, & is totally at a Loss how to proceed; not knowing what mode Congress have prescribed for Redress, in such Cases. You will oblige me exceedingly in informing me whether any Court of Vice-Admiralty is established for the Trial of Appeals from the Courts of Admiralty in the different States, & where it sits; if there is yet no such Court whether Congress, in the mean time, takes Cognisance of such Matters; in short what will be the proper Steps for Capt. Harper to take to come at Justice.

I beg my Comps. to your Colleagues, particularly to your Brother Colo. F. Lee, & my Friend Mr. Thos. Adams; & am, Dr. Sir, Yr. sincerely affecte. Friend & Sert.

G MASON

RC (Lee Papers, ViU). Five pages with outside endorsements: "No 242 George Mason 6 Letters," "G. Mason 1778," and "No. 288."

GM's optimism was probably dampened when he learned that reinforcements reached the British fleet, and that despite American valor displayed at Monmouth on 28 June, hope that A BLOW IS ALREADY STRUCK was indeed premature. Lee possibly wrote GM, as he already had written Jefferson, mentioning negotiations between Congress and the British peace commissioners, adding his opinion that their letter of authority was "a combination of fraud, falsehood, insidious offers, and abuse of France, Concluding with a denial of Independence" (letter to Jefferson, 16 June 1778, Boyd, II, 200). Americans generally interpreted the peace commission as a sign of British weakness, and GM certainly thought continued hostilities might bring to fruition the hope of Canada joining the Union, YET INCOMPLEAT, as the 14th state. LORD CHATHAM'S DEATH on 11 May 1778 surprised Americans because of consistent newspaper rumors that the elder Pitt was about to form a new cabinet (Va. Gaz. [Purdie], 10 July 1778). MRS. LEE OF BELEVIEU ("Belleview") presumably was the recently widowed Mrs. Thomas Ludwell Lee. A VERY WORTHY FRIEND . . . CAPT. John HARPER of Alexandria, had been victimized by the notorious tory privateers, the GOODRICH family, maurading along the Virginia–North Carolina coast. They had recently burned or captured nine American ships in that area (Va. Gaz. [Purdie], 19 Jan. 1778).

In the modernized text printed in Rowland, I, 293–295, CURRATUCK (Currituck) Inlet is identified as "Currabuck Inlet."

To Richard Henry Lee

DEAR SIR. Gunston-Hall August 24th. 1778.

We have such various & vague Accounts of our Affairs to the Northward, & of the Movements of the French Fleet, that I am extreamly anxious to know, with Certainty, what is doing. Is our Army drawn near to King's Bridge? Are the Enemies Out-Posts abandoned? Is N. York effectually besieged? Are or can the Enemie be prevented from foraging upon Long Island & Staten Island? Is the Cork Fleet of Victuallers arrived at N. York; or was the Report a Peice of Artifice, or has any such Fleet actually sailed? Has Lord Howe's Fleet left Sandy Hook, & gone to Rhode Island, or were the English Ships which appeared there a Fleet lately from Great Britain; & what has been the Consequence of their Meeting with the Count De Estaings Squadron? Are the french Land Forces landed upon Rhode Island, to act in Concert with Genl. Sullivan, & are they thought able to [hold] Burgoyne [and] the British Troops there? I am almost ashamed of having asked you so many Questions; I think they are nearly equal to the String with which old Colo. Cary once harrass'd Doctr. Francis, upon his coming on Show at Hampton. If L[or]d. Howe, with his Fleet, has really left N. York, the British Army must be in the most desperate Circumstances, & his Intention must be to draw off the Attention of the French Squadron, until the Troops can embark, & run down to the Southward, where they can get Provisions; for I hardly think they can have Provisions for a long Voyage.

The Money recd. for your Tobo. is sent down to Mrs. Lee at Bellvieu, as you desired. I wish the Tobo. had not been sold so soon, as the Price has risen 15/ ℔ hund. since.

If the Congress, or any of yr. Friends shou'd have Occasion to purchase a Quantity of Tobo. in this Part of the Country, I wou'd beg Leave to recommend my Friend & Neighbour Mr. Martin Cockburn. He was regularly bred to Business in a very Capital House in London, & I know no Man whose Attachment to the American Cause, or whose Integrity Diligence & Punctuality can be more thoroughly confided in. I am not fond of giving Recommendations, but I am so well acquainted with Mr. Cockburn, that I know I can recommend him with Safety. God bless you, my Dear Sir, & believe me, Your affecte. Friend & Servt.

G. MASON

RC (Lee Papers, ViU). A four-page Ms, addressed and overwritten in several hands with "Mr. Hunter," "No. 251," and "No. 289" on the margins.

AFFAIRS TO THE NORTHWARD revolved around the movements of the British after the evacuation of Philadelphia. After the Battle of Monmouth on 28 June, Sir Henry Clinton led the British across N. J. to Sandy Hook, where they embarked for New York harbor. The French fleet under the Comte d'Estaing reached Delaware Bay on 8 July but did not attack the British and an effort to evict the British from Newport, R. I., through a joint operation was abandoned. There was no real threat from Burgoyne's BRITISH TROOPS in New England, who had been marched to Cambridge as prisoners of war. Gen. Howe's dilatory tactics led to suspicions "that his real intention was to get Burgoyne's troops within the British lines and keep them as an addition to his own army" (Christopher Ward, *The War of the American Revolution,* ed. John Richard Alden [New York, 1952], II, 541). Burgoyne finally left for England without his army, which was sent to Virginia after the British were denied entrance to Boston harbor. COLO. Archibald CARY, whose nickname was "Old Iron," was a leading figure in the House of Burgesses and the Virginia Conventions of 1775-1776; however, DOCTR. FRANCIS' identity remains unknown. GM had reported the sale of Lee's tobacco for 60 shillings on 21 July at "the highest Price which has been given here," but apparently it was a seller's market if THE PRICE HAS RISEN 15/ HUND. SINCE. MARTIN COCKBURN was GM's esteemed neighbor whose estate, "Springfield," adjoined Gunston Hall.

The text printed in Rowland, I, 295-296, has been modernized and the spelling of BELLVIEU corrected.

To [Mr. ——— Brent?]

MY DEAR SIR   Virginia, Gunston-Hall, Octor. 2d: 1778

It gave me great pleasure, upon Receipt of your Favour of the 23d. of April, by Mr. Digges, to hear that you are alive & well, in a Country where you can spend your Time agreeably; not having heard a word from you, or of you, for two Years before. I am much obliged by the friendly Concern you take in my domestic Affairs, & your kind Enquiry after my Family; great Alterations have happen'd in it. About four years ago I had the Misfortune to lose my Wife: to you, who knew her, & the happy Manner in which we lived, I will not attempt to describe my Feelings: I was scarce able to bear the first Shock; a Depression of Spirits, & setled Melancholly followed, from which I never expect, or desire to recover. I determined to spend the Remainder of my Days in privacy & Retirement with my Children, from whose Society alone I cou'd expect Comfort: some of them are now grown up to Men & Women; and I have the Satisfaction to see them free from Vices, good-natured, obliging & dutiful. They all still live with me, & remain single, except my second Daughter Sally; who is lately married to my Neighbour Mr. McCarty's Son. My eldest Daughter Nancy (who is blessed with her Mother's amiable Disposition) is Mistress of my Family, &

manages my little domestic Matters, with a Degree of Prudence far above her Years. My eldest Son George engaged early in the American Cause, & was chosen Ensign of the first independent Company formed in Virginia, or indeed on the Continent, it was commanded by the Present General Washington as Captain, & consisted entirely of Gentlemen. In the Year 1775 he was appointed a Captain of Foot, in one of the first Minute-Regiments raised here, but was soon obliged to quit the Service, by a violent Rheumatic Disorder; which has followed him ever since, & I believe will force him to try the Climate of France or Italy. My other Boys have not yet finished their Education; as soon as they do, if the War continues they seem strongly inclined to take an active part.

In the Summer 75 I was much against my Inclination drag'd out of my Retirement, by the People of my County, & sent a Delegate to the General Convention at Richmond, where I was appointed a Member of the first Committee of Safety; & have since, at different times, been chosen a Member of the Privy Council, & of the American Congress; but have constantly declined acting in any other public character than that of an independent Representative of the People, in the House of Delegates; where I still remain, from a Consciousness of being able to do my Country more Service there than in any other Department; and have ever since, devoted most of my Time to public Business; to the no small Neglect & Injury of my private Fortune; but if I can only live to see the American Union firmly fixed, and free Governments well established in our western world, and can leave to my children but a Crust of Bread, & Liberty, I shall die satisfied; and say with the Psalmist "Lord now lettest thou thy Servant depart in Peace." To shew you that I have not been an idle Spectator of this great Contest, and to amuse you with the Sentiments of an old Friend upon an important Subject I inclose you a Copy of the first Draught of the Declaration of Rights, just as it was drawn by me, & presented to the Virginia Convention, where it received few Alterations; some of them I think not for the better; this was the first thing of the kind upon the Continent, and has been closely imitated by all the other States. There is a remarkable Sameness in all the Forms of Government throughout the American Union, except in the States of South Carolina & Pensylvania; the first having three Branches of Legislature, and the last only one; all the other States have two; this Difference has given general Disgust, and it is probable an Alteration will soon take Place, to assimilate these to the Constitutions of the other States. We have laid our new Government upon a broad Foundation, & have endeavoured to provide the most effectual Securties for the essential Rights of human nature, both in Civil and Religious liberty; the People become every Day more & more attach'd to it; and I trust that neither the Power of Great Britain, nor the Power of Hell will be able to prevail against it.

There never was an idler or a falser Notion than that which the British Ministry have imposed upon the Nation "that this great Revolution has been the Work of a Faction, of a Junto of ambitious Men against the Sense of the People of America." On the Contrary, nothing has been done without the Approbabtion of the People, who have indeed out run their Leaders; so that no capital Measure hath been adopted, until they called loudly for it: to any one who knows Mankind, there needs no greater Proof than the cordial Manner in which they have co-operated, and the Patience & Perseverance with which they have strugled under their Sufferings; which have been greater than you, at a Distance, can conceive, or I describe. Equally false is the Assertion that Independence was originally designed here; things have gone such Lengths, that it is a Matter of Moonshine to us, whether Independence was at first intended, or not; and therefore we may now be believed. The truth is, we have been forced into it, as the only means of self-preservation, to guard our Country & posterity from the greatest of all Evils, such another infernal Government (if it deserves the Name of Government) as the Provinces groaned under, in the latter Ages of the Roman Commonwealth. To talk of replacing us in the Situation of 1763, as we first asked, is to the last Degree absurd, & impossible; they obstinately refused it, while it was in their power, and now, that it is out of their Power, they offer it. Can they raise our Citys out of their Ashes? Can they replace, in Ease & Affluence, the thousands of Familys whom they have ruined? Can they restore the Husband to the widow, the Child to the Parent, or the Father to the Orphan? In a word, can they reanimate the Dead? Our Country has been made a scene of Desolation & Blood. Enormities & Cruelties have been committed here, which not only disgrace the British Name, but dishonour the human kind! We can never again trust a People who have thus used us, Human Nature revolts at the Idea! The Die is cast —the Rubicon is passed—and a Reconciliation with Great Britain, upon the Terms of returning to her Government is impossible.

No man was more warmly attach'd to the Hanover Family & the Whig Inter[e]st of England than I was, & few Men had stronger Prejudices in Favour of that Form of Government under which I was born & bred, or a greater Aversion to changing it; it was ever my Opinion that no good Man wou'd wish to try so dangerous an Experiment upon any speculative Notions whatsoever, without any absolute Necessity.

The ancient Poets, in their elegant manner of Expression have made a kind of Being of Necessity, and tell us that the Gods themselves are obliged to Yield to her.

When I was first a Member of the Convention, I exerted myself to prevent a Confiscation of the King's Quit-Rents; and altho' I was for putting the Country imediatly into a State of Defence, and preparing for the worst; yet as long as we had any well founded hopes of the Reconciliation, I opposed, to the utmost of my Power, all violent Measures, & such as might shut the Door to it; but when Reconciliation became a lost Hope, when unconditional Submission, or effectual Resistance, were the only Alternatives left us, when the last dutiful & humble petition from Congress received no other Answer than declaring us Rebels, and out of the King's protection, I from that Moment look'd forward to a Revolution & Independence, as the only means of Salvation; and will risque the last Penny of my Fortune, & the last Drop of my Blood upon the Issue: for to imagine that we cou'd resist the Efforts of Great Britain, still professing ourselves her Subjects, or support a defensive War against a powerful Nation, without the Reins of Government in the Hands of America (whatever our pretended Friends in Great Britain may say of it) is too childish & futile an Idea to enter into the Head of any Man of Sense. I am not singular in my Opinions; these are the Sentiments of more than nine tenths of the best men in America.

God has been pleased to bless our Endeavours, in a Just Cause, with Remarkable Success. To us upon the Spot, who have seen Step by Step, the progress of this great Contest, who know the defenceless State of America in the Beginning, & the numberless Difficultys we have had to struggle with, taking a retrospective view of what is passed, we seem to have been treading upon enchanted Ground. The Case is now altered, American prospects brighten, and appearances are strongly in our Favour: the British Ministry must, & will acknowledge us independent States, but (judging of the future by the past) if they act consistently, they will delay this, until mutual Injuries & Resentments are further agravated, until our growing Prejudices against Great Britain (are more firmly rooted, and until we become better reconciled to foreign manufactures and foreign manners. It will not require many years to accomplish this, and then the wisdom of the British councils will seize the auspicious moment to recognize the independence of America.

The present plan of the British ministry seems to be to corrupt and bribe the Congress; but in this, as they have in everything else, they will be disappointed; not that I imagine that there are no rotten members in so numerous a body of men. Among the twelve apostles there was a Judas—but they are too much in the power of the Assemblies of their respective States, and so thoroughly amenable to the people, that no man among them, who values his own life, dares to tamper; and upon this rock the safety of America is founded.

I have thus given you a long and faithful, and I fear you will think a tedious account of the political state of affairs here; my opportunities of knowing them are equal to most men's, and the natural anxiety you must have to be well informed of the situation of your native country, at so important a crisis, will apologize for the trouble.

We have had 200,000 acres of land laid off, marked and bounded in one survey for the Ohio [Company]⟩ . . .

[enclosure]

[2 October 1778]
(Copy of the first D[r]aught by G M.)

A DECLARATION OF RIGHTS made by the Representatives of the good People of Virginia, assembled in full and free Convention; which Rights do pertain to them and their Posterity, as the Basis and Foundation of Government,

[14 articles then follow, with sufficient differences between the Declaration of Rights as adopted 12 June 1776 to make it obvious that Mason blended his memory with notes and printed texts to produce an interesting but unauthentic document. It was this document, or an identical copy of it, which Mason enclosed in the 2 Oct. 1778 letter and which was displayed in Richmond during the 1840s as the original draft of the 1776 Declaration of Rights. The four-page Ms is in Mason's handwriting and also carries his comment (after the 14th article): "This Declaration of Rights was the first in America; it received few Alterations or Additions in the Virginia Convention (some of them not for the better) and was afterwards closely imitated by the other United States." Also endorsed by Mason: "Virginia Declaration of Rights in 1776." In such circumstances, it is hardly surprising that members of his family regarded the document as a great national heirloom. The full text is printed in Rowland, I, 433–436. In 1941, historian Irving Brant noticed the discrepancies in various texts and correctly perceived that the first draft of the Declaration of Rights was still another document in the handwriting of Mason and Thomas Ludwell Lee. The various drafts are more fully explained in the note below and also in the editorial note prefacing the Declaration of Rights, 20 May–12 June 1776. Marginal commentaries in another handwriting compare the text with the final version of the Declaration. The last marginal entry reads: "2 more articles were added Viz the 10th & 14th in the adopted Bill—not of fundamental nature."]

Ms (Bancroft Letter Books, NN); enclosure, Ms (Mason Papers, DLC). In 1822 the letter, which has long since disappeared, was owned by GM's son, John Mason, who permitted a copy to be made for H. Niles's *Principles and Acts of the Revolution.* The copied letter is 7 pages in length, preceded by the notation: "Fragment of a Letter from George Mason. Its address is lost. *'Believed to have been addressed to some one of the Mercer Family of Virginia, then in England, who were near connections of Col. Mason. The conclusion of the letter lost. J[ohn]. M[urray]. Mason. Selma 27 Apl. '57.'*" Also the word "Copy" and "Much of it printed in Va. Hist. Mag. ii. 28." Other copies of the letter are located at ViHi and MH.

Although Kate Mason Rowland (Rowland, I, 237) offered the suggestion that GM was writing to the discredited and improvident George Mercer, the editor believes it much more likely that this letter was addressed some younger Virginian who may have been in England (after all, the war was in full progress) upon the only justifiable excuse of the day—to receive an education. Perhaps the intended recipient was a member of the family of Robert Brent of "Woodstock," whose sister GM married in 1780. The instructive tone of the letter, at any rate, supports the idea that GM was writing to a highly regarded younger man and not to a middle-aged failure such as George Mercer. Often quoted since the appearance of Miss Rowland's volumes, the letter has been cited for the insights offered on the rationale of an American patriot who moved down the road to armed resistance with a measured gait. The Biblical quotation is from Luke 2:29. A COPY OF THE FIRST DRAUGHT OF THE DECLARATION OF RIGHTS which GM wrote out became in time a puzzlement to archivists and historians. GM's statement was long taken at face value, which made it appear that almost the entire 1776 Virginia Declaration of Rights was originally conceived by GM. A critical examination of the various texts by Irving Brant revealed that GM had in fact copied rather "a composite of the original, the committee draft and the final draft, with one word transplanted from the Declaration of Independence [viz., "created"]" (Brant, *James Madison,* I, 236). Kate Mason Rowland and the editor of these volumes were among those who accepted GM's original claim too readily, but it is now a fact beyond question that GM's zeal to explain the Revolution to an American abroad led him to an overstatement. The REMARKABLE SAMENESS of the various state constitutions was partly GM's own doing, for the Virginia Declaration of Rights and Constitution of 1776 were the first adopted after the Continental Congress recommended such a step on 10 May 1776. Both documents were quickly and widely reprinted along the Atlantic seaboard and furnished models for other drafting bodies (Rutland, *Birth of the Bill of Rights,* 41–77). The assertion that THE PEOPLE . . . INDEED OUT RUN THEIR LEADERS has since been a capsuled doctrine of far-reaching intellectual revolutions. Historian Bernard Bailyn has demonstrated "the autonomy of ideas as phenomena, where the ideas operate, as it were, over the heads of the participants, taking them in directions no one could have foreseen" (Wood, "Rhetoric and Reality," WMQ, 3rd Ser., XXIII [1966], 31). Though the question of an incipient independence movement had become in 1778 A MATTER OF MOONSHINE TO US, GM must have recalled the general anxiety present in America between 1767 and 1775 regarding Britain's own attachment to constitutional principles. Thus, to save the inherent values of the British constitution, Americans had BEEN FORCED INTO . . . [a war] OF SELF-PRESERVATION. The sentence relating ANCIENT POETS who MADE A KIND OF BEING OF NECESSITY is striking evidence of GM's memory (unless he consulted some now-lost copybook), for he used the identical words in his petulant letter to the London merchants almost 12 years earlier (6 June

1766). Whether remembered or copied, the doctrine of expediency is predominant in GM's writings from 1766 onward as a justification for the Revolution. GM's acknowledgment of his final conversion to a militant stand is fixed at the King's rejection of THE LAST DUTIFUL & HUMBLE "Olive Branch" PETITION in Aug. 1775.

Several commas in the Ms have been replaced with periods, in the interest of clarity. The text printed in Rowland, I, 297–301, includes the portion in angle brackets that is missing from the Bancroft transcript. Rowland's text of the enclosure is also modernized (I, 433–436) and fails to distinguish the handwriting variation of one commentary.

To William Lee

DEAR SIR.   Virginia, Gunston-Hall, Octor. 8th. 1778.

Your Favour from Nantes in October last, (dated in London 22d. May 1777) ℣ the Congress Capt. Skinner, was duly received, covering Accts. of Sales for my one hundred Hhds. of Tobo. ship'd you to London in 1775, Nett proceeds £1053. .11. .10. Ster: with which I am by no Means pleased. Had the Tobo. been kept up, as I desired (& put it in your Power to do, by not drawing on it for a year or two) it wou'd have produced more than double the Sum; instead of which, I observe it was sold, soon after it's Arrival, at a less price than I refused for it in Virginia; & if I was to take Paper-Money here for it, as you intended, I shou'd not receive one fifth of the Value, & will sooner submit to a Loss of the whole. I therefore imediatly return'd your Orders, one on Mr. John Mills for the Sum of £388. .17. .5. & the other on Messrs. Triplett & Thornton for the Sum of £445. .12. .10, to your Brother, Colo. Richd. Henry Lee, whose Receipt I have for them. I have certainly a legal, as well as just Right to the Benefit of the Exchange for my own Money in another Country, or to make such other Use of it as I judge best, and if you endeavour to disappoint me in doing this, I must draw Bills on you, & in Case of non-payment, order them to be regularly protested & returned; that I may seek my proper Remedie. I intreat you, my dear Sir, not to lay me under this disagreeable Necessity; for my Friendship for your Family will make it exceedingly so to me. My Bills of the 13th of March 1777, favr. Messrs. Jenifer & Hooe, for £190. . Ster: you say shall be duly paid; but take no Notice of my Bills of the 24th of April 1777 favour Messrs. J. Gruell & Company Merchts. in Nantes for the Sum of £850. . Ster: which I understand, from your Brother, you had refused to pay. Had I known of your removal from England to France, I shou'd not have drawn the sd. Bills to Gruell & Compy. having no other Motive in doing it, but to get my Money out of England; &

therefore your not paying them has not (that I know of) been any Disadvantage to me; as I had rather my Money shou'd have remained in your Hands than a Stranger's; & this Suggestion might perhaps induce you not to pay them; but I shou'd have taken it more kindly, if you had mentioned the matter openly & candidly to me, instead of studiously avoiding such an Explanation. I hope you will excuse the Freedom with which I write, as in doing so, I deal with my Friend, as I wish all Men to deal with me.

I have now to desire you will send me Goods, to the amount of the Ballance I have in your Hands, as per List on the other Side, per the first good Ship to Virginia agreeing particularly for the Freight, & transmitting me Bills of Loading accordingly; and that a proper Insurance be made on them, & in Case of Loss, the Goods reship'd.[*] As many vessels, bringing goods from Europe hither, come out not fully loaded, I shou'd hope the Freight might be reasonable; but at all Events, wish it to be firmly fixed; because great Impositions, respecting Freight, have been attempted here.

I pray you to let me hear from you speedily, and sincerely wishing you Health & Happiness, remain, Dr Sir Your most obdt. Servt.

G MASON

P.S.
If the Goods cou'd be sent to Potomack
it wou'd be more convenient to me than
any other River—

[enclosure]   [8 October 1778]
Goods to be ship'd by William Lee Esqr. on Acct. & Risque of George Mason, ℔ the first good Ship to Virginia; the Goods to be insured, & in Case of Loss, the same Articles reship'd, & again insured. The Packages containing the Goods to be mark'd G $\frac{4}{\diamond}$ M.

NB. it will be more convenient to receive them in Potomack than any other River. Rappahannock will be nearly as convenient.

One Set of good common Black Smith's Tools, to consist of-1. pr. good Bellows 1. best large Bench-Vice_____2. Hand Do.
1. best Anville ____ 1. Beake Iron ____ 1. Sledge Hammer
2 large Hand-Hammers ____ 2 smaller Do. ____
4. pr. Tongs & 1. dozn. Smith's Files sorted.
N.B. other small Tools are not wanted.

Good ozenbrigs, or strong brown Linnen, to the amount of about two hundred Pounds Sterling ____

200. pr. good Wool Cards ____ 100. pr. good Cotton Cards.

[440]

10. pr. good woolen Bed-Blankets.

1. dozn. fine Linnen Handkerchiefs ____ 1. doz: coarser Do.

3. pr. of white Sheeting, at abt. 15d. Ster: ℔ yd.

2. doz: pr. of men's thread or Cotton Stockings.

---

* And the remainder of the Balle. due G Mason, in white Linnens solid, such as usually cost in London from 1/ to 2/ Sterling ℔ yard.

* 1. lb: Nun's thread sorted—1. lb. fine Do. sorted

RC (ViHi). A three-page letter and one-page invoice.

This letter continues GM's running complaint over the ill-starred business affair which began with the consignment of 100 hogsheads of tobacco on 20 May 1775. GM was initially disappointed by what appeared to be Lee's undue haste in selling the huge consignment, but as time went by GM grew more suspicious of Lee's conduct in other ways. The complexity is increased by letters passing between Lee and his brother and GM's close friend, Richard Henry Lee. "You will probably hear some complaint from Col. Mason about not paying his bills. If you do, pray request of him to suspend his judgment 'till he hears from me, and he will then be satisfied that his money is safe, and perhaps much safer than the hands he meant to put it in" (letter to R. H. Lee, 1 Sept. 1777, Ford, ed., *Letters of William Lee*, I, 240). William Lee was by this time an agent for the Continental Congress in Europe. Richard Henry Lee's reply made it appear that GM was not disconcerted by the turn of affairs. "The Colo. says that his only reason for drawing on you formerly in favor of Pliarne Gruel & Co. was because he apprehended you still continued in London . . . but since you are in France he is Well satisfied that you did not pay the draught, as he is better pleased with the money being in your hands. . . . So the matter stands right" (letter to William Lee, 25 Jan. 1778, Ballagh, *Lee Letters*, I, 381). GM was anxious to avoid payment of his credit balance in depreciated currency, hence his insistence on THE BENEFIT OF THE EXCHANGE OF MY OWN MONEY IN ANOTHER COUNTRY. William Lee refused to honor the £850 bill of exchange (notation, Wm. Lee copybook [ViHi], 4 Mar. 1779 entry). More letters crossed the Atlantic before GM finally sued Lee and won a £2420 judgment in May 1789 (see letter to Samuel Griffin, 8 Sept. 1789).

Several colons have been replaced with periods for clarity's sake. GM was obviously distressed by this transaction, and he wrote "& if was I to take Paper-Money" by misplacing a caret. The mistake has been corrected by a transposition in this text.

To Richard Harrison

DEAR SIR.   Virginia, Gunston-Hall, Octo. 24th. 1778.

I sent you by Capt. John Sandford of the Sloop Flying-Fish, last Voyage, a few Silver Dollars, to discharge the little Bal[an]ce. you was so kind to advance for me in the Goods purchased, & sent me by him from Martinique; but he inform'd me, upon his Return, that not meeting with any safe Opportunity of sending the Money from St. Eustatia he had brought it back again. I therefore desired him to carry it out again this last Voyage, and if he did not find you at St.

Eustatia (as he told me he expected) to endeavour to give it a Conveyance from thence to you, to Martinique.

I am uneasy at not having heard any thing respecting the Goods you ordered for me last Year from France, & must beg you will let me know whether you have any, & what late advices concerning them. As Hostilities are now commenced between France & England, & they seem to be making very free with each other's Ships they will be probably in as great Danger in a french Bottom, coming to the West Indies, as to this Continent. Will it not therefore be better, if they are not yet shipp'd for Martinique, to direct your Correspondent to ship them imediatly to Virginia, in the first good Vessel, & consign them to me? In which Case, I wou'd have a proper Insurance made on them in France, & in Case of Loss, the goods reship'd as before & again insured. However I submit it thus to you; not doubting but you will do therefor the best, and remain, Dr. Sir, Your most obdt Sert.

G MASON

RC (Gunston Hall). Two pages in GM's hand, addressed to Harrison, "Merchant in Martinique, ℀ Capt. Johns, of the Dolphin."

Harrison was the Virginia agent in Martinique charged with selling tobacco on the commonwealth's account and using the funds received for French munitions and other supplies. The HOSTILITIES . . . BETWEEN FRANCE & ENGLAND began after the Franco-American mutual-assistance treaties were signed in Feb. 1778, wherein France recognized American independence and promised to give the U.S. military aid.

The printed text in Rowland, I, 303, has been modernized, and Capt. SANDFORD misspelled. Several colons were changed to periods in the interest of clarity. GM used a dash, colon, and period interchangeably and all for the same purpose.

From Richard Harrison

[[*5 Nov. 1778.* GM acknowledged this letter, which Harrison probably wrote from Alexandria shortly after his apparently unexpected return from Martinique, where he had been the Virginia business agent and also did some mercantile transactions on his own account. This letter, which has not been located, is mentioned in GM's message to Harrison dated 9 Nov. 1778.]]

To Richard Harrison

DEAR SIR   Gunston-Hall   Novemr. 9th. 1778

I have your Favour of the 5th. Inst. & heartily congratulate you on your safe Return to your native Country & Friends.

[442]

I set off to-morrow Morning for the Assembly; I expect my Stay in Wmsburg. will be pretty long; during which, if any thing shou'd occur, in which I can serve you there, it will give me Pleasure.

I hardly know what Steps will be best to take with Respect to Mr. Lemozin; it really looks as if he prefered keeping the Money in his Hands to sending out the Goods ordered. I shall be a considerable Loser by his Negligence, even if he now sends the Goods; as the Hostilities between the French & English, makes the Risque much greater, & consequently the Insurance higher; whereas if he had sent them out at first, they wou'd have come w[i]th. very little Charge to Martinique, & almost the only Risque wou'd have been from thence hither. As the Bills & Invoyce were remitted in your Name, I can't, with Propriety, write to him, or give Orders on the Subject, & must therefore beg the Favour of you to do it, by different Opportunities, desiring him to send the Goods imediatly by the first Good Vessel, to Virginia, if they are not already ship'd to Martinique; reminding him to insure, & in Case of Loss, to reship the same Articles & insure again. It will be most convenient to have them sent to Potomack, but as an Opportunity for that Purpose may not speedily offer, it they are sent to James or York River, I wou'd have them addressed to the Care of Colo. Wm. Aylett at Wmsburg, if to Rappahannock, to the Care of Colo. Thos. Jett Mercht. near Leed's Town.

I think it may not be amiss to mention to Mr. Lemozin, his very Extraordinary Delay in this Business, & the Inconvenience & Loss incurred by it, & to let him know, that if the Order is not speedily executed, the Money will be drawn out of his Hands, & put into those of some Mercht. who will be more punctual; or if you have any other Correspondent at the Place, whom you think safe, I believe it might be well to desire the favour of him to make Enquiry about it, or to send him a Draught on Mr. Lemozin for the Money, in Case the Goods are not bought when it arrives; for I presume if they are not by that time, they never will by that Gentleman.

Upon the whole, I leave it entirely to you, Sir, to take such Measures therein as you judge best; and am, Dr Sir, Your most obdt Servt.

G MASON

RC (PP). Addressed to Harrison at Alexandria and probably endorsed by Harrison.

Andrew LIMOZIN (also Lemozin) was a LeHavre merchant who disappointed GM by failing to execute the order. Fourteen months later, an exasperated GM was still wondering what had become of his money (see letter to William Bingham, 10 Mar. 1780).

In the modernized text printed in Rowland, I, 304–305, LEED'S TOWN is mistakenly called "Leed's Tavern."

To the Honourable the General Assembly of Virginia, The Memorial and Petition of the Ohio Company

HUMBLY SHEWETH   [20 November 1778]

That sundry Gentlemen of Virginia, Maryland and Great Britain in or about the year 1748 formed a Copartnership, by the Name and Stile of the Ohio Company for exploring the Country westward of the Great Mountains upon both Sides the Ohio River (at that time known only by Name to the People of Virginia) for taking up five hundred thousand Acres of Land upon the Waters of the said River and carrying on a Trade with the Indians; and thereupon presented a Petition to his late Majesty King George the second in Consequence whereof additional royal Instruction bearing Date at the court at St. James's the 16th. Day of March 1748/9 was given to Sr. William Gooch Bart. then Governour of Virginia to make a Grant or Grants, upon certain Conditions therein specified "to John Hanbury of London Merchant, the honble Thomas Lee Esqr. the honble Thomas Nellson Esqr. Colo. Thomas Cresap Colo. William Thornton, William Nimmo, Daniel Cresap, John Carlyle, Lawrence Washington, Augustine Washington, George Fairfax, Jacob Giles, Nathaniel Chapman, and James Wardrope Esqrs. *and their Associates* for two hundred thousand Acres of Land betwixt Romanettoes and Buffaloe's Creek, on the South Side the River Alleghany, otherwise Ohio, and betwixt the two Creeks and the Yellow Creek on the North Side of the said River, *or as aforesaid to the westward of the Great Mountains* free from the Payment of any Rights, as also from the Payment of any Quit-Rents for the Space of ten Years from the Date of their Grants, at the Expiration of which Term the said Petitioners are to pay the usual Quit-rent for so much of the said Lands as they shall have cultivated within that time" and upon the Terms on which the first two hundred thousand Acres were to be granted being complyed with "to make a further Grant or Grants to the said Petitioners of three hundred thousand Acres more, Residue of the said five hundred thousand Acres of Land.

That in the Month of June 1749 the following Gentlemen, whose Names had been inserted in the said Petition and Royal Instructions, vizt. the honble Thomas Nellson Esqr. Colo. Francis Thornton, (who thro' Mistake had been miscalled Colo. *William* Thornton)

William Nimmo, John Carlyle, and George Fairfax Esqrs. desired to resign their Shares and Interest in the said Company, which Resignations were accordingly accepted, and entered in the Company's Journals; and such of them as had advanced anything had their Money returned to them: And that Mr. Daniel Cresap (whose Name was inserted in the Petition and Royal Instructi[ons] and in the minutes of the said Ohio Company, never advanced a Shilling, [nor] had any Manner of Concern, or Interest whatever, in the said Undertaking, o[r] Copartnership; But the Governor and Council, not at that time having proper Notice of the before mentioned Resignations, or knowing who were the real Members of the said Ohio Company, and litterally pursueing the Words of the *Royal Instruction;* which was communicated by the Governor to the Board, on the 12th Day of July 1749 caused an Entry to be made in the Council Books, in the Names of the first mentioned gentlemen, for the first two hundred thousand Acres of Land, as aforesaid: to which Entry, as well as the Royal Instruction whereon it was founded, your Memorialists beg Leave to refer.

In pursuance of their said Plan that your Memorialists erected large Store-houses and other Buildings, at a very great Expence, upon Potomack River, opposite the place where Fort Cumberland was afterwards fixed, purchased a number of Horses, and imported several large Cargoes of Goods to the amount of several thousand Pounds Sterling from London; for the Purpose of carrying on an extensive Indian Trade.

That in the Year 1750, they employed Mr. Christopher Gist at the Expence of one hundred and fifty Pounds, to explore the Country on the North Side the Ohio River, as low as the Great-Falls, and upon the Great and Little Miamee Rivers, to discover what Tribes of Indians inhabited there, and endeavour to conciliate them to the Interest and Friendship of Virginia: And the Year following, they employed the said Christopher Gist, at the Expence of fifty pounds, to explore and examine the Country upon the South Side the Ohio River, from the Monongahaly to the Great Conhaway; as will appear by the said Gist's Journals.

That in the same Year 1751, there having been considerable Changes made by Resignations and Alienations of Shares, the Members of the said Ohio Company entered [into and] executed, regular Articles of Agreement and Copartnership for the Space and Term of twenty Years: And in the two years following, were at considerable Expence in laying off and clearing a Road from the Mouth of Will's Creek on potomack River, over the Alleghany

Mountains, to the Waters of the Ohio; and in building a Warehouse near the Mouth of Red-Stone Creek, on the Monongahaly.

That as the Location of the Company's claim, from the words of the Royal-Instruction, and their Entry on the Council-Books, was so very extensive, affecting any Lands *to the westward of the Great Mountains,* on either Side the Ohio River, where no Settlements had been yet made, or Countys establish'd, your Memorialists obtained, from the President and Professors of William and Mary College, in the Year 1753, a special Commission for the before mentioned Christopher Gist, appointing him Surveyor of the Lands belonging to the Ohio Company; and began to survey some of the Lands upon the waters of the Monongaly and Youghyoughgaine (about the Place now called the Red Stone Settlement) and at the Confluence of the Ohio and Monongaly Rivers (where Fort Pit now stands) and setled the said Christopher Gist's, and several other Families thereon. They also imported, from London, twenty new Swivel Guns, with a Quantity of suitable Ball, small-arms, Blunderbusses, Tools, and other Military-Stores, prepared Materials, and were erecting a Fort, on the Spot where Fort Pit now stands, under the Direction of Captain William Trent, the company's Agent; when about seven hundred French and Indians, commanded by a regular Officer, with several Pieces of Cannon, came down the River in Battoes, and landing within a small Distance drove away your Memorialist's Workmen and People, took possession of the place, and built their Fort DuQuesne there.

That upon this Occasion, and by the french and Indian War which followed, your Memorialists were not only prevented from proceeding further in the Execution of their Plan, but sustained very great Losses, to the amount of several thousand Pounds in their Materials, Tools, Stores, Horses, and other Effects in that Country, and even in their Houses and Property upon Potomack River; which were wantonly destroyed by our own Troops, and the Lands the Company had purchased near Fort Cumberland entirely pillaged of Timber, for the public-buildings, and for Beef, Pork & flour-Barrels; without your Memorialists ever being able to obtain the least Satisfaction or Redress. And that the Nature of the Trade your Memorialists were engaged in was such, that they were obliged to give large Credits to the Indian-Traders, most of whom were killed, captivated, or ruined in the Course of the War, and the Debts due to your Memorialists thereby lost. That by these Events, which are faithfully recited, and generally known, your Memorialists were prevented from proceeding in their surveys during the last War, as they were also, after the conclusion of the War, by the King's Proclamation, prohibiting the setling or granting any lands to the westward of the Great Mountains.

That your Memorialists finding the Land they had begun to survey about Fort Pit was appropriated to the use of a Public Garrison, and the Lands they had surveyed upon the Branches of Monongahaly and Youghyoughgaine were claimed by the Province of Pensylvania, as well as by another Company in Virginia, and not caring to contend with such Powerful adversaries, determined to take their Land lower down the Ohio, between the Monongahaly and the Great Conhaway, as soon as government wou'd permit them to make Surveys, but afterwards, at the particular Request of General Washington, and some of the Members of the Council, your Memorialists promised not to interfere with the first Virginia Regiments Claim of two hundred thousand acres of land under Gover[no]r Dinwiddie's Proclamation, and to suffer that to be first laid off; by which all the good Bodys of Land, upon the Ohio between the Great and Little Conhaway, in the Country your Memorialists had been at the charge of exploring many Years before, were taken up.

That in the year 1772, your Memorialists, apprehending that the former Proclamation, prohibiting the setling or granting Lands to the westward of the Great Mountains, was repealed by a late royal Instruction for running a western Line, presented a Representation and Petition to the Governor and Council setting forth the Difficulties they had laboured under, and how they had been prevented from surveying by the late War and afterwards by the King's Proclamation; complaining of their Agent Colo. George Mercer having undertaken, without their Consent or Authority, to make an Agreement of Copartnership between them and Thomas Walpole Esqr. and others his Associates in Great Britain; which they disclaimed; And praying for a new Order or Warrant to survey their Land. Upon which the Council was pleased, on the 27th. Day of July in the said year 1772, to order the Substance of the said Representation to be entered upon their [J]ournals, and make an Order of Council recognising, confirming, and declaring still in Force your Memorialists' first Entry and Order for the two hundred [t]housand Acres herein before mentioned, and therefore that any further or other Warrant or Order was unnecessary; to which Order, together with a letter [fr]om the Clerk of the Council, wrote by Order of the Board, your Memorialists beg leave to refer.

That in the year 1773 (their former Surveyor Mr. Gist being

dead) your Memorialists obtained, from the President and Professors of William and Mary College a special Commission, appointing Mr. William Crawford Surveyor of their Lands; who had a Year or two before, by Virtue of a like special Commission [for] that Purpose from the said President and Professors, surveyed the two hundred thousand acres for General Washington, and the Officers and Soldiers of his Regiment; upon which Surveys regular Patents had been granted and passed. And the Year following they also obtained from the said President and Professors, a Commission for Mr. Hancock Lee, as Deputy-Surveyor to the said William Crawford: And they were proceeding down the River, in order to begin their Surveys; but had the Misfortune to have their cannoes overset, in attempting to pass the Falls of Youghyoughgaine, and to lose all their Provisions Arms and Amunition, and have two of their Men drowned; which, together with the Indian War that Summer, prevented their further Progress.

That in the next Year, 1775, your Memorialists had their beforementioned quantity of two hundred thousand Acres of Land surveyed, laid off, marked, and bounded, all in one compact well shaped Tract, upon both Sides the main South Fork of Great Licking Creek, in Fincastle now Kentucky County; as will appear by the Certificate of Survey, and Plat thereof, returned under the Hands of the said William Crawford, and Hancock Lee, the Surveyors, clear of any prior Titles, or Surveys; but the Confusion of the present Troubles preventing any Land-Office being open'd, your Memorialists knew not where, or how to make Return of the said Survey. And the Term of their Partnership being expired, and several of the Members residing in Great Britain, with whom the Members in America can now have no Communication, they are utterly at a Loss how to proceed, or in what Manner to secure Lands, to which they have acquired a just Title, at so great Expence, without the Interposition of the Legislature.

That the said Ohio Company was always intended to consist, and doth at present consist of twenty Shares, of which the following Persons are at this time the Proprietors, vizt. eleven Shares belonging to Persons residing in Virginia; one held by the honble John Tayloe Esqr. one by the late Thomas Ludwell Lee Esqr. one by Richard Lee Esqr. one by James Scott Clerk, one by George Mason Esqr. one by Peter Presly Thornton Esqr. one by Thomas Lomax Esqr. one by the Heirs of John Mercer Esqr. Decd. one by the Heirs of the honble Philip Ludwell Lee Esqr. Decd. and two by the honble Robert Carter Esqr. three Shares belonging to Persons residing in Maryland, one held by Colo. Thomas Cresap, one by Jacob Giles

Esqr. and one by Pearson Chapman Esqr. And six Shares held by Persons residing in Great Britain; one held by Osgood Hanbury Merchant, one by the Heirs of Capel Hanbury Merchant Decd. one by the Heirs of the honble Robert Dinwiddie Decd. one by the Heirs of the honble Arthur Dobbs Decd. one by the Heirs of James Wardrope Esqr. Decd. and one by Colo. George Mercer; Some of which Shares in Great Britain are considerably in arrear to the Company, for their Quota of Stock not paid up.

That the Term of their Co-Partnership being expired in the present dispersed Situation of their Members, and a War carried on against America by Great Britain, your Memorialists conceiving it absolutely impracticable for them to comply with that Part of the Royal Instruction respecting the Fort and Garrison (originally intended in the Lieu of paying Right-Money) and also that the same is utterly incompatible with the Nature and Constitution of the present Government; Such of the Members of the said Company as reside in Virginia and Maryland are willing and desirous to receive a seperate Grant or Patent, each in his own Name, for his due Share or Proportion of the said two hundred thousand Acres of land, in the common Form, and in Lieu of the Fort and Garrison, to pay for the same the ancient accustomed Right-Money of ten shillings Sterling Per hundred Acres; but do not care to advance this Money for others, especially for those beyond Sea, in the present Situation of Affairs.

In tender Consideration of the Premises, of the great Charge and Trouble they have incurred, and of their having complied, as far as was practicable, with every Requisition of Government, your Petitioners humbly pray, that an Act of Assembly may pass for issueing patents, in the common Form (so soon as a Land-office shall be established) to all the said Proprietors of Shares in the said Company now residing in Virginia and Maryland, each in his own Name, for his due Share or proportion of the said Tract of two hundred thousand Acres of Land, upon their respectively paying down the Sum of ten Shillings Sterling per hundred Acres, Right-Money for the same; And for reserving the quantity or Proportion due to the said six Members residing in Great Britain, all in one Tract or Peice, subject to the further Order of the General Assembly: for which Purpose your Petitioners have prepared an accurate Plat (the outlines whereof are exactly copyed from the Surveyor's original Plat) in which all the said Shares are divided and laid off accordingly: so that the Courses of the several Patents may be ascertained with the greatest Precision.

Your Petitioners beg Leave to observe that by this Mode, such of the Members in America as are ready to pay down their Right-Money will be secured their Property, no Injustice will be done to the Members in Great Britain; and to the Public, it will be exactly the same thing, as if a Patent for the whole two hundred thousand Acres was granted to the Company, and afterwards divided among them in seperate Shares, and mutual Deeds of Conveyance for each Person's Proportion, duly executed.

Your Petitioners are not able to suggest any Method of setling this Matter so unexceptionable as that they have proposed; but thoroughly confiding in the Wisdom and Justice of this honourable Assembly, they humbly beg Leave to submit the Case to their Consideration; not doubting but that such Remedie will be granted to your Petitioners, and such Order made therein as shall be judged just and reasonable. And your petitioners will ever pray.

G Mason for the
Ohio Company P[artners]

I approve of the above Petition and in case of my absence for George Mason Esqr. to act for me.

Richard Lee

I consent to the foregoing Petition & authorize Colo. George Mason to act to [*illegible*] on behalf of myself Colo. George Mercer & the Estate of John Mercer deced.

J. Mercer

I assent to & approve of this Petition, & empower George Mason Esqr. to act for me in fixing the particular Part or lott which each Member is to have in the Survey in the same Manner as if I myself was present.

Pearson Chapman

I do highly approve the above proposition, and as Trustee for the estate of the late hon. Phil. Lud. Lee give my assent thereto. I do also hereby empower George Mason esqr. to act for said Estate in the way that shall be agreed on to fix the part that each Member is to have of said Survey.
April 25th 1778

Richard Henry Lee Administrator

I also assent to & approve this petition, & empower Geo: Mason Esqr. to act for me also in the same Manner.

James Scott

Ms (Vi). Two pages in GM's handwriting. The Ms has been folded and slightly torn in several places. The approving endorsements signed by Pearson Chapman and James Scott are in GM's hand; and it also appears that GM signed Chapman's name. The clerk's endorsement reads: "Memorial of the

Ohio Company—20th. Nov. 1778. Referred to [the Committee on Prop[o]s[itions and Grievances]. Def[erre]d to next Session."

At the preceding winter session of the General Assembly GM had hoped to guide bills providing for settlement of old land claims through to enactment, along with companion measures establishing a land office and a sinking fund on the public debt. Thwarted in these moves, GM salvaged only a resolution calling upon all claimants to "any unpatented Lands on the said western waters" to present their case during the May session. That abbreviated term was missed by GM, but he obviously had drafted this petition before Richard Henry Lee signed it on 25 Apr. It is not clear why GM withheld the petition, for he had encouraged James Mercer and other partners or executors to act with speed (in the Ohio Company advertisement of 24 Apr. 1778) and had taken the time to detail the company's history with a graphic account. In preparing the petition, GM must have used the company papers in his possession. By this stage, he was ready to forego the larger claim to 500,000 acres and he confided to Mercer that 200,000 acres were "all I have Hopes of & that I think is upon such a Foundation, as that Nothing but our own Negligence can deprive us of it" (letter to Mercer, 6 Feb. 1778). The petition was another round in the legal battle to remind Virginians that the Ohio Company intended to press its old claim in opposition to the Indiana Company. A counterclaim from the Indiana Company, led by Samuel Wharton in Philadelphia, had been presented to the legislature in 1777. A few weeks earlier in this session, the Transylvania Company had offered to compromise its claim through a proposition Richard Henderson presented the legislature (JHD, 1827 ed., 29 Oct. entry). The point, as far as Virginians was concerned, was to establish their claims before the land beyond the Alleghenies was transferred to the United States or some local jurisdiction (see R. H. Lee to [Patrick Henry], 15 Nov. 1778, Ballagh, Lee Letters, I, 451–453).

There are slight deviations in punctuation and capitalization in the petition text printed in the appendix of Bailey, Ohio Company of Virginia, 320–327. The portions in brackets are conjectures for a word or words blotted or torn in the Ms.

A Petition to the General Assembly regarding Importation Rights

[[23 Nov. 1778. At the Oct. 1777 session of the General Assembly GM had expected action on his bill "for establishing a Land Office," which recognized head-right certificates as legal entitlements to 50 acres of land under "the antient custom of importation rights." This measure had been postponed and was still pending, but meanwhile the 24 Jan. 1778 resolution which GM wrote and ushered through the legislature called upon land claimants to present their case forthwith. Thus GM wrote a petition on behalf of the Ohio Company which was presented 20 Nov., and the Journal indicates that GM on this day read a petition "setting forth, that he hath a claim to a considerable quantity of land upon the western waters, due to him upon charter importation rights, which hath been recognized by the governor and Council during the British government, as legal and valid: that conscious of the uprightness of his conduct and soundness of his title, he has proceeded to locate and survey the lands which he thus claims, in the most legal and authentic manner; and praying that his title and locations, and surveys, may be confirmed" (JHD, 1827 ed., 23 Nov. entry). GM had been buying these headrights in quantity since 1773, and his position was confirmed with passage of the act "for adjusting and settling the titles of claimers to unpatented lands" (Hening, X, 35–50). On 10 July 1779 twelve warrants were issued to GM by the state allowing him 68,900 acres for surrendered headrights (see Appendix A). The petition GM presented has not been located.]]

Settlement of Richard Henderson's Claims to Western Lands

[[*23 Nov. 1778–8 Dec. 1778*. Jefferson and GM had been designated by the House of Delegates early in 1778 to receive "a copy of the several papers filed in the office relating to the claim of Richard Henderson and Company . . ." (JHD, 1827 ed., 24 Jan. entry). Henderson's claims were based on his Indian purchase of 1775 at Sycamore Shoals, and since a resolution of the General Assembly in 1777, voluminous depositions had been submitted to buttress his extravagant claims (see Boyd, II, 68–111). GM was not present for this session until 19 Nov., and on the following day he was named to the committee considering a proper award; but by that time Henderson and his friends had made much headway in the House. Between 23 Nov. and 9 Dec. the House and Senate shifted a bill which first offered Henderson & Company up to 800,000 acres, then 400,000, and finally 200,000 acres "beginning at the mouth of Green river" (JHD, 1827 ed., 23 Nov. entry; Hening, IX, 571–572). GM's late arrival at the session makes it unlikely that he played a major role in this legislation, although he was vitally interested in the manner of the settlement since his own Ohio Company claim was still pending. "The land was so remote that it was not surveyed until 1796; as immediate compensation, therefore, it was valueless" (Boyd, II, 66). See also GM's enclosures No. 5 and No. 6 in his letter to Samuel Purviance, 20 May 1782, relating to Henderson's claims. In 1785, GM asserted that he had spent about £10 "in collecting Evidence, & cross examining Witnesses between the Commonwealth & Colo. Richd. Henderson in the Cause which I was directed to manage by a Vote of both Houses" (letter to James Madison, 7 Dec. 1785).]]

Resolution to Purchase Iron for the Cannon Foundry

[2 December 1778]

Resolved, That fifty tons of the pig iron brought down from the Buckingham furnace, and lying at the said cannon foundery, be purchased on the public account at the current ready money price, and that Richard Adams and Turner Southall, Esquires, be empowered to contract with Messrs. John Ballendine and John Revely, for the same, and that their certificate shall entitle the said Ballendine and Revely to payment at the treasury.

Printed from the JHD, 1827 ed., 2 Dec. 1778 entry.
The commonwealth was subsidizing the production of iron in Buckingham County, about 50 miles up the James River from Richmond. ADAMS and SOUTHALL were Henrico County legislators, logical persons to deal with BALLEN-DINE and REVELY (or Reveley), the operators of a foundry at Westham in Henrico County. GM probably wrote the resolution since he was ordered to carry it to the Senate. The negotiations dragged on, and in the summer of 1779 GM was trying to settle accounts between the state and Ballendine. An indefatigable promoter, Ballendine appears to have submitted substantial claims against the state in July 1780 and Feb. 1781 (see resolution of 25 June 1779 and Palmer, ed., Cal. of Va. State Papers, I, 366, 544–546).

Depositions concerning Dr. Savage's Brigantine

Virginia Fairfax County Sct.   [3 December 1778]
Lawrence Sandford Mariner, of full Age, deposeth & sayeth, that some time in the Year 1776 he this Depot. was called upon to appraise & value upon Oath sundry Sails which were taken & seized for the Use of the Potomack Navy, from a Brigantine of Doctor William Savage's then lying at the Mouth of Quantico Creek in Potomack River, that all the said Sails were in very bad Condition, & so mildewed & rotten that they were unfit for Use, or carrying a Vessel to Sea, except one, a small forestay-sail, that this Depot. Capt. Richd. Conway (who is now down the Country) Mr. Thomas Flemming & Mr. Thomas Crafts were sworn to appraise and value the said sails, which they minutely examined, & appraised at the price they were then worth; but what the exact amount was this Depot. doth not now remember, but thinks it was twenty odd pounds; that this Depot. does not think any of the said Sails, except the before mentioned small forestay-sail, was worth the charge of refitting or altering; that this Depot. at the time commanded the Brigantine Adventure in the Commonwealth's Service, loading with Tobacco at Alexandria, & was frequently on board the different vessels of the Potomack Navy, as they were fitting up for public Service; & knows that the said sails were not, nor cou'd not be made use of for the said Vessels, otherwise than as Oakum Bags, to stuff the Nettings; to which use most of them were applyed; that this Depot. knows that the Managers of the Potomack Navy were under great Difficultys in procuring Sails & other Necessaries for fitting up the armed Vessels, and were very anxious to get them equipped for

Defence, in Case any of the Enemie's Vessels shou'd come up the River, before they were compleated; which this Depot. believes was the Reason why the abovementioned Sails (as well as some others of much better Quality from other Vessels) were seized; and this Depot. further sayeth that one of the Mariners who had belonged to Doctor Savages Brig, & said he had been her Boatswain, told this Depot. that the said Brig had other & better Sails than those which had been seized but they had been secreted & kept out of the Way—that this Depot. was on board the said Brig of Doctor Savage's early in the Year 1775, that she was then in very bad Condition, & this Depot. thinks cou'd not have been ventured to Sea with any tollerable Safety, that he himself wou'd not have taken the Command of such a Vessel, or have gone to Sea in her; that she was an old Shattered Vessel, & as this Depot. understood had been purchased as a Wreck, or condemned Vessel by Doctor Savage at Norfolk; who after being at considerable Expence, sent her on a voyage to Ireland, from whence she returned, & had been laid up a long time at Quantico, when the said Sails were seized, and her Hands discharged, except one, the beforementioned Boatswain, who this Depot. understood was left to take Care of the Riggin & Apparrel of the said Vessel, which this Depot. understood & believes was unfit to go to Sea again—and further this Depot. sayeth not.

LAWR. SANFORD

⟨Alexandria April 22nd. 1778
The above deposition was taken in
the presence of & sworn to before⟩
WM. RAMSAY J. P.

Virginia Fairfax County Sct.
Thomas Flemming of the said County Ship-Carpenter; being of full age, deposeth & sayeth, that some time in the Summer of the Year 1776 he this Depot. was called upon to appraise & value upon Oath sundry Sails which he understood were taken & seized by George Mason & John Dalton Esqrs. for the Use of the Potomack Navy, from a Brigantine of Doctor William Savage's then lying in the Mouth of Quantico Creek in Potomack River; that all the said Sails were in very bad Condition & so mildewed, & rotten that they were unfit for Use, or carrying a Vessel to Sea; except one, a small Sail commonly a fore-Stay-Sail; that this Depot. Capt. Richd. Conway (who is now down the Country) Capt. Lawrence Sandford, & Mr. Thomas Crafts were sworn to appraise & value the said Sails, which

after due Examination, they accordingly did at about twenty three or twenty four pounds (this Depot. can't now recollect the exact Sum) which at the then [prevailing] prices, were the full Value of them; that this Depot. does not know what use were afterwards made of the said Sails; but does not think that any of them, except the before mentioned small fore-Stay-Sail, cou'd have been made Sea-worthy; or were worth the charge of fitting on or altering; that the abovementioned Brigantine lay some time in the Harbour of Alexandria, & this Depot. understood was a Wreck which Doctor Savage had purchased at Norfolk, & been at considerable charge in fitting out for Sea, & had made a voyage to Ireland before she came to Alexandria; that she went from Alexandria to the Mouth of Quantico, where she had been laid up a long time, when the said Sails were taken from her, & this Depot. understood was intended to sold or condemned as unfit for Sea, and further this Depot. sayeth not.

THOMAS FLEMMING

[Ramsay's endorsement also appears here.]

Virginia Fairfax County Sct.

Thomas Crafts Sail-Maker of the said County, being of full Age, deposeth & saith, that some time in the Summer of the Year 1776 he this Depot. was called upon to appraise & value upon Oath Sundry Sails which he understood were seized & taken by George Mason & John Dalton Esqrs. for the Use of the Potomack Navy, from a Vessel belonging to Doctor William Savage, then lying at the Mouth of Quantico in potomack River, that the said Sails were of different kinds, & eight in Number; that all the said Sails were in very bad Condition, & rotten, except one, a small Sail, commonly called a fore-Stay-Sail, & that no Vessel could have used or gone to Sea with them; that this Depot. Capt. Richard Conway (who is now down the Country) Capt. Lawrence Sandford, & Mr. Thomas Flemming were sworn to appraise & value the said Sails that they accordingly after a minute Examination, valued & appraised the said Sails at twenty three pounds some odd Shillings, this Depot. can't now recollect the precise Sum, but it did not amount to twenty four pounds; which according to the then Prices, were the full Value of the said Sails; that this Depot. made up all the Sails that were used in fitting the Potomack Navy, but that he did not make up or fit any of the aforesaid Sails, for that purpose; all the others being unfit for

[455]

that Use, except the before mentioned small-fore-stay Sail—and further this Deponent sayeth not.

⟨Alexandria April 22d 1778   THOMAS CRAFTS
The above deposition taken in the
presence of & sworn to before⟩

WM. RAMSAY J. P.

 Ms (Vi). Five pages, all in GM's hand, with his outer endorsement: "April 22d. 1778. The Depositions of Thomas Crafts, Thomas Flemming, & Lawrence Sandford, between the Commonwealth of Virginia & Doctor William Savage for the Committee of Propositions." A clerk later wrote: "Wm. Savage's Petition & Depositions on behalf of the State Decr. 1st. 1778. ref[erre]d to next Session of Assembly" and below that "(reasonable)."

 GM prepared this series of depositions for the May 1778 session of the General Assembly, which was of short duration and which GM did not attend. He apparently had some arrangement with DOCTOR WILLIAM SAVAGE, plainly because of his work on the Fairfax County Committee of Safety. LAWRENCE SANDFORD (or Sanford) had been a ship captain around Alexandria for a decade before the war began. Dr. Savage lived in the vicinity of Dumfries. GM was appointed to the Committee on Propositions and Grievances, which was overwhelmed with private petitions during the session. Savage's own petition, which these supported, has not been found. Almost a year later, the House of Delegates approved a £24 payment (plus interest from 1 June 1776) for the sails, but rejected Dr. Savage's other claims (JHD, 1827 ed., 19 Oct. 1779 entry).

 Portions in angle brackets are in the handwriting of William Ramsay, Fairfax County Justice of the Peace.

Resolution to Consider the Emancipation of the Slave Known as Kitt

[10 December 1778]

 Resolved, therefore, That the Governor be requested to sequester the said Kitt from his said master, until the end of the next session of Assembly; and that the said Hinchie Mabry be summoned to attend this House, upon the tenth day of the next session, to shew cause why a bill should not pass for the emancipation of the said negro Kitt, and said Hinchie Mabry receiving full compensation for the same.

 Printed from the JHD, 1827 ed., 10 Dec. 1778 entry.

 Kitt's service to the commonwealth was particularly timely, as he informed officials of a counterfeiting ring in Brunswick County which led to the capture of two men and "considerable sums of [bogus] continental Money." Counterfeiting was plaguing the state and continental treasuries to the point that some leading public men were ready to dispense swift and certain capital punishment for offenders (see R. H. Lee to [Patrick Henry], 15 Nov. 1778, Ballagh, *Lee Letters,* I, 451-453). The House was concerned that Kitt would be harmed unless he was protected "from the wrath of those whom he has offended." Six months later, GM also appears to have written the act which freed Kitt (JHD,

17 June 1779; Hening, X, 115). No manuscript of the resolution has been found, but in both instances GM carried the legislation to the Senate for action. This was the usual routine for the author of a bill or resolution.

Resolutions Calling for a Conference to Determine the Pennsylvania-Virginia Boundary Line

[12 December 1778]

Resolved, That the southern boundary offered by the Pennsylvania Assembly, is inadmissible; and that no part of the offer heretofore made by the Assembly of this Commonwealth, is, or ought to be, binding upon Virginia, unless the whole had been, or shall be, accepted by the Assembly of Pennsylvania.

Resolved, That it is now too late in the present session, to enter into proper discussion of the observations made by the Assembly of Pennsylvania, or to give a full and determinate answer to their proposals; but as the confusion, from the doubtful jurisdiction in the county adjacent to the disputed territory, may produce the most dangerous consequences to the common cause of America;

Resolved, That the Virginia delegates in Congress, be empowered and instructed to propose to the Commonwealth of Pennsylvania, to appoint commissioners on their part, to meet commissioners to be appointed by the Assembly of this Commonwealth, at such convenient place as may be agreed on by the said commissioners of both States, to confer together and endeavor to fix on the true and proper boundaries between the said States; or, if that cannot be done, to agree upon some temporary boundary, in the mean time, and report their proceedings thereon to their respective Assemblies.

Printed from the JHD, 1827 ed., 12 Dec. 1778 entry.

Wrangling over the southern Pennsylvania-Virginia boundary and its westward extension had been a discordant note since the early days of the Revolution. A temporary boundary line had been proposed by the Virginia Convention of 1776, but the problem grew more complex as settlers pushed into the southwest corner of Pennsylvania and appealed to authorities in Philadelphia for support. GM served on the committee studying the question in 1776 and his proposal was adopted by the Convention on 17 Dec. (*q.v.*). The Virginia solution conceded Fort Pitt to the Pennsylvanians but placed the southern boundary above the Mason & Dixon line separating Pennsylvania and Maryland, which Pennsylvania authorities naturally favored. GM had a double concern, both as a legislator and as champion of the Ohio Company claims which were still unsettled. Heretofore, the Virginia delegation in the Continental Congress had been negotiating with the Pennsylvanians. GM probably drafted this set of resolutions which finally brought a settlement through the conference of commissioners, an idea accepted by Pennsylvania. Commissioners from the two states met at Baltimore in Aug. 1779 and reached an agreement, although friction between rival settlers continued (see Thomas Scott to Joseph Reed, 29 Nov. 1779, Boyd, III, 208). A final survey of the boundary was delayed until 1784–1785. Details of the settlement are graphically portrayed in Paullin, *Historical Atlas*, 77–78. See also GM's accounting of the final negotiations in his letter to Joseph Jones, 27 July 1780.

An Act "to prohibit the Distillation of Spirits from Corn, Wheat, Rye, and other grain, for a limited time."

[15 December 1778]

WHEREAS the great quantity of grain consumed in the distilleries will increase the present alarming scarcity, *Be it enacted by the General Assembly*, That no kind of spirituous liquors shall be distilled from Indian corn, wheat, rye, oats, barley, buck wheat, meal, or flour, within this commonwealth, between the fifteenth day of February next and the fifteenth day of October next, on pain of forfeiting the liquor so distilled, or the worth thereof, if sold before seizure, together with the still in which the same was distilled, to be recovered in any court of record within this commonwealth, by action of debt, bill, plaint, or information, by any person who shall sue for the same, one half thereof to the informer, and the other half to the use of the commonwealth; and upon the recovery of any still or stills sued for under this act, the court by whom judgment is given shall order the sheriff to sell the same for ready money to the highest bidder, and pay one half of the money arising from such sale into the publick treasury.

Provided, That the penalties of this act shall not be extended to any person distilling wheat or rye unless he shall have refused to sell the same to some publick agent or contractor offering to purchase at the following prices, to wit, the wheat at fifteen shillings per bushel, and the rye at fifteen shillings per bushel. And wherever any dispute shall arise from what species of grain any liquor hath been distilled contrary to this act, the *onus probandi* shall lie upon the distiller.

Printed from Hening, IX, 476–477. GM wrote on a slip of paper (Vi): "Add to the end of the Bill 'provided that the Penalties of this Act shall not be extended to any Person distilling Wheat or Rye, who within one Month before such Distillation, shall have offered the Wheat or Rye so distilled to any public Agent or Contractor, at the following Prices, to wit the Wheat at   per Bushell and the Rye at   per Bushel; and who shall have had the same refused by such Agent or Contractor.[']" A clerk's hand has altered GM's Ms to constitute the second paragraph of the bill as passed.

On 8 Dec. GM had been ordered to bring this bill into the House. He presented the bill on 15 Dec., and on 18 Dec. it had been approved (JHD, 1827 ed., 18 Dec. entry). GM was ordered to carry the bill to the Senate, in itself a strong indication of his authorship even if the addition in GM's hand had not been found. The bill was written in response to entreaties from the Congress for legislation "to prohibit the converting of . . . Bread, which was meant for the sustenance of Man into a Liquid poison for his Destruction" (letter from A Committee of Congress to the [Governors of] Several States, 11 Nov., 1778, Burnett, *Letters of Continental Congress*, III, 491–492). The Committee also requested the laws dealing with monopolizing and profiteering in a similar latter of the same date (*ibid.*, 490–491).

A Bill "for the More General Diffusion of Knowledge"

[[*15 Dec. 1778*. Rowland, I, 308–309, mentions the order of the House of Delegates for GM and "Mr. Parker" to prepare a bill by this title and present it. The JHD, 1827 ed., 16 Dec. entry, records that [Richard?] Parker presented such a bill on the following day, but it failed to pass. It is highly unlikely that the bill was written by GM, although a Ms draft for the rejected legislation has not been located.]]

Report and Resolutions concerning Captain Benjamin Hoomes

[[*16 Dec. 1778*. GM served on the committee of the House of Delegates appointed to consider the hardships suffered by Capt. Benjamin Hoomes, a veteran of Brandywine, Germantown, and Monmouth. Capt. Hoomes was wounded at Monmouth and left on the field as a casualty, but was later rescued from the battlefield and hospitalized. GM reported that Hoomes had made a miraculous recovery and should be paid £216 from the state treasury. The report noted that Hoomes wished to return to active duty, but admitted that his status was uncertain. Resolutions were offered to keep Hoomes on full pay, recommend him to General Washington's attention for some kind of suitable duty, and request "that the Governor . . . be pleased to promote the said Capt. Hoomes to a majority, whenever a proper vacancy shall happen, notwithstanding the necessity of his present absence from duty." The report and resolutions are printed in the JHD, 1827 ed., 16 Dec. entry. GM was ordered to carry the resolutions to the Senate and was probably their author, but the Ms in his handwriting has not been located.]]

Resolutions concerning Trade and Profiteering

[17 December 1778]

Resolved, that it is the opinion of this committee, That all persons exporting grain or other victual, contrary to an act, passed in this

[459]

present session of Assembly, entitled "an act to empower the Governor and Council, to lay an embargo for a limited time," ought to be forever thereafter rendered incapable of carrying on any trade or commerce within this Commonwealth.

Resolved, That the master of every vessel building within this Commonwealth, or coming into the same, shall give bond, with sufficient security to the naval officer of the district, that he will not during the stay of the vessel, load or take on board any articles, contrary to the said act, other than shall be necessary for the sustenance of the crew of such vessel, for her voyage or cruise.

Resolved, that it is the opinion of this committee, That those who purchase grain or other victual, other than for the consumption of themselves, their families, or those in their employ, or for manufacture, ought to be declared by law, to be engrossers, save only that such declaration should not extend to any public agent or contractor, purchasing in pursuance of the duties of his office.

Resolved, that it is the opinion of this committee, That persons, not being public agents or contractors, and taking upon themselves that character, thereby to take advantage to themselves of those exemptions and privileges, which the laws give to public agents and contractors, ought to be made subject to exemplary punishment.

Printed from JHD, 1827 ed., 17 Dec. 1778 entry.
A day earlier, the Speaker of the House made public a letter from Gov. Henry enclosing a message from the President of the Continental Congress along with two other letters from the Virginia delegation at Philadelphia, "several resolutions of that body, and several letters from a committee of Congress." A committee, headed by GM, was charged with examining these documents and reporting back to the House. The SEVERAL LETTERS FROM A COMMITTEE OF CONGRESS dealt with four topics: an unpublicized inventory of commodities, the need for laws to punish war profiteering, a recommendation for a law to suspend distilling of spirits from grains, and a warning that some public contractors had been reaping dishonest profits on their transactions, with the observation that "This seething of the Kid in its Mothers milk, calls for the most exemplary punishment" (Burnett, ed., *Letters of Continental Congress,* III, 489–493). The House of Delegates handled all of these matters with specific resolutions or bills, and in this series of resolutions attempted to tighten the loosely-drawn law TO EMPOWER THE GOVERNOR AND COUNCIL, TO LAY AN EMBARGO (Hening, IX, 530–532). Congress may have been acting in response to Washington, who was infuriated with "those murderers of our cause (the monopolizers, forestallers, and engrossers)" and "lamented that each State long ere this has not hunted them down as the pests of society, and the greatest Enemys we have to the happiness of America" (ltr. to Joseph Reed, 12 Dec. 1778, Fitzpatrick, ed., *Writings of Washington,* XIII, 383). On the following day, GM brought in a bill from a committee which he headed that was intended to give more teeth to the previous legislation on profiteering (JHD, 1827 ed., 18 Dec. entry; Hening, IX, 474–476 [it should be remembered that laws are not printed in Hening according to their chronological order of passage, hence chapter III in this volume was passed long after chapter XV, which it amends]). GM's draft of these resolves has not been located, but his

authorship is evident from the Speaker's action in ordering him to carry them to the Senate for action.

Amendments to the Act Relating to Hoarding and Profiteering

[[*18 Dec. 1778.* At the winter session of the House of Delegates in 1777–1778, GM and Jefferson had been ordered to draft a bill that would prohibit and provide punishment for hoarding and profiteering on a variety of commodities then in short supply. The resulting legislation (see entries of 29 Dec. 1777 and 20 Nov. 1777–6 Jan. 1778) appears to have been ineffectual. Again, the two experienced delegates were placed on a committee to bring in amendments, with the "act to amend the act for preventing forestalling, regrating, engrossing, and publick vendues" brought out and presented by GM on 18 Dec. Jefferson was ordered to carry the bill to the Senate, which usually meant he was its author and floor manager (JHD, 1827 ed., 18 Dec. entry). Since a manuscript in neither Jefferson's nor GM's hand can be located, it is impossible to say the degree in which the bill was a cooperative effort. The bill as finally approved is in Hening, IX, 581–583. It enlarges the definition of engrossing, excepted "the managers of any iron works . . . ordinary [i.e., tavern] keepers . . . or persons keeping private houses for lodging or entertainment," millers, bakers, butchers, and brewers. Foodstuffs in the hands of condemned parties were liable to seizure for the use of troops or the French forces, and it also provided for the punishment of "any person pretending to be an agent of this commonwealth. . . ."]]

Preamble and Resolution Seeking Information concerning the Illinois or Wabash Land Company Partners

[18 December 1778]

And whereas, this Assembly hath come to believe, that sundry citizens of some of the United States, were, and are, connected and concerned with some of the King of Great Britain's late governors in America, as well as with sundry noblemen and others, subjects of the said King, in the purchase of a very large tract of land from the Indians, on the northwest side of the Ohio river, within the territory of Virginia;

Resolved, also, That the said delegates be instructed to use their endeavors in Congress, to cause an inquiry to be made, concerning the said purchase, and whether any, and what citizens of any of the United States, were, or are, concerned therein.

Printed from JHD, 1827 ed., 18 Dec. 1778 entry.

The background for the maze of speculation and intrigue by the various land companies is lucidly set forth in Merrill Jensen, "The Cession of the Old Northwest," *Miss. Valley Historical Review*, XXIII, 27–48. Jensen notes (p. 30) that a band of Pennsylvania and Maryland businessmen secured a grant of land north of the Ohio in 1773, and that the "same group with a few additional members including Lord Dunmore, organized the . . . Wabash Company and secured another grant of land north of the Ohio in 1775." Virginia claimed all the territory involved under its 1606 charter, and used this point as a wedge in any bargaining with other states over its boundary settlement. GM probably wrote this resolve although it is impossible to make this an absolute assertion of fact. His authorship claim rests on the circumstances of his known interest in thwarting the Illinois-Wabash and Indiana claims, and also his letter to Joseph Jones of 27 July 1780. In the 1780 letter GM's seventh point (giving details of a projected western land cession) buttresses a plea for a large military tract, and makes the point that "several gentlemen of great influence in the neighboring States were, and still are, concerned in partnership with Lord Dunmore, some other of the late American governors, and several of the British nobility and gentry, in a purchase for a mere trifle, about the year 1773, from the Indians, of a large tract of country . . . on the north-west side of the Ohio. . . ." Part of the purpose of the resolution, which had little chance of implementation in Congress, must have been to warn the land speculators in Maryland and Pennsylvania of Virginia's vigilance. A powerful association, including Robert Morris and James Wilson in Pennsylvania, and Samuel Chase and Charles Carroll in Maryland, had considerable influence in Congress and their state legislatures. GM may have seen Richard Henry Lee's letter to Patrick Henry of 15 Nov. 1778 (Ballagh, *Lee Letters*, I, 451–453) in which Lee expressed fear that Maryland would never ratify the articles of Confederation "whilst our claim remains so unlimited to the westward. . . . Some of the most heated Opponents of our claim, say that if we would fix a reasonable limit, and agree that a new State should be established to the Westward of those limits, they would be content to confederate." Lee went on to propose that Virginia acknowledge the Ohio River as the western Virginia boundary with "the Country beyond . . . settled for common good." Thus a preliminary resolution to this one possibly was GM's, for it proposed the surrender of claims to lands northwest of the Ohio, with the United States to take jurisdiction and distribute the lands "without any purchase money, to the troops on continental establishment" from those states in the Confederation without western land reserves (JHD, 1827 ed., 18 Dec. entry). Pressures from the land speculators continued and provoked GM to write his well-known "Remonstrance . . . to the Delegates of the United American States" (10 Dec. 1779). Ordinarily, the authorship could be presumed from the Speaker's designation of a member to carry the resolutions to the Senate; but in this singular instance, the House *Journal* adds to the mystery by leaving a blank space: "*Ordered*, That Mr. do carry the resolutions to the Senate."

An Act "for the more effectual execution of an act intituled An act to empower the Governour and Council to lay an embargo for a limited time."

[18 December 1778]

WHEREAS the inordinate lust of gain may tempt many persons to risk the penalties inflicted by an act passed this present session of assembly, intituled "An act to empower the governour and council to lay an embargo for a limited time," by exporting provisions contrary to the same, which during the present alarming scarcity and publick distress would be highly criminal:

Be it enacted by the General Assembly, That any and every person, who, during the continuance of the said recited act, shall export, or cause to be put on board any vessel for exportation, any sort of grain or other victual contrary to the said act, and on which an embargo hath been or shall be laid by the governour and council in pursuance thereof, shall for ever thereafter be disabled from exercising or carrying on, either by himself or by any other in trust for him, or for his use and benefit, or in partnership with any other, any manner of merchandise or commerce within this common-wealth, and from buying or selling any kind of goods, wares, or merchandise, other than what shall be necessary for the use and consumption of his own family, or those in his employ, or shall be the produce of his own estate or manufacture, under pain of forfeit-ing the full value of the goods, wares, or merchandise, which shall be so bought or sold, to be recovered by action of debt or informa-tion in any court of record, one half to the informer, and the other half to the use of the commonwealth.

And for the more effectual discovery of any provisions which may be put on board any vessel for exportation contrary to the said recited act, *Be it enacted*, That the master of every vessel now in this commonwealth, or building within the same, or which shall hereafter come hither, shall, before he presume to load any such vessel, give bond with sufficient security to the naval officer of the district, in a sum proportioned to the tunnage of such vessel, after the rate of fifty pounds per tun, that such vessel shall not, during her stay here, take on board any of the articles prohibited to be exported by the said recited act more than will be necessary for the suste-nance of the crew of such vessel for her voyage or cruise; and every vessel loading or taking on board any goods or commodities, before such bond be given, shall, together with her furniture, apparel, and tackle, be liable to seizure, and be forfeited, one half of the value thereof to the informer, and the other to this commonwealth, to be sued for and recovered as in manner before directed.

And whereas part of the trade of this commonwealth is carried on by persons who have refused to take the oath of fidelity to the same, and it may be dangerous to allow any recusant to have such oppor-tunity of injuring the republick, *Be it therefore enacted*, That any inhabitant of this commonwealth, who hath not heretofore taken the oath or affirmation of fidelity to the same, shall, after the fifteenth day of March next, carry on any trade or commerce whatever, either by himself or any other person in trust for him, or for his use or benefit, or in partnership with any other, he shall forfeit and pay the full value of his merchandise in which he shall so trade, unless he, before the said fifteenth day of March, take the oath or affirmation of fidelity to this state, to be recovered in the same manner as the penalties inflicted by this law are herein before directed to be recovered.

Printed from Hening, IX, 474–476.

The Governor, Privy Council, and General Assembly were feeling pressure from the Continental Congress, General Washington, and their constituents as the scarcity of supplies and the surplus of money played havoc with the state's economy. Moreover, it was not certain whether the "many evil disposed and designing men in the Commonwealth" were tories or pretended patriots. A committee under Gen. Thomas Nelson had been ordered to bring in the earlier bill empowering the governor and council TO LAY AN EMBARGO FOR A LIMITED TIME, but part of the necessity arose from a request from the Continental Congress that provisions be made available for the French squadron (JHD, 1827 ed., 20 and 27 Oct. 1778 entries). This urgent plea brought forth an act "to supply the armies and navies of the United States, and of their allies, with grain and flour"—a harsh measure insofar as the search-and-seizure provisions went, but without penalties for hoarders and engrossers except seizure of their goods (Hening, IX, 584–585). Similarly, the act which Gen. Nelson's committee brought before the House contained no personal penalties for the offending parties (Hening, IX, 530–532). These measures had passed the House by 29 Oct., and GM did not report until 19 Nov. It seems that delegates saw the loopholes in their earlier work and in the final hours of the session attempted a patching job that struck at both war profiteers and PERSONS WHO HAVE REFUSED TO TAKE THE OATH OF FIDELITY. GM was ordered to carry this bill to the Senate, and was presumably the chief author. Similar legislation was enacted at about the same time in Maryland, New York, and Pennsylvania, with stringent confiscation powers left in the hands of local justices of the peace (Ferguson, *Power of the Purse*, 60–64).

Resolution to Provide for Protection of the Coast and Chesapeake Bay

[19 December 1778]

Resolved, That the Governor, with the advice of the Council, be empowered to instruct the Board of Commissioners, from time to time, to have such material alterations made in [the disposition?], and arrangements of the Navy, as may be judged expedient and necessary; and also, to direct the erecting such fortifications and batteries on the Bay of Chesapeake, as may, in co-operation with the Navy, more effectually protect the trade than hath been done hitherto.

Printed from JHD, 1827 ed., 19 Dec. 1778 entry.

GM was chairman of a special committee appointed on 16 Dec. to study correspondence that passed between Gov. Patrick Henry and the Virginia delegates in Congress. Possibly one item that the committee perused was Henry's letter to the delegation dated 4 Dec. 1778 which complained of "The great distress our Trade has of late and does at present suffer from the Ships & privatiers of the Enemy which infest our Coast" (Hutchinson-Rachal, I, 272). The chief target of such complaints was not the British blockade but the family of John Goodrich, the Virginia turncoat whose small band of vessels became the *bête noire* of Virginia coastal shipping. Richard Henry Lee voiced similar distress, mentioned the Goodriches, and urged that a combined state and continental naval force rendezvous at Chesapeake Bay for their destruction (letter to Gen. [William] Whipple, 29 Nov. 1778, Ballagh, *Lee Letters*, I, 454). GM carried the resolution to the Senate.

The conjectural wording in brackets have been added by the editor because the clerk or the printer seems to have omitted several important words.

Resolutions Recommending Additional Land Bounties for Troops Serving with the Virginia Regiments

[19 December 1778]

Resolved, That it is the opinion of this committee, that a certain tract of country to be bounded by the Green river and a south east course from the head thereof to the Cumberland mountains, with the said mountains to the Carolina line, with the Carolina line to the Cherokee or Tennessee river, with the said river to the Ohio river, and with the Ohio to the said Green river, ought to be reserved for supplying the officers and soldiers in the Virginia line with the respective proportions of land which have been or may be assigned to them by the general assembly, saving and reserving the land granted to Richard Henderson and company, and their legal rights to such persons as have heretofore actually located lands, and settled thereon within the bounds aforesaid.

Resolved, That it is the opinion of this committee, that the said officers and soldiers, or any of them, may be at liberty to locate their proportions of land on any other vacant and ungranted lands within this Commonwealth.

Resolved, That it is the opinion of this committee, that the allowance of two hundred acres of land over and above the continental bounty, be given to all the soldiers in the Virginia line, who have heretofore enlisted or shall hereafter enlist for the term of three years, or during the war.

Resolved, That it is the opinion of this committee, that the several commissioned and non-commissioned officers in the Virginia line ought to have their allowance of lands increased in the same proportion as that of the soldiers are by the preceding resolution. And whereas no provision hath been hitherto made for the general officers:

Resolved, That such General officers who were inhabitants of this state, be allowed the following proportions of land, upon the same terms and under the same restrictions with the lands engaged to the officers and soldiers raised in this commonwealth, that is to say, to the commander in chief,   acres, to every Major General,   acres, and to every Brigadier General,   acres.

Printed from Hening, X, 55*n.*

A petition (or, as they said in 1778, a memorial) from the general and field officers of Virginia regiments had been referred by the House of Delegates to a special committee. GM served on the committee, but when the resolutions were brought before the House, George Lyne made the report. The House approved the first resolution but turned down the other four, and ordered GM to carry the surviving resolve to the Senate for its concurrence (JHD, 1827 ed. 19 Dec. entry). The CERTAIN TRACT OF COUNTRY was in the Kentucky district, adjacent to the 200,000 acres granted to Richard Henderson's company (Hening, IX, 571–572), earlier in the same session. The delegates were inclined toward generosity in handing out western land parcels because they hoped to fill quotas with volunteers and thus avoid "so unpopular a measure" as the draft (letter to George Washington, 22 Dec. 1778, Mays, ed., *Papers of Edmund Pendleton,* I, 276–277).

The first resolution, which was approved by the Senate on 19 Dec. and printed in the *Journal of the Senate,* is reprinted in Rowland, I, 310. There are variations in the punctuation and capitalization between each of the printed versions.

Resolution Complaining of Disadvantages in the Franco-American Treaty of Commerce

[19 December 1778]

The House [of Delegates] upon due consideration of the 11th and 12th articles of the treaty of commerce with France, are of opinion, that they are not consistent with the principles of equality and reciprocity, so wisely proposed as the basis of that treaty, and so well calculated to give that permanence thereto, which every friend to the alliance wishes to take place.

Resolved, therefore, That the delegates to the General Congress from this Commonwealth, be directed to propose to Congress that the minister of the United States at the court of France be instructed to represent the same to his Most Christian Majesty, and to use his utmost efforts that the said 11th and 12th articles may be rescinded.

Printed from JHD, 1827 ed., 19 Dec. 1778 entry.

Anyone doubting the existence of sectional rivalries during the Revolution would have to be unfamiliar with this resolution, which complains of discriminatory clauses in the Franco-American treaty of 1778 that clearly favored the northern states. THE SAID 11TH AND 12TH ARTICLES declared that no tax would be imposed on any molasses exported from the French Sugar Islands to the U.S., and in compensation for this concession promised that Americans would not tax their exports to those islands. This allowed the northern shipping states to load duty-free molasses at French Caribbean ports, but deprived Virginia and other southern states exporting tobacco, rice, indigo, ships-bread, etc., from any levy on exports. The time-honored tax on each hogshead of tobacco was a considerable source of revenue in Virginia. GM probably wrote a preamble which the clerk copied along with the resolution, but GM's draft of the resolve has not been located. The text of the treaty, as it was transmitted from the Congress to the states, is found in Ford, ed., *Journals of the Continental Congress*, XI, 419ff. Background on the treaty, which was signed 6 Feb. 1778, is found in S. F. Bemis, ed., *The American Secretaries of State and Their Diplomacy* (New York, 1955), I, 14–24.

An Act "to amend an act intituled An Act to enable the officers of the Virginia line, and to encourage the soldiers of the same line, to continue in the continental service."

[19 December 1778]

WHEREAS it is justly to be apprehended, from the scarcity and dearness of the several articles directed to be furnished to the officers and soldiers of the Virginia troops on continental establishment, or in continental service, by the act passed in this present session of assembly, intituled "An act to enable the officers of the Virginia line, and to encourage the soldiers of the same line, to continue in the continental service," that the said recited act cannot be carried fully into execution without greatly distressing the publick treasury, *Be it therefore enacted by the General Assembly*, That until the meeting of the next session of assembly, the governour and council shall carry the said act into execution, so far only as in their discretion it shall appear practicable to be done, without too great distress and injury to the commonwealth.

Printed from Hening, IX, 580–581.
This was enacted on the final day of the session. The act encouraging officers and men to remain in the Continental Army (*ibid.*, 565–567) provided a bonus of immediate payment of six months pay, guaranteed prices for vital commodities from the military commissary, and a life pension for widows. The plain truth was that t was almost impossible to find the green tea, bohea tea, coffee, chocolate, and sugar which the bill promised to troops at reasonable prices. Hence this act permitted the governor and council to suspend that provision until more food items, at normal prices, could be obtained. The rising price of chocolate indicates the difficulty. Chocolate prices in Pennsylvania, probably

about the same as those of Virginia, rose from 16/8d. in Jan. 1778 to 45/ in May 1779 and 90/ in Dec. 1779 (Anne Bezanson, *Prices and Inflation During the American Revolution; Pennsylvania, 1770–1790* [Philadelphia, 1951], 336). The Ms draft in GM's handwriting has not been located, but he was ordered to carry the bill to the Senate and is thus presumed to be its author.

APPENDIXES

*A. Mason's Land Purchases, Leases, Receipts, Inventories, and Head-
right Certificates, 1749–1791*

*B. Mason's Account with the Commonwealth of Virginia
for Munitions, Provisions, etc.,
during the Revolution, 1775–1781*

C. Mason Family Bible, 1750–1780

Consisting of Mason's land purchases and leases, receipts other than those related to wartime activity, inventories of slaves and other property, and headright or importation certificates Mason bought, sold, or redeemed. An asterisk (*) indicates the item is in Mason's handwriting. Except as noted, the appendix does not include accounts or legal matters Mason handled as treasurer of the Ohio Company, which are calendared in James, *The Ohio Company of Virginia*, 300–353.

Date	Item	Location
1749	*Fairfax County List of Titheables* shows GM owning 11 slaves	DLC
14 July 1749	GM purchased lot 53, town of Alexandria, for 7 pistoles	DLC (*Proceedings of Alexandria Trustees*)
29 Dec. 1752	Lease to Thomas Halpert for 200 acres at Accotinck for 1,050 lbs. of tobacco annual rent	*Gunston Hall
20 June 1753	Sale by GM of 627 acres lying on NW. side of Great Hunting Creek in Truro parish, Fairfax County	Morristown, N.J., National Historical Park
11 Sept. 1753	GM assigned 500 acres at Walnut Bottom in Maryland for £20. Not recorded until 25 Mar. 1756 (probably related to Ohio Company holdings in GM's name)	Maryland Land Office, Prince Georges County Surveys, No. 2241
[June?] 1754	GM purchased lot 54, town of Alexandria, for ten shillings	DLC (*Proceedings of Alexandria Trustees*)
25 Oct. 1754	Deed of 329 acres from Lord Fairfax for land in Hamshire County.	Gunston Hall
25 Oct. 1754	Deed of 220 acres from Lord Fairfax for land in Hampshire County, "Beginning at a black wallnut. . . ."	Northern Neck Grants Book H (Vi)
25 Oct. 1754	Deed of 237 acres from Lord Fairfax for land in Hampshire County, "Beginning at a Sugar tree standing. . . ."	Northern Neck Grants Book H (Vi)
25 Oct. 1754	Deed of 315 acres from Lord Fairfax for land in Hampshire County, "Beginning upon the Edge of Potomack river. . . ."	Northern Neck Grants Book H (Vi)
25 Oct. 1754	Deed of 334 acres from Lord Fairfax for land in Hampshire County, "Beginning at a White Oak. . . ."	Northern Neck Grants Book H (Vi)
10 Aug. 1756	Lease to Joseph Bennett of 100 acres	*Gunston Hall
18 Aug. 1756	Sale of Alexandria town lots recorded	Fairfax County Deed Book D-1
1 Oct. 1757	Lease to William Kitchen of 100 acres	*Gunston Hall
7 Oct. 1757	Lease to William Stone of 100 acres	*Gunston Hall
7 Oct. 1757	Lease to William Scott of 100 acres	*Gunston Hall
July 1759	GM owner of lot 55, town of Alexandria	DLC (*Proceedings of Alexandria Trustees*)

Date	Item	Location
31 July 1761	Deed for 265 acres opposite Crane Island	Northern Neck Grants Book I (Vi)
15 Oct. 1762	GM leases plot in Alexandria for one year	Fairfax County Deed Book E-1
14 Dec. 1762	Will of Ann Mason, GM's mother, entered for probate, bequeathing GM the "land lying on Goose Bay in Charles County in Maryland" and nine slaves	Rowland, I, 79
25 March 1763	GM purchased 260 acres in Frederick County, Maryland (possibly this purchase, as was case on 24 June 1763 of the 510-acre "Cove," also mentioned in Rowland, was connected with Ohio Company affairs)	Rowland, I, 117
14 June 1763	Thomas Bladen assigned 300 acres to GM after some litigation that related to the Ohio Company. A caveat was filed against the title on 6 Sept. 1763 but a clear title was not issued until after April, 1821, when GM's heirs accepted $951 for quit-claim deed (James, *Ohio Company*, 182–183).	James, *Ohio Company*, 194
16 Dec. 1763	GM and John Moncure sign two bonds for proper management of Potomac ferry in Ann Mason's estate.	Gunston Hall
13 Dec. 1763	GM and John Moncure account for Ann Mason's estate	Stafford County Will Book O
23 Aug. 1766	GM credited with delivery of 88 hogsheads of crop tobacco weighing 50,034 pounds at Piscataway landing, assigned to Alexander Hamilton.	John Glassford & Co. *Journal* *1766* (DLC)
25 Aug. 1766	GM purchased dry goods, hardware, tea, spices, etc., valued at £80.5 .7 from Alexander Hamilton of Piscataway	*Ibid.*
9 Sept. 1767	Deed for 100½ acres from Lord Fairfax on Lower Spout Run	Northern Neck Proprietor's Book O (Vi)
6 Nov. 1767	Purchase of 224 acres, formerly in Prince William, but now in Fairfax County, for £60 Virginia currency, from Philip and Francis Ellis	*Gunston Hall
16 Nov. 1767	Purchase of 276 acres in Fairfax County from Hanover Bradie for £90 Virginia currency	*Gunston Hall
[21 April] 1769	George Washington agrees to pay GM £100 for 100 acres	*Henkel's Sale Catalogue* No. 663 (Phila. 1891)

Date	Item	Location
14 Oct. 1769	GM sold George Washington 300 acres on [Little?] Hunting Creek, Fairfax County (see also memorandum of agreement signed this date in correspondence section of volume)	DLC, Washington Ledger Book A
Feb. 1772	Deed for 214 acres from Lord Fairfax for land in Hampshire County	Rowland, I, 154
22 Sept. 1772	GM loans George Washington £203	DLC, Washington Ledger Book A
26 May 1773	Promissory note: Frederick Nichols to GM and Martin Cockburn	Gunston Hall
5 June 1773	James Scott's certificate of rights of importation of 59 persons	CSmH
22 June 1773	Harry Piper to GM; bill of sale for headrights on 377 persons	CSmH
20 July 1773	Robert Adam to GM; bill of sale, headrights for 87 persons	CSmH
28 July 1773	Promissory note: Edward Smith to GM and Martin Cockburn	Gunston Hall
2 August 1773	John Smith to GM; sale bill for headrights of 28 persons for £1 8s.	CSmH
6 Dec. 1773	John Graham to GM; sale bill for headrights for 132 persons for £33	CSmH
6 Dec. 1773	John Graham to GM; sale bill for headrights of 85 persons for £21 5s.	CSmH
1774	GM buys one share in Philip Mazzei's winery.	DLC, Va. Misc. Docs.
11 March 1774	Alexander Campbell to GM; sale bill for headrights to 28 persons for five shillings	CSmH
11 March 1774	Alexander Campbell to GM; sale bill for headrights of 41 persons for five shillings	CSmH
11 March 1774	Cumberland Wilson to GM; sale bill for headrights to 17 persons for five shillings	CSmH
11 March 1774	Cumberland Wilson to GM; sale bill of headrights for 20 persons for five shillings	CSmH
May 1774	Benjamin Waller's certificate that proofs and certificates for headright importations are in due form (see GM's petition 17 June 1774)	*CSmH
6 June 1774	William Harrison to GM: sale bill for 137 headrights for £13 14s.	*CSmH
20 May 1776	Wm. Ramsay to GM; sale bill for headrights of 37 persons for £9	*CSmH
17 June 1776	Robert Adam to GM: sale bill for 84 headrights	CSmH

Date	Item	Location
21 Oct. 1776	John Dalton to GM; sale bill for head-rights of 6 persons for thirty shillings	*CSmH
21 Oct. 1776	John Carlyle and John Dalton to GM; sale bill for headrights of 66 persons for £16	*CSmH
14 Nov. 1776	James Dunlap to GM; sale bill for headrights of 7 persons for 35 shillings	*CSmH
10 July 1779	12 land warrants issued to GM to survey total of 68,900 acres: No. 1—8,400 ac. for importing 162 persons No. 2—8,300 ac. for importing 166 persons No. 3—8,200 ac. for importing 164 persons No. 4—8,100 ac. for importing 162 persons No. 5—8,000 ac. for importing 160 persons No. 6—4,550 ac. for importing 91 persons No. 7—4,200 ac. for importing 84 persons No. 8—4,100 ac. for importing 82 persons No. 9—4,000 ac. for importing 80 persons No. 10—2,000 ac. for importing 40 [?] persons No. 11—to James Scott of Prince Wm. County 2,950 ac. for importing 59 persons [sold to GM] No. 12—to Theodorick Bland: 6,050 ac. for importing 121 persons [sold to GM]	Vi (Virginia State Land Office, *Old Military and Importation Warrants,* Vols. 1 and 2)
22 Dec. 1779	53,700 acres in nine entries withdrawn from unpatented lands in Jefferson County for GM	Jefferson County, Ky., Deed Book A
23 Dec. 1779	2,200 acres on Licking Creek, Jefferson County, withdrawn from unpatented lands for GM	*ibid.*
29 Apr. 1780	37,000 acres in ten entries ordered surveyed for GM on Panther and Green creeks, Jefferson County	*ibid.*
22 May 1780	400 acres in Jefferson County ordered surveyed for GM	*ibid.*
27 Oct. 1780	8,200 acres on Panther Creek, Jefferson County, ordered surveyed for GM	*ibid.*

Date	Item	Location
27 Oct. 1780	8,400 acres on Panther Creek, Jefferson County, ordered surveyed for GM	*ibid.*
25 Oct. 1782	Bill of Exchange for £540 entered to GM's credit by Nantes office of Wallace, Johnson & Muir	NN, Wallace, Johnson & Muir Letterbook
17 Dec. 1782	2,000 acres on Green River ordered surveyed for GM	Jefferson County, Ky., Deed Book A
10 Jan. 1783	5,496 acres on Tagert's Creek, Fayette County, ordered surveyed for GM	Fayette County, Ky. Deed Book II
7 Feb. 1783	500 acres in Lincoln County ordered surveyed for GM	Lincoln County, Ky., Deed Book I
20 June 1783	1,000 acres on South fork of Big Benson Creek ordered surveyed for GM	Lincoln County, Ky., Deed Book II
9 Sept. 1783	8,400 acres on Panther Creek, Jefferson County, ordered surveyed for GM	Jefferson County, Ky., Deed Book A
4–10 Oct. 1783	13,500 acres in five entries ordered surveyed for GM in Jefferson County	*ibid.*
27 Oct. 1783	8,400 acres on Panther Creek, Jefferson County, ordered surveyed for GM	Registrar, Ky. Land Office, Frankfort, (Virginia Land Grants)
15 Dec. 1783	400 acres on Summerset Creek, Fayette County, ordered surveyed for GM	Jillson, *Kentucky Land Grants*, 85
16 March 1784	1,000 acres on Kentucky River, Lincoln County, ordered surveyed for GM	*ibid.*
17 March 1784	500 acres on Benson Creek, Lincoln County, ordered surveyed for GM	*ibid.*
21 July 1784	500 acres on Kentucky River, Lincoln County, ordered surveyed for GM	*ibid.*
30 March 1785	GM's expense account for service on commission for Chesapeake-Potomac jurisdiction, £3.16. .9	VI
17 Aug. 1785	GM requested payment of £6.18 .8 as balance due from estate of Thomas West's father	MB
3 Jan. 1786	8,000 acres on Ohio River, in Nelson County, ordered surveyed for GM	Jillson, *Kentucky Land Grants*, 85
4 Jan. 1786	2,000 acres on Ohio River, in Nelson County, ordered surveyed for GM	*idem.*
14 April 1786	GM acknowledges, in ltr. to Martin Cockburn, ownership of Loan Office Certificates with total nominal value of $3,900	Mason Papers, DLC
11 Aug. 1787	£100 bill of exchange drawn to GM's credit for service at Federal Convention	Vi

Date	Item	Location
17 Sept. 1787	£ 50 promissory note to Robert Morris for cash advanced to GM	Vi
28 Sept. 1787	£248. .8. .o account of expenses incurred at Federal Convention by GM	Vi
15 Nov. 1787	GM ordered to pay 150 to R. T. Hooe in civil suit relating to losses on board the *General Washington*	*Va. Journal & Alexandria Advertiser*
15 Feb. 1789	1,700 acres in Nelson County ordered surveyed for GM	Jillson, *Kentucky Land Grants*, p. 85
20 May 1789	GM awarded £2,420 . .1 . .6 in civil suit against William Lee (see GM to Lee, 8 Oct. 1778)	York County Order Book
May 1791	Dudley Mitchum adknowledges bonds from GM of £240 and £25	ViU

This is a far-from-complete listing, but gives at least a hint of GM's broad range of activities beyond those items mentioned specifically in his letters. A word of caution regarding the land entries is in order, because it is impossible to know when certain lands were duplicate entries or were finally deeded to GM. GM's letter to George Muter, 28 Sept. 1785, and another to Col. John Harvie, 10 Dec. 1785, cast some doubt on the extensive Kentucky District entries. It is also likely that portions of the Kentucky lands were claimed by GM on behalf of the Ohio Company. Litigation to clear the Kentucky titles was under way by GM's heirs in June 1794. As James, *Ohio Company*, 182–183, points out, some of the legal battles continued to 1821. Unhappily, GM's account books have not been found, and yet there is little doubt that a man of his methodical bent would have kept extensive records of crop sales, bills of lading, loans, and real estate transactions. The entries from George Washington's Ledger Book "A," which has survived the passage of nearly two hundred years, hint at what GM's records might have revealed for their operations were similar. Entries on pages 6 and 61 of the Ledger Book "A" (Washington Papers, DLC) cover a period from April 1759 to June 1787 and show that GM and Washington borrowed and lent each other money, carried on small personal favors for each other, and also bought and sold fish, saws, land, shingles, and linseed oil from the Mount Vernon and Gunston Hall estates. Other business with GM is noted in Washington's Ledger Book "B" (*ibid.*) for 1778.

George Mason's Account for Weapons, Supplies, and Services to the Army and Navy

Consisting mainly of entries from the Account Book of the Virginia Committee of Safety, 21 Oct. 1775–5 July 1776 (Vi), Journal of the Committee of Safety for 1776 (in McIlwaine, *Journals of the Council of State of Va.*, 14–29), and the Ms collections of the Virginia State Library. This is by no means a complete accounting of all of GM's military activity from 1775 onward, but rather a collection of information that elucidates his concept of patriotic participation in a limited role.

Date	Item	Location
1 Dec. 1775	GM paid £33. .6. .4½ for salt-peter and sulphur	Acct. Book, Committee of Safety
1 Dec. 1775	£857.17. .7 paid GM for "sundry Goods bot. for publick use"	*ibid.*
13 Dec. 1775	£12. .9. .6½ paid to GM "for collecting & purchasg. sundry Goods"	*ibid.*
10 Feb. 1776	GM and John Dalton, Fairfax County Committee of Safety, advanced £1,000 "for fitting the Potowmack Navy"	*ibid.*
23 April 1776	GM and John Dalton paid £3,000 by Lieut. Arrel	*ibid.*
23 April 1776	GM and John Dalton paid £3,000 "by order on Virginia Delegates"	*ibid.*
6 May 1776	GM and John Dalton paid £100 for "purchase of Tobacco" for state account	*ibid.*
29 May 1776	GM paid £3.10. .o for "Arms bought for Public use"	*ibid.*

[Ledger entries on page 111 of the Acct. Book indicate these sums were used to purchase a sloop from "Morris & Richards," to pay James Mercer and William Fitzhugh for tobacco, to buy the sloop *Liberty* from John and George Fowler, to pay John Tayloe for "Cannon, Shot, plank, Iron &c. furnd.," and reimburse Philip Ludwell Lee for "Sail Duck."]

Date	Item	Location
11 June 1776	GM authorized "to draw on the Commissary of Provisions" for seamen "engaged for the Potowmack River Department"	Journal, Committee of Safety
10 June 1776	GM and John Dalton authorized to contract for purchase of 2,000 blankets	*ibid.*
12 June 1776	GM issued warrant for £2.10. .o "for twenty yards of half thick" furnished to 2d. Va. Regt.	*ibid.*
14 June 1776	GM authorized to draw "so many blankets or Ruggs as he may apply for" for use of seamen and marines on Potomac duty	*ibid.*

18 June 1776	GM issued warrant for £3. .5. .0 "for two Guns furnished" to George Mason, Jr.'s "Minute Company sent to Hampton"	*ibid.*
13 Dec. 1776	GM and John Dalton to use £760. .0. .9 warrant to balance account of "Schooner Speedwell now sailed on a trading Voyage"	*Journal of Council of State*, p. 277
20 Dec. 1776	£947. .4. .0 issued to GM, "being the recruiting Money for Captain's John Allison and Samuel Arrell"	*ibid.*
28 Dec. 1777	Receipt from GM £62. .2. .6 for weapons furnished and salary as delegate	NNP
26 July 1780	Receipt for 138 pounds of bacon GM furnished for troops at $8 per pd.	Vi, Fairfax County Public Service Claims
26 July 1780	Payment order for sheriff of Fairfax County, in GM's hand	*ibid.*
21 April 1781	Receipt for 75 pds. of beef received from GM for public use	*ibid.*
22 May 1781	Order to deliver 10 bushels of public corn to Samuel Alexander (in GM's hand)	*ibid.*
7 July 1781	Receipt for three head of cattle judged to weigh 1,600 pds. received from GM for public use	*ibid.*
7 July 1781	Receipt for seven head of cattle judged to weigh 2,975 pounds from GM for public use	*ibid.*
10 July 1781	Receipt for 7,900 pounds of hay from GM for public use	*ibid.*
11 July 1781	Receipt for three head of cattle judged to weigh 1,175 pounds from GM for public use	*ibid.*
4 Oct. 1781	Receipt for 475 pounds of beef from GM for public use	*ibid.*

This listing indicates the range of GM's participation in the provisioning of troops and his work as a Fairfax County Committee of Safety member for fortifying Alexandria and guarding the Potomac navigation. Readers interested in these activities should also consult the correspondence section of this volume, e.g., the letters to the Md. Council of Safety of 31 Jan. and 15–19 March 1776, or the letters to Martin Cockburn of 23 June 1776 and Col. William Aylett of 19 April and 8 June 1777.

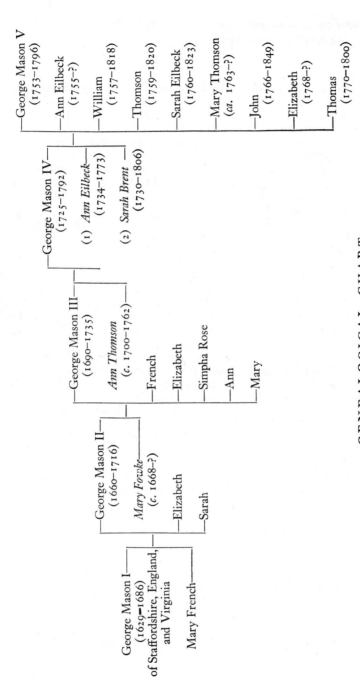

GENEALOGICAL CHART

George Mason I
(1629–1686)
of Staffordshire, England,
and Virginia

Mary French

George Mason II
(1660–1716)
Mary Fowke
(c. 1668–?)
Elizabeth
Sarah

George Mason III
(1690–1735)
Ann Thomson
(c. 1700–1762)
French
Elizabeth
Simpha Rose
Ann
Mary

George Mason IV
(1725–1792)
(1) Ann Eilbeck
(1734–1773)
(2) Sarah Brent
(1730–1806)

George Mason V
(1753–1796)
Ann Eilbeck
(1755–?)
William
(1757–1818)
Thomson
(1759–1820)
Sarah Eilbeck
(1760–1823)
Mary Thomson
(ca. 1763–?)
John
(1766–1849)
Elizabeth
(1768–?)
Thomas
(1770–1800)

Mason Family Bible Entries of Marriages, Births, and Deaths
[4 April 1750–11 April 1780]

George Mason of Stafford County Virginia, aged about twenty five Years, and Ann Eilbeck (the Daughter of William Eilbeck of Charles county Maryland, Merchant) aged about sixteen Years, were married on Wednesday the 4th. Day of April in the Year 1750 by the revd. Mr. John Moncure Rector of Overwharton Parish, Stafford County Virginia.

George Mason, their eldest Son, was born on Monday the 30th. Day of April 1753, abt. 8 O'Clock at Night, in Dogues Neck, & privately baptized the Week after by the revd. Mr. Charles Green Rector of Truro Parish Fairfax County.

Ann Eilbeck Mason was born on Monday the 13th. of January 1755, abt. 4 O'Clock in the Morning, in Dogues Neck, & privately baptized at a Fortnight old by the revd. Mr. Charles Green.

William Mason was born on Thursday the 16th: of April 1756 about 4 O'Clock in the Morning, in Dogues Neck, & baptized by the revd. Mr. Charles Green on Monday the 14th. June following; the revd. Mr. John Moncure & Mr. Thomson Mason being God-fathers, & Mrs. Sarah Eilbeck & Mrs. Margaret Green God-Mothers. N.B. At the same Time my two eldest Children (George & Ann) had public Baptism; the same Persons being Sponsors for all the[m]

William Mason died of the Flux on Thursday the 4th. of August 1757. and was buried in the Family Burying Place at Newton

William Mason (the second of the Name) was born on the 22d. Day of October 1757. abt. 3 O'Clock in the Morning, in Dogues Neck; & was privately baptized by the revd. Mr. James Scott Rector of Dettingen Parish Prince William County.

Thomson Mason was born on Sunday the 4th. of March 1759 abt. 11 O'Clock in the Fore-noon, at Gunston-Hall, & privately baptized by the revd. Mr. Charles Green.

Sarah Mason was born on the 11th. of December 1760. abt. 9 O'Clock at Night, at Gunston-Hall, & was privately baptized by the revd. Mr. Charles Green

[Mary] Th[o]mson Mason was born on the 27th. of January [1763? . . . o'c]lock in the Morning, at Gunston-Hall, & was privately baptized [by the Rev. Charles] Green.

John Mason was born on Thursday the 4th: of April 1766. about ten O'Clock in the Morning, at Mrs. Eilbeck's, in Charles County Maryland, and was privately baptized by the revd. Mr. James Scott.

Elizabeth Mason was born on Teusday the 19th. of April 1768. about two O'Clock in the Morning, at Gunston-Hall, & was privately baptized by the revd. Mr. Lee Massey Rector of Truro Parish. Mr. Martin Cockburn standing God-father & Mrs. Ann Cockburn & Miss Elizabeth Bronaugh God-Mothers.

Thomas Mason was born on Teusday the 1st: Day of May 1770. about two O'Clock in the Afternoon at Gunston-Hall & was baptized by the revd. Mr. Lee Massey Mr. Martin Cockburn & Capt. John Lee standing God-fathers, and Mrs. Mary Massey and Mrs. Ann Cockburn God-Mothers.

Richard Mason and James Mason, Twins, were born on Friday the 4th: Day of December 1773, about eleven O'Clock in the Forenoon at Gunston-Hall, & baptized the same Day by the revd. Mr. Lee Massey; but being born about two Months before their due time (occasioned by a long Illness of their Mother) they both died the next Morning, and were buried in the new Burying Ground at Gunston-Hall; being the first of the Family who are buryed in that Place.

On Teusday, the 9th. of March, 1773, about three O'Clock in the morning, died at Gunston-Hall, of a slow-fever, Mrs. Ann Mason, in the thirty-ninth [ye]ar of her Age; after a painful & tedious Illness of more than [nine months, which she] bore with truly Christian Patience & Resignation, in [faithful hope] of eternal Happiness in the World to come. She[, it may be truthfully said, led a] blameless & exemplary Life. She retain[ed unimpaired her mental faculties to] the last; & spending her latest Moments [in prayer for those around her,] seem'd to expire without the usual [pangs of dissolution. During the whole course] of her Illness, she was never heard to utter one peevish or fretful Complaint, and [constan]tly, regardless of her own Pain & Danger, endeavoured to administer Hope & Comfort [to her] Friends, or inspire them with Resignation like her own! For many Days [be]fore her Death she had lost all Hopes of Recovery, & endeavour'd to wean herself from the Affections of this Life, saying that tho' it must cost her a hard Struggle to reconcile herself to the Thoughts of parting with her Husband & Children, she hoped God wou'd enable her to accomplish it; and after this, tho' she had always been the tenderest Parent, she took little Notice of her Children' but still retain'd her usual Serenity of Mind. She was buried in the new Family-burying-Groun[d] at Gunston-Hall; but (at her own Request) without the common Parade & Ceremo[ny] of a Grand Funeral. Her funeral Sermon was preach'd in Pohick Church by the reved. Mr. James Scott, Rector of Dettingen Parish in the County of Prince William, upon a Text taken from the 23d, 24th, & 25th Verses of the 73d. Psalm.

In the Beauty of her Person, & the Sweetness of her Disposition, she was equalled by few, & excelled by none of her Sex. She was something taller than the middle-size, & elegantly shaped. Her Eyes were black, tender & lively; her Features regular & delicate; her Complexion remarkably fair & fresh—Lilies and Roses (almost without a Metaphor) were blended there—and a certain inexpressible A[ir of] Chearfulness, Health, Innocence & Sensibility diffused over her Coun[tenance] form'd a Face the very Reverse of what is generally called masculi[ne. This is] not an ideal, but a real Picture drawn from the Life. Nor was this be[autiful out]ward-Form disgraced by an unworthy Inhabitant:

> Free from her Sex's smallest Faults,
> And fair as Woman-kind can be;

She was bless'd with a clear & sound Judgement, a gentle & benevolent Heart, a s[incere] & an humble Mind; with an even calm & chearful

Temper to a very unusual degree Affable to All, but intimate with Few. Her modest Virtues shun'd the public-Eye, Superior to the turbulent Passions of Pride & Envy, a Stranger to Altercation of every Kind, & content with the Blessings of a private Station, she placed all her Happiness here, where only it is to be found, in her own Family. Tho' she despised Dress, she was always neat; chearful, but not gay; Serious, but not melancholly; she never met me without a Smile! Tho' an only Child, she was a remarkably dutiful One; an easy & agreeable Companion; a kind Neighbour; a steadfast Friend; an humane Mistress; a prudent & a tender Mother; a faithful, affectionate, & most obliging Wife; charitable to the Poor, and pious to her Maker; her Virtue & Religion were unmixed with hypocrisy or Ostentation.

Form'd for domestic Happiness, without one jarring Attom in her Frame!

[Her . . .] irreparable Loss I do, & ever shall deplore; and tho' Time I hope will [soften my sad im]pressions, & restore me greater Serenity of Mind than I have lately enjoy[ed, I shall ever retain the most tender and melancholy] Remembrance of One so justly dear.]

George Mason of Gunston Hall in Fairfax County Virginia, aged abt. fifty four Years, and his second Wife, Sarah Brent (D[aughter] of George Brent Esqr. of Woodstock in the County of Stafford) aged abou[t fifty] Years, were married on Teusday the 11th. Day of April in the Year 1780, [by] the revd. Mr. James Scott, Rector of Dettingen Parish in the County of Prince William in Virginia

Ms (Gunston Hall). Four numbered pages in GM's hand, written on extra pages placed in the Bible for such purposes. The Bible is probably the folio edition printed by Thomas Baskett in London in 1759, although the title page and all printed pages prior to that beginning with Chap. XXIX, verse 43 of Exodus are missing.

The date for GM's first marriage is according to the Julian, or Old Style, calendar. By the New Style calendar adopted in 1752, the date would be 15 April 1750. Presumably, the marriage took place in Charles County, Md., but neither GM's entry nor the newspaper notice in the Annapolis *Md. Gazette*, 2 May 1750, make this clear: "On the 3d of last Month, *George Mason* Esq; of *Virginia*, was married to Miss Anne Eilbeck, Daughter of Mr. *William Eilbeck*, Merchant in Charles County in this Province; a young Lady of distinguishing Merit and Beauty, and a handsome Fortune." The accompanying Mason Family Chart carries more information on the Mason offsprings.

Long held privately by Mason descendants, the Bible was brought to Gunston Hall in 1965, when the badly damaged Ms. portion was chemically treated to arrest further deterioration. It is likely that GM wrote or copied the twelve entries preceding that for 9 March 1773 at one time, relying on paper fragments or memory for the vital statistics thus supplied. Also, since this Bible was probably printed in 1759, six entries would pre-date publication. Kate Mason Rowland saw the Ms. while it was still in good condition, and the bracketed portions of GM's eulogy to his wife are taken from that version printed in *Rowland*, I, 162–163. Other bracketed words have been added conjecturally where the Ms. is torn, except that the editor is reluctant to guess the age of Sarah Brent at the time of her marriage, and therefore the age given in Rowland, I, 349, has been accepted. GM's eulogy was bordered in black, in the custom of the day. A similarly bordered eulogy of GM follows the final entry, possibly in John Mason's handwriting. There are also marginal commentaries in an unknown hand, chiefly setting down specific information on the deaths of GM's children.